W9-AKN-613

LIGHTNING MAN

LIGHTNING MAN

The Accursed Life of Samuel F. B. Morse

KENNETH SILVERMAN

Da Capo Press
A Member of the Perseus Books Group

For Benjamin Berkman and Eve Silverman

Copyright © 2003 Kenneth Silverman

All rights reserved. No part of this publication may be reproduced, stored
in a retrieval system, or transmitted, in any form or by any means, electronic, mechanical, photocopying, recording, or otherwise, without the
prior written permission of the publisher. Printed in the United States of
America.

Cataloging-in-Publication data for this book is available from the Library
of Congress.

First Da Capo Press edition 2004
Reprinted by arrangement with Alfred A. Knopf
ISBN 0-306-81394-7

Published by Da Capo Press
A Member of the Perseus Books Group
http://www.dacapopress.com

Da Capo Press books are available at special discounts for bulk purchases
in the U.S. by corporations, institutions, and other organizations. For
more information, please contact the Special Markets Department at the
Perseus Books Group, 11 Cambridge Center, Cambridge, MA 02142,
or call (800) 255-1514 or (617) 252-5298, or email
special.markets@perseusbooks.com.

1 2 3 4 5 6 7 8 9—08 07 06 05 04

Contents

COMMANDADOR

FINLEY

The value and rank of every art is in proportion to the mental labour employed in it, or the mental pleasure produced by it. As this principle is observed or neglected, our profession becomes either a liberal art, or a mechanical trade.

—Sir Joshua Reynolds, "Fourth Discourse on Art" (1771)

We are a people essentially active. I may say we are preeminently so. Distance and difficulties are less to us than any people on earth. Our schemes and prospects extend every where and to every thing.

—John C. Calhoun, speech in the U.S. Senate, June 24, 1812

Samuel F. B. Morse, *Self Portrait* (1812–13)
(Addison Gallery of American Art)

ONE

Geography

(1789–1811)

O N APRIL 30, 1789, Jedediah Morse was installed as pastor of the First Congregational Church of Charlestown, Massachusetts. The occasion was triply significant to him. Twenty-seven years old, he had come to his vocation by study at Yale and graduate work in theology. He felt eager to promote the interests of religion but awed to contemplate the degenerate state of his fellow mortals, who every day crucified their Redeemer anew. The labor now to be undertaken by him was worthy but daunting, "a good work," he said, "but alas who is sufficient for these things."

The place mattered to Jedediah no less than the occasion. The First Church was one of the oldest in America, a fit pulpit for a man whose ancestors had emigrated to the New World in 1635, among the first settlers of Puritan New England. The church stood, too, in the shadow of Bunker's Hill. Just fourteen years earlier, armed provincials had defended the hill against three assaults by British infantry and marines.

And for Jedediah, the date was no less symbolic than the place. On the same day, on the balcony of New York City's Federal Hall, George Washington was inaugurated as the first President of the United States and called on the new nation to preserve "the sacred fire of liberty." Jedediah revered him as an epitome of republican virtue—self-sacrificing, pious, restrained, great because he was good, indeed, Jedediah said, "the *greatest Man alive*."

Two weeks after the momentous day of his settlement, Jedediah married twenty-three-year-old Elizabeth Finley, a granddaughter of the president of Princeton College. In appearance they were unlike, to judge from a later family portrait: Jedediah tall, slender, old-fashioned–looking in his knee breeches and black silk stockings; Elizabeth stoutish, buxom, jowly—"no dwarf," she said of herself. Their personalities differed, too. Jedediah's well-bred manner and sweet voice set him off from his wife's no-nonsense practicality and tart wit. Just the same they made a close, affectionate couple. In letters home he addressed her as "*My dearest Life & Love.*" He borrowed the salutation, he explained, from a letter of George Washington to Martha Washington: "as he is an excellent pattern in almost everything, so in this I would imitate him, believing that my Love for you is as great as his for Mrs. W."

On April 27, 1791, two years after marrying, the couple had their first child, a son whom they named after Elizabeth's father and grandfather: Samuel Finley Breese Morse. Finley, as the family called him, spent his first seven years in the parsonage, a two-story wooden building near the First Church. The household included a pious Baptist servant-nurse, Nancy Shepherd. For a time, a black boy named Abraham also lived with the family, tending the horse and cow. Jedediah ministered to the black population of nearby Boston and publicly condemned the slave trade as inconsistent with republican principles.

Few details of Finley's early childhood remain. When about a year and a half old he contracted smallpox during an epidemic that struck a thousand people in Boston. At the age of four he began attending a dame school near the parsonage. Nancy Shepherd sometimes took him to Bunker's Hill and recounted its historic battle, which she had witnessed.

During the first ten years of their marriage Jedediah and Elizabeth had six more children. Only two survived, Finley's younger brothers Richard and Sidney. In the same period Jedediah became a national figure. While writing sermons and preaching about mankind's fallen state, he issued atlases, school texts, and travel guides with such titles as *The American Universal Geography* (1793) and *The American Gazeteer* (1797). He put the books to press, arranged for British editions, looked after sales and distribution, each year publishing a new geography or revision of some earlier one.

Jedediah's geographies became second in popularity only to Noah Webster's spelling books and the Bible. Producing them put him in touch with notable men at home and abroad. He dined in Philadelphia with Benjamin Franklin and at Mount Vernon with George and Martha Washington. His many, far-flung correspondents included John Adams; the Bishop of London; and the French foreign minister, Talleyrand, who also visited him in Charlestown. His publications brought him an honorary degree from the University of Edinburgh and fame as America's pre-eminent geographer. He did not hide his renown. On the title page of *American Universal Geography* he identified himself as a Doctor of Divinity, Fellow of the American Antiquarian Society, and Fellow of the Historical Society—as "Jedediah Morse, D.D.F.A.A.S.H.S."

Jedediah became prominent in political life as well. Like the rest of the Congregationalist clergy he allied himself with the Federalist party. Against the more liberal, capitalistic social order taking shape in the wake of the American Revolution, he upheld the Calvinistic faith of his New England forebears, whose piety and sense of human dependence on God he considered essential to republican life. He hoped that the new United States would be left to itself, "kept out of the Whirlpool of European Politicks." But there was no insulating the country from the long war for supremacy between Great Britain and Napoleon's France. As the eighteenth century closed, Jedediah like most other Federalists viewed with growing alarm French interference in American affairs: use of American seaports as bases for privateering, attempted bribes to American envoys, manipulation of the American press—especially the export to America of deism, skepticism, Voltairean atheism, and other forms of French Infidelity.

Such ominous political-religious issues brought out a combative side of Jedediah's personality, at odds with his usual mildness. He fought the French Antichrist from his historic pulpit, raging against France as the "destroyer of nations" that had enslaved millions and now menaced the independence of the United States. He sermonized against all the other enemies of Christian Republicanism as well: Masons, Illuminists, Roman Catholics—the last being not Christians but idolators, with a libertine priesthood. All were leagued with the French Imperium, Jedediah warned, in trying to foment revolution in America and ultimately seize the country.

Jedediah's fiery sermons had no political effect. As the new century opened he grimly watched the nation choose for its president the gallified Thomas Jefferson, a man unaccustomed to attending public worship, a professed Infidel: "Unhappy indeed must that Christian people be," Jedediah reflected, "whose Chief Magistrate is an *Atheist*." George Washington had mercifully not lived to see it all: "Ever since his death the clouds seem to have been gathering for a storm."

In 1799, as Jedediah thundered from his pulpit, Finley was sent from home for schooling. Now eight years old, he would spend most of the next decade living apart from his family. Jedediah enrolled him at Phillips Academy, in the isolated village of Andover, Massachusetts, some twenty miles from Charlestown. The well-regarded Academy had about sixty students. Its curriculum stressed classical languages, mathematics, and religious instruction suited to the sons of New England Congregationalists. The school's Overseers included Jedediah himself.

Concerned above all with Finley's growth in piety, Jedediah tried to board him with a prayerful family. He also wrote out a daily routine for his son to follow. It aimed at fashioning a Christian Gentleman—reverent, well mannered, and frugal, but aspiring to personal distinction:

> 1.   Rise early in the morning—read a chapter in the Bible, & say your prayers—Read the Bible in course. The Old Testament in the morning. The New Testament at night—
> 2.   After a serious performance of these religious duties,—comb your head & wash your face, hands & mouth—in cold water, not hastily & slightly but thoroughly—

Next came instructions for Finley's behavior at school:

> 3.   Get your morning lesson well—Behave decently at breakfast. Go regularly & seasonably to the Academy—While there, in study hours, attend to your lesson, & get it thoroughly, & try to be the best scholar in your class.
> 4.   In play hours, while at play, behave manly & honorably. Avoid every thing low, mean, indecent, or unfair—And endeavour to play in such a manner as that all may wish to have you on their side. . . .

"Take care to read your rules every day & observe them strictly," Jedediah said.

Settled in the Academy's preparatory school, Finley hastened to show his father that he understood and would obey. Probably only weeks after arriving in Andover, he sent home a scrawled reply: "I retire always by my self and say my prayers. I learn a hymn every sabbath." Lest Finley forget his routine, Jedediah repeated the rules in nearly the same words week after week. And Elizabeth in her homelier voice repeated them, week after week: "make it your Daily business to obey your kind preceptors," she wrote; "and above all things remember your duty to God pray to him Night and morning and read your chapter in the bible as often and do not read trifling books. . . . be as carefull of all your clothes as possible." Jedediah directed Finley to fold the letters neatly after mastering their content, then tie them together and preserve them in his trunk.

The long-distance family discipline included detailed instructions to Finley on how, each week, he should respond: "You must write me long letters, & vary them as much as possible—avoid sameness," Jedediah said. "Pay great attention to your handwriting." His own letters could not be said to avoid sameness, and the hand was often crooked and blotchy. Nevertheless in letter after letter he insisted that his son reply pleasingly and by rule: "Avoid vulgar phrases. . . . Hold your pen properly and keep your elbow & arm in a right position. . . . Conclude your Letters in this way 'I am your affectionate & obedient Son S. F. B. Morse.' "

The letters Finley received from home often came with long-distance kisses and concerns for his health, gifts of raisins or cake. But mostly they told him what to do and feel and think. At first, the all-seeing discipline did not take. He failed to write back. He got demerits in spelling and for whispering. A tutor reported that he had been idle and untruthful, and had ended up at the bottom of his class. "What a character, my son," Jedediah moaned to him; "if you persevere in this conduct, you will fill our hearts with sorrow." The sorrow was paternal but also personal, for Jedediah expected his children to reflect well on himself. He punished the boy by threatening to keep him at Andover during school vacations. Visits home were an "indulgence," he said, to be granted only when Finley proved "peculiarly attentive to his studies."

Jedediah rarely if ever enforced such threats, and Finley did often return to Charlestown at vacation times. But affairs at home were troubled. Angry party divisions had developed in the continued turmoil over American relations with France and England. Federalists and Jeffersonian Republicans held separate Independence Day ceremonies in Charlestown, both claiming to be the true heirs of the American Revolution. Jedediah's affairs were troubled by more than politics. In many ways he enjoyed his situation in the First Church—a pleasant house and garden rent-free, just a mile from Boston. But the salary of only $11 a week was inadequate to support him and his family, and the congregation refused him a raise. "They are a people of a very peculiar character," he complained. The congregation complained, too. As new editions of Jedediah's geographical works appeared, they objected to the time he devoted to them and his frequent travel away from Charlestown to gather information. Their griping so wounded his feelings, and parish affairs became so disorganized, that he found it difficult to faithfully discharge his ministry. He seriously thought of leaving the place.

And Jedediah and Elizabeth lost another child, their fifth—a boy named Russell who died after a siege of dysentery. Finley learned of the event through a tutor at the Academy, who drew out for him the lesson: "Remember that good children only will hereafter meet in heaven to be forever happy. Earnestly endevour [sic] to be of that number that you may meet your little brother, and all good people in a better world."

Once Finley left the Phillips preparatory school and entered the Academy proper his studies improved, some. Reading the Greek New Testament and the *Aeneid,* he sent home letters in Latin. Jedediah was pleased but, as usual, not entirely: "Write your Latin letters first on a piece of waste paper & shew them to your preceptor, for correction, & then copy them & send them to me." Another time, Finley sent him a three-page summary in English of Plutarch's life of Demosthenes: "written very well for one of his age," Jedediah conceded. "He omitted an important circumstance, however."

And Finley's improvement turned out to be temporary, or worse. He soon wrote home asking Jedediah's permission to quit Greek and Latin, to study English instead. He could not remember the lessons, he said, and was often put back. Jedediah recommended greater application and perseverance: "All good scholars have found it laborious to acquire knowledge—the 'hills of science, is [*sic*] represented as steep & of difficult ascent.' "

Of Finley's improvement in piety there was less doubt. In the evenings he began reading about and summarizing the lives of Protestant martyrs, devout ministers who for their faith had been jailed, assassinated, burned at the stake. When his younger brothers Sidney and Richard entered the Academy, he read them religious works. Sometimes he adopted with them the godly manner of their pious elders. When Elizabeth again gave birth to a stillborn child—the sixth of her children to die—he told Sidney and Richard: "Now you have three brothers & three sisters in heaven, and I hope you & I will meet them there at our death. It is uncertain when we shall die, but we ought to be prepared for it." He presented them a copy of *The Christian Pilgrim*.

While becoming more learned and pious, as his parents wished, Finley also began finding his own way. In taking drawing as one of his academic subjects, at about the age of eleven, he discovered a talent for art. He sent samples of his work to Charlestown. The much-published Jedediah had his own share of worldly gentility, and boasted about his son's gift: "he is self taught—has had no instructions." He encouraged the boy, but reminded him that art should be "your amusement merely," and that his approval was not a given but a reward. He promised Finley a drawing book—"if I find when he comes home that he is improved & grown manly & genteel in his manners." Another time he promised Finley a paint box—if he learned by heart and recited well an oration on George Washington.

Finley's talent developed quickly. By the age of twelve he was creating miniatures—small portraits painted on slices of ivory. And his handwriting began taking on the copperplate elegance it would retain to the end of his long life.

In the fall of 1805 Finley entered Yale College. The choice was inevitable. Not only was the school a Congregationalist bastion, but Jedediah had also earned two degrees there, taught there, and befriended Yale's president, Timothy Dwight. A famous Congregationalist minister himself, called by some "The Pope of Federalism," Dwight, too, had vigorously preached and written against the French peril. Under his effective administration, Yale was growing from a local college into a national university.

Finley now learned something of what it meant to have "The Father of American Geography" for his father. When he stopped at an inn during his first trip to New Haven, the owner treated him with special kindness, "more like his own son than a stranger," he wrote home, "wholly on account of my being your son." Once he arrived at the school, President Dwight took a personal interest in him. And fellow students nicknamed him "Geography."

But attending Yale also had drawbacks for Finley. From Charlestown to New Haven was 160 miles, thirty dusty hours of horseback, chaise, stagecoach, and overnight taverns. He would rarely get home to see his family. And he was fourteen and a half, while most entering students were about sixteen. Jedediah and Elizabeth feared his falling in with older boys who might corrupt him. So instead of enrolling him as a regular member of the freshman class they boarded him off campus in the family of a Yale instructor. There he would do freshman work but postpone his formal admission until the following year.

Finley felt belittled by the arrangement, as he let his parents know by again getting off to a bad start. During his first month in New Haven, Jedediah and Elizabeth received only one letter from him. "We are extremely anxious to hear from you," Jedediah informed him; "Your Mama is distressed & almost sick with anxiety lest you are sick."

When Finley at last wrote to his parents, he sent more for them to be anxious about. He protested that because he had not been regularly enrolled he had already fallen behind the other freshmen in his studies. Elizabeth was unconvinced: "I am fearful my son that you think a great deal more of your Amusements than your studies and there lies the difficulty and the same dificulty [sic] would exist were you in Colledge." Finley's letter also served notice that when he officially became a student he would want brandy, wine, and cigars for his room. "Pray is that a custom among the students," Elizabeth wanted to know; "your papa & myself positively prohibit you the use of these things." As if this were not enough, Finley also mentioned that he had gone out hunting, on a "gunning party." Elizabeth, always worried about his health and safety, gasped: "Does the Government of Colledge allow the Students to go a guning?"

The question of Finley's status at Yale became a family quarrel. In letter after letter he bemoaned his failure to progress in his studies. The regular scholars got through fifty lines of Homer daily while he did twenty-eight: "I fall behind my class every day; it makes me homesick & very unhappy." Every student that he knew advised him to get a room at the college as soon as possible. But Jedediah insisted he was "well situated" and Elizabeth told him to stop whining: "determine to be happy just in the situation that providence has plac'd you in & think that your Friends know better than you *can possibly* which situation is best for you."

Finley retaliated in his own way. His letters shrank to a half page of large script: "I am in great haste to study, therefore . . . excuse my brevity & bad writing." He had a headache, he said. An earache, a stiff neck. After months of bickering, Jedediah agreed to let Finley enter the regular class, on three conditions. First, he would have to catch up on his studies; second, Elizabeth said, "no use of Segars or Brandy or Wine or any thing of the kind"; third, their young son would have to board with a private family off campus.

The last condition set off a new struggle, fought on Finley's side with more lightly veiled threats. He lived so far from school, he now protested, that he could not hear the campus bell—causing him to miss prayers: "It is very necessary that I should room in college as soon as possible. I am absent from prayers and resitation [*sic*] very often." Living off campus made it necessary for him to go on gunning parties, too: "I need some exercise. If I walk that is no amusement & if I wish to play ball or any thing else I have no one to play with."

Around the fall of 1807, when he was sixteen, Finley did at last settle in his own room at the College. Again Jedediah and Elizabeth reminded him weekly of his fallen state and need to seek Christ. But they stressed more urgently than before the need to economize. Scrimping by on Jedediah's thankless salary, and with two other sons to raise, they sent Finley hand-me-down slippers, patches for his shirts and coats: "be careful my son not to dirt [*sic*] more Clothes than is necesary [*sic*]," Elizabeth wrote; "Washing is so Dear put on two clean Shirts a week two Neck Cloths & one pair of stockings is enough." Finley wanted to show that he understood: "You expend & have expended a great deal more money on me than I deserve," he said, "& granted me a great many of my requests & I am sure I can certainly grant you one, that of being *economical.*"

But Finley found his promise hard to keep. He ran up a staggering bill of $43 at the College Buttery—the campus outlet for ice cream, port ("for my health," he explained), and the cigars that he continued to smoke. Elizabeth rebuked his money-wasting and condemned the place as a hangout for "Idle Gluttons among the scholars." She thought no better of Finley's desire for a new, fashionable coat. His brown one for every day and blue one for the Sabbath sufficed, she said, "quite enough for any boy that is not a going to be an extravagant foolish fellow. You will remember that you have promised in your first letter to be an oeconomist."

Finley knew that his letters home often sounded grasping and manipulative. He parodied one of them for his brothers' amusement: "Please send me a pocketbook, please send me some Hale cider, please send me some kittens and young puppies. I now take this opportunity of writing to you to inform you that I am sick." But in truth one could not live at the College without spending money, and it irked him to be scolded for having his ice skates sharpened: "I think every minute I shall recieve [sic] a letter from home blaming me for not being more economical & thus I am kept in distress all the time."

Jedediah and Elizabeth prodded Finley to stay at the head of his class. Despite his lively intellect, however, his academic record was mediocre. One time or another he studied history, philosophy, English composition, Greek and French, geometry and trigonometry. But he failed to earn such college distinctions as a junior-class "Appointment" ("I am 'disappointed,'" he kidded). When his brothers joined him at Yale, about halfway through his schooling, they both outshone him. Richard was chosen to deliver a commencement address; Sidney made Phi Beta Kappa.

Finley's lusterless performance confirmed his parents' suspicion that their son was flighty. His moods and desires shifted in an unmanly way. Now he wanted to change roommates, then to room by himself, another time to drop his studies and come home for a while. Elizabeth chided him for "driving on from one foolish Whim to another." Jedediah made it clear that between a resolute and a restless spirit the difference was success in life or failure: "steady and undissipated attention to one object, is a sure mark of a superior genius," he wrote to Finley; "cease your fondness for continual change. It is a bad habit

& you must strive to break it or it will be ruinous to you. Resolve to be *steady*."

But at Yale as before at the Academy, Finley found a way to what interested him. He was drawn to science. Scientific training at most American colleges was outdated and meagerly equipped with apparatus. Through President Dwight's efforts to hire outstanding faculty, however, Yale's science offering was superior to that of most other schools. Finley attended the chemistry classes of Professor Benjamin Silliman (1779–1864), who later organized the Yale Medical School. Silliman's lectures included demonstrations of galvanic electricity, in which he explained the construction and operation of such current-producing devices as the Voltaic pile and the Cruikshank battery. Apparently fascinated by the subject, Finley spent one school vacation in the college's "Philosophical Chamber," assisting a tutor in electrical experiments. He also attended the demonstrations given by Jeremiah Day, Professor of Natural Philosophy. Day had all of the students hold hands to form a circuit, which he electrified: "it felt as if some person had struck me a slight blow across the arms," Finley wrote home; "we all received the shock apparently at the same moment."

Finley developed literary interests as well. He swapped an eight-volume set of Montaigne for a copy of *Gil Blas*, "not so much for the books contents," he tried to explain to his parents, "as its acquainting me more thoroughly with the Language." Jedediah and Elizabeth insisted that he return the book. They were no happier when after selling his gun for $4 he bought a copy of Edward Young's *Night Thoughts* and an unidentified play "which I consider as *trash*," he wrote home, "& only took them that I might sell them again." He tried writing verse himself, a dramatic dialogue in which an old Revolutionary War veteran prays to the Goddess of Liberty that "I may live forever free." For one of his college compositions he also wrote an essay on "Beauty." It treated painting and natural landscapes together, under the same three aesthetic principles of Variety, Proportion, and Uniformity.

Finley continued to paint, too, more seriously than before and now with some profit. His parents would not have approved what he reportedly sketched on the wall of his room—a scene of freshmen scrambling up the Hill of Science on their hands and knees, a burlesque of his father's admonitions to him about the labor of acquiring knowledge. But he found Yale faculty and other New Havenites willing to pay a dollar for his watercolor profiles of them on paper or $5 for ivory miniatures. He did a miniature of himself as well, a Portrait of the Artist as a genial stylish Young Man. His commissions gave him the means not only to buy his own paint supplies, but also to pay off some of his buttery bills and treat himself to a fashionable double-breasted waistcoat.

Samuel F. B. Morse, *Self Portrait* (ca. 1809)
(National Academy of Design)

Jedediah and Elizabeth badly missed their sons. By her account, they often looked at the picture of the far-off College Finley had painted for them, saying, "Now the boys are going in to prayers & now to recitation & now to commons." Nor did the couple find comfort in Charlestown. Jedediah's disgruntled congregation excluded him from a commemoration of the founders of New England, determined, he said, "to mortify and 'put me down' as they express it." And Elizabeth lost two more daughters, one a few days after birth. Eight of her children had died, leaving only Finley, Sidney, and Richard.

The world outside Charlestown offered not much comfort either. Jedediah was alarmed at the growing appeal in New England of liberal Protestant sects. Unitarianism did the most harm—"the *democracy* of Christianity," he called it, softheaded optimistic worship with no vision of human degeneracy since The Fall. "It dissolves all the bonds of Christian union, & deprives religion of all its efficacy & influence upon Society." He especially worried about the influence of Unitarianism at Harvard, the great training ground for the Congregationalist ministry: "the ancient fountain will be poisoned & its streams henceforth be the bane of evangelical religion." To combat this threat to American Calvinism he launched the *Panoplist,* a militant religious periodical designed to uphold "the truth as it is in Jesus." Relieved that his boys were at Yale and not at Harvard, he sent copies for them to read and keep for their libraries.

The political situation too had worsened. With France and Great Britain both harassing American commercial shipping in their never-ending conflict, Jedediah feared that the United States would come to war with one or the other. President Jefferson and Congress had tried to retaliate by restricting trade, forbidding any American vessel to sail from the United States to a foreign port. But the embargo crippled New England's once-prosperous maritime business and disrupted the American economy. To Jedediah, the country's future, clouded as well with Infidelism and Unitarianism, looked dismal: "Our Nation, alas, how fallen!—What is to become of us?"

Finley's graduation from Yale, in 1810, was for him a mixed occasion of delight and misery. The delight he owed to a young Saybrook woman named Jennette Hart, apparently his first romantic attachment. During the commencement season he sat beside her at tea parties, walked with her in the evenings, read Milton to her—"and while my eye was on the book my heart was with you," he said. He counted himself "the happiest mortal breathing."

The misery arose from Finley's vocational plans. He had decided, he wrote to his parents, to be a painter. The decision was chancy. America had no community of artists, no schools of instruction, no great collections, no part in the urgent continental debates on aesthetics. Paint, brushes, and other basic materials were scarce, and many Americans associated art with luxury and self-indulgence, forces that corrupted republics. Yet Finley asked his parents to arrange for him to study in Boston with Washington Allston (1779–1843), an American painter of growing prominence. Not surprisingly, "Geography" had developed a yearning to travel, and hoped that after studying with Allston in the winter he would be allowed to accompany the artist to London: "I should admire to be able to go with him."

Jedediah put off a full response until he could speak with Finley during the Yale commencement, which he always attended. Meanwhile he told the boy to do nothing: "it will be best for you to form no plans. Your mama and I have been thinking and planning for you." The plan, when he revealed it to Finley in New Haven, was for his son to become an apprentice to one of his publishers, the Boston booksellers Farrand & Mallory.

After learning the plan, Finley wrote to his mother assuring her that he would do what his parents thought best for him. "I was determined beforehand to conform to his and your will in everything." The obligation to gratify his parents had been preached to him in letter after letter from home, week after week. But within and around their demands for compliance he had followed his own inclinations and talents, not to be sacrificed without pain. "I have been extremely low-spirited for some days past, and it still continues," he added, without explaining to Elizabeth why or for what reason; "I am so low in spirits that I could almost cry."

Returned to Charlestown, Finley started work at Farrand & Mallory's bookstore at an annual salary of $400. He needed the money. He had left Yale with debts, a fact he concealed from his parents; creditors in New Haven were dunning him for payment. Lonely, he missed Jennette Hart, to whom he sent an edition of Sir Walter Scott. Evenings he spent painting, fitting up a room above the kitchen of the parsonage and working by lamplight.

Finley's training for the book business lasted only about three months. Once again Jedediah softened and gave in, this time generously and on no small matter. He would afford Finley a chance to become an artist. "His parents had designed him for a different profession," Jedediah explained, "but his inclination for the one he has chosen was so strong . . . that we thought it not proper to attempt to control his choice." The new plan called for Finley to remain at home until the summer helping Jedediah prepare his geographies, then accompany Washington Allston and Allston's wife to London for three years of study.

Washington Allston, *Self Portrait* (1805)
(Museum of Fine Arts, Boston)

It was Allston himself who had changed Jedediah's mind. He had been painting in a Boston studio, a pale, brooding, cultivated young man with large blue eyes and silken black hair. Seven years of training in London, Paris, and Rome had made him the most accomplished and promising American painter in the generation after Benjamin West and John Singleton Copley. Having seen and approved some of

Samuel F. B. Morse, *Morse Family Portrait Group* (ca. 1809)
(National Museum of American History)

Finley's works, he persuaded Jedediah and Elizabeth to allow Finley to join him when he returned to England.

While waiting out the six months before his departure, Finley informally began his studies. He attended lectures on anatomy given in Boston by the eminent physician Dr. John Warren. With Allston's guidance he also kept painting. Several works from the period of his late teens survive. They include an unfinished liny watercolor of his family, himself leaning in over his mother's shoulder as Jedediah discourses on geography. Daring to paint a historical subject in the grand style, he at first considered depicting the defeated Roman general Marius viewing the ruins of Carthage—an image of the mutability of empires and of human fortune. Instead he chose a subject that might induce not only moral elevation but also patriotic pride—the landing of the Pilgrims at Plymouth, heroic windswept figures on a canvas some four feet by five, ambitious though crudely jumbled.

Having consented to Finley's plans, Jedediah felt uneasy about them. Providing the boy's expenses for a three-year stay in London would be a hardship. American-British relations were tense, too. Presi-

Samuel F. B. Morse, *The Landing of the Pilgrims at Plymouth*
(Boston Public Library)

dent James Madison and Congress had reinstated a policy of non-intercourse that forbade American trade with England. And the boy was only nineteen years old: "what must be our solicitude for a son, at his critical age," Jedediah confided, "removed at such a distance from us, with little experience or knowledge of mankind, in a land of strangers, & exposed to the various evils & snares of the world."

Probably toward the end of June, Finley left Charlestown for New York City, there to depart for England in mid-July. Traveling first to New Haven in a stagecoach stiflingly hot under the summer sun, he stopped off at Yale to say good-bye to his brothers. His coastal packet boat to New York was becalmed for two days. And when he at last reached the city, it roasted him with its worst heat in fourteen years— 116 degrees, he claimed.

Finley spent two weeks in New York before his departure. He bought the bedding he would need aboard ship—mattress, pillows, sheets. He enjoyed passing an afternoon with Allston's Knickerbocker friend Washington Irving, just twenty-eight years old but already America's first literary celebrity. He got to meet some of his thirteen fellow passengers, an exotic group that included a Prussian, a Russian, a Scotsman, and a minor comic dramatist, John Minshull, author of *He Stoops to Conquer, or, The Virgin Wife Triumphant.*

With two piano-playing passengers and a pianoforte aboard, the voyage promised to be agreeable and Finley felt in good spirits, although once the ship got under sail with a fair wind off Sandy Hook, he admitted to feeling also a bit strange, "rather singularly," he said, "to see my native shores disappearing so fast and for so long a time."

TWO

———

No One Uninspired
by the Muses May Enter

(1811–1815)

L ONDON seemed overwhelming, "unlike any thing I had seen
before," Finley wrote. Here was the richest city in the world—
noisy, smoky, bustling with commerce and industry, ten miles of
labyrinthine streets covered with buildings, "whole forests of spires &
towers rising up in all directions."

The honored place of artists in London society also came as a
shock. Americans regarded painters as members of the "lower class of
people"; Londoners ranked painters with lords or barons, "& a person
cannot be better recommended than by avowing himself a painter."
Indeed, in London art exhibitions were resorts of the fashionable, art
was a constant subject of conversation, and no one was considered well
educated who lacked an enthusiastic love of painting.

Finley took rooms on Great Titchfield Street, in the Marylebone
district, sharing his quarters with another young American artist,
Charles Leslie (1794–1859). Only sixteen years old, Leslie had come
to London from Philadelphia to study painting for two years. "Every
thing we do has a reference to the art," Finley said, "and all our plans
are for our mutual advancement in it." Finley expected good things of
his roommate, predicting that Leslie would become an ornament to
the new nation's culture, as he hoped to become himself.

Many other artists lived in Marylebone, including Benjamin West,
Henry Fuseli, and Allston. Finley visited Allston every evening and
soon learned that London connoisseurs considered him the painter to
watch, destined to "carry the art to greater perfection than it ever has

been carried, either in ancient or in modern times." Allston was beginning work on his large *Dead Man Restored to Life by Touching the Bones of the Prophet Elisha,* a characteristic dramatization of Divine power, with elements of gothic horror, that would establish his reputation on both sides of the Atlantic. Finley cherished Allston's practical and theoretical instruction, and the example he set of high-mindedness. Allston refused to leave off a painting until it satisfied him, and scorned mere moneymaking. "Oh! he is an angel on earth," Finley wrote, "I cannot love him too much."

Through Allston, Finley got to meet the legendary founder of American art, Benjamin West. Now an amiable, white-haired sophisticate of seventy-three, West had left Philadelphia fifty years earlier as a barely literate Quaker youth, to study and paint in Rome. His progress over the next decade had been astonishing. Moving to London, he helped to create the Royal Academy of Arts, at the request of King George III. His *Death of General Wolfe* excited more interest than any other American picture that had ever been exhibited. Its use of modern dress and contemporary events constituted a revolution in the painting of history. West had never returned to America, but Finley found him eager to know the state of the arts there. Having painted some six hundred pictures in his lifetime—"more than any artist ever did, with the exception of Rubens," Finley said—West was still active, presiding over the Royal Academy and working on eight or nine different paintings at a time.

Only a few days after Finley's arrival in London, West took him to see his celebrated life-size sermon on canvas, *Christ Healing the Sick.* It was probably the first important original painting Finley had ever seen, dazzling: "A sight of it is worth a voyage across the Atlantic." He may have been less impressed by West's comment that during six weeks of exhibition the picture took in some £9000 ($50,000). Finley came to feel that he could not respect West, despite the grandeur of his thought and perfect understanding of artistic theory. He continued to seek his advice, but believed that Allston would almost as much surpass West as West had surpassed earlier American painters.

With an introduction from West, Finley was admitted as a student at the British Institution. Founded six years earlier to stimulate interest in British art, the Institution was governed mainly by connoisseurs, not artists. Probably for this reason, Finley tried to gain admission instead to the Royal Academy. That was not easy. The select Academy enrolled only about thirty students. They gained entrance by submitting a drawing that, among other virtues, demonstrated an accurate knowledge of anatomy. According to Finley, most applicants had drawn for three or four years before they ventured to submit a figure; yet some were turned down even after a second and third application. But he believed that the anatomical lectures he had attended in Boston would help, and anyway he welcomed the challenge: "the harder it is to gain admittance the greater the honor it will be should I enter."

Finley first decided to submit a drawing of a classical statue of The Gladiator. Displeased with it, he made another—from a plaster cast of the Laocoön, "the most difficult of all the statues." Allston praised this drawing as superior to most such works made by third-year students. It at least succeeded in getting Finley admitted to the Royal Academy for a year as a "probationer."

Finley entered an exclusive artistic domain, sumptuous beyond anything in the raw United States. The Academy was located in Somerset House, a monumental palace fronting the Thames, all colonnades and classical pilasters. Within the Academy were an Antique school, where students drew from casts of classical statues; a meeting room and library, adorned with paintings by West and Sir Joshua Reynolds; and a nearly fifty-foot-square Great Room for exhibitions, inscribed above the doorway, in Greek, "No one uninspired by the Muses may enter." The Academy did not teach painting, offering instruction only in drawing the human figure. Students painted at home. Older artists sometimes dropped in to draw from a model, so at the next easel a student might find, say, J. M. W. Turner.

Between study at the prestigious Academy and work at his lodgings, Finley painted and drew all day and into the evening. As practice he and Charles Leslie posed for each other in fancy costume—Finley in Scotch tartan plaid with plumed bonnet—and did portraits of acquaintances, who paid for the canvas and colors. Sometimes they painted together in the fields in the open air before breakfast, to study the effect of morning light on the landscape. On his own Finley often walked the mile and a half from his lodgings to Burlington House, residence of Lord Elgin, to draw from the celebrated Elgin marbles, fifth-century B.C. sculptured friezes that, in his view, made all later sculpture seem inferior. Although most of Finley's London works have unfortunately become lost, a profile self-portrait painted around 1812 survives—himself as a handsome romantic figure of vivid eye and curling dark hair.*

Allston oversaw Finley's progress. His blunt criticism was not easy to take, as Finley admitted:

> It is a mortifying thing sometimes to me, when I have been painting all day very hard, and begin to be pleased with what I have done, and on showing it to Mr. Allston with the expectation of praise, and not only of praise, but a score of "*excellents*," "*well dones*," and "*admirables*," I say it is mortifying to hear him after a long silence say, "*very bad Sir, that is not flesh, it is 'mud' Sir, it is painted with 'brick dust and clay.'*"

At such moments Finley sometimes felt ready to gash the canvas. But on reflection he realized that to improve he must see his own faults. And Allston invariably cheered him up by offering practical advice: "*put a few flesh tints here, a few grey ones there . . . clear up such & such a part, by such and such colors.*" Sometimes Allston took the palette and brushes and showed him how.

With Finley's growing competence came enlarged interest in painting, deeper understanding of its demands, and greater clarity about his own aims. He undertook a program of reading—"the old poets, Spencer [*sic*], Chaucer, Dante, Tasso &c &c. these are necessary to a painter." He understood that the painter must study everything in nature with minute attention, under varying conditions. Every species of tree, for instance, then its different parts, then

> the color of those different parts in light or in shade, near or at a distance, and then at the different seasons of the year, in spring when they are fresh, in summer when they are ripe and in perfection, in autumn when they fade, and in winter when without leaves, in motion or at rest, and also at different parts of the day, morning noon at night, effect of strong sunshine or of a cloudy threatening atmosphere upon them.

A tree being only a small part of a picture, and of nature, he concluded that he would count himself successful if after eight or ten

*Reproduced on p. 2.

years he could paint "tolerably." And ultimately, following the example of West, he wished to excel in "history painting," the depiction of dramatic scriptural, historical, or mythological scenes. Such works were generally held to be the highest form of the art: "as epic poetry excels all other kinds of poetry, because it addresses itself to the sublimer feelings of our nature, so does historical painting stand preëminent in our art, because it calls forth the same feelings."

Finley was not daunted by these long-term demands on his energy, intellect, and skill. On the contrary, they deepened his growing sense of consecration, that he now and for the future had a calling: "My passion for my art is so firmly rooted that I am confident no human power could destroy it."

Finley took time off from his easel to relax and to get around London. When in his quarters his main amusements were music and smoking. His father liked to sing, and before being ordained had even taught a singing school. Finley now got a pianoforte, and apparently learned to play it; he entertained fellow artists at his rooms, one of them said, with "Novels Coffee and *Musick by Morse.*" He had smuggled a supply of American cigars into England, stuffing some in his pockets and hat, and another hundred or so in his trunk. He slipped the contraband past a good-natured customs officer by giving him a few dozen "for his kindness." Allston was a great smoker, too, the mantel in his painting room fringed with cigar stubs. For Finley, puffing an evening cigar with Allston meant knowing bliss, "that if there was ever a happy being in the world, *I was that person.*"

Once settled in London, Finley saw the sights. He took in Vauxhall, the crown jewels, the races at Epsom, and the annual St. Bartholomew's Fair, with its slack-wire dancers, pickpockets, and deafening confusion of fiddles and drums. In front of St. James's Palace he got his first glimpse of royalty—the heavy-drinking Prince of Wales, "very red and considerably bloated." Over time he ventured into the countryside to shoot target practice against a tree, and visited Oxford, the cliffs of Dover, Stratford-upon-Avon. He discovered that in London, as in America, his father was known "pretty extensively." People who learned that he was an American named Morse often asked if he was related to Jedediah.

Through Allston and West, and on his own, Finley gained some entry into London's intellectual and literary society. He got to meet the liberal reformer William Wilberforce, the poet Samuel Rogers, and the essayist Charles Lamb. He was especially impressed by Allston's friend Samuel Taylor Coleridge, lecturing in London on Shakespeare and Milton but in ill health and struggling against his opium addiction. Coleridge visited Finley and Leslie in their rooms, where they reportedly tried to relieve his melancholy by drawing him out on aesthetic and metaphysical questions. It also "much pleased" Finley to befriend the colorful American playwright-actor John Howard Payne, said to be the bastard of Tom Paine. Just Finley's age, Payne had created a sensation as a boy actor in New York. In Boston he became the first American to act Hamlet, playing opposite the Ophelia of Elizabeth Poe—three months after she had given birth to the later-famous son she named Edgar.

Finley became an ardent theatergoer himself. A rebuilt Covent Garden had opened in 1809, one of the largest theaters in Europe, holding nearly three thousand spectators. Finley went often to enjoy "the best acting in the world," he said, especially the great Sarah Siddons, "the best tragic actress perhaps that ever lived." One time he made a theater party with Coleridge, Leslie, and Allston to see the opening of Coleridge's tragedy *Remorse*. He even tried his hand at writing a farce. He created the main character with Charles Mathews in mind, hoping that this celebrated comedian might consider staging his play on a benefit night. He sent a copy to Mathews, assuring him that the work had widespread approval—"not only of my theatrical friends generally, but of some confessed critics."

Finley's new way of life, with its farces, cheroots, and addicted poets, took some explaining to his pious parents. He wrote home often, assuring them of his efforts to be what his mother called a "good child." His roommate, Leslie, was exemplary, he promised, "very agreeable, industrious, steady." He himself had become a steady person, having chosen art for his life's work. He thanked his parents for having tolerated his earlier fidgeting: "They have watched every change of my capricious inclinations," he wrote home; "I hope that one day my success in my profession will reward you in some measure for the trouble and inconvenience I have so long put you to." As if to mark his new identity, he stamped the seal of at least one letter with an antique gem—a replica of the original, which had sat in the seal ring of Michelangelo.

But to Elizabeth and Jedediah, Finley's devotion to painting was itself worrisome. "He is so absorb'd in his *art* that every thing else is considered unimportant," she complained to Finley; "I hope he will not think so much of that or any thing else in this Vain World as to neglect his precious soul." His spiritual nature, in fact, remained undeveloped. He attended a Congregational church near his lodgings, but had yet to experience conversion—the quasi-mystical assurance that he truly loved God, entitling him to full church membership. "The acquisition of a *new heart,*" his father wrote to him, "would give us more pleasure than any other you could name. Fail not to be emulous of this honor & happiness in preference to every other." Their son did not seem headed in the right direction, however. Elizabeth frowned on his evenings at Drury Lane—"a most bewitching amusement," she warned, "ruinous both to soul and body." Nor did she applaud his keeping company with young Payne, American Hamlet though he was: "however pure you may believe his morals to be. . . . he is in a situation to ruin the best morals."

Parents and child scrapped about money as well. Jedediah had agreed to provide Finley an annual allowance of about $800. But Finley protested that to get by on that amount he had to deny himself necessary art supplies, and ordinary needs and pleasures: "I am treated with no dainties, no fruit, no nice dinners," he wrote home, sounding like the Yale undergraduate rather than the scion of Michelangelo; "I have had no new clothes for nearly a year; my best are threadbare, and my shoes out at the toes." His wheedling stirred compassion (guilt?) in Jedediah, who praised his thrift but urged him not to risk his health or reputation by it. "Let your appearance be suited to the respectable company you keep, and your living such as will conduce most effectually to preserve health of body and vigor of mind. We shall all be willing to make sacrifices at home so far as may be necessary to the above purposes." He raised Finley's allowance to $1000.

Finley stayed in touch with his brothers, Sidney and Richard. Both were completing their studies at Yale and helping Jedediah to ready new geographies for the press. Jedediah tried to enlist Finley as well, offering to send him a volume on American geography that he might try to get reprinted in England, retaining the copyright and the profit.

But Finley resisted being drawn into the business world: "my mind has been so habitually employed in works of fancy and imagination, that I found myself perfectly stupid, the moment I thought of the plain, dry, matter of fact, book accounts."

Jennette Hart, the young woman he had courted in New Haven, stayed on Finley's mind, too. He wrote to her recalling their cotillion parties and evening walks. But he did not commit himself, signing his letters with emphatic lukewarmth: "Your very sincere *friend.*" He apparently did not seek much female companionship. English women, compared with American, seemed to him haughty and designing: "all is reserve, affectation, and art." Besides, he had no time for romance. "I find that *love* and *painting* are quarrelsome companions, and that the house of my heart was too small for both of them; so I have turned *Mrs. Love* out-of-doors."

One feature of London life angered Finley: the general contempt for America. It had found brutal expression after Napoleon declared a blockade of the British Isles, intending to cripple England by destroying its commerce. The British government replied with Orders in Council declaring a blockade on France. Under the Orders, England freely seized American vessels supposedly trading with the French or their allies. In four and a half years, 390 American ships were taken. American merchantmen were impressed and forced to serve in the Royal Navy. Officials such as Lord Castlereagh, the foreign secretary, assured the public that America was compelled to submit because too weak to resist.

Born in the shadow of Bunker's Hill, Finley shared with the gentry of the Revolutionary generation a deep concern for personal and national honor. It galled him to read in London newspapers the names of American vessels detained or captured for trading with France. Invited to dine one evening at the home of John Thornton, a noted English philanthropist, he heard his host argue that only the British navy protected America's shores against Napoleon's obsession with conquest, that Britain was fighting for the liberties of the world, "that America was in a great degree interested in the decision of the contest, and that she ought to be content to suffer a little."

No admirer of Napoleon, Finley, too, considered British arms the best hope of preserving liberty in Europe. But this did not excuse legalized British sea robbery against America. If England did not repeal the Orders in Council, he believed, the United States should declare war, "or we cease to be an independent nation." Across the water, many Americans north and south believed the same. The New Hampshire *Patriot* called on the government to take spirited action, "or the United States will become proverbial for servility and debasement." The nation's failure to resist attacks on its commerce already called into question the vitality of its republican ideals. "Our government is despised for its want of energy," the Richmond *Enquirer* wrote, "and our people are held up to scorn for their unmanly sacrifice of rights."

Over the first half of 1812, as Finley turned twenty-one, Parliament and the British press vigorously debated the question of repeal. On May 11 an ardent supporter of the Orders, Prime Minister Spencer Perceval, was shot through the heart as he entered the House of Commons. Finley joined an immense crowd that gathered to view the scene. The following week he went to see Perceval's assassin mount the scaffold—a man genteelly dressed, who bowed to the crowd, cried out "God bless you," and drew the cap of execution over his face. The country now seemed to Finley dangerously volatile, "in a very alarming state. . . . London must soon be the scene of dreadful events."

One month later, Congress voted by narrow margins to declare war on England. As had happened to Benjamin West at the time of the American Revolution, Finley found himself living in the land of the enemy. As he sat at some coffeehouse or dinner party, he heard English gentlemen discuss sending twenty thousand troops to take New York City and deride the American navy as "*below the Chinese.*" In naval terms the conflict was wildly unequal: the U.S. force consisted of sixteen ships, Britain's of over six hundred. Given the odds, Finley exulted in reports of American victories at sea: "the *Essex* frigate has taken the Sloop of War *Alert;* bravo!—the privateer *Yankee* in the West Indies is showing them some yankee tricks." He longed to join the navy himself, to "teach these insolent Englishmen how to respect us."

Jedediah and Elizabeth did not join in their son's cheers. Solid Congregationalist-Federalists, they viewed England as the defender of the Christian civilization of the West against atheistic France. America's "mad rulers," Elizabeth wrote to Finley, had plunged the nation into chaos, "into an unnecessary War with a country that I shall always *revere* as doing more to spread the glorious Gospel of Jesus Christ . . .

than any other nation on the globe." Finley's parents not only disliked his politics. They also worried that it might be dangerous for him to discuss his beliefs with others in England. "Be the *artist* wholly," his father cautioned, "& let *politics* alone."

But for Finley there was no separating art and politics. What mattered was that America be respected abroad. This meant that while achieving its own artistic culture, the country must also show that it could not be intimidated. "The only way to please John Bull is to give him a good beating," he told his parents, "and such is the singularity of his character, that the more you beat him the greater is his respect for you and the more he will esteem you." Thus beaten by American frigates, the British were already changing their tune. "What!"—he now heard it said—"is this the cowardly, weak, inefficient race of men, we have so often sneered at." And not only the British. Italian, Dutch, and Swedish newspapers, he added, also reported the country's naval victories, and "speak in raptures of the rising greatness of America."

Finley dismissed as fantasy the Federalist charge that in waging war against England, the American government was aiding Napoleon. In fact, by convincing Americans that they needed a strong navy, the war would equip the country to also chastise France, for *its* insolence. He told his parents that, in his view, many New Englanders who decried the war did so not from political or religious principle but to prevent any interruption of their business affairs: "Is this the spirit of -'76? the spirit of -'76 was *sacrifice of individual interest for the good of the public;* their spirit seems to be, *the sacrifice of the public interest for that of the individual.*"

Finley's parents did not enjoy his lectures. Jedediah stiffened: "It is with great difficulty & self denial that we maintain you abroad. We cannot do it, for the purpose of making you a *politician.*" But two years of independence in England had made Finley more restive than ever under his parents' control. When Jedediah sent one of his recent sermons, attacking American policy for undermining "the only Christian nation beside ourselves," Finley returned an anti-Federalist tirade, nineteen closely written pages long. It came laced with hints of old resentment over inadequate financial support, attempts to maneuver him into the book business.

Now a student at the Royal Academy, a protégé of Washington Allston, Finley made it clear to his parents that he and his ideas deserved to be taken seriously. "I find I am three and twenty years old, that I am neither blind nor deaf, can hear, and I hope understand, that I have some judgment in many things, that I can trace the causes of that judgment to their sources . . . that I am in England, wide awake & that it is no dream; now having found all this I begin to exercise my judgment."

Finley worked on through the wartime tension. He decided to submit a painting for the 1813 exhibition of the Royal Academy. He began by making a two-foot-long clay model of the famous Farnese Hercules, his first attempt at sculpture. It pleased Allston, who did much modeling in clay and recommended the practice to young painters for gaining accurate knowledge of the joints. West praised it as no mere academic exercise, saying that it "displayed *thought*." Finley glowed: "He could not have paid me a higher compliment."

Finley used his sculpture of Hercules as a model for a painting of the same subject. Following West's advice to "paint *large*," he made a picture eight feet by six and a half. A Michelangelesque titan of bulging muscularity, the dying Hercules strains to lift himself from a rock. He holds aloft the lethal robe that has poisoned him, his agonized body powerfully dominating the canvas as a diagonal slash. By Finley's account, West told him that should he live to be West's own age he would never make a better composition.

The judges at the Royal Academy agreed. They rejected six hundred pictures submitted for the exhibition but accepted Finley's *Hercules,* to be displayed with canvases by West, Sir Thomas Lawrence, Turner, and John Constable. Even in this distinguished company the painting made an impression. The London *Globe* commented that several unheralded artists had shown works of "very high merit," ranking Finley and one other painter at "the head of this class." The exhibition won him more than a blurb. The Adelphi Society of Arts awarded his statue its gold medal for the best piece of sculpture. The prize was presented to him by the Duke of Norfolk before a large assembly that included the ambassadors of Turkey, Sardinia, and Russia.

Finley's parents had long and repeatedly asked him to send evidence of his progress. "We have not seen any of your handy work except the picture in India ink of yourself," Elizabeth complained, "which we did not think a good likeness." But Finley now had something to show. He sent home a flattering press clipping about his painting, a plaster cast of his sculpture, and his gold medal from the

Samuel F. B. Morse, *Dying Hercules*
(Yale University Art Gallery)

Adelphi Society. With Americans eager to be appreciated abroad,
news of his success spread quickly. He was nominated for membership
in the American Antiquarian Society; President Dwight of Yale
delighted in his "proficiency"; the Philadelphia *Port-Folio,* a literary
journal, linked him with Allston as successors to West and Copley. Lest
Finley's growing reputation puff him up, Elizabeth sent some deflat-
ing advice: "observe a modesty in the reception of premiums and
praises on account of your talents, that will show to those who bestow
them that you are worthy of them in more senses than merely as an
artist."

Hoping to earn money by his art, Finley made two extended trips to Bristol. Many opulent merchants lived in the city, and altogether he spent some eight months there. Little more is known of his first stay than that he thought the place pleasant and got some profitable commissions for portraits. But his second stay was both unprofitable and unpleasant. Almost no one called to look at his pictures, much less order a portrait. Allston was there part of the time, but did little better. Holding one of England's first one-man shows of works by a living artist, he sold a single picture—to his uncle, the American consul.

Finley decided that businessmen were brutes—"grovelling, avaricious devotees of mammon, whose souls are narrowed to the studious contemplation of a hard-earned shilling." One Bristol patron, a man worth a hundred thousand pounds, ordered three paintings from him and then declined to take them. He gave no other reason than that he had enough pictures already. Finley regretted that he had catered to such "miserly beings" until it almost seemed to him no longer repugnant to treat his noble art as a mere trade: "Fie! on myself, I am ashamed of myself."

Finley drew a second conclusion from the merchants' treatment of him. They were in no mood to encourage an American artist, being absorbed in "the *conquest of the United States.*" He had arrived in Bristol for his second stay just as extraordinary dispatches from America reached England: British troops had invaded the city of Washington, torched the Treasury Building and Navy Yard, burned President Madison's furniture in his parlor, and set fire to the Capitol.

Outraged, Finley looked for guidance to the hero he had been taught to emulate: "Oh! for the genius of Washington. Had I but his talents with what alacrity would I return to the relief of that country which . . . is dearer to me than my life." He did what he could. He assisted Americans who had been stranded in London, gave money to American prisoners of war. Meanwhile the British press boasted that England would reduce the United States to unconditional submission. The national prejudice had become deadly, Finley thought: "They no longer despise, they hate, the Americans."

Finley appealed to his parents for another year's support, beyond the three they had granted. He said that he needed the extra time in order to become a history painter: "I cannot be happy unless I am pur-

suing the intellectual branch of the art. Portraits have none of it." Allston backed him up. He wrote to Jedediah that Finley's progress had
been "*unusually* great." But should the young man be obliged to
return to America, his progress might be squandered in work unworthy of his potential: "It is true he could there paint very good portraits,
but I should grieve to hear at any future period that on the foundation
now laid, he shall have been able to raise no higher superstructure
than the fame of a portrait painter."

Jedediah's reply is not known, but Elizabeth was unconvinced. She
was certain that Finley could not survive as an artist in America by
offering the public wall-size spectacles of Marius before Carthage.
"You must not expect to paint anything in this country, for which you
will receive any money to support you, but portraits," she warned;
"That is all your hope here, and to be very obliging and condescend-
ing to those who are disposed to employ you." However unkindly
expressed, the warning was not groundless. Few artists even in England managed to support themselves as history painters, the notable
exception, Benjamin West, having had the patronage of the King. And
forward-looking America had no kings and paid not much homage to
history. Anyway, Finley's request for new funds was badly timed.
Already in debt and forced to borrow, Jedediah had accumulated new
debts of $4000 and feared bankruptcy—"in consequence," Elizabeth
let her son know, "of his endeavors to establish you in the Book Store
of Farrand & Mallory . . . which failed."

Finley did not help his case by telling his Federalist parents that
he wished to spend the extra year in France. He had rejoiced in the
Russian-Austrian-Prussian attack on Paris during the spring of 1814
that forced Bonaparte into exile and raised Louis XVIII to the throne
of France. When Louis visited London, Finley stood for five hours in
Piccadilly to see the new French king, craning his neck for a look and
joining the crowd's cries of "*Vive le roi! Vive Louis!*" A month later, as
other European potentates arrived in London preliminary to the
Vienna peace congress, he strained to get close to Czar Alexander,
who recently had led a review of mounted Cossacks down the Champs-
Elysée—"truly a great man," he thought, vanquisher of "the most
alarming despotism that ever threatened mankind." He got hold of a
ring on the door of Alexander's coach, and kept pace for a quarter
mile as the Czar rolled along.

Finley explained to his parents that the crushing of Napoleon augured a new Renaissance. With Europe once again open to study, art seemed destined to revive as it had in the fifteenth century. "I long to bury myself in the Louvre," he said. There he would no longer have to bear daily insult to his feelings as an American. He could improve in drawing, where he was still deficient, and undertake a serious histori- cal work. Scarcely any of his fellow art students remained in England; all had gone to liberated Paris. And the thought of them reveling in opportunities to view the Old Masters, while he might be forced to return to Charlestown, brought back his adolescent spells of gloom: "for the first time since I left home," he told his parents, "have I had one of my desponding fits."

But to Elizabeth, Paris was no place for a Congregationalist son— "the seat of dissipation," she called it. Finley had mentioned the possi- bility of visiting Russia, too, a harebrained notion demonstrating that he had yet to conquer his restlessness: "You must not be a schemer, but determine on a steady, uniform course." How the issue got resolved is unclear. But in the end Jedediah and Elizabeth agreed to support him for one more year of study, until the fall of 1815. In England, they insisted. Even so, providing another thousand-dollar stipend meant large sacrifices. "We shall have no more left us, when you & your brothers have got through with your educations," Jedediah protested, "than will carry us comfortably through life—it may not be even that, shd. this dredful war continue much longer."

Late in December 1814, Londoners learned that representatives of their battle-weary country had met with an American delegation in Ghent and worked out an agreement ending the War of 1812. Finley no sooner heard the welcome news than, with shipping lanes less risky, he packed up and sent home his eight-by-six-foot painting of *The Dying Hercules*. The picture was admired, "highly approved by all who examine it," Jedediah informed him, including for once even Eliza- beth, who had a handsome frame made for the large canvas, at the substantial cost of $100. She and Jedediah said they would try to get the painting publicly exhibited in Boston, Philadelphia, and perhaps Charleston—a step toward making Finley financially independent by gaining him a reputation.

Finley's pleasure at the return of peace was dampened by the unexpected death in February of Allston's wife, a woman refined and angelically sweet. Particularly because of the political situation, he had viewed her, Leslie, Allston, and himself as a domestic circle, a family: "we became in a manner necessary to each others happiness . . . we could meet, and talk of our beloved country, mutually rejoice in her successes, or lament at her reverses." He felt "overwhelmed" by the loss, but Allston seemed broken, "almost bereft of his reason." Finley and Leslie tried to relieve their mentor's distraught state. But despite their support Allston fell into a year-long depression that brought on something like a religious crisis, in which there was "revealed" to him the divinity of Christ.

Finley still fretted over the lost chance to study in Paris, "letting an opportunity slip," he said, "which is irrecoverable." Astoundingly, however, by springtime France was once more under the control of Napoleon. Arising once more from defeat, he had escaped from the island of Elba, raised an army, and put King Louis XVIII to flight. He seemed determined to "again set the world by the ears," Finley said; "I fear we are apt yet to see a darker and more dreadful storm than any we have yet seen." That did not happen. In June, now a wheezing forty-five-year-old with a paunch, Bonaparte engaged the Duke of Wellington's army in the savage battle at Waterloo that left some 25,000 French troops dead or wounded. This time, Finley exulted in British victory. "I wish the British success against everything but *my country*." In July he saw and heard the flash-boom of the Hyde Park guns, confirming news that the allies had again entered Paris and that Napoleon had been captured, ending twenty years of European warfare.

During the year, Finley worked on an ambitious picture he planned to submit for the history-painting prize at the Royal Academy's 1815 exhibition. He chose a subject from mythology, the judgment of Jupiter in the case of Apollo, Marpessa, and Idas. He depicted the shamefaced Marpessa throwing herself into the arms of her husband, Idas, while her spurned lover, Apollo, looks on in surprise and chagrin. The three-by-four-foot canvas required much study, but the Academy rejected his petition to enter it for the prize. The exhibition rules required his presence in London during the show, held in December; he was scheduled to depart for America in August. Allston denounced the Academy's decision as based on a mere formality that could have been waived: "they resist all kinds of improvement from too great a dread of innovation." West liked the picture enough to encourage Finley to stay on in England. Instead, Finley packed *The Judgment of Jupiter* to take home with him.

In depicting Marpessa's choice to abandon the god of artistic inspiration and return to her mortal husband, he perhaps had in mind a question that his return to Charlestown raised about himself. Did he belong to domestic life, or to his artistic career? To art, he believed. Either way, he felt it necessary to tell his parents that he did not want to endure in person the scoldings they had administered by mail. "I have not, that I recollect since I have been in England, had a turn of *low spirits,* except *when I have received letters from home.*" The letters came with affection and solicitude, he knew. But they also contained so much nagging, distrust, and doubt that after reading them he felt miserable for a week, "as though I had been guilty of every crime."

Finley set down for Jedediah and Elizabeth the terms on which he was returning. He would linger only a year, earning enough money by painting portraits to go abroad again to continue his studies. He would not pursue a permanent career as a portrait painter. He would never abandon his long-range aim of becoming a successful history painter: "My ambition is to be among those who shall revive the splendour of the 15th century, to rival the genius of a Raphael, a Michael Angelo, or a Titian; my ambition is to be enlisted in the constellation of genius which is now rising in this country."

Finley's manifesto struck Elizabeth no more agreeably than had his teenaged pleas from New Haven to have brandy in his room or go gunning. He addressed his parents from on high, she said, as "poor shortsighted worms." She sent back pages of reproof, with what she called "a word of kind advice":

> we may and ought to tell you, and that with the greatest plainness, of anything that we deem improper in any part of your conduct, either in a civil, social, or religious view. . . . and it will ever be your duty to receive from us the advice, counsel, and reproof, which we may, from time to time, favor you with, with the most perfect respect and dutiful observance.

Whether in England or America, that is, Finley remained his parents' child and would have to listen and obey—even, she added with a sting, "when you are head of a family, and even of a profession, if you ever should be either."

Jedediah returned a softer answer. He accepted without argument Finley's decision to remain in America for only a year. But he added his hope that "artists in your profession, and of the first class"—as he respectfully referred to Finley's situation—might soon be so well supported in the country that they would not have to study and paint abroad. "In this case you can come and live with us," he said, "which would give us much satisfaction."

Although Finley considered his return a pause before a fresh start, he brought with him a mission as well. He would do what he could to establish the arts in the United States so that, as his father hoped, the nation's painters would not have to become exiles and expatriates. What Americans needed was Taste, he believed, the ability to appreciate different kinds of excellence and to separate the real from the meretricious. Such Taste, after all, was acquired; it could be had by anyone of common sense who took a serious interest. Creating it meant introducing first-rate pictures into the country and forming institutions such as the Royal Academy. Sometime before leaving England, he entered a resolution in his journal: "On returning to America, let my endeavor be to rouse the feeling for works of art."

The speed of sailing ships in 1815 was about the same as it had been for the last century. Finley's trip to England from New York had taken twenty-six days, and what with the piano playing, flying fish, and buffoonery of the British dramatist Minshull, had been a delight. "I am sometimes at a loss to understand," he had written, "why so much is made of a voyage across the ocean."

Now he found out.

Finley sailed from Liverpool in the *Ceres,* bound for Boston. The ship crashed through one howling storm after another. Its foremast almost toppled under winds so fierce they could not be faced. Sometimes the sea became a rocky precipice, with tangled black clouds overhead riven by lightning and rolling thunder. Other times the sea turned into a roaring foam-storm, the hurricane-churned white surge carried into the air like clouds. Ominously, wreckage of other storm-battered vessels drove past, in one case an entire ship, belly up. "Lord who can endure the terror of thy storm," Finley prayed, "we are in the hands of a merciful God; in whom let us trust, and he will deliver us from all our fears!"

Night after night he went sleepless in his smelly cabin, tossed about in darkness, oppressed by the creaking bulkheads, dashing of glass bottles, and distressed cries of the sailors. "If we should arrive at length in our port," he wrote in his journal, "what great reason shall I have for praise & thanksgiving." One sunset he was on the cabin stairs when the heaving sea rose over the *Ceres*, drenching him as it flooded the stairwell. After something more than a month, provisions began running out. The surly captain rationed what potatoes and moldy bread remained. Soon the water supply ran short. The passengers, washed in seawater, looked solemn and barely spoke to each other.

But on October 18, a Wednesday, the *Ceres* came in sight of Cape Cod. And fifty-eight days—nearly two months—after leaving England, Finley returned to Charlestown, from an absence of four years. "Thanks to a kind Providence who has preserved me through all dangers," he wrote from aboard ship, "I have at length arrived in my native land!"

THREE

A Terrible Harum-Scarum Fellow

(1816–1823)

L ITTLE OF FINLEY'S vision of his next few years survived his return to America. As he had planned to do, he set out at once to
earn money for further study in Europe. First he rented a large room
in Boston to mount a show of his paintings. The ten canvases represented much of his best London work, including a scene from *Don
Quixote,* John Howard Payne in costume, and the large *Dying Hercules*
and *Judgment of Jupiter.*

Finley's exhibition drew visitors and brought him publicity in the
local press as an "accomplished young painter" with a "poetick imagination." After hearing that the Pennsylvania Academy of the Fine Arts
had purchased Allston's *Elijah* for $3500—the most ever paid for an
American painting—he offered his *Hercules* to the Academy for display
and possible sale in Philadelphia. The directors accepted, remarking
that *Hercules* showed "uncommon powers in an artist so young."

With his most ambitious works on view in Boston and Philadelphia, Finley took to the road as an itinerant portrait painter—the
drudging routine of most American artists since colonial times.
Sketching along the way, he toured New Hampshire and Vermont. He
put up in town only long enough to complete what commissions he
could acquire, mostly for "cabinet" portraits painted on small mill-
boards. The wandering by stagecoach, horse, or on foot was no more
pleasant than he might have expected—muddy roads and loose
wheels, animals that kicked and snorted, breakfast in a "hovel." Just
come from London, he thought some of the towns despicable: the

natives of Windsor, Vermont, mistook "*drunkenness and noise,* for *good humor, gambling,* for *sociability,* and *filth* for *wit.*" Painting his sitters rapidly for about $15 a head, he did not much more than clear his travel expenses. He often thought of Allston, particularly when smoking an evening cigar.

In getting about New England, Finley called on Jennette Hart. His letters to her while abroad had spoken of their prospects in an offputting tone of possibly-but-possibly-not, sounding much as if he wanted to wriggle out. He did not have to, for when he visited Jennette she "undeceived" him. Their college romance, she declared, could not become a marriage. Relieved, but eager to display sincerity and preserve his dignity, Finley told her brother-in-law that he would remove himself to Europe, "where I shall probably spend the greater part, if not the remainder of my life."

Far from doing that, he quickly found a wife. Early in August 1816, while seeking portrait commissions in Concord, New Hampshire, he met Lucretia Pickering Walker, the daughter of a local lawyer. She knew of his arrival, having heard of him as "a celebrated painter lately returned from London. . . . very eminent in his profession." He had enjoyed good health while overseas, and a resident of Concord later remembered him as strikingly attractive—tall, elegant in person, pleasing in address, with piercing eyes and black hair. A month later he and Lucretia became engaged.

Lucretia was seventeen, Finley twenty-five. Her youth appealed to him for its beguiling combination of modesty and frankness. And beauty. Her friends spoke admiringly of her delicately pretty features—rosy cheeks, slightly upturned nose, overflowing masses of dark curled hair. Altogether he counted Lucrece, as he called her, a special gift of Providence: "Never, never was a human being so blest as I am."

In fact, Finley was swooningly in love. Arriving alone at another of his itinerant stopovers, he recollected in tearful detail a walk with Lucrece, their conversation in a garden, a parting kiss. He confessed to her his yearning: "As I write, the moon shines on my paper, as if to remind me that last night at this hour it shone on both of us to-gether; Oh, when, dear Lucrece, shall I again see you? When shall the moon shine again on both of us together?" He asked her to look at the moon for half an hour on Sunday evening, beginning precisely at eight o'clock. Precisely at eight o'clock he would look at the moon for half

an hour, too, and think of her. When on the road, he poured out letters to her; when back in Charlestown he sometimes walked to Boston
early in the morning to get her replies.

Considering that he had recently parted with Jennette, Finley realized that his parents might accuse him of haste in his engagement as
in much else, thinking him "a terrible harum-scarum fellow." Despite
his many complaints about their attempts to control his life, he consulted them about his marriage plans often. They advised him to go
slowly. Elizabeth stressed the "*absolute necessity*" of his becoming financially independent before settling down: "Remember it takes a great
many hundred dollars to *make* and to *keep* the pot a-boiling." She also
had her own ideas about the characteristics of a good wife, including
common sense, a decent dowry, and domestic skills—"a slutt is a terrible trial to a man." In addition, it helped, she said, if "you love each
other better than all the world beside."

One thing about Lucrece troubled Finley: her religious life. Her
father was unreligious; her younger brother, a Harvard student, was
infected with the school's Unitarianism; and her many friends were
"all of the gay kind," given to waltzing. She herself was surely open to
genuine piety, but she had no adequate idea of it: "She seems willing
to know *the truth,* but I fear she has not yet experienced a true change
of heart. She believes in the truth of the gospel, but I fear it is only a
speculative belief."

As Finley's qualms suggest, his nights at Covent Garden left his
religious being unchanged. Spiritually he remained the adolescent
who summarized the lives of Protestant martyrs, a descendant of the
Calvinist-Congregationalist piety of New England that stretched back
150 years from Jedediah Morse to Jonathan Edwards to Increase
Mather. And with his return to America and to his family he had been
experiencing signs of conversion, "serious impressions," Jedediah
called them, marks of a "lively Christian." Jedediah had undergone
conversion at around the age of twenty—"a secret, inexpressible Pleasure arising in my Breast," as he described the process at the time,
"with a certain awe & reverence, of God." To feel such a powerful
change of heart, receive such an influx of divine grace, had been his
parents' fondest hope for Finley since the day of his birth.

While undergoing his own arduous conversion, Finley ministered as well to Lucrece's "*unrenewed heart.*" In one way he felt uncomfortable presuming to lead her to experiential knowledge of the love of God. One might never be certain that one's feelings had genuinely changed. His own ardor for God often waned, and he castigated himself for self-deception and spiritual sloth, "my coldness and indifference, my neglect of duty, & attachment to the world. Oh, that I could feel more heavenly mindedness." Such backsliding and self-doubt, however, were normal, even conventional parts of the process. On his travels he sent Lucrece many letters of religious instruction, his swoony trifles about moonshine giving way to somber moralizings about dying unconverted—a fate that damned the soul to an "endless existence" without hope, he pointed out, "no offers of mercy, no chance of salvation . . . *forever, through eternity.*"

Finley found Lucrece eager for his teaching. It included tests by which she might recognize whether she had a truly gracious heart: "Do you love to pray? Do you hate sin? . . . Do you dread above all things *lest you decieve* [sic] *yourself?*" He emphasized the last, crucial question because saving grace might begin not as a sense of purgation, but the opposite: "the first indication of a renewed heart," he explained to her, "is a willingness to believe the worst of ourselves." Indeed the more she grew in grace, the more sinful and unworthy would she appear to herself. As a further test, he recommended that she write down her secret thoughts each day so as to bring them starkly before her eyes, a method of meditation he practiced himself. He sent her pious works to study but emphasized the all-important truth that they were merely incidental to faith, which consisted in sole and utter reliance on Christ for salvation.

Lucrece dutifully reported to Finley on her progress in the elusive work of self-examination. "I once knew nothing of the depravity of my own heart," she admitted to him. But with his guidance she had begun to perceive her wickedness, "that dreadful opposition of the heart which we all feel towards the truths of the Gospel." As she came to this understanding of her true state, much that had seemed innocent now appeared sinful. She began turning down invitations to the dances and card parties she used to attend—"the height of folly," she now called them, "idle amusements." She began quoting Scripture. She was beginning to understand, too, the central truth that grace is no human achievement but a miraculous gift of God: "I feel the dawning of religious joy in my soul," she wrote to him, "and that my only hope of acceptance is through the merits of my Redeemer, with a sincere conviction of my entire inability to save myself—Your letters, dearest love, first awakened my attention."

To foster Lucrece's religious growth, Finley proposed that she stay awhile with his parents in Charlestown. They were eager to meet their future daughter-in-law, and the town was in the midst of a religious revival. Jedediah wrote to Lucrece's father, formally requesting his permission for the visit, which lasted at least a month. With Finley away painting, Jedediah spoke with Lucrece often about her spiritual condition. He perceived that she was indeed undergoing gracious enlightenment, though the signs were at present faint: "She evidently relishes what no unrenewed heart ever relished, & dislikes what no such heart ever disliked." Lucrece grew fond of Jedediah: "he is so mild and amiable." And as she began joining in the Morses' daily life, they more and more enthusiastically approved their son's choice: "We think she has the right disposition & talents to make you, & us, happy," Jedediah wrote to Finley; "All the family love her."

Finley's own conversion process fed and was fed by his preaching to Lucretia. On December 8, 1816, he presented himself for examination to the Charlestown First Church—his father's church. His profession of faith satisfied the church officers that he had attained a grateful heart, and they admitted him to full communion—the passage to a new, enlarged participation in religious life.

Five months later, Lucrece felt convicted enough of her own conversion to also desire to take communion. "Oh, my dear Lucrece," Finley wrote to her, "you cannot concieve [sic] the pleasure which it gives your Finley to think that his dear Lucrece, will shortly be a professor at the same table of the Lord." Troubled by fresh doubts about the reality of her conversion, she delayed two months. But on Sunday, July 6, 1817, supported by divine grace, she took communion and was fully admitted to a Congregational church in Concord: "Oh!," she wrote to Finley, "that I could serve him better and be enabled to make more suitable returns for his great goodness unto me a sinner."

While Finley's spiritual life flourished, his plans for studying in Europe collapsed. The *Judgment of Jupiter*, on display in Boston for a year, found no buyer. Neither did his *Dying Hercules*, on exhibition at the Pennsylvania Academy; the painting was too large for any private house, he was told. Some of his pictures had also been shown in New York, but a downturn in the city's commercial affairs left no prospect of selling them for a reasonable profit. There were other discouragements. A Philadelphia bookseller commissioned from him a portrait of ex-president John Adams, to be engraved and included in a biographical encyclopedia of distinguished Americans. Finley produced a harsh memento mori of Adams in old age, shrunken and rheumy-eyed. The bookseller refused to publish it, advising Finley that those who saw the picture "universally disapproved" of it.

Anyway, Finley's engagement to Lucrece had turned his attention from study in Europe to earning a dependable family income. He began to rethink his career. Before leaving England he had announced that he would never become a portrait painter. Now he thought that he should perhaps return to London to perfect himself in commercial portraiture. He had an even more extreme thought. He had announced that as a history painter his aim would be to lend his own Raphaelesque luster to America's rising "constellation of genius." Now it occurred to him that he should, perhaps, just give up art altogether.

Finley tried invention. Americans were becoming known for their "improvements": new trusses for hernias, machines for making suspender buckles—better bobbins, doorknobs, pessaries, music stands. "There is no clinging to old ways," a German visitor to the country remarked; "the moment an American hears the word 'invention' he pricks up his ears." Finley set out to make a perhaps profitable "improvement," together with his brother Sidney. Three years younger than Finley, Sidney too had recently undergone conversion, and he too was trying to find his place in the world. Finley believed that his brother had a gift for "philosophical research," demonstrated in Sidney's efforts to build a kite for human airborne navigation.

Experimenting together in the spring of 1817, Finley and Sidney invented a flexible leather piston. The device could be adapted to various methods of raising and forcing water—a bilge pump in ships, a machine for watering gardens. (Sidney satirized it as "Morse's Patent Metallic Double-Headed OCEAN-DRINKER and DELUGE-SPOUTER VALVE *Pump-Boxes*.") The brothers secured an American patent for their invention, sought an overseas patent as well, and tried to interest foreign investors in promoting the device.

Finley's and Sidney's most promising use for the piston was in fash-

ioning an improved fire engine. Simpler and easier to work than current engines of the same capacity and power, and half the price, it
would bring fire-fighting machinery within the means of every village
in the country. Finley showed a model of the engine to Benjamin Silliman, his former science professor at Yale. It interested Silliman so
much that he asked for a set of drawings and specifications to print in
the first issue of his new periodical, the *American Journal of Science,* soon
to become the country's main channel for scientific papers. Finley also
got a valuable endorsement from the famous inventor Eli Whitney,
who pronounced the engine superior to those in common use. "Every
one thinks we shall make our fortunes if it succeeds," Finley wrote.

But at the same time he felt pulled toward an entirely different
sort of work. His conversion had broadened and deepened his religious interests. He wrote a sermon-like essay about the false promise
of Universal Salvation. He began teaching a Sunday school in
Charlestown. The religious revival in the town, and reports from London that several deistic young artists he knew were turning to God, led
him to suspect that the Millennium might be dawning: "not a wind
blows but brings intelligence of the increase of the Redeemer's King-
dom." He now regretted his behavior overseas: "I am ashamed of
much . . . very much of my life in England, but hope for forgiveness
through the merits of my Savior." The regrets came to include Covent
Garden: "I am conscientiously opposed to the Theatre."

In the summer of 1817, seven or eight months after his admission
to the church, Finley made a startling announcement to Lucrece. He
had new plans—"a *change of profession,*" he said, "for *Divinity.*" As a minister he could be more useful to others than as a painter. He was prepared to sacrifice his noble profession for the sake of duty and
conscience. "The salvation of a soul! who can tell its worth!" he
explained; "Oh that I might be made the instrument of turning many
from the error of their ways unto the Lord."

Finley planned to study at the Andover Theological Seminary for a
year, then at the new Episcopal seminary in New York City. He would
take orders in the Episcopal Church, whose form of worship he considered close to that of the Primitive Church, as described in the New
Testament. Congregationalist friends and clergy approved his decision, he said, and he felt no misgivings except those arising from a
sense of his own insufficiency to undertake so high an office. He
would complete his remaining portrait commissions—as "the *Painter*

Clergyman," he joked. But after beginning his ministerial studies in the fall, he would abandon art, at least as a profession.

Finley kept to his new course barely two months. He began having serious doubts: his mediocre record at Yale implied that he did not have a scholarly temperament; his eight years of training as an artist had given him habits wholly different from those of a divine. After discussing the situation with his family and friends he concluded that it was not his duty to change professions.

Lucrece had affectionately approved Finley's decision to enter the ministry, and affectionately accepted his counter-decision to go on as a painter. But his conscience accused him of rushing thoughtlessly into new schemes—shuffling about, he told himself, like "the most *fickle* being in the world."

To restart his painting career Finley headed south. He had several ties to Charleston. His father had preached there and knew such prominent Charlestonians as Charles Cotesworth Pinckney, who invited him to visit. His mother was the niece of a prominent Charleston physician, James E. B. Finley, who thought him destined as an artist for America's "earliest lists of its Great Men." Charleston was the birthplace of Allston, too, and patronage in the city was said to be lively, with much demand for Northern painters.

Finley timed his arrival in Charleston to coincide with the beginning of the annual social season, in late January. From then through March the prosperous rice and cotton planters brought their families and slaves to town to enjoy the horse races, concerts, and theatrical performances. Finley's impression of the place was mixed. The people seemed hospitable, their elegant brick homes graced with balconies and piazzas; gardenias and olive trees thrived in the sultry climate. On the other hand, the moral climate of the South seemed debased—"all the dirt, and indolence, and inconvenience, and comfortlessness, inseparable from slave population." Both slaves and people of fashion in Charleston used the Sabbath not to pray or study but to pay visits. And with the social season came brothels and gambling tables—a "torrent of dissipation, and ungodliness."

Staying with his uncle James, Finley established a studio on King Street, near the tall white steeple of St. Michael's Church. This time his search for a living to support himself and Lucrece was repaid. He soon became a sought-after painter in Charleston, earning $60 and $70 apiece for his portraits—four or five times what he got for the same painting in New England. Over time, one rice and indigo planter hired him to do nineteen family portraits; in appreciation, Finley presented to him as a gift the still-unsold *Judgment of Jupiter.* By mid-March Finley had completed twenty-seven portraits and had commissions for forty more: "with application," he wrote to Lucrece, "I can make a fortune in a few years." He planned to return to Charleston for the next social season, this time bringing Lucrece as his wife.

With his first commercial success as a painter, Finley could afford to act on his pious belief in charitable giving, especially to religious causes. He sent $20 to the theological seminary at Princeton, another $20 to the Board of Missions—"little enough considering how abundantly the Lord is pouring wealth into my lap." He forwarded several hundred dollars to his parents, as a loan to help them pay off their many debts.

Capable now of earning a thousand dollars a month, he wildly believed, Finley stopped peddling his and Sidney's inventions. Although he had taken along a model of their fire engine to display in Charleston, he had become "heartily sick" of the whole business: "it yields much vexation, labor, and expense, and no profit." Inquiries about foreign patents for the flexible leather piston revealed that a French patent would be costly, and that someone in England had already patented what appeared to be the same device. Moreover, a New Hampshire demonstration of the fire engine had failed, he learned, prompting a spectator to comment, "Mr Morse better stick to his brush, *he will do well enough then* but as to Engines he'd better let them alone."

Finley's plentiful commissions came with a price. His customers were demanding, in the way that made artists in the "higher branches" of painting look down on portraitists as mere servants, hired flatterers. One patron gave him an engraving of Chief Justice John Marshall and specified that he wanted his son depicted in the same attitude. And dressed in a black coat and white waistcoat. And seated in a beautiful chair at a handsome table—against a backdrop of magnificent scenery. Another patron required that the subject's right hand must nestle in a partly buttoned coat, "his *left arm* being entirely exposed and the left *hand* with *glove on,* resting on the hilt of the sword." Not all his employers were satisfied with the results, either. Some thought his pictures good likenesses but painted hastily.

Finley did tend to leave his portraits unpolished. Yet his popularity was the deserved reward of matured skill and insight. Despite his loving admiration for Allston, in depicting his sitters he departed from his arch-Romantic mentor. Where Allston suffused his paintings with an aura of moonlit fantasy, Finley clung to some advice by Gilbert Stuart: "Be rather pointed than fuzzy. . . . you cannot be too particular in what you do to see what sort of an animal you are putting down."

Samuel F. B. Morse, *Rev. and Mrs. Hiram Bingham*
(Yale University Art Gallery)

Accordingly, he emphasized candid observation and concrete detail, conveying his sharp sense of character through careful representation of posture, hair, facial contours. He acknowledged his patrons' wealth, elaborately rendering their clothing and jewelry. But he usually granted their faces no flattery. He bluntly depicted his sitters as lack-luster, gawky, porcine, or whatever else his eye recorded, as in his por-trait of the New England missionaries the Reverend and Mrs. Hiram Bingham.

During Finley's six-month absence in the South, Lucrece remained with her family in New Hampshire. She missed him badly and wrote often: "*dearest love*," one letter began, "how painful this separation is to me who love you with so *much* tenderness and affection." But Finley's return to Charlestown in the early summer of 1818 meant another three-month separation before their marriage. He had brought with him some unfinished portraits, and after visiting Lucrece briefly in Concord he went back to his parents' house in Charlestown to com-plete them. "Oh my *dear* Finley how I do miss you," she wrote after see-ing him, "I was wholly overcome by my feelings, I felt ashamed of my weakness and strove to subdue my sorrow."

As their separation continued and the wedding approached, Lucrece sent more professions of ardor and longing. They made Fin-ley uncomfortable, perhaps representing to him a sexual challenge, certainly raising the danger of Idolatry. He instructed Lucrece that God caused their affections to flow out toward each other, but com-manded their supreme affection to Himself: "let us not then idolise the gift instead of the Giver; let us be more earnest in our prayers that God would so direct our love as not to interfere with our Love to him." Lucrece tried to show that she understood. "I view you, love, as the gift of God," she replied, "and pray that in infinite mercy I may be pre-served from setting my heart too much upon you or any other earthly blessing."

Marriage also raised the more mundane but no less disturbing question of Lucrece's dowry. Here Finley's hope of becoming finan-cially independent clashed with his fear of becoming worldly, the result being a draw. "I consider my *Lucrece* a *fortune* in herself," he told her; "still," he added, "for her sake I hope there will be something handsome for her." Lucrece shrank from questioning her father, mindful that he had other children to support. From speaking to her mother she learned only that he would furnish the newlyweds' house—should they get one. And when she did at last confront her father, he gave her nothing more encouraging to tell Finley than a promise to "*fix me out.*" Finley's often proclaimed scorn of material things allowed no protest: "I can cheerfully leave all to the direction of our Heavenly Father who careth for us."

The approaching wedding date made them both anxious. Their self-condemnations multiplied—attachment to vanities, want of confidence in God. Lucrece also suffered physical distress—exhaustion, colds, headache. She asked to postpone the marriage a week. The delay or loss of a letter brought on tiffs, as when Finley became unable to complete a certain portrait because he had not heard from her: "I cannot but feel, strongly too, this inattention," he huffed, "you will not think that I am grieved without cause." Jittery and impatient, they both literally counted the days.

Finley and Lucrece married in Concord on September 29, and settled before the end of the year in Charleston, for his second season. They lodged at a $10-a-week boarding house, a short walk from his painting room. Downcast at first to be living among strangers, Lucrece soon came to enjoy the hospitality and attention she received. The agreeable climate put color in her pale cheeks and she gained some needed weight: "she is esteemed quite a *belle,*" Finley noted. He learned that some local gossip criticized her clothing as ostentatious, but he dismissed it, knowing that her dresses had been made under his mother's supervision. Perhaps, although in the portrait of Lucrece that he painted near this time, she wears a flouncy pink and yellow gown with a fur-lined satin cape, surely no couture of Elizabeth Morse.

The new social season brought Finley even richer returns than his first. In scarcely more than two months he booked over $4000 in commissions. "I am in the *fashion,*" he whooped. Already as prosperous as he could wish, he sent another few hundred dollars to his parents and raised his price for a portrait from $60 to $80. He earned the money, working long hours and trying hard to improve. He experimented with achieving delicate lighting effects by dropping a scrim of black gauze between himself and the background while he painted. He explored colors, mixing yellow ochre with chrome yellow to produce a flesh yellow that was effective for painting shadows of white drapery. He gathered a small collection of antique sculpture—an imported

Samuel F. B. Morse, *Lucretia Pickering Walker Morse*
(Mead Art Museum)

cast of the *Venus de Medicis,* a patched-together figure of Apollo, frag-
ments of hands and feet. They made "a very good academy," from
which he drew two hours in the evenings, much as he had in London.

As summer approached, the air in Finley's studio became oppres-
sively close, and Lucrece found the city so hot that she badly wanted to
leave. Even with a dozen other painters working in Charleston, however, his waiting list had kept growing—enough patrons to justify his
returning for another five or six seasons. And he had a choice commission for later in the year. The city council, recognizing his ability,
offered him $750 to paint a full-length portrait of President James
Monroe, who was coming to town. Finley had a long interview with
him but the President's time was so taken up that no sittings could be

arranged. Instead, Monroe agreed to have Finley paint him during the winter in Washington.

Lucrece was pregnant when she and Finley returned to Charlestown. As she came to term she was looked after in the Morses' parish house by Elizabeth and by the aging family nurse, Nancy Shepherd, who nearly thirty years ago had attended Finley, too, and told him about Bunker's Hill.

Jedediah had preached from the First Church pulpit since his settlement in 1789, on the day of George Washington's inauguration. Now nearly sixty years old, his temples sunken, he was being forced out. Twenty-five members of his flock had requested him to convene a council to discuss whether he should be removed from his ministry.

The basis of the request was a new edition of one of Jedediah's geographies, further evidence of his indifference to church matters. A deacon of his flock charged that he trifled away whole months, "without producing scarcely one, original, well studied discourse." Elizabeth understood the situation differently: "if every Old woman in the Church & parish is not visited as often as she thinks she ought to be . . . there is a hue & cry raised and it is made the subject of constant reproach till we are sick of hearing it." Jedediah viewed the objections to his geographies as a pretext, the dissenters' real motive being to convert his church to Unitarianism.

Finley encouraged his father to leave. Although born in Charlestown he had never grown attached to the place or even spent much time there. Except for a few friends, he did not care to see Charlestown and Boston again, nor their provincial, self-important residents—"the meanest, most selfish, most narrow-minded set of beings in the world." He thought of moving his parents to Charleston. In their advancing age they would benefit from the climate. And Jedediah could combat the *"Unitarian Hydra"* now rearing itself in Charleston, too, an indulgent place well suited to the sect's easygoing religion.

But to Finley's dismay, his father resisted leaving. Wounded and angry, Jedediah wanted to deny his enemies the triumph of making him seem cast out. He went along with a plan by supporters in his church to put off his departure and hope for an end to the dissent. To Finley, with his touchy sense of personal honor, the delaying tactics seemed "idle and mad," certain to make Jedediah appear crafty. "Do determine speedily to go, dear Father, if you value your own reputation, peace, and usefulness and that of your loving family."

But Jedediah, and everyone else, clearly understood that he must sooner or later resign his pulpit. He wanted to have at least the satisfaction of not being present when the congregation installed his replacement. So he informed the church board that he intended to seek a government commission to investigate the state of the Indians on the country's borders. Just the same, he and Elizabeth felt evicted, thrown out of their only and lifelong home. They decided that, next year, they would pack up and move to New Haven, near Yale, his alma mater, a town with no trace of Unitarianism.

Over the summer, despite the turmoil in the church, Finley completed the portraits he brought from Charleston. He had the pleasure and advantage of guidance from Washington Allston. Although presumed to be next in line for the presidency of the Royal Academy, Allston had chosen to live and paint in Boston. He believed he saw signs of encouragement for the arts there, which he owed it to his country to foster. Finley did not share his faith in Boston: "I think it will be the last in the arts," he once remarked. Nevertheless he went to Allston thirstily, "as to the sun to imbibe light."

Probably inspired by his mentor's presence, Finley painted an Allstonesque full-length of a girl wandering in the ruins of a Gothic abbey, emblematic of her failing health: "I always thought he had a great deal in him," Allston commented. Allston himself began a mammoth painting of *Belshazzar's Feast,* the canvas stretching across nearly the entire back wall of his studio. He expected to finish the picture in six or eight months, then put it profitably on exhibition. A perfectionist, however, he would do and undo *Belshazzar's Feast* the rest of his life.

In September, Lucrece gave birth to the couple's first child, a daughter they christened Susan Walker Morse. Finley was able to enjoy his infant barely two months, however, his here-and-there commissions making for a back-and-forth existence. He had to leave for Washington to do his portrait of President Monroe, and head from there to Charleston for the social season. His brother Sidney, now a ministerial student at the Andover Seminary, accompanied Lucrece, baby Susan, and nurse Nancy to the home of Lucrece's parents in New

Hampshire, where they stayed until Finley returned from Charleston some six months later.

The addition of Susan made this parting from Lucrece more than usually wrenching—"and I don't care to try it again," Finley said. Washington did not much lift his spirits. The nation's capital had a "very mean *aspect*"—badly built houses scattered over a windy space of uneven ground without connecting streets, the landscape blotched with swamps and vacant lots. And the work was frustrating. The President treated him without formality, inviting him to dinner three times, and to tea. But the subject was often called away during the sittings, too busy to pose longer than ten or twenty minutes at a time.

Finley managed to do no more than take the President's face, leav-

Samuel F. B. Morse, *James Monroe*
(White House Collection)

ing his body to be filled in. He made a bust-length copy of the face for one of Monroe's daughters, vividly rendering the President's ruddy complexion and deeply cleft chin. She said that her father thought it the only portrait that really looked like him—although he had also been painted by Gilbert Stuart, many of whose portraits Finley ranked with Vandyke's. When later completed, the full-length portrait won admirers too, despite its fuzzy unfinished-looking torso. The New York Academy of Arts asked to exhibit it, "presenting you to the New York public in the most graceful way."

From Washington, Finley set out for South Carolina through a violent December snowstorm that nearly upset his creaking coach, the horses toppling under their crust of ice and icicles. The tough going made an apt prelude to his season in Charleston. The city he returned to early in 1820 was in economic decline. Since the war with England, Americans had turned much of their attention from foreign affairs to internal improvement and domestic manufactures, with seemingly unlimited opportunities for average but energetic people to make money. The country was growing, too, at a rate that stirred hopes for national greatness—its territorial claims extending to the Pacific Ocean, more and more new states seeking admission to the Union. In 1819, however, the intense economic development withered into a financial depression that would last almost a decade. Businesses failed, some half-million workers were left without means of support, philanthropic groups doled out soup.

Finley discovered that the depression had reached Charleston, where cotton prices had plunged. He got some commissions, although the city swarmed with unemployed painters: "I wish I could divide with some of them, very clever men who have families to support, and can get nothing to do." To save money he slept in his painting room. But he had fewer invitations than before, lost weight, yearned for Lucrece and little Susan. In letters from New Hampshire, Lucrece sent an unfolding account of the infant's growth: Susan's eyes follow her around the room; Susan has become afraid of strangers, especially if they wear black. "How often do I wish her dear Father could see her," Lucrece wrote, "oh my husband I do long to see your dear face again, and once more hear the sound of your affectionate voice."

Lucrece also reported her recurrent illnesses—more headaches, dizziness, pain in her side and breasts. Worries about Lucrece's health intensified Finley's yearning for her, so that for all his effort to center his affection on God, he was making her an idol: "My impatient longings to be with you as though you were not safe out of *my presence* tells me this, my constant fears of bad news from you tells me this, my dreams." A steamship had come into service between New York and Charleston, and he sometimes felt tempted to drop everything and immediately return home.

Finley's discontent may not have been much relieved by several visits from his brother Richard. Now twenty-five years old and a licensed minister, Richard was preaching for a while at the Presbyterian church on John's Island, near Charleston. Even more restless than his brother, he had come out of their closely regimented childhood with no clear sense of what he wanted. Having failed as a schoolteacher, he accused himself of one defect after another—timidity, selfishness, impiety, a "moping melancholy" that made him unsociable and unpleasant. He still consulted his mother about how to get a new coat—a "quere [*sic*] creature," Elizabeth thought him. Finley assured him that he would succeed in anything he undertook, "with a little self confidence"—a trait Richard wholly lacked. While in Charleston, Richard wandered about to relieve his ennui, bit his nails, brooded in his journal: "This evening I felt as if every one was my enemy."

At the end of his dismal season, Finley returned not to the parsonage but to his parents' temporary new home—a rented cottage in New Haven. Lucrece was there with little Susan, although now, a married woman and mother, she felt uncomfortable living with her in-laws: "I wish I could receive you at *our* own house," she told Finley. Scraping by himself, he had sent what money he could to help pay for his parents' move from Charlestown. They found some comfort in at least having their furniture with them. Jedediah borrowed $400 to have a studio built for Finley, and counted on loans from his son to partly finance the construction of a house in New Haven to accommodate the entire family.

Only a few months after relocating, Jedediah left for distant Buffalo and Detroit. Through highly placed officials in Washington who admired his geographies, he had obtained an appointment to collect information on the numbers, location, and institutions of all the Indian tribes outside the Northeast—"400,000 of our fellow beings," he said. In this way he managed to be far from the Charlestown First Church when its new minister was installed in his place. Instead of

preaching the customary farewell sermon, he sent a letter to be read
to his flock.

Jedediah's appointment took him to new scenes that he found fascinating—Mackinaw, with its waterside lodges and birch canoes, most
of the villagers filthy, many naked, some in war paint. But he remained
bitter at having been driven from his ministry by people he had
counted friends—"conduct *cruel* as the *grave*," Elizabeth called it. He
fell prey to "depression of spirits," developed an obscure numbness,
constriction in his chest. The thought of separation from his wife and
from the home he had had for thirty years sometimes made him weep.

Finley tried one more season in Charleston, then never went back. He
lowered the price of his portraits and boosted his efforts to please. But
most people who had once paid much attention to him now ignored
him. His few patrons were harder than before to please, too, and
slower to pay. "Cotton and rice are so dull," he told Lucrece. "I know
not how much I shall bring home." He reminded himself to view his
frustration from a religious perspective: should he receive good from
God and not also evil? Still, he heard out advice from his parents and
brothers that he think about spending the winters not in Charleston
but in New Orleans, Savannah, or Washington. He reassured Lucrece
that he favored New York: "if I can get established there I think it will
be much better for me than to be so far from home."

Finley considered another way out. At the moment, aspiring artists
in America taught themselves or worked in the studios of established
artists. He might open a school for painting and sculpture in New
Haven, based on what he knew of the Royal Academy. He already
owned nearly enough casts, prints, and books to equip such a school
himself. Together with portrait commissions, ten or fifteen pupils at
$100 a year would provide a livable income, especially if he also gave a
course of public lectures on the fine arts. In the evenings he began
devising a format for the talks, certain he could make them "highly
popular."

Finley realized that the whole scheme might seem another of his
impractical flights. But teaching and lecturing in New Haven would
keep him together with his family. And it would, after four years of distraction, return him to his vocation, "the higher branches of poetical

and Historical Painting which it is high time I should begin to think of again if ever I mean to pursue them with success."

Perhaps simply to test his idea, Finley tried to lay the groundwork in Charleston for a South Carolina Academy of Fine Arts. Collaborating with the Comptroller General of the state, an amateur painter-sculptor named John Cogdell, he drew up rules for the Academy and submitted a resolution asking the city council for a building site in the public square. He felt no great certainty that the Academy would win public support. "It looks *prosperous now*," he wrote to Lucrece, "but I am not sanguine as to its success." With good reason. Many of the subscribers he enlisted failed to pay up, a lottery to purchase plaster study-casts yielded little money, and the completed building ultimately cost three times the estimate. The Academy languished for a decade before vanishing in 1830, its property sold to pay debts.

Finley had planned to return home at the end of March, earlier than usual. Business was slack, and Lucrece was pregnant, expecting the birth of their second child. Some new commissions kept him in Charleston until April, however. Meanwhile Lucrece caught a severe cold that lamed her arm. "I *dread the trial*," she said, "still I trust I can wait with humble submission to my heavenly Father." Finley soon received news that he had another daughter, named Elizabeth Ann. "God did help you," he wrote to Lucrece, "he made your trial short." They asked God for grace to bring up their children in the admiration of the Lord. But fourteen days out of the womb the infant became critically ill and died, medicine having failed to cure her "canker of the bowels."

Still without a home or an income, Finley returned briefly to New Haven then went off seeking portrait business in Massachusetts, Vermont, and upstate New York. Another rootless six months on the road, with the lonely wait for letters reporting that little Susan looked for him when she awoke, saying, "Papa all gone he don't *been* in Mama's bed now."

During his tour, Finley conceived a bold new painting, the most novel and complex he had ever attempted. Its subject would be the monumental interior of the House of Representatives, newly rebuilt since the British torched the Capitol in 1814. The great canvas, eleven feet wide by over seven feet high, would include portraits of all the House members. The ambitious idea grew out of his experience and hopes. He considered architecture part of his province as an artist, and had even offered to design a library and chapel for Andover Theological Seminary. He had reason to hope, too, that he had conceived an aesthetically satisfying historical subject that might also be a popular success. A painting of the interior of the Capuchin Church in Rome had drawn crowds when shown in America, and the recent traveling exhibition of John Trumbull's *Declaration of Independence* had reaped more than $4000. A comparable painting of the House of Representatives might be sent around the country—"one of the most popular subjects I could possibly undertake."

Finley began the work in November 1821, in Washington. Well known in the city through his father and on his own, he was cordially received, given a painting room in the Capitol, so close to the House chamber that he could hear the sound of debate through the wall. President Monroe advised him to paint the House members first, then the room: "he seems pleased with the idea of all the pictures," Finley wrote home, "and thought they would be popular." But Finley chose to do both at once, taking the congressmen when they could sit for him in his studio, painting the chamber when they could not. He intended to depict the scene in the legislature as it appeared by lamplight, "when the room already very splendid will appear 10 times more so." The venerable doorkeeper of the House agreed to light the chamber's great chandelier for him two hours each evening, so that he could make sketches.

Up at dawn, Finley worked sixteen hours a day on the painting, he said, so intently that he confused one day with another. The subject required him to make small portraits of sixty-seven congressmen, and of another nineteen figures as well—Supreme Court justices, newspapermen, doorkeepers, servants. He was able to get in six sittings a day, of two hours each; one day he held eleven sittings, equivalent to painting five ivory miniatures. The sessions went well, the House members being not just willing to pose but deeming it an honor.

Yet the painting progressed far more slowly than Finley anticipated. The semicircular House chamber presented "Herculean difficulties" in perspective—an art, he realized, in which he had little skill. He tried using a camera obscura to puzzle out the technical problems, sometimes spending a whole day erasing and re-erasing. Three weeks passed before he drew a line of the chamber on his canvas. But he solved the problems, "by the assistance of God's grace," and in the process gained a satisfying new ease in drawing backgrounds. "I am certain, that with diligence & perseverance," he wrote to Lucrece, "I can make a popular & profitable picture."

Lucrece had expected Finley to return to New Haven late in December. But his labors stretched on through January, then beyond. He asked her whether he should finish the portraits and come back briefly in February, or complete the entire painting and return permanently in April: "*Can you spare me till April dearest? . . .* You shall decide for me, my dear wife, and dear little daughter." Lucrece had never written her husband a letter even remotely critical of him, but the question for once angered her. During his absence her mother had died, an event not unexpected yet devastating. She was pregnant again, too, and felt drooping and dizzy. "I cannot feel *at all* reconciled to the thoughts of your absence for several months longer," she replied. "Shall I tell you husband, that your letter made me feel dull and unhappy?"

Finley returned to New Haven in February, bringing some eighty heads he had painted on small panels, and the giant canvas on which he would copy and arrange them. In April Lucrece gave birth to a daughter, whom they named Lucretia Ann. Born one year after the death of their second child, the infant survived only twenty-five days. How the couple dealt with their new loss is unknown. Little information about such intimate crises appears in the extant letters and journals of Finley and his family; if more at some time existed, it may have been culled from the documentary record by a descendant. However affected, Finley strenuously resumed work on his picture, which he now believed he could complete by the fall.

He saw encouraging signs of how his efforts might be received. During his stay in Washington, the painting had become a town topic. After he left, notices of its progress appeared in several newspapers, anticipating how it would finally look and praising "the assiduous labour and distinguished talents of the artist." As he worked on through the fall, he moved the estimated completion date forward to January. But by the new year he was at last done, having toiled over the canvas some fourteen months.

The House of Representatives shows a silhouetted figure lighting the thirty Argand oil lamps of the great three-tiered chandelier. Members

Samuel F. B. Morse, *The House of Representatives*
(Corcoran Gallery of Art)

of the House face the viewer as they stand around the glowing hall singly or in small groups, preparing to assemble. Finley intended not so much to portray the congressmen, however, as to show the American public its seat of government, to make "a faithful representation of the national hall, with its furniture and business during the session of Congress." In doing so, he convincingly depicted the tricky-to-render half-dome and sloping concentric circles of seats, and minutely reproduced the chamber's yellow curtain fringes, wall clock, inkstands, letterbox, and distant firelit lobby.

Regarded as a history painting, *The House of Representatives* lacks the memorable narrative content of such predecessors, and likely influences, as Trumbull's *Declaration of Independence* or Copley's *Death of Lord Chatham*. But it offers something as novel in its way as West's *Death of Wolfe*—a history painting without history. Finley discovered a material symbol for his sense of America's growing might and the superiority of its institutions, for the cultural nationalism that in London had animated his fierce denunciations of British policy. The somberly lit cavernous chamber and its twenty-two monumental columns, dwarfing the legislators who prepare to work into the night, dramatize the young republic's seriousness, stability, and unostentatious grandeur.

Connecting the present with the foundational principles of the Constitution, the justices of the Court stand on a raised platform to the left. On the wall behind them, in a massive bronze-colored frame surmounted by an eagle, hangs a copy of the Declaration of Independence. Connecting the country's destiny, too, with the Morse family, in the scarlet-draped gallery overlooking the legislative throng stands Jedediah Morse. Returned from his expedition to the Great Lakes as an Indian commissioner, he peers down upon the scene, near the Pawnee chief Petalasharo.

After displaying *The House of Representatives* briefly in New Haven, Finley sent it to Boston for exhibition in February, going along to help unpack the 640-pound canvas. Even Allston's critical eye admired the perspective, the well-drawn figures naturally disposed, especially the exquisitely colored architecture—"really a very beautiful thing. . . . he has brought out more in this picture than I ever anticipated." Were it shown in London, he said, Finley would be made an associate at the

Royal Academy. Still, he suggested some small improvements, which Finley made, delaying the opening for two days.

The Boston exhibition took in some $40 the first day, including the sale of printed keys that identified each of the eighty-six figures. Admission was twenty-five cents, but Finley also sold thirty-five or so season's tickets, for fifty cents. "Things look well," he wrote to Lucrece, "every thing indicates success." Having launched the show, he went back to New Haven and gave over its management to Henry Pratt, a young artist just out of his teens who had assisted him in Charleston and Washington.

In the changeable March weather, alternately cold and warm, Pratt averaged only about $3 a day. As receipts fell, he hired a man to distribute five hundred handbills around town; yet one day he took in only seventy-five cents. Finley instructed him to light the show in the evening, to extend the viewing time. Pratt put up tin lanterns, but attracted only one customer. Three further evening viewings produced $1.50. By mid-April, Finley ordered Pratt to close up.

Allston urged Finley not to be discouraged. Although the painting had brought in little cash it had gained him much praise, from the best judges. In Allston's aristocratic logic, the meager cash return meant that the worst judges had ignored it: "the lower classes must have been wanting in curiosity, and as they make up the mass of the town, if it does not attract them, the receipts must of course be small." The life of the painting had just begun, he said. "Be of good heart then. I have no doubt of your success."

At the end of April, Pratt moved the heavy *House of Representatives* to Salem, Massachusetts, for display at a local coffeehouse—small but the best he could get. The local press took notice, the public did not. In two weeks he made just over $40, his expenses amounting to nearly $60. He sent the picture on for exhibition to New York City, where Finley went to receive it, now in no hopeful mood. "I cannot predict any thing concerning it, but I don't expect much."

Under Pratt's management, *The House of Representatives* was presented to New Yorkers through June and July. Although he circulated seven hundred handbills and kept the hall open each evening, his receipts in the first twelve days averaged only about $4; on one day only $1.50 came in. The trouble this time, he believed, was that the painting faced too much competition—not only from simultaneous shows by Rembrandt Peale and Thomas Sully but also from the city's many theaters, circuses, and pleasure gardens. "Exhibitions are so multiplied that people begin to think them not worth seeing," he informed Finley; "it is worse than it was at Salem; as far as I can judge, there is not the least interest taken in the subject." It did not help that the street outside the hall was being torn up and repaved, leaving stony rubbish that made it impassable. By the time Pratt closed the show, in July, he had only three and a half cents on hand, together with bills for rent and advertising amounting to $110.

After the miserable seven-week run in New York, Finley signed over to a man named Curtis Doolittle the right to exhibit his picture anywhere in the United States—Doolittle to pay costs, Finley to receive half the profits. But there were no profits. After trying out the painting in Albany, Doolittle reported that receipts were so small he blushed to relate them. When he moved it to Hartford and Middletown, Connecticut, he lost $20 to $30. Finley released him from their contract. Doolittle transported the eighty-square-foot canvas back to New Haven and gave up.

Lucrece worried about how the series of failures might affect Finley. "My dear husband I trust will not give way to any anxious, desponding feelings," she said; "it has pleased our heavenly Father for wise reasons to disappoint our expectations in regard to your large Picture, and it is our duty to submit to the disappointment." But although he had very often preached the same to her, he found submission difficult. He came to feel that most people who attended exhibitions had no ability to appreciate his picture: "its merit is of too refined and unobtrusive a character." To achieve that subtlety he had given the painting his all—all his improving skill, all his hopes for becoming a history painter, all his commitment to the nation's promise, all the little money he had saved from his itinerant portrait painting and from the liberality of his Charleston patrons—all this and more than a year's work. He understood well enough what it all meant: "this picture has ruined me."

FOUR

An Affection of the Heart

(1823–1829)

THE FAILURE of his *House of Representatives* left Finley nowhere. "My plans for the future are in much confusion," he told Lucrece. "I dream of this plan & that." For a while he took to the road again. He tried Albany, but wound up reading in his room, without business. People told him he had come at the wrong time—"the same tune that has been rung in my ears so long!" He tried New York City, boarding cheaply for $2.25 a week and sleeping on the floor of his studio. But New Yorkers were devoted to making money, not spending it. "No business at all," he recorded; "All the artists agree there's nothing doing." Over one twelve-day period only two people came to see his samples. "I wait, and wait, and wait." His clothes needed patching and he borrowed money for his necessities. Once again spending New Year's apart from Lucrece, and alone, he listened to the city greet 1824 with an all-night din of trumpets and kettles.

Finley tried to revive his artistic career by changing its course. "I could easily be a sculptor," he decided. After all, his statue of Hercules had taken a prize in London, and he could now apply to sculpture all he had since learned of painting. Sculpture was an art little practiced in America, too, "a field in which I cannot have, in the nature of the case, a single competitor." As a move in that direction, he had conceived a lathelike device for carving in marble or another substance a replica of any statue or vase. He built a small model and got a New Haven mechanic to construct the working machine. But it proved wearying because turned by foot, and so heavy with its marble block as to make the floor tremble. Finley also learned that a marble-carving machine had already been patented. The truth was that America at the moment simply could not afford artists: "All are poor & discouraged, some are leaving the profession others leaving the country."

Finley thought he might join the exodus, however. Perhaps to Mexico. The country was Americanizing its government, ready to adopt its first federal constitution, choose representatives, and elect its first president. It would enjoy the protection of the United States, too; in his annual message to Congress, President Monroe had declared that the Americas were no longer to be considered subjects for colonization by European powers. Given the current friendliness of Mexico toward the United States, Finley thought of pursuing his profession there, taking along *The House of Representatives* for exhibition. He might also become an art dealer. The upper classes of Mexico City lived lavishly, and the country probably harbored some important paintings. He might be able to interest speculators in buying them for resale in the United States, the profits to be split.

Finley began by seeking a position as private secretary to the new American minister to Mexico, Ninian Edwards, a former governor of Illinois. He wrote to several congressmen trying to enlist their influence, noting that his work as a painter would not interfere with his government duties: Rubens, for example, had done some of his finest portraits in England while serving as ambassador to the court. It turned out that Edwards already had a secretary. But he invited Finley to at least accompany the legation to Mexico, the American government providing free passage from New Orleans to Vera Cruz.

Finley's latest scheme alarmed Lucrece: "How can I consent to have you be at such a distance?" She had given birth again, this time to a son named Charles Walker. Sickly at first, the infant vomited incessantly, and once even seemed to be dying. A frightened letter from her had brought Finley rushing back from Albany. But the episode left her feeling so guilty that she resolved to keep to herself whatever she suffered that might interrupt his work. She did suffer, her already frayed health worn down by the fatigue of caring for two young children: "I sometimes despair of ever enjoying any thing like health and strength again." She feared opening letters from Finley lest they contain more news about Mexico, with the possibility of his being gone for two or three entire years.

The first week in April, however, Finley left for Mexico—the worst but one of their many separations. Lucrece and Jedediah went with him from New Haven to New York, where he took the steamboat for

Philadelphia—the first leg of his journey to Washington, where he would join the legation, accompany it to New Orleans, then on to Vera Cruz. Lucrece planned to move back to her family's home in Concord, but expected little solace: "no one can supply that place in my affections which you have ever occupied." On his trip to Philadelphia, Finley himself was overcome by recollections of leaving his mother and little Susan and Charles in New Haven: tears and kisses; his children frolicking, too young to understand; his desolate last look at every room, "farewell, farewell, seemed written on the very walls."

When he reached Washington, Finley learned that he had set out for his long journey badly unprepared. He was told that he would not find bed and bedding on the road to Mexico, and should have brought them along. He should have brought a saddle, too, and his own provisions. And he would not be able to wear the black suit he had packed: to Mexicans, a man dressed in black meant either a priest or a Freemason. He bought a bed in Washington and sent the suit back to New Haven, asking for a blue one and for a keg of crackers to sustain him on the road.

A week later, still in Washington, Finley received jolting news. The legation's departure for Mexico would be long delayed. Perhaps suspended. Ninian Edwards had been detained on a warrant while a House committee investigated serious charges of fraud he had presented against a congressman. In some desperation, Finley went to see the Secretary of the Navy, to find out whether the vessel, too, was to be detained. If not, he might proceed to Mexico himself, leaving the legation to follow after the House inquiry. But neither staying nor going seemed a good idea: "to go back seems ruin, and forward hazard."

Finley went back—all the way to New Haven. Sending to New Orleans for the baggage he had shipped on, he felt more dejected than ever. To what was his latest defeat due if not to his own religious failings?—failure in his duties toward others, failure to pray enough, failure to keep his religious resolves: "I must plead *guilty, guilty;* and feel that it is but perfectly just that God should desert me, when I have deserted him."

Whatever the cause, the sudden death of his Mexican venture left Finley where he was after exhibiting *The House of Representatives*—without prospects. "I can form no plans for the future, they have all been frustrated," he wrote to Lucrece; "all is darkness and gloomy suspence before me." He could bear hopelessness, if his thwarted plans affected only himself. But on his success had hung the well-being of Lucrece and their children, who deserved better of him: "when I see before me poverty & neglect, the deepest, severest pang I feel is that I am a *married* man."

For a few months Finley painted in New Hampshire and Maine, disgusted with scrambling for commissions: "I have run about long enough." But where to stop running? New York beckoned, although he had had little success in the city. "If I am to live in poverty it will be as well there as any where, and if to make money, why there is the place." New York had yet to reap the profits of the soon-to-open Erie Canal, connecting its trade and busy harbor to the fastgrowing West. But it would be wise, he believed, to make himself known in the city before the wealth began pouring in. New York was booming anyway, everywhere putting up new hotels and banks and shops and publishing firms, on its way to becoming the London of the New World. And with the city's best-known artist, John Trumbull, growing old, he would have no serious rival in painting.

Finley was further drawn to New York by the presence of his brothers. They had moved there the year before to publish a large four-page weekly, the New York *Observer*. An immediate success, it attracted some 2400 subscribers in the first three months, aimed at 10,000, and would become the most widely circulated religious paper in the country. Its news and articles focused on the state of Protestantism worldwide—"The Sabbath in Scotland," "The Bible in the Prussian Army." The *Observer* offered much of secular interest as well—book reviews, commodity prices, speeches in Congress. Finley had designed a vignette for the masthead, a dove with olive branch and rainbow, and the national motto *e pluribus unum.*

Unlike Finley, his brothers were thriving. Work as a full-time religious journalist gave Richard an uncharacteristic sense of purpose. Regarding the paper as "an incalculable service to the Christian public," he energetically rounded up subscribers and composed advertising circulars. Sidney, trained in the law, needed no such steadying. Jedediah once compared him and Finley to the tortoise and the hare: Sidney phlegmatic, Finley impulsive. The most prudent member of the family, Sidney, unlike Finley, distrusted visionary prospects: "new schemes have been the ruin of the Morses," he said. As the *Observer*

Sidney E. Morse (ca. 1860)
(New-York Historical Society)

flourished, he and Richard detached themselves from New Haven and
stopped working on their father's geographies: "we have shone long
enough with borrowed light," Sidney explained, "& wish now we may
shine for ourself."

Finley settled in New York in mid-November, renting a studio at 96
Broadway, a few blocks from his brothers' Pine Street newspaper
office. To his surprise and relief he did well. The new demand for his
painting may have been due to his altered view of it. Instead of trying
to line up and dash off many commissions, he sought only as many as
he could handle while painting carefully. "I have no disposition to be
a nine days' wonder, all the rage for a moment and then forgotten forever." At the same time he took on a few promising pupils, such as the
nineteen-year-old rustic portraitist Erastus Field. "My storms are partly
over," he wrote, "and a clear and pleasant day is dawning upon me."

With the pleasant day came some good luck as well. Three months
before Finley settled in the city, the Marquis de Lafayette
(1757–1834) had arrived in New York harbor to begin a year-long
farewell tour of the country that would take him to all twenty-four

states. Now the only surviving general of the American Revolution, he came at the invitation of Congress and of President Monroe, to a tumultuous reception. A flotilla of seven decorated steamboats manned by two hundred sailors swept him from Staten Island to the Battery, where he was welcomed by ringing bells, roaring cannon, and a crowd of more than fifty thousand.

To Finley as to Jedediah, Lafayette was a near-mythical figure, scarcely less beloved than Washington himself. Lafayette incarnated the fact that the American Revolution, in rejecting monarchy and aristocracy, marked the beginning of modern world history. And he remained a leading international spokesman for representative institutions and the universal right of liberty.

New York City planned to commemorate Lafayette's visit by ordering a life-size portrait of the general. Enthusiastic for the idea, Finley wrote to the chairman of the portrait committee, nominating himself. He sent along testimonials from Charleston, and offered to submit samples of his pictures of New Yorkers. The intense competition for this uniquely important commission brought applications from such well-known artists as Rembrandt Peale and Thomas Sully. But the honor went to Finley, with a fee of about a thousand dollars. An engraving of the portrait would be made, certain to be popular, for which he would receive half the profits.

"We must begin to feel proud of your acquaintance," Lucrece wrote to Finley. His extravagant success also heartened her by its promise of ending their separation. "I think now that we can indulge a rational hope that the time is not very far distant when you can be happy in the bosom of your much loved family, and that your dear children can enjoy the permanent advantage of an affectionate father's counsel and care." Finley spoke of renting a house and settling his family in New York—a possibility all the more desirable to Lucrece because she was pregnant again. She felt worse than usual, but to spare him anxiety said little of her chest spasms and other distresses. Instead, she urged him to take advantage of his sudden good fortune, and return home only when business allowed. "I trust I shall be safely carried thro' *all* that I shall be called to suffer."

Lafayette had moved on to Washington. Before going there to paint him, Finley made a quick trip to New Haven, apparently arriving about two weeks after the birth of his second son, named James Edward Finley. When he reached Washington, around February 8, there was no time to lose, for Lafayette was scheduled to leave soon on a triumphal southern tour, taking him as far as New Orleans.

On first shaking hands with Lafayette, Finley saw a tall man with a florid complexion who walked with a slight limp. He was professionally pleased by the nobility of Lafayette's massive face, and personally over-awed: "This is the man now before me, the very man . . . who spent his youth, his fortune, and his time, to bring about (under Providence) our happy Revolution; the friend and companion of Washington, the terror of tyrants, the firm and consistent supporter of liberty . . . this is the man, the very identical man!" They breakfasted together, and Lafayette introduced Finley to his son as, inevitably, "the son of the geographer." Finley started on the full-length portrait by making an oil study of Lafayette's face. But after three days of sittings he felt he had not done the general justice, and asked to have another few sittings when Lafayette returned to New York from his tour of the South.

Finley's presence in Washington allowed him to witness a historic political event—the debates in the House to resolve the contest for the presidency between John Quincy Adams and Senator Andrew Jackson of Tennessee. In the recent election Jackson had won a majority of the popular vote, but fell short of a majority in electoral votes. In such a case, the Constitution provided for the president to be chosen by the House of Representatives, voting by states. In what became infamously known as the "corrupt bargain," the Speaker of the House, Henry Clay, threw his support and the vote of Kentucky to Adams, electing him president—and later receiving from Adams an appointment as Secretary of State.

Finley not only heard the debates in the House, but also attended President Monroe's levee the evening after the decisive balloting. In a large crowd that included Lafayette, he looked on as Jackson shook the hand of President-elect Adams and cordially congratulated him on his victory. For some Americans, Jackson was the hero of the War of 1812, a man of the people; others saw him as a hotheaded brawler, a potential Napoleon. To Finley it seemed that in bearing his defeat manfully, Jackson showed a "nobleness of mind" that commanded respect. Actually, the enraged Jackson believed that Adams and Clay had stolen the presidency from him.

Excited at being in the Washington whirl, Finley sent Lucrece a lengthy account of these events. But there was no reply. Instead, he received a letter from Jedediah. "My Affectionately-Beloved Son," it began. "My heart is in pain and deeply sorrowful, while I announce to you the sudden and unexpected death of your dear and deservedly-loved wife."

Just twenty-five years old, Lucrece had died in New Haven three weeks after giving birth—only a few days after Finley's visit. While painting Lafayette and hearing the House debates, he had been unaware of her passing. As Jedediah described it to him, Lucrece was about to take to her bed in the late afternoon, still convalescing from her delivery. She spoke cheerfully of before long joining Finley in New York. Stepping into bed, she struggled momentarily then fell back on her pillow: "her eyes were immediately fixed, the paleness of death overspread her countenance, and in five minutes more, without the slightest motion, her mortal life terminated." All attempts to revive her failed. She apparently suffered a heart attack, what Jedediah called an "affection of the heart."

Finley received the agonizing news too late to return for Lucrece's funeral, which was held without him. But on the long slow stagecoach trip back to New Haven he paused in Baltimore to observe the Sabbath, and sent a letter to his parents: "Oh, is it possible—is it possible? shall I never see my dear wife again?. . . I fear I shall sink under it." Every day made evident to him another bond to Lucrece he had taken for granted, which now was all too plainly ruptured. "Oh, what a blow! I dare not give myself up to the full survey of its desolating effects." His attachment had been strengthened, too, by her ardent affection for him, and by her piety. In her trunk he discovered a personal journal recording her arduous self-examination for grace and her delight in at last feeling qualified to take communion. He had guided her through the conversion process, their souls wrapped together. No wonder he now felt heartsick, empty, "as if my very heart itself had been torn from me."

And what would become of his children, "one of the darkest points in my future"? He left young Charles and his infant son in New Haven with his parents and Nancy Shepherd. He took Susan to live with him in New York, where the family with whom he boarded looked after her. Perhaps with some thought of also moving the boys to New York, he rented a three-story house on Canal Street, planning to let part of it to a couple rent-free in exchange for cleaning, washing, and some cooking. But Susan felt homesick, cried, wanted to see her little brothers. After two months he brought her back to New Haven. Much as he wanted the children with him, it seemed impossible to manage. He sent money for their upkeep and often thought of paying them a short visit, "but dare not think of it," he said.

As he tried to get back to his painting, Finley felt tired and preoccupied, "ready almost to give up." Once he got going, however, he threw himself into the work relentlessly. Sitting before his easel all week from seven in the morning until past midnight, by the Sabbath he felt "exceedingly nervous," he said, "so that my whole body and limbs would shake." Lafayette had sent him a sympathizing note on Lucrece's death, promising to finish the large portrait they had begun in Washington. The general came to New York in July, after laying the cornerstone of a fiftieth-anniversary Bunker's Hill monument in Boston, before a throng of forty thousand. The many demands on his time, however, allowed Finley no more than a "few casual glimpses" of him before his return to France.

Although still uncompleted, the prestigious commission brought Finley other important orders for portraits. During the winter and spring of 1825–26—"pumping hard," he said—he created several memorable images of distinguished contemporaries, including the Knickerbocker poet-journalist William Cullen Bryant and the popular governor DeWitt Clinton, chief sponsor of the just completed 350-mile-long Erie Canal. The carefully painted pictures have not only historical value but also a fascinating presence—of vulnerable sensitivity in Bryant, in Clinton of bullnecked combativeness.

Finley's commission also brought him election as an Associate in the American Academy of the Fine Arts. The rank entitled him to participate in the Academy's annual exhibitions and to enter its gallery free of charge. This relatively minor bit of recognition may not have provided much relief from his sorrow. "There are times," he wrote, "when I realize her loss with as much intensity as ever." But his election to the Academy now figured in earning him a unique place in the history of American art.

Like Finley's ill-fated Charleston Academy, the American Academy had mostly languished since its founding in 1802, installed for the last decade behind City Hall in a converted almshouse. The idea of an

Samuel F. B. Morse, *William Cullen Bryant*
(National Academy of Design)

academy devoted to the discussion and teaching of art had been alive
in Europe since at least the sixteenth century. But the wealthy New
Yorkers who founded the American Academy and owned its property
had little interest in training practicing painters and sculptors. Rather,
they sought to bring refinement to America by cultivating public interest in the arts, at the same time keeping alive their upper-class values.
To that end they imported and exhibited antique casts, copies of European masterpieces, works by contemporary European artists. Thirty-
two oil-on-paper sketches of the ruins of Herculaneum by Piranesi had
been donated by the Academy's first Honorary Member, Napoleon
Bonaparte.

The Academy's current president was the distinguished history

Samuel F. B. Morse, *DeWitt Clinton*
(Metropolitan Museum of Art)

painter and Revolutionary War veteran, Colonel John Trumbull. One of very few American artists with an international reputation, he alone held together whatever art community existed in New York at the time. He had studied with Benjamin West in London and had personally known many of the Founding Fathers, many of whose faces he had taken from life in depicting such events as the signing of the Declaration of Independence. He got along easily with the directors of the Academy—bankers, merchants, physicians, and other New York gentlemen of taste and fortune.

Trumbull had liabilities as well, including a scandalously hard-drinking wife and an illegitimate son who had joined the British army. Nearing seventy, his energy waning, he was quick to sense and resent disrespect. And unlike Reynolds and West at the Royal Academy, he had no interest in developing art theory or nurturing young artists. "I would sooner," he remarked, "make a Son of mine a Butcher or a shoemaker."

In October, about six months after his election as an Associate, Finley was given a petition to the Academy drafted by some disgruntled students. The Academy offered no art classes, but during certain morning hours it allowed students to draw from its collection of antique casts, which included models of the Apollo Belvedere and the Laocoön purchased from the Louvre. The students who composed the petition had gone to the Academy one morning to draw, but found the door locked. The doorkeeper reportedly said he would open up when it suited him. Trumbull reportedly approved and commented, haughtily: "These young men should remember that *the gentlemen* have gone to a great expense in importing casts, and that they [the students] have no property in them. . . . beggars are not to be choosers." The students' petition asked the Academy to honor the privileges it had extended.

The document seems to have come to Finley with the request that he present it to the Academy. Stress "seems": the several surviving accounts of the events that followed over the next three months are fragmentary, biased, and contradictory. But Finley's increasing prominence and his standing as an Associate did make him a likely choice to present the petition. And after his abortive attempts to found an academy in Charleston and New Haven, it did occur to him when settling in New York that he might replace the aging Trumbull as head of the American Academy. Nor had he forgotten the resolution he entered in his journal when he left England ten years before: "On returning to America, let my endeavor be to rouse the feeling for works of art."

Finley seems to have invited some Academy students to his Canal Street house to discuss the situation, with two results. The petition was dropped, and a Drawing Association was formed, headed by Finley. The members proposed to meet three evenings a week to draw together from casts, for mutual improvement. Enrolling such well-known New York painters as Asher B. Durand and Thomas Cole, the club presented itself not as a competitor to the American Academy but an extension of it. Trumbull said he was "delighted." He lent the artists some of the Academy's casts, and arranged for them to use rooms at the New-York Historical Society, of which he was vice president.

Finley was pleased by the drawing club's atmosphere of cooperation, especially as the members attributed it to him. "There is a spirit of harmony among the artists," he said, "which never before existed in New York." He considered solidarity among American artists essential for gaining them a voice in American life and challenging the cultural authority of monied patricians. Its membership trebling within weeks, the Drawing Association asked Trumbull for the use of larger quarters. He again agreed. But, not unreasonably, he began to sense a threat to his Academy.

Finley seems not to have been present when, around mid-December, Trumbull turned up at an evening get-together of the club. With the artists drawing from casts he had loaned them, in a room he had provided for them, he apparently wished to reassert the sway of the American Academy over them. As one of the artists, Thomas S. Cummings, recorded the event, Trumbull "took possession" of Finley's seat. Looking around "authoritatively," he asked all the artists present to sign the Academy's student register, which he had brought with him. "The Colonel waited some time," Cummings wrote, "but receiving neither compliance nor attention, left in the same stately manner he had entered; remarking aloud, that he had left the book for our signatures." After Trumbull left, the artists gathered in groups to discuss the confrontation. They agreed that they were not his students, and unanimously refused to sign.

Finley led an effort to restore unity between the drawing club and the Academy. Aware that the mutinous artists wanted to remain in the Academy but have a greater say in its management, he discussed the standoff amicably with Trumbull over dinner. A few weeks later, he chaired a three-man committee from the Drawing Association that conferred with a comparable Academy committee. He reported back to the club that the meeting produced a valuable agreement: in the upcoming vote for a new board of directors, Trumbull's Academy would elect a slate of six artists chosen by the Association—"ensuring us," he said, "that share in the direction which we desire."

Finley's peacemaking, however, may only have touched off total war. The thirty-five Academy members who voted for their new board, on January 10, did elect six artists, but not the six chosen by the drawing club. Surviving explanations of this result differ irreconcilably. In one, Finley misunderstood the committee agreement and thus misrepresented it to the Association. In another, the Academy members betrayed the agreement, voting as if it did not exist. For whatever reason, Trumbull's Academy chose for its board of directors only two of the artists selected by the club—A. B. Durand, and Finley himself. Both resigned.

Four days after the election, Finley addressed a memorable meeting of the Drawing Association. "We have this evening assumed a new attitude in the community," he told the members; "our negotiations with the Academy are at an end." He formally proposed that for the sake of elevating the condition of the arts in the United States they form a new institution, modeled on the Royal Academy. It would differ from Trumbull's conservative Academy in being geared not to the interests of rich patrons and collectors but of artists, managed not by physicians or politicians but by artists—an institution by artists, for artists: *every profession in society knows best what measures are necessary for its own improvement.*"

On January 19, 1826, Finley called to order at his house the first meeting of the National Academy of the Arts of Design. In its earliest form the National Academy consisted of four divisions, each supervised by a prominent artist: Painting, Sculpture, Architecture, Engraving. At the Antique School, about forty students, male and female, could draw from casts and compete for prizes of gold or silver palettes. Plans were soon made for an annual exhibition, a library of standard European works on art, and weekly lectures on such matters as anatomy and perspective.

The members elected Finley as their first president. Committed to painting full-time, he debated with himself whether to accept. He had long hoped to see in America a republican version of the Royal Academy—an American school for training American artists. And New York City was the ideal home for it, "the capital of the country, and here the artists should have their rallying point." But with nothing less than "professional freedom" at stake, the president would bear heavy responsibilities, "more than a balance for the honor." Seeking advice from above, as always, he prayerfully decided that he had a calling to the office: "the cause of the Artists seems under Providence to be in some degree confided to me, and I cannot shrink from the cares and troubles." He agreed to serve as president—as he would every year for the next fifteen years.

By his essential part in creating the National Academy of Design, Finley did much to give American artists a sense of identity and lay a foundation for the modern New York art world. Over the next decade, some four hundred students received instruction at the Academy, which over the next half century remained the most influential art institution in America. Thomas Cole, Rembrandt Peale, William Dunlap, the architect Ithiel Town, and the other original members were succeeded by such distinguished National Academicians and Associates as Winslow Homer, Thomas Eakins, Mary Cassatt, John Singer Sargent, and Frank Lloyd Wright.

The idea of lecturing on art had been with Finley since the time of his seasons in Charleston. Amid the wrangling that brought the N.A.D. into being he tried putting together four lectures. Reading widely and taking copious notes, he found the writing difficult and often thought of postponing the talks, or giving only two. But a desire to enlarge his growing reputation kept him at it: "if well done, they place me alone among the artists; I being the only one who has yet written a course of lectures in our country."

Finley delivered his lectures over four nights in March and April 1826, in the chapel of Columbia College. They were sponsored by the New York Athenaeum—one offering in a series of talks by writers, philosophers, and scientists meant to enrich the city's intellectual life. As literature Finley's lectures are undistinguished. He borrowed freely from the many books he consulted, especially Sir Joshua Reynolds' *Discourses,* and strained to achieve a highfalutin tone. His first lecture, for instance, opens with a convoluted by-your-leave:

> If those of your Lecturers who have been in the habit of addressing a popular assembly have felt a diffidence in appearing before so refined and intelligent an audience as I now have the honor to address and have claimed your indulgence, well may I feel a diffidence in submitting to you the composition of one more accustomed to address the public through the eye than through the ear, and consequently inexperienced in the facilities of arranging a written discourse.

Despite the wearisome formality, in the history of American art Finley's lectures have the primacy of Edgar Allan Poe's attempts, a few years later, to educate the American public in sophisticated standards for judging literary works.

Finley took as his main subject the affinity of painting to poetry, music, and landscape gardening, and their mutual dependence on the eternal principles active in Nature. He began, that is, with the ancient doctrine of the sister arts, but gave it an important twist: "the other Arts of the Imagination have hitherto been more cultivated in our country than Painting, and I presumed that the latter would be better understood by showing it in its connexion with the former." His lectures were a simile, comparing the unknown to the known. Unlike a European audience, his listeners in New York had had little experience of serious painting. So to suggest its features he described congruent features of carefully wrought poetry, music, and landscape gardening, kindred arts more familiar to them.

In his first lecture, Finley distinguished the Practical Arts from the Fine Arts, the aim of the latter being to please the Imagination. His second lecture set out a theology of the Fine Arts. Created in the likeness of God, humanity desires to create; not being God, however, it cannot create out of nothing. The artist can only combine into new forms the existent God-given "*principles*" of nature, such as Motion, Order, Unity, and Mystery. Lecture Three demonstrated how painting's sister arts use these principles to stir the Imagination. To reproduce natural effects of Motion, for instance, poets divide their language into metrical feet, musicians vary their tempi, landscape gardeners build brooks. In his final lecture Finley showed how painters too reproduce these familiar principles. Much as poets render natural forces through words, painters use lines, chiaroscuro, and color. The painter imitates Motion, for instance, by arrangements of color that move the viewer's eye from point to point, or imitates Mystery by contrasts of light and dark. To illustrate, Finley held up and analyzed engravings of works by Titian, Rubens, Poussin, and other masters.

While speaking of general principles and old masters, Finley obviously had his own situation in mind. By refining American taste he hoped at the same time to create American buyers for the sort of pictures he wanted to paint, to overcome the indifference that had doomed his *House of Representatives:* "what use is it for the Artist to cultivate his own taste," he asked his audience, "if those around him are incapable of feeling and appreciating the beauties which are spread before them." He generally excluded the lower classes from the future ranks of the tasteful, confining his instruction to persons such as he considered his listeners to represent, "the intelligent and well educated in all countries and ages." In their disdain for the emergent democratic masses, at least, his lectures offered nothing to offend the patrician founders of Trumbull's American Academy.

According to Finley, each lecture drew a larger audience than the one before, his final lecture attracting the largest audience ever assembled in the Columbia chapel. He found not much time to enjoy his success, being obliged to prepare for another important event—the first exhibition by his National Academy of Design. A private opening was held on May 13, attended by Governor Clinton, the mayor of New York City, the Columbia College faculty, and other dignitaries. Next day the Academy members welcomed in the public—the artists identifying themselves by wearing white ribbons in their buttonholes, shaped into roses. Housed on the second floor of an ordinary dwelling on lower Broadway, the exhibit stayed open through June from nine in the morning to ten at night (lit by six gas lamps). Finley contributed three portraits; Trumbull himself sent a painting, as did Allston. All of the 180 oils, watercolors, engravings, and architectural drawings were new works by living artists, not previously displayed in public—an important innovation that led Thomas Cummings to call the N.A.D. show "the first solely artistic effort at Exhibition in the country."

Probably only a day or two before or after the opening, Finley received a letter from his mother saying she had never seen Jedediah so feeble. He would be glad to see his sons, "if they can break away from their numerous cares." Although often tempted to drop everything for a "short look" at his children, Finley had not visited New Haven for three months. A few days after receiving his mother's letter, he received another from her, with the news that Jedediah was now unable to get out of bed without help: "He will be much gratified to see his dear children when they can conveniently come." Finley replied that he was tied down, "painting away with all my might," the city Corporation pressing him to finish his full-length portrait of Lafayette: "Nothing but the most imperious necessity prevents my coming immediately. . . . like our good father, all his sons seem destined for most busy stations in society . . . not for themselves alone, but for the public benefit."

With the news early in June that his father had only a few days to live, Finley tore himself from business. He seems to have arrived in New Haven on June 9, only hours before Jedediah's death. He found several young people gathered around his father's bed. Sinking but tranquil, Jedediah said to them: "You see how a Christian can die, *without fear.*" Calvinist tradition cherished such demonstrations of how a Christian faced death, especially a minister. Finley joined in by catechizing his father. What was his mental state? "I have a *hope full of immortality.*" Did he at all doubt the truth of the doctrines he had long preached? "O no; I believe them to be the doctrines of the Bible."

At one moment Jedediah shuddered, laboring for breath. Finley assured him that the Savior would not desert him in his hour of trial. "O no, he gives me already a foretaste of heaven," Jedediah replied earnestly; "I have not strength to express the joy I feel." In what Finley believed was an allusion to Lucrece, his father added: "I feel no gloom about the grave knowing . . . in whose company I am to rise." A few minutes later, with Richard and Sidney still en route from New York, Finley closed his father's eyes. Next day he recalled Psalms 37: 37, "Mark the perfect man, and behold the upright, for the *end* of that man is *peace.*"

But Jedediah's end had not been so peaceful. He died convinced that his labors had gone unappreciated. He had prepared a 500-page report on his tour of Indian villages, but the government refused to publish it—"to mortify & wound your feelings," Elizabeth said. Lamenting the loss of his ministry, his geographies no longer selling as well as before, he had had to mortgage his house and borrow to keep up appearances.

Jedediah's will testified to the deepening financial failures of his last few years. To his three sons he left only $50 each. Noting that Finley had received his portion through his training in England, he gave the copyrights of his books to Richard and Sidney, requiring them to pay a third of the income to Elizabeth. The remainder of the estate went to her, but this amounted to less than nothing. At the time of his death Jedediah had $7000 but owed $14,000. As Elizabeth summed up her situation soon afterward, "At age 61 years I have three little motherless children to take care of besides three young men all without wives who have never yet been from under my care at home or abroad."

Throughout Finley's life, "Morse" had meant Jedediah, the "Father of American Geography." But by his lectures and his activities as president of the National Academy, "Morse" was beginning to mean himself—

New York City's, perhaps the nation's, chief spokesman for American art. Artists elsewhere noticed and sent congratulations. "The progress of your Academy has produced a sensation," Thomas Sully wrote. The Philadelphia painter John Neagle hurrahed: American artists had at last shown themselves to be self-sufficient, "qualified to preside over and govern '*An Academy of Arts*' without the adventitious & aristocratic influence of the MD'S, LLD'S or ASSES!" The news reached even London: "Morse," said his old friend Charles Leslie, "seems to be a great man among them at New York."

Finley's completed *Lafayette* brought further notice and praise. The eight-by-five-foot canvas was displayed at the N.A.D.'s second show, held this time in the city's best exhibition room, the skylighted upper floor of the handsome Arcade Bath building. The portrait depicts the thick-waisted sixty-eight-year-old general standing at the top of a flight of stairs. In his black coat and yellow pantaloons he looks baggy-eyed, a bit mournful, quintessentially Gallic. Several newspapers hailed the painting for accurate likeness, but it aims, rather, at symbolic representation. Finley explained some of the many symbolic touches: a glowing sunset sky, marking the glorious evening of Lafayette's life; a heliotrope facing the sun, alluding to his unswerving consistency; an empty pedestal beside busts of Washington and Franklin, waiting to complete the national trinity by receiving a bust of the Marquis himself. Concerned more with the thought than the thing, Finley painted not so much Lafayette as the Idea of Lafayette— an authentic American hero who happened to be French.

Finley's *Lafayette* did not please everyone. One reviewer wrote that he "might have made a much better picture of any thing or any body." As Finley's prominence more and more exposed him to public scrutiny, he won detractors as well as admirers. The New York *Mirror* put down a portrait he displayed in the third annual N.A.D. exhibition, for "the unskillful manner in which the colours have been laid on." Another viewer derided Finley's portrait of William Cullen Bryant as vapid, "too much like a common man—Mr. Morse never could have understood and felt his genius." Still another critic sensed in Finley— correctly—pretensions to having attained rank in an aristocracy of talent. Much as Jedediah had styled himself "D.D.F.A.A.S.H.S.," Finley now signed himself "P.N.A.," President of the National Academy—as if, it was said, he wanted to make artists princes or knights.

Barely two years old, Finley's Academy also came under attack,

Samuel F. B. Morse, *The Marquis de Lafayette*
(City of New York, Office of the Mayor)

some of it intense. He had advised the members not to lash out at
Trumbull's American Academy, indignant though many felt over its
past treatment of them. Further controversy, he said, would be expensive, and a distraction from their studies: "*silence* is undoubtedly the
best defence."

Without intending to, however, Finley himself touched off a mean-
spirited public battle between his organization and Trumbull's. It
began with a lengthy commencement address he delivered at the conclusion of the N.A.D.'s first academic year, published with notes as a
sixty-page pamphlet entitled *Academies of Arts* (1827). His arguments

are too many and complex to be summarized briefly. But in essence he contended that from late-medieval Venice to the present, art academies had two features in common: instruction for students and governance by the artists themselves. Throughout their history, academies served especially to teach students to draw, accurate representation being the foundation for all the arts of design. But American students would face public insensitivity and ignorance, the country being as yet unable to appreciate genuine merit: "Bold pretension will be successful, while more retiring merit will be neglected, for it will not be understood." And American patrons preferred buying supposed European masterworks—most of them fakes—to works by living American artists, a practice certain to "retard the progress of modern art."

Finley's pamphlet provoked a seventeen-page reply in the *North American Review*, New England's most prestigious intellectual journal. The anonymous author was a Boston lawyer and amateur painter named Franklin Dexter. More sympathetic than the classicist Finley to new currents of Romantic thinking, he argued that when artists govern an academy they tend to establish a school, systematizing what should arise from the student's observation of nature. By emphasizing accurate drawing, too, academies teach students to make dull copies of what happens to be before them, ignoring poetical conception. Dexter also countered Finley's pessimistic picture of American taste. The enemy to national progress in the arts is not a snobbish preference for European works, but the utilitarian spirit of the present age: "Eloquence, poetry, painting, and sculpture—do not belong to such an age; they are already declining, and they must give way before the progress of popular education, science, and the useful arts."

Finley published a thoughtful rebuttal to Dexter's article. Writing for a New York newspaper, he argued among other things that the very progress of practical arts in America reflected a national energy that would at some future date also elevate painting and its sister arts: "Their place in the march of civilization is in the train of the *useful* arts, and these, their *avant couriers*, have long and eminently occupied a distinguished place in our country." The elegant arts would someday thrive in practical America, he prophesied, because they need the atmosphere of a free government in which to breathe. America, "from its very freedom, is the natural habitation of these arts."

Had it ended there, the well-mannered exchange between Finley and Dexter might be remembered as the country's first substantial public debate on art, touching many issues of long-range importance to the arts in America. The Academy question having been opened for discussion however, others took it up. Under such pseudonyms as "A Patron," "Middle Tint," and "Joe Strickland" of "Memphremagog," they turned out a score of pamphlets and newspaper articles that dragged into public view conflicting and often bitter accounts of how the National Academy of Design came to be.

One side attacked the breakaway artists as "*seceders*," the other defended them as patriots, acting "as much from principle as our Republican Government." Both sides grumbled about backstabbing and snakes in the grass, and spoke out for or against Finley or Trumbull personally. One side said Trumbull turned artists into sycophants, fawning on the rich in hopes of patronage; his exhibitions at the American Academy, showing the same pictures year after year, were a joke ("Have you seen the exhibition this year?" "No, I saw it last year"). Finley, the other side said, inflated himself "with the pompous title of President"; proceeds from exhibitions of the National Academy went to line his own pockets.

Becoming a storm center, Finley held still until the appearance of an article in the New York *American* by "A Lay Member." The writer charged him with having published a series of inflammatory articles under the names "Boydell" and "Denon." This duo had denounced Trumbull's American Academy for among other things holding fraudulent elections, faltering under a load of debt, and being useless to the city's artists. Insulted to be accused of hiding behind pseudonyms, Finley replied in the *Evening Post,* dismissing the charge as "*entirely mistaken*" and for the first time publicly laying out his own version of the founding of the N.A.D.

This "Exposé," as Finley called it, enraged Trumbull. Answering back in the same newspaper he blasted Finley as a "wretched pettifogger," damning his "gross perversion and suppression of truth." It was Finley, he said, who had excited students at the American Academy to revolt, who had masterminded a plan to deprive the Academy of its charter of incorporation, rob it of its property. In any circumstances Trumbull was quick to take offense. But the violence of his response suggests that he may have been the "Lay Member" who sniffed out Finley behind "Boydell" and "Denon." Invoking his advanced age and long service to the country, he told his readers that he felt duty-bound to speak plainly: "in the spirit of the olden time, I have called a Cat a Cat, and not a pretty pussy."

Finley remained calm, at least before the public. Addressing Trumbull through the *Evening Post,* he said that he had "too much self-respect to spend many words in answering." He would rest content with drawing a comparison: "The National Academy, sir, is a real Academy for the promotion of the Arts of Design. . . . The American Academy of Fine Arts, sir, is *not* an Academy."

The controversy died down in the summer of 1828. But Finley did not forget the harsh words written against him. Later in the year an upstate newspaper editor asked him to review an exhibition at Trumbull's Academy. He declined, explaining that he could give no lengthier appraisal than to comment that most of the pictures were junk—"*execrable trash,* the vile daubings of *old-picture* manufacturers, or the crude copies of students . . . *But don't say I gave it to you.*"

Amid the public exhibitions and quarreling, Finley lived the drifting life of a homeless widower. He changed residences several times, moving from Canal Street to Cedar Street, Murray Street, Grand Street. With New York City becoming the country's publishing center, he befriended Bryant, the poet Fitz-Greene Halleck, and other writers no less eager to establish a professional class of American authors than he to win respect for American artists. He joined James Fenimore Cooper's literary society, the Bread and Cheese, and when it disbanded in 1829 joined its successor, the Sketch Club. The Club's twenty-five members met weekly at one another's quarters, in alphabetical rotation, the host providing sandwiches, mulled wine, hard-boiled eggs. Meetings were announced cabalistically in the daily press. "S.C.:S.F.B.M." meant that Sketch Club members would gather that evening at Finley's, as they did several times.

The atmosphere of the Club was mock-solemn. Members discussed the "evolvement of sardonic iced gas," the propriety of "discumgarigamfrigation." Finley fully entered the farcical fun. The club minutes record that he at one time or another made a motion that "whereas this is moving day, the Secretary be removed"; exhibited a new portrait from life of Oliver Cromwell; and offered a hanky to a leaking fellow club member, "which on examination turns out to be a modification of a mixture of purple and pea green—no go." The host of each meeting selected an object or phrase for the members to illustrate in a poem or drawing. Revealingly perhaps, when the host suggested "The Emotions," Finley chose to depict "Indignation."

Finley had done some writing since his undergraduate days—poems, essays, scriptural exegeses, a few newspaper articles, a farce. Friendly now with the Knickerbocker literary lights, he became a part-time literary man himself. Writing anonymously in his brothers' *Observer,* he assailed the Bowery Theater for presenting Madame Hutin, a scantily clad danseuse whose performances amounted to smut, "the *public exposure of a naked female.*" The articles made such a stir that he was invited to write the prospectus for a new daily newspaper that would not, as he said, "pander to the appetites of the depraved by enticing them to scenes of licentiousness"—a journal dedicated to the moral reform of New York City. He named the paper the *Journal of Commerce* and may even have managed it awhile before finding a permanent editor. He wrote poetry, too: a sonnet to Lafayette, who "freely brav'd our storms"; an insipid "Serenade," about "magic notes/In visions heard."

Finley also found time to edit the literary remains of a precocious Plattsburgh girl named Lucretia Davidson. She had died at the age of seventeen, leaving over three hundred poems in manuscript. He published the collection as *Amir Khan,* sending copies to Sir Walter Scott and Robert Southey. Lucretia Davidson's name was of course resonant for him. The memories it stirred register in his description of her as an example of "exquisite beauty . . . perishing in its bloom."

Finley thought often and tearfully of Lucrece. People he knew urged him to remarry and make a new home for his children, but he lacked the "*shopping* disposition," he said; "I cannot look for a wife as I would for a pair of gloves." In his most dejected moments he believed he had no prospect of ever marrying again, or having his family around him; other times it seemed at least not impossible.

Such a moment arrived in the fall of 1828, a few months after his newspaper squabble with John Trumbull. Traveling upstate to paint some commissioned portraits, he met a young woman named Catherine Pattison (or Patterson), the daughter of a Troy, New York, businessman. She seemed a "lovely, noble minded girl," having the qualities of mind and heart that he sought. After much prayer he proposed to her. Not much more can be said about how their close relationship developed; relevant passages in his surviving correspondence have been deleted and entire letters lost or removed. What is known is that Catherine agreed to marry him, although apparently half his age—a schoolgirl in her teens and ill at ease in the world, "so different from other people," she told him, "that I almost despair of ever being like the rest of the human family."

But Catherine's father strongly disapproved the match and forbade Finley to visit or communicate with her—"Nor would her father see me, or explain to me, or suffer me to personally explain to him." He considered Finley unsuitable as a widower with children and, more so, as a painter. The second objection startled and angered Finley, given that he was also the son of The Geographer, a graduate of Yale, devoutly pious, and president of the National Academy: "Family, education, talents, habits, character, standing in society, all it seems are of no weight against the single fact that I am an artist."

Although tempted to defy Catherine's father, Finley did nothing. His own principles condemned any interference with a child's duty to obey parental commands. And he believed that Catherine's father would repay disobedience by disinheriting her—"on my own account it would not weigh a straw, yet I feel it to be too great a sacrifice on her part to risk." But replacing Catherine would not be easy. The ending of the affair left him devastated: "since the death of my dear Lucretia I have had nothing occur so overwhelming."

The end of the affair had another powerful effect. It quickened Finley's long-unfulfilled desire to visit Paris and Rome. He had planned to take Catherine, but decided to go himself—not for sightseeing but to complete his artistic education. American painters had looked longingly toward Italy since Benjamin West's pioneering trip there in 1760. Cut off from the Continent during the Napoleonic Wars, they were once again making their way to Italy, where they could live cheaply while painting, and see the masterworks they knew only from casts and engravings. To Finley, his present miserable moment seemed the right time. Now in his late thirties, he would soon be too old to profit much from further study. And Europe promised renewal, another beginning in a lifetime of fresh starts.

Finley tried to raise enough money to cover the cost of his visit. The *Journal of Commerce* invited him to serve as a correspondent, travel articles being popular in the American press. But he thought the effort would too much reduce his painting time. He solicited subscriptions for a large picture that he proposed to paint while abroad. It would remain the subscribers' property until its exhibition in America paid back the money they advanced, with interest. Considering the public's indifference to exhibitions of his *House of Representatives,* the idea seems starry-eyed, and in any case failed to inspire patronage. He tried the government. Congress was thinking of hiring American artists to complete the group of paintings it had authorized years earlier, pictures of American history to be hung under the huge dome of the United States Capitol. Four 12-by-18-foot canvases had been commissioned in 1817 from John Trumbull, who spent eight years producing them.

Securing a commission for one of the Capitol pictures represented to Finley far more than a means of getting to Europe. In the work's subject, scale, and placement he saw the realization of his highest ambitions as a history painter. He wrote to Senator Robert Young Hayne, whom he had painted in Charleston, frankly recommending that Congress hire him. "I have been preparing myself in all my studies for many years for such a work," he said, "and am burning for an opportunity to execute one work at least which shall reflect credit on myself, and I hope on my country." Announcing that he was about to leave for Europe, he asked to be given the commission now, so that through his advanced study abroad he might perfect his ability to fulfill it.

No government commission arrived. But Finley did manage to finance his trip, by lining up orders to paint landscapes, portraits, or copies of works by Poussin, Tintoretto, and other European masters. In all, he acquired pledges for some thirty pictures amounting to about $3000, enough to support him modestly in France and Italy for three years.

Before departing in November, Finley got a letter of introduction from Secretary of State Martin Van Buren, and another to the American minister to France. Settling his affairs, he resigned as president of the National Academy. But the Council persuaded him to retain the office and allow the vice president, Henry Inman, to perform its duties in his absence. And he had to arrange for the care of his children—Susan, Charles, James. Their material well-being seemed assured.

Lucrece's father, their grandfather, had recently received a large inheritance and promised to provide for them.

As to leaving his children for three years, Finley reasoned that all his artistic labors aimed at having a home for them. Since his study abroad would ultimately be to their benefit he need not feel guilty: "I think no one will accuse me of neglecting them." But he had not often visited the children during his four years in New York, either. Instead he sent them instructions indistinguishable from those his parents had sent him many years before, bartering love for obedience: "tell Susan if she loves her Papa, she will gratify him by behaving so that he shall hear good accounts of her." The conflict between domestic life and an artistic career was of course nothing new to Finley. As a student at the Royal Academy he had painted a *Judgment of Jupiter,* showing a young woman in flight from her lover Apollo, god of inspiration, to her mortal husband. For himself he had long ago chosen Apollo, finding some comfort and warrant in religious scruples about the "danger of idolizing the family circle."

Following the deaths of Lucrece and Jedediah, Finley's children had been looked after in New Haven by Elizabeth Morse and nurse Nancy Shepherd. But Elizabeth herself had died while he was caught up in preparing the third annual N.A.D. exhibition. At first she had shown symptoms of dropsy. When he learned that her legs were swollen he sent a letter of sympathy—and news that the exhibition was thronged, "the first people in the city, ladies and gentlemen." Two weeks later he wrote again. "I am so situated as to be unable to leave the city without great detriment to my business," he said. "I will come, however, if, on the whole, you think it best." Whether he then returned to New Haven is unknown, but ten days later Elizabeth was dead, at the age of sixty-two. She had been a difficult woman, a difficult mother—embittered by the loss of eight children, sharp-tongued, quick to find fault. Still, her death left him counting the toll of the last few years: "my wife, my father, my mother all in their graves."

After Elizabeth's death, Finley's children were placed with various caretakers, with whom they would remain during his absence. Charles, seven and a half years old, was boarded with a clergyman near New Haven. James, two years younger, early on developed some serious illness: "I can't but hope he will yet be a well child," Finley said; "he seems to have an unusual share of troubles." James was moved around, boarded awhile upstate with Richard Morse's new bride and her aunt, then taken by Sidney Morse to Brooklyn and put in an "Infant School," then reunited with his brother Charles at the home of the clergyman. Finley placed ten-year-old Susan with Lucrece's sister and her husband in Concord, New Hampshire—"without expence to me," he noted.

The couple considered adopting Susan, not out of affection for her, it seems clear, but out of respect to the memory of Lucrece. Lucrece's sister complained to Finley that the girl had been improperly reared, too much given her own way: "when I commanded her to do any thing, she would not be very ready to mind." She applied herself to breaking Susan's bad habits by denying her walks or visits and sending her to a "man's school," in which almost all the students were boys. "If there is any thing that is painful to me," she said, "it is to see a child, made completely wretched by selfishness and indulgence." Susan keenly felt her separation from Finley and wrote to him imploringly from New Hampshire: "I hope you will not go to Europe my dear Father. You must come and see me." At the bottom of the letter she added: "When this you see/Remember me."

Finley was not deaf to such cries, nor indifferent to the uprooting of his children. But long practice in a self-pitying fatalism helped him justify his failure to relieve their situation: "my children scattered, separated from each other, and from me, and I alone," he wrote; "I feel this trial most severely, it is a dark dispensation but I know it is right, for He has done it who cannot err." Yet however much he trusted the design of Providence, when just about to leave his country he sank into depression, "great depression," he said, "from which some have told me they feared for my health and even reason."

MORSE

We have listened too long to the courtly muses of Europe. The spirit of the American free-man is already suspected to be timid, imitative, tame.

—Ralph Waldo Emerson, "The American Scholar,"
address delivered August 31, 1837

The invention all admired, and each, how he
To be the inventor missed; so easy it seemed
Once found, which yet unfound most would have thought
Impossible.

—Copied out by Morse in 1839 from *Paradise Lost*, VI, 498–501

Horatio Greenough, *Samuel F. B. Morse* (1831)
(National Museum of American Art)

FIVE

Il Diavolo

(1830–1832)

A FTER A twenty-six day voyage, Morse reached Liverpool on December 4, in cold that frosted his eyebrows and the fur on his cape. He stopped two weeks in London, then caught the small, dirty cross-Channel steamer to France, arriving in Paris at dawn on New Year's Day. The icy weather had frozen the Seine. From Paris he headed for Rome by diligence, a clumsier vehicle than American stage-coaches, he thought, the cheap rear seats occupied by "low people."

Even in his own well-cushioned compartment, Morse found the trip south jangling. Snow clogged the iron wheels of the diligence, forcing it to make sudden stops. No guardrail shielded the carriage from plummeting off the winding precipitous mountain roads, often blocked by rocks washed down from the heights. To cross the swollen streams he sometimes had to step out and be carried over on the shoulders of "brawny watermen." Irksomely, as the diligence passed through the ten "dominions" of divided Italy he again and again had to present his papers and luggage for inspection. And there was talk of bandits, avalanches.

Journeying through France and Italy, Morse sometimes thought of Napoleon. In reading biblical prophecy while at college, he believed he saw Bonaparte foretold in Daniel and Revelation. He took time when in Paris to see the robes and golden cups used in the Emperor's coronation. Drawing closer to Rome, he stopped at an inn near Antibes and breakfasted in a room Napoleon had occupied as he withdrew into exile on the island of Elba. Although he had exulted in Bonaparte's defeat, he knew something himself of frustrated ambition, and felt if not kinship at least sympathy with the banished

Emperor. He lay down on the bed and looked out on the room, which had been kept as Napoleon left it: "I . . . endeavored to conceive for the moment how he, who had in that very situation seen the same objects when he woke, then viewed the reverses of life, to which he had apparently hitherto believed himself superior."

Then, Rome. Encircled by walls, without modern buildings, the city survived as a mausoleum of the classical world, Middle Ages, and Renaissance—to Morse a promised land, overpowering: "All the classic story of our school boy days, history and fable, truth and fiction . . . are now reality," he wrote; "*Rome,* the very spot, *Rome* . . . once the seat of the Arts, the seat of the empire of the world."

Morse settled into a shuttered four-story house at 17 Via dei Prefetti, a narrow cobblestoned street just off one of Rome's main thoroughfares, the busy Via del Corso. Shelley had lived nearby in 1819, and a few streets away was the Piazza Colonna with its sculpted Egyptian column, taken as a trophy by Augustus after his victory over Cleopatra.

At first Morse established a daily routine of visiting the Vatican galleries, the Palazzi Borghese, or some other dizzyingly lavish collection. There the poorest Italian could experience aesthetic pleasure more refined than any available to even the wealthiest American. Despite his fifteen years' experience and study, Morse felt unprepared for the scarcely imaginable magnificence he beheld, room upon spectacularly opulent room of marble walls and rare inlaid woods, packed floor to ceiling with stupendous frescoes, exhaustless stores of supremely gifted painting and sculpture by Caravaggio, Bernini, Botticelli, Michelangelo.

As he gazed and gaped, Morse took rapturous notes, listing the scores of paintings he saw and occasionally making small outline sketches of their composition. He made many discoveries, for instance finding painterly strengths in such "early masters" as Giotto and Ghirlandaio. To a modern eye their works seemed "rude, and stiff, and dry," yet he saw much worth studying, especially "variety of attitude character and expression," strong points of his own portraits as well. Other canvases leaped out to him as revelations, such as a portrait by Veronese: "proves that harmony may be produced in one *color,*" he noted, excitedly; "Curtain in the back ground *hot* green, middle tint sleeves of the arms *cool,* vest which is in the mass of light as well as the lights of the curtain *warm,* white collar which is the highest light cool!!!!"

Morse soon got down to business, copying paintings by Poussin, Rubens, and others to fill the commissions that made his life in Rome possible. In sending the completed pictures back to his patrons in the United States, he rolled up the canvases, coating them with a special varnish to prevent sticking. The commission that occupied most of his time involved a work by the artist considered in America to be the greatest painter of them all—Raphael's *School of Athens.* The fifty or so figures in this summit of Western art include Plato, Aristotle, Pythagoras, Euclid, Ptolemy, and Raphael himself. Morse often worked at the copy all day, sitting in the famous Stanza della Segnatura of the Apostolic Palace and trying to shrink Raphael's intricate wall-size fresco onto a canvas thirty by forty inches.

When he could, Morse visited the studios of some of the many European artists in Rome, not without envy. Students at the French Academy painted in a villa on the Pincian Hill overlooking the city, their ateliers provided rent-free by the French government, with a stipend for living expenses. Could he live that way, Morse felt, not forced to support himself by copying the works of others, "I too might paint the picture I have so long desired to paint." He also saw the extensive studios in the Palazzo Barberini of the Danish sculptor Bertel Thorwaldsen, an old man with wild gray hair straggling over his ears, yet honored by the potentates of all Europe—"the greatest sculptor of the age," Morse thought. The classical simplicity of Thorwaldsen's work seemed to him no mere imitation of the antique but a reincarnation of its spirit. He got to walk with Thorwaldsen for recreation and to paint his portrait. In his diaries he noted but crossed out the information that the great man had taken an English noblewoman for one of his mistresses and fathered two children by another.

Thorwaldsen presented Morse with a cast of his Venus to send back to the National Academy of Design. From artists and patrons in the Rome art community Morse rounded up other benefactors for the N.A.D. as well. He shipped to New York such gifts as a ten-foot-high cast of the Farnese Hercules and scores of prints and books containing heads by Raphael, views of Pompeii, sulfur impressions of gems. The donations turned out to be costly, however. Freight charges from Rome to New York ate up funds set aside for operating expenses, and ran the N.A.D. into debt. Word came back to Rome to send "NO MORE PRESENTS."

Morse found the Roman summer scorchingly hot, with a glaring sunlight that pained his eyes. He made several excursions into the surrounding countryside, including a month-long tour of Hadrian's Villa and the Sabine Hills, a popular trail for plein-air sketching. He carried his painting gear slung over his shoulder, taking along a field chair and tall umbrella. The villa, with the decayed splendor of its amphitheater, temples, and fountains, was peerless, "the finest ruins I have ever seen." Snacking on a basket of cherries, he sketched all day, the solitude broken only by the sounds of crumbling architecture and green lizards rustling through the leaves and ivy.

From Hadrian's Villa, Morse traveled to Subiaco, about forty-five miles from Rome, bobbing along part of the way on a donkey over the steep twisting rocky paths. As many other artists had, he found the place uniquely picturesque—flocks of goats, twanging guitars, ruined convents, peasants in sugarloaf hats. He sketched in oil a rustic outdoor chapel, from which he made a larger landscape that shows a *contadina* kneeling before a shrine to the Virgin.

Morse got around Rome, too. He often attended concerts, and took in performances of *The Barber of Seville* and Bellini's *Romeo and Juliet*. He visited the Protestant cemetery, where he copied down the odd inscription on a stone marking the burial of "a young English Poet . . . whose name was writ in water." He was entertained one evening at the house of the painter Joseph Severn, but may never have realized that the peculiar grave was that of Severn's dear friend, John Keats. In some fear of being mugged, he entered the Colosseum on a still night. Surrounded by broken moonlit piers and arcades, he seated himself in the center of the arena, where once stood a colossal statue of the sadistic Nero.

Apart from the superb art and antiquities, most of what Morse saw of Italian life disgusted him. He had arrived in Rome during the carnival season, in time to observe some of the festivities in the Via del Corso. The decorated thoroughfare was mobbed with revelers costumed as bears, harlequins, and even Satan, pelting each other with flowers and imitation sugar plums. Travel writers romanticized the scene, he thought. In reality it represented only degenerate chaos, "where man

Samuel F. B. Morse, *Contadina of Nattuno at
the Shrine of the Madonna*
(Virginia Museum of Fine Arts)

seems to delight in the opportunity to demonstrate to his fellowman
how near he can approach in appearance and manners to the beasts
he imitates." During the previous year's carnival a murderer had been
publicly drawn and quartered; the merrymakers carried on in full view
of his severed festering limbs.

Morse found evidence of the country's "low state of moral feeling"
not only in Roman decadence but also in the thievery at all levels of
society. Customs inspectors extorted money by slapping on imaginary
duties. Merchants asked for their goods three or four times what they
were willing to take, trying to grab what they could. Morse learned
how to handle price-gougers: "treat them like slaves, hold a haughty
domineering manner towards them, you will then get civility." Worst,
at the bottom of the social ladder, were the beggars. Everywhere he

had to fend off these "squalid and hideous objects," including children beseeching him for treats. Once he found himself circled by a whole begging swarm—"such devouring eyes such pushing and bawling . . . so disgusting a sight."

And farther south the moral climate was still more sordid. Visiting Naples in the fall, Morse enjoyed the gorgeous bay, and ascended the thundering cone of Vesuvius, the sea of hot lava inside sending up suffocating fumes and showers of hot cinders. He also visited the notorious private rooms of the museum, with their pornographic frescoes and statues, "evidence of the most depraved state of morals." Far more offensive was the public burial place, which every day opened one of its 365 stone-covered pits to receive corpses of the poor. Holding a handkerchief to his nose and peering into the vault he beheld carcasses of men, women, and children of all ages. Thrown together in heaps, they had been stripped naked and left to corrupt in a mass like offal from a slaughterhouse. "So disgusting a spectacle I never witnessed," he said. "Never I believe in any country Christian or pagan is there an instance of such total want of respect for the remains of the dead."

What Morse experienced of Neapolitan filth and noise sickened him hardly less. Bored and mindless, people ate macaroni while delousing each other's heads; children of both sexes went naked; vendors screamed cockles and figs; vagrants shat in public. The city had no libraries, no newspapers, no literary societies. And there was the loathsome local specialty, "a species of most nauseating looking cake . . . covered over with slices of pomodoro or tomatos, and sprinkled with little fish and black pepper and I know not what other ingredients, it altogether looks like a piece of bread that had been taken reeking out of the sewer." Here Morse may well have written the first description in American literature of an anchovy pizza.

Nothing else in Italian life so much repelled Morse as the bizarre, menacing power of the Catholic Church. Hatred of Popery had been common in the New England of his youth, brought there from England nearly two centuries earlier by the first colonists. And now, despite a swelling population of twenty-one million, Italy was economically stagnant, dependent on an old-fashioned agricultural system, its work force largely illiterate. Like nearly every other American who visited Italy at the time, Morse blamed the country's poverty and moral debasement on the "darkness and ignorance and superstition" of the Church.

Like his compatriots, too, who flocked to Catholic worship as to a circus, Morse made himself a connoisseur of ritual. Attending Catholic services became his chief entertainment in Rome. Mystified, he watched an attendant ceremonially open a prayer book: "bows, turns round, bows each side," he recorded in his journal, "advances one side of the altar, and kneels; advances to the altar, bows, and kneels again; lays the book on the altar, bows, and kneels again." He observed nuns taking the veil, the installation of several cardinals, the baptism of a converting "Jew man." Upon the death of Pope Pius VIII he viewed the corpse lying in state at the Quirinal Palace, clad in an ermine cape and gold-embroidered crimson stole. Later he endured the motley crowd of beggars and nobles at St. Peter's, to be present for the first appearance of the new Pope, Gregory XVI, trumpets blaring.

What Morse saw of monastic life appalled him as a macabre blend of deathly asceticism and leering sensuality. A group of brown-frocked Franciscans and Capuchins, heads shaven, seemed to him as haggard as disinterred corpses, yet libidinous-looking: "it needed no stretch of the imagination to find in most the expression of the worst passions of our nature." Intrigued by ceremonial kissing, he recorded one faintly wanton instance after another: virgins kissing the hem of a cardinal's garment; cardinals kissing the Pope's toe; nuns kissing nuns; hundreds kneeling to kiss a crucifix; the foot on a bronze statue of St. Peter worn away not by kissing but by wiping preparatory to kissing, "sometimes with the coat sleeve by a beggar."

Morse experienced the frocks and altars as a lineal descendant of New England Puritanism. Unlike the intellectual religion of his father and ancestors, he decided, Catholicism addressed the imagination but not the understanding: "No instruction was imparted, none seems ever to be intended." Catholicism was not religion but theater. Like actors speaking their parts, worshippers at Mass mouthed the words of priests—priests he often caught yawning, and whose rushed, inarticulate recitation of Latin prayers struck him variously as "whining," "drawling," "brawling," and "gurgling." Indeed the playhouse was but the secular offspring of the Church, a "daughter of this prolific

Mother of Abominations, and a child worthy of its dam." Both pretended to teach morality by scenic effect and pantomime, "and the
fruits are much the same."

But much in Catholic culture pleased Morse's ear and eye. He
enjoyed the liturgical music, often going out of his way to hear the
singing in some church. The architecture of the great cathedrals
seemed "gorgeous beyond description." And his color-sense delighted
in the crimson-gold-and-ermine spectacle of Catholic worship, the
shining mitres, flambeaux-lit processions, fans of peacock feather. Not
to mention the unexcelled painting and sculpture, however its
madonnas and eroticized cherubs offended his Calvinist sensibility.

In the landscape he painted at Subiaco, Morse managed to
divorce such iconography from its meaning and to treat a shrine to
the Virgin as little more than a picturesque rural object. Still, the
strain between his religious and aesthetic responses to Catholicism
sometimes left him benumbed. One night, for instance, he attended
an illumination at the Vatican. Upon a signal, the thousands of spectators lighted candles, suddenly making visible in the darkness the vast
piazza with its surrounding colonnade and the immense dome of St.
Peter's. Morse reached for language to describe the effect: "like
enchantment . . . overpowering in brilliancy . . . truly sublime." He
reminded himself, however, that the magical event had been staged
on a Sunday—the Sabbath treated as carnival, desecrated. "I never
wish to spend such another," he concluded glumly; "St. Peters is a
world of magnificence . . . and to what purpose!"

Such uncomfortable reminders of the seductive power of the
Church led Morse to question the power of his own art. His painting
aimed, after all, at promoting moral refinement and respect for
republican ideals. But might the sensuous appeal of color and form
promote instead, as Catholicism did, a "religion of the Imagination"?
He remained persuaded that when properly employed by the painter
the medium would communicate truths to the Understanding. But
there was clearly a danger. Without an "enlightened piety," a love for
art could sink into "heartlessness and frivolity." And if it came to
choosing, he preferred sermons on The Fall to Raphael: "I had rather
sacrifice the interests of the arts, if there is any collision, than run the
risk of endangering those compared with which all others are not for
a moment to be considered."

What Morse regarded as his deepest insight into Catholicism came during a walk on the Corso. Out to get some air, he paused to observe still another ceremony, a celebration of the Corpus Domini. A procession advanced toward him, several men upholding a canopy above the Host. As the canopy passed, spectators uncovered their heads and genuflected. Instead of doing either, Morse began writing some notes about the scene. Suddenly his hat flew off as he staggered under a bash to his head. The blow had come from the rifle of a soldier, one of the guards of honor for the officiating cardinal. The soldier pressed a bayonet against his chest and began cursing him, with "the expression of a demon," Morse said, "pouring forth a torrent of Italian oaths." He asked why the guard had struck him, but was answered only by more oaths, unintelligible to him except for the words *il diavolo*.

Morse often recalled the savage moment, and later wrote about it several times for publication. The soldier, he believed, must have been under orders to see that people knelt and took off their hats in respect to the display of the Host. That taught him something. Catholicism sustained its beguiling-horrifying dumb show by coercion. It was above all a "religion of force."

Morse's first trip abroad, eighteen years earlier, had landed him in a country at war with his own. Remarkably, he soon realized that his second trip had taken him to a country under revolutionary siege.

In the time between Morse's two journeys—since, that is, Napoleon's defeat at Waterloo—most of the rulers displaced by Bonaparte's imperial armies had regained their thrones. The kings, emperors, and statesmen who gathered in 1814–15 for the Vienna Congress hoped to prevent any country from again dominating Europe, as had Napoleonic France. To establish a lasting balance of power they rearranged the Continent, making some domains larger, some smaller, combining or creating others. Yet the European political order remained volatile. Its aristocratic leaders governed uneasily, aware of massive unemployment, democratic aspirations, and a widespread sense of grievance.

Morse had been in Rome only about six months when the political system contrived at the Vienna Congress began to rupture. In July 1830, three days of revolutionary street fighting broke out in Paris, killing about two thousand people. Forced to abdicate, King Charles X fled the country. Parliament offered the throne to his cousin Louis-Philippe, a successful businessman. This blow to the ancien régime sparked uprisings in Belgium, Switzerland, Germany, Poland, and much of the rest of Europe.

Hopes for a new order soared in the Italian states, too. These hopes threatened not just the city of Rome but also the far larger region governed by the Pope, spread across the country from Venice to Naples. The zeal of the Italian insurrectionists was fed by the declared readiness of Lafayette and other French liberal politicians to block any attempted intervention by reactionary Austria, which governed the north of Italy. Austria at the time was a formidable power, a conglomerate of kingdoms, duchies, and earldoms personally possessed by the Hapsburg dynasty, which in addition presided over the union of German states.

Morse welcomed the historic moment as a contest between New World republicanism and an Old World alliance of kings, a "great contention . . . between liberty and despotism throughout Europe." But the uprisings left him vulnerable in Rome, much as he had been years before in London. "Persons are frequently missing," he observed, "no one knows what has become of them." By mid-February, a year after his arrival, news reached Rome that rebels in Bologna had proclaimed the United Provinces of Italy, set up a provisional government, and declared the Pope's temporal power at an end. Within a few days other cities revolted: Ravenna, Ferrara, Perugia, Urbino.

Morse recorded in his diary the growing alarm in Rome over a possible invasion by revolutionary forces, or insurrection from within. "The streets are filled with the people," he wrote, "who gaze at each other inquisitively, and apprehension seems marked on every face." As both an American and a painter, he feared for his safety. Some opponents of the uprisings blamed them on *forestieri*, foreigners such as himself. The galley slaves and lower-class Trasteverini were rumored to have been secretly armed by the government in order to massacre all foreigners in Rome. Artists were particularly suspected of being liberals. Near him in the Corso, soldiers took two French artists into custody; a Swiss artist had reportedly been roused from bed at midnight and imprisoned.

And the tension steadily increased. "A proclamation was issued last night requiring all persons to be at home in the evening," Morse noted on February 15. "Arrests occur every night of suspected persons," he wrote four days later; "I was told that not less than 8000 passports had been granted to leave Rome within a few days. Rome begins to look like a deserted city." Those in flight included nearly all the Americans in Rome.

Morse closely followed events at the Vatican, to see how Gregory XVI dealt with the threat to his temporal power. High-ranking persons in the Church, he heard, had been arrested, among them the secretary of a cardinal; deserters from the Pope's army had been captured and executed. Rumors circulated that to quiet the popular unrest, Gregory was disposed to grant a constitution—was even prepared to resign his mighty office. However much Morse despised the papacy, he admired Gregory's willingness to sacrifice his dignity for the public good: "he is entitled to great respect for his personal character."

On February 24 dependable reports arrived that a revolutionary army from the provinces was approaching Rome. Morse decided to flee north, and next day went to get his passport visaed. The consul advised him that the roads outside Rome were militarized and risky, infested with brigands: days before, a courier had been shot five times in the head. Just the same Morse packed up his trunk, painting case, and portfolio, and set off for Florence.

His escape from the Pope's domain into Tuscany was nerve-wracking. He traveled by *vettura*, a slow-moving carriage capable of making only three or four miles an hour. Both he and his fellow passengers, two American men, carried pistols. Leaving Rome at four in the morning, they arrived around sunrise at Civita Castellana, where papal troops, on the alert and expecting a battle, took their passports and detained them for five hours.

Incident then succeeded incident so quickly that Morse had little time to think. Passing from town to town, through two hostile armies, he encountered soldiers asleep in the streets; crowds crying "Viva la libertà"; prisoners under escort, tied by the wrists; priests sporting the tricolor revolutionary cockade—dragoons, scouting parties, clusters of artillery, a singular air of alarm and sadness. Constitutional rebels or troops of the Pope often stopped the *vettura* to question him and his companions about the number and position of the enemy. The rebels liked Americans, he discovered. At a stop about fifty miles north of Rome, the commander of the Revolutionary Army, General Sercognani, even welcomed him and the others, "pleased to meet with citizens of a country which had taken so distinguished a part in promoting the liberties of the world."

Morse slipped out of papal territory just in time. He later learned that he and his companions had no sooner left Civita Castellana, after their five-hour detention, than an order was issued for their arrest. And had he lingered in Rome he would have joined some English artists on their outing to the noted Grotto Ferrata. All the artists became gravely ill, he learned, some revolutionist having mistaken them for Germans and poisoned their wine with a solution of copper—"a most diabolical attempt."

Reaching Florence was a relief. While living in Rome, Morse had longed for the amenities of bourgeois Protestantism, holding his nose for the sake of seeing the art. It cheered him to be in a culture that valued neatness and industry. "Everything in Northern Italy appears superior to the South, the cities, the people, the roads, the cultivation."

During Morse's two months in Florence, his relief turned to joy. His experience of Italy had meant a day-by-day readjustment of aesthetic standards, each discovery of some dazzling collection dimmed by the discovery of another still more dazzling. And in Florence he reached pure radiance, the city of Dante, Michelangelo, Leonardo, "the *beautiful city*." While working on commissioned copies of self-portraits by Rubens and Titian, he studied paintings in the Pitti Palace and other collections that outshone anything he had seen in Rome, climaxed by the incomparable Tribune Room of the Uffizi Gallery— "the richest collection of art I have ever seen, every picture and statue is of the highest class."

Morse took apartments in a house at 14488 Via Valfonda, where Thomas Cole and the Boston artist Horatio Greenough also roomed. Cole, an early member of the National Academy of Design, was developing a distinctive landscape style rich in historical reference, a hybrid landscape/history painting. Morse had met Greenough two years earlier in New York, through their mutual mentor and idol, Washington Allston. A bewhiskered six-footer, Greenough was on his way to becoming America's first sculptor of international reputation. While in Florence he executed a perceptive marble bust of Morse. It records the furrows beginning to show at the corners of Morse's mouth, lending his sensitive face a clenched determination that makes him seem at once gentle and severe.*

*Reproduced on p. 96.

Morse admired Greenough as someone "wholly bent upon one object, *excellence in his art*." But their friendship was uneasy. A Harvard graduate with an irreverent wit, Greenough disdained academies of art as pompous and joked about "my natural depravity of heart." He teasingly called Morse "wicked Morse" and breezily advised him not to stay unmarried: "a man without a true love is a ship without ballast, a one-tined fork, half a pair of scissors." He twitted Morse on religious issues too. His own "stubborn head," he said, refused to "believe infants are born charged and primed with sin." For Morse, art, sex, and original sin were solemn matters, as he evidently made clear to Greenough, who apologized: "Pardon, I pray you, anything of levity which you may have been offended at in me."

Morse received a rebuke of sorts himself, from news that the uprisings in the Papal States had been squashed. He had welcomed Gregory XVI's rumored disposition to end the tumult by granting a constitution. On the contrary, the Pope requested military aid from Austria, which sent some 15,000 troops to Rome. They quickly restored order, the rebels having no forces that could hold out against them. In foreseeing liberty triumphant over despotism, Morse had also put too much faith in declarations by France that it would block any Austrian intervention. The French failed to act, unwilling to be dragged into a war against the powerful Hapsburgs.

Headed ultimately for Paris, Morse left Florence in the middle of May for a two-month stay in Venice. Approaching from the sea and being poled through the Grand Canal, he thought the place a wonder: "we seemed to be rowing through an inundated city." Yet another world of art opened up for him, the Venetian school of Titian, Tintoretto, and Veronese that in subordinating drawing to color had deeply influenced Allston. The city was friendly to artists. The Accademia and the gallery of the Palazzo Ducale stayed open from six in the morning until dark, "so that an artist can spend all his time to advantage, which is not the case in Rome or Florence." He spent much of his time at the Accademia, copying on a small canvas Tintoretto's monumental *Miracle of the Slave*.

Morse enjoyed the strangeness of Venice, not least the gondolas, "very like our Indian canoes." Drinking his coffee each day in Piazza San Marco, he watched the Austrian officers promenading with their ladies, and the exotically costumed Greeks and Turks seated under awnings outside the cafes, smoking nonstop. His life was made the more agreeable by the British consul general and his family, devout Protestants with whom he often spent evenings singing hymns, praying, and reading Scripture.

But as Morse stayed on in Venice, he came to detest the place. The Venetians of the north began seeming no less indolent than Neapolitans of the south: "how many hours and days are wasted by this people in perfect sloth, in a dreaming, dosing reverie, or in actual sleep; the bustle, the restless activity, the enterprize so conspicuous with us is wholly unknown here." The all-day lounging in San Marco was not merely an "empty heartless enjoyment," either, but something darker, repressive. People socialized under surveillance, "surrounded by police agents and soldiers, to prevent excess." In a bloody-walled dungeon of the ducal palace he saw and sketched a machine for strangling prisoners. He began to feel languid himself, a result of the sirocco-swept climate and, perhaps, the odoriferous canals—"excessively offensive," scorpion-breeding.

It became evident to Morse that Venice was moribund, a place without a future: "No one can conceive without visiting Venice, the melancholy dullness of a decaying city, every thing going to ruin trade languishing, and the leaden hand visible everywhere; it is truly . . . a *città morto*." In this it typified much of the rest of Italy, a stricken wasteland of reliquary bones, catacombs, and vats of stinking corpses. He passed July 4th with the only two other Americans he could find in Venice, talking about home, grateful to have been born in the United States—"the happiest of countries. . . . one bright spot on earth."

Before heading for Paris, Morse crammed in the aesthetic and historic sights of other northern cities, taking notes on works by Carpaccio and Crivelli, quick sketch-copies of Velázquez and Brueghel ("small figures exquisitely finished"). In Ferrara he inspected the cell that had confined the mentally ill Tasso, noticing on an arch the large autograph of a previous sightseer, Lord Byron. He visited the geometric classical villas of Palladio in Vicenza, and Leonardo's nearly ruined *Last Supper* in Milan—the disappointing "tameness" in the faces and "clumsiness" in many of the hands redeemed by strong composition and subtle narrative details, such as the overturned saltcellar in front of Judas.

Morse's journey to Paris, in mid-September, turned out to be even more harrowing than his flight from Rome. Moving north through

Switzerland and Germany, sketching mountains along the way, he learned that he would not be allowed to enter France. The French government had established a cordon sanitaire at the German border, hoping to protect the country from a cholera epidemic advancing from Asia through eastern Europe. A fellow passenger on Morse's diligence, a young French-speaking German officer, offered to get him into France by sharing the expense of a well-placed tip (*douceur*) at the blockade.

Morse went along with the plan, which to his understanding involved little more than a routine bribe. One dark cloudy daybreak he found himself descending from the coach and following the officer and a guide through plowed fields wet with rain, while the diligence sped on with his luggage. He asked where they were going, but received in reply only the caution to go softly. "It then for the first time," he wrote later, "flashed across my mind that we had undertaken an unlawful and very hazardous enterprize that of running by the cordon."

Terrified of being arrested or shot, Morse managed to sneak across the frontier. He was rejoined by the diligence, which had gone through customs without him.

Two trials remained, however, the more difficult one a psychological trial. When the diligence stopped at a small village to change horses, some gendarmes asked Morse for his papers. He realized that his passport contained no signature verifying that he had officially been granted entry into France. He presented it, fearful that the omission would be discovered. But the much-traveled document contained the signatures of so many guards and customs officers that the puzzled policeman let it through.

Further on toward Paris, at Metz, Morse's passport was demanded again. This time it was taken to the station-house for examination. Guiltily recalling the *douceur*, the guide, the slinking around at daybreak, he felt doomed. "The more I reflect the more I regret the step I have been ignorantly led to take," he wrote, "and shall be much surprized if I am not yet a sufferer for it." Instead, the police gave him a provisional passport to Paris. Just in time. His conscience had been telling him to confess that he had crossed the border illegally.

Paris at the time Morse returned was in some ways still a medieval city, a maze of narrow winding streets, wet and smelly from open sewers that ran in the gutters. Many of its three-quarters of a million inhabitants lived in crowded tenements, fetched their water from public fountains, endured the droppings of the city's tens of thousands of horses. Yet the Napoleonic triumphal arches proclaimed the recent past and there were signs of the future as well—department stores, an elegant new Bourse, experiments in street lighting by gas.

During his year in Paris, Morse enjoyed the company of a politically engaged artistic and social circle. He took rooms at 29 rue de Turenne, a house owned by a *comtesse*, whose distinguished friends he met. Caustic Horatio Greenough lived there for two months, sculpting a bust of the Marquis de Lafayette although disdainful of the "frippery" of Paris and unimpressed by French taste: "They are in Art but the slaves of fashion." Morse spent time with him, "now talking seriously," as Greenough put it, "and now letting ding anyhow." Ding as they would, Morse was miffed when Greenough sent home a statue for exhibition at Trumbull's American Academy.

Settled only a few doors from Lafayette's Paris mansion, Morse got to know the General more intimately than before. Now seventy-five, Lafayette greeted him warmly, the complexion of his massive face that of a vigorous young man. Morse had preserved with "religious care" letters to Jedediah from George Washington; he locked away letters from Lafayette to himself with similar reverence for their "high moral value," intending to have his children read them as models of virtue. He relished visits to Lafayette and rides with him in his carriage—opportunities to hear firsthand anecdotes of the War for Independence and discuss the failed revolution in Italy.

Members of the American colony asked Morse to preside over an Independence Day celebration at Lointier's restaurant, at which Lafayette was the guest of honor. Some eighty Americans attended, including the U.S. minister to France, William Rives. Morse rose after the first of thirteen toasts to salute the General as a countryman: "Yes, gentlemen, he belongs to America as well as to Europe. He is *our* fellow-citizen." Oddly echoing his family's frequent criticism of himself, he praised Lafayette for the consistency that set him apart from the "fickle class" of humanity: "He is a Tower amidst the waters; his foundation is upon a rock; he moves not with the ebb and flow of the stream." According to newspaper accounts, applause interrupted nearly every sentence of his panegyric, topped at the end by nine cheers and a band playing the *Parisienne*. In the toasts that followed,

Lafayette proposed *"Republican Institutions: the prolific Daughters of American Independence."* Morse received a health as "The worthy representative of the artists of the country."

Practically every evening Morse spent with James Fenimore Cooper (1789–1851) and his family. A close friend of Lafayette, the novelist was in his early forties, tall, with a rich voice and military bearing. His manner was brusque—"unconciliating," people called it, "uncompromising," "like a bluff sailor." With his wife and daughters he occupied two floors of a house in the elite Faubourg St. Germain, in view of the Hôtel des Invalides. His much-translated Leatherstocking tales were widely read in France and throughout Europe, taken as realistic pictures of American life. He worked so intently at his writing that his hand sometimes shook. But his literary efforts brought him nearly $20,000 a year, probably more than any other American writer had ever earned.

Morse admired Cooper for proving to the world the value of American culture, refuting "the disgraceful taunt that is hurled at us by foreigners of being destitute of genius." He also saw embodied in Cooper his own ideal of the American gentleman, someone of simple manner but superior mind and bearing, "equal to any title of rank in Europe, Kings and Emperors not excepted." Cooper understood the hollowness of European political systems, and spoke on behalf of American principles with fearless dignity. Yet he was more courted abroad by the great than those who truckled and cringed to foreign opinion. Unknown to his friend, Morse wrote to Professor Benjamin Silliman in New Haven suggesting that Yale award Cooper an honorary M.A. degree: "Such a man ought to be cherished and supported by his countrymen."

For his part, Cooper rated Morse "just as good a fellow as there is going." Fancying himself a connoisseur of art, he accompanied Morse around Paris looking at old paintings for sale on the street. They argued whether some cheaply priced begrimed canvas was or was not a Teniers, Cooper interpreting along the way since Morse spoke little French. Morse also gave painting lessons to Cooper's daughter Sue, in whom he was rumored to be interested. Cooper denied this: "Morse is an excellent man, but not just the one to captivate a fine young woman of twenty."

Nevertheless, the rumor was probably true. Morse seems to have had no female company while in Italy, and did not consider looking for a wife abroad. Only America, he said, could produce "the *beau ideal* of woman in all that gives dignity and loveliness to the sex." He apparently found such a prospect in young Sue, for he admitted taking a "deep interest" in Cooper's family, "not merely on the father's account." Sue was half his age, but so was Catherine Pattison when he proposed marriage to her. On the other hand, that Sue was also the daughter of an esteemed friend may have aroused guilt. For whatever reason, he backed away. Horatio Greenough sent discreet congratulations on "your sound conscience with regard to the affair that you wot of."

Through Cooper and Lafayette, and on his own, Morse gained a clearer understanding of the political situation in Europe. It seemed to him that between his two visits to Paris, the government of France had been transformed. When stopping in the city nearly two years earlier, en route to Italy, he had joined a crowd in the Tuileries to gaze at King Charles X dining off gold and silver plates. But the revolution of July 1830 had forced the ultraroyalist Charles to abdicate. "How changed are the circumstances of this city," Morse found, "blood has flowed in its streets, the price of its liberty." The values of the current monarch, Louis-Philippe, had been shaped by three years of exile in America, which he toured from Maine to Louisiana. This middle-class "Citizen King," Morse believed, had brought France a new, progressive political order. During his earlier visit, too, Lafayette had little influence and was out of favor at court. Now he seemed a key figure, "second only to the king in honor and influence as the head of a powerful party."

Cooper thought otherwise. To him, a royal reception that he attended typified the nature of Louis-Philippe's government. A woman sat in a corner of the room throughout the evening, conspicuously sewing. She had been placed there, Cooper decided, as evidence of the king's simplicity. But the plebeian touch was a "mummery," like the rest of Louis-Philippe's supposed republicanism. In reality, France was rapidly returning to aristocracy. Cooper also believed that his friend Lafayette had been outmaneuvered by the party around the king, manipulated to keep republican enthusiasm under control. Nevertheless Louis-Philippe was losing popularity every day. France had become a "Volcano."

Morse learned that Cooper was right. Soon after he arrived in

Paris, news came of the fall of Warsaw, ending Poland's attempt to win independence from the rule of Czar Nicholas I of Russia—the state where the ancien régime had been most unbudgingly preserved. France failed to aid the Polish rebels, against whom the Czar sent an army of 80,000. To many it seemed that Louis-Philippe had once again first encouraged then betrayed hopes for political emancipation. Despite the four days he had spent at Mount Vernon with George Washington, he remained reactionary, no more willing to fight Russia for the independence of Poland than he had been to fight Austria over Italy.

Parisians protested the new regime's cowardice and perfidy, giving Morse a second glimpse of revolutionary strife. One day in the early fall of 1831 he saw shops closing down, troops assembling, cavalry on the move. People quietly filled the streets as if expecting a parade, in defiance of police notices advising them to disband. That night the tense mood erupted. On the boulevard de la Madeleine near his house, Morse watched a crowd surge toward the gates of the hotel of General Sebastiani, Louis-Philippe's minister of foreign affairs. Trampling horses and a corps of gendarmes approached to scatter the rioters, helmets glittering in the streetlights, swords drawn: "orders were given for the charge," he recorded, "and in an instant they dashed down the street, the people dispersing like the mist before the wind." His fear that blood would eventually flow was realized a few weeks later with the killing of about thirty people in an uprising near the Palais-Royal.

Morse became an active sympathizer with the cause of Polish independence. He joined the American Polish Committee that met Wednesday nights at Cooper's apartments. Among other responses to the crisis the committee raised $6000 in the United States for the relief of the many Poles exiled in Paris. Morse did his part by investigating the financial prospects of a group of exiles who wished to emigrate to America, perhaps to found a colony in Ohio. He also went with Cooper to see Minister William Rives, hoping to obtain the release of the committee's chairman, Dr. Samuel Gridley Howe of Boston. While on a mission to supply distressed Polish exiles in Germany with 20,000 francs, Howe had been seized by the Prussian government and jailed incommunicado in Berlin. Morse and Cooper gave Rives documents which they asked him to lay before the Prussian

minister, showing that Howe's mission had been charitable, not political. Howe was released, taken in a cart to the French border, and
dumped across. His fate again demonstrated to Morse that the European powers took America for granted: the Prussians "would not have
dared to treat a citizen of any other country in so cavalier a manner."

Morse also wrote up for the American press an eyewitness account
of the melancholy celebration held in Paris on November 29 to mark
the first anniversary of the Polish revolution. The event brought the
American Polish Committee together with a similar group from Poland itself and a French-Polish Committee organized by Lafayette,
who attended in the uniform of the Polish National Guard. Pained by
what he saw, Morse described for American readers the woe on the
faces of the more than sixty exiles present—"the close pressed mouth,
the frowning brow, and the downcast fixed eye." The prominence of
some of the exiles emphasized the pervasive sense of defeat. Among
those in the flag-draped hall were the last president of the Polish government at Warsaw, the former principal of the University of Warsaw,
"nobles, men of science, literature and art, and officers and soldiers,"
Morse reported, "outcasts in a foreign country, housed by strangers,
and living on their charity."

Most of his time and energy in Paris, Morse devoted to painting at the
Louvre. In easy walking distance of his house, the museum stretched
more than a quarter of a mile along the Seine. Napoleon had swollen
its holdings with the spoils of his military campaigns, masterpieces pil-
laged from churches and palaces throughout Europe. Much of the
fabulous booty had been returned, but perhaps a fifth was left, in addition to the treasures of the French royal collections.

The museum's mammoth Grand Gallery, lit by glass skylights, ran
on for perhaps five city blocks. From one end to the other artists sat
silently copying at their easels, soldiers motionlessly on guard. "It is a
long walk simply to pass up and down the long hall," Morse wrote, "the
end of which, from the opposite end is scarcely visible, but is lost in
the mist of distance. On the walls are 1250 of some of the chefs d'oeu-
vres of painting." He saw works by Piero della Francesca and Murillo,
staggering historical epics such as Veronese's *Wedding Feast at Cana*,
the dusky golden atmosphere of Caravaggio. Here was yet a further

aesthetic standard, in one respect surpassing even that of Rome and Florence—gems not only from Italy but also from France, Germany, and Holland, "the most splendid, as well as the most numerous single collection of works of art, in the world."

Morse painted at the Louvre throughout the winter cold, hindered by the short days but filling his many commissions. Cooper ordered a copy of Rembrandt's *Angel Leaving Tobias* and often stopped by to banter: "Lay it on here, Samuel—more yellow—the nose is too short—the eye too small—damn it if I had been a painter what a picture I should have painted." Others also paused at Morse's easel, including Baron Alexander von Humboldt, author of *Kosmos*, a "physics of the world" fifty years in the making. Sometimes called the last universal genius, he had corresponded with Jedediah and praised his geographies, and now "took pains," Morse said, "to find me out." Morse toured the gallery with him at his request, awed by Humboldt's ability to speak not only German, French, and English, but also Spanish, Turkish, Swedish, Danish, and Russian.

Sometime around the new year, Morse decided to refuse further commissions and apply himself to a single ambitious work. It would depict the Louvre's Salon Carré, as if the room had on display many of the museum's chief treasures. A tour de force, six feet by nine feet, it required him to copy in miniature thirty-seven masterpieces. Painting on a high stand from nine each morning until four, with "the closest application" and without interruption, he wore himself down and felt he had damaged his health. Yet he could hardly bear to be away from the canvas. "I have become so interested in it that I believe I should risk my life in finishing it." He did not let up even when, in March, the cholera epidemic that had been raging through eastern Europe reached Paris, ultimately killing 18,000 people. Carts piled with corpses moved through the city; the deaths from cholera of two Liberal leaders touched off two days of renewed political street fighting. "I have remained at my post through the whole scene," Morse wrote, "not without danger, not without great apprehension, but . . . with confidence that all was safe in the hands of Him to whom I have confided all for time and for eternity."

Morse considered his *Grand Gallery of the Louvre* worth all the danger and effort, "a great labor but it will be a splendid and valuable work. . . . I am sure it is the most *correct* of *its kind* ever painted, for

every one says I have caught the style of each of the masters." His incessant toil over the complex canvas attracted crowds of onlookers. "He
really has created a sensation in the Louvre," Cooper wrote, "having a
little school of his own, who endeavor to catch his manner." One
French nobleman was so impressed that he presented Morse an
expensive folio of the monuments of France containing hundreds of
engravings.

Morse planned to complete the miniature copies in Paris, adding
the frames and the ten foreground figures when he returned to America in the fall. What to do after that was unclear. Despite the failure of
his *House of Representatives* he thought he might send the *Gallery* on a
traveling exhibition, beginning in New York City. Cooper advised him
against this. Harshly criticized by some New York newspapers for med-
dling in European politics, he urged Morse to display the painting in
Philadelphia, then in Baltimore and Washington: "Your intimacy with
me has become known, and such is the virulence of my enemies in
New-York, that I have no sort of doubt, of their attacking your picture
in consequence." As an alternative to either plan, Morse thought he
might sell the painting to someone else for exhibition—or that
Cooper himself might buy it.

Morse spent fully fourteen months on *The Grand Gallery of the Louvre.* The completed canvas reproduces in miniature the *Mona Lisa,*
Raphael's *Belle Jardinière,* Murillo's *Beggar Boy,* and Veronese's tremendous *Wedding Feast at Cana,* as well as pictures by Leonardo, Poussin,
Rubens, and other masters, whose manner he convincingly rendered.
To the left appears Cooper's daughter Sue, copying a painting, with
her parents behind her; beside her easel hangs Rembrandt's *Angel
Leaving Tobias.* Morse stands in the center, legs crossed, instructing a
young female artist. Although this painting-about-painting belongs to
an established genre of works that depict galleries, its inner subject is
Morse's experience of Europe and his hopes for the future—his pro-
ductive encounter with the richness-beyond-measure of Western art,
and preparation to paint a major historical work of his own.

As he got ready to return home, Morse assessed what he had learned
during nearly three years abroad, and how it had changed him. His
thinking about politics had been kept "at boiling heat," he said, mak-

ing more apparent than ever before the contrast between America and Europe. Europe was, above all else, sinister. Everywhere he had felt the oppression of Church and State, with their attendant ignorance and squalor. The Continent was but a larger version of the Roman soldier cursing him as *il diavolo*—one great garrison, preserving peace at the point of a gun. "The *sword* and *bayonet* are every where. . . . the habit of dread operates very powerfully to preserve order, but such order is purchased at the expense of the dearest rights of man."

Morse also appreciated more keenly than ever how America's precious political liberty depended on its foundation in Protestantism—"a religion of *persuasion* not of *force*." In America, worshippers on the Sabbath were treated to a reasoned discourse that trained and encouraged them to think, immunizing them from the sophistical reasonings of demagogues. By contrast, the people of Catholic France had no means of acquiring habits of sober investigation, the Sabbath for them being distinguished from other days only by more billiard playing. Lacking a moral authority to sustain its political institutions, a "truly *rational* intellectual practical Christianity," France was sinking back into despotism, making another, general European war inevitable.

Morse had also come to understand why European governments so often criticized the United States. They dreaded change. They feared that America's example of people ruling themselves would threaten class privilege and possibly foment revolution. "Our simple existence keeps hope alive in the breasts of patriots." He had often heard Europeans speculate that in fifty or a hundred years the United States would split into several different domains, some returning to monarchy. But Americans universally preferred republicanism, and sought political relief by changing administrations, not forms of government. The opposite was more likely to happen: over the next century all Europe would be revolutionized into constitutional governments, then republicanized, adopting "the principles of liberty promulged 60 years ago in America, and proved sound by 60 years experience."

But three months before Morse's departure, news from America tested his confidence in the country's future. South Carolina cotton producers had blamed a serious decline in cotton prices on the high protective tariffs levied by the federal government. A South Carolina

Samuel F. B. Morse, *Grand Gallery of the Louvre*
(Terra Museum of American Art)

convention had declared the tariffs null, and warned that if President Jackson tried to enforce them, the state would secede from the Union. Morse deplored this "blindness and madness." It encouraged European enemies of civil liberty, who claimed that republics were inherently unstable. He remained convinced that Americans were committed to enduring as a single people, the United States: "As to the Union," he told Lafayette, "let the simple question 'Shall this Union be dissolved?' be so put that the *nation* must decide it, and but one voice will be heard from Maine to Mississippi, *Never!*"

About his own future, Morse was less optimistic. He had learned much about brushwork and color harmony from Europe's canvases aglow with centuries of ambition, skill, and genius. But what he had seen only recalled to him his still-frustrated longing for distinction as a history painter. Where was *his* School of Athens?

When he left America, Morse had been depressed, his career faltering. The thought that he was not improving as an artist but going backward, he said, "unremittingly tormented me." He had hoped while abroad to rekindle his ardor and regain his proficiency, so that he might at last "execute some *great* subject." He now felt better than ever prepared to do so, conscious "of the power to do more than I have ever been *able* to do." But all told he had not accomplished much in Europe. Lack of money had forced him to spend his time copying. Not even *The Grand Gallery of the Louvre* had demanded the full range of his talents. As Greenough said, his gifts and most of his time had been wasted, "dribbled away in little things."

Where was *his* School of Athens? The answer left Morse feeling no less futile than when he left America. His only hope lay in obtaining from Congress one of the still-uncommissioned history paintings to be hung under the dome of the Capitol. He had decided that the perfect subjects for him would be the departure and return of Columbus— "on these two I will stake my reputation as an artist." Greenough implored him not to give up: "Hang on like Columbus himself. . . . These subjects are yours, you are theirs."

But hanging on was not so easy. At times Morse felt that for too long he had spent too much energy dreaming of the commission from Congress: "I see year after year of the very vigor of my life wasted in this vain expectation." And time was running out for him. He was forty-one; Raphael had painted all his wonders by the age of thirty-seven, "I ought to use the remaining few years of life in that department of art which will leave bread to my children." When he returned to America it would be best to confine himself to portraits and copies. Europe had taught him much, not least by raising a question that could not be ignored. Why, after all, go on acquiring skills and knowledge he could never use?

SIX

Anomalous, Nondescript, Hermaphrodite

(1832–1837)

M ORSE'S RETURN to New York began hopefully. A month after arriving, he accepted an appointment as Professor of Painting and Sculpture at the just-opened University of the City of New York. Founded by a small group of patricians, the school aimed at educating sons of the rising middle class. Morse was appointed without salary, expected to receive his pay in the form of fees from his art students for their instruction.

On reaching New York, Morse stayed several weeks with his brother Richard. But eventually he lodged, handsomely, at the university itself. Outgrowing its rented quarters in congested lower New York, the school joined a larger exodus of city residents northward to what would become Greenwich Village. In 1835 it erected a permanent building on parklike Washington Square, an impressive Gothic struc-ture of white marble that inspired a fashion for "college Gothic" on other campuses. Morse rented five rooms in the northwest tower, and was given a sixth gratis—plenty of space to live, paint, and teach. Some of the rooms he rented to his five private students.

With the building still under construction, Morse's quarters at first proved troublesome. The ceiling of the tower leaked and the walls dribbled, "perfect shower baths" that drove two students from their apartment. Forced to suspend his painting and teaching, Morse lost the fifty-three cents per day he charged each pupil for instruction. Three months after moving in he presented a bill for $50 in damages, including harm to his and his students' health.

New York University
(New York University Archives)

Despite the fuss Morse valued his professorship. He praised New York University—as the school quickly became known—for creating a separate department of the Arts of Design, the first in America. He recorded his high regard in an unusual architectural fantasy, *Allegorical Landscape Showing New York University.* It depicts the new Gothic edifice standing across a lagoon from Mount Helicon, the abode of the Muses. The key to the allegory is perhaps the powerfully rising morning sun that begins to illuminate the scene. The rising sun image had often been used during and after the American Revolution to symbolize the inevitable movement of the arts and sciences westward from the classical world to Europe and, inevitably, to America. Read in this way the painting presents the university as one locus of a cultural progress in America that is as certain as sunrise.

Morse also took charge again as president of the National Academy of Design, energetically. His absence had been felt: the number of lectures had dropped, instructors had missed classes. He threw himself into readying the annual exhibitions, advising Philadelphia

Samuel F. B. Morse, *Allegorical Landscape Showing
New York University*
(New-York Historical Society)

artists on their conflict with the Pennsylvania Academy, delivering a
reworked version of his talks on the affinity between painting and the
other fine arts. He tried to raise money for the widow and daughter
of Gilbert Stuart, living destitute in Newport. In touch again with Allston, he arranged a $500 loan to his mentor—by now considered the
greatest living American artist, but debt-ridden and still struggling
with his unpaintable *Belshazzar's Feast*. All his efforts treated art as an
exalted cause. They were noticed, too, bringing him election to such
select groups as the Académie des Beaux Arts of Anvers, the Belgian
Royal Academy of Fine Arts, and New York's St. Nicholas Society,
whose membership boasted families celebrated in the city's history—
Stuyvesants, Fishes, Roosevelts.

Shortly after resuming his presidency, Morse was approached by a
director of John Trumbull's American Academy, David Hosack, about
the possibility of uniting the two associations. Unknown to Morse,
Hosack came at the behest of Trumbull, who understood well enough
that the breakaway N.A.D. had cost his Academy interest and support.

Although Morse had feuded publicly with Trumbull at the time he founded the N.A.D., he approved the union if it could be made without compromise. Every academy he had seen in Europe was managed by artists, strengthening his conviction that any other plan of governance was "perfectly absurd."

In January 1833, Morse, A. B. Durand, and William Dunlap met several times with a committee from Trumbull's American Academy. On the crucial issue of governance, they agreed to unite by creating different classes of membership, one of academicians, another of lay members, with authority over separate matters. Morse and a representative of Trumbull's committee drafted a description of the new, united academy. But when it reached Trumbull he rejected it. The plan, he said, denigrated and disempowered the propertied benefactors who had founded the Academy, and contributed its building and collections. Without the patronage of such men as John Jacob Astor, who recently donated two marble busts by Canova, the arts could not flourish in America: "never, while I live and have my reason," Trumbull said, "will I . . . consent to such a violation of their rights."

Morse spent two weeks writing a reply, an exercise in cultural politics published as *Examination of Col. Trumbull's Address, in Opposition to the Projected Union.* He denounced the American Academy as "antirepublican," subjugating artists to a monied aristocracy: "The Artist, poor, helpless thing, must learn to *boo* and *boo* in the halls and antechambers of my lord, implore his lordship's protection, advertise himself painter to his majesty." Privately he wrote off Trumbull as the dead hand of the past—"an old man," he told a friend, "in an institution formed for the promotion of the arts, but which has been an incubus on them." Three years later the American Academy again tried to interest the N.A.D. in a union; its communication was read and filed.

Returning to his easel, Morse put finishing touches on some commissioned paintings he had brought back from Europe. Local awareness of his studies abroad created much curiosity about what his new work would be like. William Cullen Bryant promised readers of his *Evening Post* that their "talented countryman" would prove that America had artists the equal of any in Europe, and "earth and skies as fitted to inspire the poet or the painter as Italy can boast." Morse's many striking portraits in this period retain a precisely observed visual real-ism but reach beyond it for what he called "*Intellectual Imitation*"—not likeness but analysis, inner revelation. The sitters' unconventional poses and unusual facial expressions seem emblematic of their being, as in his strongly composed portrait of the Reverend Thomas Harvey Skinner of Andover Theological Seminary. Not everyone agreed with Bryant, however. To New York's former mayor Philip Hone, attending an N.A.D. exhibition, some of Morse's new work looked frigid: "the warmth of the sunny skies of Italy does not appear to have had any effect upon the worthy president. He is . . . well acquainted with the principles of his art; but he has no imagination."

However Morse's European study affected his painting, it made the art scene in America dreary by comparison. Feeling for the arts in New York was low—or rather, he said, there was "*no feeling.*" In explaining to the public the failure of the N.A.D.'s proposed union with Trumbull's Academy, he had had to rehash elementary matters he had

Samuel F. B. Morse, *Rev. Thomas Harvey Skinner*
(Museum of Fine Arts, Boston)

made clear years before: "It is mortifying to find on my return home, that the very first principles of encouragement, the A. B. C. are to be taught." The New York exhibition of his ambitious *Grand Gallery of the Louvre* was a commercial failure. Several city newspapers published laudatory reviews, the *Mirror* acclaiming the "magnificent design, the courage which could undertake such a herculean task. . . . We have never seen anything of the kind before in this country." So few people attended the show, however, that Morse removed the *Grand Gallery* and displayed it in New Haven, where it failed to earn enough to pay for the exhibition room. William Dunlap explained that the painting charmed connoisseurs and artists but "was caviar to the multitude."

Despite his professorship, his presidency, his vision of the rising glory of American culture, after a year back in New York, Morse again felt seriously depressed: "I have more mental suffering, more hopeless despondence in regard to the future, than I have ever before suffered." He often fell ill, and once was confined for three weeks, under a physician's care for boils on his legs. His brother Richard was also liable to such "fits" of "*the blues*"—and their father before them. Morse wondered whether something in his physical system might be awry, capable of producing in him "such settled conviction of hopelessness."

He decided not. The real and the apparent causes were the same: his inability—for twenty years now—to survive as the sort of painter he wanted to be: "my profession is that of a *beggar*, it exists on *charity*." His resettlement in America had only confirmed what he gloomily sensed in Paris: "My life of poetry and romance is gone. I must descend from the clouds and look more at the earth."

Perhaps to begin his descent, Morse decided to sell the *Grand Gallery of the Louvre*. He gave it up reluctantly: "As a record of studies made in Paris, it was particularly calculated to be a treasure to me." He considered asking $2500. But being again broke and in debt he offered the picture at half that amount to an upstate New Yorker, George Hyde Clarke, whose portrait he had painted five years earlier. He got more than he bargained for. When he told Clarke that after reducing the price to $1300 he had been offered $2000 by someone else, Clarke offered to release him from their deal. On the edge of losing a badly needed sale, Morse squirmed out: "I prefer your note for 1300 to his for 2000." He even offered to paint Lafayette into an unfinished space in the foreground of the *Gallery*. This, too, was a mistake, for Clarke wrote back cursing the General as a Jacobin—"a Philosopher that only comprehended one half of Liberty merely personal freedom, & neglected the other more essential half the protection of Property." Morse offered instead to fill the space—there beneath miniatures of Raphael and Murillo and Rubens—with hundred-dollar-apiece portraits of Clarke's family, full-length.

Morse's domestic situation offered little to lift his fits of the blues. On returning to America he seems to have placed his children under the guardianship of Sidney Morse, perhaps only as a legal convenience so that his brother could administer the bequests to them from Lucrece's now-deceased father. But physically and emotionally he remained distant from the children, as his parents had been from him. His constant separation from them disturbed his brother Richard, who thought it "unnatural."

Morse visited Susan at least once at her school in New England. At least once she also visited him in New York, when he likely painted *The Muse,* a monumental five-by-six-foot portrait of her at about the age of seventeen. She had been taking drawing lessons, and he depicted her holding a pencil poised over a large sketchbook on her lap, awaiting inspiration, clad in a lace cape and richly painted butterscotch-colored dress. Susan was also taking music lessons, learning to play "The Caliph of Bagdad"—an interest he encouraged by sending her sheet music for a waltz. Meeting his daughter now in her teens, after a three-year separation, he found her likable, "an affectionate, sweet dispositioned fine girl." But he less often described her qualities as a credit to her than as a consolation to him, "a great comfort to me amidst my anxieties, cares, and disappointments." She wrote to him of her desire to be with him: "I want to see you very much, dear father, and wish you would surprise me again." But by contrast with his voluminous letters to Lafayette and Cooper, he replied with what barely amount to notes, one ending "I am in great haste."

Morse's son Charles was about thirteen, two years older than his youngest child, Finley—as James Edward Finley had become known. The boys stayed for a while with their grandmother's family, the Breeses, in upstate New York. Mostly they seem to have been at school in New Haven, Morse paying off part of their school bills in copies of

Samuel F. B. Morse, *The Muse—Susan Walker Morse*
(Metropolitan Museum of Art)

self-portraits by Rubens and Titian. Charles took Latin and French, achieving many grades of Excellent. Finley did less well, his mind and senses dulled. At some time in his early years he had contracted measles and scarlet fever. The diseases reportedly produced convulsions that damaged his brain and, among other impairments, left him partly deaf. The boy's schoolmaster told Morse that with a little more strength Finley probably would make "respectable improvement" in his studies.

Morse still felt the shock of Lucrece's death ten years earlier, and still spoke of "the wounds which one such blow sends through all the affections of the heart." But he wanted to remarry, and courted several women, without success. He still loved young Catherine Pattison— only as a daughter, he told himself, "not with that kind of love which were we nearer in age I could not help indulging. Such a love is now forbidden by every consideration." Just the same he kept writing to her. And his avuncular warnings about the traps of this world came scented with gallantry:

> I have seen but few such as you, except in the ideal creations of Romance, and I can only liken the concern with which you have inspired me when I see you entering into Society to that which one feels on seeing a beautiful young fawn fearlessly gambolling on the borders of a forest where its natural enemies of every kind lurk.

Catherine too knew how to play yes-and-no: "whatever you may say," she replied, "will be looked upon as *destiny*."

Morse found a more suitable prospect in New York City, but became put off by her character. He found another in Boston, whose "inexorable friends," as James Fenimore Cooper described them, forbade her to marry him. Cooper and his family, returned from Europe with four Swiss servants, had rented a splendid town house on St. Mark's Place, a half-dozen streets from Morse's tower at New York University. A rumor went around that Morse had become engaged to Cooper's daughter Sue—"which he laughed at, of course," Cooper said.

Morse's experience of Europe had intensified his already fierce nationalism. With his artistic career stalled, he gave much of his time to writing about the threat to America of foreign despotisms. While abroad he had kept extensive journals, full of political observation and commentary. He revised them for publication in the *Observer*, where they appeared as a series of "Sketches of France, Italy and Switzerland." He also honored a request from Lafayette to publicize the reactionary nature of Louis-Philippe's government. In an article for the New York *Commercial Advertiser*, he described how gendarmes "invaded" Lafayette's country estate, seized a leading Polish exile Lafayette had been housing there, and drove him off as a prisoner to Tours. "Thus you will see what kind of *liberty* is enjoyed [in France]," he told American readers, "and you may well ask, whether the cause of freedom has gained any thing by the three days' revolution."

Morse tried to show that Louis-Philippe menaced freedom in the

United States as well. Writing for the *Journal of Commerce,* he addressed the long-simmering issue of the payment by France of some $13 million in damages to American merchants for shipping that had been seized or destroyed during the Napoleonic Wars. American representatives in France had been trying to arbitrate the issue with the French government for years. A breakdown in the negotiations had recently produced a buzz of war talk in Paris and Washington. Morse proposed that the issue could be settled in ten minutes, except for Louis-Philippe's effort—in concert with the sovereigns of Austria, Russia, and Prussia—to suppress aspirations for popular government. The king's aim in leaving the indemnity unsettled was to push France into war with America: "The feelings of hostility towards the United States which a war will inevitably beget in the masses, will be a natural and effectual antidote to all that love of republicanism among them, which is engendered by admiration of American institutions."

Morse's encounter with Europe left him particularly concerned to warn about the spreading influence of Catholicism, sustained by increasing numbers of foreign immigrants. He clipped scores of newspaper articles marking the inroads of the Church in America—"Popery in Kentucky," "Romanism," "Real Principles of Modern Papists." The anti-Catholic novels, pamphlets, and journalism that deluged the country included his brothers' *Observer.* It published anti-Catholic news in every issue and ominously measured the Church's rapid advance. By 1833, it calculated, the United States had become home to 11 bishops, 35 seminaries, 320 priests, and 500,000 worshippers, "a greater number of communicants than are attached to any other denomination in the country."

To Morse, the danger was already evident in the growing number of violent confrontations between Catholics and Protestants. The most notorious erupted in his own birthplace, Charlestown. On August 10, 1834, a warm Sunday evening, forty or fifty Boston truckers, bricklayers, and volunteer firemen ransacked the Ursuline Convent School, an imposing red building occupied by twelve nuns and fifty-seven girls. Shouting "No Popery," the men smashed furniture, burned the altar ornaments and cross, and at last set the building itself ablaze.

Morse deplored the violence, but sympathized with the indignation behind it. In his version of the widely reported events, the rioters believed that a young woman had been abducted, brought to the school, and subjected there to a "secret tyrannical punishment." So the indignation, he said, was honorable to the Charlestownians: "had they viewed such an outrage with indifference, they would have shown themselves unworthy of American citizens." What most worried him was the threat allegedly made by the Mother Superior. Confronting the crowd that first gathered at the convent, she promised that if they dared to damage the building the bishop would order "20,000 foreigners" to rise up in vengeance. For Morse, here in effect was Pope Gregory XVI summoning the myrmidons of Austria, but on American soil—a faithless betrayal of the nation "uttered *in sight of Bunker's Hill.*"

Morse's disgust was widely shared. Within a week after the burning of the convent, two new anti-Catholic newspapers appeared, the Philadelphia *Downfall of Babylon* and the New York *American Protestant Vindicator.* Attacks on Catholic churches in New England soon became so frequent that many posted armed guards to protect their property.

In this atmosphere of alarm, Morse carried forward the work of his father thirty-five years earlier, when Jedediah defended the Republic against imported Infidelity and Jacobinism. Under the pen name "Brutus," he wrote for the *Observer* twelve articles on the Catholic peril, published serially in August and November 1834. Revised and expanded, the articles soon appeared as a nearly two-hundred-page tract, *Foreign Conspiracy against the Liberties of the United States.* In a tone of alternating sweet reasonableness and anxious fury, he revealed that European governments, in their long effort to forestall their own overthrow, were now plotting to bring down republican America by means of the Catholic Church: "Yes, the King of Rome, acting by the promptings of the Austrian Cabinet . . . has already extended his sceptre over our land."

The Pope, Morse explained, is but a "creature of Austria," whose Emperor recognizes the dangers to his country's "principles of darkness." Behind them both stands the archreactionary Austrian chancellor Prince Klemens von Metternich, guiding spirit of the Congress of Vienna—"the master of his Master, the arch contriver of the plans for stifling liberty in Europe and throughout the world." To subvert America, Metternich and his Emperor, with the Pope's blessing, have created the Leopold Foundation. Its funds support the work of Jesuit missionaries in America—"a *secret* society, a sort of Masonic order, with superadded features of most revolting odiousness, and a thousand times more dangerous." Sent here to prey on ignorance and inflame passion, ready to spread riot upon a signal from Vienna or Rome, the

Foundation's terrorists were quietly putting in place the mechanisms of the country's destruction. "The serpent has already commenced his coil about our limbs, and the lethargy of his poison is creeping over us."

In its main elements, at least, the foreign conspiracy Morse described was not unfamiliar to Americans. Austria's large holdings in Italy and intervention against Italian revolutionaries at the Pope's behest had been kept in public view through newspaper articles headed "Austrian Horror of Republics," books such as the Transcendentalist Elizabeth Peabody's *Crimes of Austria against Mankind*. And a belief in secret societies as hidden managers of political upheaval had been constant in Western culture since at least the Middle Ages. It activated Jedediah Morse's charge in the 1790s that clandestine Bavarian Illuminati were fomenting counterrevolution in America. It revived with the European political uprisings of the early 1830s, in which the Italian Carbonari, the French Societé des Droits de l'Homme, and similar underground organizations did in fact operate. The Leopold Foundation also existed, created in Vienna in 1828 with official approval of Pope Leo XII. Its members contributed money for missionary work in America, such as funds for the college that became Fordham University. In so doing, the Foundation helped to establish Catholicism in the country, especially in the West.

The detailed workings of the conspiracy that Morse depicted, however, were less familiar to his Protestant readers, and more chilling. Drawing on published and unpublished correspondence of the Leopold missionaries, he tried to demonstrate that Jesuit cells were even now infiltrating the American press, insinuating themselves into American political councils, inveigling American children into Catholic schools. Consider St. Joseph's College in Kentucky with its priest-trustees, a college thus "under the exclusive control of the Pope, and consequently for an indefinite period under that of Austria!!" Consider the recent consecration of the Cathedral of St. Louis: artillery pieces thundering, a paramilitary "guard of honor" stationed around the church. The scene, Morse said, might have been not the western United States but Rome. He fully recounted his Corpus Domini confrontation—how once, as a canopy shielding the Host passed by him on the Via del Corso, a soldier knocked off his hat, pressed a bayonet to his chest, and cursed him as *il diavolo*.

At stake for America was what Morse called "Protestant republi-

canism." Which is to say, as he understood the phrase, liberty of conscience, liberty of opinion, liberty of the press—the fruits of the country's homogeneous white Protestant culture. "Our religion, *the
Protestant religion,* and *Liberty* are identical." ("The foundations which
support Christianity," his father had preached in 1799, "are also necessary to support a free and equal government like our own.") He
urged Americans to fight Catholicism not by its low methods of persecution and intrigue, but by their own distinctive means—the tract, the
Sabbath school, the open discussion of the free press. But war is waging and fight they must: "THE WORLD EXPECTS AMERICA,
REPUBLICAN AMERICA, TO DO HER DUTY."

Morse's *Foreign Conspiracy* became controversial. Widely circulated
and often extracted in the anti-Catholic press, it spurred the formation of such anti-Catholic groups as the New York Protestant Association, dedicated to exposing the inconsistency of popery with civil
liberties. Its narrative of the *il diavolo* episode made Morse's defiled
hat something of a symbol to anti-Catholic activists. Some newspapers
dismissed his revelation of foreign conspiracy as a "chimera." But he
replied that during his years abroad he had observed the network first-
hand, and that parts of the press itself might be even *"unconsciously"* a
victim of Jesuit arts. "I have the fullest persuasion that this Conspiracy
exists, that it is no chimera, and that all Americans of all parties religious and political should be aware of this new danger to our institutions."

Living proof of the conspiracy, Morse believed, arrived in the fall
of 1835 at his very doorstep. He was visited at New York University by a
young German, about twenty-four years old, named Lewis Clausing.
Formerly a medical student at Heidelberg, Clausing had just come
from Pittsburgh—by way of Brussels, London, and Boston. He was in
flight from Jesuit spies, he explained. They had been sent to pursue
him because of his membership, while at Heidelberg, in a secret
republican association. No longer knowing whom to trust, he sought
out the author of *Foreign Conspiracy.*

By his account, Morse helped Clausing find a place to live, and to
divert the young man from his troubles gave him tickets to lectures at
the University and a pass to the N.A.D. exhibition. But Clausing's troubles persisted—maps stolen from his room, he said, seductive women
set in his path, a mysterious deaf man. Jesuits tracked him to his job at
a New York printing office, plotting to make him seem a petty thief.

Morse soon began to suspect that Clausing was mentally unbalanced. He frankly told the young man that he saw no reason for the Jesuits to relentlessly pursue someone his age. But Clausing produced a copy of a German magazine entitled *Der Geächtete* (The Proscribed). It contained a list of political outlaws drawn up by the Austrian Central Committee and sent to all police officers in Germany. Clausing's name appeared sixteenth on the list. "I saw by this document that his *proscription* was indeed not a dream of the imagination, but a truth," Morse said. Nor could he discount as irrational the young man's belief that he was under surveillance. Jesuits adept at espionage were being sent to America by the hundreds and "disposed all over the land, in the pay of the Austrian Leopold Foundation."

Eventually Clausing also revealed to Morse the crime for which he was proscribed and pursued, which had nothing to do with membership in a secret society. Morse recounted without comment what Clausing told him. But as the author of *Foreign Conspiracy* it surely must have astonished him.

Clausing's story was this: While a student at Heidelberg he went to see the revival of a long-discontinued ceremony—the "*procession of the host*"! Ignorant of the appropriate behavior, he did not remove his pipe from his mouth or his cap from his head. An ecclesiastic, in a passionate manner, left the procession—and struck off his cap! Unlike Morse in Rome, Clausing retaliated. Feeling humiliated before his fellow students and their code of honor, he went to the priest's home and shot him through the face.

During Clausing's final visits to him, Morse found the young man increasingly paranoid, construing the most ordinary events as evidence of a cabal. Clausing tried to see him at the University on July 2, 1836, but he was away. The same evening, in the Battery, the young man put a gun to his head and killed himself. Whatever else Morse felt about Clausing's death, he considered his literary remains valuable in the crusade against foreign conspiracies. He printed from manuscript Clausing's "Treatise on the Jesuits" and turned the unfortunate young man's personal papers into a fifty-eight-page anti-Catholic biography of him, published in 1836 as *The Proscribed German Student*. He also wrote a biographical sketch of Clausing, published in several New York newspapers.

Some of Clausing's fellow workers denounced Morse's accounts of his life. In an article for the *New Era*, they denied his "atrocious calumny" that after a Corpus Domini procession their friend had attempted to murder a priest. One shopmate, born near Heidelberg, noted that the city is Protestant, and had witnessed no such ceremony since the Reformation. They all maintained that Clausing's proscription had strictly to do with his membership in a republican organization that corresponded with Polish rebels. Morse investigated the matter and replied through the press. He quoted a letter to him from Charles Follen, professor of German at Harvard, affirming that Heidelberg celebrated the procession of the Host and was about half Catholic. Information he received from Heidelberg itself, however, forced him to acknowledge that Clausing's tale of having shot a priest was untrue.

Morse completed his warnings about the Catholic menace by uncovering sexual corruption in the Church. He edited from manuscript a 250-page account of ecclesiastical lechery, published in 1837 as *Confessions of a French Catholic Priest.* The book appeared amid a burst of similar exposés inspired by Maria Monk's *Awful Disclosures of . . . Five Years as a Novice and Two Years as a Black Nun in the Hotel Dieu Nunnery at Montreal* (1836). Her slim but sensational volume became the all-time American bestseller before *Uncle Tom's Cabin,* its first buyers grabbing up 20,000 copies in a few weeks, later sales surpassing 300,000. A novice claiming to be a Protestant convert to Catholicism, Monk told a sado-Gothic tale of her sexual abuse in a conventual system designed, as she put it, to "comfort the priest"—illegitimate offspring being baptized then strangled. Morse credited Monk's account, as many people did not, and may even have interviewed her.

A sort of male Maria Monk, Morse's French priest presented himself as a refugee from popish tyranny and licentiousness, seeking shelter in America. He revealed how the Church's vow of celibacy served only to inflame the passions of its priests beyond control. To quench his own lust he had worn vermin-infested clothing and drunk potions of water lilies, yet became attracted to one of his young female confessants. His fellow priests spoke as freely about their girlfriends as about theology. One killed his lover and cut her body into pieces; another made love to his mistress's corpse. The French priest's alarum summed up Morse's own message to Americans about the militant fanatics among them: "Open your eyes and see: Popery overflows, invades you, and you are not aware of it; it strides with the steps of a giant to the conquest of your glorious land, and you do not resist, yea, you stretch out your hand to it."

Morse's anti-Catholic campaign led him for the first time into the rough-and-tumble of American party politics. Whatever the exact influence of *Foreign Conspiracy* and his similar works, they fed the closely related but broader fear of immigration. During the 1830s more than half a million immigrants from Great Britain, Ireland, and Germany arrived, in New York City alone.

The hope of controlling the tide gave rise, in the early summer of 1835, to the Native American Democratic Association—the country's first explicitly nativist political party. It declared opposition not only to the Church, but also to the immigration of paupers and criminals and to office holding by foreigners. Based in New York, the Native Americans got the support of several city editors and sponsored their own penny journal, the *Spirit of '76*. But they meant to do more than write. Claiming to stand apart from existing political parties, they organized ward committees and ran Native American candidates in the 1835 local elections. The party polled an impressive 9000 votes out of 23,000 cast. Similar nativist organizations sprang up outside New York—Paterson, Washington, Cincinnati, New Orleans.

Morse became one of the Native Americans' chief spokesmen. Although a longtime Democrat, he considered independent opinion his privilege as an American. And at the moment he saw little more in the bickering between Democrats and Whigs than the defensiveness of officeholders and frustration of office seekers. The Native Americans had got hold of a momentous issue, vital to "all true patriots, whatever may be their party predilections."

America, in Morse's view, had fought itself free of Kings, Emperors, and Czars. But the new immigrants retained the mentality of subjects, bringing with them the same sinister anti-republican forces he had seen produce squalor and maintain oppression on the Continent. He believed that America properly welcomed "the intelligent and persecuted of all nations." But on his moral-aesthetic scale the new arrivals stood beside the pizza-eating *lazzeroni* of Naples: "Filthy and ragged in body, ignorant in mind, and but too often most debased in morals . . . a loathsome picture of degradation, moral and physical."

Morse's visceral revulsion was felt by many others in New York's older Protestant community, such as the diarist George Templeton Strong: "It was enough to turn a man's stomach—to make a man abjure republicanism forever—to see the way they were naturalizing this morning. Wretched, filthy, bestial-looking Italians and Irish . . . the very scum and dregs of human nature." And more were on their way. "All Europe is coming across the ocean," Philip Hone grumbled, "all that part at least who cannot make a living at home; and what shall we do with them?"

In support of the Native American Democratic Association, Morse wrote a series of impassioned letters for the *Journal of Commerce*, published separately as *Imminent Dangers to the Free Institutions of the United States Through Foreign Immigration*. He took as his occasion a rise in public violence that "sadly degraded" the American character. He mentioned no specific events, but in recent memory a New York physician had been trampled to death during a clubs-and-brickbats clash between a Bowery gang and some Irishmen, the mayhem spreading in the city until put down by two hundred police. Some might view the lawlessness as a byproduct of democracy, Morse said. But the real cause was immigration, "foreign turbulence imported by shiploads."

Morse scourged three immigrant groups in particular. First, predictably, the Hapsburg-Vatican Manchurian candidates, the "hundreds of thousands of human priest-controlled machines." Next, the "outcast tenants of the poorhouses and prisons," paupers and convicts whose immigration European governments in fact sometimes subsidized. He took special aim, however, at newcomers who weakened the coherence of the Union by resisting assimilation. He had in mind clannish Germans, Italians, and, especially, Irish who called the old country "home," living in America as neither foreigners nor natives— "anomalous, nondescript, *hermaphrodite*."

Among the national clubs they often formed, Morse singled out an Irish organization founded by a Bowery saloon keeper, the O'Connell Guard. He considered the name offensive and incendiary. It honored the Irish Catholic patriot Daniel O'Connell, who often publicly contrasted America's reputed democracy with the reality of slavery in the South. At a crowded anti-slavery meeting in London's Exeter Hall, he stood beside the Abolitionist leader William Lloyd Garrison and damned the United States as "the vilest of hypocrites— the greatest of liars." To Morse, the new Abolitionist movement was "rife with danger to our country," and in naming their paramilitary club the O'Connell Guard, Irish immigrants had "thrown a firebrand into the *Slavery* question."

Morse acknowledged that not all immigrants were ignorant, vicious, or unpatriotic. But the present, "when the country is invaded by an army," allowed for no nice discrimination. The innocent and the guilty come over together and live together: "We must of necessity suspect them all." To protect the Republic he called for changes in laws concerning citizenship. He proposed extending the five-year probationary period for naturalization and denying suffrage to naturalized aliens. Since the immigrant came to America, and stayed, by permission of the people, the people could also withdraw permission and the privileges that accompanied it—"*can take away his liberty, yes, and even his life.*"

In addition to his influential tract, Morse wrote many signed and unsigned newspaper articles on immigration. Typical is a letter to the editor he composed for the *Native American Citizen,* asking Americans not to vote for naturalized office seekers: "depend upon it, the insolence of foreigners will no longer be endured." The *Observer* published many like-minded articles, some of them probably by Morse himself. Readers of the paper learned that the Irish were "the most ignorant and turbulent people of Europe," and were told what to expect from the onrushing boatloads: "We shall soon have more Papists in the North than they have slaves in the South. And who would not prefer two million slaves."

In the spring of 1836, after a long search for a candidate, the Native American Democratic Association asked Morse to run for mayor of New York City. At first he for some reason declined. Mayors at the time served only a one-year term, but after all he still taught at the University; still presided over the National Academy; still painted, however much discouraged. And he had become engrossed in a possibly important new venture, as will appear. The Association asked him to reconsider, however, and in the end he accepted the nomination. The party's demand for revised naturalization laws convinced him, he said, that it was his duty "to make the sacrifice to which I am called, and place myself at its disposal."

Morse quickly got a taste of practical politics in New York. The conservative Whig party—descended from the now-defunct Federalists—fielded no candidate in the mayoralty race, expecting that Whig voters would support the Native American candidate. But only two days after Morse's official nomination, the Whig *Morning Courier* disowned him. Its editor explained to the public that he had intended to vote for Morse, but he discovered that Morse backed the presidential nominee of the rival Democrats, Martin Van Buren. Morse had been "imposed" on the Native Americans, he charged, by "*designing Van Buren men*." With the election only a day away, the startled Whigs hurriedly nominated a candidate of their own.

Morse admitted in print that he favored Van Buren for the presidency, someone he knew and had painted. "I have always avowed this preference," he announced, "but it is subordinate to *principles* which are superior to any man." He would not support Van Buren or anyone else, he said, who did not fearlessly espouse the principles of the Native American Democratic Association.

Morse's explanation did him little if any good. The *Courier*'s revelation and the ticketing of a Whig candidate surely lost him votes, perhaps from among the Native Americans themselves. In the three-day balloting he ran last in a field of four, receiving 1496 votes, while the last-moment Whig candidate received 5989, and the victorious Democrat, C. W. Lawrence, received 16,101. "The fellow actually got 1500 votes," as Cooper put it, "and would have been elected could he have got 15,000 more."

The beating Morse took did not disenchant him with the Native American cause. The following year he attended the party conclave to again choose a mayoral candidate. He wrote an adjunct to the party platform, a call-to-arms addressed to all the citizens of America: "Shall the alternatives of riot and outrage, or order and tranquillity depend upon the yea or nay of a Foreigner? Shall they longer brow beat you at the polls, or dictate to you your rulers?—No! No! NATIVE AMERICANS OF LIBERTY, LOVERS OF LAW, LOVERS OF ORDER." His shouting may have been heard. In the new city elections, a nativist ticket swept into office a mayor of New York and complete Common Council.

Morse's shift to politics offered nothing to deny his parents' criticism, years before, that he was fickle, unable to settle down: "one can never *fix* him," Cooper said. Even his fond teacher Allston recognized something scattershot in Morse that limited his achievement. "I know what *is in him,*" he told William Dunlap; "If he will only bring out all that is *there,* he will show powers that many now do not dream of." Greenough, too, urged him to focus: "give us at least one picture which should embody all your acquirements."

But in addition to turning his career on and off, Morse was falling out of step with the direction of American art. Among the younger generation, his friend Thomas Cole was maturely developing the historiographic and ideological possibilities of landscape painting in his five-canvas *Course of Empire* series (1836). Oblivious to high culture, the genre painter William Sidney Mount was depicting scenes of ordinary Americans in everyday situations, designed for the many not the few. The theoretical superiority of history painting in the grand manner continued to be stressed. But under the influence of genre painting, many history painters began representing not major historical events but historical anecdotes such as the marriage of George Washington to Martha Custis. Morse had no wish to paint American scenery, American society, or kitsch Americana. Nor was he sympathetic to the Romantic call for a national art of raging originality, as propounded for instance by Emerson, who considered even Allston's works genteel and complained that "all the American geniuses . . . lack nerve and dagger."

But however behind the times or diverted by politics, Morse had hung on to one hope of succeeding as an artist on his own terms. The commissions for four paintings to adorn the Capitol rotunda remained open. The problem of assigning them had dragged on in Congress the whole time since his return to America, but was finally resolved early in 1837, just before the new city elections. In March 1834, Morse had presented his views on the matter in letters to a half-dozen influential members of Congress, including Daniel Webster, John C. Calhoun, and John Quincy Adams. He said he would be honored to be chosen for one of the commissions, and laid out his imposing credentials: "I have devoted twenty years of my life of which *seven* were passed in England, France, Italy and Switzerland studying with special reference to the execution of works of the kind proposed."

But the signs were unfavorable. When the House debated the issue in December 1834, Congressman (and ex-president) John Quincy Adams questioned whether America could supply artistic talent worthy of decorating the seat of its government. He doubted, he said, "if four native artists could be found of eminence in the profession so transcendent as to ensure the performance of four master-pieces." His colleagues took this to mean that the country might be better served if they hired at least some European painters. Adams later confided in his diary that he had spoken "somewhat inconsiderately," but his snide remarks provoked an outcry. A representative from Virginia, Henry Alexander Wise, rose to object: "Sir, I am proud to say and believe, that this country—the great masters dead—is richer now in native talents in the fine arts than any country on the globe." Cooper replied through Bryant's *Evening Post*. He argued that the U.S. Capitol was destined to become a historic building and should display paintings by native artists, if only as moments in the record of the country's cultural development, "links in the History of American Art."

Further congressional action, in 1836, brought Morse months of painfully seesawing hope and disappointment. A select committee decided to ask seven artists to present sketches of possible subjects for the Capitol paintings. Morse was not included. His hope revived, however, when the committee abandoned this plan, and he heard that two of its members were favorably disposed to him. But nothing happened for another nine months. Then the committee at last chose four artists to paint the rotunda pictures: John Chapman, Robert Weir, John Vanderlyn, and Henry Inman.

For Morse, the decision to pass him by contained an added sting. Vanderlyn would paint a subject he had considered his own, the landing of Columbus. Something like hope flickered early in 1837, when Inman unexpectedly declined the commission. Several artists and newspaper editors advised Congress how to fill his place. "The rare qualifications of Mr. Morse for a work of the character contemplated," the *Journal of Commerce* wrote, "are well known to all who are acquainted with the progress of the arts in this country."

But Morse felt humiliated by the situation. Even if chosen to replace Inman, he could take no pleasure in being a leftover, "selected as a sort of fifth wheel." He was tempted to save face, and spare himself further misery, by anticipating the committee's decision and declining the commission in advance. He did not need to: Inman reversed himself and agreed to paint the one remaining picture. However indifferent Morse may have grown to the whole business, the turnaround came as a further humiliation: "even this back door way is closed to me." He decided that Inman had been persuaded to change his mind by John Quincy Adams, whose seeming personal hostility he found unaccountable: "I never gave him the slightest cause of personal offence." He came to believe that what turned Adams against him was a long-nurtured dislike of Jedediah, who had spent time with Adams in Washington fifteen years earlier.

Rejected beyond hope or appeal, Morse became more seriously depressed than ever. Having trained himself to do a grand historical work since at least his graduation from college, and having made himself one of the most conspicuous artists in America—probably too conspicuous for noisy politicking—he experienced his rejection as total defeat: "the object of my studies for 26 years, and the special mark at which I have aimed for 15 years, are forever removed before me." He spoke of resigning his presidency of the N.A.D. and abandoning painting altogether. Friends tried to cheer him up. "To you our Academy owes its existence & present prosperity," Cole wrote; "You are the Key Stone of the Arch." Allston sent reassurance: "You have it still in your power to let the world know what you can do. Dismiss it from your mind, and determine to paint all the better."

But Morse felt battered. "I staggered under the blow," he said. He took to bed, "quite ill," Cooper reported. The litterateur N. P. Willis, who had known Morse in Paris, later recalled him saying around this time that he was weary of his existence, and had he "divine authorization" would terminate it.

Morse's near-collapse apparently lasted several weeks in the early spring of 1837. While abed in his sickroom, he was visited by a committee of artists, who brought an encouraging proposal. They represented artists in New York and Philadelphia, and some New York gentlemen, who formed a sort of stock company that would hire him to paint a historical picture of his own choice. Selling subscriptions at $50 each, and receiving $1000 from an anonymous New Yorker, they raised over $3000. The fee hardly compared with the $12,000 offered by Congress for the rotunda paintings, but Morse accepted the commission gratefully: "is not this noble? Is this not honorable to the character of our profession? Will it not tell to the credit of American artists?" In addition, the subscribers planned for him to keep the painting, for his own use and profit.

His depression lifting, Morse chose his subject. In Charlestown, while still in his late teens, he had painted the landing of the Pilgrims at Plymouth—probably his first ambitious history work. He would return to the subject now, but with a difference. The new painting would depict the Pilgrim fathers in Cape Cod harbor aboard the *Mayflower*, signing the Mayflower Compact—in his view "the first written constitution." Entitled *The Gem of the Republic,* it would be massive—eighteen feet by twelve feet, the size of the rotunda paintings. It would take years to complete, but he planned to sacrifice everything else, and hoped to visit England and Holland for special study. Some of the figures, he decided, should be women. He thought he might paint in his young friend Catherine Pattison.

Morse's plans and hopes had a way of dissolving, however, and *The Gem of the Republic* no sooner took shape than it became unreal. . . .

SEVEN

High Attribute of Ubiquity

(1837–1838)

THE STARTLING news evidently came to Morse through his brothers. On April 15, 1837, their *Observer* reprinted an item that had run a few days earlier in the Baltimore *Patriot*. It reported that two Frenchmen, named Gonon and Serval, were in the United States demonstrating a revolutionary system of long-distance communication. They claimed that their telegraph was capable of operating as fast as a person could write or even speak. Fast and far. A hundred-word dispatch might be sent from New York to New Orleans in half an hour.

The claims were amazing. The world measured communication-time in terms of transportation time, by how long it would take anything or anyone to get from here to there. Except by smoke signal, semaphore, and the like, sending words was the same as sending a package. Earlier in the century this meant that a letter went out no faster than ponies could gallop or sails could waft a schooner—or, by mid-century, no faster than coal-fed boilers could push steamships and railroad cars. The identity of communication with transportation had existed for millennia. News of Andrew Jackson's victory in the Battle of New Orleans in 1815 took as long to reach Washington as news of Alexander the Great's victory at the Battle of Arbela took to reach his capital in 331 B.C. But Gonon and Serval redefined the possible. As the newspaper item exclaimed, "The imagination is overpowered in contemplating the consequences of such an achievement of human ingenuity."

Morse felt overpowered, too, but for a different reason. He had in his rooms at New York University, he believed, the same system the

Frenchmen were promoting in America. As far as he knew, no one but himself had even dreamed of such a device. Not only that. He had been quietly developing it for five years. He had allowed a few people at the University to see preliminary stages of his invention, and had sent a few correspondents a few oblique hints about it. But he seems to have kept only his brothers fully informed. As far as the world knew, since returning from Europe he had spent his time painting, teaching, or fighting immigration and Catholicism.

Through experiment Morse had often changed the design of his telegraph. The apparatus that existed around 1837 remained so crude that he was reluctant to have it seen, and perhaps ridiculed. It consisted of two main elements: a transmission device that he called the port-rule and a receiver called the register. The port-rule was activated by a printer's composing stick (M)—about three feet long, made of wood, and grooved. Flat metal blanks could be set into the groove, each having from one to nine V-shaped notches. (An unnotched blank represented a space.) When the crank (L) was turned, the composing stick glided beneath the balanced lever overhead (O-O). A projecting tooth dropped into the valleys or rose to the peaks on the notched metal blanks. At the same time, the two-pointed copper prong at the other end of the lever dipped in and out of two thimble-size cups of mercury (J, K), which were connected to a battery (I). As the composing stick passed underneath, the seesawing lever opened and closed an electrical circuit, in a rhythm dictated by the notched blanks.

This circuit activated Morse's register. He built the device into a wooden frame otherwise used for stretching canvas (X). A clockwork mechanism (D) slowly fed out a ribbon of paper over a drum (B). From the top of the frame, suspended above the paper, hung a pyramid-shaped pendulum (F) with a pencil at the lower end (g). Its movement was governed by a device set in the middle of the frame: an iron armature, and a bar of soft iron coiled in wire that led back to the port-rule (h). As the copper prongs dipped into the cups of mercury they closed the circuit, sending an electrical current into the wire, which magnetized the bar, which attracted the armature, which caused the pendulum to swing, which made the pencil zigzag along the moving paper. When the circuit opened, the armature, mounted on a spring, moved away from the magnet.

In operation, then, as the composing stick passed beneath the

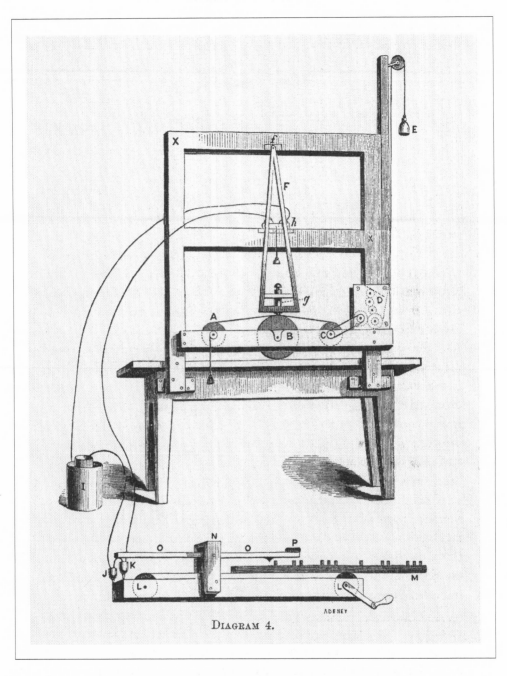

Morse's original telegraph apparatus (ca. 1836)
(Samuel I. Prime, *The Life of Samuel F. B. Morse, LL.D.* [1875])

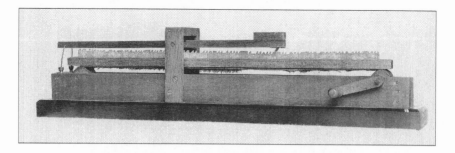

Reproduction of Morse's original port-rule
(Smithsonian Institution)

seesawing lever, opening and closing the circuit, the register reproduced in pencil on its paper ribbon the pattern of the V-shaped
notches cut into the metal blanks. The Vs signified numbers: VVVVVV
represented 6, for example, VV VVV 23. To decode the message the
recipient looked up the word numbered 6 and the word numbered 23
in a dictionary expressly compiled for the purpose.

However crude, Morse's telegraph was accurate and, once the type
was set, fast. That it might not be unique, however, had never occurred
to him. To counter the boasts of Gonon and Serval, he and Sidney
immediately made his five-year-long effort known to the public. In
reprinting the Baltimore article about the French invention, Sidney
informed readers of the *Observer* that rapid communication over long
distances was stale news. The feat had been suggested to him "several
years since," he said, using an electrical battery and fine wires. Surely
to avoid any hint of Morse family self-interest, he identified the inventor only as "a gentleman of our acquaintance." Instead, he had his
brother's identity revealed in a companion article in the *Journal of
Commerce:* "The Gentleman alluded to by the editor of the New York
Observer, as the inventor of the Electric Telegraph, is Professor Samuel F. B. Morse, the President of the National Academy of Design."

Whatever dismay Morse felt in learning about Gonon and Serval was in
one sense excessive and in another not enough. The system of the two
self-styled "Professors of Graphy" was not an electrical telegraph at all,
but an alleged improvement on the optical telegraph, a semaphore.
France had a working system of such semaphores, windmill-like towers
of adjustable arms and flaps, built about six miles apart. Signal opera-

Chappe semaphore
(Musée de la Poste, Paris)

tors used ropes and pulleys to position the arms according to a code. Messages were read by telescope from station to station and passed on. The system spanned all of France, extending into Holland, Germany, Italy, and Spain. It was to this complex visual semaphore that, in 1794, the word "telegraph" was first applied.

Morse soon learned, however, that although he had supposed himself to be the first person who ever put the words "electric" and "telegraph" together, scientists of several countries had been experimenting with electrical signaling systems for about twenty years. And in the fall of 1837 the American press began reporting a sudden surge in the production of such devices abroad, and of interest in them. "Scarcely a journal arrives from Europe which does not contain some notice of the *Electric Telegraph*," the *Journal of Commerce* said, "which now seems to have excited the attention of the scientific world as the wonder of the age."

Morse clipped and preserved articles depressingly headed "ELECTRIC WIRE TELEGRAPHS," "NEW AND BEAUTIFUL INVENTION." He read that in Scotland a William Alexander proposed laying insulated copper wires, one for each letter of the alphabet, under the turnpike from London to Edinburgh. In Munich a Professor Steinheil was stringing iron wires between the cathedral and the observatory of Bogenhausen; he conjectured that Lisbon could communicate to St. Petersburg in two seconds. In London an "eminent scientific gentleman" was perfecting a device to send an electric current through five wires that activate needles, whose positions on a dial denote letters of the alphabet: "the discovery will perhaps be the grandest in the annals of the world."

Such reports described methods and devices akin to what Morse had produced himself. He received the news with not only pained disbelief but also suspicion. "There is not a thought in any of the foreign journals relative to the Telegraph," he said, "which I had not expressed nearly 5 years ago." Knowing well enough how Europe and England feared America's example and wished to curb its growing power, he worried that before he could perfect his own apparatus the innovations it embodied would be stolen from him, "that other nations will take the hint and rob me both of the credit and the profit."

Morse set to work establishing himself as *the* inventor of the electric telegraph. First he tried to verify the date of his discovery. When and how had news of his invention leaked out? Word of mouth travels fast: "a hint flies from mind to mind and is soon past all tracing back to the original suggester." He traced the progress of his own hints back to his return voyage from France in October 1832, aboard the ship *Sully*. It was then and there that the idea of an electric telegraph first occurred to him, and he had divulged it. "It is certainly by no means improbable," he thought, "that the excitement on the subject in England has its origin from my giving the details of the plan of my telegraph to some of the Englishmen or other fellow passengers on board the ship."

To confirm his suspicions and establish his originality, Morse prepared a circular letter addressed to the captain of the *Sully* and four passengers:

There is to be a contest, it seems, for priority of invention of this Electric Telegraph between England, France, Germany and this country. I claim for myself and consequently for America priority over all other countries in the invention of a mode of communicating intelligence by electricity.

His object in writing, he said, was to ask whether his shipmates recalled his speaking about an electric telegraph during the voyage five years ago. If so, he asked them to fully state what they recalled. He also asked the captain, William Pell, to answer a more specific question: had Pell mentioned the telegraph to others after the voyage? The ship had carried twenty-six passengers, mostly Americans, plus seven or eight French farmers in steerage, presumably immigrants. In addition to Captain Pell, Morse addressed his letter collectively to fellow-passengers Francis J. Fisher, a Philadelphia lawyer; William Rives, the American minister to France; Charles C. Palmer; and the Boston physician-geologist Dr. Charles Jackson.

Morse may not have sent Jackson a copy of the letter—for reasons to be explained—and Palmer seems to have left the United States. But his other hoped-for defenders replied quickly, and their accounts of the voyage bore out his most significant assertion. "I have a distinct remembrance," Captain Pell wrote, "of your suggesting as a thought newly occurred to you, the possibility of a telegraphic communication being effected by electric wires." The passengers agreed, with slight variation. "You spoke of a *single wire*," Fisher wrote, "and *letters* or *signs* were to be indicated by a quick succession of strokes or shocks."

Morse's respondents also agreed that his telegraph generated discussion, among other things of how to protect the wire conductor when strung across rivers. Morse had solved the problems proposed to him, Rives recalled, with "great promptitude & confidence." Captain Pell believed that the give-and-take helped Morse refine his vague original idea, so by the end of the trip he had conceived a workable instrument. "I sincerely trust," Pell added, "that circumstances may not deprive you of the reward due to the invention, which, whatever may be its source in Europe, is with you I am convinced original." He mentioned, however, that since the voyage he had indeed spread the word and told others of Morse's telegraph.

Morse's own recollections of his discoveries aboard the *Sully* were minutely particular. He clearly remembered, he said, "the manner, the place, and the moment when the thought of making an electric wire the means of communicating intelligence first came into my mind and was uttered." He and Dr. Charles Jackson had just dined and were sitting across a table from each other. "We were conversing," he said, "on the recent scientific discoveries in electro magnetism and the experiments of Ampere." Another passenger asked whether a lengthy wire did not retard the passage of an electric current. Jackson replied No, that Benjamin Franklin had demonstrated long ago in London that electricity travels at once through any known length of wire. This, Morse said, triggered his crucial realization: "I then remarked . . . if the presence of electricity can be made visible in any desired part of the circuit I see no reason why intelligence might not be transmitted instantaneously by electricity."

By Morse's account, the possibly world-changing idea took posses- sion of his mind and kept him from sleeping. He tried to work out methods of regulating the current, drawing in his sketchbook what became the notched blanks of his port-rule. He pondered ways of using electricity to inscribe: the current might be made to puncture some paper by a spark or mark it by chemical decomposition. Regard- ing the second notion he consulted Jackson, who suggested that the current would leave a brown mark on paper stained with turmeric and treated with sulfate of soda. They agreed to experiment with the idea after reaching home.

Some at least of Morse's account is confirmed by the pocket-size sketchbook he kept aboard the *Sully*. What survives is only a certified copy of a certified copy of the original. But it has an authentic look and feel of Morse's return from his three years abroad, containing sketches of Havre and notes for his Capitol rotunda painting of Columbus. Quite as Morse maintained, he evidently was preoccupied while at sea with thoughts of a telegraph system. He sketched some of its main elements: a tube for burying conducting wires under the earth and tall poles for stringing them above ground; an electromag- net actuating an armature to move a stylus against a roll of paper. He also composed a newsworthy dispatch to be sent by number-word code, perhaps his first conception of what a telegraph message might be like: "War. Holland. Belgium. Alliance. France. England. against. Russia. Prussia. Austria."

Of Morse's work on the telegraph between his first inklings on the *Sully* in 1832 and the port-rule/register of 1837, only glimpses remain. Twenty years after the voyage, his brothers testified that they met him when the ship docked. As soon as they greeted him he announced that he had discovered a means of communicating intelligence by electricity. Moving in for several weeks with his brother Richard, he made a mold and used the parlor fireplace to cast blanks for the port-rule. In the process he spilled molten lead on a chair and rug, severely burning a finger.

Some of Morse's colleagues and painting students at New York

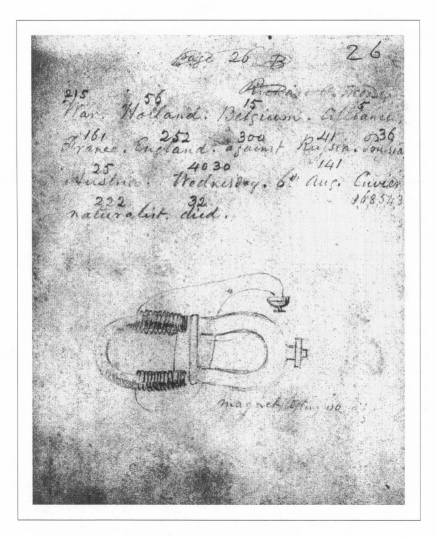

Page from Morse's *Sully* sketchbook
(Smithsonian Institution)

University later recalled seeing telegraph apparatus in his rooms in 1835–36, months after he moved into the tower. They remembered galvanic batteries, wire lying about the floor or suspended on the walls, the clockwork paper dispenser feeding out a white ribbon that became covered with Vs. "We grieved to see the sketch upon the canvas untouched," one student added. "We longed to see him again calling into life events in our country's history."

To further secure his title to the invention, Morse began publicizing his telegraph through the press. Articles about his ongoing work soon appeared, headed "Morse's Telegraph" and "Morse's Magnetic Telegraph." The *Journal of Commerce* commented that while American newspapers had been copying from papers abroad ecstatic notices of telegraphs in Europe, they seemed unaware that "the honor of the first discovery" belonged to America. "Prof. MORSE . . . some *five years* ago, on his passage home from France, conceived the idea of communicating intelligence by electricity, and matured his plan." In published letters to the editor of several newspapers, Morse pointed out that Europeans asserted only what their devices "*may*" do; he asked for proof that they had actually sent intelligible communications. Meanwhile the *Journal* reproduced an example of what his port-rule had provably transmitted—a ribbon of Vs representing the numerically coded message "Successful experiment with telegraph."

Suspecting that foreigners had stolen his ideas, Morse was astounded when his new publicity aroused charges of theft against himself—from an American. The accuser was Dr. Charles Jackson, his fellow passenger on the *Sully*. At the time of the voyage Jackson had been a twenty-eight-year-old physician with a Harvard M.D., returning from study of medicine and geology in Europe. Now he operated a private chemistry lab in Boston and served as state geologist of Maine. He wrote to Morse saying he rejoiced in the success of "our Electric Telegraph." He had read notices of the device in the press, but he missed seeing himself mentioned: "I suppose that the reason why my name was not attached to the invention of the Electric Telegraph is simply that the editors did not know that the invention was our *mutual* discovery."

The intensity of Morse's reaction to this can be measured by the dozens of furious pages he wrote in reply. Going over in detail what seems every moment of his acquaintance with Jackson, he adopted a tone of gentlemanly respect for Jackson's honor and fairness—broken, however, by poisonous accusations of delusional thinking, faulty memory, bad faith, and theft of intellectual property.

"I lose no time in endeavoring to disabuse your mind," Morse began, "of an error into which it has fallen." Rehearsing all their encounters aboard the *Sully*, he reminded Jackson of the after-dinner conversation that had inspired his crucial realization. Jackson had spoken of Franklin's demonstration that electricity passes at once through any length of wire. This had been the moment of Morse's epiphany: "I see no reason," he had told the company, "why intelligence might not be transmitted instantaneously by electricity." Jackson considered himself a partner in the telegraph, it seemed, simply because they had agreed to experiment together with marking turmeric paper by electricity. In fact, Jackson had no conception of the port-rule and register Morse had devised. "All the machinery has been elaborated without a hint from you of any kind in the remotest degree. I am the sole inventor."

"I have always entertained the highest opinion of your honour & fairness," Jackson came back, "& should be very sorry to have any reason to change my opinion of your character." He challenged point by point Morse's version of what was becoming The *Sully* Story. The all-important suggestion for communicating intelligence by electricity had come not from Morse, he said, but from himself. During the after-dinner conversation he mentioned having seen a demonstration at the Sorbonne in which an electric spark traveled instantaneously around the lecture room four hundred times, an experiment anticipated by Franklin. Then one of the passengers, either Rives or Fisher, said "*it would be well if we could send news in the same rapid manner.*" At this, Morse asked, "*Why cant we?*" Jackson then explained how it could be done, using the spark to perforate ordinary paper or mark chemically treated paper—an experiment he had made himself. "I do claim to be the principal in the whole invention made on board the Sully," Jackson concluded. "It arose wholly from my materials & was put together at your request by me."

Too enraged to bother seeming polite, Morse replied with a threat of legal action. Certain that Jackson, an American, meant to steal his work, he again appealed to his acquaintances from the *Sully*, whose testimony he had sought against thieving Europeans. "I little thought when I made this request in order to prepare myself against *foreign* claimants," he wrote, "that I should be under the necessity of again troubling you for evidence to defend myself against an attack *at home.*"

Morse asked Rives and Fisher whether either of them had remarked, as Jackson alleged, that "*It would be well if we could send news in the same rapid manner.*" He also asked Captain Pell, "Was there on board ship any other person than myself the inventor of the Telegraph?" Their responses were heartening. Rives and Fisher both disowned the remark: "such a conception had never entered my mind," Rives said; "it was a complete novelty to me when first presented to my contemplation by your conversations." Pell admitted that he could not remember every conversation about the telegraph during the voyage, but one impression stayed with him forcefully: "*you only* on board of that ship was the originator . . . *your mind alone* seemed interested in it with any seriousness of purpose, even after its first suggestion by you."

In sum, Morse denied that he was indebted to Jackson in any way—"for any single hint of any kind whatever which I have used in my invention." He did however owe to Jackson some of his thinking about telegraphs, how much is uncertain. Jackson was one of the few Americans acquainted with current European research in electricity and magnetism, of which Morse knew nothing. Jackson's assertion that he made rough drawings of electrical apparatus for Morse is substantiated by Morse's sketches of an electromagnet, an electrical generator, and similar devices in the *Sully* sketchbook. Such unacknowledged influence may explain another suspicious matter. As noted earlier, Jackson's name appears in the heading of Morse's first circular letter, asking fellow passengers to confirm that he had thought up an electric telegraph in 1832, years before the outburst of comparable European inventions. Jackson later contended, correctly it seems, that Morse never sent him the circular, as if aware that his reply would be damaging.

On the other hand, whatever Morse may have learned from Jackson, the design of the cumbrous but effective port-rule and register was his own, evolved over five years. And the co-creator of "Morse's Patent Metallic Double-Headed OCEAN-DRINKER and DELUGE-SPOUTER VALVE Pump-Boxes" was not exactly a stranger to technology. Some of the bitterness between the two men arose from their shared conception of the Lone Inventor, creating *ex nihilo* from his lofty imagination, an ideal in Morse's case reinforced by his imperious conception of The Painter, independent of all ties to patrons. This dubious notion—to look ahead—would bedevil Morse the rest of his life, burdening him with neverending disputes that many times multiplied the entire days he must have spent trying to refute Jackson. And the brilliant Jackson's account of what he told Morse would become ever more suspect as his craving for celebrity led him to appropriate other inventions and discoveries.

If nothing else, Morse's set-to with Jackson was instructive. "The condition of an inventor," he had found out, "is, indeed, not enviable." To protect his rights and the further development of his work, he applied in October 1837 to the Commissioner of Patents in Washington, Henry L. Ellsworth, a friend and Yale classmate. He said he wished to have a caveat. This document granted statutory protection to an inventor's claim of priority, even before his work was matured enough to be patented. If the inventor did not file a patent within a year, he forfeited the protection. Morse's application described in detail what was now his invention-in-progress—port-rule, register, numbered dictionary, the elements of "a new method of transmitting and recording intelligence by means of Electro-magnetism."

The application and Morse's $20 fee secured him a caveat for the improbable-looking composing stick and canvas stretcher he chose to call the "*American Electro Magnetic Telegraph.*"

Engrossed now in his invention, Morse set out to substantially improve the apparatus and demonstrate it to the public. He sought the advice of a scientific colleague at New York University, Professor Leonard D. Gale, author of *Elements of Chemistry* (1835). Morse's device worked perfectly, Gale found, but through a wire circuit of only forty feet. For the telegraph to become practicable, the distance obviously had to be greatly extended.

Gale knew how to do that. He saw that Morse's telegraph used a one-cup galvanic battery—that is, a pair of zinc and copper plates immersed in a cup of acid. Such a battery generated low voltage, incapable of producing a current over a long distance, which demanded a battery of many cups. Gale had one, a so-called intensity battery of forty cups that he substituted for Morse's single cup. Gale also saw that Morse had wound the electromagnet loosely, with a few turns of wire. Gale had read a scientific paper published in 1831 by Professor Joseph

Henry of Princeton, the pre-eminent American physicist, describing how the power of an electromagnet could be greatly increased by winding it tightly in hundreds of turns of wire. No physicist himself, Morse expressed "great surprise" at the idea, Gale said. But on Gale's advice he rewound the magnet, girdling it a hundred times or more.

With the powerful new battery and magnet, Morse soon had his telegraph operating not through 40 feet but through 200 and shortly after through 1000. On September 2, 1837, he gave his first public exhibition of the apparatus, at New York University. He set up a circuit of 1700 feet, one-third of a mile. The wire stretched many times back and forth across a long room that served as Gale's lecture hall and housed the University's mineralogy collection. The spectators included a Fellow of the Royal Society, Charles Daubeny, Professor of Chemistry at Oxford. Morse reported the success of his presentation in the *Journal of Commerce,* remarking that it showed the practicability of his telegraph, and its superior simplicity "over any of those proposed by the Professors in Europe."

Increasingly confident and ambitious, Morse wrote three weeks later to the Secretary of the Treasury, Levi Woodbury. At the direction of Congress, Woodbury had issued a government request for information and advice about the possibility of erecting a telegraph in the United States—that is, a network of semaphore towers such as existed in France. Morse's response to Woodbury reconceived the whole project. Optical telegraphs, he said, were inaccurate, slow, and useless at night or in fog. Instead, he had invented a new mode of telegraphic communication that was precise, nearly instantaneous, and operable day or night in any kind of weather.

Morse described in detail his port-rule–register-dictionary. But he emphasized that the interest of Congress in a nationwide telegraph system inspired him to now think beyond it. He suggested that miles of wire might be interred in iron tubes or strung above ground on stout spars, thirty feet high, fifteen to the mile. He told Woodbury that he was now experimenting with very long distances, along with Professor Gale, "a gentleman of great science, and to whose assistance . . . I am greatly indebted." He promised to send their results to the Secretary, and demonstrate his invention in Washington before the new year. If the government wished to use it he was ready to make any sacrifice of time and energy to help create a national system, "which may justly be called the American telegraph."

Morse's unusual response impressed Woodbury. The Secretary submitted to Congress seventeen of the replies he received. All but one, he explained, concerned semaphores, the single, striking novelty being Morse's. Woodbury soon passed along to the House the progress reports Morse had promised. By late November they contained news that Morse and Gale had transmitted a message through a circuit of ten miles—"and we have now no doubt of . . . effecting a *similar result* at *any distance*." At this point Morse told Woodbury that he wished to delay his appearance in Washington in order to refine his crude hardware and present for the government's evaluation "as perfect an instrument as possible."

Morse knew no more of toolmaking, however, than of electrical science. Having turned to Gale for help with the batteries and magnet, he now enlisted an experienced machinist—one of his former pupils at the University, a recent graduate named Alfred Vail (1807–1859). Thirty years old, considerably older than most of the other students, Vail had previously studied at a seminary. Morse knew him fairly well. They had lived for a while in the same boarding house, and they attended the same Presbyterian church, on Mercer Street. More important, Vail's family owned a foundry and machine shop, the Speedwell Iron Works. Vail had worked there, cutting screws and handling a drill press.

Vail had been present on September 2 for the public debut of Morse's telegraph at the University. By one account he was greatly impressed, and then and there offered Morse his assistance. By another, he returned a few days later to discuss the invention, skeptical that it could work over long-enough distances to be commercially useful. Morse was aware of the problem, and had already talked it over with Gale, who believed that a current could not be produced strong enough to mark characters on paper at a hundred miles. The problem did not affect Morse's upcoming demonstration before Congress. But against the distant prospect of developing a system that might have to reach hundreds and thousands of miles, he had invented a new device. "*It matters not how delicate the movement may be*," his thinking went, "*if I can obtain it at all, it is all I want*." However weakened at, say, twenty miles, the current might at least be strong enough to close and open another circuit, sending the signal on with a fresh impulse for another twenty miles. The signal could be repeated from one twenty-mile circuit to another for the required distance—even around the globe.

Alfred Vail
(New York University Archives)

This so-called relay was an elegantly simple device that used an electromagnet to close and open an independent circuit having its own battery. It marked a huge, essential advance in the utility of Morse's telegraph, and had many other possible applications. Given his little knowledge of mechanics and electrical science, the relay seems miraculously ingenious. One historian of technology has called it "a creative engineering achievement of the first order."

Morse's description of his relay convinced Vail. He agreed to take on the job of refining Morse's machinery, in exchange for a share of

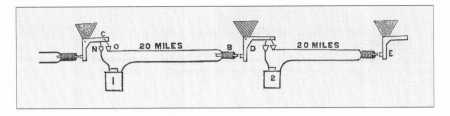

Morse's 1837 relay plan
(Samuel I. Prime, *The Life of Samuel F. B. Morse, LL.D.* [1875])

the profits. The partnership had other mutual benefits. Seeking his place in the world, Vail had thought of entering the Episcopal ministry or opening a religious bookstore—or working at the Philadelphia mint. In the telegraph he believed he had found his future. "I disided [*sic*] in my own mind," he said, "*to sink or swim with it.*" On his side, Morse valued not only Vail's mechanical skill but also his financial assistance, for Vail offered to ask his father and brother to pay for building the apparatus to be shown to Congress. The offer came as a deliverance. A hike in rent at the University had forced Morse to give up four rooms that he rented to his pupils. Even more than usually strapped for funds, he accepted money from Sidney and Richard to support his work on the telegraph. And the year, 1837, had brought one of the worst economic depressions of the nineteenth century, bankrupting hundreds of businesses and throwing thousands of people out of work.

Morse and Vail signed formal articles of agreement. By its terms, Vail would construct a perfected telegraph for exhibition before Congress "*at his own proper costs and expense*"—the money coming, in reality, from his family. He/they would also defray all incidental expenses, including the costs of obtaining a patent. In exchange, Morse granted Vail a one-fourth financial interest in the apparatus in the United States, and one-half interest in the foreign rights—provided Vail also paid the costs of taking out patents abroad.

Beyond his know-how and family resources, Vail was a young man to Morse's taste—artistic, literary, and pious. He played the violin and had led the school's literary society, the Eucleian. He was preoccupied with Sabbath-keeping, self-examination, and other means of becoming a "perfect Christian." As was true for Morse also, his religious, aesthetic, and political views flowed together. In his commencement oration he depicted God as the origin of beauty in the universe and of the human impulse to improve nature—of both the fine and the useful arts. Nor could Morse have disapproved Vail's statement, in an undergraduate essay, "If America is free, she must obey the laws of God."

With the agreement signed, and the Vail family sending checks, Morse and his team got to work in earnest overhauling the telegraph for demonstration in Washington. He and Gale stayed at the University, Vail returned to the Speedwell Iron Works, in Morristown, New Jersey. The surviving documents provide only sketchy information about the time and exact nature of their various improvements. But now and over the following months Vail streamlined the register. He got rid of the canvas stretcher and pendulum, and reinstalled the recording apparatus on and within a flat box. The register became a horizontal, not a vertical, device, no longer standing up but lying down. At the same time he simplified the operation of the electromagnet and of the clockwork that moved the paper.

Meanwhile Morse and Gale prepared the conducting wire, no easy task. Plans called for showing Congress an instrument that could operate over ten miles—commonly the distance between the stations of optical telegraphs. Frustratingly, the wire arrived slowly in batches from its Connecticut manufacturer and proved to be made of inferior copper. The brittleness made it difficult for Morse and Gale to solder the segments together. Their efforts were further delayed in awaiting the arrival of heavy storage reels from Speedwell. And the entire ten miles of wire had to be wound in cotton for insulation. By November, Gale had a strong current working through the whole length—a triumph—but the current burned the mercury in the small cups. A so-called Cruikshank's battery had to be built to overcome the problem: a tar-coated mahogany trough filled with acid, holding sixty pairs of large zinc-copper plates.

At the same time, Morse labored over the giant dictionary, "a most tedious, never ending work," he said. "I am up early & late, yet its progress is slow." He had in mind a compendium of 30,000 handwritten words, but whether he achieved this length is uncertain. He completed two copies late in October, on oversize pages about two feet square. To judge from his later dictionaries, he divided each page into five columns, fifty words per column, in alphabetical order and several grammatical forms. The number 36, for example, meant "abash," 37 "abashed," 38 "abashing," 39 "abate," and so on. However grueling the effort, Morse glowed over the result. Operators could now transmit, by numbers alone, "*any intelligence whatever* in the *fullest manner.*"

Over the first three months of the new year, Morse unveiled his refurbished telegraph in a series of public exhibitions, climaxed by his presentation to Congress. Vail or someone in his family suggested that he first try out the apparatus at Speedwell, about thirty-five miles from New York City. Morse and Gale stripped from one of the reels, and sent on to New Jersey, two miles of wire—a length sufficient to prove the efficiency of the remodeled telegraph over substantial distances.

Set in rolling hills along the Whippany River, the Vails' foundry and machine shop converted iron bars into screws for ships and crankshafts for railroad cars, its clanging forge room a world of burning cedar and white-hot fagots. In addition to Vail and his brother George, the place was worked by several slaves and indentured servants, sometimes personally whipped by a stout old gentleman in Quaker garb—Alfred's father, Stephen Vail, a skilled mechanic who was also a lay judge of the Court of Common Pleas.

Morse had visited the ironworks once before to test an earlier model. But he fell ill and became bedridden for ten days, with "one of my bilious attacks." A young assistant at the place later recalled that he seemed glum over his painting career, and had a "facility of becoming 'ill' " when problems arose: "if we were meeting with difficulties, he succumbed to the blues and left us to work our way out as best we might." Ill or not, Morse managed during the trip to paint portraits of Vail's parents, for a fee.

Returned to Speedwell, Morse conducted a private trial on January 6, using the vacant second floor of a barnlike factory building. Through the two miles of wire coiled around the room he sent a message suggested by Judge Vail: "A patient waiter is no loser." Morse repeated the demonstration four days later, this time for hundreds of local people and some who had come from Newark for the event. He transmitted a quite full letter, which was deciphered with but a single minor error. "The success is complete," he cheered, "the talk of all the people round."

Two weeks later, accompanied by Vail, Morse tried some further experiments at New York University. For each performance he sent

Speedwell factory building
(Smithsonian Institution)

out engraved invitations requesting the presence of a select audience "*to witness the operation of his* ELECTRO MAGNETIC TELEGRAPH . . . *previous to its leaving the City for Washington.*" For the first time in public he attempted a transmission through the entire ten miles of wire. Disastrously, in three days of public tryouts the system repeatedly failed. As reportedly had happened at Speedwell when he faced difficulty, Morse fell ill (or "ill"). He recovered when still another attempted transmission worked. Better than that, he succeeded in the related test of using his markings to represent not numbers but letters. Surviving accounts do not make clear his means of doing so, beyond mentioning that he cast some sort of new type for the port-rule. But he learned that in this way he could transmit ten words per minute, twice as many as before. Among the messages he sent, one began, appropriately: "ATTENTION, THE UNIVERSE!"

Morse and Vail went on to Philadelphia, where Morse exhibited his ten-mile circuit before the Franklin Institute. Founded a decade earlier as the nation's first organization "for the promotion of the mechanic arts," the Institute sponsored lectures, published a distinguished journal, and looked into new inventions.

Morse demonstrated both his numerical method of marking, and his just-introduced method of marking letters that came to be known as Morse code. What seems to be the first mention in print of this famous dotdash alphabet appears in the Institute's lengthy report on the demonstration:

> Two systems of signals were exhibited, one representing *numbers,* the other *letters.* The numbers consist of nothing more than dots made on the paper with suitable spaces intervening. Thus ··· ·· ····· would represent 325, and may either indicate this number itself, or a word in a dictionary prepared for the purpose to which this number is attached. The alphabetical signals are made up of combinations of dots and of lines of different lengths.

The still-controversial code has sometimes been attributed to Alfred Vail. On the contrary, Vail at this time told his father, significantly: "Professor Morse has invented a new plan of an alphabet, and has thrown aside the Dictionaries." He also had reservations about Morse's "new plan." When improved it would outperform the numerical dictionary method, he thought. But the alphabetical signals required that the port-rule be cranked by machine, Morse's hand being too unsteady. And Morse's freshly cast type seemed to him imperfect. Even Vail's criticisms, it deserves emphasis, indicate that the contriver of Morse code was Morse.

Following the Philadelphia exhibition, Vail boxed up the telegraph and forwarded it to Washington by railroad—a technology less than a decade old in the United States, and just beginning to flourish. Meanwhile the Franklin Institute sent a copy of its report to the Secretary of the Treasury. The report warmly endorsed Morse's apparatus, calling it practicable, pointing out its superiority to European semaphoric and electromagnetic systems, and declaring it "worthy of the patronage of the Government."

Arriving at the capital early in February, Morse and Vail put up at Gadsby's Hotel for $17.50 a week. Vail had grown used to shelling out family money for Morse's expenses—$35 to $75 here and there—but the steep rate dictated a move to some less expensive boarding house. Vail found such lodging for $10 a week, but Morse decided to stay at

Gadbsy's—for the sake of having servants to cater to him, Vail believed. He did not mind the separation, for he had become miffed at Morse. Morse had printed up invitations to the Philadelphia performance—without asking the Vails, but at their expense, and in his own name. And now in Washington, Vail discovered, when invited to meet with President Van Buren or other distinguished people, Morse was inclined to go alone, "unwilling that I should accompany him to see any of the Great Folks."

A week at Gadsby's taught Morse that despite its enormous prices the hotel offered poor service. But his move to Fuller's, a $9-a-week boarding house, made Vail no less disgruntled. It galled him that, although they had signed articles of agreement, Morse called him an "Assistant." When he protested the title Morse apologized and explained, not convincingly, that he "supposed it synonymous with Partner, Colleague." Many inventors of the period, imbued with the ideal of the Creative Genius, failed to credit the mere craftsmen and mechanics who were essential to their work. Vail nevertheless felt used, resentful at being handed such menial chores as packing and shipping: "Professor Morse is indisposed when there is anything to do." And his brother George griped that Morse failed to keep the family posted and granted them no recognition. Vail did not turn away, certain that he had embarked on a great and noble adventure. But he was beginning to see his former teacher as imperious, exploitative, and vain, a hierarch who gave him the dirty work, let his family pay the bills, and took the glory for himself.

Morse's Washington demonstrations apparently began around February 15 and lasted several days. He used the numerical code rather than trust his alphabetic method. The city was cold, the ground covered with a half inch of ice, boys and men skating over the streets. Morse and Vail performed in the carpeted room of the Committee on Commerce, warmed by a hickory wood fire, the wire circuit spooled on two five-mile reels. Despite the stormy weather, members of Congress crowded into the room, some bringing back other witnesses, who came again and again. John C. Calhoun alone sent down a dozen other senators. Morse gave a special showing, upon request, for President Van Buren and members of his cabinet, including the Secretaries of State, Treasury, War, and the Navy. He had the President convey a message to him silently, which he then set up on the port-rule, in numbers, for Vail to decipher. Van Buren sent "The enemy near."

But to Morse's delight, there were no enemies, only dumbstruck admirers of his telegraph. "Members of Congress who, when told of its operation, scouted it as impossible and visionary, come and are for a while mute and then go away with exclamations of wonder." To Vail the events seemed unreal, "as though some strange thing had happened." He recorded some of the amazed comments he heard: "what would Jefferson think, could he arise up . . . where will improvements and discoveries stop . . . it is the most wonderful discovery ever made . . . it must belong to the government." Patent Commissioner Henry Ellsworth, from whom Morse had obtained a caveat, reportedly said that "nothing has ever been in Washington that has produced such a noise."

The Committee on Commerce asked Morse to draw up a full report on his invention. They planned to recommend that Congress appropriate funds to test the device over a much longer distance. Morse believed that if the experiment succeeded, the government would buy his telegraph and amply reward him. He submitted two reports, a week apart. Trying the telegraph over fifty miles, he said, would show whether it could operate over a thousand or ten thousand. He estimated that the circuit and instruments could be built in three months, at a cost of $26,000.

Looking further ahead, Morse addressed the sensitive question of ownership. Given its immense power, the telegraph would become a tool for good or for evil, as properly or improperly used. If some speculators monopolized it, for instance, the device might enrich them but bankrupt thousands. He therefore suggested that the government retain sole right to use of the telegraph, granting individuals or companies the right to build lines between two points. By making the telegraph a joint public-private venture the government could both reap a vast revenue for itself and nourish the "enterprising character of our countrymen."

The Committee on Commerce gave Morse more than he asked. They recommended that Congress appropriate $30,000 for a fifty-mile test—the extra $4000 to be used for meeting unforeseen expenses. The committee chairman, Francis O. J. Smith, submitted an ecstatically zealous report to the House. Morse's telegraph, it said, could transform the nation's commercial, political, and social condition, bringing about "a revolution unsurpassed in moral grandeur by any discovery that has been made in the arts and sciences." Among its other benefits, the tele-

graph could enable people all over the widely extended country to communicate with each other instantaneously. In a manner that inspired
religious reverence it could endow the American citizen with a power
approaching the "HIGH ATTRIBUTE OF UBIQUITY."

F. O. J. Smith (1806–1876) was himself so keen on the telegraph's
possibilities that he asked Morse to take him in as a partner. He suggested that they go to Europe together and apply for foreign patents
while waiting for the appropriation bill to pass Congress. Morse hesi-
tated: such an alliance with a public official might be misunderstood,
giving rise to charges of improper influence. At the same time he recognized how valuable Smith could be to the suddenly flowering enter-

Francis O. J. Smith
(Maine Historical Society)

prise, not only by his connections in Washington but also as a lawyer. He explained his misgivings to Smith, who replied that, as the session of Congress was ending, he would take a leave of absence. A thrice-elected congressman from Maine, he would also send a letter to his constituents declining to stand for reelection. On these terms Morse agreed to a partnership.

Commissioner Ellsworth reportedly discouraged Morse from making the trip abroad. The time had passed for obtaining foreign patents, he said; telegraphs were already well known in Europe. He had reason to think so, for stories about European devices continued to appear in the American press. But by now Morse dismissed them as kowtowing, signs of "a slavish dependence on *foreign opinion,* not yet eradicated from American hearts, the old colonial feeling of inferiority." Ellsworth advised him instead, while in Washington, to approach the foreign ministers of various countries and try to interest their governments in purchasing his device. Morse did speak with the minister of Turkey, and with Gail Hunt of the then-independent Republic of Texas. But he decided to head for Europe anyway, together with Smith.

In March, Morse drew up new articles of agreement embracing himself, Smith, Alfred Vail, and Leonard Gale. Smith would seek patents for the telegraph in Great Britain, France, and other countries; negotiate with foreign governments and private persons the right to use the invention, and act as legal counselor and attorney for the other partners. Morse agreed to accompany him abroad for three months, to aid in demonstrating the telegraph, his expenses to be paid by Smith and refunded from the proceeds of sales. Smith would acquire a one-quarter interest in the American patent and a five-sixteenth interest in any foreign patent. Vail agreed to a two-sixteenth interest in both patents, Gale to a one-sixteenth. Morse retained the major stake, but not by much: a nine-sixteenth interest in America and half interest abroad. All the parties bound themselves to another, essential principle: no partner could sell rights to the invention without consulting the others and having their consent.

Before leaving for Europe in mid-May, Morse got ready several complete telegraphs to take along—transmitters, receivers, dictionaries, batteries. Given the difficulty of moving it all aboard ship and between countries, he decided to take a setup capable of working through only two miles. The apparatus included a once-again-improved port-rule and register, created by Vail after much thoughtful experiment.

Morse also gathered up letters of introduction and recommendation from well-placed politicians and other notables to their counterparts in Europe, including Russia. He impressed on them that in going abroad he hoped not only to profit from his telegraph, but also "to claim for my country the honor of the Invention." At the same time he prepared a U.S. patent application, working together with F. O. J. Smith but making the elaborate drawings himself, a "most arduous and tedious process." Foreign governments would not patent his telegraph if he had already patented it in America. So he asked the Patent Office to delay issuing the document until he returned from abroad—a request that would bring him grief.

While developing his telegraph, Morse had stayed in touch with his artist friends and painting pupils. As President of the National Academy of Design, too, he had continued to deliver the annual address and look after the awarding of premiums. On the eve of his departure the members once again elected him president, commissioning him to make purchases for the Academy while abroad. Before setting off he also attended to *The Gem of the Republic,* his giant history painting of the signing of the Mayflower Compact. After his wounding elimination from the Capitol rotunda project, a group of artists had raised subscriptions to commission the work, hoping to rally him. Getting started, he had visited Boston and Plymouth to search for remains of the *Mayflower* and of the furniture of the Pilgrims.

Morse sent the subscribers a printed letter, admitting that he was in a "state of suspense." He hoped while in Europe to pursue "some studies connected with the Picture," he said. But his commitment to the telegraph might make it a duty, "to myself and to my country," to put off the painting for a while, perhaps eventually to give it up. For the moment he asked his sponsors to collect no more money until he returned, when he would more certainly know what to do. What he *wanted* to do was clear, he concluded: "If possible I wish as soon as practicable to relieve myself of the cares of the Telegraph, that I may have my time to devote more strenuously than ever to the execution of my picture." In fact, however, his lifelong and once-consuming ambition to paint was dying.

Morse's brother Richard decided to accompany him and Smith,

not to transact business, but for the healthful effects of an overseas voyage. Sometimes vomiting after meals, he had been experiencing again the emotional pain that had darkened his adolescence and young manhood, what he described as "depression of mind, irritability of nerves & irresoluteness."

As he embarked for Liverpool, Morse himself felt anxious. "I am risking all my professional business by this act," he told Vail, "and if it should turn out nothing, I shall be in a bad situation." His artistic career had taught him much about hopes that turned out nothing, or worse. Although pleased by the rousing and unanimous approval of his telegraph in Washington, he recalled his last stay in the city thirteen years before: while painting Lafayette he had received the news of Lucrece's death. He must stay guarded, he thought, even though the prospect before him now was of fame and wealth, "the tide of prosperity at its full flow." Human affairs were inconstant, and just ahead on such tides often lay defeat: "in this world a continued course of prosperity is not a rational expectation."

EIGHT

Traveling on a Snail's Back

(1838–1839)

SEEKING A BRITISH patent first, Morse settled with Richard and F. O. J. Smith in Bloomsbury. London seemed jammed with people of every rank, pickpockets to princes, wholly given over to the upcoming coronation of the new English monarch, Queen Victoria. Soon after arriving Morse witnessed the public ceremonies, from seats temporarily set up near Westminster Abbey. The bell ringing and twenty-one-gun salutes, the shouts and hand clapping, the gold-laced silver-buttoned coachmen, struck him as brilliant, "the most gorgeous pageant that our times have witnessed." But in London as before in Rome, Morse the republican came back at Morse the artist, tempering aesthetic pleasure with scorn: "Is it possible, I thought, that the English are children, to be duped by these gew-gaws?" He kept his hat off during the proceedings—not out of respect, but so that people behind him could see.

Morse experienced many more emotional swings in trying to get foreign patents. In England the process was expensive and complicated, normally taking six to eight weeks and an outlay of a few hundred pounds. Over four days in June, Morse went about to the offices of a half-dozen or more clerks, paying the required fees. Smith drafted a petition to the Crown describing Morse's invention, and Morse's intent to obtain patents in Scotland and Ireland as well. A hearing was set before the Attorney General, Sir John Campbell, at which the petition would be compared with the descriptions in any previously filed caveats.

Morse took his apparatus to the hearing in order to explain to the

Attorney General the difference between his system and those of his competitors. But Campbell refused to even consider granting a patent. Instead, he confronted Morse with the February issue of the London *Mechanic's Magazine,* where Morse's method, he declared, had already been published. Because of the prior publication he told Morse he could not proceed.

Having expected his application to be approved, Morse was "certainly surprised." To his knowledge nothing of his invention had appeared in print beyond the results—accounts of what his telegraph did, but with no description of its operation that would enable a mechanic to reproduce the apparatus. Returned to his lodgings he drew up an essay-length letter to Campbell, probably with Smith's advice and help, defending his right to a British patent. He trod daintily, suggesting that some key points in his case had perhaps been misapprehended by the Attorney General because of "the imperfect manner in which I presented them." He exhaustively described what he considered the unique, and still unpatented, features of his telegraph, and submitted drawings of them.

On the basis of his patiently detailed letter, Morse was granted a second hearing before Campbell, which he attended with Smith. He discovered, however, that the Attorney General had not read the letter. Carelessly turning over its pages, Campbell asked whether he had not applied for a patent in the United States. Morse said he had. As he recalled the exchange, Campbell snapped at him: "America was a large country and I ought to be satisfied with a patent there." He protested that the point at issue was whether legal obstacles existed to granting him letters patent in England. Campbell shrugged him off. "He observed that *he considered my invention as having been published* and that he must *therefore* forbid me to proceed." The Attorney General's "most gross injustice," Morse believed, had nothing to do with the merits of his case, but sprang from "*national or other motives.*" Either way, it killed any hope of profiting from his telegraph in Great Britain.

During his first interview with the Attorney General, Morse came face-to-face with one of his foreign competitors. In Campbell's anteroom he encountered Charles Wheatstone (1802–1875), whose telegraph had been written up in the *Journal* of the Franklin Institute in May 1837. At the time, Morse was laboring to send messages through a circuit of 1700 feet; Wheatstone was transmitting across nineteen

Sir Charles Wheatstone
(The Science Museum, London)

miles. Now in his mid-thirties, Wheatstone looked "quite young,"
Morse thought, an impression that Wheatstone's small features and
painful shyness also left on others. Shortsighted and fast-talking, too,
he had been born into a family of musical-instrument makers. He himself later invented the concertina—as well as a solar clock for arctic
expeditions, an effective typewriter, and the rheostat. Interested also
in pure scientific research, he worked with Michael Faraday on ther-
moelectricity and was elected to the Royal Society. Currently he taught
at King's College, London, as Professor of Experimental Philosophy.

    Wheatstone invited Morse to visit him at the College and inspect
his telegraph. Together with William Fothergill Cooke (1806–1879),

a maker of anatomical wax models, he had developed a receiving apparatus that indicated letters by deflecting five needles in various ways on a diamond-shaped plate. For example, two counterclockwise deflections stood for A, one counterclockwise and three clockwise deflections stood for T. Wheatstone and Cooke had been granted a patent a year before—the first English patent for an electrical telegraph.

Morse found Wheatstone likable and intelligent, "a most liberal generous hearted man. . . . decidedly a man of uncommon genius." He admired the clever and handsomely built telegraph, too, but thought it overly complex. It required five wire conductors between transmitter and receiver, and the signals were evanescent: the position of the needles on the dial had to be observed on the instant or be lost for ever. By comparison, his own telegraph used only one wire and imprinted its messages permanently. Except that both devices sent an electrical current over a circuit, Morse saw, the two systems had nothing in common. And a signaling telegraph such as Cooke-Wheatstone's was intrinsically slower and less accurate than his recording telegraph.

During his seven weeks in London, Morse also learned something about two other rivals—the London surgeon Edward Davy and, especially, Karl Steinheil, a professor of mathematics and physics in Munich. He saw Davy's six-wire telegraph in operation, and heard that the surgeon was attempting to add a recording device. It would produce a "bungling imitation" of his original zigzagging Vs, he thought, illustrations of which Davy must have seen in some newspaper. Steinheil's telegraph represented a greater challenge. Morse did not see the instrument, but it was described to him as actuating two needles, which carried small reservoirs of ink and could mark a paper with lines resembling the dotdash code. It used a single circuit, like his own telegraph. Indeed he was told that Steinheil had copied this improvement from him. Later he learned that in reality Steinheil used two circuits.

Before coming to London, Morse had known about European telegraphs only through accounts in the press. His personal investigation of them enabled him for the first time to define the uniqueness of his own system, the ground on which his claim of originality could solidly stand. "My time has not been lost," he wrote, "for I have ascertained with certainty that the *Telegraph of a single circuit* and a *recording apparatus,* is mine."

Denied a British patent, Morse left for France, "not sanguine," he said, "as to any favorable pecuniary result." He took rooms on the rue de Rivoli, pleasantly overlooking the Tuileries gardens. The city had been turbulent during his visit six years before, following the July revolution. In the meantime his esteemed friend Lafayette had died, and with growing prosperity, new roads, the opening of the Arc de Triomphe, and at least a facade of parliamentary government, organized resistance and street rioting seemed things of the past.

Morse quickly obtained the French equivalent of a patent, a *brevet d'invention.* Since the semaphoric French system was state-controlled, however, the *brevet* meant nothing unless he sold his invention directly to the government. "The Telegraph is a government monopoly, and therefore I am dependent wholly on them." He counted on being allowed to demonstrate his apparatus to Louis-Philippe—even though, five years earlier, he had accused him of conspiring with the despots of Austria and Russia to push France into war with the United States. "I am hourly in expectation of a message from the King to show the Telegraph before him," he said.

It turned out to be a long hour. As the hoped-for invitation failed to arrive, Morse attributed it to the royal family's preoccupation with the recent birth of the young prince, whom he saw ("he looked very much like any other baby"). But Louis-Philippe's prestige and popularity had fallen, and he had been the target of several assassination attempts—one using a machine constructed of two dozen rifles that left fourteen people dead.

Morse's prospects brightened when he was introduced to the celebrated astronomer-physicist Dominique François Jean Arago (1786–1853). Catalonian by birth, with dark curly hair and bushy sideburns, Arago was director of the Paris Observatory and permanent secretary of France's elite national scientific society, the Académie des Sciences. Keenly interested in electromagnetic phenomena, he had been awarded the Royal Society's Copley Medal for his discovery that nonferrous metals could display magnetic properties. He invited Morse to exhibit his telegraph at the observatory and, impressed by what he saw, asked him to exhibit it again before the *savans* of the *Académie.*

The Academy met at the Institut de France, on the Left Bank of the Seine. Seven years before Morse had spent his time just across the river—at the Louvre, perched on a high stand to paint his *Grand Gallery.* For the telegraph demonstration, on September 10, he sent messages some four hundred feet in the alphabetic code of dots and lines. He used a battery recently invented by the British chemist John Daniell, capable of delivering a constant and powerful current—a major, permanent improvement to his system.

Morse wrote out some notes for Arago to use in serving as his spokesman and translator. Arago would explain to the academicians that the exhibition instrument was imperfect, deliberately made about as large as a little desk (*"petit bureau"*) to endure the knockabout of travel, although the actual instrument could be made only one-third the size. Morse's notes included a short version of The *Sully* Story and points for Arago to stress in explaining the uniqueness of the system: it requires only one circuit, uses no magnetic needles, writes in permanent characters, needs no attendance at the place of delivery, and is relatively inexpensive. He also had Arago mention his yet unused receiving magnet, by which intelligence could be "written at any number of intermediate places between any two distant points, and simultaneously with its reception at the most distant points."

Morse felt that his demonstration went off no less effectively before the French Académie than it had before the American Congress. And Arago's verbal presentation of it was lucid and convincing, as Morse judged from the Academicians' faces and surprised cries. "A buzz of admiration and approbation filled the whole hall," he wrote later, "and the exclamations, '*Extraordinaire!*' '*Très bien!*' '*Très admirable!*' I heard on all sides." These were no ordinary mortals, of course, but "the most celebrated scientific men of the world." The spectators included Gay-Lussac, famous for his work on the volume of gases, and the brilliant Baron Humboldt, who arose after the demonstration, Morse said, and taking his hand congratulated him before the entire Academy.

Full accounts of the event appeared in the *Courier Français,* the *Moniteur,* and other Paris newspapers, as well as the *Annales de Chimie et de Physique* and the Academy's weekly bulletin, the *Comptes Rendus,* which went out not only to members but also to foreign scientific societies and libraries. Several papers regretted that Morse's ignorance of French made it impossible to interview him; a few misidentified him—as a Philadelphian, or as "Un savant étranger, M. Moss." Nevertheless, they reported that even the most incredulous spectators became convinced that a dispatch could be sent over France end-to-end in half an hour. They envisioned Morse's lines replacing the older semaphores, and within fifty years crisscrossing all of Europe.

Some of the journalists observed that questions of priority, Europe vs. America, were at the moment being debated fiercely ("*avec acharnement*"). They drew up genealogies of the telegraph, charting a history of active European experiment and invention over the last thirty years. The names and events were becoming familiar to Morse, although he had known nothing of them when he began. They included Samuel T. Sömmering, president of the Bavarian Academy of Sciences, who in 1809 demonstrated a thirty-five-wire telegraph driven by the electrolytic decomposition of water; the Danish scientist Hans Christian Oersted, who initiated the study of electromagnetism by discovering, in 1819, that a wire carrying a current deflects a compass needle; André Marie Ampère, a French physicist who saw the possibility of using Oersted's deflected needles to transmit alphabetic signals (an idea he published but did not pursue); Baron Pavel L. Schilling, one of Sömmering's assistants, a Russian who developed a prototype of the needle telegraph, perhaps as early as 1825; and the Germans Carl Friedrich Gauss and Wilhelm Eduard Weber, who in 1833 built the first telegraph to come into practical use, an electromagnetic needle device with a two-wire circuit. The *Courier Français* commented that "in reality there does not yet exist an inventor of the telegraph. The Inventor will be the first *constructor* who shall make it operate upon a very extended line."

Morse enjoyed the publicity and enthusiasm. He noted that the Théâtre des Variétés was presenting a skit in which the characters conversed by telegraph over hundreds of miles. The Paris town talk not only established his name in France, but also put him ahead of his British and German rivals. Cooke and Wheatstone had obtained a French *brevet*, but Morse learned that his own telegraph was preferred, "pronounced far superior in simplicity and practicability." Steinheil's two-needle telegraph was shown in Paris, and Morse was also pleased to note that because of its complexity "mine is considered . . . having a decided advantage." The news got back to America, where the Washington *National Intelligencer,* for one, reported that their countryman had the Englishmen and German beat: "It is said . . . to be very manifest that our Yankee Professor is ahead of them all in the essential requisites of such an invention."

The acclaim brought Morse a new chance to realize his ultimate hope of demonstrating his telegraph to the King. Following the Academy exhibition, he was visited by Alphonse Foy, administrator of the current network of semaphores. Foy told him that the government now meant to test the practicability of a nationwide electric telegraph. He said he would recommend Morse's apparatus: "*I have examined carefully the system of Steinheil, of Wheatstone, and many others, French and German, and . . . yours is the best.*"

Foy's endorsement would go to the influential Minister of the Interior, Count Marthe de Montalivet, who was personally close to Louis-Philippe. Hoping to reinforce his case, Morse got a letter of introduction to Montalivet from General Lewis Cass, the American minister to France. Drafted by F. O. J. Smith, it explained that Morse wished to bring before the government a method of telegraphy that was simple, cheap, fast, and accurate, capable of being extended to every point in the country. If the government preferred, he could begin by building an experimental line connecting the royal palaces alone.

Having gained influential support, Morse awaited an interview with Count Montalivet, leading to a presentation before Louis-Philippe. But Montalivet's secretary put him off from day to day by one excuse after another: Foy had not yet submitted his recommendation to the minister; the recommendation had been received but a synopsis had to be written; the synopsis had been written but Montalivet had not yet seen it. During one particularly aggravating period Morse called eight or ten times at the bureau and was unable to see even the secretary. At times he doubted that Louis-Philippe would ever get to see his telegraph: "some of the most essential improvements have lain for years in the portfolios of the Ministers." But he kept hoping for a summons from the Palais-Royal, which would be decisive: "If I could but once get them to look at it, I should be sure of them, for I have never shown it to anyone who did not seem in raptures."

The problem, Morse believed, was not one person or another but the French mentality. "I find delay in all things, at least, so it appears to me, who have too strong a development of the American organ of 'go-ahead-ativeness' to feel easy under its tantalizing effects." The shipment from London of some new clockwork for his telegraph took more than two weeks, going through a dozen customs officers, commissionaires, and administrators demanding papers, receipts, drawings, sureties. The ponderous bureaucracy was only a sign of the larger, moral problem: "there is no such thing here as *conscience.*" Knowing themselves to be untrustworthy, the French had no confidence in others. They did not delegate authority to subagents, certain that it would be abused—"consequently the regular military muster-roll mode must supply the place of conscience, and all its circumlocutory, cumbrous powers. . . . Happy, thrice happy America!"

There were other frustrations as well. While waiting to hear from Montalivet, Morse also awaited word from home that Congress had passed the $30,000 appropriation bill. No news arrived. Hoping to goad the legislators into action, he wrote to the House Committee on Commerce describing his success abroad. Several European governments, he said, had in view adopting an electrical telegraph. And in France the *"American Telegraph"* was being recommended as the best: "I am at this moment awaiting the orders of the Minister of the Interior." He implied that a similar interest in his apparatus existed among capitalists in America. He needed to know the government's wishes because they would determine for him whether to go public, committing his telegraph to "the control of associations of private individuals." The pressure on Congress, he hoped, might also work the other way, exciting action in the Paris bureaucrats: "I should be exceedingly glad to hurry these people by telling them that my services are wanted at home."

A new possibility opened for Morse when he was called on by a director of the St. Germain railroad, a twelve-mile line outside Paris. This official inquired whether a telegraph could be contrived to report the location of the company's trains along the road. Morse worked out a detailed plan featuring small electromagnetically operated bell towers that would register the arrival of the cars at a given point and notify every station over the whole route. He took a *brevet* for his new invention and made a working model.

The directors of the railroad, however, failed several times to show up for the demonstrations Morse arranged at his lodgings. "They are famous here for not keeping appointments," he told Smith; "I have only to exercise patience and wait." He needed more than patience.

When the directors finally came they approved his plan—all but one of them, who objected to the enormous cost of building a trial line, an estimated 60,000 francs. Morse proposed an economy: instead of stretching the wire circuit underground, in protective tubes, it would be laid down above ground in grooved bricks. He waited for a reply, but heard nothing. Like the rest of France, the railroad officials proved to be "as dilatory as the Government." In the end the company simply dropped the project.

Morse also tried to interest the French military, although his efforts are known only through his considerably later account of them. The Minister of War, he recalled, put him in touch with an elderly Marshal of France. Through an interpreter, he described for the *Maréchal* his strategy for using telegraphs on the battlefield. The instruments and a reel of fine insulated wire would be transported in a few light wagons: "when required, the wagons with the corps of operators, two or three persons, at a rapid rate should reel off the wire to the right, the centre and the left of the army . . . and thus instantaneous notice of the condition of the whole army, and of the enemy's movements, would be given at headquarters." Morse's pitch got nowhere, the Marshal objecting that his plan would overburden the army with matériel.

Despite his many frustrations, Morse kept seeking new outlets for his invention. Smith drafted for him a letter to the famed international banker Baron Rothschild. It solicited the interest of "gentlemen of enterprise & intelligence," promising that by Morse's telegraph they could send messages in perfect secrecy. Morse also arranged with a wealthy Vermont capitalist then in Paris, Mellen Chamberlain, to market his system outside England and France. Smith drew up an agreement by which Chamberlain would bear the costs of travel and of procuring new instruments, and after deducting them from the proceeds return to Morse and his partners half the profits. Chamberlain meant to look for buyers or agents not only throughout Europe, but also in Asia and Africa.

Morse had intended to stay abroad only three months. But with some projects still alive and new ones developing he decided to linger. Meanwhile his brother Richard and F. O. J. Smith returned to the United States. Having taken the waters at Vichy and consulted physicians in Switzerland, Richard felt he had overcome his constant "sadness & dejection." But the cures were short lived. Ever pessimistic—set on shutting out, as he realized, "every agreeable view of any object"— he began to think that whatever he had gained he would soon lose. He decided he must leave New York and withdraw from his partnership in the *Observer*.

Morse now saw Smith as a mixed blessing. He valued him for drafting letters that required legal expertise and for managing business deals. "I am not a business man," he confessed, "and fear every movement which suggests itself." But on other important matters he found Smith unreliable—especially in supplying the money the former congressman had promised to cover expenses in Paris. Jobless, his purse emptied by "a kind of perpetual diarrhoea," he often complained to Smith that he had had to borrow: "I hope by an early answer you will relieve . . . the embarrassment I am in and have funds at my command sent me without delay." To economize he built needed apparatus himself, spending hours in his room "like any mechanician." In some degree he also blamed Smith for holding up the demonstration of his telegraph at court. "If I had the funds the King should have seen this long ago, and the government too have given me an answer."

The stalled funds and bureaucratic delays often left Morse glum, his bright hopes in reach but never secured. He tried to "keep myself loose," confining his expectations "at the lowest point, that is, at *nothing*." But at times he slipped into one of his fits of "*the blues*," certain that he was destined to be purse-poor forever, "never to realise even a competency." He considered returning to America and moving permanently to the South, where he could resume his career in solitude as a portrait painter, "live secluded, without being burdensome to my friends." But some encouraging chance for his telegraph always turned up to revive and strengthen his hopes. "My confidence increases every day in the certainty of the eventual adoption of this means of communication throughout the civilized world." He reproved himself for mistrusting Providence, which in countless ways deserved his gratitude.

The black moods always returned, however. Or worse, when to the silence from the Palace and from Washington he added the state of his personal life. In his absence his affairs in America were becoming deranged beyond repair, his children parentless: "they are orphans, and orphans they are likely to be," he admitted to Sidney. "I know they suffer in this forming period of their lives for the want of a home, of the care of a father and a mother, and that no care and attention from friends, be they ever so kind, can supply the place of parents." Having soared on visions of fame and now sunk in hopelessness, he again felt unraveled, his "acute mental trials" all but unbearable—"so severe as almost to deprive me of reason, though few around me would suspect the state of my mind."

Morse had cause to brood over his children's well-being. Eighteen-year-old Susan lived with Sidney for a while in New York, but not happily. Full of business cares, Sidney sometimes forgot to dole out the money he was obligated to provide from her grandfather's bequest. And despite Susan's many economies he considered her extravagant. She reported to Morse that when she asked for money to buy Christmas presents, Sidney gave her a lot of his old books to bestow, "which I did not like much, as my friends gave me such handsome presents." Mostly Susan was unhappy over living as the ward of friends and relatives. While in New York she also stayed part of the time with a family named Peters, and when they moved was left uncertain where to go next. She ended up with an aunt in New Haven, where, she said, "I do not feel *exactly* at home." Her great wish, she wrote to Morse, was that someday "my dear father will have a sufficient competency to enable us to live in a home together."

Morse usually offered Susan little consolation. "I look to God to take care of you," he wrote. She lacked a home, true, but he reminded her that he himself was deeply bereft: "You cannot know the depth of the wound that was inflicted when I was deprived of your dear mother, nor in how many ways that wound has been kept open." What hope of family life he held out for her seems, at least in one letter, no more than disguised self-pity, designed not to reassure Susan but to elicit her sympathy:

> Tell Uncle Sidney to . . . have a little snug room in the upper corner of his new building, where a bed can be placed a chair and a table, and let me have it as my own that there may be one little particular spot, which I can call home. I will there make three wooden stools, one for you, one for Charles, and one for Finley, and invite you to your Father's house.

Morse's repeated depiction of himself as poor and helpless obviously made Susan feel guilty. She asked him to bring back a music box she might listen to while sewing—"that is, if you can afford it." Like the

rest of her letters to him since childhood, those she sent to Paris usually ended with a plea: "How I long for your return, my dearest father!"

However insensitive to Susan, Morse was even further cut off from
his sons. "I feel quite unfit to advise with regard to them," he told Sidney. "I know neither their dispositions nor their necessities." For a time
the boys were put up in Claverack, New York, with their uncle Richard
and his wife, Sarah. Charles was nearing college age. Thirteen-year-old
Finley, his mind stricken, seems to have had trouble dressing himself
and may have developed a violent clumsiness. Richard described him
as "mild, sweet-tempered, destructive." He believed Finley should be
put out to "some kind-hearted farmer in the country, where he could
amuse himself with work or play." In his emotionally ragged state,
Richard cannot have been an adequate caretaker for Morse's sons.
And his wife seems to have been no better. Winter was coming on, and
the boys lacked coats and had outgrown their pantaloons. Yet she told
Richard, "Don't bother about the children. Let them remain till their
father comes home, or makes provision for them."

Sidney planned to send Charles and Finley to school in Vermont.
Susan was dismayed by the idea: "Poor boys! They are *truly wanderers*,"
she protested to Morse. "I cannot bear the thought of their going so
far away from us all," she wrote to her father in Paris; "I long to see
them have a home. And be with me again."

With the New Year came a new hope of demonstrating the telegraph
at court. Morse was visited by the Prefect of the Seine, Count Ram-
buteau, whose power he considered next only to the King's. He
worked the apparatus for the Count, who sent the words "Louis-
Philippe" and was so impressed that he promised to speak to the King
the same evening. But as usual nothing happened. A promised visit
from the Chief of the King's household, Count Bondy, apparently
never happened either. And early in the new year Morse lost his closest contact with the palace when the government formed a new cabinet, deposing Count Montalivet as Minister of the Interior. "I cannot
bear this *standing still*," Morse groaned. "I have been dealing too much
in lightning lately to feel easy travelling on a snail's back."

Morse got some further discouraging news from Mellen Chamberlain, the Vermont capitalist who was trying to sell rights to the
telegraph elsewhere on the Continent, and in Asia and Africa. Cham-

berlain reported from Athens that he had demonstrated the invention to important persons in the city, including the King and Queen of Greece. All were captivated, he said, none was willing to risk money: "Fame is all you will get . . . in these poor Countries." Still, he was off to Alexandria to show the telegraph to Mehemet Ali, Sultan of Egypt, "and hope to get something worth having."

But Morse was beginning to feel that he must confine his hopes to America. The Old World and its old systems made Europeans unwilling to try new things however promising: "There is more of the '*Go-ahead*' character with us, suited to the character of an electro-magnetic Telegraph." Some doubt was cast on this too, however, when Morse learned that Bavaria had put in operation on part of its railroad system the apparatus of Steinheil—the first government to give its support to electrical telegraphs. Morse regretted that the American Congress had not taken the lead. But he managed to see in the event a sign of approaching vindication: "this first adoption gives the assurance of . . . *universal adoption* and if mine is best as all continue to affirm, mine must supplant all."

This depended, however, on the meaning of "mine." Morse learned that an article in the Boston *Post* had declared the electromagnetic telegraph "entirely due to our fellow citizen Dr. Charles T. Jackson." Jackson himself had supplied the information in the article. His spokesman in the *Post* explained that aboard the *Sully* Morse "pretended to feel a great interest in the invention," and later "undertook to monopolize the credit." Morse replied from Paris, threatening Jackson with public disgrace unless he immediately published a retraction: "For your family's sake, and for your friends sake, I would wish to spare you this mortification; an indulgence on my part, which you must be conscious you do not deserve."

Far from retracting, Jackson took aim at Morse's reputation among the *savans*. He wrote off a blast to the Académie des Sciences: "I am pained at the undeserved patronage which the French philosophers have accorded to Mr. Morse. The invention which he has shown them belongs entirely to me." ("*L'invention qu'il leur a montrée mi appartient en entier.*")

In reopening his war on Morse after five years, Jackson triggered a transatlantic cross fire of angry letters between them, as well as charges and countercharges in the *Observer* and other American newspapers. Morse found out that Jackson had recently been accused of plagiarism. Now a geological surveyor for the U.S. government, Jackson had allegedly pilfered from an unacknowledged source the substance of his published report on the mineralogy of Nova Scotia. Just the same, his tale of technological theft and deceit was much talked about in Paris. Morse countered it by publicizing the testimonials from fellow passengers on the *Sully*, which he had brought with him to Europe. They produced "a pretty strong tide of indignation raised against Jackson," he said. He also assured his partner, F. O. J. Smith, that the battle in the American press would not hinder but promote their interests. Many people who would not bother to read dispassionate descriptions of the telegraph would devour controversy about it. So the fracas would serve as "one of the best advertisements."

Toward the end of February Morse received an exciting proposal from a surprising direction. He had moved into new quarters, 5 rue Neuve des Mathurins. To save money he shared the space with a French-speaking Protestant minister from Boston, Edward Kirk. With Kirk acting as translator, he demonstrated his telegraph at home every Tuesday afternoon. He opened the levee to Paris scientific and government circles, but many other Europeans crowded in—Counts and Lords, as he carefully noted, Dukes and Duchesses, the Infante of Spain. All exclaimed over his system. He recorded the broken-English praise from one bigwig: "Are you not *glorious*, sair, to be the author of this wonderful discovery?"

The exciting proposal came from another of his enthusiastic distinguished guests—a Baron Meyendorff, agent of Czar Nicholas I of Russia. Meyendorff said he would immediately advise his government to establish a twenty-mile line of Morse telegraphs from St. Petersburg, laid underground. His right-hand man, an experienced scientist named Amyot, could experiment with Morse to ascertain the effects of temperature on the conductibility of long lengths of buried wire. The Czar had 80,000 men at his command, Meyendorff pointed out, so the trench for interring the circuit could be dug in only a week. Over several further meetings, he and Morse discussed the possibility of an eight-hundred-mile line to Warsaw.

Meyendorff's Czar was of course the same autocratic Nicholas I who eight years earlier had crushed the Polish uprising and absorbed Poland into the Russian empire. Outraged, Morse had joined the American Polish Committee in Paris and written sympathetic newspaper articles describing the woeful situation of Polish exiles. But with the chance of Morse lines serving the great Russian capital, outrage made room for buttering up. Czar Nicholas, he told Meyendorff, was "well known to be both just and liberal."

Morse, Meyendorff, and Amyot worked out detailed financial arrangements and a schedule. The Russian government would pay all expenses, including an advance of 4000 francs to Morse and a per diem allowance from the time he embarked for Russia. The contract was dispatched by courier to St. Petersburg for approval by Nicholas. Aware that Morse was planning to return home, Meyendorff promised to send him the Czar's reply through the Russian Ambassador to the United States, between May 10 and 15. Morse could leave from New York around June 1, be in Paris a month later, and reach St. Petersburg by July 15.

Morse immediately booked return passage to America for March 23, a month hence. He quickly wrote to Smith, asking his partner to have six or eight new telegraphs made that he could take to Russia, embodying all the recent improvements: "our whole energies must be directed to having *this first adoption of our System,* a successful one; all hands must go to work."

Morse's last two weeks abroad were intense. Since the beginning of the year his telegraph had been competing for public notice with another invention, by the stage designer Louis Jacques Mandé Daguerre (1789–1851). Daguerre operated a celebrated diorama in Paris, huge transparent paintings brought alive with props and lighting effects, such as a view of Mont Blanc, changing from night to day, an Alp horn sounding.

After many years' labor, Daguerre and his now-deceased partner, Joseph Nicéphore Niepce, had discovered a chemical process that could fix an image in the camera obscura (literally, "dark room"). The camera was a light-tight box commonly used as an aid to drawing. A convex lens at one end projected an image of the outside world onto a screen at the other end. An artist could peer into the box and draw from the image. When painting in New Haven around 1821, Morse had experimented with fixing camera obscura images on paper treated with silver nitrate. But he managed to produce only different degrees of shade, and gave up the idea as impracticable.

Daguerre's invention competed with Morse's telegraph not only for public attention but also for government support. His remarkable success had been described to the Académie des Sciences by Arago in January, although in general terms. Daguerre was keeping his process secret, offering to disclose it to the French government in exchange for a pension. The Chamber of Deputies was discussing whether to grant the pension, on the condition that Daguerre's process would be made public for anyone to use, as a boon to humanity. Morse was well aware of the competition, but supposedly not fazed by it. A Deputy remarked to him, he said, that of the "two great wonders of Paris" the telegraph was of "vastly more importance than the Daguerreotype."

Anxious to meet Daguerre before leaving France, Morse sent him a note asking to see his images, and inviting him in turn to inspect the telegraph. On March 7 he visited the French inventor for two hours at his rooms in the Diorama, a man with curly blondish hair and small dark mustache. Whatever superiority to Daguerre he may have felt before gave way to wonder when he saw the pictures, on metal plates about seven inches by five.

Morse was startled by the "exquisite minuteness of the delineation," the inconceivable fidelity to physical reality: "No painting or engraving ever approached it." The image of a boulevard contained a distant sign, on which the eye could discern letters but not read them. Examined with a powerful magnifying glass, however, every letter became distinct, "and so also were the minutest breaks and lines in the walls of the buildings and the pavements of the street." Similar examination of Daguerre's picture of a spider showed an intricate organization never before seen, opening a new field of research for the naturalist. And the images of interiors were Dutch paintings, "Rembrandt perfected." As both a painter and an inventor Morse considered the new process "one of the most beautiful discoveries of the age." He sent a lengthy narrative of his interview with Daguerre to his brothers in New York. Part of it was published in the May 18 issue of the *Observer*—the earliest firsthand account of photography to appear in America.

Daguerre's return visit, the following day, ended badly. He spent more than an hour examining Morse's telegraph. Meanwhile a fire broke out in his Diorama building, during a show. The audience escaped, barely, but his highly inflammable paintings were consumed. Sparks threatened to ignite his nearby house as well. Some neighbors saw the danger and carried off to safety his daguerreotype apparatus.

A notebook containing his experiments, at first believed to be lost, turned up ten days later.

Probably a few days after Daguerre's visit, Morse received a letter that prompted a last-minute change in his travel plans. It came from Lord Elgin, whose famed classical sculptures he had seen when studying in England twenty-five years ago. Elgin had attended Morse's afternoon exhibitions twice, impressed both by the telegraph and by its inventor being president of the National Academy of Design. He brought along such splendid friends as the young Earl of Lincoln, later one of Queen Victoria's Privy Council. Morse let his British guests know how coldly the Attorney General had dismissed his application for a patent. Elgin's letter now informed him, however, that his telegraph had become well known in London, and influence might be used to obtain a patent for him. He urged Morse to return to London: "a short delay in your proceeding to America may secure you this desirable object immediately."

Morse was reluctant to extend his stay abroad. He was scheduled to depart from Liverpool in only about ten days, and an expected summons from the Czar demanded his presence in New York. He decided to leave Paris immediately and spend as much time as remained in London. The day after arriving he sent his card to the Earl of Lincoln, who at once invited him to bring the telegraph to his house in Park Lane. On March 19 Morse exhibited its operation to an illustrious audience of Admiralty Lords, members of Parliament, and fellows of the Royal Society.

The heady appeals and flattery from on high produced no more action, however, than the rest of Morse's dealings with the British and French, which had crept along or gone nowhere. Elgin promised him an introduction to the influential former Lord Chancellor of England, Lord Brougham. But when Morse applied to see Brougham the answer was a formal note of compliments and regrets. His Lordship was engaged at the House every day until dinner, and could allow him only a few minutes some morning before ten.

Morse sailed back to the United States on March 23 aboard the *Great Western,* one of the new screw-propelled iron steamships that were all but eliminating the centuries-old tedium and danger of ocean travel, capable of crossing the Atlantic in only two weeks. He made it to New York in three, despite stormy weather, anxious to hear from the Czar and move on to St. Petersburg.

NINE

Beware of Tricks

(1839–1842)

HAVING BEEN gone eleven months instead of the intended three, Morse found his affairs at home even more chaotic than he expected. In his absence the University had dismissed seven professors and reduced student enrollment from a hundred or so to forty. His own professorship had become "merely nominal." Dr. Charles Jackson was still attacking him. Congress had done nothing toward financing a long-distance trial of his telegraph. And he had arrived broke—owing for rent, borrowing for meals, "not even a farthing in my pocket."

Morse saw his one hope of relief in selling his telegraph to the Russian government. As he awaited the promised message from Baron Meyendorff, announcing the Czar's decision, he tried to work out problems in his apparatus, to have it in top condition for presentation in St. Petersburg. Leonard Gale, his partner and consultant on scientific questions, was away in New Orleans. So he sought advice from Joseph Henry (1797?–1878), the formidable Professor of Natural Philosophy at Princeton. Son of an alcoholic day-laborer who died in a seizure of d.t.'s, Henry had made himself a world-class investigator of electricity, and the only American physicist with an international reputation.

Morse wrote Henry a deferential letter asking to meet with him at Princeton. He would come strictly as a learner, he said, but in advance he raised a general question: had Henry's research and experiment uncovered anything that seemed to make the Morse system impracticable? Henry wrote back encouragingly. He said he knew of nothing that might prevent the success of Morse's mode of telegraphy: "on the

Joseph Henry
(Chicago Historical Society)

contrary I believe that science is now ripe for this application and that there are no difficulties in the way but such as ingenuity and enterprise may obviate." One such issue, he said, was the length of wire between stations. If the length were great, something would have to be done to develop sufficient power at the far end. Meanwhile he invited Morse to Princeton.

Morse visited Henry for a few days in May. Blue-eyed and rosy-cheeked, Henry himself had recently returned from a year's leave in Europe, where he met Wheatstone and Michael Faraday, and sat in on a meeting of the Académie des Sciences. (A reader of the Romantic poets, he also heard Wordsworth lecture on poetry.) Morse wrote out several key questions to ask Henry. For one, Would a succession of magnets introduced into the circuit diminish the magnetism in each? Here he obviously had in mind his relay, although he does not seem to have mentioned the invention during his visit.

Henry freely gave his opinions on Morse's telegraph and Morse generally thought him amiable—an opinion he would drastically revise. They evidently discussed unrelated scientific topics as well, for Morse afterward sent him comments on the phenomenon of prismatic arches observed at morning and twilight. Morse was beginning to care about being, and seeming to the world, not simply a gimcrack inventor but a serious investigator of nature.

Morse expected to hear from Baron Meyendorff between May 10 and 15, but no answer came. For once he welcomed the delay. He wanted time to test his apparatus at home before embarking, "to have every thing in prime order, so as to surprise the czar." He decided to build two new instruments, still further improved. Among other things, he overhauled the port-rule so that the metal blanks no longer had to be laboriously set by hand and cranked under the lever. Instead, he devised a small keyboard with a key for each letter, something like a miniature piano. Pressing the key closed the circuit and produced on the tape dots and dashes representing that letter. The new port-rule, he felt, overcame the one advantage of Wheatstone's system to his own, that of showing a letter instantly, without having to set it up in type.

While streamlining his apparatus, Morse wrote again to Baron Meyendorff. But he received no news about the thinking in St. Petersburg. The Secretary of the Russian legation called on him in July to say that a message was expected by steamship. But none arrived: "the state of suspense," he told Meyendorff, "is becoming exceedingly painful as well as disastrous to me in forming my plans for the future."

The news finally arrived in August, and came from Amyot, the Baron's assistant. No, the Czar had decided, no telegraph. It troubled him, Amyot explained, that electrical communication might easily be interrupted by acts of malevolence. Morse had discussed such concerns with Meyendorff while still in Paris, and refuted them to the Baron's satisfaction. No matter. As Amyot dismally concluded, "The despotic countries and the free countries, my dear M. Morse, have therefore equally rejected your setting up a telegraph system." Morse hoped to get from Meyendorff a fuller account of the Czar's reasons, "*if Emperors give reasons.*" He comforted himself by recalling that leading scientists at home and abroad believed that his invention would be established all over the world. But the defeat was hard to take: "I cannot believe that all my time and anxiety, and risk, and labors are to end in nothing."

Prospects looked darker still when Morse learned, at around the same time, the fate of Mellen Chamberlain—the agent who had exhibited his telegraph to the Greek royal family and had been about to take it to Asia Minor and Egypt. During a pleasure-boat excursion on the Danube, Chamberlain and his party of nine drowned. No one knew what if anything he had managed to accomplish in Constantinople or in Alexandria.

Morse decided to take a break: "Perhaps it is the part of wisdom to let the matter rest and watch for an opportunity, when times look better." Early in the fall, burdened by debt, he began making himself into a full-time photographer.

Morse had kept in touch with Louis Daguerre, whose process had been receiving excited coverage in the American press, headlined a "Remarkable Invention," an "Extraordinary Chemical and Optical Discovery." He invited Daguerre to exhibit in the United States and proposed him for honorary membership in the N.A.D.—to which Daguerre was unanimously elected, with "wild enthusiasm." Morse also championed Daguerre against the Englishman William Henry Fox Talbot, a member of the Royal Society who had independently invented a rival method using photosensitive paper instead of metal plates. "Should any attempts be made here to give to any other than yourself the honor of this discovery," he wrote to Daguerre, "my pen is ever ready in your defense."

Morse set to work by acquiring a copy of Daguerre's seventy-five-page manual, *Historique et Description des Procédés du Daguerréotype*, which described the new process step by step, with diagrams of the necessary equipment. Later in life he claimed to have bought the first copy of Daguerre's manual to reach America, and to have been the first American to make a photograph—claims now either disputed or discarded. As with the telegraph, and most matters of technological priority, the early history of daguerreotyping in America is beclouded by mythology, competing claimants, and unresolvable controversy. Other Americans obtained copies of Daguerre's pamphlet too, or knew what it contained, and several newspapers published Daguerre's (and Talbot's) procedures, including the *Observer.* As Morse undertook his work, so did others in Boston, Philadelphia, or Cincinnati, experimenting with different chemicals, finding ways to speed up exposure times, making and selling photographs. The French invention became internationally popular, although in America more than anywhere else. By one estimate, over the next twenty years as many as thirty million photographs would be made in the United States. "In Daguerreotypes," Horace Greeley said, "we beat the world."

Morse brought a copy of Daguerre's manual to a maker of scientific instruments, George Prosch, who built him a camera according to Daguerre's diagrams, for $40. Daguerre's process, which Morse followed closely, consisted of four steps: sensitizing a silver-coated plate with iodine vapor; inserting the plate in a camera and exposing it to light; treating the exposed plate with hot mercury vapors to bring up the latent image; and fixing the image by bathing the plate in sodium thiosulfate. There were problems: the fragile surface of the image could easily be marred or tarnished, the highly toxic chemicals could cause blindness.

At first Morse used playing-card-size plates of silvered copper bought at a hardware store. Thinly coated with impure silver, they proved defective, and he began ordering plates from France. He reported his progress to Daguerre. One time he mentioned that he had discovered superior material for the important preliminary polishing of the plates, which he proposed calling Daguerreolite. Another time he said he had attained only "indifferent success" in picture-making, for want he believed of a proper lens.

But once he got going Morse delighted in the "photographic paintings," as he called them. According to one of his several accounts of the subject, he made his first successful daguerreotype in September 1839: a view of a Unitarian church taken from a staircase on the third story of the New York University building, with an exposure of about fifteen minutes. (The earliest surviving American daguerreotype, however, is of Central High School in Philadelphia, taken on October 16, 1839.) He made many other pictures as well: interiors with busts, books, rugs; views of Brooklyn, of rooftops in Manhattan, of City Hall; experiments to capture an impression of motion. Like most other early daguerreotypes, Morse's no longer exist. With two exceptions, one including his daughter, Susan,* they have all become lost or destroyed.

Hoping to learn the fine points of Daguerre's process, Morse took some lessons from a pupil and business associate of Daguerre's named François Gouraud. Gouraud was introducing the new art to America, beginning with demonstrations, lectures, and private instruction in New York late in 1839. He also showed a collection of photographs, some made by Daguerre himself, steeply priced for sale at from $40 to $300. Attracting much attention in the press, he planned to tour the other major American cities, working his way south to Charleston and New Orleans, and from there to Havana.

During January and February 1840, Morse took lessons from Gouraud in making proofs. He observed, asked questions, and took down for future reference Gouraud's teachings on the acidizing process, the mercury bath, the calculations involved in figuring exposure time. He put the instruction to use in making many experiments on his own. He recorded in some detail their often disappointing results:

Jan 25. Friday, very cold, clear, cloudless sky. arranged for interior. plate a little streaked with acid, which became in those parts purple in the iodine box; placed plate in camera at 12:10 . . . time in the camera 30 minutes. result very imperfect. the acid mark showed streaked. . . .

Feb 7. Thermo 66. 20 min to 12. Interior. bright sun. Camera 15 minutes. result bad scarcely any impression.

Another. 5 min. to 1 . . . Thermo. 63. Arranged objects on the roof in the open air, just without the window. bright sun. 15 minutes. result very fair shadows too dark and light solarized.

Another. 1 h. 28′ Thermo. 63. small plate. 10 min. no result.

Another. 2h. 4. Ther. 63 a little wind agitates the drapery and prints, after 5 minutes a gust of wind deranged all the prints. no result.

Another. 3. 26. Ther. 63. Exterior, view towards Brooklyn. same plate, used no acid on any plate this day. 24 minutes in Camera. Result. *Nothing!*

*See p. 298.

Morse was joined in his work by the recently appointed Professor of Chemistry at New York University, John William Draper (1811–1882). Twenty-eight years old, a chubby, broad-faced man with a dimpled chin, he had published several sophisticated scientific papers on the chemical effects of light. Broadening his interest in photochemistry, he now devoted himself fervently to the daguerreotype. He and Morse experimented together, Draper concentrating on the scientific problems, Morse the artistic, "as more in accordance with my profession."

Morse and Draper especially hoped to make photographs of people. According to Morse, Daguerre had discouraged the idea when he proposed it to him in Paris. Pictures of still objects required an exposure of fifteen to twenty minutes, and Daguerre believed it impossible for anyone to remain immobile that long. But Morse and Draper both succeeded in making portraits by Daguerre's process. Who produced one first became a matter of friendly disagreement between them. Morse later said that around September or October 1839, he took ten- to twenty-minute portraits of Susan and some of her friends. This seems unlikely, since the *Observer* did not announce his feat until April 1840, remarking that "Europeans have not succeeded in taking Daguerreotype likenesses of persons." This too seems unlikely, since according to François Gouraud, Parisians were making portraits only two weeks after Daguerre published his process. Morse later settled, or at least smoothed over, the issue by granting both himself and Draper something. Draper, he said, succeeded first "in taking photographic portraits *with the eyes open,* I having succeeded in taking portraits previously with the *eyes shut.*"

Whoever did what first, in the spring of 1840 Morse and Draper opened a primitive portrait studio atop the New York University building, consisting of a workshop and a shed with a glass roof. By using two mirrors—one to reflect sunlight on the other, which threw the light on the sitter—they achieved fast exposure times of from forty seconds to two minutes. On sunshiny days they made pictures of prominent New Yorkers and on darker days gave lessons to student daguerreotypists. Morse of course had always scorned portrait painting. Ironically, his chief pride was now his notable ability to produce portraits photochemically. He even went to New Haven for the thirtieth reunion of his Yale class and took two group pictures of the others who attended, eighteen men arranged side by side in the yard of the President's house. In doing so he apparently inaugurated a popular and profitable line of commercial portrait photography. "How valuable," the *Observer* commented, "would such a momento [*sic*] of early friendship be to every class, on leaving college for the busy scenes of life."

The surviving evidence about Morse's alliance with Draper is too skimpy to judge their individual contributions to its success. Both by himself and with Morse, Draper did pioneering work in photography. Among other achievements, he took daguerreotypes by artificial light, applied photography to microscopy, and made the first known photograph of the moon, launching astronomical photography. On the other hand, Morse's personal acquaintance with Daguerre and his standing as head of the N.A.D. made him more conspicuous than Draper and many other daguerreotypists. Aspiring photographers wrote to him from all over the country, wanting to know how he managed to take likenesses in so few seconds, in diffuse light; inquiring where to get Tripoli powder for polishing plates. Many persons interested in the art looked to him as the head of photography in the United States—in effect Daguerre's American representative.

How long Morse and Draper operated their University gallery is unclear. Draper withdrew to concentrate on scientific research, and in the fall of 1840 Morse moved into new quarters at the *Observer*. Despite the economic depression, Sidney was prospering, his newspaper now printing 16,000 copies—"beyond our most sanguine expectations," he said. He had purchased the six-story building that housed the paper, on the corner of Beekman and Nassau Streets. At a cost of $500 he built his brother a rooftop studio, "entirely of glass," Morse said, "so that I have nearly the effect of outdoor light." The light especially pleased Morse, for he had been experimenting with reduced exposure times, and believed he could ultimately take a portrait in two seconds, if not in one. The rapidity also depended on the shortness of focus in the lenses, and he put together a series of lenses that provided a focus of four and a half inches.

Morse worked hard to make his photographs pay. "I am tied hand and foot through the day," he said, "endeavoring to realize something from the Daguerreotype portrait." The "something" amounted to enough to get him out of debt, but not enough to repay Sidney for the cost of the studio, as he promised to do. He increased his income by taking on pupils, charging $50 for one quarter's instruction. They learned from him not only Daguerre's process, but also ideas about

lighting, posing, and facial expression he retained from years of training and practice as a painter. His pupils soon formed a corps of American photographers. It included the famous Mathew Brady, who later
praised his teacher as "the first successful introducer of this rare art in
America."

Like all of Morse's endeavors, the latest one drew him into debate and
controversy. Exhibitions of daguerreotypes provoked much public discussion of how photography might redefine art. Most believed that its
eerie exactitude would diminish the value of painting and painters.
The *New-Yorker,* reviewing François Gouraud's exhibition of French
daguerreotypes, commented that by comparison the most beautifully
painted miniature seemed "a miserable daub." "You would be led to
suppose that the poor craft of painting was knocked in the head,"
Thomas Cole wrote, "and we [artists] nothing to do but give up the
ghost."

Morse disputed such beliefs in a speech to the National Academy
of Design. The daguerreotype was bound "to produce a great *revolution* in art," he said. But its influence would be "in the highest degree
favorable." The artist would no longer have to paint from imperfect
sketches that had taken him days or weeks to execute. Now he could
furnish his studio with exquisite models, facsimiles of scenes and figures—not copies of nature, "*but portions of nature herself.*" Such images
would offer unsurpassed lessons in perspective, light and shade, and
other problems of optics. For the public they would form a new school
of taste, teaching how to discriminate between true artists and the
merely chic: "Will not the artist, who has been educated in Nature's
school of truth, now stand forth pre-eminent, while he, who has
sought his models of style among fleeting fashions and corrupted
tastes, will be left to merited neglect?" He saluted Daguerre as a dis-
coverer comparable to Columbus and Galileo: "Honor to Daguerre,
who has first introduced Nature to us, in the character of *Painter.*"

No honor, however, to Daguerre's pupil and associate François
Gouraud. The lessons Morse took from him occasioned a bitter war of
words between them. It began when the New York press praised some
of Morse's daguerreotypes. Gouraud wrote to the city's *Evening Star,*
implying that much of the success of the pictures was owing to himself,
since he had "given Mr. Morse all the instruction in my power." Morse

already ached from slaps at his gifts as an inventor and painter, and was in no mood to suffer criticism of his talent for photography. He shot back in the same newspaper, saying that he had produced several photographs "of more or less perfectness" three weeks before Gouraud arrived in New York. Everything useful that Gouraud showed him in two months of so-called instruction was already available in Daguerre's manual. Gouraud's additions to it only hindered him: "all the instruction professed to be imparted by M. Gouraud I have felt it necessary to forget."

Gouraud and Morse began attacking each other through lengthy letters to the editor, in what the press played up as the "Daguerreotype Controversy." Gouraud evidently had taken a personal dislike to Morse, whose Christian-republican manner of dignified benevolence seemed to him (and to some others) an off putting combination of self-importance and obsequiousness. He portrayed Morse as an oily American Tartuffe, "a man of *honied* aspect, of such *affectionate* grasping of the hand, of such open and *heavenly* smiles." Having learned about Charles Jackson's quarrel with Morse, he accused Morse of trying to "appropriate to himself the fruits of the genius of his fellow citizens." And now Morse was falsely claiming to have improved Daguerre's process—"one more in his long list of self-illusions. . . . after having *invented* the Electric Telegraph."

Gouraud portrayed Morse as not only hypocritical and larcenous but also vicious. Morse was representing him to Daguerre as a shady financial schemer, "IN ORDER TO RUIN ME IN THE MIND AND ESTIMATION OF THAT GREAT MAN!" As evidence he published a letter to him from a devoted Paris Daguerrian, Abel Rendu. It confirmed that Daguerre had received defamatory statements about Gouraud from Morse. Rendu speculated that in making Daguerre an honorary member of the N.A.D., Morse hoped to give his slanders against Gouraud greater effect, "*and secure for them a more certain triumph.*" Gouraud followed up by leaving a petition at the office of a French-language newspaper in New York, the *Courier des États Unis,* which he invited his sympathizers to sign. With its hundreds of signatures the petition would be forwarded to Daguerre in Paris: "We shall then see whether M. Daguerre will conceive himself to have been so highly honored by the reception of a diploma which makes him the colleague of Mr. Morse."

Morse denounced Gouraud as an "unblushing falsifier," and

denied that he had ever written Daguerre, or anyone else in Europe, a single word about him. The Morse-friendly *Journal of Commerce* turned Gouraud's charges inside out. It alleged that he had invented his story of persecution by Morse in order to rob him of Daguerre's friendship and confidence: "A storm is thus raised which threatens for a moment to bear down a worthy citizen, who has made himself poor by his devotion to the Fine Arts."

In the end Morse was vindicated. Rendu, a minor government official, resented Gouraud's publication of his private letter. He wrote to Morse apologizing for having unwittingly been used to injure him. He explained that Gouraud had duped him into becoming an accomplice, and gave Morse permission to publish his apology. Later he revealed to Morse that although Gouraud identified himself as a "Docteur de Science" and professor at the Sorbonne he was neither.

Morse happened to meet Gouraud about a year after their public free-for-all. The Frenchman seemed to feel "*deep regret.*" Others had deceived him, he said, and being excitable he got carried away by his feelings. Morse promised to forget the affair and extended his hand. Gouraud remarked, "you are indeed a christian." For his brother Sidney, Morse drew the appropriate lesson: "How cautious it is necessary to be with these foreigners!"

Morse's photographic work did not keep him from closely watching political affairs, ever alert to threats against America's "Protestant republicanism." Calls for public support of New York Catholic schools particularly disturbed him. The matter affected some 70,000 German and Irish Catholics in New York City alone, nearly a quarter of the population.

Governor William H. Seward, in his 1840 annual address, had expressed concern for the quality of education being offered the children of immigrants—an important consideration if they were to be assimilated into republican life. He invited foreign-born New Yorkers whose children attended parochial schools to petition for a share in state funds for public schools. A group of Catholic churches in the city immediately applied to the Common Council, which administered the funds. According to the *Observer,* they demanded a third of the school budget, about $45,000 out of $140,000. The *Observer* warned of what was afoot: "a wide spread, long concerted, deep laid and powerfully sustained conspiracy is just breaking out, to make this land what Italy and Ireland are, so far as popery is concerned."

To Morse's relief, the Council turned down the request for public funds. "Their vote," he said, "deserves to be recorded by the side of the Declaration of Independence." But the issue stayed alive, too dangerous to ignore. In October 1840—about when he opened his studio atop the *Observer* building—Morse chaired the founding meeting of a new national association, the Society for the Diffusion of Useful & Religious Knowledge into Italy. It planned to evangelize the country by sending Protestant missionaries and distributing Protestant books and tracts. Addressing the new group in the chapel of Union Theological Seminary, Morse reminded them that his warnings of foreign conspiracy, a few years ago, had often been dismissed: "many if not most of you deemed it a false alarm, the visionary fears of a morbid imagination." But the warnings were being borne out, indeed the half had not been told: "How is it now? . . . Popery has reared its head boldly in our midst, and stalks with giant strides over the land . . . has even dared to dictate in the politics of the country." To help the Italian people toward their spiritual regeneration would be at the same time to "attack the monster in his den" and protect the homeland.

Angry and divisive, the school funding issue gave new life to the Native American Democratic Association. Quiescent since 1836, when it had run Morse as a mayoral candidate, it regrouped to field candidates in the April 1841 city elections. As a prominent New Yorker and leading spokesman for the party, Morse was again nominated as its candidate for mayor. His surviving papers do not explain why he chose to drop photography and return to political life. Catholic influence was a grave issue to him, of course, and he had often before shifted directions. Most likely, however, he considered himself to be still biding his time while waiting for Congress to act on the telegraph. Whatever his reasons for accepting the nomination, he hardly knew what he was letting himself in for.

Running as a third-party candidate, Morse was regarded as a spoiler. Whigs had felt confident about winning the city election, riding on the recent victory of the first Whig president, William Henry Harrison. Fearing that Morse would draw off enough votes from their party to elect the Democrat nominee, Robert H. Morris, they set out to obliterate him.

The political dirty tricks began on April 8, one week before the election. The *Express,* a Whig paper, reported that the Native Americans had met at a city hotel and withdrawn Morse's name from the mayoralty race. That was news to Morse indeed. Not until reading the paper did he learn that he had been scuttled. The Executive Committee of the Native American party published in the *Sun* a formal letter to him, explaining that the "meeting" was a sham, held without knowledge of the officers and attended by only a few members and strangers. To restore his candidacy, the Committee also took out two ads in the *Sun.* One included a letter from Morse asserting that he remained actively in the race. The other restated the party's endorsement of him for mayor: "The friends of American principles—all opposed to foreign influence . . . will vote this ticket. Our fellow citizens are warned against all the arts of politicians to defeat this nomination."

But the Whig tricksters had not finished with Morse. On April 12 three Whig papers in the city ganged up on him. The *Commercial Advertiser* revealed that his nomination as a third-party candidate was a Democrat scam—"a mere *ruse* of the enemy. The design is to create a diversion in the Whig ranks. . . . we say to the Whigs beware! Mr. Morse IS A VAN BUREN MAN." The cry echoed accusations during the 1836 election that although running as a Native American, Morse supported the Democratic nominee for president, Martin Van Buren, as Morse admitted he did. The Whig *Tribune* joined the attack: "BEWARE OF TRICKS . . . The wire-workers in this business will doubtless vote themselves for Morris, after decoying all the Whigs into voting for Morse that they can humbug." The same day, the Whig *Express* reported that the Native American party had met and once more withdrawn Morse's name as a candidate.

In the space of one week, Morse read in the city press: first, that his party had disowned him; second, that Democrat conspirators had nominated him; third, that his party had disowned him a second time. Next he read an announcement by himself that he had backed out of the race. The day before the election, the *Express* and the *Advertiser* published a counterfeited letter to the editor, with Morse's name attached as the author:

Dear Sir—Seeing the discord among the friends of the Native American Party, and that no good can result from their running a

separate candidate at this election, I have come to the conclusion
to withdraw as their candidate.

The *Advertiser* congratulated Morse for stepping down, the "tempestu-
ous sea of politics" being no place for his high qualities of mind and
artistic gifts: "He *is* a gentleman—every inch of him. He is more—
being a man of genius and talent—both of which have been highly cultivated." Next day, Election Day, many other city newspapers reprinted
Morse's "letter of resignation," every word a fake.

The flimflam succeeded in confusing voters about whether Morse
was or was not a candidate. In the close election, the Democrat and
Whig nominees almost evenly divided the 37,000 votes cast, the Whig
receiving just over 18,000 and the victorious Democrat, Morris,
about 18,500. Morse polled a ridiculous 78. In about a third of the
city's seventeen wards he received no votes at all. Nastily bamboozled,
he was left privately denouncing the "unprincipled tricks and forger-
ies."

But the Catholic threat represented by parochial school funding
continued, and became a key issue in the fall state elections. In May,
Morse was chosen President of a new group called the American
Protestant Union. It apparently consisted of no more than the old
Native American Democratic Association reorganized and renamed to
give it a fresh look following its dismal showing in the city elections.
The Union styled itself a "national defensive society" and aimed at
consolidating opposition to "the perversion of the Common School
Fund to sectarian purposes." As the election approached, school funding was argued caustically in the press and in public forums. Morse
probably wrote some articles anonymously for the *Observer*, which
printed a warning by him on its front page:

> Americans, when you shall have become tired with your liberty,
> when you shall envy the fate of Ireland, Spain, and Italy; when
> you wish that your children and your descendants may become
> superstitious slaves, introduce Catholic schools . . .

The *Observer* described several meetings of Catholics in which abuse
had been heaped upon Protestants, "our cherished institutions and
sacred doctrines denounced."

The most notorious such meeting occurred at Manhattan's Carroll Hall on October 29, less than a week before the state election. The meeting was addressed by the fiery bishop of New York, John Hughes—a "cunning, flexible, serpent tongued priest," the young reporter Walt Whitman called him, supported by "scullions from Austrian monasteries." The bishop told the crowded assembly that their only hope lay in fielding their own ticket. To loud applause and cheers, he presented an independent Catholic slate, and urged its election.

For Morse and for the *Observer*, the spectacle of an ecclesiastic nominating candidates for the New York State Senate and Assembly gave unmistakable evidence of Catholic intentions to seize political control of America. It raised the supreme nightmare of "Protestant republicanism": an American president holding his power from the Pope. "The mask was off," the *Observer* jeered. "The foot of the Beast was trampling on the elective franchise, and his High Priest was standing before the *ballot box*, the citadel of American liberties."

Two days after the Carroll Hall meeting, Morse, as president of the American Protestant Union, presented a rival nativist slate. Once again the Whig press opened fire on him. The *Commercial Advertiser* mocked him as a nativist version of Bishop Hughes. He had sent inquiries to Whig candidates asking their views on the school system, the paper said, then published only the replies that might be taken as support for the Protestant Union: "Why oppose Catholic juggling in one breath, and indulge in Protestant juggling in the next?" The *Tribune* denounced the Union ticket as a swindle, contrived to scare Irish citizens into voting for Democrats—who in the end won a sweeping victory. Morse's Union ticket proved not much more popular than Morse the mayoral candidate. Of some 35,000 votes cast in New York City, the party received only 400, the all-Catholic Carroll Hall ticket got more than five times as many.

Morse continued to speak out against granting public school funds to Catholic schools, but his opponents soon won a partial victory. In the spring of 1842, the state legislature passed a bill giving over supervision of New York City's schools to commissioners elected by each ward. This move toward community control brought mobs into the streets of Manhattan, who pursued Irishmen and stoned the house of Bishop Hughes. The militia was called out to protect Catholic churches. The *Observer* reviled the bill as "the most serious blow which has ever been struck at the citadel of religious liberty in this Western world." The head of the Leopold Society, the paper reported, was on his way to the United States to help celebrate the advancing march of papal power in America.

Now fifty years old, Morse sometimes felt spent: "my prime is past; the snows are on my temples . . . my eyes begin to fail, and what can I now expect to do with declining powers." Since returning from France he had been lonely, too: "trouble in various shapes . . . has shut me up within myself for two years past. I have made no visits, and scarcely have seen any one." Fourteen years after Lucrece's death he still marked the anniversary of her passing, recalling on every February 7 her faultless features, refined mind, devoted affection. The years, he said, "have scarcely healed the wounds which the loss of a most lovely wife on that day, first opened in my heart."

The shock of his wife's death, probably, and some later failed overtures to women made Morse wary of romantic attachments. "The burnt child dreads the fire," he observed, "and I have been so scorched from my tinder box of a heart, that I have learned a little prudence." So much ardor checked by a little prudence may explain why after more than a dozen years he still wrote to Catherine Pattison. When they first met, in 1828, she was in her teens, half his age. Now she was in her early thirties, unmarried, apparently available, and more desirable than ever for having undergone conversion: "Woman never appears in so lovely an attitude," he wrote to her, "as when bending at the foot of the cross." Yet he still presented himself ambivalently, expressing deep interest by emphasizing his desire to overcome it: "The more I have thought about you friend C. the more I felt disposed to keep my thoughts locked up, for I am not so ignorant of myself as not to know that my too sensitive feelings were not always under the control of a judgment which ought to be mature from years." Sending mixed signals, he left it to Catherine to decipher his impassioned prudence.

Despite his fear of being burned again, Morse for a while pursued an eligible widow, identified in his correspondence only as "Mrs. Y." They met at a dinner party in Sconondoa, an upstate village about twenty miles from Utica. Following his defeat in the New York mayoralty race, Morse had gone there to visit his mother's family, the Breeses. He was enough interested in "Mrs. Y." to give her his edition of the works of Lucretia Davidson, and write to her afterward to find out how she might be disposed toward him. He received no answer, however, and wrote to her again. Again she did not reply.

Uncertain how to interpret the "most perplexing silence," Morse apparently returned to Sconondoa to see "Mrs. Y.": "I do not give up until every effort has been made which I can make." To younger members of the Breese family, their cousin's "dismal courtship" seemed risible. "We tickle our sides well," one of them wrote. They thought Morse pompous and hoped to see him fall on his face, "have his laurels a little bit ruffled, his plumes a little picked." They got what they wanted. Returned to New York City he waited three months for a letter. None came, and he gave up. The rejection left him alone with "the blue gentlemen," more solitary than ever, persuaded that he should stay single the rest of his life: "I feel in my despondency that no one cares for me."

The Breese family had taken in Morse's unfortunate son Finley, but Charles and Susan still had no home. Morse sent Charles long-distance bromides and instructions, identical with those he had once received from his own father: "You have a character to maintain. . . . Take care to deserve praise. . . . keep an accurate account of every cent you expend." When his son entered Yale, Morse felt too preoccupied in New York to help the boy get settled in New Haven, "and must therefore," he said, "leave him to be directed by the kindness of friends." Charles was left scrounging for money to buy necessary books and winter coal, borrowing a quarter to pay postage, sending his father the same plaint as his sister Susan—"I wish you would come to see me some time."

Susan shuffled among a pack of friends and relatives from one place to the other. Off and on she stayed with Lucrece's sister in New Hampshire, with a family named Denison in New Haven, a Wickham family in New York City. The lifetime of vagabondage had its effect. Like her father, Susan had spells of deep depression. "I feel sometimes as if I had no desire whatever to live," she wrote to him, "life seems without one cheering spot to me. I know, dear father, it is very wrong to indulge such feelings, and I pray that my Heavenly father will take such wicked thoughts of my heart, and make me a better Christian."

Without meaning to, the prosperous Sidney became the medium for at last providing Susan with a home. When he married—for the first time, at the age of forty-seven—she fantasized that he and his bride might set up house in New York and take her in, so that "poor me will have some abiding place." Instead, in the late fall of 1841, the couple took her along on a trip to Puerto Rico, where they planned to spend the winter. Now twenty-two years old, Susan had had a few suitors but rejected them, one because his religious faith was shallow, another because she thought him "*countryfied.*" While on the island, however, she gained a new beau, a young man named Edward Lind. She wrote about him to Morse, who approved what he read. Lind came from "one of the first families" in the West Indies, was partners in a flourishing firm in St. Thomas—and was not a Catholic. In the summer of 1842, Susan and Edward Lind were married in New Haven. "Why it was only yesterday I was married myself," Morse reflected; "It must be a dream. I am growing old."

Having not painted a picture for several years, Morse wondered whether he still could: "I presume that the mechanical skill I once possessed in the art has suffered by the unavoidable neglect." A young artist who visited his studio at the University saw a few crayon drawings pinned around, but otherwise everything seemed neglected and unused. Dust covered the plaster models, canvases faced the wall, stumps of brushes littered the floor. Finished with his career or not, Morse still brooded over having been denied a commission for the Capitol paintings. The never-to-be-won prize had preoccupied the best part of his life, "animated me to sacrifice all that most men consider precious, prospects of wealth, domestic enjoyments, and not least the enjoyment of country." The disregard of Congress, he said, had killed his enthusiasm for painting.

Morse apparently had done no work on *The Gem of the Republic*, the history painting commissioned by some well-wishers to console him for what Congress had done. To his horror, a subscriber to the painting placed an anonymous notice about it in the New York *Mirror:* "Not having heard any thing of this picture for upwards of a year, it has just occurred to us to inquire what has become of it? Is Mr. Morse engaged upon it? and when is the picture to be done?" Morse drafted a seven-page reply, rehearsing the long history of his connection with the rotunda project, including his studies in France and Italy, followed by a brief history of his misfortunes with the telegraph, including its rejection by the Czar.

Wisely, Morse did nothing with this anguished moan. Instead, he printed up a circular addressed to the subscribers, announcing that he now planned to return all the money they had given him—"*not that I abandon my enterprise,*" he insisted. On the contrary, he intended to free his imaginative powers from the sense of financial obligation that had inhibited it, "the first necessary step to the final accomplishment of my design." This can have been nothing more than a hope-against-hope or attempt to save face, for privately he despaired of ever being able to paint again.

Fellow artists still treated Morse as a respected member of the guild. In 1841 the National Academy of Design ordered a bust to be sculpted of him and placed in the Council Chamber. While abroad he had sent back books on art for the N.A.D. library, and he took at least some part in its activities. John Trumbull's long-failing American Academy had ceased to exist, its property sold off, including about twenty casts of antique statues and sixty-three busts bought by the National Academy.

A serious rival to the N.A.D., however, arose in 1839 with the formation in New York of the American Art-Union. Morse and a committee of the N.A.D. met with representatives of the new group to discuss the possibility of cooperating to advance the fine arts in America. But the committees clashed over the issue of exhibitions. The Art-Union maintained a free public exhibition of works by living American artists. Morse feared that this show would deprive the N.A.D. of some good pictures and reduce public interest in its annual exhibition—the Academy's main source of support. "We have no stockholders," he pointed out, "no subscribers to create a fund for our use; our sole Revenue is the Exhibition." His committee therefore asked the Art-Union to confine its exhibitions to copies of famous paintings, works by deceased artists, and works previously shown at the National Academy. Here the negotiations broke off.

Morse remained proud of having founded the N.A.D. The Academy had a new room devoted to sculpture, and now owned the country's largest collection of studio models, affording rich means of study. When asked to supply information on the history of the arts in New York, for an official state survey, Morse observed that when the Academy began, Philadelphia, Boston, and Baltimore led New York City in taste and enthusiasm. But currently about seventy professional artists connected with the N.A.D. lived in the city. The Academy was on its way to realizing part of the mission of its founders, "that of making New York the great centre of the Fine Arts as it has long been of the Commerce of the country."

During his two-year engagement with daguerreotyping and politics, Morse had held himself ready to go to Washington if summoned by the government to discuss his telegraph. But as he often complained, he was not. And what news he received about the invention showed him not simply standing still but losing ground.

Morse learned that the Cooke-Wheatstone needle telegraph had been put in successful operation over thirteen miles on the Great Western Railway in England. More menacingly, the British partners were seeking an American patent for an improved version of their apparatus. Seemingly unaware of Morse's lifelong distrust of English intentions toward America, they invited him to become their agent in the United States, obtaining the patent for them at his own expense in exchange for a half share in it. Oblivious also to Morse's belief in the superiority of his own system, Wheatstone promised him more than financial profit: "you might have the merit of introducing into America the only invention of the kind of which the success has been put beyond all doubt."

Stung and worried by the insensitive offer, Morse asked F. O. J. Smith for legal advice: "Does not our Patent secure us against foreign interference? Or are we to be defeated not only in England but in our own Country by the subsequent inventions of Wheatstone?" In fact, however, Morse had filed for but not yet received his patent. He wrote off inquiring about it to his friend Henry Ellsworth, Commissioner of Patents: "unless something is done to help me forward, the more wealthy Englishmen will have it in their power not merely to deprive me of the profit of my discovery in my own country, as they have already in their own, by a gross act of injustice, but . . . the Telegraph will be an English, not an American invention." Ellsworth reminded him that the granting of the patent had been postponed at Morse's own request, so that he could first secure European patents. Since the Patent Office had heard nothing further from him, it still had not issued the patent but would do so now.

There were vexing delays, however. The Office asked Morse to make several corrections in his drawings. It also belatedly discovered that he had neglected to fill in the date on his oath, requiring him to prepare a new affidavit, sworn before the mayor of New York. The certificate was finally issued on June 20, 1840, as U.S. patent No. 1647: "a new and useful Improvement in the mode of communicating information by signals, by the application of Electro Magnetism." Since the first U.S. patent statute had been signed into law by President Washington in 1790, the provisions had been several times revised. Present law protected Morse's invention for a term of fourteen years, with the possibility of a seven-year extension.

Not only the English, but French telegraphers, too, were looking for business in America. Early in 1841, Congress received a memorial from M. Gonon, one of the two so-called Professors of Graphy whose demonstrations in America four years earlier had prompted Morse to first unveil his own telegraph. Gonon now offered to establish a line of twenty-seven semaphore stations connecting Washington with New York, for a total cost of $15,000. He submitted endorsements from businessmen and politicians who had seen his system. He also laid out for Congress the disadvantages of supposedly superior electrical telegraphs: unsolved problems in crossing rivers and swamps, vulnerability to vandalism, enormous expense, "and, after years of gigantic work to establish a line of little distance." The House Committee on Commerce reported a bill for $5000 to test Gonon's plan, an attractive saving over Morse's petition for $30,000.

It was in part Morse's resentment of English and French trafficking in America that brought him back to telegraphy—"sick at heart to perceive how easily others, *foreigners,* can manage our Congress and can contrive to cheat our country." A stronger inducement came in a long letter he received the first week of August 1841 from a Washington lobbyist named Isaac Coffin. Coffin knew that Morse's petition for an appropriation to test the Electro-magnetic Telegraph had been before Congress many years without being acted upon. He explained to Morse that the main obstacle was the expense. Many members favored the cheaper plan of Gonon, who had just placed a working model of his semaphore atop the Capitol. There were other obstacles. The press of national business meant long delays in gathering quorums and getting bills reported out of committees to both houses of Congress, where they had to again await their place on a docket and then be debated. "A claim," he told Morse, "therefore needs the most constant, unceasing and untiring and vigilant attention to see that it is not neglected."

For a commission, Coffin offered to act as Morse's agent in seeing the petition through. He said that he had the "warm friendship" of many congressmen, understood patent law, knew something about electromagnetism, and had much experience in forwarding bills. Sending along a testimonial from an influential House member, he promised to use "the most strenuous, untiring and energetic exertions to get Reports from the Committees in accordance with the prayer of the petition and to get the claim through both Houses of Congress." If he failed, he asked no commission.

After two years of stagnation and hopelessness, Morse was enthusiastic about Coffin's offer. "I at length have some nibbles at the Telegraph." The other nibble arrived at about the same time. Some private individuals, "men of capital," proposed financing a telegraph line of about 120 miles. Morse immediately consulted his partners, with whom he had fallen out of touch. Leonard Gale was in New Orleans, F. O. J. Smith back in Maine; Alfred Vail had married, become a father, and moved to Philadelphia. Morse asked Gale and Vail for a power of attorney so that he could act on their behalf. Recognizing Smith's expertise in business, he asked him to come to New York: "I should prefer to have your business tact at hand to see that I did not defraud myself."

Taking advantage of the nibbles proved not so easy. The capitalists' proposal disappeared—"another of those ignes fatui," Morse lamented, "that have just led me on to waste a little more time, money and patience and then vanished." Coming to an agreement with his partners on Coffin's offer meant three letters to write on each trivial point, then a week or ten days to receive an answer. Gale sent a power of attorney, but Vail wanted to consult his brother George. George had supplied most of the Vail money for Morse's telegraph work so far, and like Alfred he resented Morse's turn to photography. The Vails eventually granted a power of attorney, but negotiations about it hobbled on for four months.

Smith, an experienced Washington pol, was skeptical about Coffin's assurance that he had enough influence to get the petition through Congress. Nevertheless he agreed to give Coffin a $2000 commission if he succeeded. But Coffin held out for $3000, "low enough," he said, "especially as I have to take the risk after infinite labor of no remuneration." He warned Morse that the Committee on Commerce had reported in favor of Gonon's semaphore system: "Probably he and his friends will make great exertions to have it adopted, which once adopted, will be the death of yours."

After months of this wearying back-and-forth, Morse felt futile, "almost ready to cast the whole matter to the winds, and turn my attention forever from the subject." He thought of going to Washington himself to push his petition, but more than usually lacked funds. "I have scarcely (indeed I have not at all) the means to pay even the postage of letters on the subject." The same want of money that kept him from acting, however, demanded that he act. Only his telegraph, he believed, could at last provide him a livelihood. And he had now become too deeply committed to its success to quit. "I have an invention which is to mark an era in human civilization, and is to contribute to the happiness of millions."

Morse decided to start all over again. With the arrival of 1842 he launched a second, and more vigorous, campaign to get an appropriation from Congress for an experimental line. He began, in January, by seeking testimonials to send on to Washington. He wrote to Professor Joseph Henry, whom he had visited at Princeton, asking for "a letter expressive of your views." Henry returned a solid recommendation. He commented that the time was ripe for the telegraph and that he preferred Morse's to Wheatstone's or Steinheil's: "I have not the least doubt, if proper means be afforded, of the perfect success of the invention."

Morse wrote the same month to several congressmen asking their help. A few expressed vague interest or doubt. But a member from Connecticut, William W. Boardman, agreed in effect to reintroduce Morse's petition. In February he placed before the House a resolution calling on the Commerce Committee to "inquire into the expediency of establishing a system of electro-magnetic telegraph for the use of the Government of the United States." The Committee would not address the issue for months, and meanwhile Boardman advised Morse to publicize the cause: "It may be worth while to keep the matter before the public eye, and excite an interest in it."

To create a stir that might impress Congress, Morse prepared a new series of public demonstrations. He built several improved instruments, and experimented again to work out problems in transmitting over long lines. "I retire early and am up early and at work again so that days weeks and I find even months have slipped by almost unconsciously." He devised a new battery, "the most powerful of its size ever invented," he claimed, and succeeded in passing a usable current through thirty-three miles of wire.

Morse exhibited his system in New York City throughout the summer and early fall, reaping much new notice in the press. Journalists from the *Tribune* witnessed one trial. They wrote a rhapsodic account for the paper, calling the apparatus "among the most wonderful and, prospectively, the most useful applications of science to the great purposes of life which the present age has seen." Most important, they asked Congress to immediately grant Morse the appropriation. Several weeks later Morse performed before a committee of scientists from the American Institute. The committee's report, reprinted in the press, concluded that the instrument was admirably adapted to sending long-distance messages at high speed—"a most important practical application of high science, brought into successful operation by the exercise of much mechanical skill and ingenuity."

The Institute awarded Morse a gold medal, and chose to include his apparatus in its annual fair at Niblo's Garden. At this exposition of American progress in manufactures, agriculture, and invention, New Yorkers could see Morse's system in operation all day. Reviewing the fair on its front page, the *Herald* predicted that his telegraph would prove "the great invention of the age," and expressed pleasure in hearing that Congress might underwrite a large-scale test of it.

Morse gained sensational publicity, most of it unwelcome, in teaming up with twenty-eight-year-old Samuel Colt (1814–1862). Colt had received a patent for his famed revolver, the first multi-shot firearm. But he was struggling financially and personally, his gun company having gone bankrupt and his brother, convicted of murder, having committed suicide. He and Morse met at New York University, where Colt had a laboratory sponsored by the Navy Department. Colt experimented there with methods of detonating gunpowder underwater by electricity, in effect creating an arsenal of undersea mines to destroy enemy ships and defend American harbors. What interested Morse were Colt's attempts to transmit electrical currents through water—a difficulty that had to be overcome if the telegraph was to work across the nation's rivers. They shared wire and other equipment and commiserated on problems of getting financial support.

In October, Morse joined Colt for a two-day demonstration off Castle Garden, in New York harbor. From a galvanic battery on the U.S. brig *Washington*, Colt lay underwater cable to a ship aptly named the *Volta*—stripped but mined, one of its masts topped by the effigy of a man. Before a crowd estimated at 40,000—including the Secretary of War and Commodore Perry—he blasted the ship into the air, enveloping the sinking wreck in a thunderous cloud of mist: "Bang! bang! bang!" as the *Herald* described it, "combusti-blowup eruption! . . . 1,756,901 pieces."

The same day, Morse gave a private demonstration of his telegraph for the Nautical Committee of the American Institute. He tried to send a message underwater from the tip of Manhattan to Governors Island, a distance of about a mile, using copper cabling insulated with tarred thread. His battery proved too weak, however, so that he had to exchange it for Colt's large battery—"neither entire failure," the *Herald* remarked, "nor entire success."

Morse's public demonstration the next day, however, left no doubt. The *Herald* promised a major event, bound to convince those who questioned the power of Morse's telegraph: "All such may now have an opportunity of fairly testing it. *It is destined to work a complete revolution in the mode of transmitting intelligence throughout the civilized world.*" A crowd gathered at the Battery to watch Morse send a message electrically through a mile of water. He got off several characters, but without warning the transmission went dead. A merchantman had been getting underway, and its anchor fouled the submerged cable. As Morse looked on, the ship's crew hauled in two hundred feet of his carefully insulated copper wire and severed it. The crowd at the Battery scattered—with jeers, by one account. Humiliated by his abrupt and complete failure in public, Morse was unable to sleep.

Morse's new campaign to influence Congress brought other discouragements. He had hoped to personally exhibit his system in Washington, but learned that the House was in bad humor. By midsummer he stopped hearing from the lobbyist Isaac Coffin. He supposed that Coffin had rejected the partners' offered terms, and had abandoned the idea of representing him: "Well so be it." He felt deserted by his partners, too. During the year several entrepreneurs proposed plans to him for raising private capital to build a telegraph line. But his partners squandered the opportunities in slow, endless consultation by mail—Maine, New York, Philadelphia, New Orleans— and by their unwillingness to meet with him in New York. "I find myself without sympathy or help from any who are associated with me," he complained to Smith. One time when Smith came to New York to advise on some legal matters, he promised to call on Morse but did not. Nor did he say where he was staying, leaving Morse to search at several hotels without finding him. Ahead, Morse saw only more delay, "another year of anxious suspense."

The worst of it was that his partners contributed no money to the enterprise. While he spent his every last cent perfecting the system, often unable to pay everyday expenses, they claimed to be suffering from the long economic depression. Alfred Vail spoke of being "awfully poverty stricken"; his brother George pleaded that "my means are nothing at the present time." Morse told Smith that without some financial assistance from someone, he would be compelled to return to painting, "and if I get once engaged in my proper profession again, the Telegraph and its proprietors will urge me from it in vain."

A turning point for Morse came through the efforts of a New York City congressman, Charles Ferris, a member of the Committee on Commerce. To him had been referred the resolution introduced in the House by William Boardman of Connecticut, calling on the Committee to explore the possible usefulness to the country of communication by electromagnetic telegraphs. Ferris was excited about Morse's invention and eager for the government to back it. When they spoke in New York, he asked Morse for an account of the system to use in winning over the Commerce Committee. He apparently also suggested that Morse support his efforts by demonstrating the telegraph in Washington.

Morse did both. He wrote a detailed history of his work on the invention from the time he first petitioned Congress, five years earlier. In eight printed pages he summarized his recent improvements of the telegraph, made clear its difference from Wheatstone's and Steinheil's needle versions, and carefully itemized the cost of erecting a line— about $400 per mile if strung on spars, $600 if enclosed underground in tubes. He also computed the revenue the government might expect from operating only a single circuit from New York to New Orleans: annual gross receipts of $300,000.

Morse journeyed to Washington early in December, putting up at a Missouri Avenue boarding house. How he financed the trip is unknown, perhaps by borrowing from Sidney. No help came from his partners. As a former congressman, F. O. J. Smith might have been especially useful; he promised to show up but did not. Vail did not come either; obtaining the necessary funds, he said, was "out of my power." But Morse found Ferris, Boardman, and several other congressmen working energetically on his behalf, as well as his Yale chum, Commissioner Henry Ellsworth. However grown used to failure, he felt hopeful.

The enthusiastic response to Morse's demonstrations justified his hope. With Alfred Vail unable to assist, he had brought along a colleague from the University, James Cogswell Fisher, Leonard Gale's replacement as Professor of Chemistry. Over a few weeks they set up and performed three related tests. Stretching a wire circuit between the rooms of the House Committee on Commerce and the Senate Committee on Naval Affairs, they sent and received messages for any who cared to see and hear. They also showed that two or more currents could be made to pass at the same time on the same wire—a discovery they had made shortly before leaving New York, hinting at the possibility of multiplex telegraphy. And they successfully demonstrated submarine transmission. According to Morse, during a sleepless night following his mortifying failure in New York harbor, he devised a new method of crossing water. Fisher assisting, he tried it out on Washington's Susquehanna River Canal. He immersed a pair of large copper plates on one bank, facing a similar pair immersed on the opposite bank, and successfully used the water itself to conduct the electrical current.

Morse believed that everyone who saw the tests admired them, a judgment confirmed by rave reviews in the Washington press. "This invention has truly been placed among the greatest of this or any other age," the *National Intelligencer* commented. "The mind is scarcely prepared to pursue even in speculation the mighty results which are soon to follow its practical demonstration."

On December 30, in the wake of Morse's demonstrations, Charles Ferris submitted to Congress a five-page recommendation on behalf of the Committee on Commerce. It praised Morse's telegraph as "decidedly superior to any other now in use." Developing his system would lay no burden on the people, for the revenue to be derived from it would far outrun the building costs. Equally at stake were fairness to Morse and national pride:

> Your committee are of opinion that it is but justice to Professor Morse, who is alike distinguished for his attainments in science and excellence in the arts of design, and who has patiently devoted many years of unremitting study, and freely spent his private fortune, in inventing and bringing to perfection a system of telegraphs which is calculated to advance the scientific reputation of the country, and to be eminently useful, both to the Government and the people, that he should be furnished with the means of competing with his European rivals.

Ferris bolstered the Committee's case by including the impressive endorsements Morse had received from Joseph Henry, the American Institute, and Alphonse Foy, administrator of the French telegraph system. The report closed with the language of the appropriation bill itself, calling for a grant of $30,000 to Morse so that he might "*test the Practicability of establishing a System of Electro-Magnetic Telegraphs by the United States.*"

Morse took a deep breath. "I am told from all quarters that there is but one sentiment in Congress," he said, "and that the appropriation will unquestionably pass."

TEN

Hurrah Boys Whip Up the Mules

(1843–1844)

JANUARY and February 1843 were the most anxious months Morse had ever experienced. Staying on in Washington, he awaited the fate of his bill as it went through Congress, "painful and trying to me," he said, "but there is no help for it but patience." Every day, tantalizing gossip reached him from the Capitol: his bill might be moved as an amendment to a military bill; might be referred to a committee of the whole; might be opposed by some members from Maine. He asked Sidney to get notices placed in the New York *Journal of Commerce* and *Evening Post,* saying that the American press and public supported the appropriation: "it will be read here and produce an effect." Prodded or not, the representatives felt obliged to "*define their position*" by idle speechifying, so the House moved with agonizing slowness.

Morse tried to talk himself into the right mood, not pessimistic yet prepared for the worst—although the worst, if it came, would be "disastrous in the extreme." Deeply as he wished to trust in Providence, he found it difficult, "easier to say 'Thy will be done' than at all times to feel it." And his long stay in the city had used up everything he had. Nearly his every last cent was in his pocket. He steadied himself by thinking that his hard work could not have gone for nothing, that he could not have been brought to Washington, at the urging of congressmen and others in government, merely to be deluded. But he often felt oppressed and headachy, "still *waiting, waiting.*"

The suspense eased a little on February 21, when the appropriation bill at last came up for vote in the House. Twenty years earlier,

Morse had impressively painted the House chamber as a symbol of republican ideals. But the day's proceedings had less the spirit of Washington and Lafayette than of Punch and Judy. Cave Johnson, a congressman from Tennessee, rose to say that since Congress had done much to encourage science, he did not wish to neglect the science of Mesmerism. He therefore proposed an amendment to the bill: half the $30,000 should be given to a mesmerist, enabling him as well as Morse to experiment. As reported in the *Congressional Globe,*

> Mr. [Edward] Stanly said he should have no objection to the appropriation for mesmeric experiments, provided the gentleman from Tennessee was the subject. [A laugh.]
>
> Mr. Cave Johnson said he should have no objection provided the gentleman from North Carolina [Mr. Stanly] was the operator. [Great laughter.]

A more sober congressman objected that the amendment demeaned the character of the House, and asked the chair to rule it out of order. The chair refused, rousing more laughter by quipping that only scientific analysis could show the analogy between the electromagnetic telegraph and the "magnetism of mesmerism."

Two days later the appropriation bill passed, barely. Aided by a Whig majority in the House that favored internal improvements, it squeaked through by 89 votes to 83. Morse put the best face on it— "six votes are as good as a thousand"—but he had undergone an ordeal: "I can truly say that I have never passed so trying a period." And the vote in the Senate remained. There, with only eight days of the session remaining, and six inches of snow on the ground, the bill faced a crowded legislative calendar that included conflicting U.S. and British claims to the huge Oregon Territory.

On March 3, the final day of the session, Morse's appropriation passed the Senate unopposed and was signed by President John Tyler. His two months of faith and patience had paid off, especially his faith. Often verbose and self-dramatizing, he summed up his reaction in two words: "Laus Deo."

Morse leaped in to begin work on his experimental line, the first feat of electrical engineering attempted in the United States. He hoped to finish in about eight months, in time for the opening of the next session of Congress, in December. He decided to run the line between Washington and Baltimore, a distance of about forty-four miles, installing it alongside the route of the Baltimore & Ohio Railroad. Having in mind often-expressed opinions that exposed wires invited vandalism, he chose to inter the circuits in a trench two and a half feet deep. He had considered simply insulating the wires, winding them in rope, and binding the bundle in asphalt. Now, however, he decided to string the wires out in tubes made of lead for cheapness and durability.

Once Morse got the appropriation, including annual salaries for a staff, his partners returned happily, even greedily. He assigned each a particular task. For a salary of $1000, Vail would make and help operate the instruments. Gale, returned from New Orleans, would receive $1500 and oversee the pipe—inspecting the metal for defects, checking the soldering joints, testing the effects of the soil on the lead. Smith would handle the legal work. He would draw no salary, but profit by contracting for the tubing and trenching, besides his one-quarter share in hoped-for profits from the patent. Morse also invited his Washington assistant James Fisher to join the team, for $1500, to superintend the preparation of the wire from its manufacture to its placement in the tubes. Morse as overall superintendent would receive $2000—more money than he had seen in years.

The superintendence burdened Morse with endless paperwork. The appropriation required him to submit to the Secretary of the Treasury a detailed monthly account of expenses, and keep all vouchers in duplicate (more than eight hundred, it turned out). He had to register weekly salaries for lab assistants, brass and iron workers, varnishers, solderers, a battery man, assorted mechanicians and laborers. He also had to account for elephantine quantities of material: 160 miles of No. 16 copper wire, weighing five tons; 25 dozen glazed stone cups to hold mercury for the batteries; 200-pound bales of twine; 70,500 yards of lead pipe—not to mention screws, stationery, and other incidentals. Morse meticulously documented every payment and purchase, well served by having earlier submitted to his father penny-for-penny accounts of his school expenses. The drudgery of bookkeeping was perhaps offset by pleasure in sporting a new title. He now routinely signed himself "Superintendent of the Electromagnetic Telegraph."

Morse planned to begin the trenching no later than October 1, hoping to proceed at the rate of two and a half to three miles a day. Before that, contractors had to manufacture the insulated wire circuits and lead tubing. The production of the circuits went smoothly, except for minor delays owing to an imperfect batch of solder or weak vinegar. By late July, Morse had 160 miles of wire, insulated by windings of colored cotton thread and two coats of varnish. He decided to test it, once more taking on the old problem of the action of galvanic electricity through long wires. Twenty years earlier, the English electrician Peter Barlow had made experiments which showed that the current along a wire diminishes approximately as the square root of its distance from the battery. He concluded that a long-distance telegraph was theoretically impossible. Morse believed, however, that his still-under-wraps relay system overcame the problem.

Early in August, Morse invited several prominent scientists to witness an experiment in long-distance telegraphy, at a ropewalk on the outskirts of New York City. He used a so-called Grove battery, recently invented, consisting of a hundred cells of nitric acid, one pair of its plates being made of platinum. By far the strongest battery available, it sent Morse's current effectually through all 160 miles of wire, even when he reduced the number of cells by half. The wire came in two-mile units on eighty spools. In a further experiment, Morse joined the units to make not a single 160-mile circuit, but several circuits of different lengths. He used them to test and compare the lifting power of a magnet and the falling off in current at various distances from the battery.

Morse wrote up his experiments for Benjamin Silliman's *American Journal of Science*—his one substantial piece of published research, and a bid for scientific respectability. Professor John Draper, his former partner in daguerreotyping, appended a mathematical analysis of the results. They illustrated, Draper wrote, "the law of the conducting power of wires": as the length of the wire increased, the diminution in electrical effect decreased and at a certain point became insignificant. Thus if Morse's telegraph could operate over 160 miles, it could also transmit over far greater distances: "It is . . . possible to conceive a wire to be a million times as long as another, and yet the two shall transmit quantities of electricity not perceptibly different."

In reporting his long-distance experiments to the Secretary of the

Treasury, Morse invoked Draper's "law" to prophesy the future. He had become fond of making such predictions, and in this case, as he would often point out, he was not mistaken: "a Telegraphic communication on my plan may with certainty be established across the Atlantic! Startling as this may seem now, the time will come when this project will be realised."

While the insulated wire worked nicely, serious problems developed with the lead tubing. F. O. J. Smith had contracted for its manufacture with a young New Yorker named James Serrell. In Serrell's patented process, lead was first cast into eighteen-inch ingots, through which ran a lengthwise hole. The ingots were threaded on a mandril (a cylindrical rod) and passed between rollers that pressed the lead around the mandril, shaping it into half-inch tubes. But in August, with the wire insulated and ready to be inserted in the tubing, Serrell failed to deliver—"not *one foot*," Morse moaned. Serrell explained that an unusual rainstorm had flooded the basement in which he manufactured his pipe. To Morse, however, the problem seemed to be that the young man lacked drive, "a yankee contriving go ahead management." A few weeks later, Serrell reported that he was halted again, this time by damage to the furnace that powered his steam engine. In the end he admitted that he could produce no more than ten of the forty miles of pipe that Morse required.

Badly set back in his schedule, Morse had Smith hire a different manufacturer for the remaining thirty or so miles. Smith contracted with Benjamin Tatham & Company, which agreed to deliver all of the tubing, in three installments, before November 20. Morse had planned to demonstrate his Baltimore-Washington line when Congress convened in December. Tatham's delivery date would at least allow him to demonstrate it before Congress closed, at the beginning of March—though the timing would be close and meant working into the early winter. He got Tatham to use a hollow mandril that he and James Fisher had invented. The insulated wires could be laid in the mandril beforehand and inserted into the tubes at the moment they were shaped from the lead ingots. Morse appointed Fisher to inspect the results at Tatham's New York manufactory, using an air pump to make sure the tubing was free of leaks and cracks before shipment by schooner to Baltimore.

To get things moving, Morse decided to put down the existing ten miles of pipe. The trenching—the last of the three major steps in constructing the line—gave no less trouble than the manufacture of the tubing. To excavate the forty-mile-long trench, Smith contracted with a New Yorker named Levi S. Bartlett, who happened to be his wife's brother. Morse objected, not because of the nepotism but because Bartlett's rate of $153 per mile exceeded the estimate he had given the government. He had stayed painstakingly within his budget. He hoped to produce the Baltimore-Washington line for the government and the country as cheaply as possible. What most threatened the future of his telegraph, he believed, was that it might be seen as an extravagance.

Smith took offense, but arranged for his brother-in-law to subcontract the trenching to a different excavator, Ezra Cornell (1807–1874). Born to a Quaker family in Westchester, New York, but now settled upstate in Ithaca, Cornell had had a rural upbringing and little education. Like Morse, he had scrambled for a living—in his case for a wife and nine children. Off and on he had worked as a potter, carpenter, sheep raiser, machinist, millwright, and real estate speculator. Having recently bought the rights to a new sort of plow, he traveled the country to market it, sometimes doing forty miles a day on foot. In Portland, Maine, he met F. O. J. Smith, who persuaded him to design a machine for laying pipe underground. Cornell saw Morse's telegraph enterprise as his financial salvation. If the new line worked, lines would be laid all over the country, and his trenching machine would be worth a fortune.

Morse went to Portland for a few days to inspect Cornell's machine, liked it, and authorized its use. In essence the machine was a combination plow and cart, drawn by a team of eight mules. The plowshare, rather like a hatchet blade, cut a deep narrow slit in the earth. Atop the cart stood a large drum wound with lead pipe containing the wire circuits. As the plow advanced, tubing was at the same time fed behind it into the just-dug trench. The narrow furrow collapsed into itself, covering the tube with earth. Almost simultaneously, the machine cut the trench, laid the pipe, and buried it.

The trenching got under way at eight o'clock on the morning of October 21, three weeks behind Morse's schedule. Working from Baltimore toward Washington, Cornell began laying the ten miles of Serrell pipe from a hill on which stood the depot of the Baltimore & Ohio Railroad. Because of the city terrain, he and his men had to entrench the first two thousand feet by hand. Once outside the depot area, early in November, Cornell set to work with his machine. He discovered that while the mule team could lay from half a mile to one mile a day, the plumbers who soldered together the drum-length sections could join no more than a quarter of a mile. As a result, the two crews worked out of step, the time lag increasing day by day. Morse applied to Washington for permission to hire extra solderers. But to his grief, the new pipe manufacturer, Tatham & Company, announced that they were running late and could not produce the rest of the tubing before early December.

Existing documents leave the sequence of events during the first few weeks in December unclear. By then Cornell had laid the Serrell pipe from the Baltimore depot to a point about ten miles outside the city. But Morse's troubles were piling up, money running out, winter coming on. "I shall need driving able faithful men," he lamented, "men capable of bearing the cold weather if it should so happen." This excluded Leonard Gale, who fell ill; too thin and weak to work outdoors, he resigned. Worse, a section of the entrenched Serrell pipe was found, ominously, to contain water.

Much worse, when the new pipe from Tatham & Company arrived, the insulated circuits inside turned out to be severely damaged. Unlike Serrell, Tatham had shaped the lead tubes from hot rather than cold ingots. The heat had in many places charred the varnished cotton that insulated the wire. Morse blamed Fisher, having carefully instructed him to visit Tatham's New York manufactory to examine the tubing and test the wires before they were shipped. Believing that Fisher had simply neglected to do so, Morse discharged him—reluctantly, since he felt grateful to Fisher for his help in Washington the year before.

Sometime in early December, Morse suspended the trenching in order to study his deteriorating situation. Thirty years later, Ezra Cornell recalled that Morse took him aside and confided that he did not want the newspapers to know that work had been deliberately stopped; he needed an excuse. Cornell said he could manage that. Stepping back to his machine he called out "hurrah boys whip up the mules." His teamsters cracked their whips. As the mules started off, Cornell grasped the handles of the trenching machine and intentionally steered it into a rock, breaking it. Cornell's recollections are often unreliable, and Morse may have given out a milder explanation of the stoppage. The Baltimore *Patriot* reported that having laid his circuit ten miles, Morse was now "making a trial in order to ascertain its capacities before going further."

During the time-out Morse seems to have weighed several possibilities. He might withdraw the defective wire from the Tatham tubes and revarnish it. Or lay down a short line in Washington between the Patent Office and the Capitol, to have at least something to show. Or try putting the conductors above ground. His friend Ellsworth advised him against making major changes, which might weaken public and government confidence in the telegraph. With cold weather setting in Morse resigned himself to storing his materials and halting work until the spring. "I have difficulties and trouble in my work," he told Sidney, "but none of a nature as yet to discourage."

Discouragement was not far off, however, plenty of it. Work on the line no sooner stopped than Morse got into a heated quarrel with Professor James Fisher. Fisher resented having been summarily fired "without a hearing, without any examination of the facts." In fact, he said, he did test the wire in the pipe from Tatham & Company, but had been given a weak battery that did not reveal its defects. Condemning Morse's "imperious manner," he not unreasonably reminded him of his labors in Washington to secure the appropriation. At a time when Morse's partners had deserted the venture, he had left his family and borrowed money to get to the capital: "you were willing to avail yourself of my assistance to obtain that which you wished & then to whistle me off as of no further use."

Though fond of Fisher, Morse did not take well to what he regarded as insolence from a subordinate. He got off a high-toned reply sternly charging Fisher with "*unfaithfulness to your trust.*" Opinion in Washington was that Fisher had done more harm than good, "that where you gained one friend for the telegraph you made two enemies." Fisher slashed back, demanding that Morse pay him $55 for his board in Washington the previous winter, at the home of a Reverend Rich. Morse checked with the minister and learned that Fisher had been a welcome guest, at no charge. He refused to pay. Fisher demanded the money again, this time adding interest as a late penalty:

"I wish you . . . no longer to trifle with me." To convince Morse that he meant to be taken seriously, he threatened to show their correspondence to "leading scientific gentlemen" and to publish part of it.

At the same time, Morse began squabbling with F. O. J. Smith. Although about fifteen years younger than Morse, the ex-congressman was far shrewder. From his marriage into the wealthy Bartlett family—whose members included a signer of the Declaration of Independence and a governor of New Hampshire—and from his own questionable bank deals and land speculation, he had built a mansion on thirty-four acres near Portland, crowned by a dome of colored glass. He passed through the city's streets in a fine carriage driven by a black coachman and drawn by expensive blood grays. His political foes had often accused him of double-dealing and chicanery. One dubbed him "F. O. J. Smith, L.S.C."—Liar, Scoundrel, and Coward.

Morse discovered that Francis Ormond Jonathan Smith knew something about wheeling and dealing. In arranging contracts for the tubing and trenching, Smith had seen a chance to make some fast cash at government expense. He had bargained for an advantageous rate with Tatham & Company, a savings in Morse's cost estimate of about a thousand dollars. He proposed to Morse that they split the money—"all perfectly fair," he said. Morse was less certain, and after consulting Sidney he said no. Smith pocketed $500, while Morse credited the rest to the government as so much saved from the appropriation.

On another bit of financial legerdemain, Smith tried to cut in his brother-in-law, Levi Bartlett. Clearly with Smith's connivance—probably at his urging—Bartlett protested that the work stoppage violated his contract. The trenching, he said, had been halted after ten miles not through any fault of his or of his subcontractor, Cornell, but because of damage to the lead pipes. He therefore insisted on being paid in full for trenching the entire forty miles, some $4600. Smith wrote out a letter to the Secretary of the Treasury for Morse to sign. Morse would say that he had vouchers for all of Bartlett's work, and in effect ask the government to pay him the full amount.

Morse's scrupulous sense of personal honor gasped at the crude scheming. Smith asked him, he said, for "a sacrifice of what to me is dearer than life." Nothing if not brazen, Smith in response took the high moral ground. He grandly accused Morse of casting "undeserved reproach" on his motives: "I fear not the strictest scrutiny. I have done nothing secretly." In reality it was Morse who had a "*secret* purpose," he charged, namely, to evade the Bartlett contract altogether, as if it had never existed. Smith prepared a substitute letter for Morse's signature, asking the Secretary of the Treasury merely to pay Bartlett proper damages.

Morse had been inclined to do something like that. But in Smith's offensive tone of injured innocence he detected a clawing opportunist who held in contempt his own ideal of public service. He told Smith he had read his reply with "much surprize," unable to reconcile it with "the professions of regard you have so often expressed towards me." He would tell the Secretary no more than how much of the trenching had been completed, and how much money paid out for it; the Secretary could decide whether to award damages to Bartlett. Not to be denied, Smith personally took his case to the Secretary, complaining about Morse's superintendence. As it happened, the Secretary had no authority to investigate the merits of Bartlett-Smith's case or to entertain any claims for damages. Smith denounced him as a "knave at heart" and asked Morse to join in an appeal to the President.

Morse declined, but as the new year approached he again began to feel desperate. "I was never so tried," he wrote to Sidney from Washington. "Troubles cluster in such various shapes, that I am almost overwhelmed." He had come to realize that he was locked in partnership with a slick-tongued finagler, a bully on the make: "where I expected to find a *friend* I find a FIEND." It appalled him that he had nearly fallen for Smith's attempt to skim government money from the Tatham contract. And now, for having repulsed his shabby trickery, Smith was hounding him: "because I refused to accede to terms which, as a public officer, I could not do without dishonor and violation of trust, he pursues me thus malignantly." The recognition that he now had a hell-raising enemy made prospects for the Baltimore-Washington line look dark, "but I know," he said, "who can bring light out of darkness, and in Him I trust."

While uneasily waiting to resume work in the spring, Morse spent most of the winter in Washington. He put up at the house of Henry Ellsworth, who allowed him to store the telegraph apparatus and materials in the basement of the Patent Office. Alfred Vail and Ezra Cornell remained in the capital too, busy but discontented.

Vail roomed near the Patent Office, indulging before breakfast his mineralogy hobby, collecting petrified hickory from nearby streams and railroad beds. Mostly he spent the interlude studying Michael Faraday's *Experimental Researches*, laboring as always to improve the components of Morse's ever-more-demanding system. While working on the line he had invented many perhaps useful devices, such as a machine for winding magnets in fine, silk-covered copper wire. Skilled in mechanical drawing, he set down detailed illustrations of them in his lab books. But he still griped that his salary was inadequate and confided to his wife that Morse's management was inefficient and indecisive: "I should not at all wonder if the appropriation is exhausted before we are able to do a thing, such is his manner of proceeding." He stayed cheerful and lost no sleep, he said, but he also thought of quitting.

Cornell too read up on electricity, in books he withdrew from the Library of Congress. Mostly he looked after the mules, enthusiastic about being part of the government project—and grateful. He saw a real chance of improving the hand-to-mouth existence of his much-loved family by getting a permanent place with Morse, who had put him on the payroll as a full-time "Assistant" to replace Fisher. Just the same, in debt and patching his work pants he considered peddling his pipe-laying machine in Washington and grumbled that he was treated unfairly: "I do more work myself than the other men that Professor Morse has attached to the Telegraph put together and one of them at least [i.e., Vail] receives as much pay as I do."

During the break, relations between Smith and Morse grew so tense that they could no longer speak to each other without wrangling. Morse's first mistake had been to involve himself with the conniving Smith. His second was to rile him, for Smith was rabid about settling scores. It seems certain that it was Smith who prodded Tatham & Company to now demand full payment for their lead tubes, as Bartlett had for his trenching. Tatham claimed (not unreasonably) that the charring of the wires inside was the result of the hollow mandril devised and supplied to them by Morse and Fisher. Smith backed up the Company in a letter to the Secretary of the Treasury, attributing the damage to "the error in Professor Morse's whole theory of laying his wires."

Smith also took sides against Morse with the dismissed Fisher—unjustly accused of negligence, he said, when the real fault was

Morse's "supposed knowledge of electric current." He stirred up further trouble by protesting Vail's receipt of a government salary, on the ground that Vail's agreement with the other proprietors of the patent required him to give his personal services without pay. Aware of friction between Vail and Cornell regarding which "Assistant" had the higher authority, Smith played on it by advising Cornell to badmouth Vail to Morse: "I would just take Professor Morse aside, & tell him in plain terms how utterly worthless Vail is in all the practical matters of constructing the work." Needling Morse more directly, he asked reimbursement now for postage, cabs, and other alleged expenses during his legal service in England and France six years earlier.

Morse still hoped to settle their differences amicably. For all his intelligence and imagination, he was easily flustered by worldly men, fearful that they might undo his prestige and his financial independence. And he had yet to fathom Smith, whom an adversary described as "one of the most heartless and vindictive villains that ever trod in shoe leather." To inject real torment into the petty feuding, Smith joined Charles Jackson and François Gouraud in branding Morse an intellectual thief. Morse's inventions, Smith told him, were shams, "pieces of deception & humbuggery" filched from Steinheil and others. "The day of exposure in this matter is fast approaching," he threatened. "You have driven me by the interest of self protection & self defence to hasten it." He reportedly began knocking Morse's telegraph to others, calling it "not such a great affair"; "it will be superseded by other plans." In his reckless rage, Smith apparently did not care that his threats to destroy Morse recoiled on himself, that as one of the proprietors of Morse's patent he stood to lose if the telegraph failed. "He seems bent on his own ruin," Vail said.

Morse replied to the bullying with a dozen dignified letters, lecturing Smith on every issue between them in a controlled, unperturbed tone. But his wounds showed. Waiting out the winter at Ellsworth's house he sometimes went sleepless, and became bedridden with a bad cold. To Vail he seemed more than usually overbearing and irritable, making a "great fury" if one of his crew was absent even when there was nothing to do. Morse understood that Smith's assaults had shaken him. "I am fully aware that of late I have evinced an unusual sensitiveness," he told Ellsworth. "My temperament, naturally sensitive, has lately been made more so by the combination of attacks from deceitful associates without and bodily illness within."

Morse also understood that his difficulties in constructing the line had inspired criticism and unfavorable publicity. To counter it he placed a notice in the *Journal of Commerce:*

> In an enterprise so entirely new, it can hardly be expected that every part can be conducted with that precision and perfectness which is gained only by experience. Unforeseen difficulties will be encountered and are to be overcome, and delays will of course be incurred. There are no intrinsic ones as yet of a nature to shake the confidence of the most sanguine in the final triumph of the enterprise.

Morse meant to reassure the public, but his statement was no mere cover-up. Every new technology encounters unforeseen problems and undergoes a process of refinement. Quite as Morse said, his work on the line had been a hands-on education that by exposing defects and raising unfamiliar questions produced practical understanding. The confidence he expressed in "the final triumph of the enterprise" was also no twaddle. He, Vail, and Cornell had an almost impersonal faith in the possibilities of the telegraph that transcended failures, setbacks, and bickering, a zeal beyond ambition and desire to see it succeed.

In mid-March, Morse and his crew set to work again on building the Baltimore-Washington line. His experience during the fall with punctured tubes and burnt insulation had left him skeptical of interring the circuit. In addition, Leonard Gale warned that acid in the soil would corrode the pipes, and Joseph Henry said he believed that contact between the wires inside would cause a short circuit. Morse decided to experiment with the alternate method he had described to Congress six years ago, when first requesting an appropriation— stretching his conductors in the air on poles.

Proceeding this time from Washington toward Baltimore, Ezra Cornell headed a work gang of more than twenty-five men to bore auger holes in the earth and set up the posts. These were mainly rough-hewn chestnut trees, barks left on, cut to a height of 30 feet, planted to a depth of 4 feet, about 200 feet apart. Two wires ran on from post to post, attached to cross arms. The fastening of the wires presented a critical problem in insulation. Morse adopted Cornell's idea of wrapping them at the point of contact in shellac-saturated cloth. The packet was sandwiched between two plates of glass, kept in place by a wooden cover nailed to the post.

By the last week in March, Cornell's gang had put up some seven miles of timber—distance enough for trials to determine whether to extend the line all the way to Baltimore. The short-range tests were successful, and early in April construction began in earnest. Cornell toiled from six in the morning to six at night, sometimes in rain and wind, shuttling back and forth between Washington and Baltimore on the railroad cars, in which some of his men also ate and slept. Morse remained mostly in two rooms assigned him in the Capitol building, where a transmitter and receiver had been set up.

Each day, as the line of poles marched eastward, Morse tested the ever longer circuit for several hours. He telegraphed back and forth with Vail or Cornell at the other end in some town or village ever closer to Baltimore—Bladensburg, Beltsville, White Oak Bottom:

> [April 27] . . . day rainy and cold wind N. E. 60 pairs, nitric acid twice used. Mr. Vail at Bladensburg. Much perplexed in the morning to arrange connections, but about 30 minutes past 10 found all right. Corresponded till 12 then disconnected and tried long circuit to the Junction 22 miles, had slight indications for a few moments, when all action ceased . . . Either the rain affects it, the battery is too weak, or there is defective connection somewhere in the line.

Experiments continued, for instance with using the earth itself as part of the conducting circuit. And in fine-tuning the line, adjustments were continually made in batteries, magnets, and other apparatus. Yet construction of the overhead line went briskly, better than a mile a day. Worries persisted that someone might maliciously damage the exposed wire. No one did, although at least once the wire broke at a faulty joint. "Professor Morse is on tiptoe," Vail observed.

On May 1, Morse staged a dramatic stunt that gave the public a peek at what was to come. The Whig national convention was meeting in Baltimore to choose candidates for President and Vice President. Morse stationed Vail at Annapolis Junction, a train stop some twenty-two miles from Washington. There Vail would intercept the results of the balloting as they were being forwarded to Washington by railroad. Vail would then telegraph the results to him, so that the much-awaited news would reach the capital an hour and a quarter before arriving by train. Vail reported by wire that the Whig delegates had nominated Henry Clay for President and Theodore Frelinghuysen for Vice President. As the news spread through the capital, Morse found himself "over run" with visitors. Some asked him to have Vail transmit their names, which they could say had been written down in Washington by someone at Annapolis Junction.

As the line neared Baltimore over the next three weeks, Morse arranged other means of "exciting wonder." He again had Vail intercept the train, this time to send on to Washington items from New York or Philadelphia newspapers, and short sentences by the passengers. Messages flew back and forth, Morse beamed, "with the rapidity almost of common conversation." While sending the messages, he and Vail tried to improve their transmission of the still unfamiliar code. "Separate your *words* a little more," Morse instructed him in one case. "Strike your *dots firmer,* and do not separate the two dots of the *O* so far apart. Condense your language more; leave out '*the*' when ever you can, and when h follow t, separate them so that they shall not be 8."

As public curiosity and excitement swelled, Morse's mood, never very stable, fluctuated wildly. "He changes oftener than the wind," Vail complained. "Now he is elated up to the skies, then he is down in the mud." Vail said he had his hands full trying to keep his employer from becoming ill: "Professor Morse is a complete granny." Some of Morse's downswings may have been brought on by F. O. J. Smith. He kept pressing Morse to persuade the Secretary of the Treasury to settle with him and his brother-in-law for the unfinished trenching, even though the Secretary had made it clear that he lacked authority to do so. Morse scoffed at Smith's demand as a "hallucination." But Smith had bought a half interest in Cornell's pipe-laying machine, and now was also miffed by Morse's decision to string the wire on posts. He chafed like "a wild boar," Morse said, determined to be "as ugly as he can."

During the last week of construction, Morse petitioned the mayor of Baltimore for the right to plant twenty-five or thirty posts within city

Register used in the Baltimore-Washington trials
(Smithsonian Institution)

limits. The system now nearly in place differed beyond recognition from the printer's composing stick and crude frame-stretcher that Morse had cobbled together a dozen years earlier. Vail had reinvented the cumbrous port-rule, replacing it with the simple classic telegraph key that opened and closed the circuit, sending a sequence of dots and dashes. After much experiment, Morse or Vail or both together

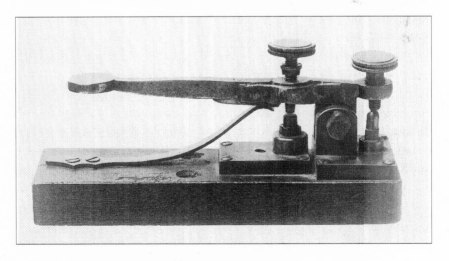

Telegraph key of the 1840s
(Smithsonian Institution)

had also transformed the unwieldy register into a compact clockwork machine that embossed incoming signals on a paper tape.

Morse powered his instruments by a bulky Grove battery, eighty cups of nitric acid. The use of an overhead line allowed him to at last introduce his relays. He also installed his so-called receiving magnets. Kept hidden from the general public until now, these relay-like devices actuated registers at local telegraph stations along the main line. According to Cornell, the receiving magnets weighed 150 pounds and were housed in yard-long boxes about two feet wide and eight inches deep. Renewing the current, passing it along, and switching in intermediate circuits, Morse's relay system promised future networks of enormous versatility and range.

Morse's Washington-to-Baltimore telegraph line officially opened on May 24, 1844. For the inaugural transmission Vail brought his apparatus to the so-called upper depot in Baltimore, about a mile outside the city. Morse set up his instruments in the chamber of the United States Supreme Court.

Morse invited Annie Ellsworth, the commissioner's daughter, to compose the first message. He spoke of her as "my dear young friend" and was rumored to be romantically interested. But the invitation, he explained, was a form of thanks. When Congress passed the appropriation bill, it was Annie who brought him the news. In thinking up an appropriate message she consulted her mother, who suggested the exclamation of the prophetic Balaam in Numbers 23:23: "What hath God wrought!"

Unfortunately, no graphic account of what transpired in the Supreme Court chamber survives. Morse tapped the message to Vail in Baltimore, who tapped it back to him. Next morning, Vail removed his apparatus to the railroad warehouse in the lower depot, within city limits. Morse again transmitted the same biblical text. He kept the line open for several hours, allowing the perhaps two dozen spectators in Washington and Baltimore to exchange names and send compliments to each other.

The now-famous transmission on May 24 attracted little more attention in the press than an item Morse himself wrote for the *Observer*, headed "The Electric Telegraph Triumphant." The acclaim began three days later, as the Democratic convention convened at Baltimore's Odd Fellows' Hall, the city's largest auditorium. Because of intense interest in the proceedings, the place was jam-packed. Delegates strenuously contested the nominations for president, one major issue being the annexation of Texas and what it would mean for the controversial extension of slavery. With the nomination deadlocked between Martin Van Buren and Lewis Cass, the convention picked the first presidential dark horse candidate, James K. Polk.

Morse generated enormous publicity by having Vail telegraph news of the raucous proceedings to Washington. Mobbed by people eager to watch the transmission, Vail had to keep the door locked so as to admit only fifteen or twenty spectators at a time. "Hundreds begged and pleaded to be allowed mearly to look at the instrument," he told Morse. "They declared they would not say a word or stir and didn't care whether they understood or not, only they wanted to say they had seen it." At the same time, Morse in Washington found himself surrounded by politicians eager for results of the balloting. A Washington correspondent of the New York *Herald* reported that "little else is done here but watch Professor Morse's Bulletin from Baltimore, to learn the progress of doings at Convention."

Those seeking up-to-the-minute news of the convention were not disappointed. Vail's dispatches to Morse, recorded in his detailed transcript of them, included the choice of Polk on the ninth ballot, and the rush of state delegations to change their vote in order to demonstrate loyalty to the party's compromise choice:

V[ail] Mr. Brewster of Pa is speaking in favour of Buchanan
M[orse] yes. . . .
V Mr Brewster says his delegation go for VB but if VB's friends desert them, the Delegation go for Buchanan. . . . The vote taken will be nearly unanimous for J K Polk & harmony & union are restored
M Is it a fact or a mere rumor
V Wait till the ballot comes. . . . Illinois goes for Polk . . . Mich goes for Polk. Penn asks leave to correct her error so as to give her whole vote for Polk. . . .
M Intense anxiety prevails to . . . hear the result of last Balloting
V Polk is unanimously nom

At this point Morse telegraphed back to Baltimore the effect on those around him of Polk's nomination:

M 3 cheers have been given here for Polk and 3 for the Telegraph.

By Morse's account, the hundreds of people outside the room, mostly members of Congress, called for him to appear at the window, where they added three cheers for him. He and Vail closed up shop on a less stirring note:

V Have you had your dinner
M yes have you
V yes what had you
M mutton chop and strawberries.

Morse created more excitement the following day by making his system part of the process for selecting Polk's running mate. The Baltimore convention nominated Silas Wright, an anti-slavery senator. The delegates' choice was telegraphed to Wright, who immediately telegraphed back from Washington that he declined. A second message went out from Baltimore asking him to reconsider, but he wired back that his mind was made up. A third message informed him that the convention had adjourned for the day but that five delegates had been appointed to confer with him in the capital, where they would arrive next morning. The long-distance political bargaining, the *National Register* reported, went on "with *lightning speed.*"

Morse kept the line in operation after the Democratic convention closed, with spectacular results. Like New York, Philadelphia had been riven by nativist debates about the relation of Catholic citizens to the public schools. A week after the convention, Catholic-Protestant fighting with fists, knives, and pistols broke out in Philadelphia, eclipsing in violence the sack of Boston's Ursuline Convent School in 1834.

Vail intercepted news of the bloodletting as it arrived by express train in Baltimore. Then he telegraphed reports to Morse, who brought them personally to Secretary of State John C. Calhoun: "continued riots at Philadelphia. . . . The mob has possession of the city . . . Gen Cadwallader has fled for his life . . . 40 or 50 killed and wounded." With two Catholic churches and many Irish homes burned to the ground, Morse's line also showed its potential by sending on to President Tyler a request for aid from the mayor of Philadelphia. Throngs gathered around Vail and Morse to watch the urgent transmissions: "The Rooms are crouded with gazing spectators," Cornell wrote to his wife, "whose countinances are not unfrequently distorted with wonder and amazement."

In June, Morse opened the line to selected members of the public. A Washington post office employee was informed of the birth of his Baltimore grandson: "Mother and son doing well." From Baltimore, the incendiary Samuel Colt detonated a fuse of gunpowder in the antechamber of the Supreme Court building. Members of the Washington Chess Club played Baltimoreans an intercity over-the-wire match, "with the same ease," Morse remarked, "as if the players were seated at the same table." The celebrated Antarctic explorer Captain Charles Wilkes conducted a three-day experiment in the more exact determination of differences of longitude.

Morse had suggested this scientific use for the telegraph five years earlier. Establishing longitude meant knowing the time in two far-apart places at once, a one-hour difference representing fifteen degrees of longitude. Wilkes was able to place Battle Monument Square in Baltimore 1 m. 34 sec. 868 east of the Capitol, correcting former measurements by .732 of a second. "Your Telegraph," he told Morse, "offers the means for determining *Meridian distances* more accurately than ever before within the power of Instruments and Observors." The improvement mattered because communities all over America defined their own local time, and travelers had to readjust their watches from city to city. By making possible the all but instantaneous synchronization of distant places, Morse's telegraph augured the introduction of a uniform national time.

Morse produced his most impressive show during the fall presidential elections. He assigned Vail to the Washington station and positioned a new assistant, Henry Rogers, at the Baltimore end. As election returns from the southern states arrived at the capital, Vail sent them on to Baltimore. At the same time, Rogers tapped out from Baltimore incoming returns from the northeastern states. Expectant crowds collected around the telegraphs in both cities, including cabinet members and other government officials.

Into the late evening, Vail had the tallies announced out the window of his Washington office. Morse cautioned him to give only official results, not mere rumors, and in announcing them to leave no impression of political partisanship. Vail estimated the number of Whig and Democrat voters gathered outside at three to four thousand: "their shouts go up like peals of thunder," he said. "It is royal sport to see the breathless interest felt just before the telegraphic communication is announced. . . . Then the 3 cheers from one party or the other as the case may be."

In proving the efficiency and usefulness of his invention, Morse revealed the coming into being of a remarkable new technology. His telegraph was the subject of relatively as much discussion in the newspapers and magazines of the mid-1840s as the Internet became in the mass media of the 1990s. Americans could not read enough about his "Lightning Line," as they began calling it. The press published his dot-dash code in full; explained in elementary terms his conductors and galvanic batteries; offered capsule histories of the discovery of electromagnetism—matters little if at all known to American readers. "Is this mysterious power a substance or an effect?" asked the New York *Daily Times*. When Morse tried to explain his invention to several members of Congress, a bystander observed, they looked blank, "as if he had spoken in Hebrew."

Bafflement was the common reaction to Morse's system. It seemed to operate by "an almost supernatural agency," one newspaper said; "we stand wonder-stricken and confused." Americans compared it to a bottle-imp, a spell, a classical myth, something from the *Arabian Nights*. The wonderment stemmed in part from the awesome harnessing of power they believed the telegraph represented. Most conceived the electric current in Morse's circuits not in terms of batteries but in terms of lightning. In many minds, he had "chained the very lightning of heaven," commanding his wires to program and propel the most destructive force in Nature. Marveling at his invention as the "climax of all human might," they experienced something of the all-transforming awakening that later accompanied the dawn of the atomic age.

Just as bafflingly, Morse's telegraph "annihilated space and time." No other description of his device was so often and so widely repeated. Through his before-unthinkable lightning-wires, information could hurtle across forty miles instantaneously (actually, at nearly the speed of light). Better than that: given the difference in clock-time between cities, a message could arrive at one before being sent from the other, transmitted in "*less than no time.*" Americans conceived telegraphic transmission not so much as communication, however, than as a sort of teleportation. Morse had transmuted Thought, abstract human Thought, into metal strips and jars of acid. A congressional report on the telegraph noted: "If machinery don't *think,* it does that which nothing but severe and prolonged thinking can do, and it does it incomparably better." Americans spoke of creating a "new species of consciousness" separated from the body, a discorporate electronic telepresence. Dizzyingly, Mind could be at one place but also at another: "this extraordinary discovery leaves . . . no elsewhere—it is all *here.*"

For the United States, the annihilation of space was as much a political as a scientific achievement. From the beginning, the spread of the American people over so large a territory had raised doubts about whether the Republic could be governed. Such concerns became acute as the population increased during the first half of the nineteenth century by about 450 percent, and the nation expanded westward across the continent. And the five years after the opening of the Washington-Baltimore line would enlarge the problem. Into the Union would come Texas, the huge Oregon Territory, and the half-million square miles of land including the present states of Nevada, Utah, and California, most of New Mexico and Arizona, and part of Wyoming and Colorado.

But Morse's "magic chords" put to rest any fears that the swelling United States was doomed to burst apart. As a government report explained:

> Doubt has been entertained by many patriotic minds how far the rapid, full, and thorough intercommunication of thought and intelligence, so necessary to a people living under a common representative republic, could be expected to take place through-out such immense bounds. That doubt can no longer exist. It has been resolved and put an end to forever by the triumphant success of the electro-magnetic telegraph of Professor Morse. . . .

Many likened this interconnectedness to the central nervous system: "Touch but one nerve with skilful hand, / Through all the thrill unbro-ken flies." Now American institutions could be extended indefinitely, the nation becoming a lightning-bound network of communities within minutes' reach of each other, a single neuro-electropolis. Despite the vastness of the territory across which their tens of millions were spread, Americans would become more and more one people, thinking and acting alike.

In forecasting other social changes that Morse's invention might bring, antebellum futurologists adapted their thinking to the Gospel of Progress. The New York *Sun* proclaimed the telegraph "the greatest revolution of modern times and indeed of all time, for the amelioration of Society." It would create civic order, strengthen domestic ties, bring harmony among nations, and redeem mankind.

In this spirit, the Utica *Gazette* anticipated an "immense diminution" in crime. Felons would give up hope of escaping justice: "fly, you tyrants, assassins and thieves, you haters of light, law, and liberty, for the telegraph is at your heals [*sic*]." Domestic joy and sorrow would thrill along the wires: "the absent will scarcely be away," rhapsodized the Philadelphia *North American*, "the mother may, each day, renew her blessing upon her child a thousand leagues away; and the father, each hour, learn the health of those around his distant fireside." The author of "The Song of the Telegraph" promised that war would cease:

> *With the olive branch extended,*
> *Swift I go to every shore;*
> *Soon all nations shall be blended,*
> *They shall learn of war no more.*

Ultimately nations would be wired to each other, making the planet a neural map, what the *Christian Observor* called a "sensorium of communicated intelligence." Acting through the global cyborg, God's grand processes would realize His grand design of leading humanity toward salvation. As the New York *Herald* put it, "What a future!"

In its more practical effects, the telegraph would whet the appetite for news, strengthen national defense, and boost the country's go-ahead businessmen, transforming the press, the military, and the marketplace. News of the Declaration of Independence had taken more than two weeks to reach Williamsburg, Virginia, from Philadelphia. In the near future, by contrast, "the events of yesterday throughout the entire land will be given, as we now give the occurrences at home today." Should European despots threaten an invasion, the government would activate the "mystic meshes," instantly alarming the entire country and raising three million fighting men: "no power of a foreign country could long have a foot-hold among a people who possess such combined and prodigious means of concentrating its great strength." With the country pulling out of its long economic depression, the telegraph would carry complex business deals, in secrecy if desired, making commerce no longer dependent on snail-paced mail or agitated by rumors. Guarantees sent at lightning speed would take the place of precious metals and banknotes: "gold and silver may stay at home . . . or be laid aside in flower pots and old stockings. The lightning will have taken up their task."

Whatever their particular hopes, all those who praised Morse's apparatus agreed in viewing it as a surpassing marvel. It was "the most wonderful climax of American inventive genius," the "greatest of the great inventions of the modern times"—even "the most magnificent effort of the mind of man."

To its enthusiasts, this opening of the modern era of communication marked a new start, a dividing line between generations. According to the *Herald*, those who resisted it would count for nothing:

> Steam and electricity, with the natural impulses of a free people, have made, and are making, this country the greatest, the most original, the most wonderful the sun ever shone upon. . . . Those who do not mix with this movement—those who do not become part of this movement—those who do not go on with this movement—will be crushed into more impalpable powder than ever was attributed to the car of Juggernaut. Down on your knees and pray.

Some Americans, of course, refused to pay tribute. To Henry David Thoreau, for one, it seemed that sender and receiver might have "nothing important to communicate." Refining human instruments but not human beings, electromagnetic telegraphy represented only "improved means to an unimproved end."

The social consequences of the telegraph, like those of every other technology, would of course depend on the people who owned and used it. It needs no saying that despite the vision of a national sensorium uniting the continent, the United States would soon implode in civil war. Nor that for all the techno-utopian hoopla about reduced crime and family values, lightning-fast information processing in the era of cyberspace might also be a boon to credit-card fraud, child pornography, and international terrorism.

In the "Lightning Man," as they often referred to him, Morse's fellow citizens discovered a new national hero, a second Benjamin Franklin:

> *On the same tablet with our FRANKLIN'S name,*
> *Thine, MORSE, in blazing characters shall flame!*

In Washington, a House member rose in Congress to say: "His name is immortalised and will remain as long as time shall endure." "Fame will build a new Pillar in her Temple," a fan wrote to him, "higher & more magnificent than all of the others, & on the top of it inscribe the name of Morse." Newspapers such as the *Southern Standard* acquainted Americans with their hero's appearance and manner:

> This eminent individual—the inventor of the last and greatest wonder of the age—is under forty-five [actually fifty-two]. He is a little above the common height [actually, just under five feet ten], and rather thin; his hair slightly grey, complexion dark and sallow, eyes brilliantly black, with a peculiarly soft and gentle expression.

The *Home Journal* subjected Morse's head to phrenological analysis. Its readers learned that his well-developed organs of Constructiveness and Ideality revealed him to be hard and soft: "forcible, persevering, almost headstrong, self-relying, independent, aspiring, good-hearted, and eminently social, though sufficiently selfish to look well to his own interests."

Invitations, honors, and flattering requests poured in on Morse. The British minister asked him to dine. The French Académie de l'Industrie awarded him its silver medal. He was elected to membership in the literary society of Marshall College, the Belgian Academy of Archaeology, the National Institution for the Promotion of Science. Admirers importuned him to act as agent for the Syro-Egyptian Society; to speculate in a new photographic process; to lecture to the Irving Literary Association of Baltimore; to furnish material on his modus operandi for an engineering journal. They sought his permission to demonstrate the telegraph in classrooms, his instruction in operating the invention, his political endorsement, his advice, a job ("I am a sober industrious man & can give my reference").

Morse had always longed to be a national figure, like Joseph Henry in science or James Fenimore Cooper in literature—as his father had been in geography. He fully understood that his position in the world had changed: "my praises," he told Sidney, "ring from one end of the country to the other." The homage made him think of the hopeless darkness a year ago, the painfully slow labor of improving his instruments, the pie-in-the-sky offers extended then withdrawn, the suspense of waiting for an out-of-humor Congress to act, the indifference or perfidy of his partners—not to mention the many mornings before that when he arose not knowing where to find money for common expenses of the day, and his still earlier years of frustration as a painter. Reflecting on what he had survived and overcome, he told Sidney, he found himself constantly exclaiming, "What hath God wrought!"

Scarcely if at all remarked on at the time, the scriptural message would owe much of its later historical radiance to Morse's invocations of it throughout his life. For him, it marked not the event but the gestation of the event. His work on the telegraph had all along been sustained by his belief that technology and theology were two sides of the same thing, that the inspiration and end of his invention was the greater glory of God, and secondly of God's country. The conviction expressed in the text suggested by Annie Ellsworth's mother had been in his mind day and night: " 'What hath God wrought!' It is his work, and He alone could have carried me thus far through all my trials and enabled me to triumph over the obstacles, physical and moral, which opposed me." His uplifting had come in answer to prayer, had come from God's right arm which brings salvation. In recalling how his many trials had issued to his advantage, he felt his faith strengthened and believed he might never again mistrust the future.

Beginning with his arduous conversion, however, Morse's long and deep religious experience had taught him that such assurance was often short-lived. The heart was deceitful, the future uncertain. Only three weeks after the triumphant inaugural demonstration of May 24 he took a bad fall, wounding his leg. He had injured his leg years before, as a boy studying at Phillips Academy. This time the painful wound confined him to bed in Washington. Though repeatedly dressed by a physician, it took six weeks to heal.

Not only failure, but prosperity, too, Morse could see, was a trial. The applause he heard so eagerly might rouse the natural pride of his heart, tempt him to take too much credit for what he had achieved, forget that without Christ he could do nothing. It was proper for him to rejoice, and he did. But he rejoiced, he said, with fear. In his new station in life he would need new strength to fortify him against the temptations of self-love: "If I am to have influence, increased influence, I desire to have it for Christ, to use it for his cause; if wealth, for Christ; if more knowledge, for Christ. I speak sincerely when I say I fear prosperity."

SAMUEL F. B. MORSE

I jump'd aboard the tel-e-graph and trabbled down de ribber,
De lectrick fluid magnified, and kill'd five hundred Nigga.

—Stephen Foster, "Oh! Susanna" (1848)

[T]his volume of Moby Dick may be pronounced a most
remarkable sea-dish—an intellectual chowder of romance,
philosophy, natural history, fine writing, good feeling, bad
sayings.

—*Literary World,* November 22, 1851

The great difference between Young America and Old Fogy, is
the result of Discoveries, Inventions, *and* Improvements.

—Abraham Lincoln, "Lecture on Discoveries
and Inventions" (1859)

Samuel F. B. Morse, at about sixty
(Princeton University Library)

ELEVEN

Mere Men of Trade

(1844–1845)

T HE MUCH-APPLAUDED success of the Baltimore-Washington telegraph left Morse with a question: What next?

As one possible move, Morse considered giving the commercial development of his system to private investors. He had many bids from capitalists and speculators, some wanting to buy rights to the line, others seeking to build new lines themselves. Still others asked him to build lines for them—not only locally but to and from Buffalo, Richmond, Mobile, New Orleans. A Baltimore merchant wanted to buy out the entire patent. Morse offered to sell his nine-sixteenths share in it for $110,000—a sum not half the value of his invention, he reasoned, but it would free him to spend his time perfecting and superintending the system, "unembarrassed by the business arrangements." The deal faded but Morse remained willing to sell his patent right for a relatively modest sum, the competence that had eluded him all his life.

Morse also weighed, and generally favored, selling his invention to the American government. The press took up the question of whether as a matter of public policy the new technological marvel should be nationalized. The Washington *Union,* for instance, argued that the government would distribute its benefits impartially, while in private hands it might become a "dangerous monopoly." But the New York *Evening Mirror* and other papers condemned such thinking as patronizing and unrealistic; it regarded the people as "a set of knaves and swindlers, and the officials of the government as being alone worthy of holding any trust." The *Mirror* foresaw congressmen misusing the wires for their private convenience, at public expense: "The Hon. Mr.

Hopkins will send word to his wife in Buffalo, that he had a comfortable night's sleep." To Morse the issue was neither economic nor political but essentially moral. Being "an engine of power, for good or for evil," the telegraph would be safer under federal control. He hoped the government would buy his patent outright, expand and manage the system on its own, and keep him in place as superintendent.

With a half-dozen options before him, Morse was uncertain what to do. "Professor Morse is so constantly changing his plans," Vail wrote, "that it is impossible to say what will be the next suggestion." Morse's attempts to confer with F. O. J. Smith, his partner, did nothing to relieve his indecision. As often in the past, Smith failed to answer letters and managed to be unavailable for consultation. Having come to despise Morse as narrowminded and sanctimonious, he cursed him as "the 'puritan'" and ridiculed him for wanting to consult. Morse behaved, he said, as if he "could not start an inch until I came. It is provoking to witness such selfishness & effeminacy combined."

Not that letters or meetings helped. In one exchange of views, Morse suggested that they sell the patent to the government, asking a quarter of a million dollars: "would you not be satisfied?" Smith was not satisfied. Nor could they agree on bargaining terms when discussing possible deals with private investors. Again and again Morse proposed divisions of profits, outlined responsibilities for bookkeeping, named prices for the sale of side lines. Again and again Smith rejected Morse's terms and submitted counterproposals, all of which Morse found unsatisfactory and rejected in turn.

Their angriest clash arose over Morse's hope of getting an additional appropriation from Congress. He wanted the money in order to extend the Washington-Baltimore line to New York City, with intermediate stations at Wilmington, Philadelphia, and Trenton—a distance of about two hundred miles. He planned to once more enlist Smith to write the contracts for the construction, while he once more superintended the work, which on completion would be offered to the government for purchase. But he seems to have understood that Smith had not forgiven his handling of the Bartlett contract—that Smith remained incensed over his refusal to ask full payment from the government for brother-in-law Bartlett's never-completed trenching. Smith was "determined," he suspected, "to defeat all application for an appropriation if I am to have the management of it."

Since Smith at once dismissed any terms he proposed, Morse

apparently invited him to name his own figure for the appropriation: $100,000, Smith said, to build a line of four wires. But Morse sensed and feared that Smith's interest in the project was limited to using him as a respectable front for finagling a large grant. Then Smith would again subcontract work for less than the cost estimate to Congress and pocket the difference.

Morse may have been right. Smith became enraged when he visited the Committee on Commerce and learned that Henry Ellsworth, the Patent Commissioner, had proposed to its members a two-wire line, for only about $50,000. Smith protested violently to Morse that Ellsworth's "mousing visits" to the committee had killed any chance of a congressional appropriation. "The intermeddling of your supposed friend . . . puts an end to all possibility of any further concert among the proprietors," he said. "You will live to see these unpleasant truths verified to your sorrow." Morse saw in Smith's rant "the darkest designs upon us all," menace that left him "sick at heart." More than heartsick, Ezra Cornell now found Smith and Morse mutually envenomed, "entertaining the most perfect hatred towards each other."

Smith had other ideas about how to cash in on Morse's success. He offered to take over all telegraph negotiations for the next six years— "selling, leasing, constructing, & using"—putting his partners on salary and giving them a share of his profits. "It is unnecessary to say," Morse remarked, "it was at once rejected as absurd." Alternatively Smith proposed a geographical division. He would control the New England states, his partners New York, New Jersey, Pennsylvania, and Delaware. Morse greeted this with no less disdain. "I can hardly think you intended the proposition seriously," he replied. "I cannot of course accede to a proposition so manifestly unequal."

Some such division, however, appealed to Morse as possibly freeing him from Smith. He granted Smith the right to contract separately for a line from Boston to New York—not a promising venture since Smith understood little about telegraphy. Smith sent Cornell to Boston to exhibit Morse's telegraph, hoping to raise money for his line from local "Merchant Princes." As Smith's one ally in the enterprise, Cornell helped him to aggravate Morse. Aside from long-standing gripes about salary and workload, Cornell believed, very improbably, that Morse had seen drawings he made of a new register and had stolen his design. Smith cheered on Cornell's dislike of Morse, and they swapped abusive comments about him by mail.

Morse's efforts to take advantage of his bright prospects antago-nized not only Smith but also Alfred Vail, his other partner. Vail, too, nursed a list of grievances—that Morse was overbearing and erratic, broke promises, took him for granted. It distressed him that Morse had still not officially registered with the Patent Office his two-sixteenths interest in the patent. If Morse died, he might not be able to claim his share—and he had a wife and children to think about. He repeatedly asked Morse to register his name. But Morse nonchalantly said he would see, it wasn't necessary, it could be done at any time, "putting off this matter of so much importance to me, and my depend-ent family."

Morse's handling of the new business opportunities deepened Vail's resentment. He complained that Morse set terms for the sale of patent rights without consulting him, offering the rights cheaply even though people in Washington said the telegraph was "worth millions." He also deplored Morse's consent to Smith's Boston–New York line. Smith was a "cunning deceitful man" bent on freezing him out: "I have no mind to give Mr. Smith any advantage in making money out of the Telegraph." Besides, Morse's decision to allow private individuals to own a major line would discourage Congress from purchasing the patent on behalf of the nation. All of Morse's business dealings, Vail decided, betrayed his gullibility: "Professor Morse has confidence in . . . everybody till they cheat him."

Vail probably kept his disgust to himself. Behind the scenes, his brother George kept reminding him that the family's profit from their substantial investment in the telegraph depended on Morse's good will: "upon every consideration," George advised, "keep Morse your partic-ular friend." Meanwhile, through connections of his own, George qui-etly looked into the possibility of establishing a Vail telegraph line in Austria.

Despite Smith's scheming and raving, Morse managed to get before Congress an appropriation bill for extending the Washington-Baltimore telegraph to New York City. The bill encountered both opposition and apathy, however. Congress ended its current session, in June, without taking final action. Recently glorified by public and press as the equal of immortal Franklin, the Lightning Man was ingloriously forced once again to anxiously wait out government indecision, this time for six months, until Congress reconvened in December.

Staying in Washington, Morse used the time for important new experiments. He and Vail worked at slimming the bulky Grove battery that powered the Washington-Baltimore line. They succeeded in reducing the necessary number of cups from eighty to twenty, promising great savings in the cost of material and maintenance. Morse looked into the possibility of dispensing with batteries altogether by using the "magneto-electrical machine," a primitive generator designed by Charles Page, Chief Examiner of the Patent Office. Page's device proved its enormous potential when it successfully operated the line in a test on Christmas Day, without the clutter of acid and plates and cups. Morse kept Page on as an adviser but did not alter the power supply in his system, probably because of the expense of manufacturing as many magnetos as he would need to replace his batteries.

Morse and Vail again addressed the problem of river crossings, a difficulty that at some time would have to be decisively faced and overcome. Morse had twice before attempted to conduct electricity underwater: by wire in New York harbor, inconclusively; and successfully across the eighty-foot-wide Susquehanna Canal, using the water alone as a conductor. At the canal he had been assisted by James Fisher, the New York University colleague he hired, then fired. Distrusting Fisher's results, he decided to repeat the experiment, now aided by Vail and Cornell. On one bank of the canal they stretched a wire four hundred feet long, parallel to a wire of the same length on the opposite bank. To the four ends of the wires they attached copper plates, which they immersed in the canal. When a battery connected to the wire on the near shore was activated, it moved a galvanometer connected to the wire on the far shore, proving that current had been conducted through the water from one pair of plates to the other. In one of many further tests, Vail and Henry Rogers, Morse's newly hired assistant, sent a current wirelessly across the Susquehanna River at Havre de Grace, a distance of nearly a mile.

Morse's experiments made news, as did his fanciful suggestion that a telegraph line might be constructed along the Connecticut shore of Long Island Sound, electromagnetically linking all the neighboring towns "without the necessity of any other connection but the water of the Sound. It is even hoped," the *Journal of Commerce* reported, "that a telegraphic communication may be made with Europe, and at no very great expense." Despite the impressive trials and the fanfare, Morse wondered whether a more practical way of traversing rivers might be to stretch wire circuits across the water on lofty spars.

Morse and his assistants also tried to learn how telegraph lines might be affected by electrical storms. During one test, in a Washington office, a terrific lightning flash outside roiled the apparatus, spattering liquid mercury and shooting jets of snapping sparks. Onlookers were alarmed, and the dangerous accident found its way into the press. Morse and his crew said little, concerned that such reports might warn off insurance companies and scare landlords, whose permission was required before planting telegraph poles near their buildings. The indoor fireworks had a benefit, too. They led Morse and his helpers to devise a lightning arrester to protect the instruments and operators.

Hoping to improve the operators as well, Morse directed Vail to experiment with transmission speeds. Vail could telegraph 20 letters per minute; Morse, working as fast as possible, once managed to send 48 (or, in another trial, 122 *s*'s). But excitement over the invention was beginning to attract many young men who saw employment for themselves as telegraphers. Some took training from Vail, for $25. The learners included a whiz named Louis Zantziger, just fifteen or sixteen years old. Hired to work for Morse in Washington, he soon could transmit some 60 letters a minute, and within a year was tapping out 101.

As usual, Vail also experimented on his own. Among other things, he tried substituting a permanent magnet for the electromagnet, making a railroad track serve as a conductor, and using the earth itself to generate a galvanic current. He also devised a method of operating two independent circuits with one battery. "My mind has become so entirely engrossed in all that relates to the Telegraph," he said, "that I almost feel unfit for anything else." He also felt, however, that although his research had reduced the expense and difficulty of operating Morse's system, it went unacknowledged and unappreciated. "*With all these improvements, I got no credit* from Professor Morse," he told his brother. He intended to keep his current experiments to himself, and later make their results public: "Not even Professor Morse knows what I have in my possession." But his family believed they knew—and they would long remember.

With Congress not in session, Morse left Washington for a few days in May to see his daughter, Susan. She came to New York from Puerto Rico, bringing his first grandchild, a boy named Charles. The reunion does not seem to have gone very well. Susan had developed chronic health problems. She spoke of her move to Puerto Rico as a "great sacrifice" and hoped to return permanently to the United States. Although her husband, a sugar merchant, had made a lot of money as sugar prices advanced, he lost much of it in speculations. And Morse seems to have treated his grandson with no more warmth or finesse than he had shown to his children. He left Susan feeling "sometimes sad," she said, to think that he had been disappointed in the boy and found him unhandsome. Returned to Washington, Morse wrote to Sidney, asking his brother to reassure her—if the comment can be called reassuring—that while he considered his grandson handsome indeed, "I think more of disposition which is of most consequence and he appears to have a fine disposition."

Whether or not his grandson Charles disappointed Morse, Charles his son certainly did. Now about twenty years old, the young man had done poorly at Yale—his father's and grandfather's alma mater—finding algebra and other subjects difficult and getting harder. He told his father he wanted to quit college and become a farmer. Morse consented, although "almost heart broken" by his son's dropping out of school. Gradually, however, he came to think the move desirable for Charles' health. And if Charles had a farm it might provide something like a home for Finley, who was showing an interest in gardening.

Sidney Morse vigorously publicized his brother's telegraph system in the *Observer*. He himself had contrived a method of printing maps by engraving on wax—"cerography"—that Morse considered no less valuable than the telegraph. "It is rare," he told Sidney, "that two of a family should be so favored, as to be the instruments of bringing before the world, such important revolutionizing inventions." The two brothers also stood together in opposing the ever-noisier crusade against slavery. Sidney published a pamphlet, *Letter on American Slavery*, assailing the radical tactics of the Abolitionists. Morse said he agreed—"demons in human shape," he called the Abolitionists; "a more wretched, disgusting, hypocritical crew, have not appeared on the face of the earth since the times of Robespierre."

By contrast with the robust Sidney, Morse's bookish brother Richard went on enumerating his plague of ailments—"indigestion, tendency of blood to the head, wakefulness, needless anxieties." Married and the father of ten children, he had withdrawn from partnership in the *Observer*, doing no more for the paper than light writing and translating. Meanwhile he wandered in restless desolation from upstate New York to New Haven to Long Island—"not a well man," he said, "and never expect to be." Morse believed that, rather like himself, Richard was cursed by a "constitutional predisposition to low spirits." He urged his brother to resist: "go round with your children to see amusing exhibitions."

Although Morse surely would not have taken such advice himself, he did still long to have a family life. "I feel my loneliness more and more keenly every day," he lamented. "Fame and money are, in themselves, a poor substitute for domestic happiness." He quietly courted his "young friend" Annie Ellsworth, to whom he addressed some verse:

> . . . *when I review all the scenes that have past,*
> *Between me and thee, be they dark be they light.*
> *I forget what was dark, the light I hold fast.*

Nothing is known of the "scenes" that passed between Morse and Annie Ellsworth. But they or Morse's accounts of them were intimate enough to convince Susan that her father meant to marry the young woman: "you seemed so fondly attached to her." Morse also kept up his cryptically flirtatious correspondence with Catherine Pattison. She sent congratulations on his success, hopes of seeing him, and the (beckoning?) news that she was not engaged.

Morse stayed in only distant touch with his former colleagues in art, and presided over the National Academy of Design as a figurehead. In July 1843 he had been obliged to call a special meeting of the N.A.D. to mark the sudden death, at the age of sixty-three, of Washington Allston. Allston had been unwell for a few years, struggling to climb his painting ladder, his face inflamed with erysipelas. Morse delivered an affectionate eulogy, honoring him as "our great American Painter," a Christian gentleman of delicate sentiment who held to the highest standard of artistic excellence—"my long known, long tried, most valued friend and master." At the family's request he journeyed to Allston's home near Boston to discuss arrangements for the uncompleted wall-size *Belshazzar's Feast* that his mentor had made and unmade for twenty-five years. Looking through the paintbrushes Allston had last used, he chose one and accepted it from the family as a token.

In January 1845, Congress at last returned to deliberating on Morse's request for an appropriation to extend the telegraph to New York City. Having already waited six months for a decision, he waited two months longer, in "unpleasant suspense," as the bill made its way out of committee and into the House, then to the Senate. With his original grant about to expire he applied for a separate appropriation of $8000, for salaries and material to keep the Washington-Baltimore line in operation another year. He took pride in the fact that during its first year the line had been out of commission only one day, despite winter storms that had strewn the seashore with wrecks and halted railroad traffic. Many newspapers supported both his applications and even called on Congress to run the line to all large cities along the Atlantic coast.

Savvy and cynical about the workings of Congress, Smith doubted that the extension bill would pass. "A good feeling exists on all sides towards it," he told Cornell, "yet it is like universal charity that fixes upon nothing in particular and helps nobody." If the appropriation failed, as he believed, he intended to insist on a geographical division of the patent rights. As for the additional $8000 Morse asked, he considered the figure inflated, calculated only to provide another year's salary for "the 'puritan' " and Vail, with nothing for himself. Still well connected in official Washington, he let it be known that maintenance of the line required no more than $2500. The award of any larger grant would amount to a "sinecure."

Morse's eight-month wait ended mostly in defeat. The bill for running the Washington-Baltimore telegraph to New York failed. As Smith understood, Congress had little real interest in extending the line. Development policy in Washington had in general turned away from public financing of internal improvements, leaving them to be made by private enterprise. Morse did at least receive the requested $8000 to keep the line in service a year longer, with himself as the salaried superintendent. Congress assigned control of the line to the Post Office Department, making it a branch of the mail service. Ironically, this brought Morse under the authority of the Postmaster General, Cave Johnson, the former congressman from Tennessee who in the early House debates over funding the line had mockingly compared him to a mesmerist.

On Morse's recommendation, Johnson boosted Vail's salary and appointed him operator of the Washington station, now set up in the post office. "His time and talent," Morse said, "are more essential to the success of the Telegraph than any two persons that could be named." Transmissions were opened to the public, at the rate of one cent for every four characters. In securing salaries for himself and Vail, Morse inflamed Smith, who demanded part of the "sinecure" for himself, as one-quarter proprietor of the patent. Morse pointed out to Johnson that the original grant from Congress made no reference to paying the proprietors. Smith, he said, "has done nothing in the invention but throw obstacles in the way of its success ever since he had any connection with it."

Morse's defeat brought him back to the question raised the year before by his triumph: What next? With the government unwilling to develop his invention he might turn to private investors. But dealing with them meant asking help from Smith or trying to act as an entrepreneur himself. Both prospects repelled him. In his lifetime the American economic scene had changed dramatically. The earlier world of small farms and workshops supplying local needs had been taken over by competitive financiers, corporations, and wholesale commission houses geared to national and world markets. The distinctiveness of America was now to be measured by its New Men, as one commercial magazine declared: "it is the BUSINESS-MEN OF AMERICA that have made us what we are; and it is their enterprise that will still further advance our national power and greatness."

Morse did not share the enthusiasm. "Money is the main thing to be got," he complained, "*character* is of secondary & very trifling consideration." He still lived for a personal glory unthinkable and unattainable without obedience to Christ, loyalty to artistic values, and pride in America's Protestant Republicanism. His contempt for the scramble of moneymaking, his naiveté, his tendency to become easily vexed and discouraged—all disabled him for marketing his telegraph in the no-holds-barred world of buccaneer capitalism. He disdained the economic and social forces that might realize his hope of bringing his invention into universal use.

Morse's deliverance from this bind was at hand. It appeared in the improbable shape of a short, emaciated-looking man of fifty-six—a "little whiffet of a man," as a contemporary described Amos Kendall (1789–1869). Shoulders stooped, cheeks sunken, hair prematurely white, he had a cadaverous appearance that suggested disease. And

Amos Kendall
(The Library of Congress)

indeed he coughed asthmatically and suffered chills, though some-times bundled in an overcoat on even the warmest summer days.

But Amos Kendall's spindly fragility was deceptive. He was among the most influential politicians of the day, his name constantly before the public. At the time he and Morse met in Washington, around February 1845, Kendall had grown weary of government, but was deeply involved in Native American affairs, acting as a lawyer for one faction in a bitter dispute within the Cherokee nation. Betweentimes he worked on a biography of his political idol, Andrew Jackson. Jackson had brought Kendall to national prominence, appointing him Postmaster General—a cabinet position overseeing twenty thousand postmasters and a corrupt, mismanaged agency some half a million dollars in debt. By demanding efficiency and rectitude, Kendall quickly improved mail service, reduced expenses, and produced a $100,000 surplus.

Kendall became Jackson's close friend and adviser, invited to dine with the family, entrusted with writing and revising state papers. He served Jackson brilliantly in the administration's war on the Bank of the United States, the privately owned bank that managed the government's funds. Sharing the President's hatred of the bank as a manipulator of public credit for private enrichment, he outlined and publicized a phased removal of federal deposits to state banks. When Congress passed a bill to recharter the bank in 1832, it was Kendall who drafted Jackson's impassioned veto message, concluding with an attack on the rich and powerful. Nicholas Biddle, the bank's president, denounced the message as "a manifesto of anarchy—such as Marat or Robespierre might have issued to the mob." But the veto helped Jackson win reelection, and gave Kendall the reputation of being the power behind the throne. "He is supposed to be the moving spring of the whole administration," Harriet Martineau wrote, recounting Washington gossip; "the thinker, planner, and doer; but it is all in the dark."

Contemporaries of this sickly, intelligent, complex man had sharply different opinions of him. Andrew Jackson praised his "stern and unflinching honesty." Others called him "suspicious and Jesuitical," Jackson's "writing machine—aye, and his lying machine." For Morse there was no question. Seeking to establish his telegraph system nationally but contemptuous of those he called "mere men of trade," he saw Kendall as an invaluable ally. Kendall knew the top people in government. His tenure as Postmaster General had given him knowledge of the country's routes of communication. He had legal training, managerial skill, understanding of finance, long experience with the press, and even a real interest in inventions, having himself devised something he called a cylinder steamboat. And Kendall was sensitive to Morse's loathing of the marketplace. "It is my earnest desire," Kendall told him, "to see you in a condition not to be annoyed and discomforted by the unpleasant incidents which must be encountered in a business so ramified."

No less important to Morse, Kendall was someone of his own background, social views, and temperament. Just two years Morse's senior, Kendall had been born into a Congregationalist family that went back five generations in Massachusetts. "No man is more ready than I am to say God's will be done," he remarked, "and to submit to that will without a murmur." Dubbed "the Deacon" in boyhood because of his sobriety, he frowned on the efforts of Washington society to ape the manners of London and Paris. As Postmaster General—and the owner of three or more slaves—he had treated abolitionist pamphlets as incendiary printed matter, so local postmasters in the South were forbidden to deliver them. He had read Byron and written a tragedy, "The Fall of Switzerland." The death of his first wife left him with four children; when he remarried three years later, at the age of thirty-seven, it was to a woman barely sixteen years old.

In a decision that would redirect his energy and change his life, Morse turned over the financial management of his telegraph system to Kendall. He had found, he believed, "perhaps the most competent man in the country to manage such a concern." As it happened, he had also found his longest-lived and, except for Allston, deepest friendship. Kendall's existence would be affected no less, for he pledged to Morse his wholehearted commitment: "My earthly all, my time, provision for my family, now and when I am gone, are embarked in this enterprize, for which I have resigned all other business."

One month after meeting Kendall, Morse signed an agreement granting him full power to transact all telegraph business "in as full and complete a manner as I myself could do." The agreement covered Vail and Leonard Gale as well, so Kendall represented in his person three-quarters of the patent right to Morse's invention. He would get a commission of 10 percent on the first $100,000 he realized from the sale of rights, and a commission of 50 percent on further sales. "And I shall do my best," he promised Morse, "to make my agency more prof-itable to you than it will be to myself."

Morse's agreement did not cover the one-quarter interest in the patent owned by F. O. J. Smith, whose permission Kendall would need in order to convey the rights to others. Kendall planned to interest pri-vate capital, organize the investors into companies, and issue stock to the members. At the same time he intended to hold open the option of selling the patent outright to the government. In his first encoun-ters with Smith, Kendall found him adamantly opposed to such a sale unless Washington paid for the Bartlett contract. "In matters of trade with the Government," Smith said, "I would feign no patriotism." Unlike Morse, Kendall could speak Smith's own language as a capital insider and match him cynicism for cynicism. "I have the same object in view," he replied, "to make the most money in the shortest time that we honestly can."

Kendall was also tenacious in forceful, intelligent argument. He gave Smith a dozen reasons to keep government purchase a possibil-ity. For one, although a million dollars might ultimately be made through private investment, doing so would take years of perplexing toil. But an outright sale to Washington would at once reap "all of wealth the human heart ought to desire." He stressed to Smith the importance of working together: "It is only by harmony in action that we can do any thing, and to preserve it we must make concessions where we cannot agree in opinion." Kendall managed to pacify Smith, but by no means to convert him into a team player. Smith worked only for Smith: "I have no idea of going ahead of my necessities," he said, "to serve the wishes of other folks."

For the first six months after his agreement with Kendall, Morse be-came little more than a bystander to the development of his inven-tion. Kendall rapidly set to work forming or licensing companies to build new telegraph lines, with most of the capital raised in small amounts from people located along the routes. Three companies were especially important as representing the foundation of a national net-work, with New York City the hub. In May, Kendall organized a joint stock association called the Magnetic Telegraph Company—the nation's first telegraph company. The Magnetic took subscriptions for carrying on the Baltimore-Washington line through Philadelphia to

Ad for the Magnetic Telegraph Company
(Washington *Republic*, February 1, 1852)

New York. Kendall himself served as the salaried president. The same
month he concluded an agreement with some upstate operators of
stagecoaches to form the New York, Albany & Buffalo Telegraph Company. Capitalized at $200,000, the company intended to build a line
from New York City through Albany, Syracuse, and Rochester to Buffalo,

with a link at Springfield, Massachusetts, to Smith's New York–
Boston line.

Kendall drew up his most far-reaching agreement in mid-June, with
a Rochester group later called the Atlantic, Lake & Mississippi Telegraph Company. It was led by Henry O'Reilly (or O'Rielly, 1806–1886),
a rosy-cheeked, chin-whiskered immigrant from County Monaghan,
Ireland. Now forty years old, he had come to America at the age of ten
with his mother and sister; his father remained behind, in debtor's
prison. Weighing only 124 pounds, he was a bantam dynamo, the prototype of the Go-ahead American driven more by the promise of gain
and advancement than by the fading ideal of self-sacrificing republican
virtue. By the age of twenty he had made himself editor of the
Rochester, New York, *Daily Advertiser*, the first newspaper between the
Hudson and the Pacific. Identifying his own and the city's future, he
served as its postmaster and president of its Young Men's Association,
worked to improve its public schools, and wrote a history of the place.

Henry O'Reilly
(Rochester Historical Society)

He saw in himself the frontier spirit of western New York, "where *Yankee* enterprise," he liked to say, "is quickened by the energies of a *newer* country."

In his agreement with Kendall, O'Reilly committed himself to raise money for the construction of two mammoth trunk lines extending thousands of miles. One would connect at or near Philadelphia with the in-progress Washington–New York line, running to Harrisburg, Pittsburgh, and on through Cincinnati to St. Louis, with branches into Kentucky and Tennessee. The other line would carry the in-progress New York–Buffalo line to Cleveland, Detroit, Chicago, and principal intermediate cities. Stretching westward from the Atlantic seaboard to the Mississippi River and the Great Lakes, O'Reilly's system would open to the telegraph the sprawling continental interior, rapidly being settled. O'Reilly also undertook separately to build the Baltimore to Philadelphia segment of the Magnetic company's Washington–New York line. "There is some field for *ambition* here!" he whooped; "some hope for *position* & *profit!*"

The high-risk, high-gain O'Reilly approached what he called the "Great Enterprise" with swashbuckling ebullience. He enlisted as a "soldier for life," he said; his partners were "a band of brothers." He so much admired Morse that he wanted the terms "telegraph" and "telegraphy" changed to "*Morsograph*" and "*Morsography*." Full of pep and can-do, he hustled back and forth from Rochester to New York City to Harrisburg, shipping wire, setting timber, selling stock, printing circulars, talking up railroad officials, cultivating newspaper editors, getting his exertions boosted and avidly reported in the press.

Kendall worried that O'Reilly might be overreaching himself: "Doubts are entertained whether he will accomplish anything." The doubt grew when O'Reilly proposed constructing a line north from New York through Quebec and then to Halifax. From Halifax it would communicate with the Magnetic company's seaboard line by semaphores, to give intelligence of the progress of coastal shipping along hundreds of miles. O'Reilly assured Kendall that this northern line would not retard the building of his western system but quicken interest in it, forming "a magnificent outline of Telegraphic communication over a large section of North America." Kendall restrained him: "my dear Sir, are you not suffering your mind to take too wide a range? Is not the field opened to you by your contract broad enough?" He advised O'Reilly to concentrate on realizing his already colossal plans.

Although Kendall spoke in a high-pitched voice and wrote in a trembly, spidery hand, his energy equaled O'Reilly's—its mode, however, being not effervescent but focused and intense. He quietly took on a mountain of legal, political, and commercial problems that would have overwhelmed Morse. He negotiated rights-of-way with railroads and farmers, arranged for issuance of stock, saw to the sale of short-distance side lines off the main routes—a separate, further world of bargaining and aggravation—even looked into difficulties about purchasing augers and delivering chestnut posts. The work entailed writing hundreds of letters to the now-many members of the companies he had formed. Yet the ailing Kendall also took on the emotional burden of dealing with grumbling from Vail and shows of independence from Cornell. Polite but firm he took no nonsense. "To cut the matter short," he said regarding Cornell, "he will have to follow my directions or seek employment elsewhere."

Kendall patiently explained to Morse all his complex business arrangements and kept him closely informed on their progress. But for all his managerial skill and stamina, the multiplication of companies and lengthening of lines across the country meant an exponential increase in the number of persons involved in developing Morse's system. Among many lesser promoters, for instance, Samuel Colt organized a New York and Offing Magnetic Telegraph Association, running a line from New York City to Coney Island that provided notification in Manhattan of ship arrivals off Sandy Hook. Each major or minor player had his own agreements, angles, and demands, complicating the overall situation well beyond the ability of Kendall or any other single person to keep in view, much less control—and beyond the scope of this biography to describe in any detail.*

Kendall admittedly found the work a great burden. "I do not know when I shall be with you again," he wrote to his wife from New York. While in New York, unwell, he received appalling news. His twenty-two-year-old son, William, had been on a street in Washington joshing with a friend. The kidding deteriorated into a quarrel, during which William's friend shot him dead. The calamity left Kendall uncertain whether he could continue his agency for Morse. But his piety and

*The development of the companies is comprehensively and brilliantly described in a classic work, Robert Luther Thompson's *Wiring a Continent: The History of the Telegraph Industry in the United States, 1832–1866* (1947).

faith absorbed his agony: "thank Heaven," he was able to say after a week, "I am resigned and have become calm." The news came to him partly by telegraph, through the astounding electrical communication network now building across the United States.

Kendall's agency gave Morse an unfamiliar sense of freedom. Surviving documents do not reveal his exact profits from the new telegraph companies, now or later. But after years of scrounging and borrowing, he stood in reach of financial security. For granting some group of businessmen rights to the patent, he and the other partners got a modest cash payment plus 50 percent of the stock issued. By taking patent fees in stock rather than cash, Kendall hoped to demonstrate confidence in the telegraph and encourage capitalists to invest. Looking further ahead, he believed that if the patentees retained half the voting stock in every company they would be able to promote unified policies and procedures that would bind the separate lines into a coherent and powerful national system.

At the moment Morse's holdings represented future prospects, dependent on the success of telegraph entrepreneurs in making their stock pay dividends. But now or later he was the largest shareholder in the New York, Albany & Buffalo company, with 585 shares. He also held 256 shares in the Magnetic; most other shareholders had fewer than 20. He soon began to tithe his assets for "religious benevolent objects." He donated stock certificates in Morse companies to Protestant churches of various denominations, and to such organizations as the American Tract Society, the Foreign Evangelical Society, the Cleveland Female Seminary, and the American Temperance Union. He also contributed $2000 in stocks to New York University and $1000 in cash to Yale.

With his budding telegraph empire under Kendall's command, Morse returned to the idea of marketing his invention in Europe. His futile trip to England and France six years earlier had reinforced his sense that the Old World feared change, that he must confine his hopes to America. But his now-proven success had excited new interest abroad, bringing many feelers from European agents and governments. A "Dr. Bergman" offered to secure exclusive telegraph rights through the whole German confederacy. The French consul in Boston, named de Burgraff, advised him that the government was testing electric telegraphs and asked for the plans of his system. The Russian minister promised to write home in his favor and invited him to dine at the ministry in Washington. There Morse shared a twenty-five-foot-long table, all candelabra and flowers, with Daniel Webster and several Supreme Court justices.

Similar European enticements had once before come to nothing, but Morse anyway decided to take a short trip abroad. His departure gave Alfred Vail another reason to feel wronged. Vail was about to publish a monograph on the nature and history of Morse's invention. "If the book comes out, I may as well stay at home," Morse complained to him. He seems to have feared that Vail's explanations and drawings might be used against him if he tried to secure foreign patents, as had happened years before in England. Vail had spent six months and more than $700 producing the work. He protested that chances of its being read in Europe were 100 to 1, and that everything in it was already well known, "explained to thousands, who have seen the instrument in operation;—and . . . published in the newspapers over and over again."

Morse offered a trade. He would permit immediate publication of the work, in exchange for all of Vail's contractual interest in overseas rights to the telegraph. Vail scoffed at the lopsided proposal—another case of his former teacher still seeing him as an undergraduate. "None of your nonsense Professor Morse," he griped to his brother George; "I have some of my eye teeth cut now. . . . *No you don't.*" While Morse was in Europe, the well-known Philadelphia house of Lea & Blanchard published Vail's two-hundred-page monograph, entitled *The American Electric Telegraph.* Morse was not wrong in expecting it to cause trouble.

For demonstrations Morse took with him overseas two telegraphs. He planned to spend time in London and Paris, then go on to Stockholm and beyond. In preparation for a visit to St. Petersburg he gathered letters of introduction to American merchants in the city who could put him in touch with "Christian friends" there, and from Secretary of State James Buchanan. His prospects in Russia, however, once more proved phantasmal. During his three months abroad he got no farther north than Hamburg, Germany, and toured for a while in Holland as well.

In setting out, Morse centered his hopes on England. "If our Telegraph can be once successfully established on a line in England," he told Vail, "we command the Continent also." England mattered most because it had produced the only serious rival to his own system—the needle telegraph of the British inventor-scientist Charles Wheatstone, which several European countries had begun to adopt. The priority and comparative virtues of the two systems were at the moment subjects of cultural warfare in the British and American press. The rancor was intensified by competing national claims to the Oregon Territory, which for nearly forty years had been jointly occupied by both countries.

London journals such as the *Globe* and the *Literary Gazette* declared that everything accomplished by Morse in his Washington-Baltimore line had been done earlier and better by Wheatstone. "The English reader need scarcely be informed," said the London *Mechanics Magazine*, "that Mr. Morse has . . . only *re* discovered what was previously well known in this country." American newspapers fought back in articles typically entitled "The Magnetic Telegraph—*American and British*," making the same claims for Morse: "the *Electro-Magnetic Telegraph* of Prof. Morse is the *first realization* of a *practicable Telegraph on the Electric principle*," one wrote; "thefts of new inventions and bold plagiarisms of whole works, the offspring of American minds, have been so common in England, that we deem it almost a matter of course that no acknowledgement will ever be made in English works of indebtedness for any thing of the kind to America."

Morse had inspected the British telegraph when he visited Wheatstone at King's College, London, in 1838. Now he carefully observed it in public operation at railway stations and ticket offices in London and Hamburg, and along a ten-mile route in Holland between Haarlem and Amsterdam. What he saw confirmed his earlier sense of the superiority of his own system. Wheatstone had simplified his apparatus, reducing the number of needles from five to two. But transmission remained complicated. As part of a description in the London *Pictorial Times* suggests, it demanded a sort of bifocal gymnastics:

> The left hand needle moving to the left twice gives *a*, three times *b*, once to the right and once to the left *c*. . . . The order is then taken up by the right hand needle, moving once to the left for *h*, twice for *i*, three times for *k*, once to the right and once to the left for *l*. . . . The remaining signs are made by the two needles working conjointly, so that the simultaneous movement of the *two*, once to the left, indicates *r*, twice for *s*, three times for *t*, once to

Cooke-Wheatstone double-needle telegraph
(The Science Museum, London)

the right and once to the left for *u*, once to the right for *w*, twice for *x*, and three times for *y*.

At the Paddington Station in London, Morse gave the operator a name of nineteen letters to send and have sent back. The result was several failures to spell the name correctly.

And as in Wheatstone's earlier apparatus, the jerking needles had to be observed or their meaning lost. "The advantage of recording is incalculable," Morse noted, "and in this I have the undisputed advantage." In Hamburg he learned, for the first time, that Wheatstone's system could not accommodate additional instruments along a route, as his own system could by using receiving magnets. "If anything is done in the way of Telegraphs," he decided, "I think there is little doubt mine will be adopted." He also learned that Wheatstone had become aware of his presence abroad and was putting down his telegraph as inferior—"as indeed *impracticable!!* and *absurd!!* Is not this truly laughable?"

Laughable or not, Morse made no headway for his system in England. While in London he managed to interest a start-up British association, the General Commercial Telegraph Company. He offered his invention to them for a thousand pounds sterling, plus a return on receipts. They required that he obtain an English patent, but he believed he could now secure one by treating his relay system—still undescribed in print—as an integral part of the apparatus. The group delayed making a decision, however, and the possible deal expired in brusque letters between lawyers for both sides.

Morse was anxious to get on to Paris, where a government commission was determining which one of several electrical telegraphs should be adopted in France. Besides, he wanted to get out of England. The tense dispute over title to Oregon had created more than the usual prejudice against America. In the outfitting of some naval expedition or fortifying of some dockyard he believed he saw signs of preparation for war. If so, the British would find it hard going: "we are better prepared than they have any idea of." Whereas he always felt alien in England, the French made him feel welcome. "How deep this welcome may be I cannot say," he added, "but if one must be cheated I like to have it done in a civil and polite way."

Morse was well positioned to present his telegraph in France. In shifting from the old Chappe system of semaphores to electrical telegraphs, the government was using for its first trials Wheatstone's needle apparatus. But the head of the government commission was Morse's good friend Arago, Secretary of the Académie des Sciences. Morse wrote to Arago before coming to Paris, saying he had examined "the English system" and could confidently affirm that his own was much simpler, far more efficient, and less expensive. As used in the French trials, Wheatstone's apparatus had been redesigned by a scientific-instrument maker named Louis Bréguet, whose grandfather had assisted Chappe. (Wheatstone, Morse noted with pleasure, "may crow on his own dunghill, but the French cock crows here.") An experimental line of the Wheatstone-Bréguet telegraph had been installed on the Paris-Rouen railroad—the first electrical telegraph line in France.

On the last day of October Morse went to inspect the line, accompanied by Bréguet himself. He took careful notes and made drawings of the stubby ten-foot-high posts and the dial-plate receiver, whose needles registered incoming signals in a code adapted from the old Chappe semaphores. Like some other British and continental instruments, Bréguet's seemed to him beautifully made. Where his own functional-looking equipment had the spare concentration on essentials of his neo-Calvinist portraits, Bréguet's and the others had fancy dial faces and handsomely carved wooden cabinets. And like them, too, it seemed to him inefficient. In one minute it could display about twelve signals transiently; in the same time, his own telegraph could record permanently "at least *120!!!*" Moreover, Bréguet's Chappe-like code was no less hectically complex than Wheatstone's. A day after inspecting the line, Morse penned a nineteen-page letter to Arago, recommending that the French government substitute his own system: "*with simpler means,* I can give *a greater amount of intelligence in a given time.*"

Arago arranged for Morse to demonstrate his telegraph for the Chamber of Deputies. However the showing may have impressed the parliamentarians, it displeased the *Revue Scientifique:* "The way the signs are produced, the writing carried out at a distance, the . . . composing of the alphabet, all these elements are essentially defective [*essentiallement defecteuses*], and it will be necessary to abandon them." Morse's inconclusive visit to Paris left at least some hope that the French might adopt his system. On that chance he left behind a telegraph with the American minister, Robert Walsh—"witnesses for me in France should attempts be made to encroach on my invention."

Concerning the most fascinating adventure of his telegraph in Europe, Morse unfortunately left no record. While he was abroad, the Continent was also being toured by his friend Charles Fleischmann, an agent of the U.S. Patent Office gathering information about foreign agriculture and mechanic arts. Morse gave Fleischmann one of his instruments, to show to bigwigs he might encounter. Fleischmann happened to arrive in Vienna around October, just when the Austrian government was considering whether to put up electrical telegraphs along its railroad routes. He thus managed to secure an audience with Prince Klemens von Metternich.

Metternich, of course, was Morse's Devil-of-all-devils, mastermind of the Leopold Foundation for supporting Catholic missionaries in America, the super-reactionary he once called "the arch contriver of the plans for stifling liberty in Europe and throughout the world." Interested in telegraphy, Metternich invited Fleischmann to set up Morse's apparatus in his palace. There Fleischmann demonstrated it to the corps of foreign diplomats in Vienna—including the ambassador of the Pope, who transmitted a brief message.

Metternich expressed astonishment at the simplicity of Morse's "beautiful Telegraph," as he called it, and opened the way for Fleischmann to demonstrate it in November before the imperial family. In the red-velvet royal reception room, Metternich himself, speaking in Italian, explained the workings of Morse's invention to Empress Maria Theresa. One can only imagine how Morse received the news, early in the new year, that the first European country to adopt his system, for a 320-mile line from Vienna to Prague, was to be Austria, that serpent entwined with the King of Rome to Jesuitize America.

TWELVE

Tantalus Still

(1846–1848)

R ETURNING to America, Morse first gave his attention to completing the Magnetic company's all-important line from New York to Washington. "The moment that is done," Kendall told him, "the telegraph will be worth *millions*." In Morse's absence, Henry O'Reilly had nearly put up the Baltimore-Philadelphia section, and Vail and Cornell had nearly finished the leg from Philadelphia to New York. With Smith's New York–Boston line almost completed too, the moment was exhilarating. Before spring, the *Observer* announced, it would be possible to speak by lightning directly from Boston to Washington.

A massive physical obstacle remained, however. The tail end of the line, the final link from Washington to New York, had to be stretched to upper Manhattan from a two-hundred-foot-high cliff in Fort Lee, New Jersey, and operate effectively across nearly two-thirds of a mile of the Hudson River. Cornell at first tried insulating the wire with india rubber and laying it across the river in pipes. He and Vail succeeded in communicating between the shores of New York and New Jersey. But a few weeks later, Morse tested the setup more rigorously by transmitting from Vail in Philadelphia, through Cornell in Fort Lee, to himself across the river in Manhattan. No current came through, as he frustratingly recorded:

> At 11.25 reduced battery to 14. Still nothing from ft. Lee.
> At 25 min to 12 I wrote "I get nothing from you" and also gave
> (26.) but received no indication.
> At 5 to 12 reduced battery to 10 cups. No indications.

274

At 12 h 5 increased battery again to 26 cups. No indications.

1. PM tried the instrument as before and with the same result.

The failure, Morse speculated, might be due to broken or twisted wires, perhaps to faulty insulation in the pipes. In any event, Cornell's submarine line was problematic. The pipe and wires might be broken at any moment by the anchors of vessels getting underway in the Hudson River.

Morse considered or tried other methods of bridging the two shores. The wires could be run on high masts erected on either side of the river, but they might be struck by lightning or blown down by wind. Morse and his assistants tried changing the locations, extending an insulated wire across the river from Jersey City to lower Manhattan. A promising solution, but after four days a vandal severed the wire. An experiment to make the Hudson itself carry the electricity, as had been done successfully on the Susquehanna, produced a current too feeble to move the instruments. "You may judge of my anxieties," Morse said. "The river I think will be a serious hindrance to us."

A different problem hindered the western line of O'Reilly's Atlantic, Lake & Mississippi company. Receiving magnets sold to him by Cornell—that is, devices that switched-in telegraph stations along the main line—were defective in themselves and incompatible with other equipment, causing long delays. A register he bought from Cornell was also "botch-work," he said, screws working loose, cogs failing to mesh. Morse discovered that Cornell had designed the equipment himself and was going into business as his competitor. Cornell offered a defense—that his instruments embodied improvements that would benefit all the patentees. But the argument was fraudulent. Privately he believed that the public expected more from Morse's system than it could deliver and would react against it, opening a market for his own inventions. Kendall warned him that he was exposing himself to prosecution.

Morse felt doublecrossed and angry. "Cornell has so bewitched, and befouled every thing he has touched . . . that I have hard work to restrain my indignation." He regarded Cornell's receiving magnets as no more than a "*clumsification*" of his own, using four magnets instead of one—sold without his permission, too, and without compensating him. Installing Cornell's instruments on Morse lines would also corrupt the desired uniformity of operation. Telegraph companies would be hard put to replace defective parts and shift operators from one part of the country to another. Cornell's treachery left Morse reeling, "almost sick," he told Vail. "Let us get along as quietly as we can with the plague till we can cut loose from him." He had learned a lesson, too. After years of keeping his own receiving magnet under wraps, he now took out a patent for the device, at last describing and diagramming it in a public document.

With whatever difficulties, the country's powerful new communication system kept expanding. Several new lines were completed by early summer. Morse enjoyed a triumph on May 12, when the Baltimore *Sun* printed an exclusive—three full columns of President Polk's address to Congress the day before, requesting a formal declaration of war against Mexico and authority to call up troops. Taking more than two and a half hours to transmit, the important speech was by far the lengthiest document ever sent by telegraph. Morse sent a copy of the *Sun* to his friend Arago in Paris. The Chamber of Deputies was debating whether the worth of the electrical telegraph had been proved enough to justify government construction of a line from Paris to Belgium. "In the United States the matter is settled irresistibly," Arago told the Chamber; "here is the President's message printed from the telegraph in two or three hours . . . it could not have been copied by the most rapid penman in a shorter time than it was transmitted." Impressed, the Deputies voted an appropriation of nearly half a million francs.

A month later, the crucial New York–to–Washington lightning line was functioning. The potential nucleus of a continental network, it was capable of leaving off dispatches at Baltimore, Wilmington, and Philadelphia. With the problem of crossing the Hudson still unsolved, messages arriving in New Jersey had to be steamboated across the river to Manhattan Island. Still, the press treated the event as extraordinary. The Washington *Union* reproduced at length the telegraphic interchange among Vail, Morse, and two unnamed operators—a nearly simultaneous four-way conversation across 260 miles:

> Washington.—Baltimore, are you in contact with Philadelphia?
> Baltimore.—Ay, ay, sir; wait a minute. (After a pause.) Go ahead.
> You can now talk with Philadelphia.
> Wash.—How do you do, Philadelphia?
> Phila.—Pretty well. Is that you, Washington?

Wash.—Ay, ay; are you connected with New York?

Phila.—Yes.

Wash.—Put me in connection with New York.

Phila.—Ay, ay; wait a minute. (After a pause.) Go ahead. Now for it.

Wash.—New York, how are you? . . .

New York.—Ay, ay. Washington, write dots. (Washington begins to write dots.) That's it; O.K. Now I have got you.

The newspaper assured its readers that the seemingly imaginary event it recorded had actually occurred—such a scene as "has never had its parallel on this earth." News of the marvel reached England as well, for once impressing the British press, at least faintly: "The Americans appear to be going rather ahead of us in this branch of enterprise."

On June 27, F. O. J. Smith opened his Boston–New York line, heralding instant communication between major American cities along some 450 miles of the Atlantic coast. Put up crudely and hastily, however, the line went out of commission more than half the time during its first months of operation. Sagging wires got in the way of passing trains, causing at least one death, and a single storm left 170 breaks. Alfred Vail had warned Smith that constructing the line would be more difficult than he supposed, advice Smith had laughed off as "quackery." Morse recalled Smith's arrogance with satisfaction: "A little less boasting a little less self complacency . . . would not have been of any harm." On the other hand, given Smith's full-time scheming, it occurred to him that Smith may have deliberately bungled the construction, hoping to buy up stock in the line at fallen prices: "A more perfect specimen of satanic possession, I do not believe exists."

The first week in September, Morse officiated as New York became electrically linked to another major city. By turning a screw he opened the pioneer 507-mile line to Buffalo, constructed by the New York, Albany & Buffalo company. Operators at intermediate stations in Troy, Albany, Utica, Syracuse, Auburn, and Rochester all saluted him over the magic wires:

> *Buffalo* sends compliments to Prof. Morse . . . and presents *Lake Erie* to *Old Ocean*.
>
> *Rochester* Office sends compliments to Prof. Morse . . . and presents *Erie Canal* to *Croton Aqueduct*

Auburn presents *State Prison* to the *Tombs.*

Syracuse sends compliments to Prof. Morse and asks how are the Yorkers.

"Is not this *the* feature of the age?" asked one amazed newspaper; "The visitant to Lake Erie holding confidential converse with his friend in New York!"

The publicity and acclaim brought Morse a new round of ambitious proposals. Telegraph lines for Mexico, Cuba, and Chile . . . a system for the new state of Texas . . . intracity telegraphs for New York's firehouses, police stations, and watchtowers. The enthusiasm did not move Congress, however. The legislators still showed no interest in nationalizing the telegraph, ending Morse's hope that the government might purchase his patent. From now on, Kendall told him, "private enterprize must carry out what it has begun." Leaping in, Kendall sold patent rights to a New York restaurant owner for organizing the Washington & New Orleans Telegraph Company. This group planned to carry the New York–Washington line south through Richmond, Charleston, and Mobile to the port of New Orleans. The commercial promise of the route was vast, as the company told potential investors: "If you want to be a *Millionaire,* take hold of this thing."

Morse's new revelations of the networked future also swelled his list of honors. "The nation's idol," as a friend described him, was elected to membership in the American Philosophical Society and awarded an LL.D. degree by Yale, its first honorary degree for work in science or invention. The twenty-six-year-old Sultan of Turkey, Abdul Mejid, conferred on him the country's Nishan Iftichar, or Order of Glory. Morse had made two instruments especially to be taken to Turkey by the president of the American Scientific Association, Professor John Laurence Smith, headed there to advise on the country's mining resources. Smith demonstrated the telegraph at the Sultan's palace on the Bosporus, running a wire from its main entrance to the royal harem. Morse's Order of Glory represented the first and only decoration the Sultan had bestowed on an American. As will appear, it took a year arriving.

Morse was further rewarded in seeing the many newspaper columns now headed "By Magnetic Telegraph." In fact, his invention was beginning to transform news gathering and to reshape American journalism. With the completion of the New York–Washington line,

New Yorkers who bought the morning edition of James Gordon Bennett's popular *Herald* could read southern news telegraphed from Washington the evening before. Bennett planned to establish permanent bureaus of reporters and editors in Buffalo and Boston to promptly report the latest eastern and western news as well.

To the press and the public, Morse's ever-lengthening lines gained a more urgent importance with the onset of the Mexican War, in May 1846. Americans eagerly waited to learn about troop movements in Texas and Mexico. News from the front arrived in Washington by pony express and steamboat, where it was tapped out over the wires. As Superintendent of the line Morse drew up regulations to ensure that all interested parties had equal access to the incoming dispatches, which could be copied at the rate of two words for one cent. Among eastern papers, competition to get out the war news first was intense and wasteful. Bennett agreed with the editors of five other New York papers to receive the news in common and share the expense of transmitting it—the beginnings of the Associated Press.

Morse stayed aloof from the business problems of his developing empire, living most of the time in Washington as Superintendent of the original line, "pleasantly situated," he said. He boarded in a room across from one occupied by the social reformer Robert Dale Owen, whom he got to know. An amiable man, he thought, but in his efforts to improve society without reference to Christianity, a "subject of pity." Morse invented a useful device for locating breaks in the lines, experimented with using not one but several electromagnets in his register so that several pens could record messages at the same time. Other inventors submitted ideas to him, many of them harebrained: plans for suspending telegraph wires across rivers by balloons, transmitting "Grammalogues" through a "Phono-Magnetic Alphabet," rendering people weightless by means of the "anti-gravitating power."

Despite Morse's distaste for the marketplace, events forced him back into its push and shove. The trouble began, in the late fall of 1846, with a clash between F. O. J. Smith and Henry O'Reilly. O'Reilly, to recall, had contracted to build two mammoth lines from the eastern United States to the Mississippi River and the Great Lakes. He also built separately for the Magnetic company the Baltimore to Philadelphia segment of the Washington–New York line. The segment had cost $4000 more and taken longer than O'Reilly planned—results of using iron instead of copper wire, and of the many rivers and creeks to be crossed. The delays set back his work on the western lines for six months to a year. Always quick to scent an advantage, Smith claimed that by failing to meet several construction deadlines, O'Reilly had violated his contract with the patent owners.

Smith charged that O'Reilly had violated his contract in a more serious way as well. The language of the contract was in many places ambiguous. But in essence O'Reilly was required to turn over what funds he raised for the western lines to trustees, appointed to disburse the money and manage the business for the mutual benefit of the subscribers and the patentees. Instead, Smith charged, O'Reilly had formed his own stock association, the Atlantic and Ohio Company, and had issued stock in Baltimore—without the patentees' knowledge. O'Reilly tried to explain that he meant his company to be "merely temporary," a way of setting things in motion, "matter of form rather than substance." He vigorously denied that he had issued any stock in Baltimore—"except *one certificate* was sent to the *one subscriber* in that City." His several accounts of the stocks, however, are inconsistent and fuzzy, some conceding that he had also distributed certificates as gratuities to helpful newspaper editors.

Whatever the truth of these matters, Smith declared O'Reilly's contract forfeit, putting him out of business. Kendall had been willing at first to negotiate the cost overrun with O'Reilly and to forgive the missed deadlines. But he could not ignore the charge that O'Reilly had formed a private stock association, in which the patentees themselves were not members. And when O'Reilly turned down an invitation to meet with him and Smith to discuss the situation, Kendall, too, had had enough. He joined Smith in declaring the contract a nullity. "I see storms ahead," he said.

They came, for the cancellation incensed O'Reilly: "Never was a more dastardly attempt of things in the shape of men, to crawl out of a contract." He had thrown himself into the telegraph business with visionary fervor, erecting posts, defying floods, overseeing operators, his eye fixed on Louisville, Kentucky, gateway for his western line to the Mississippi Valley. The thought of being compelled to abandon his quest seemed unreal. "It is like being out of the world," he said, "to be away from telegraphs." A proud man, he was also pained to disappoint the large public expectations he had aroused. A man of feeling as well, for all his braggadocio he had labored chiefly for his tenderly loved wife and sorely missed seven children. And creditors were pressing him to be paid for labor and material.

O'Reilly directed his rage at F. O. J. Smith. He believed that Smith's aim in canceling the contract was to negotiate a more profitable deal for the western lines. Under the terms of O'Reilly's contract, the patentees received a quarter interest; contracts that the patentees negotiated later with others gave them a half interest. O'Reilly believed that Smith was trying to get a half interest in the western lines as well. He also suspected that Smith wanted to cut in yet another brother-in-law, this time a Cincinnati newspaper editor named Eliphalet Case. "I for one will not tamely yield to one jot of any such scheme," O'Reilly made it known; "I will hurl it back." Attorneys having assured him that he had not violated the contract, he pressed on defiantly with the construction of telegraph lines to the West.

The "*Napoleon of the Telegraph,*" as the press tagged O'Reilly, soon won an impressive victory. Late in December, his line from Philadelphia reached Pittsburgh, making it possible to electrically transmit a message three hundred miles across the Allegheny Mountains. To mark the achievement, newspaper editors in Pittsburgh exchanged greetings with colleagues in Philadelphia, and a message went out to Washington informing President Polk that a regiment of Pittsburgh militia would soon be ready to leave for the Texas battlefront.

Morse got drawn into the quarrel at the end of the year, when Kendall and Smith filed an injunction to prevent O'Reilly from extending his line beyond Pittsburgh. O'Reilly laid no blame on Morse, with whom he had had no business contact, and even sympathized with him "for being in the hands of such men." He credited a friend's report that Morse was indignant over the situation, and had exclaimed "It is all the doings of that phantom, that spectre, F. O. J. Smith, who has haunted me like a phantom in this enterprize!" Morse may have said something to that effect, for he considered Smith's attack on O'Reilly's contract questionable, "not *morally* right if it was *legally* so."

Morse went to Philadelphia for the trial, in February 1847. It was a bleak occasion for him. His appropriation from Congress to maintain the original Baltimore-Washington system had run out, leaving him not a Superintendent but a man with no salary. And he felt alien to the scene—a U.S. circuit court. Never before had he been party to a lawsuit: "I confess to great ignorance even of the ordinary, commonplace details of a court." Attending the proceedings throughout the day, he for the first time learned the details of his contract with O'Reilly. Vail had often accused him of being a "granny," and indeed he sympathized with O'Reilly's situation and wished to make "every possible allowance" for him. If the court granted an injunction, he told Kendall, it would be decent to show leniency: "O'Reilly may have acted hastily, under excitement, under bad advisement, and in that mood have taken wrong steps." When his lawyers advised him that the case would undoubtedly go for the patentees, he arranged to have $20 sent to O'Reilly's wife, keeping the source secret: "I could not bear to think that an innocent wife, and inoffensive children should suffer."

Morse got no chance to show O'Reilly his fellow feeling and generosity. The judge, named Kane, dismissed the motion for an injunction. His ground was narrowly technical: at the end of the year, the patentees had conveyed to Smith's brother-in-law the construction rights to O'Reilly's Philadelphia-Pittsburgh line. Ignoring the charge that O'Reilly had formed his own stock company, the judge ruled that since the patentees had given up their interest in his line, they could not appear as complainants against him. "An injunction cannot be awarded at the instance of a stranger," Kane observed, "and a patentee who has assigned away his interest is nothing more."

The ruling jolted Morse. Although disposed to let O'Reilly off easily, he had also been led to believe that O'Reilly's contract violations were so manifest that an injunction would be granted as a matter of course. "I never was more deceived in regard to a case," he told Kendall. A committed believer in the law, he now questioned whether it could protect his rights. "I feel there is no security . . . the effect has been to make me doubt every thing, and whether in the eye of our laws I have any rights at all." In the aftermath of the trial, he wrote to O'Reilly in a friendly spirit, hoping to arrange a peaceful settlement. But he also girded himself: "I am preparing for the worst."

Morse much needed to be prepared. Emboldened by his victory at court, O'Reilly forged onward with his lines, using Morse's system, contract or no. *"We are nobly vindicated! . . . Now, indeed, for the Great West."* As his poles began marching west from Pittsburgh through Cincinnati to Louisville, the press disclosed that he was also building from Buffalo to Chicago. Morse was stunned. "Pray what does it all mean?" he asked Kendall. "Is the effect of the Philadelphia decision to give O'Reilly and his associates the construction *of all the Telegraphs in the Union?*" O'Reilly thought so, and believed that further efforts by Kendall and Smith to nullify his contract would backfire, destroying public confidence in Morse's system: "they may find that, like Sampson [*sic*] of old, they have pulled down ruin around their own heads."

To win public support, O'Reilly mounted an unrelenting advertising campaign. Dispatching agents into towns and cities where he planned to build, he blitzed the country with pamphlets, memorials, handbills, addresses to local legislatures, daily letters and notices in newspapers and magazines, broadsides and circulars with booming headlines: "TO THE PEOPLE OF THE UNITED STATES." Each communiqué lambasted the patentees and assured existing and potential stockholders that he had the legal right to use Morse's system. Kendall's partisan writing as a political journalist during the Jackson era had trained him in riposte. He and Smith answered O'Reilly's forces ad by ad, circular by circular—"TO THE PEOPLE OF THE WEST"—documenting O'Reilly's violations of the contract, warning investors against subscribing to his lines, threatening to prosecute any of his operators who used Morse equipment.

Publicly and in private the two sides scourged each other as "Molochs," "hyena-like personages," "damned Skinflints," "guerilla speculators." Morse-ites routinely ridiculed O'Reilly as "the Great O'Reilly," greatest humbugger of a humbugging age. O'Reilly-ites lampooned the wizened somber Kendall as "Old Amos," "Amos the Pious," or "Pope Amos." F. O. J. Smith they impaled as "F. O. G. Smith" or simply "Fog"—names that stuck.

Morse abhorred the brawling and name-calling. But with the press sometimes identifying O'Reilly's foes as "Morse & Co.," he, too, came within the crossfire. "Notwithstanding my matters are all in the hands of agents and I have nothing to do with any of the arrangements," he groaned, "I am held up by name to the odium of the public." So recently a national hero, he saw himself become something like a national villain, "a target for every vile fellow to shoot at." And he looked on as his invention, the so much praised wonder of the age, became derided and discarded.

O'Reilly had used Morse instruments on his west-moving lines. But he now began seeking out devices by other inventors to replace them. He favored the telegraph of a Vermonter named Royal House. It used a piano-like set of keys to transmit messages, one key per letter of the alphabet. The messages were reproduced at the receiving station by a type wheel that stamped the letters on a paper tape. Several newspapers highly praised House's method. "Instead of an arbitrary character, like that which is used in Professor Morse's machine, there is the letter of the alphabet," reported the New York *Herald;* "It is . . . decidedly superior to any other telegraph ever used." O'Reilly gave House money to develop his system, and secured rights to it for his western line. At the same time, he publicly belittled Morse's telegraph, making known its supposed line breakdowns, errors in transmission, and other shortcomings. Morse and his associates had "diddled Uncle Sam out of $30,000," he snickered; "There is more genius, twenty times, in House, than there is in Morse."

House printing telegraph
(Smithsonian Institution)

Morse examined a model of House's invention at the Patent Office. He was certain that it infringed his patent and could be stopped in the courts or, if not, would prove to be "all humbug." The printing of common letters seemed to him not only no advantage but a serious disadvantage. It called for twenty-eight keys instead of his one, and depended on a dense machinery of springs, magnetic coils, and clock trains, plus a hydraulic pump. Untested over long distances and slower than his own telegraph, it represented an "improvement *backwards.*" He lumped House with Cornell and others who were trying to capitalize on the success of his system, "to avail themselves of its popularity to make something for themselves." Just the same, an editor of the New York *Evening Post* told him that after witnessing the device in operation he decided that its importance had been not exaggerated but underrated.

Though he thought House's invention no more than a fussy gadget, Morse wished to protect himself against it. He filed a caveat with the Patent Office for a printing telegraph of his own. "I shall proceed to make it for curiosity's sake, and to defeat these *would-be* infringers on their own ground." But O'Reilly's ground was always wide. He asked associates in Washington to speak with foreign diplomats and urge them to consider adopting some other telegraph than Morse's for their countries. Morse believed that O'Reilly was also actively promoting House's system in England. He prepared an article for the press that incorporated a letter "from a gentleman of distinguished mechanical science in London to his friend in America." The scientific gentleman avowed that the English considered printing telegraphs "*philosophical toys,* of *no practical value.*" The gentleman was his brother Sidney, then visiting London. The friend was himself, but he preferred "not being known in the matter," he explained, withdrawal from bare-knuckle capitalism seeming more desirable than ever.

O'Reilly understood that House's invention might infringe Morse's patent. To head off any attempt to attack the printing telegraph on that basis he turned the legal question into an ideological issue. He had always looked for investors not among bankers and financiers but among farmers, shopkeepers, and small traders who had only tens or a few hundred dollars to spare. He mustered their support for House's telegraph by calling his line "The People's Line" and depicting Morse and his associates as monopolists, enemies of the competitive economy that would stimulate the development of new and better systems. "We take the *strongest Anti-monopoly ground,*" he proclaimed; "*Equal Rights* to *all* modes of Telegraphing." A broadside ditty set his message to the tune of "Dan Tucker":

The "People's Line" has just begun,
When we get thro' we'll have some fun. . . .

CHORUS
—Get out of the way with your monopoly,
Get out of the way with your monopoly. . . .

O'Reilly especially aimed his propaganda at westerners, picturing Morse's supposed monopoly as part of the eastern stranglehold on the burgeoning frontier.

Behind O'Reilly's efforts to turn him into an "odious monopolizer," Morse saw a quite different object: "It is to destroy any feeling of sympathy in the public mind, from the gross robberies committed upon me." To his grief, the efforts worked. After years of threadbare hanging on, he found letter writers to the daily papers perversely deriding him as a "nabob," comparing him to Nicholas Biddle, estimating his wealth at half a million, a million, "far beyond what any other patentee has ever obtained in this country."

As Morse feared might happen, the press itself turned against him, "giving currency to falsehoods, and magnifying troubles." Editors had come to depend on the telegraph and hoped to get cheaper rates from O'Reilly than from him: "they join in the cry of 'monopoly,' 'no monopolies,' to profit by the competition." New York papers stood to profit most from lower rates, especially Horace Greeley's *Tribune,* a leading consumer of telegraph news: "Shall [the telegraph] be republican and free," the *Tribune* asked, "or an agent of aristocratic despotism—shall it be American or shall it be Russian?" Among the few New York papers that defended Morse, the *Day Book* accused O'Reilly of bribing editors with gifts of stock: he "has made half the editors in the country his partners. Why shouldn't they think him one of the greatest men of the age?"

O'Reilly found other powerful allies in shielding House's telegraph from charges of infringement. He spoke with America's leading scientist, Joseph Henry. Henry had grown angry at Morse after reading Alfred Vail's *Description of the American Electro Magnetic Telegraph,* a popular pamphlet version of the book Vail had published while Morse was abroad. The pamphlet gave a flattering account of how Morse created his system, but did not mention the contribution to it of Henry's work in increasing the distance through which electromagnets could be actuated, or of Henry's advice, encouragement, and endorsements. Henry blamed Morse for the omission, supposing that he had reviewed and approved Vail's work. He denounced the pamphlet to one of his classes at Princeton—"HENRY sticks it into MORSE," a student reported. He also discussed his opinions with O'Reilly, as O'Reilly informed the public: "some of the most competent judges in the Union, (such as Professor Henry,) familiar with House's as well as Morse's Telegraphs, declare that House's system does not infringe on Morse's."

Greatly though he had once admired Morse, O'Reilly now craved revenge against him—"that cypher *Morse*," as he said, with his "crocodile tears & lamentations." Trying to wipe out the public's image of Morse as The Lightning Man, he announced a competition for the best essay on the "Progress of Electric Discovery, with reference to the Telegraphic system." He promised a $300 prize to the writer who most clearly proved that neither Morse nor any other single person could be said to have invented the electromagnetic telegraph. He also revived the *Sully* squabble, enlisting Morse's old nemesis, Dr. Charles Jackson: "you are said to have been present when Professor Morse claims to have invented the 'first practicable Electric telegraph' . . . I invoke your aid, in the name of truth and justice, to rebuke charlatanism grown rampant."

At the moment Jackson was caught up in a violent dispute with the medical profession. In October 1846 a surgeon at Massachusetts General Hospital had performed the first-ever operation on a patient anesthetized by ether. The surgeon had been persuaded to try the procedure by a former pupil of Jackson's, a Boston dentist named William T. G. Morton. Jackson stepped forward to claim that he himself had first conceived anesthesia, and to demand one-fourth of the profits from licensing the invention.

Embroiled as he was in what would be a lifelong battle, Jackson lent himself to O'Reilly's vendetta. "Those who know Mr. Morse," he said, "are aware of the fact, that he had no knowledge of electromagnetism previous to his voyage in company with me in the packet ship Sully." Pseudonymous articles appeared in the press, recounting and supporting Jackson's version of The *Sully* Story. In a Detroit newspaper, "Horicon" declared: "It was on this passage that he explained and illustrated to Mr. Morse the principles of the Magnetic Telegraph." "Morion"—a.k.a. Henry O'Reilly—complained in Greeley's

Tribune that "our learned countrymen, Drs. Henry and Jackson, are deprived of the honor and credit justly their due."

Morse had no appetite for renewing his war with Jackson: "The most charitable construction of the Dr.'s conduct is to attribute it to a monomania induced by excessive vanity." Feeling he must protect his reputation, however, he investigated Jackson's claims to the discovery of Letheon (as the anesthetic was called). He also wrote to several Bostonians asking whether, years before, Jackson had ever shown them a model or drawing of an electrical telegraph. He particularly wished to disprove Jackson's charge that he had known nothing about electromagnetism before meeting his adversary aboard the *Sully*. In fact, six years earlier he had attended lectures on the subject at the New York Athenaeum. The lecturer, Professor James Freeman Dana, had died. But Morse located the very magnet Dana had used for his demonstrations. This magnet of 1826 had stayed in his mind, and in its shape and wiring was identical with the magnet he had drawn in his notebook on the *Sully* in 1832. The comparison proved that he had had a general knowledge of electromagnetism long before meeting Jackson: "The first application of the electro magnet to Telegraphic purposes was by one S.F.B. Morse and no mistake."

O'Reilly launched his most intense attack where he thought Morse was most vulnerable and had most to lose—the legality of the patent. "We have now the 'bull by the horns.' Let him roar!" He and his associates challenged the patent on every conceivable ground, among them the refusal of the British Attorney General, Sir John Campbell, to grant Morse an English patent. "His failure to secure a Patent . . . was ascribed to *national prejudice*," O'Reilly said, "but this falsehood is exploded by the fact that Great Britain readily granted to Professor House, who is a Yankee, a Patent for his American Letter-Printing Telegraph." He also seized on a technicality in Morse's patent application. Morse had signed the document on April 7, 1838. But O'Reilly found that the date when the Committee on Commerce recommended Morse's appropriation for the Baltimore-Washington line was April 6. He publicized the discrepancy, implying that Morse had gulled Congress into supporting an invention that had no legal existence. "Here was a deliberate falsehood," a Louisville newspaper pointed out, "a palpable and blushing fraud practiced on the Representatives of the people for the purpose of getting thirty thousand dollars voted to Professor Morse and his associates."

Even worse, O'Reilly charged, Morse had conned the government into granting him ownership of a force in nature, a so-called general principle. Contemporary patent law was ambiguous on the question of whether an inventor could patent the general application of a natural force, or only a specific application of it embodied in some machine. Morse's patent claimed "the use of the motive power" of electromagnetism "as a means of operating or giving motion to machinery, which may be used . . . in any desired manner for the purpose of telegraphic communication." As O'Reilly interpreted this for the public, it meant that Morse had pilfered exclusive right to a "general principle." "If this general principle could be patented," he jeered, "please lose no time in applying for Patent Rights for your Schuyl-Kill water running down a man's throat so glibly when aided by a little Coniac [*sic*]."

The press and public debated the "general principle" issue. A writer to the Troy, New York, *Daily Post,* for instance, took up and reinforced O'Reilly's indictment:

> Suppose a man who had obtained a patent for a water wheel to propel machinery, were to set up the claim that no one could use water to propel machinery by any kind of wheel subsequently invented, though it might differ from his in every particular, would not even Mr. Morse treat with contempt so absurd and preposterous a claim; and yet, is it more preposterous than his attempts to monopolize Electro Magnetism. . . .

The editor of another paper compared Morse and his associates to hucksters, "venders of wooden nutmegs, proclaiming that everything else except their wares are humbug and frauds! As if the laws of Electro-Magnetism have not an infinite variety of application!"

Morse answered the attack on his patent point by point. He assured the public that he asserted no exclusive right to electromagnetism, but only to its use in transmitting and recording intelligence over long distances. As the fight over legal terms raged on, however, O'Reilly made new deals, built new lines, and enjoyed new triumphs. In August 1847 his poles reached Cincinnati. By late December, thrillingly, they stood opposite St. Louis, on the east branch of the great river: "Thank Heaven! The Mississippi is now reached," he exulted; "Hurra for the '*Atlantic, Lake & Mississippi*' Line—visionary as people once tho't it!" He applied to the corporation of the city for permission to erect posts in town, determined to march on to Louisville.

O'Reilly paid a price for his victories. At one point he had not seen his wife and seven children in Albany for thirteen months: "there is no person on our whole lines who *suffers, deeply suffers,* as I do," he told a friend. Even when one of his sons became seriously ill, "pining away to a skeleton," he felt too swept up to return home: "I can hardly write to the family, much less be with them." Each day's progress, too, meant overcoming the same heap of problems that confronted Morse's companies—how to interest investors, cross bodies of water, deal with shipping delays and snapped wires. A friend noticed that the struggle had worn on him, "changed your usually warm & generous disposition to a somewhat more bitter & less generous condition."

To Morse it seemed that O'Reilly meant not only to defraud but also to torment him. "It cannot but be painful to witness the vindictiveness with which I have been personally assailed, and the reckless manner in which my patent has been denounced." It depressed him to think that in leaving his painting career to become an inventor, he had simultaneously won applause and contempt, fame and disgrace. Depressingly too, he learned at the end of the year that a $1500 debt of his father's, of which he had known nothing, remained unpaid after twenty years. At 7 percent interest, there was owing $8000, for which he remained responsible. His whole life seemed cursed by such a pattern of cancellation, a stasis of self-negation that got him nowhere—profit came with loss, success with failure, attraction with repulsion. "So the world goes," he told his brother Richard. "It is as Sidney says, '*Tantalus still.*' "

A showdown in the conflict came late in 1847, when O'Reilly organized the People's Telegraph Company to build a line from Louisville through Nashville to New Orleans. The route unmistakably violated his contract with the patentees, which placed the termination of his western line at St. Louis. Kendall challenged O'Reilly by forming a rival group, The New Orleans & Ohio Telegraph Company. Tauntingly, it planned to mirror the movement of the People's company, building alongside it from Louisville to Nashville, thence to the Crescent City. Kendall formed companies to construct other lines in direct competition with O'Reilly's from Buffalo to Detroit, Detroit to Milwaukee, and elsewhere. "We must be *everywhere,*" he said.

On the New Orleans route, O'Reilly intended to use what he advertised as "A NEW AND IMPROVED AMERICAN TELEGRAPH (and NOT Morse's plan)." Not Morse's, or House's either. While publicly beating the drum for House's telegraph, he had always privately thought it "not simple enough." For his potentially lucrative line to New Orleans he chose an instrument called the Columbian telegraph, designed by two young telegraphers in his Cincinnati office, Samuel K. Zook and E. F. Barnes. Admirers of the Columbian alleged that it differed from Morse's system in two ways. Its register used permanent magnets instead of electromagnets; and it had a novel galvanometer-like relay that supposedly protected transmission during thunderstorms. O'Reilly-friendly newspapers played up the device as "the greatest discovery of the present day." The St. Louis *Reveille* congratulated its creators for teaching that "there are other minds in this country than Mr. Morse's."

Probably so, but it was less certain that the "other minds" included Zook and Barnes. Morse thought their apparatus unquestionably illegal, "a manifest and direct infringement of my Patent." Here he did not differ greatly from O'Reilly. For all the hoopla in the press, several of O'Reilly's associates and legal counsel told him frankly that the Columbian telegraph violated Morse's patent rights—advice that did not deter him from using it.

By January 1848 a gang of twenty-five Irish workmen were erecting Morse wires and posts on the road from Louisville to Nashville, alongside a gang of fifteen erecting a Columbian line for O'Reilly. Morse's contractor, a Louisville lawyer named Taliaferro P. Shaffner, expected fights and prepared for a "real 'hug.' " "My men are well armed," he told Morse, and "I think they can do their duty." Morse implored him to avoid violence: "It would give me the deepest sorrow if I should learn that a single individual, friend or foe, has been injured in life or limb." The harm, it turned out, went no further than some yelling. The rival crews worked side by side for fifteen miles, when Shaffner's pulled ahead and in another four days left O'Reilly's men twenty-five miles behind.

As the competing lines proceeded, pro-O'Reilly newspapers in Kentucky treated Morse and Kendall to withering scorn. The Massachusetts-born Kendall had spent ten years in Lexington and Frankfort as a lawyer, newspaper publisher, and politician. Old animosities against him had lived on. The Frankfort press mocked him as a "venomous reptile," "poor driveller," or "demented old man"—a hireling of "the blood-sucking calves that are hanging on the teats of Morse's monopoly." Kendall took it all with suave cynicism, as ravings sufficient, he said, "to excite the sympathy of every kind heart." Morse, as he often did, met the abuse of himself on the Washingtonian high ground of disinterested patriotism: "Through these reckless attacks upon me," he wrote to the editor of the Louisville *Journal,* "the merit of inventions, rightfully belonging to our own country (as in the present case) is given to other nations."

Morse's genteel replies made subscribers to his lines uneasy. The director of one company told him their concerns: "Many of our stockholders ... begin to think you cannot protect our interest in your patent. They say you let O'Reily [*sic*] go on with impunity." Although prodded by many others to take legal action, Morse considered O'Reilly's course self-destructive. And he believed in bearing abuse with Christian meekness, leaving chastisement to God. Indeed his brother Richard suggested that God perhaps had made him eminent so that he might bear his cross before the public, affording "an illustrious exhibition of the christian character."

By early spring, however, Morse had exhausted his humility. "It is high time these infringers should be brought up to the Bull ring," he admitted, "and the sooner a case is decided in the courts the better." Soon after O'Reilly opened the Louisville-Nashville section of his New Orleans line, Kendall sued him for infringing Morse's patent. O'Reilly replied in a fiery pamphlet entitled *"Letter of* HENRY O'RIELLY [*sic*] *to Professor* MORSE." Announcing that by early summer his lines would be in operation over four thousand miles from the Canada frontier to the Gulf of Mexico, he said he welcomed, indeed invited, indeed compelled Morse to sue him. He addressed Morse as a greedy hypocrite who bemoaned the "suffering poverty of genius" while teaming up with Smith and Kendall to extort money from him, "to blackmail me into the allowance of DOUBLE PRICE BEYOND WHAT YOUR CONTRACT REQUIRED FROM ME." In defense this time of the Columbian telegraph, he charged that Morse had twice been denied a British patent "for *want of originality*" and challenged him to find a single rational American citizen "who believes that your Patent includes the lightning of Heaven." He therefore welcomed a judicial inquiry. "The facts ... will prove whether you or I most thoroughly deserve the 'piratical' reputation of plundering other men."

For weeks Morse scarcely found time to sleep and eat as he prepared exhaustively for the trial, to be held in Frankfort, the state capital of Kentucky. "All my time has been occupied in defense," he told Sidney, "in putting evidence into something like legal shape that I am the inventor of the Electro-Magnetic Telegraph!! Would you have believed it ten years ago that a question could be raised on that subject?" He tried to document as fully as possible all of his early work on the telegraph. He obtained affidavits from the Captain and some passengers on the *Sully*. Through an ad in the *Observer* he turned up the physician who had treated the finger he burned with molten lead when casting type for his primitive port-rule. He gathered decade-old newspaper items and notes for experiments, facts and dates about his demonstrations at the Speedwell Iron Works, accounts from painting students and daguerreotype customers who had seen his in-progress apparatus at the University. Kendall spurred him to "push the adversary to the wall" and tried to cheer him up: "The troubles you encounter are but the tax a man has to pay for wealth and fame."

Morse attended all fifteen days of the trial, which opened in Frankfort on August 24. A district judge presided, the Honorable Thomas B. Monroe, who took several hours delivering his opening statement. Three lawyers represented each side, collectively an impressive group of three former circuit judges, two professors of law, and one U.S. district attorney. More than a week was consumed in reading depositions and examining various telegraphs. The depositions on Morse's behalf included two by current chief examiners in the U.S. Patent Office: Charles Page, who had served him as a consultant; and Leonard Gale, his colleague and collaborator at New York University in 1836–37, and formerly a patentee, although Morse had recently bought out Gale's one-sixteenth interest. The O'Reilly depositions included one from Charles Jackson, who swore that when he mentioned electromagnetism to Morse aboard the *Sully*, Morse exclaimed: "*Electro-magnetism! What is it?*"

The competing telegraphs were demonstrated in court, and explained to the judge by Morse and by E. F. Barnes. O'Reilly's lawyers contended that the Barnes-Zook Columbian was an independent invention that did not violate Morse's patent. They also assailed the patent. They argued, among other things, that Morse had obtained a French patent for the same invention; that his specifications claimed a monopoly on the "general principle" of electromagnetism; and that he had copied his apparatus from those of Edward Davy and Karl Steinheil. O'Reilly enjoyed and approved his lawyers' presentation: "Plucked Jackdaw never looked *nakeder* than did the 'learned Professor.' "

Judge Monroe rendered his opinion around September 13. It took several hours to read in court and when published ran sixty pages of small type, double columns. He ruled that the French patent had no bearing on the American patent; that the objection to Morse's claim of a "general principle" was itself too general; and that in its structure and mode of operation the instrument demonstrated by Barnes infringed on Morse, who was the true and only inventor of the telegraph. He awarded Morse an absolute injunction against O'Reilly's line—"so broad and comprehensive that nothing is left for evasion," the Frankfort *Yeoman* commented; "O'Reilly will see he has no means of going on."

O'Reilly did not blink. He promised to take his case to the Supreme Court, and meanwhile to keep his southern line in operation using some other instrument than the Columbian. In Louisville, the pro-O'Reilly *Courier* predicted that the judge's unfair decision would inflame public opinion against Morse's telegraph: "From one end of this Union to the other the people will speak out on this subject, and this monster can never now be smuggled through Congress. It is dead, dead, dead." To bring on the outcry, O'Reilly floated stories of high-level conspiracy. He hinted or alleged in print that a "Morse clique" controlled the Patent Office; that Judge Monroe had been appointed by Kendall; that one of Morse's lawyers, also named Monroe, was the judge's brother. He howled for the judge to be impeached and demanded an investigation: "*a more extraordinary case . . .* has never characterized the history of any invention in art or science."

Morse had learned from experience that O'Reilly responded to loss by raising the stakes. Still, the nature and ferocity of the attack stunned him. "Every effort of corruption is making, to rob and *murder* me, (murder I mean my reputation,) for if they can destroy that, they hope to be justified in *robbing a thief.*" He again felt at a loss what to do. Given the hostility toward him of many newspapers, he could not appeal through the press. Nor was he certain that he could rest on his reputation, preserving a dignified silence.

O'Reilly's overreaching, however, only increased his losses. He tried to skirt the injunction by strictly applying its definition of Morse's telegraph as a device for recording long-distance messages. He instructed operators of his Columbian telegraphs in Louisville to make themselves the recorders. They would receive incoming messages by ear and take them down by hand, listening to the click of the iron armature striking the electromagnet. The underlying idea had occurred to Morse at least a decade earlier, and at present many of his own operators could aurally "read" off the clicking magnet whole columns of incoming newsprint. Since the "Columbian" telegraphs no longer recorded long-distance messages, they no longer infringed Morse's invention. Morse's counsel fought O'Reilly's dodge by moving for a writ of attachment, successfully. The court called O'Reilly's attempt a palpable evasion of the injunction. He could not be located, but E. F. Barnes, his business manager in Louisville, was arrested for contempt and ordered to pay court costs.

O'Reilly tried again, and lost more. Since the injunction covered only Kentucky, he moved his Louisville office and apparatus across the Ohio River to Jeffersonville, Indiana. In this way he could use his wires in Kentucky to telegraph through to Nashville, while no longer sending messages to or from Kentucky or stationing an operator there. Once more Morse's lawyers went to court against him. This time the judge ruled that O'Reilly's sidestepping constituted an aggravated contempt of the injunction. Incensed, he ordered a U.S. marshal to seize enough of O'Reilly's wires and posts to halt all Columbian transmission through Kentucky. O'Reilly was again away from the scene, but learned that if he came within reach of a writ the judge would imprison him for six months.

The end of 1848 brought Morse some additional healing for his wounds. In November, newspapers for the first time printed the results of a presidential election reported by telegraph. Readers of the morning *Herald* in New York could find out how voters in fourteen states, nearly half of the nation, had voted the day before. And the following month Morse at last received the Nishan Iftichar, or Order of Glory, awarded to him twelve months earlier by the Sultan of Turkey. The delay was in part due to the English legation in Turkey, which protested that Morse had not invented the telegraph, and in part to the American naval commander who brought the decoration overseas but for some reason failed to deliver it. It turned up in December at the Boston Custom House, with import duties to be paid.

Morse's Order of Glory was worth waiting for—a gold brooch said to be studded with two hundred diamonds. The accompanying diploma stated that he now bore the Imperial Monogram, and praised him as a man of science, "a Model of the Chiefs of the Nation of the Messiah—may his grade be increased." He asked the U.S. minister to Turkey to convey to the Sultan his profound appreciation: "no attention I have ever received, has excited such grateful emotions as this from the illustrious and truly noble head of the Turkish Empire." Fifteen years earlier, in depicting the Catholic peril, he had warned that Americans were vulnerable because of their "*anti-republican fondness for titles.*" Just the same, in trying to achieve a sense of self-importance he had always sported such titles as Professor, President, Superintendent. He told the minister that he also wished to learn what distinguished persons had received the decoration, and what rank it conferred upon them.

Morse discovered once again that, as Sidney said, the world was Tantalus still. Several newspapers reported that his glittering Nishan Iftichar gave him the rank of Pasha. They pointed out that Article 13 of the Constitution required a U.S. citizen to obtain the consent of Congress before accepting a title of nobility or honor from any "emperor, king, prince or foreign power." On an American who had not received consent, as Morse had not, the Constitution imposed a severe penalty: "such person shall cease to be a citizen of the United States." A New York paper speculated that when "Pacha" Morse became "denationalized," his telegraph would revert to the people for their benefit.

And O'Reilly's go-ahead whirlwind was back. His circulars blared that he had sent a memorial to Congress proposing to establish a spectacular new line of telegraph—to the Far West, bringing the rest of the Union in touch with Oregon and California, "*connecting the Atlantic and Pacific coast by lightning intercourse.*"

Whatever Morse might count up as a satisfaction without a sting appeared in a brief newspaper notice: "Professor Morse, the lightning man, as he is called, was married on Thursday last, to Miss Sarah E. Griswold, of Louisiana."

THIRTEEN

The Great Telegraph Case

(1849–1853)

S ARAH Elizabeth Griswold, Morse's second wife, was the daughter of an army officer, born on Christmas Day at a military fort near Lake Superior. Not much more is known about her past, and very little about her married life with Morse. If they wrote to each other, the letters were not preserved or have been removed from surviving papers of the Morse family. In the few extant daguerreotypes of Sarah she looks plain but amiable—medium height, oval face, tightly coiffed chestnut hair parted in the middle, a pencil-line smile on her narrow lips. In two ways Morse's choice of her seems unusual. She was thirty years younger than he. And she was deaf.

Morse first saw Sarah at a relative's house a half-dozen years before their marriage. "I was exceedingly struck with her beauty, her artlessness, her amiable deportment. . . . I found myself in love with her then before I was aware." His financial situation ruled out any thought of marrying, however, and she was then barely twenty. He stifled his feelings and thought no more of her until—"accidentally shall I say? no providentially"—he saw her in Utica at the wedding of his son Charles in June 1848.

Sarah had matured, and her character impressed him. The wedding party included his partly deaf son Finley, whose "defects" kept him apart, seated alone in a corner. "I saw Sarah go to him, and taking his hand drew him up and putting her arm in his, she walked the room for some time with him endeavoring to amuse him, and then seated herself by him and in every way she could devise amused him for a long while." Sarah's kind sympathy fixed itself in his mind. Two months later they married.

Sarah and Susan Morse at Locust Grove (Daguerreotype by
Samuel F. B. Morse)
(New-York Historical Society)

Sarah had been deaf since the age of one, owing to a fall or perhaps to scarlet fever. Early in adolescence she attended for three years
the state-run New York Institution for the Deaf and Dumb, where she
learned to communicate in sign language. Morse believed, or more
likely only wanted to believe, that she had gradually been recovering
her hearing. He said that he found no difficulty conversing with her,
but this may have been due mostly to her proficiency in lipreading:
"the simple movement of the lips seen across the room, without a
sound being uttered she understands perfectly." Although her speech,
too, was impaired, he deliberately did not learn the sign alphabet, certain that if she conversed with him her articulation would improve: "I

have little doubt that I can with God's help teach her to speak as plain as anyone." About two years after their marriage, he put her under the care of a physician named Turnbull, well known for his treatment of ear and eye problems. Turnbull tried to persuade him that as a result of the therapy Sarah could hear better than ever. But Morse's own senses provided no evidence of improvement, and he wrote off Turnbull as a fake.

Sarah's impairment deepened Morse's feeling for her: "her misfortune of not hearing, and defective speech only excited the more my love & pity." He recalled Sidney remarking, before his own marriage, that he intended to choose a respectable poor girl, who would feel for him not only affection but also gratitude for befriending her. Sarah's situation at the time of their marriage was similar—"portionless" and partly dependent on the beneficence of her sister's husband. He increased Sarah's debt to him by taking in her mother to live with them. Such bonds of need, he believed—"guarantees of affection aside from mere *personal* love"—augured well for the solidity of their marriage.

Morse felt no less indebted to Sarah. She had come to him in an up-and-down, "singularly checkered" existence. As a widower he had courted a succession of young women, each time ending up frazzled and dejected: "how many several trials I have passed through on this subject of another wife . . . how many times I have been thwarted and disappointed till almost in despair." But having bowed in submission to God's will, he now had everything in a wife he could have desired. "She is noble hearted, considerate, most anxious to please me in all things," he beamed. "I say every thing when I say that my dear Lucretia could not be more so." He relished the aura of content Sarah gave off—always busy with her needle or with a book, the very pattern of neatness in her person, sensitive to the beauties of nature. "I am almost overwhelmed with gratitude. His Gifts are worthy of himself. I have looked to him for this precious gift for twenty years."

Sarah attended an Episcopal church, but in Morse's view she lacked genuine piety. He instructed her in true religion, as he had done years earlier for Lucrece, praying that she might come to experientially know what it meant to have an interest in Christ's death and salvation. "Love him, dear Sarah, pray for the Holy Spirit to take of the things of Christ and show them to you. By his aid you can be taught truly to love him." She showed serious concern for her soul, and he drew improving lessons for her from events. In one instance he mentioned a man who had been killed by a train while attempting to save a horse that balked on the tracks. "Let it have its effect my precious Sarah, on your own heart," he counseled. "How would the summons find you, supposing it should come as suddenly as to the poor man . . . *Faith in Christ alone* calms every fear."

Morse brought Sarah into comfortable circumstances. His wealth can only be estimated, but in 1852 he held nearly $400,000 in stock in six telegraph companies, besides cash he earned from the lines as dividends and from income-yielding real estate in Utica. For $17,500 he had bought a 100-acre farm property about two miles from the village of Poughkeepsie. It included an unpretentious but substantial house fronting the Hudson River. The landscape pleased his painter's eye: "every variety of surface, plain, hill, dale, glens, running streams and fine forest . . . the Fishkill Mountains towards the south and the Catskills towards the north; the Hudson with its varieties of river craft, steamboats of all kinds, sloops." The farm gained in commercial and personal value from a soon-to-be-built railroad line that would bring him within two and a half hours of New York City.

To manage the large place, Morse hired several domestics, a cook, and a live-in farming family named Teller. When asked at a court trial to state his occupation, he replied: "I . . . am at present a farmer." In time the place did become a working farm with a stable of horses, producing milk and butter, hogs for slaughter, and prizewinning wine, as well as potatoes, corn, and other vegetables, some of which he donated to a "Home of the Friendless." He took a pew in the local Presbyterian church, a fifteen-minute ride away. Indulging his love of music, he had a pianoforte and stool shipped from New York City by barge.

Morse gave his estate the same name contrived for it by some former owners: Locust Grove. After years of nomadism he was happy to have a home—at least "as far as we are permitted to call any place this side heaven home." He grew fonder of Locust Grove every day. Two years after settling in he decided to enlarge and transform his house. For the remodeling he hired the eminent New York architect Alexander Jackson Davis, designer of the influential Gothic building of New York University and author of *Rural Residences* (1837). He also hired Davis to shape the grounds according to the latest texts on landscape gardening, creating an ideal illustration of Nature. Among other things this meant landscaping the approach so that, from any one point, only portions of the house could be seen peeping through the verdure, teasing the imagination with suggestions of an infinite variety of "picturesque beauty."

Morse himself made many sketches of the house he desired. Davis' plans went through several stages of design and redesign before the remodeling was completed early in 1852. He encased the original Federal-style house in an octagonal Tuscan-style villa, featuring a dramatic four-story tower that afforded panoramic views of the lordly Hudson. The numerous rooms included a large library, into which Morse conducted a telegraph wire from a nearby line for his personal use.

Morse and Sarah quickly produced a family. Within four and a half years after their marriage, they had two sons and a daughter at Locust Grove, whom they named Samuel Arthur Breese Morse, Cornelia Livingston Morse, and William Goodrich Morse. As children of his old age, Morse looked on them as unmerited gifts from heaven: "My own unworthiness seemed more than ever great, so great that I was tempted to cry out, Why is all this to me a sinner?" Much as he enjoyed hearing their cheerful voices, however, he cautioned Sarah not to make them playthings: "Remember they have souls, and these are infinitely valuable, while the perishing body, though to be suitably cared for, is in comparison utterly worthless." He attended personally to their religious training, as he had done with his first brood, and as Jedediah and Elizabeth had done with him. In language that by now had passed through several generations of Morses, he set out for them the doctrine of original sin, the quintessential importance of the Bible as God's revealed Word, and the superiority of Christianity to other religions.

Morse's children by Lucrece had become adults without ever having lived with their father. But now, for the first time in twenty years, he was able to have all of them around him, at least temporarily. Charles moved into Locust Grove for a while with his pretty wife, Manette. Morse had given them $5000 in Magnetic company stock as a wedding present, and Charles said that he counted himself blessed to have "such a kind and affectionate father." The young man felt down, however. He had quit Yale to take up farming, but had given up that fancy and now was having trouble finding work. Lucrece's deceased brother had left him some money, which he apparently misspent.

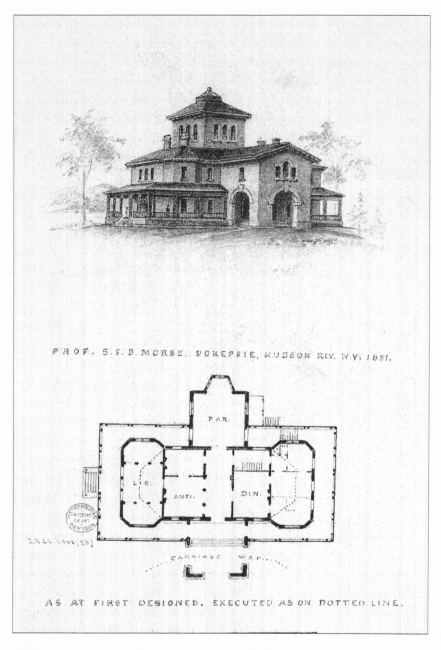

PROF. S. F. B. MORSE. POKEPSIE, HUDSON RIV. N.Y. 1851.

AS AT FIRST DESIGNED. EXECUTED AS ON DOTTED LINE.

Alexander Jackson Davis, plan for Morse home at Locust Grove
(Metropolitan Museum of Art)

Morse had little sympathy for his son's floundering. He thought Charles talented, but disorganized and careless with money, a soft touch for "any plausibly spoken man." Charles had thrown away hundreds of dollars—"and if he had millions it would be the same." He therefore refused to help Charles out financially. At the same time he contributed $1000 to Yale, but that was a different matter, he told Charles, a "religious duty." He intended, he added, to spend his money on "benevolent purposes" and Charles "should rejoice at such a prospect." As for the future disposition of his estate, he planned to keep a close watch on his son: "it will depend on his acquirement of *safe* habits, whether I leave him anything."

Finley, too, lived for a while at Locust Grove, working the farm, fishing, being helpful. Twenty-five years old, he missed his uncle Sidney, who for most of his life had served as a stand-in father. To Morse, Finley seemed a sort of sacred fool, handicapped by his condition but also elevated by it. "There is no improvement in the character of his mind, and I despair of ever seeing any," Morse wrote, "but this affliction comes with so many alleviations of . . . docility, moral if not religious principle, health &c., that it is scarcely an affliction." Lucrece's brother had apparently left money for Finley, too. Morse planned to invest it in the Locust Grove farm, paying his son interest while making certain that he would always have a home.

Susan—"my *ancient* daughter," Morse called her—remained in Arroyo, Puerto Rico, sending monkeys as gifts for his new children. But she visited Locust Grove annually, bringing his grandson, also named Charles, who to his delight showed an aptitude for drawing. At thirty, the daughter who had spent her childhood longing to be with him was now two years older than his wife. Her life in Puerto Rico seems to have been often unhappy. Contending with ants and lizards that chewed her plants, she referred to the island as "this horrid place." Her husband, Edward, had established a distillery to make puncheons of rum. But he met with uneven success, rich one moment, poor the next. Probably to help out, Morse gave Susan $10,000 worth of telegraph stock. On one annual visit he took her to the Catskill Mountain House, a well-known resort. She was thin and in poor health, and he hoped the excursion might restore her flesh and color.

Morse had intently followed the progress of the politically divisive Mexican War. What many Americans condemned as a war of aggression aimed at extending slavery, he saw as a chance to prove the nation's military valor and open a field to Protestant evangelism: "The Mexican race is a worn out race; and God in his Providence is taking this mode to regenerate them. . . . Our Bible & Tract Societies and Missionaries ought to be in the wake of our Armies." He also gave credence to long-existing rumors of plans abroad to install a French or Spanish—that is, Catholic—monarch on the throne of Mexico: "how far these designs are connected with the Leopold operations in our own country, may be guessed at." An American victory would halt the further spread of popery and teach European despots not to interfere in American affairs. He looked forward to an honorable peace with the Mexicans, he said—"after we have given them a thorough thrashing."

Morse had also kept an eye on the revolutions overtaking Europe. In February 1848 a Paris mob clashed with a detachment of troops, who opened fire, killing or wounding some fifty people. The mayhem touched off massive civil disorder. More than a thousand barricades went up throughout the city; crowds overran the Tuileries Palace, tossing the throne into the courtyard. Leaders of the insurrection proclaimed that the people would not again allow the government to betray republican principles, as had happened under Louis-Philippe, who was forced to abdicate. The upheaval in Paris inspired popular uprisings in Italy and central Europe as well, driving the Pope from the Vatican and Metternich from Vienna.

Like many other Americans, Morse rejoiced in the revolutions, which President Polk called the most important event of modern times. Morse wrote to Arago congratulating the French on what they had achieved. "In a most important sense," he said, "France now holds the destiny of the world in her own hands." The question was whether she would succeed in finding a "*moral basis*" for maintaining republican government, or again relapse into anarchy and despotism. The first amendment to the American Constitution offered a model, he told Arago. An act similarly forbidding the French state to make laws concerning religion would "lay the Corner Stone of Liberty and happiness in France and throughout the world." That, of course, did not happen. Napoleon's conservative nephew, Louis Napoleon, staged a coup d'état, proclaimed himself Emperor, and suppressed the liberal constitution. One after another the other uprisings collapsed or were beaten down. "All is crushed," the *Observer* lamented, "trampled under foot, rent at the point of the bayonet: justice, law, liberty, honor."

As for his aesthetic life, Morse had taken scarcely any interest in painting for many years: "the very name of *pictures* produces a sadness of heart I cannot describe." He visited the National Academy of Design with Sarah, but before leaving for Europe in 1845 he had declined reelection as president, and not once during his stay in Paris had he visited the Louvre. He blamed his withdrawal from art largely on John Quincy Adams. He still believed that it was Adams who had denied him a commission for one of the Capitol rotunda paintings out of ill will toward Jedediah Morse. And he still reflected bitterly on what the former president had done by thus blocking his development: "he killed me as a painter, and he intended to do it. . . . May God forgive him as I do."

His eyesight deteriorated, Morse no longer wished to be remembered as a painter. By his own high standard, he felt, he had never been one. Of the more than three hundred canvases he had produced, some family portraits remained valuable to him for their likeness. But he retained only *The Muse*, the full-length portrait of teenaged Susan in a butterscotch-colored dress. Otherwise, nothing: "I could wish that every picture I ever painted was destroyed."

Morse's disgust did not take in his adventurous work in photography, which many still appreciated. "It was through him," recalled the Brooklyn *Daily Freeman*, "that Daguerre communicated his invention to the people on our continent." The *Photographic Art Journal* asked him to head a committee to award prizes for the best daguerreotypes. He was also remembered by a former Baptist clergyman named Levi L. Hill (1816–1865). Severe bronchitis had forced Hill to abandon his ministry. He became a professional photographer, supposing that the chemical fumes given off by Daguerre's process would benefit his afflicted lungs.

They did not, but Hill made an improvement no less questionable. Some daguerreotypists had been hand-coloring their pictures. A few, notably in France, experimented with producing colored plates directly. Hill claimed that he had invented a method of photographing colors accurately, brilliantly, and permanently. Secretive, he vowed to let no one see specimens of his work until he had perfected the method and could, as he said, "dress the child of light for the public gaze." Gossip about his hillotypes, as the pictures became known, gave rise to speculation about them in the photographic journals and the general press. Many daguerreotypists regarded him as an ignorant pretender.

Hill wrote to Morse about his invention, virtually begging him to visit his home in Westkill, New York, a hamlet about sixty miles from Poughkeepsie. Morse seldom left Locust Grove, and invited Hill there instead. But Hill declined, explaining he was too ill to make the trip, suffering what he oddly called "nondescript derangements of the billiary and nervous systems." Morse finally did venture to Westkill, though it meant a seven-hour drive in a gig through a wild region of the Catskill Mountains. Hill had been physically threatened, so he said. He protected himself at home with a guard dog, revolver, and warning system. And he showed Morse no samples of his yet-imperfect invention: "*Extreme Caution* has been my motto . . . applying it to honest men as well as rouges [*sic*]."

Despite the bunker atmosphere, Hill impressed Morse as no crank but rather a retiring, sensitive "man of genius." Either he had genuinely discovered a method of photographing colors or was under an "honest delusion" that he had. More than that, Morse saw him as a pious prayerful man, exclaiming in his own way What Hath God Wrought: "I am rejoiced to know that you specially recognize the hand of our heavenly Father in making you the honored instrument of its introduction to the world." He gave Hill some stock certificates to help finance his further experiments.

Grateful for Morse's trusting friendship, Hill wrote to him often as he tried to perfect his process. He made twenty-five to fifty pictures a day, "verily and truly," he said, "heliotyping the actual natural colors." His letters sound paranoid, full of suspicions about a photography establishment out to "crush" him and a world conniving to deprive him of title to his invention ("the French *Savans* . . . are preparing to pounce upon my prize"). Far from discounting Hill's fears Morse identified with them. He assured Hill that piracy and calumny were to be expected: the new process after all would make Daguerre's obsolete and put daguerreotypists out of business. Burned by his own rub with O'Reilly, he advised Hill not to take out a patent but to maintain his secrecy. "He shall not be plagued with lawsuits, have his life shortened and made miserable, and his just right in the property of his discovery snatched from him, if I can prevent it."

Around September 1852, a year after Morse's first visit, Hill again asked to see him. He said he feared he would not live much longer, having sustained a violent hemorrhage, seemingly from his lungs. Morse again made the trek to Westkill. This time Hill showed him some twenty specimens of his work. Most seemed dubious. But two were "exquisitely beautiful" color portraits, another a color full length of a child, a fourth a color landscape. Moreover, the French specimens Morse had heard about were evanescent and soon perished; the colors of Hill's images were fixed and no exposure to light faded them. He concluded that Hill had indeed discovered a process for rendering and holding the colors of the camera image.

That may or may not have been so. Most standard histories of photography dismiss Hill's claim to have produced colored images. On the other hand, although many hillotypes survive they have yet to be scientifically analyzed. Justifiably or not, Morse championed Hill in a published letter to the Washington *National Intelligencer,* proud that in the history of the new art, America could take a place beside France. "The magnificence of this discovery," he wrote, "is as remarkable as the original discovery of photography by Daguerre."

A second, more complex cycle of lawsuits disturbed Morse's pleasure in his new marriage and the peace of Locust Grove, ending late in 1853 at the United States Supreme Court. Many important inventions of the time were repeatedly litigated: Cyrus McCormick's harvester nine times, Eli Whitney's cotton gin fourteen times—Morse's telegraph, ultimately, fifteen times. As an associate of Ezra Cornell's remarked, "When the Angel proclaimed 'peace on earth & good will to men,' there was no telegraph." Standing to gain by the most efficient development of the telegraph at the cheapest rates, newspapers and magazines covered Morse's intricate hearings and trials in detail, as a cause célèbre: "THE GREAT TELEGRAPH CASE."

Morse's new legal troubles commenced with O'Reilly. O'Reilly had run himself ragged getting up dozens of handbills and a vast correspondence—on one day nineteen letters, filling forty-eight pages. He was almost broke, too, behind in his rent and unable to pay his grocer's bills. Heavy legal costs drove him to sell a house and forty-acre tract overlooking Long Island Sound, which he had purchased as the possible site of a "Great Hotel" for "the fashionable world."

Burdened or not, the "Napoleon of the Telegraph" had no intention of allowing Morse's mere patent to obstruct his conquest of North America: "Every wrong and outrage strengthens my resolution to accomplish all and more than I ever promised." Much more. Along his announced line to Oregon and California he proposed erecting stockades twenty to thirty miles apart, manned by troops and connected by express riders. The stockades would serve not only as points of supervision for the continental line but also as a "people's highway," protecting settlers as they migrated westward and eventually flowering into towns. Still more: why not also, he wrote to the Russian ambassador, a system from St. Petersburg to the Pacific Ocean?

O'Reilly found a new telegraph to compete against Morse's. With many promoters beginning to enter the telegraph market, many new instruments appeared for them to appraise: Henley's "Magneto-Electric Telegraph," needs no batteries; Hume's "Electro-Phonetic Telegraph," registering letters of the alphabet as different tones; Bakewell's "Copying Electric Telegraph," a proto-fax. Only months after his defeat in Kentucky, O'Reilly bought rights to a device invented by a British electrician-watchmaker named Alexander Bain. Bain's electrochemical telegraph used the decomposing power of electricity to mark a revolving paper disk treated with potassium prussiate or other suitable compound. The message to be sent was punched beforehand on a perforated tape. The chemically treated disk recorded the message as blue dots and dashes. Once the tape was perforated, transmission flew—up to three times faster than by Morse's instrument.

Morse saw in Bain's telegraph "a new chapter of troubles." Concerned, he made a rare excursion from Locust Grove to New York City, where Bain was exhibiting his system. What he saw reassured him. In the time it took a Bain operator to punch out the tape for transmission, his own telegraph could send three times as much text as the operator was preparing. And his patent, as he told Bain, covered the recording of signals by dots and dashes. Bain challenged this, alleging that a dotdash alphabetic code had been devised in 1827 by a Philadelphian named Swain, published in a book entitled *Mural Diagraph*.

Morse dug up a copy, and found that Swain had not at all been thinking of long-distance communication or of recording. Rather, as the title implies, Swain had designed his code for parley through a wall, by invalids and prisoners knocking and scratching upon it. Moreover, although he had represented the knocks by dots, he indicated the scratches as perpendicular lines, not dashes. Morse believed that the patent protecting his own code remained valid. Bain's telegraph was an outright infringement, like the others—"*mine made complicated.*"

Morse tried to stop Bain from getting an American patent by beating him to it. He had conceived an electrochemical telegraph as long ago as the *Sully*. Over the years he had experimented off and on with methods of causing an electric current to mark paper treated with iron sulfate, potassium iodide, and other chemicals. He abandoned the idea as inferior to his electromagnetic instrument. But with Bain arrived on the scene he filed an application to patent a method of sending signs "by means of the decomposing, colouring or bleaching effects of electricity acting upon any known salts that leave a mark as a result."

Bain filed for a patent about two months later. He had obtained an English patent for his electrochemical telegraph the year before. When he filed for an American patent also, Morse's old colleague Leonard Gale, now an examiner in the Patent Office, turned him down. Gale refused to accept the date of Bain's English patent as evidence of priority, and declared that his application "interfered" with Morse's already submitted application, a ruling upheld by the Patent Commissioner. As American patent law allowed, Bain appealed the controversial decision to the federal courts.

Morse attended *Bain v. Morse,* heard in February 1849 before the chief justice of the District of Columbia Circuit Court. Bain's counsel portrayed their client as "a poor Scotch clock-maker." They portrayed Morse as John Jacob Astor plus Prince Klemens von Metternich, a potentate with "numerous and powerful supporters in all parts of the Union . . . a man residing in one of the most beautiful villas in the State of New York, and revelling in all the luxuries which wealth, united with taste, can bestow." The lawyers' characterization of him so much inflamed Morse that at one point he protested from his seat in the courtroom.

Kendall no longer practiced law, but he argued Morse's case himself, making a three-hour speech before the judge. The ruling surprised him:

Samuel F. B. Morse is entitled to a patent for the combination which he has invented, claimed, and described in his specifica-

tion, drawings, and model. And . . . Alexander Bain is entitled to
a patent for the combination which he has invented, claimed,
and described in his specification, drawings, and model.

The Patent Office, that is, did not err in accepting Morse's application
but did err in refusing Bain's application as an "interference" with it.
Both parties were entitled to a patent for an electrochemical telegraph. Kendall explained to Morse that the judge had not compre-
hended his arguments: "The old man is really incapacitated for his
duties by deafness and I must suppose, did not understand me." The
decision left open, however, the far more significant question of
whether Bain's electrochemical telegraph infringed Morse's patent
for an electromagnetic telegraph, particularly in using the dotdash
code.

The press reargued *Bain* v. *Morse,* partly as a now thrice-told tale
involving the *Sully,* Morse's burnt fingers, and the rest. The New York
Sun located chemists in the city who could testify that many years ago
they had sold Morse acids and salts to make his first attempts in electrochemical telegraphy. Bain being a Scotsman, the issue became
embroiled in the techno-nationalist war. A Rochester paper bashed his
telegraph as a "cast off British affair." "We 'go in strong' for our own
country," the *Sun* added; "We are determined . . . that American
inventors shall not be deprived of their just fame."

In the patent granted to Bain, O'Reilly saw huge new opportunities for himself. It freed him to build competing electrochemical lines
on Morse's major routes between New York City and Boston, Albany,
and Washington. He opened a Bain telegraph office at 29 Wall Street,
elegantly fitted up with plate glass and mahogany furniture, virtually
next door to the office of Morse's New York, Albany & Buffalo company. Morse heard that at least one Bain line was using his relays. But
Kendall advised him to do nothing, at least for the present. If
O'Reilly's Bain lines proved inefficient they would be no threat;
meanwhile they would quiet outcries against the Morse patentees as
monopolists. "But we should be ready to attack them if they are likely
to be formidable," Kendall added.

Using Bain's system, O'Reilly also planned to resume work on his
potentially lucrative line to New Orleans. He went to court seeking
release from the 1848 injunction that had forbidden him to build in
Kentucky. Morse wrote out a twenty-page deposition for the trial. But

O'Reilly won. "The good time has come," his latest circular proclaimed; "Mr. O'Rielly [*sic*] has triumphed, and completely at that, for he has cut loose from Morse."

Morse and Kendall tried to convince the public that the triumph had no other existence than in O'Reilly's say-so. The judge's narrow decision, they pointed out, stated only that an earlier court's injunction against O'Reilly's use of the Columbian telegraph in part of Kentucky did not apply to his use of Bain's telegraph. It might turn out that Bain's dotdash code infringed Morse's patent. For that reason the judge had ordered O'Reilly to provide bond with securities. Should an infringement be determined, O'Reilly would have to pay Morse costs and damages. So the *Observer*, too, issued a proclamation: "Professor Morse has been fully sustained."

The rival cries of victory confused the public, but not O'Reilly. By mid-1850 he succeeded in opening his sure-to-be-moneymaking thousand-mile People's Telegraph between Louisville and New Orleans.

In his handsome Tuscan villa with his young wife, Morse often felt deeply depressed. The piracy of his patent and unending legal tumult, he said, "leave me but little enjoyment of my life." The thousands of dollars paid out to lawyers hurt too, leaving him without cash. Kendall wanted to engage full-time counsel. But with one topflight lawyer asking $2000 in cash and $2000 in stock, Morse estimated that legal fees would amount to $10,000 annually: "We may almost as well give up."

Morse also faced attack from within. Jittery stockholders in Morse lines badgered him to guarantee the validity of his patents. He felt neither obliged nor inclined to do so. When their complaints came by mail he sent them on to Kendall, only to have the complainers appeal again over Kendall's head to him. The board of directors of one Morse company voted to withhold dividends from him and the other patentees, retaining the money as security pending the validation of his patent. When he vehemently protested, the company president told him off: "Your want of knowledge of the method of doing business . . . is too apparent to need any thing further than a passing remark."

And try as he might to keep out of the courts, Morse was engulfed by paperwork in readying himself over and over for trial. Again and again, with wearying sameness and vexation, he had to sift through growing piles of correspondence, affidavits, depositions, contracts, bills, and newspaper clippings destined for citation in shelves full of trial records, an "interminable labarinth [*sic*] of evidence, requiring the utmost minutiae of details & of hair splitting logic to defeat the cunning & knavery and persevering machinations of the pirates." Hundreds of manuscript pages survive in which he repeatedly tried to narrate the history of his invention and define its essential originality in such a way as to make it invulnerable to attack or imitation.

The definition was crucial. All of Morse's opponents in court argued that his patent protected only the particular instruments and alphabet he had fashioned from scientific discoveries made by others. Morse wished to argue the opposite: that his patent protected a vision of electrical communication. As he often put it, he had invented a genus as well as a species. In draft after draft, deleting, inserting, correcting, he strove to formulate the essence of what he alone had accomplished. At one time:

> I *do* claim to be the first person known, who ever *even conceived the possibility of marking or printing intelligible characters at any distance by means of any power whatever.*

Another time he tried out:

> *Telegraphic Speech by Electricity,* as the *principle of my whole invention.*

Or again:

> . . . *the first application of magnetism produced by electricity to the imprinting of characters at a distance by which intelligence is communicated.*

Until the end of his life, Morse went on adding this and crossing out that, revising his definition to account for and annul new objections raised by his opponents.

It upset Morse that his legal foes counted Professor Joseph Henry as an ally. He had made several attempts to placate the famous scientist, who still resented the omission of his name from Alfred Vail's history of the telegraph. Morse drafted a letter for Vail to sign and send to Henry, explaining that if the history gave offense none was intended.

Henry did not reply. Morse wrote to Henry in his own person, promising that he had no share in writing Vail's book: "I am sure of entertaining only the most exalted opinion of your genius, and your labors." Henry acknowledged the letter and promised a fuller response, but never sent one. When Henry was chosen to preside over the just-created Smithsonian Institution in Washington—the most distinguished scientific post in the country—Morse tried to make amends by publishing a letter in the *Observer* supporting the choice: "no man in the country," he wrote, "has all the qualifications for this high trust in a greater degree." But as president, Henry excluded Vail's history from the Smithsonian library. (He also refused to provide a room at the Institution for a talk by Frederick Douglass, saying he "would not permit the lecture of the coloured man.")

Morse's opponents used Henry's testimony against him at court, with damaging effect. In one deposition Henry swore that Morse based the telegraph "upon the facts discovered by myself and others." To his knowledge, he added, Morse had never "made a single original discovery, in electricity, magnetism, or electro-magnetism." Henry's antagonism saddened Morse. He so much respected Henry as a scientist that he had considered giving him several thousand dollars to pursue his electrical experiments. The respect survived, and however injured by Henry he resisted striking back. "I would bear & forbear to the last endurable moment, for the sake of science, & lest his relatives and friends should be innocent sufferers with him in his exposure."

And to deepen distress there was always F. O. J. Smith—"Professor Morse's worst enemy," Kendall called him. Morse had hoped to cut loose from Smith almost from the time they became partners. Four years earlier, the hope had seemed realized. At the time, Kendall and Smith had joined forces in fighting O'Reilly. But they began to disagree on how to carry on the war with him. Kendall then negotiated a territorial division with Smith that divorced their business interests. The agreement was complex, involving a series of contracts. Basically Smith gained control over Morse telegraph lines in New England, New York, and the Old Northwest (Michigan, Wisconsin, and most of Ohio, Indiana, and Illinois). Morse and Vail would receive stock in Smith's western lines, and control the rest of the Union. At last Morse had freed himself of Smith, "this arch-fiend."

But that was four years ago. Instead of cutting Morse loose from Smith, the agreement had generated heated quarrels about the meaning of its terms. At present, Morse found himself as much as ever the victim of Smith's lust for the upper hand, his desire to gain advantage for the sake of advantage. Kendall charged that in violation of the separation agreement Smith was granting contracts for lines outside his assigned territory and failing to give Morse stock in the lines he built. After exchanging dozens of irate letters with Smith, Kendall informed Morse that they would have to sue him.

As he usually did, Morse tried to stay out of the dispute and urged Kendall to compromise: "the excitement of such perpetual litigation as we have to encounter," he said, "sometimes distorts in our own minds the sense of right." Kendall warned him that Smith would view their desire for a settlement as a sign of weakness, and exploit it to make them give up rights: "the effect *on such a man* can only be to confirm and strengthen him in his fraudulent course." He pressed Morse to confront Smith in court. For Morse the situation came down to a choice between miseries. On balance he preferred Smith's troublemaking to the worse exasperations of the law. "Let us bear it as agreeably as we can," he told Kendall, "make up our minds to suffer a little for our want of caution." Trying to bring the two men together, he wrote to Smith several times, addressing him with polite impartiality. "Much allowance should be made on both sides," he typically began.

But Smith allowed Morse nothing. Instead, he made several new enemies for him by granting Ezra Cornell a patent right to build a 400-mile line from New York City to western New York State, in competition with the existing and profitable line of the New York, Albany & Buffalo company. Its directors angrily (and groundlessly) accused Morse of colluding with Smith, like a "double faced Judas." Smith aroused further hostility toward Morse by enraging New York's Associated Press. He had taken an intense dislike to its agent in Halifax, where transatlantic steamships first stopped when they reached the coast of North America, carrying news from abroad. Smith closed his Boston–New York line to the agent, refusing to allow him to telegraph the eagerly awaited international news to papers in New York City. The *Herald* warned that Smith's blockade would "injure more seriously the prospects of Mr. Morse, than any ten men in the country, with all their original inventions at their back, could do."

Kendall pleaded with Morse to take legal action: "The alternatives left are only submission or resistance." Kendall's threat of a lawsuit infuriated Smith: "Let him sue," he told a friend; "I will blow Morse's Patents

Sky high, when I open my books. Nobody but myself, Professor Morse & the Almighty know what the facts are." The supposedly explosive "facts" amounted to Morse's delay in patenting his receiving magnet—an attempt, Smith called it, at "fraudulent & designed suppression and concealment." Morse laughed off the trumped-up charge as "stuff of gossamer." It proved that Smith should not be taken seriously. "F.O.G.—F.O.G. F.O.G. F.O.G. F.O.G. F.O.G. whew," he told Kendall. "He threatens like a venomous serpent, but it is only the forked tongue not the fangs."

But Smith's threats were no bluff, as Morse learned in the hectic late summer and fall of 1850. At the time, Smith's Boston–New York line itself faced competition from a man named Hugh Downing. Downing planned to build a line along the same route, installing Royal House's piano-like printing telegraph. Smith decided to apply to the courts for an injunction to stop Downing, on the grounds that House's apparatus infringed Morse's patent. Downing meant to fight back by contesting the validity of the patent, using the well-worn testimony of Dr. Charles Jackson.

Smith wanted Morse to appear as a witness at the injunction trial to rebut Jackson. But Morse declined: "The idea of a *monomaniac's* testimony weighing a feather . . . is ridiculous." His disdain was not unreasonable. Jackson had recently added a new achievement to his invention of the telegraph and discovery of surgical ether. As principal U.S. geologist for the mineral lands in Michigan, he claimed that it was he, not a colleague, who had determined the age of the sandstone of Lake Superior. (The government soon discharged him, for neglect of duty and familiarity with alcohol.) Since Morse refused to appear in court, Smith decided to rebut Jackson by quoting self-incriminating passages in the many letters Jackson had written to Morse over the years. Morse had loaned him the letters to use as evidence in a recent suit in Ohio, and his lawyer still had them.

Through a farcical combination of circumstances that only the self-annihilating force of Smith's vengefulness could have brought into being, Jackson's letters became the object of a three-way struggle—Smith, his lawyer, and Morse against each other. The bizarrely tangled series of events, to merely outline them, began when Smith refused to pay his lawyer's fees, calling them extortionate. In return, his lawyer refused to release Jackson's letters for use in the injunction trial. With record-setting gall, Smith insisted that Morse pay the fees, since the suit against Hugh Downing was in defense of his patent. Morse replied that he could hardly be expected to compensate a lawyer he had not employed. But that was a moot point. In disgust, Smith's lawyer insisted on having his money from Smith, not Morse. Only then, he told Morse, would he return Jackson's letters: "I will *not permit you to pay his bill.*" Morse was left in a weird stranglehold: Smith demanding that he pay fees to a lawyer who would not accept them.

Smith threatened to break the impasse by unleashing what he called "war to the knife and the knife to the hilt." He brutally informed Morse that during the upcoming trial he would not challenge Jackson. No, he would take Jackson's side. He would expose Morse's "hitherto supposed well founded patented rights." He would show that Morse had stumbled on to his telegraph by guesswork, being otherwise limited—quite as Jackson had always said—by "a *profound ignorance* of the laws of Electro-Magnetism, by *ignorance* of the science of conducting agencies, by *ignorance* of what men of *true learning* had previously developed and established." Morse really knew only one thing well: how to hoodwink his associates. "I think," he told Morse, "we may all begin to see now the end of telegraph glory."

Smith v. *Downing* was heard at a U.S. district court in Boston by a judge named Woodbury. With his patent being tested, Morse attended the trial. Jackson's letters to him were submitted before the court, an arrangement having been made to take copies of the originals. Woodbury spent more than three months reaching his decision, which he announced in October 1850. He noted that the case was difficult. Determining whether House's printing telegraph infringed Morse's patent, he said, involved scientific ideas not well understood except by the few who had devotedly studied them. Here Woodbury echoed a growing concern in the legal profession that few judges, much less juries, were qualified to hear such cases of intellectual property. Sensibly, he declared it unnecessary to resolve the byzantine conflict between Morse and Jackson in order to settle the main issue. That he did by denying Smith an injunction to prevent his competitor from using House's system. In essence he ruled that Morse was entitled to his machinery and to his code but not to an exclusive application of electromagnetism to convey intelligence.

Whether the decision hurt or helped the self-destructive Smith is debatable. But it outraged Morse, who believed that Smith had sabotaged his own case for the sake of revenge. Since it seemed obvious to him that House's telegraph infringed "the principle, and essence" of his own, he also suspected that in trying to do him in, Smith may have reached the judge. "I can come to no other conclusion than that [Woodbury] is either corrupt and has been bribed in some way, or that he has exhibited a profoundness of ignorance of the nature of the subject." Smith being engaged in ongoing battle with the Associated Press, many newspapers applauded the outcome: "For the interest of Dr. Morse, we are sorry," the *Herald* wrote, "and are glad that Fog Smith, a most troublesome personage, is effectually put down. Fog has been a thorn to the invention since the discovery was made."

Having sided with Charles Jackson, Smith next formed an alliance that to Morse seemed unimaginable. He teamed up with their mutual enemy, Henry O'Reilly. The terms of the arrangement are unclear, partly owing to Smith's always slippery language and nearly indecipherable handwriting—"foggy hieroglyphics," Morse called them. Smith apparently conveyed to O'Reilly the right to use Morse's telegraph on certain routes that had been granted to himself under the 1847 separation agreement. In exchange, O'Reilly would give Smith one-quarter of all the stock of these lines. O'Reilly would also have the advantage of the ex-congressman's Washington contacts to advance his ballyhooed project of a lightning connection to California.

To Morse, Smith's sadomasochistic partnership in Morse telegraphy with the despised O'Reilly proved him to be more viper than human being, "the double refined and concentrated essence of rascality." Having long balked at Kendall's insistence that they sue Smith, he at last gave in. He applied for an injunction to stop Smith from transacting any further business under their five-year-old separation agreement and from conveying any more rights to his patent. Smith said he welcomed the fray: "Very well—let litigation be the order of our lives."

Morse v. *Smith* was heard in a superior court of New York City. Morse toiled twelve to fourteen hours a day for three days writing his affidavit. His lawyers argued that in the Boston trial against Hugh Downing, Smith had deliberately failed to make out a bona fide case, having on the contrary threatened to "blow Morse's patents sky high." Morse called the court's attention to a "singular fact": every prosecution instituted by himself in defense of his patent had succeeded, "whilst in every instance in which the said Smith has attempted to vindicate my patents by a judicial determination, he has in every instance been unsuccessful." He brought other charges of fraud as well, among them that during their 1838 trip abroad, Smith did not fulfill and never intended to honor his contractual obligation to seek foreign patents.

Morse suffered a humiliating defeat. The judge refused to grant the injunction, ruling that Morse failed to show that Smith had any intention of defrauding him: "there is no such clear proof of any of the acts of omissions alleged with the motives imputed." He also declined to rule on Smith's behavior abroad, deeming it immaterial to the present case. Morse felt miserably deflated by the result, and by Smith's glorying in it: "F. O. J. crows at the top of his voice." He learned that Smith went on a spree with a crony, who was seen on Broadway drunk, "boisterously huzzaing for F. O. J. and cursing me and my telegraph."

In reality, Smith had not much to crow over. Back home in Maine he was battling the boards of directors of a gas company and two railroads in which he was heavily invested. The local press portrayed him as money-mad, acting from "the lowest cupidity and lust for gain." He had also gotten up a navigation company that launched an eighty-five-foot steamboat to ply the Androscoggin River, whose shoals proved so dangerous that the boat had to be taken out of service and left to decay. His domestic life was in no better shape. While married he had carried on a ten-year-long affair with a Boston divorcée; their two illegitimate sons closely resembled him. When his wife died he left his mistress and married someone else—"for my happiness," he explained. Remarried, he soon began chasing still other women.

Looking into the future, Morse saw himself hideously coupled with Smith forever, "bound for life to a corrupted corpse." With thousands of dollars spent to no purpose on litigation, and with his telegraph stock not paying dividends, he worried that he might have to sell Locust Grove and resettle in a humbler home, "suited to my change of circumstances. It will indeed be like cutting off a right hand." And how would he make a living? Having been a painter, a university professor, and an inventor, having nearly entered the ministry and taken up political office, he might have to find altogether different employment, "and begin life again when on the downward side of the hill of life." "If ever demoniac possession belonged to an invention," he told his brother Richard, "not *seven* but *seventy* have crept into the Telegraph."

Morse's expensive but fruitless court trials also left him disillusioned with American institutions, though lifelong he had held them up to despotic Europe as examples of American liberty. The American press, "relentless unscrupulous," had poisoned public opinion against him, wholly in self-interest—"because *cheap despatches* must be had by the press, and the press must be indulged." He blamed the American government, too, for woefully defective patent laws that failed to protect the nation's inventors. Invaded and robbed, the inventor sues, then waits in vain for redress until the entire fourteen-year term of his patent has gone by, "exhausted in endless suits, and ruinous expense." "It is not the way to encourage the Arts," he concluded, "to drive the Artists into exile or to the insane hospital or to the grave."

Becoming one of the most controversial men of his time in America, Morse wished above all to get out of the spotlight, to retire "from public gaze, from public notice, from public mention." He rejoiced that through the blessing of God his telegraph had blessed the world. But the best return the world could make him would be to forget his name. After his long quest for glory what he most sought, he said, was "*Obscurity.*"

Ultimately, inevitably, The Great Telegraph Case came before the United States Supreme Court. It was axiomatic at the Patent Office that no patent was of value until the Court sustained it. Morse's chance arrived through Henry O'Reilly, who had long vowed to appeal the judgment of a Kentucky circuit court that his Zook-Barnes Columbian telegraph infringed Morse's patent. The Supreme Court agreed to review O'Reilly's case, its first scrutiny of the epoch-marking technology.

O'Reilly was in less than fighting condition. With several expensive suits pending against him, his financial situation had further deteriorated, not to mention, he said, "the losses & mortification (I might say, *agony*) which I have suffered." Morse was content to remain at Locust Grove, but Kendall and several other friends and associates insisted that he attend: "the judges are men, and are influenced no little by your presence," one wrote from Washington. "This point is the pivot of all your life's affairs and you must be here."

Morse spent two weeks in Washington at the end of December 1852, when *O'Reilly* v. *Morse* began. At the time, the Supreme Court's chamber was located on the ground floor of the Capitol, north wing. Chief Justice Roger B. Taney presided, a scrawny man with a bulging forehead who would soon rule, in *Dred Scott* v. *John Sanford,* that slaves and their descendants had no rights as American citizens. Kendall had worked closely with him during the Jackson administration, when Taney served as Secretary of the Treasury. Morse was at least acquainted with the Chief Justice, on whom New York University had conferred an honorary LL.D. When Morse opened the Baltimore-Washington line in 1844, too, Taney had sent a ceremonial message over the astonishing wire to President Tyler.

Six hours were allowed each side to argue before the seven justices, including the demonstration of telegraph apparatus. The hundreds of pages of argument defy brief summary. The lawyers covered much familiar ground—the history of electric telegraphy since the eighteenth century, The *Sully* Story. They also presented depositions from prominent scientists (including Joseph Henry, on behalf of O'Reilly), and cited scores of American and English legal precedents. Then as now, legal debate about information technology proved to be of mind-numbing intricacy. In trying to clarify the confusing issues, the lawyers explicated in detail, and often in deadly legalese, the meaning of terms such as "principle" or "improvement"; phrases such as "motive power of the electric current"; dizzying distinctions between "art" and "mode," "arm" and "lever," "characters" and "letters."

For Taney and the other justices, the case resolved itself into two basic questions. Most important, was Morse the "first and original inventor" of the electromagnetic telegraph described in his patents? If so, was O'Reilly's Columbian telegraph "substantially different" from it?

Morse's side tried to show that the Columbian infringed every claim in Morse's patent, being identical with his telegraph "in object, beginning and ending." O'Reilly's distinguished counsel, Senator Salmon P. Chase of Ohio, addressed the Court's basic questions by arguing that the "first" telegraphs had been invented abroad by Wheatstone, Steinheil, and Davy. He conceded that Morse had created the first practicable electromagnetic "*marking*" telegraph. But he emphasized how much Morse's apparatus owed to earlier scientists and inventors:

[Morse] did not invent the art of telegraphing by electro-magnetism. He did not invent the battery; nor the circuit of wire, or wire and earth; nor the electro-magnet. He did not discover the transmissibility of the electric current through a long circuit. He did not invent the combination of the battery and its circuit with an electro-magnet, or electro-magnets placed in any part of it so as to move levers or soft iron bars suspended near their poles and thus produce mechanical results at a distance. He did not invent the process of marking paper. . . .

Using the same available technology, Chase told the justices, other inventors had devised telegraphs no less useful and ingenious than Morse's and as much entitled to patent protection. This included the Columbian telegraph, which he defended as an improvement upon Morse's apparatus, not an infringement.

Morse considered the outcome in the Supreme Court critical to his future. "It involves wealth on the one side and comparative poverty on the other to me. If the decision is against me, I shall be compelled to sell my pleasant home." After hearing both sides, however, the justices chose not to rule on the matter in their present session, but to ponder its complexities while in recess. As Morse waited, false reports and rumors about their opinions leaked out constantly. It was a long wait. The Court did not render judgment for a full year.

The decision would test Morse's long-held view of himself as the sole creator of the electromagnetic recording telegraph. All achievements in the arts and sciences are in many respects connected and cumulative, of course. And his invention was constituted and forwarded by the work of pioneer electrical experimenters, contemporary scientists, academic colleagues, skilled mechanicians, continental inventors—by Volta, Henry, Gale, Vail, Bréguet, to name only some. Morse's image of himself as the Lone Inventor took off from his earlier sense of being the "Son of the Geographer," scion of a family whose intellectual independence he saluted in jotting down a brief scroll of honor:

First Geography of the United States. Jedd. Morse
First Religious Society in house of Jedd. Morse
First Religious Newspaper Sidney E. Morse
First Telegraph (in the literal sense of the term) S. F. B. Morse
First Course of Lectures on Fine Arts in U. States S. F. B. Morse

Much in Morse's later experience and the thought of his era also disposed him to think himself the Lone Inventor—his Washingtonian ideal of national honor; his heroic conception of The Painter, independent of patrons; the antebellum ethic of the Self-Made Man; romantic notions of Genius.

Ironically, Morse's claims for himself as an innovator rest most convincingly on the part of his work he valued least, his dogged entrepreneurship. With stubborn longing, he brought his invention into the marketplace despite congressional indifference, frustrating delays, mechanical failures, family troubles, bickering partners, attacks by the press, protracted lawsuits, periods of depression. Whatever the demands for recognition by Charles Jackson or Alfred Vail, neither of them produced a marketable telegraph. Joseph Henry set scientific investigation on an intellectual plane infinitely above its practical application, and thought himself superior to mere utilitarian inventors. Morse allowed his associates too little recognition, but they expected too much.

An editorial in the recently established New York *Times* put Morse's case fairly:

> Grant that MORSE was, as is claimed, indebted to the suggestions of others. . . . MORSE was *the man* who was publicly experimenting, in our midst, on this subject—inviting scientific gentlemen to witness his progress, who besieged the doors of Congress for an appropriation to enable him to demonstrate the practicability of his invention; who entered his caveat and obtained his patent; who, in 1844, laid down the first line of Electric telegraph in this country, from Washington to Baltimore, and sped the first aerial message on its electric path. . . . If others knew that electricity could be used for recording language at a distance, and kept the knowledge from the public, or were too indolent or careless to reduce it into practice, we think they are too late to claim the credit, after another, by labor and devotion, has accomplished the work.

With the help and collaboration of others, a normal situation for inventors, Morse created a telegraph system that against many competitors repeatedly proved itself to be the cheapest, the most rugged, the most reliable, and the simplest to operate. By perseverance that would not be denied he made it a commercial reality—the catalyst, to look ahead, of an entire industry and the beginning of a worldwide network.

The Supreme Court spoke in February 1854. Its thirty-seven-page decision gave Morse total victory—nearly. The justices ruled that, legally, Morse's telegraph preceded the devices of English and Continental inventors. In using the scientific research and experiments of others, including Joseph Henry, Morse did no more than all inventors do in creating a machine with several elements: "the fact that Morse sought and obtained the necessary information and counsel from the best sources, and acted upon it, neither impairs his rights as an inventor, nor detracts from his merits." On these grounds the Court unanimously declared Morse "the first and original inventor of the Telegraph described in his specification." The Columbian telegraph, they said, had the same object as Morse's and used substantially the same means, thereby infringing his patent. They imposed upon it a "perpetual injunction."

But on the important matter of Morse's right to a "general principle," the justices split four to three. They had in mind the eighth claim of Morse's reissued patent. It reserved to him the exclusive use, as he put it, of "the motive power of the electric or galvanic current, which I call electro-magnetism, however developed, for marking or printing intelligible characters, signs, or letters, at any distances." Chief Justice Taney, in his majority opinion, ruled that the claim was too broad, inhibiting improvement and innovation. Some inventor might discover an even simpler or less expensive means of telegraphic recording by electricity, without using any part of Morse's system. The Court declared this one item in Morse's patent illegal and void. The close vote dramatized the conflict in contemporary patent law between concern for protecting an inventor against piracy, and concern for the public benefit and economic growth that might result from improvements on his invention—a conflict that would lead to extensive reform of the law.

Kendall, in Washington, telegraphed to Morse the substance of the Court's decision. "Though not all we hoped for," he said, "it is for you a signal triumph." Morse thought so too. He believed that in validating his patent at the highest level, the justices not only killed the

Columbian telegraph. They also "utterly annihilated" House's printing telegraph and Bain's electrochemical version, and protected him
against "all other recording Telegraphs as yet given to the world."
Morse's glee is understandable, coming after five years of legal warfare
in Kentucky, Massachusetts, New York, and Pennsylvania. But the
invulnerability of his patent remained to be proved, and meanwhile
the denial of his eighth claim required him to withdraw or refine it.
He revised its language, restricting his exclusive use of electromagnetism to the specific instruments described in his patent.

Having narrowed his claims, Morse applied for a seven-year extension of the patent. At the time, the Patent Office granted an extension
only if the inventor could show that he had failed to receive a just
remuneration during the usual fourteen-year term. For Morse this
meant proving that he had made little or no money from his telegraph
despite its steadily growing use and enormous public value. He spent
six woeful months not only re-collecting correspondence, redrawing
diagrams, and retaking depositions, but also figuring the economic
value of his telegraph to stockholders and the public, and computing
his experimental expenses and legal costs over the last fourteen
years—at the same time fending off suits by O'Reilly and other competitors opposed to granting him the extension. "I never had any anxieties so tried as in this case of extension."

But Morse succeeded here, too. The Patent Office calculated that
over the years his patent had earned him a profit of $200,000. The
Commissioner characterized this as "abundant compensation," ordi-
narily. But some of the amount, he added, was doubtful because tied
up in litigation, and "benefactors of their race" such as Morse were
entitled to something beyond the "proper measure." He therefore
granted seven additional years of patent protection. To Morse the
extra time seemed less a renewal than a beginning. It gave his invention a first life, a first real chance in the world: "it is, in fact, the
moment to reap the harvest of so many years of labor, and expense,
and toil."

FOURTEEN

A True Social Fraternity

(1854–1856)

T HE DECADE since Morse opened the Baltimore-Washington line had been an economic boom time, stimulating enormous growth in the telegraph business. In 1855 an estimated 42,000 miles of telegraph wire thrummed across the United States. Most messages were sent by businessmen, who in the expansion of capitalist enterprise needed new communication services to stay in touch with far-off markets. Their "telegrams"—the word entered the language in 1852—contained orders to buy or sell goods, instructions to pay money, reports of freighting and shipping. Operating synergistically with railroads, the steam press, and other new technologies, the telegraph was part of an emerging infrastructure for distributing goods throughout the growing nation.

By 1855, the telegraph had also spun off collateral businesses and a new technical and professional community. The ever-lengthening lines gave rise to firms that produced wires and poles. Although Morse and Vail continued to manufacture instruments embodying their ongoing improvements, Morse met the greatly increased demand for apparatus by licensing its manufacture to instrument makers, who found a new market for their skills. Mechanics and engineers developed more sensitive relays, primitive versions of duplex transmission, and other refinements and innovations. Those involved in telegraphy were kept informed by a specialized technical press that issued such journals as the *American Telegraph Magazine* and the *National Telegraph Review.*

The occupation of telegrapher emerged as part of a new lower-middle class of white-collar workers. Each of the twelve New York City telegraph offices employed about four young men as telegraphers and clerks. On the Morse lines, devices to produce a clear loud click ("sounders") had replaced many of the paper-marking registers, increasing transmission speeds. With as many as six machines going at once, the noise in telegraph offices struck one visitor as a polyphonic clatter, like "a watchmaker's shop—a sort of Babel-like confusion."

The fifty or so small American telegraph companies were consolidating into a few large regional companies. The mergers came in response to several pressures. Local, independent control had meant inefficient service, cutthroat competition, and reduced profits. The thriving Associated Press sought a smooth-working, national system for gathering news. And despite continued celebration of a free market, the nation was tending in many other branches of its economic life to interstate corporations with centralized managements. A particularly ambitious company was formed in 1851 by a group of Rochester businessmen. They aimed at acquiring and consolidating all telegraphic interests west of Buffalo, using House's system. Organized as the New York & Mississippi Valley Printing Telegraph Company, they reorganized and reincorporated in 1857 as the Western Union Telegraph Company, and set out to dominate the industry.

At the same time, Morse's user-friendly telegraphs were spreading outside the United States. Prussia installed them, sometimes with modifications, on important lines from Berlin to Aachen, Frankfurt am Main, and Hamburg; the Prussian government awarded him its gold medal for scientific merit, presented in a gold snuffbox. In 1853 a Morse line went up between Stockholm and Uppsala, the first telegraph in Sweden. Next year, a short line of Morse telegraph was strung between Melbourne and Williamstown, Australia, with plans for a thousand-mile line from Sydney to Melbourne to Adelaide. By 1855, a 5000-kilometer Morse network in India linked Calcutta, Bombay, and Madras. Morse telegraphs began clicking in the Russian empire. And there was discussion of the daunting problem of how to transmit Chinese ideograms.

The simultaneous movement of consolidation and expansion came together in the most complex technological feat ever attempted, and one of the great farsighted adventures in human history—the laying and operation of a submarine telegraph cable across the Atlantic

Ocean, electrically connecting the Old World with the New and opening the present era of global communication.

Early in 1854, while in Washington enjoying his success in the Supreme Court case, Morse received a letter from a New Yorker named Cyrus W. Field (1819–1892). The son of a New England Congregationalist minister and a mother memorably named Submit, Field was slight, nervous, boyish. Yet he epitomized the go-ahead spirit of the American marketplace. Starting out as a teenaged dry-goods clerk he had worked his way into the business of merchandising paper, an important commodity with the growth of the American press. By the age of thirty-five he ranked among the wealthiest men in New York. Grossing a million dollars a year, he dwelt in a Gramercy Park town house crammed with Persian rugs and Greek statuary. At the time he wrote to Morse he had just returned from a six-month trip to the rubber forests of the Amazon jungle, partly for relaxation and partly to explore commercial possibilities. He arrived in New York with a flock of screeching parrots and a jaguar on a leash.

Field's letter to Morse concerned the possibility of submarine telegraphy. A beginning had been made in 1852, when a British company successfully opened electrical communication between London and Paris, by a cable laid across the English Channel. Field wanted Morse's opinion about whether a cable could be laid across the Atlantic Ocean. His idea was to span the two closest points between Europe and North America—Ireland and Newfoundland, a distance of about 1700 miles. From Newfoundland, the line could be run down through Maine to New York City.

Before replying, Morse visited the National Observatory in the capital to speak with its head, a short, stout naval lieutenant and oceanographer named Matthew Fontaine Maury. Maury had conducted a program of transatlantic soundings, and Morse inquired about the depth and contour of the ocean floor between Ireland and Newfoundland. He learned that the floor was deep enough to keep a cable beyond the reach of anchors or icebergs. And miraculously, perhaps providentially, the floor was shaped like a flat or gently sloping shelf, "which seems to have been placed there," Maury added, "especially for the purpose of holding the wires of a submarine Telegraph." Morse wrote back to Field from Washington expressing his "perfect faith" that the lightning could be made to traverse the Atlantic.

Field moved quickly. He interested several big investors, who in

Cyrus W. Field (ca. 1860) (*Carte-de-visite* by Mathew Brady)
(New-York Historical Society)

the spring of 1854 sent a delegation to Newfoundland. The group
secured from the provincial government a grant of fifty square miles
of land and a fifty-year monopoly on the construction and operation
of telegraphs, plus £5000 for building a road across the province. The
legislature granted a charter incorporating Field and his partners as
the New York, Newfoundland, and London Telegraph Company.

Field's oracular venture became a major topic of the day. It drew
some ridicule: "All idea of connecting Europe with America by lines

extending directly across the Atlantic," an American newspaper remarked, "is utterly impracticable and absurd." Far more often, however, Field's plan was hailed as a mindboggling fulfillment of modern commerce and technology: "it is impossible to contemplate the probability of such an achievement," the New York *Tribune* said, "without a glow and a thrill at its sublime audacity and its magnificent uses." The prospect of instant communication between continents stirred utopian fantasies of universal brotherhood, promising what another paper called "a more sympathetic connection of the nations of the world than has yet existed in history."

Morse shared this ideology of redemption through communication and predicted an end to war "in a not distant future." Together with his patent extension, an association with Field's daring project meant a fresh start, a new beginning of his career. He invested $10,000 in the New York, Newfoundland, and London Telegraph Company, a one-tenth interest. Enthusiastically, he gave the company patent rights to his system for a line between Maine and New York City—free of charge. He also agreed to promote the company's efforts to induce other American telegraph companies to transmit messages sent by the transatlantic cable at half price. The company placed him on its board of directors and advertised him as its "Electrician," an honorary title.

Morse tried to make it generally known that he had been interested in suboceanic communication for more than a decade. He reminded many correspondents that in 1842 he had publicly attempted to telegraph across the East River. He often quoted the prophecy he had made a year later in a letter to the Secretary of the Treasury: "a Telegraphic communication on my plan may with certainty be established across the Atlantic! Startling as this may seem now, the time will come when this project will be realized." But the many experimenters on both sides of the Atlantic now tackling problems of submarine telegraphy included several claimants to priority in the idea of a transoceanic line. Morse rebuffed them with smarmy graciousness, professing "the most respectful and kindly feeling" before laying out the crushing evidence against their delusions. "You will not feel offended if I give you facts," he wrote to one rival, "though they may be fatal to your honest supposition . . . that you can claim priority in the suggestion of a *Telegraph across the Atlantic.*"

Morse took up eagerly the many practical questions raised by the cable-laying enterprise, some of great theoretical significance. He arranged to use part of the New York–Buffalo line for new experiments to determine the battery strength needed to communicate over very long distances. He examined various types of cable and insulating material, and offered Field detailed speculations on which would serve best. He suggested using one-eighth-inch wire of the purest copper, wound in shellac-saturated cotton or linen thread, then coated with gutta-percha—a latex that retains its plasticity under extreme pressure, previously used to insulate the cable across the English Channel. So prepared, one or more copper strands would be drawn into a lead tube loosely wound in iron wire.

Morse sent descriptions and drawings of his proposed cable to the experimental genius Sir Michael Faraday. Twenty-five years earlier, Faraday had generated electricity by rotating a copper disk in the field of some horseshoe magnets, a demonstration of electromagnetic induction that pointed the way to the creation of electric motors and dynamos. Morse hailed him as a fellow scientist. He said he had noticed that a prospectus from the British side of Field's New York, Newfoundland, and London company identified Faraday as "Electrician." "I have been elected to a similar office," Morse explained. In his eleven-page letter he boasted of his pioneer cable-laying in New York harbor and his prophecy of transatlantic communication, but mostly sought Faraday's views on what problems underseas operation might present.

Faraday did not reply. In seeking recognition as a fellow scientist from him, Morse miscalculated. The theoretical level of Faraday's investigations was unapproachably beyond Morse's expertise or even comprehension. And he learned from an acquaintance in England that Faraday took offense at being addressed as an "Electrician" to a company. From love of science and a sense of civic duty Faraday freely imparted his knowledge, but he stayed out of the marketplace: "no consideration would induce him to take part in any Company of a speculative or commercial character." Morse's acquaintance nevertheless relayed Faraday's view that a current could no doubt be sent across the ocean. The chief problem, Faraday believed—correctly—would be the weight and strength of the cable, and the difficulty of laying it.

Morse quickly learned that he may also have misjudged his new business associates. Given the steep cost of lawsuits, many telegraph companies bought or leased rival lines rather than fight them in court.

For the same reason, Field wanted to acquire some small eastern companies that used Royal House's printing telegraph. Morse liked Field personally, but the idea of Field's group operating Morse lines together with House's "rotten affair" insulted him. "I will on no account consent to put an inflated, bepuffed, lying abortion, on the same footing with my invention," he told Field. He still intended to sue House for infringement, and believed that in the wake of the Supreme Court ruling he would be awarded heavy damages: "I do not feel like *paying* them money instead of *receiving* it."

Kendall too was disturbed by Field's willingness to consolidate with House companies. What troubled him even more, however, was the risky and one-sided agreement Field had extracted from Morse. Morse's grant of patent rights at no charge to the New York, Newfoundland, and London company would be resented by Morse companies, which had paid for the rights. Also, Morse's attempts to persuade other lines to transmit Field's international messages at half price created a conflict of interest, since Morse himself owned stock in many of those lines. The other stockholders would suspect him of sacrificing them to serve his interest in Field's line. Kendall warned Morse that the agreement would bring him distrust and ill will, and implored him to cancel it. "They ought never to have asked you to enter into it," he said; "I have reason to doubt the sincerity but none to make me doubt the utter selfishness of these people."

But Morse felt flattered to be treated by Field's associates as the "great high priest" of telegraphy, and viewed the transatlantic cable as a noble philosophic-scientific-humanitarian endeavor. Field and his colleagues were "honorable men," he told Kendall. They would not try to "entrap" him. Having made his agreement he would stand by it: "I shall feel myself bound in honor to bear this sacrifice myself and penalty of my folly, if folly it is."

It took an entire year to ready the first stage of Field's heroic undertaking—a land-and-water line connecting Newfoundland with the American continent. Telegraph wire had to be strung through a dense wilderness across Newfoundland, an area larger than Ireland. Eighty-five miles of submarine cable had to be manufactured to connect Newfoundland through the Gulf of St. Lawrence with Cape Breton Island, adjoining Nova Scotia, from where the line would pass into the United

States. Field sailed to England to oversee manufacture of the cable, and to consult with the men who had telegraphically spanned the English Channel.

As he waited out the year, Morse took another of his occasional intermissions, in part to reorder his business affairs. His tormentors no longer included Henry O'Reilly. However colorfully bold, the "Napoleon of the Telegraph" was in his own way no less naive about business than was Morse. Wildly overextended, his People's Telegraph to New Orleans a financial disaster, he went bankrupt, his furniture and other property seized and sold to pay his debts. The lines he had owned passed into other hands. Many of the lines had been poorly built and often broke down, so many of the companies that bought them also went bankrupt. His days as a power in the frantic telegraph business ended, O'Reilly took a clerical job in New York City, accepting daily wages to meet his family's needs.

Not only O'Reilly was out of the way. Morse believed that the patent extension dissolved his contractual links to his partners in the original patent, leaving him free to act without consulting them. Alfred Vail could legally claim no interest in the extension, but on Kendall's advice Morse gave him a continuing one-eighth share. Vail had decided anyway to quit telegraphy. He owned nearly $50,000 worth of stock in eight telegraph and railroad companies, but only about a fifth of it paid dividends. And he could find no more lucrative job than superintending a line from Washington to Columbia, South Carolina, at a demeaning annual salary of only $900. "I have made up my mind to leave the Telegraph to take care of itself," he told Morse, "since it cannot take care of me." Not an easy person to get along with—full of "morbid suspicions," Morse said—Vail left gloomily: on bad terms with Kendall, feeling cheated by Smith, resentful toward Morse for failing to publicly acknowledge his contributions to the telegraph. His health had declined as well. The cares and worries of his service to Morse cost him what he described as "a termination of blood to the brain." His physician advised him to "seek a rustic life."

Vail returned to Morristown, New Jersey, site of his family's Speedwell Iron Works. Semi-retired, he spent his time doing electrical experiments, compiling a mammoth Vail genealogy, annotating the many sermons he read, and arranging his scrapbooks and correspondence. He stayed in touch with Morse, occasionally meeting with him in New York. Rummaging around, he discovered some cast-off equipment from the early days of their partnership—a roll of the first telegraph paper they used, the model of the classic transmission key he had invented in Washington. He returned them to Morse, obviously still feeling some bond with his former teacher. Upon the death of his wife of thirteen years—a "crushing affliction," he said, that left him weeping "bitter tears in loneliness"—he offered Morse $250 to design a monument to her.

Morse believed that the extension also voided Fog Smith's share in his patent. "Consequently," he said with vast relief, "the annoyances of Smith are at an end, so far as the necessity of consulting him is concerned." Hoping to keep the peace, however, on Kendall's advice he offered Smith an interest in his extended patent, as he had done with Vail. "The animal," as Morse called him, brusquely rejected the offer and sued him for the same share in the extended patent as in the first.

And Smith won his case. A "legal swindle," Morse moaned, but not exactly surprising, "for he is in his element, and I am not." Having won his suit, "that *incubus*," as Morse also called him, announced that he, too, would make a new start. Acting under what he conceived to be the terms of their 1838 contract, he intended to sell patent rights on his own, without consultation. "I do not perceive any safe course," Kendall reported dolefully to Morse, "but an application . . . restraining him by injunction, getting a receiver appointed and going in for an annulment of the contract of 1838. The thought of another suit is revolting; but what can we do?"

Morse thought of disengaging from Amos Kendall as well. Since the extension dissolved their ten-year-old agreement, he told Kendall, it might be in their mutual interest to "close up our business relation." As Morse's agent Kendall had worked long and hard on his behalf. He not only fulfilled the terms of their agreement but also provided assistance and favors well beyond it—defending Morse at length in print, trying with Christian fellow-feeling to lift him from his blue periods. But Morse was irritated by Kendall's attempts to steer him away from Cyrus Field. And Kendall's never-robust health was worse than usual. Having suffered an attack of pleurisy and the death of another child, he could write for barely an hour without feeling exhausted; his hold on life, he said, was "very precarious." Moreover, when business records were gathered to apply for the extension, they revealed that for a long time Kendall had kept the accounts on loose slips of paper. Among other results of his carelessness, money owed to Morse had apparently never been paid to him.

Morse sent Kendall an aloof letter, setting forth his terms for continuing their arrangement. "I have felt the want of a systematic keeping of our Telegraphic accounts," he said. "This want has been felt most seriously when apprized of your often recurring illnesses, to which all indeed are more or less liable." For years he had impressed on Kendall his indifference to mere trade. Now he required documentation of all the business Kendall had conducted as his agent over the past decade, with dates and amounts of every payment and receipt, and full details of the transaction. "Such a statement is, I conceive, a necessary prerequisite to any negotiation for setting up the business of your Agency, to which it seems the 'extension' has unexpectedly put an end."

Morse's tone sounds thankless, suggesting that he took Kendall's devoted agency for granted, as if entitled to it. It turned out, however, that the extension did not alter Morse's legal agreement with him, which remained in force. Kendall had experienced far worse in his life than thanklessness, and did not gloat. He continued selling patent rights and taking on the aggravation and legal mess that often followed. "Indeed," he told Morse, "what is there connected with your patents and your telegraph property, that I have not to attend to? I do not complain, but do it all cheerfully." A quick tally of debits and credits apparently revealed that a considerable amount of money was owing—not to Morse but to Kendall, who offered not to take it. A lawyer and clerk were hired to sort through heaps of correspondence and scraps of paper, assisting Kendall as he attempted to organize the business records, prodded now and then by Morse for a definitive statement.

In a final gesture of casting off the past, Morse tried to exorcise Joseph Henry. He had not replied publicly to Henry's damning court testimony against him. But recently the testimony had been quoted at length in several new books on telegraphy, such as Alexander Jones' *Historical Sketch of the Electric Telegraph* (1852), which cited Henry in attempting to show that Morse had contributed nothing essential to the invention. Morse answered in a ninety-page tract, *The Electro-Magnetic Telegraph, A Defence against the Injurious Deductions Drawn from the Deposition of Prof. Joseph Henry, (in the Several Telegraph Suits).*

In private, Morse accurately referred to his *Defence* as his "*Attack!*" Dropping his usual polite deference to Henry, he walloped him as a befogged academic whose testimony in court misrecollected and misrepresented their meetings. Henry's supposed scientific discoveries were based on discoveries by others and/or were no help: "the impression that I derived *any* aid from him . . . is utterly fallacious." With a barrage of damaging dates, names, and facts he assailed Henry's reputation for impartiality, his credibility as an expert witness, his qualifications for heading the Smithsonian Institution. Then he sweepingly summed up the evidence: "*the Magnetic Telegraph owes little if anything to Professor Henry's labors or discoveries.* The truth of History should no longer be allowed to suffer from so erroneous an impression."

While at Locust Grove waiting out preparations for laying the Atlantic cable, Morse also reentered politics. He accepted an invitation from Democrats in the district to run for a seat in Congress. He did so without much enthusiasm, uncertain whether if elected he would be able to satisfy his constituency. As he put it, for forty years he had "cordially acquiesced" in Democratic policies—assented to the policies, he seems to mean, without espousing them. He disapproved the party's "bargaining for Catholic votes," and during the 1836 New York City mayoralty race he had run as a candidate of the Native American party.

In the congressional election, in November 1854, Morse received about 5000 votes, losing to the victor by just over 3000—a respectable showing: "I came near being in Congress," he said. Defeated or not, he got a chance during the two-month campaign to make his views public. The paramount issue remained European designs on America. With the Revolutionary generation dying off—only about a thousand veterans of the war were left—he hoped to keep alive its ideal of an America purged of Old World corruption: "I am content to stand on the platform . . . occupied by Washington in his warnings against foreign influence."

Morse had always thought the Abolitionists dangerous to the nation, comparable to the bloodsoaked Jacobins of the French Revolution. And European intriguants, in their latest attempt to divide the country, were insinuating into every public issue great and small the "rabid Abolition spirit." The Kansas-Nebraska Act of 1854, for instance, permitted settlers in the newly created territories of Kansas and Nebraska to decide through their territorial legislatures whether to allow or prohibit slavery, repealing the thirty-year-old Missouri Compromise, which had excluded slavery from the same area. Morse believed that the act would pacify the now-tumultuous agitation over slavery and produce "lasting good to the slave as well to the country." But Abolitionists had drummed up so much excitement over it as to shut out of public view vastly more important issues. And among the foreign inciters of Abolitionism, the most disruptive was the Catholic Church, now more than ever to be abhorred. "The reckless spirit of a wild and truly un-Christian *abolitionism,* is that which I believe Jesuits may, and do, use as one of the most efficient means to accomplish their great end, and the end for which they have been sent here, to wit, *the dissolution of the Union.*"

Despite efforts by Morse and others in the 1830s to warn Americans about subversion from abroad, Nativism had been quiescent for a decade. But it revived following waves of European immigration that from roughly 1845 to 1855 brought to America nearly three million foreigners, more than had come in all the time since the American Revolution. "It is a problem yet unsolved," Morse said, "how far our moral strength can withstand the shock of such an avalanche."

Morse felt the effects himself. He allowed an Irish railroad laborer named Brien to erect a "shantee" on his land at Locust Grove. Returning from a trip to Washington he found not only the Brien family but a whole shantytown on his property, "a complete Irish village" of railroad workers who had cut down his trees and burned his fences. "An incursion of savages could not have done so much injury in so short a time," he howled. "I declare I almost cried when I looked at the scene." He ordered the shanties removed and demanded "heavy damages." With forecasts in the press of further large Irish immigrations soon to come, he theorized that England intended to drive the Irish out of Ireland, recolonize the country with Englishmen, and leave America to take care of the wretched refugee population it had created. In seeking a coachman, a laundress, and other domestic help he specified Protestants only: "I do not wish Irish," he added.

Morse became a rallying point for the revived nativism. With new Catholic churches being built and new Catholic calls for an end to Bible reading in the public schools, he permitted nativist groups to reprint his *Imminent Dangers to the Free Institutions of the United States*

Through Foreign Immigration (1835). He also agreed to sit on the Council of the Order of United Americans, an organization of self-described "ultra kind of Americans" opposed to immigrant-borne "*jesuitism.*"

Although running for Congress as a Democrat, Morse boosted the Know-Nothing party, the most visible and successful manifestation of resurgent anti-Catholicism. The party's platform included a resolution to restrict political office to native-born Americans ("AMERICANS ONLY SHALL GOVERN AMERICA")—a cause Morse had espoused for twenty years. Rapidly gaining support throughout the country, the Know-Nothings elected eight governors by the end of 1855, and the mayors of Boston, Philadelphia, and Chicago. "The American mind," Morse wrote, "is at length awake."

Morse drew most attention to the cause by dueling in the press with the American-born Catholic bishop of Louisville, M. J. Spalding. At issue was a statement supposedly made by the Marquis de Lafayette more than twenty years earlier: "*American liberty can be destroyed only by the Popish clergy.*" Lafayette's warning had been often and widely quoted since first appearing in Morse's *Confessions of a French Catholic Priest* (1837). Morse had included it on the authority of the ex-priest whose manuscript he edited for publication.

About ten days before the November 1854 election, an article made the rounds of American newspapers, denouncing the quotation as a "*Disgraceful Forgery.*" Reprinted from the Cincinnati *Enquirer,* the article maintained that Lafayette's statement had been taken out of context from a letter he wrote, in a way that reversed its meaning. What Lafayette actually said, according to the *Enquirer,* was: "the fears . . . *that if ever the liberty of the United States is destroyed it will be by Romish priests*—are certainly without any shadow of foundation whatever." Morse publicly called the *Enquirer* quotation spurious, a forgery itself, and demanded that the newspaper produce the supposed letter. He claimed that he had often personally heard Lafayette, who had been born a Catholic, warn against Catholic influence in America.

Soon Morse was trading insults in the press with Bishop Spalding, who attributed the reversal of Lafayette's meaning to deceitful anti-Catholics. In their eight-month-long exchange of published letters and comments, the bishop sneered at Morse's faulty memory and fondness for academic titles. Morse sneered back that it baffled "moral science" to account for so contradictory a thing as an American-born bishop:

that one who, with his first moral breath, inhaled the purified air
of a Bible Christianity; that one whose infancy was nurtured amid
the sound heads and honest hearts of a Kentucky community,
should voluntarily shrink away from the day-light that surrounded him and deliberately prefer to grope for enlightenment
in the foreign dens of a decaying and festering superstition. . . .

Mostly Morse tried to out-argue the bishop, "Jesuit as I presume he is,
and eel like as he may be." With no less intensity than he brought to
demonstrating the priority of his telegraph, he chased down evidence
of the authenticity of Lafayette's statement—writing to Paris booksellers, scanning old newspapers, contacting persons who had known
Lafayette and historians who had written about the period, including
Washington Irving and George Bancroft.

Morse's months of research did not greatly help. Over the course
of the controversy he shifted ground. Eventually he contended not for
the genuineness of Lafayette's statement but of the "sentiment" it contained: "The precise words," he conceded, "are comparatively of little
moment." Just the same, sympathizers from all over enjoyed and
approved his thrusts at the bishop. His letters, he learned, delighted
readers in Georgia who believed that the Church was using Abolitionism to destroy the Union. An admirer in western Pennsylvania sent
congratulations: "You have . . . layed the Bishop out as Cold as a wag-
gon tire [sic]." The news reached the Protestant press abroad: "by the
world-renowned Professor Morse," the Edinburgh *News of the Churches*
reported, "Bishop Spalding is pilloried in Kentucky."

Despite his passion for the nativist cause, Morse felt no more at
home in the movement than in the Democratic party. Unexpectedly
he found himself leaving the Order of United Americans, and no
longer endorsing the Know-Nothings. Like other political parties, the
Know-Nothings were split by sectional loyalties. Many northern members aligned themselves with the Abolitionists, believing that the
Catholic Church and nearly all Irish immigrants supported slavery. To
Morse, the Know-Nothings were in this way "neutralizing" their influence, and he withdrew his support: "I cannot thus identify myself
while there is any likelihood of my giving my influence to the ruinous
anti-Slavery movement of the North against the South."

To a lengthening list of disillusionments with the country that
included the American press and American patent laws, Morse added

the American party system. The Whig party having collapsed, the Democrats being sharply divided by the "dangerous ultraisms" of the day, and the new, anti-slavery Republican party being contemptible, he began to feel disenfranchised altogether: "my own views . . . are not in accord with the platforms of any present political organization, nor can I be identified entirely with any of them."

During Morse's year-long intermission, the first, North American stage of the transatlantic telegraph had been nearly completed. Six hundred workmen had built a road from one end of Newfoundland to the other. It wound around bays, and through rocky gorges and dense forests roamed by bears and herds of caribou—a giant causeway of telegraph poles eight feet wide and four hundred miles long. Simultaneously a 140-mile telegraph line had been strung through Cape Breton Island, about sixty miles away across the Gulf of St. Lawrence. What remained was to lay a cable in the gulf electrically linking Newfoundland with Cape Breton Island, where transmissions would pass through nearby Nova Scotia into the United States. A land-and-water line of telegraph would then be in operation some 1200 miles from Newfoundland to New York City, waiting to be attached to the undersea cable from Ireland.

On August 7, Morse and Sarah sailed from New York City to witness the laying of the gulf cable. For the critically important event Field chartered a sleek sidewheel steamboat, the *James Adger.* He invited fifty-eight guests as passengers—clergymen, doctors, lawyers, reporters, as well as the other directors of the New York, Newfoundland, and London company with their wives and children. The atmosphere was party-like. The flag-decked *Adger* left its Hudson River pier amid steam whistles, three-gun salutes, and displays of the Stars and Stripes. The first night out, Field's guests heard a concert of airs from popular operas and selections of minstrelsy, such as "The Colored Fancy Ball." Morse brought along and demonstrated a telegraph apparatus. When thunderstorms struck that evening, guests jokingly blamed them on the Lightning Man.

On August 20, Morse and the others aboard the *Adger* reached Port-aux-Basques, Newfoundland, from where the submarine cable would be laid to Cape Breton Island. They were scheduled to meet up with a vessel from England bearing the cable and paying-out equipment. But the vessel had been delayed. On Field's order the *Adger* steamed around the southern end of Newfoundland to the capital city of St. John's, for a four-day goodwill call on officials of the provincial government. Field distracted his guests with a shipboard banquet, whose several toasts included a flattering quatrain to Morse:

> *The steed called Lightning (say the Fates,)*
> *Was tamed in the United States;*
> *'Twas Franklin's hand that caught the horse,*
> *'Twas harnessed by Professor Morse.*

Morse replied by acknowledging his dependence on Field for his "favorite dream," cherished for twenty-three years—"that universal humanity is to be bound in a true social fraternity by instantaneous intercommunication of thought."

Humanity would have to wait, however. The *Adger* returned to Port-aux-Basques, where it at last met up with the sailing bark from England, the *Sarah L. Bryant,* loaded with copper cable. Morse left no account of the fatal mishaps over the next week, which are known only through reports in the press. On August 22 rafts bringing ashore lumber to build a telegraph shack were split by breakers. The lumber was rescued by spectators who rushed armpit-deep into the water, and some dogs that clenched planks in their teeth and swam with them back to the beach. Three days later the ships started out across the Gulf of St. Lawrence to lay the cable. But they collided; the *Adger* carried away the *Bryant's* shrouds. On a second attempt, the *Adger's* four-inch-thick towline jammed in its side wheel; in trying to disengage the line the *Bryant* lost its anchor.

The ships resumed their attempt to lay the cable on the twenty-seventh, a beautiful morning although with a strong northwest breeze. Late in the afternoon, after about forty miles of cable had been put down, a gale swept the Gulf of St. Lawrence. The *Bryant* pitched violently, in danger of being pulled under. It held on for hours, but near seven o'clock in the evening, a cry went up from the deck: "*The cable is gone!*" All forty miles of it sank, irretrievably. The expedition to complete the first stage of the transatlantic telegraph was over, a failure.

Morse and Field's other guests returned to New York aboard the *Adger* the first week in September. Some at least stayed in a gala mood, holding a costume party and dancing the schottische. However battered, Field was determined to keep going. But he and his associates had lost about $350,000, a quarter of their capital. And manufacturing a new cable for the gulf would require several months, while the larger enterprise would be set back an entire year.

Morse had grown close to Field and his family. When writing to him, he sometimes sent a kiss for one of Field's children; Field named a new son after him. What he found out a week or two after returning from Newfoundland therefore came as a nasty surprise. Field and his associates, he learned, had paid $100,000 for patent rights to a new telegraph, invented by a London-born Kentucky music teacher named David Hughes. Like the earlier House telegraph, it used a piano-like keyboard of twenty-eight keys, and printed letters of the alphabet. Its workings were complex, involving the synchronous movement of corresponding parts in the transmitter and receiver, kept in tandem by a spring that vibrated to produce a musical note of a certain pitch.

Field's sudden interest in a rival telegraph upset Morse. But Field explained that he and his associates had bought the patent right preemptively. They simply wished, he said, to forestall the purchase of Hughes' system by others who might use it in competition with the Morse system. Having been banqueted and toasted aboard the *Adger,* Morse accepted Field's story. He assured Kendall that Field and his colleagues were acting openly and in good faith. "I am confident their designs towards me and also towards you, are of the most friendly and liberal character in their acquisition of the Hughes patent," he said; "it was for the purpose of keeping it out of the hands of such men as . . . would not scruple to use it to my detriment, and to have it in the hands of *friends.*"

But two weeks later Morse's restored confidence in Field turned to new concern. An article in the New York *Herald* entitled "Astounding Telegraphic Improvements" acclaimed Hughes' apparatus as "the most wonderful instrument for telegraphic purposes ever invented . . . far ahead of any machine now in use." The article had even worse news for Morse. It reported that Field had organized a new group, the American Telegraph Company, to build Hughes lines west and south—"a network of wires radiating in all directions from New York to every prominent business place in the Union."

Morse knew about this company. He had given it his blessing, in the understanding that Field hoped to join the submarine cable to a national network, and therefore planned to lease or buy existing lines along the Atlantic seaboard and bring them under a unified management, including Morse lines. But his understanding of what Field hoped to do had not included the building of new lines worked by Hughes telegraphs. Such lines would put Field's American Telegraph Company in direct competition with the Morse companies. He worried anew about Field's intentions: "I hope collision may & will be avoided. Yet alas! my experience of men leads me to distrust the promises of the best of them."

Morse calmed down again after a few days. He decided that the *Herald* article amounted to no more than another of those self-interested jeers at his system by the press, aimed at getting Morse lines to cut their rates for telegraphic dispatches. It strengthened his belief to learn that the article had been written by an agent of the Associated Press, Daniel Craig. Craig was the journalist whose transmission of international news from Halifax had been blockaded by F. O. J. Smith. A forty-year-old New Englander, Craig had a shady reputation. He sabotaged Smith's Boston–New York line—Smith claimed—by sending a mistress to cut the wire. On several grounds Morse discounted the *Herald* article. To clinch the matter, he heard directly from Field that the article in the *Herald* was untrue. Field said that he and his associates in the American Telegraph Company had no intention of building new Hughes lines. "They were as much surprized as any one," Morse told Kendall, "and as indignant of such misrepresentations."

Kendall was less convinced. Suspicious of Field from the beginning, he again warned Morse that Field's friendliness was a snare, designed to gain his confidence in order to exploit him. This time, he said, Field would use the fanfare about the Hughes telegraph to drive down the value of stock in companies that ran Morse equipment. Then Field's American Telegraph would buy or lease the Morse companies at bargain prices. "It was not friendship to us which induced them to buy the Hughes instrument," Kendall said; "it was in fact, say what they will, to hold it *in terrorem* over our heads and the heads of our companies to induce us to let them have our lines at a reduced rent."

But Morse was by nature trusting—of an "unsuspicious disposition," as Kendall put it. He also felt too deeply committed to the "great enterprize" of a transatlantic telegraph to risk alienating the men who made it possible. He conceded no more than that the motives of Field and his allies might be mixed. "They are kindly and I believe generously disposed towards me," he replied to Kendall, "but they are business men too."

Morse agreed to accompany Field over the summer on a trip abroad. Field wanted to enlist English capital and the English government in laying the cable across the Atlantic. He asked Morse to come along in order to experiment on submarine conductors, "of which," Morse noted, "we have none of any great extent in this country." A friend advised Morse to have the New York, Newfoundland, and London company pay for the trip: "the stockholders are a few wealthy men & you are to go to great expence for the benefit of the line & they bear none of the burden . . . is that liberal, or selfish?" Morse would hear nothing of Field's supposed selfishness, however. Besides, he meant to take advantage of the trip by seeking payment for the ever-increasing adoption of his system abroad: "not a mile contributes to my support," he complained, "or has paid me a farthing."

But the spring months of 1856, as Morse prepared to depart, brought more disquieting signs. New articles glorifying the Hughes telegraph appeared, these too by Daniel Craig. Implying that he wrote with the sanction of Field's American Telegraph Company, he reported the imminent construction of Hughes lines in New Jersey, Pennsylvania, and elsewhere along the Atlantic coast. Morse fulminated against Craig as a "low-bred profane wretch." But he could not ignore the possibility that Craig was covertly writing on behalf of Field. Kendall pushed him to ask Field bluntly whether American Telegraph, owners of the Hughes patent, had authorized the use of Hughes instruments on the lines reported by Craig—in competition with the key New York–Washington line of Morse's Magnetic company: "This much you have a right to claim as due to you."

Morse made his uncomfortable relation to Field no easier by endorsing a new British organization, the Transatlantic Telegraph Company. Finding the group composed, he said, of "substantial and honorable men," he swallowed their tale that they did not intend to interfere with Field's great undertaking but to aid it. Field and his associates quickly disabused him. Becoming "quite warm on the subject," Morse said, they made it clear that Transatlantic Telegraph was in fact a rival. The British group had widely publicized Morse's sponsorship, obliging him to take out a notice in the New York *Herald* announcing his withdrawal from them, "undoing today what I did yesterday."

Morse may have undone too soon, for only a week later he received depressing evidence of Craig's secret involvement with Field's company. How it arrived and its exact nature are unclear. But Kendall described the information as certain proof of "some degree of contact" between Craig and "*some* members" of Field's American Telegraph. "They have . . . confessedly been dealing with Craig," he said, "knowing that he entertained designs hostile to the interests of the Magnetic Line in which you are so deeply interested, and yet, with all their professions of friendship, concealed those designs from you and me." He told Morse flatly that Field and Field's associates had betrayed them.

Against his every wish and inclination to consider Field a friend, Morse was beginning to lose faith in him. "I confess," he told Kendall, "there has been so much mysterious manoeuvering." More than that, he had joined Field's enterprise not for gain but for the good of humanity, to help realize "the great plan of uniting the two continents by Telegraph." Flattered as he felt to be treated as the "high priest" of telegraphy, advertised as "Electrician" of the transcendent adventure, the evidence of schemes harmful to himself and to the Morse lines could not be wished away. He told Kendall that they would continue to negotiate with Field and his associates for the sale or lease of the lines. But he would "get away from all connection with them," he said, "the moment I can do so without too great sacrifice."

Morse and Sarah were scheduled to depart for Europe with Field in early June, now only about a month away. He still meant to make the trip, but before leaving he visited Boston and walked over to Charlestown, his place of birth. He had not seen the town for eighteen years, and then for only a few hours. The landmarks were so changed he scarcely recognized them. A pump in the square had vanished, a tavern stood in place of a mansion, the church where his father had preached was gone, together with the parsonage and garden.

But his first home, a two-story wooden house, still existed. Allowed in by the present owner, he viewed the room in which he supposed he was born, the walls unsubstantial, the ceiling low. At another house in town he discovered the watercolor portrait of his family he had painted in his teens.* He had wondered where the picture might be—his young self, his brothers, his mother and father gathered around a Chippendale table, on which stands a globe of the world.

Jedediah was much on Morse's mind. About two weeks before leaving for Europe he wrote a biographical sketch of "my venerated Father." He remembered not primarily Jedediah's acts of benevolence—as when he gave the profits from his geographies to the needy—but more strikingly his Christian forgiveness of injuries. He recalled how his father addressed the flock who had driven him from his pulpit, quoting the words of Paul to the Ephesians: "Let all bitterness and wrath, and anger, and clamor, and evil speaking be put away from you with all malice." His memory could summon up no more vivid image of his father than of Jedediah praying with choked tears for those who had injured him.

Morse and Sarah departed for Europe on June 7, taking with them their six-year-old son, Willie. They had to make the voyage without Cyrus Field, however. Field telegrammed to say he had moved his own passage up to July, owing to the illness of his eldest daughter. He said he could arrange for Morse to make the same change, so that they could still cross the Atlantic together. "My arrang. are now so fixed," Morse telegrammed back, "I fear I can't wait."

* See p. 18.

FIFTEEN

Can't! Sir, Can't!

(1856–1857)

F ROM THE TIME Morse and Sarah arrived in London, his four months abroad were a personal triumph. He knew that his telegraph had been widely introduced overseas, but the extent came as a surprise. Putting up at Fenton's Hotel in St. James, he was lionized, "overwhelmed with calls and the kindest and most flattering attentions." When he visited a London telegraph office he saw his own instruments at work, sending and receiving messages across the Channel to and from Paris, Vienna, and elsewhere on the Continent. He also learned that British telegraph companies were thinking of substituting his system for Wheatstone's over long internal lines. "Thus the way seems to be made for the universal adoption of my Telegraph throughout *the whole world*."

After about ten days, Morse and Sarah moved on briefly to Paris, and a welcome no less heartening. He discovered that France still used a dial system designed by the scientific-instrument maker Louis Bréguet. But it was beginning to be replaced by a modified Morse apparatus, and an international Morse line already served between France and Germany. In a large telegraph office he saw twenty Morse telegraphs all operating at once, "my own children . . . chatting and chattering as in our American offices." His friend and advocate Arago had died, but the current head of French telegraphs complimented his system as "the simplest and the best." And during his stay Emperor Napoleon III, Napoleon's grandnephew, awarded him one of France's highest honors, the Légion d'Honneur.

Morse's journey north toward Denmark brought further homage. Railroad travel on the Continent had greatly expanded since the time when he perforce rode by diligence and *vettura*. Tracks had been laid or nearly laid from Vienna to Prague, Paris to Marseilles, Venice to Milan. And at the railroad stations, he said, "I found my name a passport." He bought second-class tickets but got seated in first-class cars; his luggage passed customs with only a show of inspection. Officials at the telegraph stations told him they used his and only his apparatus: "We have tried others, but have settled down upon yours as the best." At the royal castle in Frederiksberg he was courteously received by Frederick VII, King of Denmark. A thickset man in a blue frock coat, Frederick asked his opinion of the idea of a transatlantic telegraph, which Morse assured him was practicable and certain to be realized. The King later conferred on him the Cross of the Order of Dannebrog, "in acknowledgment of the services you have rendered the world by the invention and successful establishment of the Electrical Telegraph." A significant honor, membership in the Order was the modern equivalent of a knighthood.

Morse considered his visit to Copenhagen a pilgrimage. He spent several hours at the tomb and museum of Bertel Thorwaldsen, whom he had painted in Rome twenty-five years earlier and still rated as "the greatest sculptor since the best period of Greek art." The same day he visited the study of "the immortal Oersted." He sat at the table on which the Danish scientist had observed that a wire carrying a current deflects a compass needle—a discovery, he said, that "laid the foundation of the science of electro-magnetism, and without which my invention could not have been made." He bought a bust of Oersted at the Porcelain Museum, where by luck he encountered Oersted's daughter—the living likeness of the bust and of her celebrated father.

From Copenhagen Morse and Sarah proceeded to St. Petersburg. Fifteen years earlier he had offered his telegraph for sale to the autocratic Czar Nicholas I. The Czar refused it, but the Russian government had nevertheless been using his system the entire time—without acknowledgment or compensation. Now St. Petersburg was getting ready for the coronation of Nicholas' reform-minded son, Alexander II, who in five years would emancipate the serfs. Morse thought the city the most sumptuously splendid he had seen in all his travels, its churches and palaces displaying profusions of gold and pearls, nosegays of emeralds and sapphires.

Through the American minister to Russia, Morse met Alexander at Peterhof, the luxurious royal estate founded by Peter the Great, seventeen miles from St. Petersburg across the Gulf of Finland. Arriving at the Peterhof quay about nine-thirty in the morning, he was drawn in a coach by richly caparisoned black horses to one of the palaces, part of which had been assigned to American guests. He found his name written on the door of an apartment already prepared for him, where servants in gold lace presented breakfast on silver plates. The same afternoon, a coach emblazoned with the imperial double-headed eagle sped him to the Czar's palace. Passing through a long anteroom lined on both sides by liveried attendants, he joined the deputations for the coronation ceremonies, a glittering company of princes, nobles, and distinguished persons from all over the Continent.

A Master of Ceremonies mustered Morse into a receiving line to meet the thirty-seven-year-old Czar, who wore military costume, a blue sash across his breast. The M.C. identified him to Alexander as "Mr. More." When Morse repeated the name correctly, the Czar exclaimed: "Ah! that name is well known here; your system of Telegraph is in use in Russia." Alexander said he hoped Morse enjoyed St. Petersburg; the line moved on, into the drawing room of the Czarina.

Among the forty-seven guests at dinner that evening Morse was seated next to one of the wealthiest noblemen in England and opposite three European princes. Nearby sat the former British foreign minister, Lord Granville, and Prince Esterházy of Hungary, the scabbard of his sword blazing with diamonds. Twenty servants in Imperial scarlet set out every variety of costly food and wine. Morse lingered over coffee before accepting an invitation from Granville to board his steam yacht for a sociable excursion back to St. Petersburg, along with Sir Robert and Lady Peel.

Passionate republican though Morse was, it delighted him to be hobnobbing with royals and bluebloods. His denunciations of them had always conflicted with his reverence for social hierarchy and his aesthetic enjoyment of panoply. And he welcomed their tasteful polite company as relief from the angry turmoil of much of his current life in democratic America—the fractious Abolitionists, the brawling immigrant Irish, the Fog Smiths and Daniel Craigs barking at his heels. He left Russia full of praise for the grandees he had mingled among, the "truly amiable and kind-hearted" Czar and Czarina, the affable and intelligent titled Britishers, "with none of the hauteur which we attach in America, sometimes unjustly, to English noblemen."

Before leaving St. Petersburg, Morse presented through the American minister a thirty-page petition to the new Czar, setting forth a claim to some compensation for the use of his telegraph. Uncertain about how much to ask, however, he withdrew the petition before it reached Alexander. Instead, he hired an agent to negotiate an indemnity with the Russian, French, and other European governments. The agent, a Paris attorney named Frederic Van den Broek, would receive a third of any sums granted.

Returned to London at the end of September, Morse began serious experiment on the cable—his original purpose in making the overseas trip. His resolve to break off with Cyrus Field and Field's business associates was not easy to keep. In fact, he worked eagerly to ensure Field's success, tolerating the ambiguities and indignities of their relationship for the sake of having not only his telegraphs but also himself present at the epochal cable-laying. Two Englishmen joined him for the experiments: Charles Bright, the brilliant twenty-five-year-old Superintendent of British telegraphs; and Dr. Edward Whitehouse, a physician who had given up all other work to devote himself to problems of cable transmission.

Morse and his colleagues took over a telegraph office on Old Broad Street, working at night when the system was not in commercial use. Since the great length of the undersea cable would retard the current, they particularly wanted to find out how rapidly a signal could be sent through. In one experiment, Morse and Whitehouse connected 10 gutta-percha-insulated cables of 200 miles each, making a continuous length of 2000 miles. Using a Morse recording instrument, and working through the night without sleep, they were able to send between 210 and 270 signals per minute—a rate fast enough to be commercially feasible. An insulated cable with a single conducting wire, Morse reckoned, could transmit at least 8 to 10 words a minute between Ireland and Newfoundland, over 14,000 words a day. Whitehouse believed that by changing the signal code an even faster rate could be achieved.

The test results exhilarated Morse: "the doubts are resolved," he wrote to Field, "the difficulties overcome, success is within our reach, and the great feat of the century must shortly be accomplished." He accompanied Field in making a business call at the Foreign Office, where they spent an hour discussing the transatlantic venture with the

Foreign Secretary, Lord Clarendon. The call evidently went well. The British government offered to supply ships for laying the cable, and agreed to pay £14,000 a year for using it, in effect subsidizing its operation for a guaranteed twenty-five years.

Morse's stay abroad ended a week later, no less triumphantly than it had begun. Several British telegraph companies threw a lavish dinner for him at the Albion Hotel. In honoring Morse they also meant to encourage the friendlier Anglo-American relations implicit in the transatlantic cable. But in three ways the occasion was touchy. Within living memory, British troops had burned the city of Washington. Cultural warfare still raged, too, over the priority and comparative virtues of Morse's system and Charles Wheatstone's needle telegraph. And to preside over the ninety invited guests, the sponsors chose Wheatstone's former partner, W. Fothergill Cooke. The partnership had degenerated into a bitter feud. Cooke charged in print that Wheatstone had stolen for himself the credit for their joint invention. Wheatstone had not been invited to the dinner but remained conspicuous by his absence.

The evening opened with toasts to Queen Victoria and Prince Albert, and to "The President and People of the United States." In introducing Morse, Cooke carefully gave him his due and then some, without granting him everything. He observed that England and Europe could claim to have invented the telegraphs used in their countries. But the American version was "conceived, worked out, and perfected" by Morse, "depending on his own scientific knowledge. . . . He stands alone in America as the originator." Cheers and laughter followed Cooke's admission that the simplicity of Morse's telegraph had brought it into use all over the Continent, "and the nuisance is that we in England are obliged to communicate abroad by means of his system."

After the downing of three toasts to him, Morse rose to speak, amid loud applause. He acknowledged the awkwardness of the moment. For a long time "part of England" had denied praise or even recognition to American inventions. And British disdain had become "a festering thorn in the hearts of some of the most cultivated in the land" (including, although he did not say so, of course himself). He therefore considered the evening not only a gratifying testimonial to him but also a sign to his fellow Americans of a new British generosity, a new "disposition to show them both justice and honour." And the Anglo-American telegraph, he declared, would produce "a firmer peace and a better understanding," even a global solidarity: not "E pluribus unum"—many in one—but "E *omnibus* unum," all in one.

London newspapers reported the evening's events in detail. Many condemned the studied absence of any reference to Wheatstone. One criticized Morse's dig at the supposed British failure to honor American inventors: "on the contrary, there was a strong disposition in England to give Americans credit for a great deal more than they are justly entitled to." But generally the London press praised Morse and the transatlantic cable endeavor as healers of old wounds: "The guest at the Albion," the *Times* remarked, "has deserved well of the world, and in his generation has done much to advance the cause of human progress. We rejoice to see England and America united in a project so honourable to both nations."

Morse and Sarah returned home in the late fall. He planned to stay in the United States only about six months, returning to England next spring as "Electrician" for the climactic laying of the cable. The interlude lasted just long enough for his pleasure in his overseas triumphs to evaporate.

F. O. J. Smith was suing again for alleged rights in the extended patent—"the appointed thorn," Morse called him, "to keep a proper ballast of humility in S. F. B. M. with his load of honors." But others also questioned his honors, as happened a half-dozen years ago after the Sultan of Turkey made him a Pasha. Under the headline "HAVE WE A KNIGHT AMONG US?" one newspaper reported his receipt of the Danish Order of Dannebrog and razzed him as "Sir SAMUEL." Another paper reported (correctly) that his grandfather on his mother's side was an Irishman. He learned that Joseph Henry was preparing a rebuttal to his *Defence* (*Attack!*).

The assaults left Morse gloomy, "much depressed in spirits from the state of my affairs." Czarist St. Petersburg had seated him among princes; monarchical London had toasted him as an agent of human progress. America sued and mocked him, preyed on him with the rapaciousness of a "money-worshipping society," as America was becoming. For years he had railed at French Louis-Philippe and Austrian Metternich, British abolitionist and Italian pope. But now a woeful thought occurred to him. He might be better off living there him-self: *there—Europe.* "I am sometimes disposed to offer all my property in America for sale at auction, take the proceeds, and retire into some nook of Europe for the remainder of my life."

Morse sought relief in continuing his cable experiments, "study-ing & solving problems with the intent of removing all the probable or possible difficulties." It was no place to seek relief. He learned that Daniel Craig had again been boosting the Hughes telegraph in the press, undermining Amos Kendall's ongoing negotiations with Field's American Telegraph Company for the lease or purchase of Morse lines. Kendall pleaded with Morse to give up the idea of going out on the cable-laying expedition. "Your true friends do not comprehend how it is that you give your time, your labor and your fame to build up an interest deliberately and unscrupulously hostile to all their inter-ests and to your own."

Morse still hoped that the Hughes-Craig-Field connection might prove to be illusory or benign. He inquired about it again in a seventeen-page letter to the wealthy industrialist-inventor Peter Cooper, Field's partner and president of American Telegraph. Cooper's eighteen-page reply was in a sense balanced: half reassurance, half threat. He reaf-firmed Field's promise that the company had bought the Hughes tele-graph only to prevent others from using it against Morse. Having said that, he lectured Morse about standing in the way of progress in telegraphy:

> it is our wish, and it should be yours, to encourage improvements
> in all the machinery requisite to facilitate this most wonderful
> mode of rapid communication regardless of any and all selfish or
> merely personal considerations.

Next Cooper denied that the company had any connection to Daniel Craig. Having said that, he denied that it had any responsibility to counteract what Craig wrote:

> we have been wholly unable to appreciate the propriety and more
> especially the necessity of the American Company's coming out
> publicly in the newspapers as you have desired, and disclaiming
> his unsolicited sayings or doings in favor of our Company or its
> interests.

Finally Cooper reassured Morse that the directors of American Telegraph were his "best friends." And having said that, he insisted that friends or not they would go on acquiring a network of lines to connect to the transatlantic cable: "Their progress is onward: they cannot if they could stand still, nor can they go backward."

A few days later, Morse learned that Cooper meant what he said. He read in a New York newspaper that, in competition with the Morse New York–Albany–Buffalo line, Field's group had contracted with the Harlem Railroad to build a line along the train route between New York and Albany, using the Hughes telegraph. Astonished, Morse immediately wrote to Cooper again: "I am most reluctant to believe, and will not believe, that gentlemen of the high character which you all hold in the community . . . are capable of playing with me the deep game of duplicity." Litigation must follow, he said, unless American Telegraph contradicted the report. And meanwhile his important work on the cable was being disrupted: "I confess, Sir, that I am deeply mortified and much depressed, at the necessity I am under of turning off my mind from experiments bearing upon our Great Ocean Enterprize, to ask for explanations of the most mysterious conduct of those whom I had confidently believed to be my friends."

But other mysterious doings also needed explaining. While in England with Morse, Field had raised £350,000, nearly $2 million, to form a British partner to American Telegraph called the Atlantic Telegraph Company. The two organizations would join in financing construction of the transatlantic Anglo-American system. Field appointed Morse an Honorary Director and offered to sell him one or more shares, at par.

Field's non-offer appalled Kendall. Morse surely was entitled to a financial stake in the new British company, without having to buy it. After all, he had given Field free patent rights; at his own expense he had gone abroad to perform valuable experiments on Field's cable—experiments that continued, also at his own expense. "They have made use of your time, labor, name and reputation in their transatlantic scheme," Kendall reminded him, "and now . . . they will allow you to *purchase* 'one or more shares' of their stock '*at par*'!" As Kendall saw it, Field was diddling Morse, taking advantage of his high-minded enthusiasm in the belief that he would demand nothing more solid for his services than honor and praise, membership in another Order of Dannebrog.

Morse thanked Field for the "kind offer" but explained that he had no surplus funds to invest in shares. He inquired politely about what he called "a point of some delicacy"—namely, as he delicately put it, "should there not be something." What moved him to ask about the "something" was the concern for him of others. Friends asked almost daily how much he stood to earn from the transatlantic enterprise:

> I have been somewhat embarrassed in replying that "as yet no interest has been definitely assigned, but I had the promise made verbally to me of my friend Mr. Field that when the company was organized, I should proportionately share with the rest. I am in the hands of friends." This answer has not always satisfied them; they have remarked, "This is not a business way of doing things." My reply has been, "Mr. Field's word is as good as his note."

Morse's craven request for "something" was unlikely to waken fear and trembling in a rip-snorting capitalist who had brought back a jaguar from the Amazon. But Morse considered his appeal decisive. It would "bring the whole matter to a head," he told Kendall: "I shall know definitely how I am to stand in my relations with these gentlemen, and am prepared to cut loose if necessary, at almost any sacrifice."

Morse's ever more desperate efforts to stay on good terms with Field strained his bond with Kendall. Impatient, perhaps disgusted, with Morse's timorous trust in Field, Kendall said it might be best if he gave up his agency and resumed the "sacred obligation" of completing his biography of Andrew Jackson. Morse had suggested as much himself two years earlier, when he told Kendall it might be in their mutual interest to close their business association. But Kendall's eagerness to now take up the suggestion jangled him. "I fear my 'bluish' letters have given you more uneasiness than they ought. . . . Pray overlook the infirmity." Without Kendall to protect his interests he could not survive in the marketplace: "you form such a contrast in all your feelings and acts to the cold and selfish and sordid doings of others that were you to withdraw I should truly feel widowed and alone and exposed to the arts of mere men of trade."

Morse anxiously longed to compose his differences with Field's company before departing for England to lay the cable. In March, with only a month to go, he met face-to-face with president Peter Cooper, the vice president, and one of the directors. "I wish if possible," he told a friend, "to avoid rupture with them on all accounts." The wish was probably intensified by Field's success, the same month, in getting aid from Washington. Congress voted by narrow margins to grant Field's company an annual subsidy of $70,000 for the government's use of the completed cable—equivalent to the British crown's £14,000. It also supplied two steamships of the American navy to join the British ships in laying the cable. Peter Cooper offered Morse passage to England aboard one of the official U.S. Navy ships.

The offer cannot have diminished Morse's yearning for a prominent role in Field's extravaganza. He apparently came away from his meeting with the leaders of American Telegraph willing to believe that Craig was promoting the Hughes telegraph without their blessing and that they had no intention of building Hughes lines. Willing to believe, that is, without exactly believing. In this half-hopeful mood he offered to put aside for a while any request for a financial stake in Field's new British company. "Whatever claims equitable or otherwise I or my friends may think are just on my part upon the company," he told Cooper, "let them *for the present* be waived. I shall not thrust before the company, at this moment when the harmonious action of all is necessary to carry forward the enterprize to a successful result, any private or mere personal object to embarrass our united action."

Morse did not say so to Field or Cooper, but he revealed to others that despite the concessions and seeming amity, on certain points he remained "not satisfied." Later on, it might be necessary to call together the directors of the major Morse lines to exchange views on a plan for defense. It could be that Field's group, he had to admit, "is thinking to swallow us all up."

As a world-historic event, the attempt to lay the transatlantic telegraph cable aroused an intense, international air of expectancy. Newspapers ran full-page stories headlined "THE GREAT WORK OF THE AGE," calling the expedition "a voyage more important than any in marine annals since the days of Columbus." Every feature of preparation became a subject for description and comment, as much so as before the launching of *Apollo 11* toward the moon a century later: "where in the annals of the world," one newspaper asked, "have we the evidence of a stride the one-millionth part as sublime as this in its immensity?"

Morse received extensive notice and credit, especially in the

American press—interviews, biographical sketches, engraved portraits. An interviewer for *Harper's Weekly* remarked to him that many
people doubted the line could be laid: " 'Can't! Sir, can't!' replied the
venerable Professor, quickly: 'I have forgotten the meaning of that
word. We must succeed.' "

Morse shipped for England aboard one of the vessels contributed
by the American government, the steam-and-sail frigate *Niagara*.
Designed by George Steers, builder of the famed clipper yacht *America,* it was deemed for size, speed, and armament the finest man-of-war
in the world. Its huge black hull was 375 feet long and 56 feet wide, its
28-foot engine room housed four boilers, its mighty guns could blast a
270-pound shot four miles with the accuracy of a rifle. Morse greatly
liked the "noble" ship. He remained in high spirits during the passage,
socializing with the captain and the two Russian naval officers who had
come as observers. While he sat having tea in a heavy rolling sea, his
table came unfastened, knocking him to the floor and throwing a
chair on top of him, painfully bruising his hip and leg: "if we are in the
Niagara," he quipped, "we must expect *the Falls.*"

After a passage of nearly three weeks, Morse arrived on May 14 at
Gravesend in the Thames estuary. The appearance of an American
warship in the Thames, and the ship's mission, drew crowds of visitors
day and night as the *Niagara* awaited the arrival of its British counter-
part, the *Agamemnon.*

A serious problem developed. Plans called for each ship to take on
1250 miles of the cable, which was being produced by two different
British manufacturers—one at Greenwich near London, the other
near Liverpool. The *Niagara*'s great length made it difficult to bring
her alongside the wharf in front of the Greenwich cableworks. And
other peculiarities of the ship's design made it impossible to stow the
cable properly. Morse saw that the very features of the *Niagara* that
had impressed him also unsuited her: "She is by far too splendid a ship
for the purpose." To overcome the problem, the *Niagara*'s interior
would have to be cut up and reshaped. The ship was sent to
Portsmouth, where workmen began breaking partitions and taking
down staterooms. Instead of returning to the Thames, the *Niagara*
would then go to Liverpool to receive cable.

Despite the setback, it excited Morse to be part of the venture,
"rejoiced that I have come out." The remodeling of the *Niagara* and

stowing of its cable would take at least six weeks. He took advantage of the delay by making an unforeseen business trip to Paris. He had hired an agent to negotiate indemnities from individual European countries that used the Morse system. But while in London he learned that France's Minister of the Interior had proposed that the French government take the initiative and arrange a joint indemnity from them all.

Morse enthusiastically approved the idea, and went to Paris hoping to forward it. A collective European grant shared in by several countries would be a unique honor, "a distinction never before conferred on an Inventor." Holding himself as always above vulgar materialism, he treated the amount to be given as a matter of greater concern to the governments involved than to himself. "This is not an ordinary transaction for them; they have an historic character to maintain, and its issue is to stamp that character indelibly on the pages of history." The logic of Washingtonian aestheticism thus allowed him to hope that the nations of Europe would contribute handsomely to the indemnity—not for his sake but their own: "A petty sum would not satisfy the world, however willing I might be to accept whatever they shall deem just and proper to give."

To reinforce the French efforts on his behalf, Morse published while in Paris a twelve-page pamphlet entitled *A Memoir Showing the Grounds of my Claim to Some Indemnity.* It described the spread of his system throughout the Continent, and his thwarted efforts to obtain some financial reward from European governments. "I conceive, however, that this justice will not be withheld," the pamphlet concluded. "I do not permit myself to doubt that when these simple facts of my case are fairly brought before them, they will honorably and promptly sustain severally their character for justice." He sent copies to Secretary of State Lewis Cass, asking him to pass them on to American ambassadors in Europe, with instructions to promote the indemnity at court. Prospects looked hopeful, but Morse had become well schooled in disappointment: "My dependence is not on man, but on one who knows the *end* from the beginning, who will give if it is for his glory, and withhold if it is not."

Providence in some degree repaid Morse's trust. Cass forwarded the pamphlets to American ministers in various countries. He told them that if they wished to present Morse's claims to government authorities, the State Department did not object. But he instructed them to do so unofficially and discreetly, "without putting into jeopardy the dignity of your own government."

Morse spent the rest of his time in Paris agreeably. He roomed at the American legation, by courtesy of the American minister, with whom he smoked an after-breakfast cigar. He glimpsed the Emperor, noted the universal fashion for carriage-filling crinolines. It dismayed him, however, to hear current opinion about the political strife in the United States. "The European mind," he found, "is sadly abused by the gross falsehoods of our violent Abolitionists. The Abolitionists have a terrible responsibility for evils they have brought upon the world, the North, the South, and the poor African himself."

Morse returned to England at the end of June, as the cable was being stowed in the American and British ships. The huge *Niagara* lay near Liverpool, anchored in the Mersey, but even after its alterations could not draw near enough to the cable factory for direct feeding. At considerable expense the cable was being ferried to it from shore aboard auxiliary ships. The British man-of-war *Agamemnon* lay moored about two hundred yards from the dockside factory at Greenwich, near London. Cable was being fed to it from the factory yard, drawn over pulleys fixed on intervening, pontoon-like barges, and packed into the ship's hold in one vast coil. This massive operation proceeded at the rate of about two and a half miles an hour, some sixty miles a day.

Morse and his fellow electrician, Dr. Edward Whitehouse, worked in Greenwich, testing the cable aboard the *Agamemnon*. The cable consisted of seven strands of thin copper wire, sheathed in three layers of insulation and protection. First the wires were coated with gutta-percha, making a tube about half an inch in diameter. The tube was then wrapped in tarred yarn. Finally the layer of yarn was encased in protective spirally wound iron wire. The resulting cable weighed just under one ton per mile and was ropelike—light and flexible enough to be tied around the arm. Morse and Whitehouse tested the cable each day as it was being stowed, by sending signals through its entire length. They used a 24-plate zinc-silver battery, and handsome Morse instruments made by the Berlin electrical engineer Werner Siemens. Michael Faraday stopped by one day, and seemed "quite delighted" by the stowing operation, Morse said.

The directors of the Atlantic Telegraph Company, Field's British partner, consulted Morse about a proposed change in strategy for laying the cable. The original plan called for the *Niagara* and the *Agamemnon* to depart from Ireland together, each bearing one half of the cable. They would proceed to the mid-Atlantic, where the two halves would be joined. One ship would head back to Ireland, paying out cable. The other ship, paying out cable, too, would head in the opposite direction toward Newfoundland, where a land-and-water line to the United States was now in operation. Under the proposed new plan, the ships would leave Ireland together, but the *Niagara* would begin at once laying cable to mid-ocean. There its end would be joined to the cable on the *Agamemnon,* which would lay the rest of the cable to Newfoundland.

Morse met with the directors at the elite Reform Club in London's Pall Mall. Dining elegantly on *Aiguillettes de Canetons* and *Caille Bonne Bouche,* he recorded the names and titles of those present, including several MPs, the mayor of Montreal, and the Lord of the Admiralty. He believed that under the new plan it would take longer to lay the cable, raising the risk, as fall approached, of encountering stormy weather. He nevertheless recommended the plan because it made ship-to-shore communication possible over the entire distance. The progress of the expedition could be continually reported to the company in London. And the working of the circuit could be continually tested all the way from Ireland to Newfoundland. He submitted two lengthy statements on the proposed change, which the company featured in a pamphlet, *Reports and Opinions in Reference to the Selection of the Best Point for Laying the Cable.*

The new plan was adopted. The revised schedule called for the *Agamemnon* to leave Greenwich late in July and meet up with the *Niagara* in Queenstown, Ireland, where both ships would take on coal and be joined by escort ships. From Queenstown the ships would steam together to the island of Valentia, where a cable-end aboard the *Niagara* would be attached to a telegraph onshore. Then the squadron would set out across the Atlantic, the giant American frigate paying out cable behind it.

Morse reboarded the *Niagara* in Liverpool, where he spent a Sunday with brother Sidney and his family, then traveling in Europe. When the American vessel left Liverpool harbor, British tars in the rigging of nearby warships cheered, flags of other nations dipped in salute, cannons fired, crowds on the quays waved handkerchiefs. Next day the *Niagara* reached Queenstown, picturesquely set on green hills over-looking the Cove of Cork, "one of the most beautiful harbors in the world," Morse thought. The *Susquehanna,* the largest paddle steamer in the American navy, dropped anchor close by, having been ordered from the Mediterranean to serve as an escort. Two days later the *Agamemnon* arrived from London with its British tenders *Cyclops* and *Leopard.* A steamer plied all day between the assembled British-American squad-ron and the shore, filling the streets of Queenstown with rambling sailors, and the ships with inhabitants of Queenstown and Cork—"wildly enthusiastic," reported a Queenstown correspondent: "This country is now filled with some of the most distinguished scholars and philosophers in the universe, all having in view the ambition of being eye witnesses of the grandest undertaking history can record."

On July 30 Morse performed an important experiment. With the *Niagara* and the *Agamemnon* lying a few hundred yards apart in the har-bor, the two 1250-mile halves of the cable were to be temporarily joined, to test whether the line functioned through its entire length. Climbing down the side of the *Niagara,* Morse stepped in and out of a pontoon of several small boats, making his way toward a tug that car-ried the span of connecting cable. The small boats rocked in the rough water. Morse misstepped. His left leg went down between two boats, scraping several inches of skin from near the knee. He had sim-ilarly injured his legs several times over the years: in 1830 a fall in Washington had lamed him for six weeks; in 1846 he fell into a coal chute on Broadway, taking off from his leg three inches of skin with some flesh and bone; only recently he had bruised his hip and leg in a heavy rolling sea. A surgeon dressed the wound, leaving Morse mobile enough to assist in connecting and testing the cables. To his great sat-isfaction a signal sped through the 2500 miles in half a second.

Morse's injury confined him to his berth on the *Niagara* for about three days, lying on his back. He emerged on August 4, when the ship steamed into Valentia, an island of neat cottages on gently sloping hills in the far southwest corner of Ireland, two and a half miles from the rock-bound coast. He delivered a speech at a public breakfast, at which the Lord Lieutenant of Ireland, who had come down from Dublin, pronounced the venture a consummation of the voyage of Columbus and prophesied an end to European bloodshed.

Next day Morse stood beside Sidney on Valentia to watch the cable on the *Niagara* being attached to a telegraph on the mainland. The bay was studded with small craft and yachts. Some two thousand persons who had gathered from all over Ireland huzzahed from shore. As they all looked on, sailors carried the cable by hand through the surf, depositing it in a trench dug in the sandy cove. The sailors brought the end into a tent temporarily erected to house the batteries and other telegraphic instruments. The connection was secured and tested both ways from ship to shore, communication passing freely.

Landing of cable from the *Niagara*
(*Illustrated London News*, August 22, 1857)

Morse left no record of his reaction to the public observances that followed. But given his view of Irish immigrants to America as little less odious than savages, he could not have been pleased. The people of Valentia island had suffered fearfully during the famine of the late 1840s, hundreds dying of starvation. The Lord Lieutenant—Queen Victoria's representative—received twelve cheers when he reflected on how many Irish families had left the country and found "hospitable shelter" in America. Cyrus Field had joined Morse aboard the *Niagara*, and he too spoke, promising that if any Irish came to his door across the Atlantic, they would have "a true American welcome." The evening's festivities included a ball, a bonfire of peat piled two stories high, and a dinner attended by the Roman Catholic Bishop of Kerry.

Early next morning, August 6, the *Niagara*, the *Agamemnon*, and their escort ships headed out over the Atlantic, close enough together to hear each other's bells.

News that the historic squadron had set off arrived in America by August 18, creating thrilled expectation. "The attention of the whole world," the *Herald* reported, "is now fixed upon the movements of that small combined fleet of American and English war steamers . . . every ship of which will be memorable for all time." What might be the content of the first transmission? Cyrus Field had received a letter from President James Buchanan, saying he would be honored if the first transatlantic message came from Queen Victoria to him. Morse decided that if he were allowed to send the first message, it would consist of two scriptural texts: "Glory to God in the highest, on earth peace and good will to men. . . . Not unto us, not unto us, but to Thy name be all the glory."

An immense coil of 130 miles of cable dominated the *Niagara*'s deck, even larger coils lying below. It stood amidst what Morse described as a bewildering mass of other equipment, some of which would be dumped before the ship reached mid-ocean: "steam-engines, cog-wheels, breaks, boilers, ropes of hemp and ropes of wire, buoys and boys, pulleys and sheaves of wood and iron, cylinders of wood and cylinders of iron, meters of all kinds—anemometers, thermometers, barometers, electrometers,—steam-gauges, ships' logs." Equally prominent on the ship's deck was the paying-out machinery: four massive iron wheels, about six feet in diameter, deeply grooved to support the cable.

The squadron had moved out barely five miles from Valentia when the cable caught in the paying-out machinery and snapped. The mishap forced the *Niagara* to turn around and reanchor in the bay so that the broken ends could be lifted from the water, spliced, and reinsulated with gutta-percha. Morse tested the splice the same afternoon and informed the ship's captain that the electrical connection per-

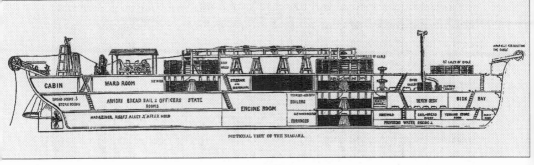

Cross section of the *Niagara*, ca. 1855
(New-York Historical Society)

formed well: "*not likely again to occur,*" he noted. But departure was delayed a full day.

When the *Niagara* steamed out again, on August 8, it did so at no more than two miles an hour, going slowly to avoid another accident. Over the next few days the ship and crew would face three critical moments. The shore end of the cable was a sort of eight-mile-long tail, deliberately made thicker than the main cable to withstand the rocky bottom of the coast. Soon the vulnerable connection point between the heavy tail and the much lighter main cable would pass through the paying-out machinery. About a day later, the first, on-deck coil of cable would run out and have to be replaced, its work taken over by a second coil, belowdecks. And after that the *Niagara* would begin making its way through much deeper zones of the Atlantic.

Operations resumed on the 8th, but without Morse. His activities in Valentia had so much inflamed his injured leg that the *Niagara*'s surgeon restricted him to his berth. He could not sleep that night, kept awake by the ruckus overhead of the paying-out wheels, scrunching like jumbo coffee grinders. He sensed, too, that the juncture was near—the point where the shore cable, weighing 18,000 pounds per mile, was spliced to the nine-times-lighter main cable. Soon he heard the machinery stop. Then voices, one saying, "The cable is broke." The unequal sections had come apart. Prudently, care had been taken to buoy up the end of the shore cable so that, by bright moonlight in the moderate sea, the connection was repaired in half an hour: "the joyous sound of 'All right' was heard," Morse noted, and "the machinery commenced a low and regular rumbling."

For about the next twenty-four hours the *Niagara* steamed smoothly through the pea-green water, uncoiling cable day and night at the rate of three miles an hour, in fine weather. Telegraphic communication was kept up continually with Dr. Edward Whitehouse at the station in Valentia.

The morning of August 9, a Sunday, brought the "critical point of change," as Morse called it. The *Niagara* had almost completely paid out the first (and smallest) of its five coils, some 120 miles of cable. Coil two had to be fed onto the wheels from beneath the deck—a worrisome moment when the cable might kink. But as the last loop of coil one unfurled, the captain slowed the ship slightly. The crew handled the slack cable deftly, and in two minutes made the changeover without accident. The new cable came up uncrinkled from the hold, unwound itself easily, and passed through the machinery over the stern into the sea.

Morse telegraphed to Whitehouse onshore: "214 miles out. All well. Beautiful day. Everything going right." His leg apparently improved, he attended Sunday services on deck, impressed anew with the workings of Providence. "The more I contemplate this great undertaking, the more I feel my own littleness, and the more I perceive the hand of God in it, and how he has assigned to various persons their duties, he being the great controller, all others his honored instruments."

Next day provided the third and more critical test of control. The *Niagara* had passed beyond the shallow waters of the coast. Paying out cable at an increased rate of five miles an hour, the ship was approaching a point where the ocean floor gradually dropped to about 400 fathoms, then suddenly fell to 1700, then to 2050—nearly the greatest depth of the Atlantic over the entire route. The paying out would have to be closely watched: increased depth tended to accelerate the flow of cable.

Morse was lying in his berth at six o'clock that evening when he heard alarmed voices calling "Stop her! Stop her!" Going up to the deck he saw the cable, fallen off the feeding wheel, running out at great speed. In the confusion a cool-headed engineer managed to halt the surge by using ropes. But the cable strained so mightily it perspired drops of tar.

About three hours later, telegraphic communication with shore suddenly went dead. Morse speculated that the strain to which the cable had been subjected after it fell off its wheel had split open the gutta-percha, destroying the insulation. For two and a half hours he tried without success to send a signal. With the circuit defunct there seemed nothing to do but cut the cable and wind back all of it that had been laid. The decision to do so was no sooner made, however, than the electrical current again came alive. No one could explain how or why.

The two crises, only a few hours apart, left behind them an atmosphere of foreboding. And at about three-forty-five in the morning, the cable began racing out again, this time over the feeding wheels. The paying-out machinery was equipped with brakes to slow or halt the flow. As Morse recounted what happened next, the chief engineer of Atlantic Telegraph, Charles Bright, ordered the application of an extra hundred pounds of braking force. The brakeman questioned the wisdom of his order, but Bright had designed the paying-out machinery himself and he persisted.

As the *Niagara* steamed on, the length of cable on its deck was stretched taut. Held by the brake, it pulled against the hundreds of tons of cable lying on the ocean floor behind the ship. The already rending tension increased as the *Niagara*'s stern rose and fell in the moderately heavy sea. "Such circumstances," Morse wrote, "would have parted a cable of 4 times the strength. Hence it is no wonder that our cable subjected to such a tremendous & unnatural strain should snap like a pack thread."

One end of the broken cable swung loosely over the stern. The other end dropped in the Atlantic Ocean and vanished—together with three hundred miles of five-strand, triple-sheathed copper wire. With the sun beginning to rise, everyone aboard the *Niagara* rushed to the deck, gathered in groups, conversed in subdued voices. "I believe there was not a man in the ship," Morse said, "who did not feel really as melancholy as if a comrade had been lost overboard."

Also lost overboard was the Columbus-rivaling, God-glorifying Event of the Age. News of the ruinous accident reached America two weeks later, evoking both sympathy and skepticism. Many judged the expedition a noble failure: "When we consider the courage which could undertake this Herculean feat," the *Tribune* editorialized, "we are almost as proud of our age as if everything had gone on smoothly, and the lightning were now leaping from continent to continent." Others found a sobering lesson for Americans: "we cannot but fear that the success so much hoped for, will not be so easily and so readily attained as our always over sanguine people seem to expect." Some suspected a coverup, wondering whether "the failure of the undertaking was more complete than has been reported, and . . . there is some disagreeable fact connected with it, not yet given to the public."

Morse contributed to public uncertainty about the cause of the failure. As he retold the *Niagara* affair, it was "the fatal mistake of Mr. Bright, which caused the breaking." His account was published in the *Observer,* widely quoted, and accepted as authoritative. *Scientific American,* a popular weekly founded twelve years earlier, repeated in a lead editorial Morse's condemnation of the "*fatal mistake of Mr. Bright*" and gibed that "Mr. Bright is evidently not bright enough to lay a telegraph cable." The young engineer, although barely twenty-five years old, was at least bright enough to have patented two dozen inventions, and to defend himself. He wrote to Morse denying that he had ordered any change in the force of the brakes. "I gave the man at the brake no orders to alter the adjustment," he said, "nor did he demur to any, nor make any such observation as you allude to." The accident occurred, he insisted, while he was in the electrical room belowdecks.

In fact, Morse's accusations against Bright were irresponsible. At the time the cable ruptured, Morse was in his berth, confined there again by his leg injury. His report of the braking incident represented not what he saw and heard, as he implied, but what others told him. After Bright challenged his hearsay narrative, he publicly acknowledged through the *Observer* that he had not witnessed the "fatal mistake." He had given his account in a private letter, he said, and had not intended it for publication. With this embarrassing admission he dropped the matter, although he still suspected Bright. He told a few correspondents—"entre nous," he said—that Bright's official report contradicted his public statements. "As I wish not to engage in controversy on the subject, I shall let others find this out."

Morse remained on the *Niagara* as it steamed to Plymouth, flags at half-mast, there to await instructions from the Atlantic Telegraph Company. His leg injury proved to be far worse than he had thought. He had not simply abraded the skin below his knee, but had also bruised the bone. With the *Niagara* anchored in Plymouth harbor he was forced to stay in bed on his back, unable to sit up without pain.

After two weeks he managed to go up on deck, where he lay on some netting to watch target practice by warships anchored in the harbor.

Meanwhile the company's directors met in London to discuss what to do next. Should they order new cable and immediately try again? Should they first improve the paying-out machinery? The company asked Morse to attend their meetings, but being hobbled he offered his views in a letter. He advised them to put off a second expedition until next year: with fall weather coming in, the Newfoundland coast would be blustery. Still convinced that no insurmountable obstacle existed, he reminded the directors that misfortune was to be expected in any great enterprise. The failure of the first trial provided a lesson in how God dispenses all things for good; it should be seen as "a providential interference to ensure final success." For much had been learned from the attempt, and a postponement would give time for further experiment and more learning.

Having sent his recommendation, Morse waited impatiently to hear from the directors about their plans. Again and again they promised he would have their decision "tomorrow": "So it goes; to-morrow, and to-morrow, but to-morrow never comes." As it happened, the directors were deluged by advice and proposals, including an offer from a clairvoyant to divine the undersea location of broken cables. After more than three weeks in Plymouth harbor, Morse still had heard nothing from the company. Others on the *Niagara* grumbled, too: the alterations of the ship compelled officers and men to sleep, wash, and dress wherever they could. Increasingly restless, and longing to see Sarah and their children, Morse decided that if his slow-healing leg improved enough he would simply up and leave.

News from home deepened Morse's frustration. A letter that Kendall had written from America six weeks earlier caught up with him. It described meetings in New York of representatives from the principal Morse lines, to work out a union for mutual protection. Members of such an alliance might pledge, for example, to connect their lines only with each other. Cyrus Field had attended the meeting before sailing to London to join the cable squadron.

Kendall gave Morse an unnerving report of Field's behavior. In a "defiant tone," he wrote, Field declared that his American Telegraph Company would not enter the union unless the other members purchased from him the patent for the Hughes telegraph, for $60,000.

Field also alluded to the power his group would have by its exclusive connection to the transatlantic cable. It seemed evident to Kendall that Field hoped to divide the Morse companies and prevent them from uniting, weakening them so that they could not stand in the way of his ambitions. "This conviction is a serious drawback upon the satisfaction I should feel at the success of the Atlantic Cable," he told Morse. "Indeed, I apprehend the utmost danger to all our Telegraph property from the power which success will place in the hands of these gentlemen."

Morse was already peeved at Field's London partners for making him "wait their convenience." But Kendall's letter revived all over again the nagging feeling, never put to rest, that for all the promised glory of the cable adventure, it was his duty to disengage himself from it. The owners of Morse lines had dealt honorably with him, and he could not act equivocally toward them: "I shall do nothing that can lead them justly to charge me with doing anything adverse to their interests." Still, he meant not to act hastily and hoped there might have been some misunderstanding.

The second week in September, after a full month of waiting, Morse at last heard from London. As he had advised, the Atlantic Telegraph Company decided to put off a new expedition about six months, until the spring. For the present, the *Niagara* would unload the thousand miles of cable still in its hold at a dockyard in Plymouth harbor—a labor, Morse foresaw, that could keep the ship there until November. He had hoped to take the "noble" warship home again, but given the possibly two-month-long wait he settled on the steamer *Arabia*.

Morse was accompanied on his passage home by Cyrus Field. His feelings about Field had grown more conflicted than ever, a welter of affection, distrust, respect, and dependence permeated with guilt over compromised loyalties and the shame of self-betrayal. He looked forward to soon joining Field on the second cable-laying endeavor. Nevertheless, during the voyage he brought up his "great uneasiness" over the letter from Kendall. He asked blunt questions. At the New York meeting of representatives from the Morse companies, had Field used "defiant language"? Was there some "intrigue" afoot to prevent a union among the companies? Would the cable be open to all the established Morse lines? Field denied the charges and assured him that the negotiations for an alliance were "going on favorably."

A little relieved, Morse offered to help Field secure government aid for the new cable attempt by composing a public endorsement, explaining why he expected it to succeed. Kendall's report had an effect, however. Morse said he would write nothing until he had investigated the situation and become "properly posted upon the state of affairs at home."

Morse's 140 fellow passengers included a Quaker, an Episcopalian, and members of other Christian denominations, with whom he enjoyed exchanging views on religious subjects. But as he settled in he found the *Arabia* wet and dirty, a miserable contrast with the formidable *Niagara*. And heading across the Atlantic the ship battled gales as fierce as he had ever experienced, twisting crosscurrents that made it near impossible to get about. "Our meals are thinly attended, every one complaining of soreness from such incessant tossing," he recorded, "the sea every now and then breaks over our bows, and deluges every thing from stem to stern."

SIXTEEN

Forward

(1857–1860)

AFTER ONLY A few days at home, Morse learned that the threat to his business interests was even deadlier than he had thought. Actions had been taken after the date of Kendall's letter to him that all but ended his control over the future direction and organization of the American telegraph industry. As he lay bedridden in Plymouth harbor, he now learned, five major companies, including Western Union, had made a separate peace with Field's American Telegraph. Meeting clandestinely, without notifying Amos Kendall, they agreed to purchase the Hughes patent from Field and form an alliance with his group.

The signatories to this so-called Six Nation Treaty, Morse learned, had large ambitions. As mutual owners of the Hughes telegraph they contemplated building a line from New York to Washington rivaling the inaugural Morse line. They also boasted of plans for new lines all the way to California. Each member of the North American Telegraph Association, as the group called itself, would be sovereign of the large area allotted to it. The Western Union Company, for example, would control rights to the Hughes telegraph in every state north of the Ohio River and parts of Iowa, Minnesota, Missouri, and Kansas.

Kendall had obtained a copy of the treaty and read its provisions. He informed Morse that the treacherous Field and his new associates had simply parceled out the United States among themselves, monopolizing the country's telegraph business. The treaty not only excluded Morse, he said, it made him disappear: "no one would know from the face of the paper itself, that *such a man as Saml F. B. Morse ever existed.*"

Morse had had enough. He accepted what before he had only

understood, that he must give up his part in the historic cable drama, however painful to quit: "I have contributed so much of my time, and made so much sacrifice." His resolve was tested only a few weeks after his return home. Field asked him to make good his offer to write an endorsement for publication, particularly supporting Field's appeal to Washington for the use once again of the naval frigate *Niagara*. In the circumstances, Morse bitterly resented Field's request: "they who have made the arrangements for hostility to me and my invention," he told Kendall, "ask me to aid them in their hostility to me." He was being taken for a fool, "as willing to commit a sort of suicide, for their benefit. It is asking a little too much." Kendall had his own plans for answering Field, and advised Morse to do nothing.

But before Morse could do or not do anything it was done to him. Atlantic Telegraph, Field's British partner, declined to appoint him an "Honorary Director" of the second cable attempt. In doing so the company deprived him of more than another mark of distinction. It was precisely his standing as "Honorary Director" that had entitled him to join the official party aboard the *Niagara*. The decision banished him from the expedition.

Field explained that under British law only stockholders in a company qualified for directorships. Morse doubted this: after all, he had owned no shares in Atlantic Telegraph when it named him an Honorary Director for the first attempt. "If they really desired me to be present, as I was last year," he told brother Sidney, "they could easily have found the means of making me an Honorary Director without violating the spirit of any rule." He believed that Field had represented him to his London partners as hostile to their company. "I hope Mr. Field can exculpate himself . . . before the world and especially before his own conscience, for the course he has taken."

Hurt and angry, Morse told Field he still wished the new expedition success. But he added that he had no part in attempts others might make to obstruct it. "I am not responsible for the schemes or plans of self-defence and self protection of those interested in the established lines," he said; "I hear of plans, the details of which are not imparted to me, for I have shut my ears." This was both quietly menacing and disingenuous. Morse well knew that Amos Kendall felt double-crossed by the Six Nation Treaty and was doing everything he could to undermine Field's preparations: "I feel a zeal to punish this perfidy," Kendall had told him, "even if my own interest suffer in the process."

Kendall was pressing his many influential friends in Washington to oppose Field's request for further government aid. He also presented a formal "Memorial" to Congress, condemning Field's cable enterprise as an enormous scheme of monopoly, "aiming to control the telegraph business of the two hemispheres for the purpose of securing, directly and indirectly, inordinate gains to a few individuals." The memorial asked Congress to pass a law requiring the cable's owners to offer connections on equal terms to all telegraph lines in the United States.

Morse companies excluded from the Six Nation Treaty shared Kendall's outrage. They unanimously agreed, he said, to " 'carry the war into Africa.' " New Morse circuits began going up in the South and West in competition with lines of the Six Nations, and patent rights to the Morse system were sold in the seven-year-old state of California.

Morse had always striven to emulate his father in forgiveness of enemies, but he too wanted to get even. "I would foil them with their own weapons . . . let there be *another Atlantic Telegraph,* which shall connect only with the excluded Morse lines." He thought of forming a rival company to lay a transatlantic telegraph from the Azores, running to both the Continent and the United States. He asked Kendall to speak with the Portuguese minister in Washington about landing a submarine cable on the islands, in exchange for a grant of priority in sending government dispatches. As Morse viewed this wild-eyed undertaking it would both set back his enemies and realize his humanitarian hopes: "if this single point can be gained to me I shall have the means of holding these intriguants in check . . . but shall be carrying out my original plan of connecting the nations of the earth together, on a more enlarged and efficient scale."

Field's exact part in dumping Morse is unclear. Peter Cooper and other leaders in his companies were involved in making decisions, and probably had a say. They would not have been the first of Morse's associates to be put off by his shifting moods of whining self-pity and imperiousness. However culpable or not, Field expressed surprised hurt at Morse's unfriendliness. "I am totally unconscious of having deserved it," he told Morse. He attributed their break to Kendall and Kendall's cronies, "persons of more worldly cunning than enters into your own nature, and who have been glad to put forward your great and honored name for the advancement of mere selfish objects."

Morse replied by recalling their discussion aboard the *Arabia* when returning to the United States. Field had assured him that negotiations between the American Telegraph Company and other Morse companies were "going on favorably." Instead, on returning home he had found Field's company promoting the Hughes telegraph and aiming at "*the utter extermination of my system. . . .* Do you say this is not so? Can you be so blind as not to perceive it?" He did not blame his expulsion from the cable project on Field, he said, but on Field's allies: "Be this as it may, I was thrown out." As happened twenty years earlier when Congress refused him a commission for the Capitol rotunda, the richest reward of his labor had again come in sight and been snatched away.

Hopeful news from France eased Morse's distress. His agent Frederic Van den Broek informed him that, under the direction of the French government, representatives of ten European countries had met in Paris late in April to discuss compensation for their use of the Morse system. This unusual international gathering agreed to propose an indemnity of 400,000 francs, payable to Morse in four annuities, each country contributing in proportion to the number of Morse instruments it had in use. The delegates had returned home to present the recommendation to their governments, but would convene again that fall in Paris to report the decision.

"My faith in those who now rule the destinies of France has not been misplaced," Morse said. He had in mind the éclat rather than the cash, which he thought small—about $80,000, of which a third would go to Van den Broek. Kendall had suggested an indemnity of at least half a million dollars, and considered the amount "niggardly": "I know not how to express my contempt of the meanness of the European governments in the award they propose to make you as *the* inventor of the Telegraph." But for Morse what mattered was that the brokers of his indemnity were not men of trade but Counts and Ministers Plenipotentiary. "I accept the gratuity," he wrote, "with tenfold more gratification than could have been produced by a sum of money, however large, offered on the basis of a commercial negotiation." The U.S. minister in France urged him to come to Paris when the delegates adjourned again in August. "My friend," he wrote, "you are about to have awarded to you a higher honor than COLUMBUS lived to receive."

Morse and Sarah sailed in July aboard the steamer *Fulton*. He planned to make a lengthy trip, including a visit in Puerto Rico with his daughter Susan and her family. He leased out Locust Grove and sent Finley, now thirty-four years old, to live with cousins in the Adirondack Mountains of upstate New York. Since the railway journey involved several train changes, he wrote a note for Finley to hand to conductors along the route, asking them to "see that he takes the right train." Given the magnitude of the honor that might await him in Paris, he took along his two young sons, a nursemaid, his mother-in-law, and other members of Sarah's family, making in all a celebratory entourage of fifteen people.

Morse had rarely traveled with his children, and a few weeks *en famille* in Switzerland drained him. "It was a great mistake I committed in bringing my family," he wrote from Interlaken; "I have scarcely had one moment's pleasure, and am almost worn out with anxieties and cares." In heading for Paris, he left ten-year-old Arthur with Sarah's mother in Geneva, to be educated by a tutor. "Children require to be early and sometimes frequently transplanted, like some plants," he explained. He had after all been sent from home himself at the age of eight—a "judicious beginning." Arthur had shown signs of rudeness, disobedience, and pleasure in low company, for which Morse had recommended a few days' "severe discipline." The boy evidently did not take well to being left in Switzerland, for Morse received from the tutor a report of new misbehavior. "I hope Mr. Binet has no occasion to punish you," he wrote to Arthur, "but if there is occasion I hope for my sake and your good he will punish you. . . . I shall thank him."

Morse and Sarah reached Paris about the first week in August. The international meeting on the indemnity was scheduled to convene in the city on the twenty-third, but meanwhile he and millions of others thrilled to breathtaking news. Using Morse instruments, Cyrus Field's group had successfully flashed a telegraphic message 2500 miles through the Atlantic Ocean.

The miracle had not come easily. Earlier in the summer the *Niagara*, with revamped paying-out machinery, had again started out with its Anglo-American squadron to the mid-Atlantic. In fierce storms and forty-foot-high waves, the frigate nearly capsized, injuring some of the crew. The cable broke three times, with a loss of 540 miles of line. The *Niagara* and the *Agamemnon* had rendezvoused again late in July and successfully spliced their cable-ends together. Speeding apart from each other, they spooled out cable toward their appointed shores. The *Niagara* reached Newfoundland on the same day the *Agamemnon* reached Ireland, August 5.

After ten days of testing, the cable pulsed with the first official transatlantic message. In part it consisted of one of the two scriptural texts Morse had chosen for the failed expedition the year before: "Europe and America are united by telegraph. Glory to God in the highest, on earth peace, good will toward men." Some days later, Queen Victoria and President James Buchanan electrically exchanged congratulations. On August 27 the New York *Tribune* reported the signing of a three-way peace treaty by China, England, and France, in a story headlined "The First News Dispatch by Ocean Telegraph."

Americans greeted the event as a rebeginning of history, remaking the idea of human society. "A mighty though silent transformation in the conditions of human existence has just been effected," the New York *Tribune* announced; "we have been thrown into the immediate intellectual neighborhood of the whole civilized and a large portion of the semi-barbarous world." Mind could now be "Shot through the weltering pit of the salt sea," Ralph Waldo Emerson exulted in a poem: "We have few moments in the longest life/Of such delight and wonder." The delight broke out in festivities across the country: a torchlight procession in Detroit; barrels of tar set afire at every street corner of Cincinnati; a nighttime regatta in Pittsburgh; a 100-gun salute on Boston Common, the city's bells rung for a full hour.

New Yorkers closed their businesses, put up triumphal arches, and enjoyed what the city's noted diarist George Templeton Strong called an "orgasm of glorification." Vessels in port flew the Stars and Stripes, Union Jack, and flags of all nations. Houses and shops were festooned and illuminated, some by special gas pipes laid for the occasion, Fifth Avenue's Brevoort House by 1500 spermaceti candles. Strangers poured in from every direction off railroads and ferries. They jammed Broadway to watch a jubilant parade: kilted Highlanders, pioneers in bearskin shakos, butchers in snow-white aprons, veterans of the War of 1812, horsedrawn floats bearing a twelve-foot bottle of ink, a grand piano (being played), a model of the *Niagara*. Banners covered the city with catchwords and slogans, the front of the Astor House being lengthily inscribed: "The Atlantic Telegraph transmits the Lightning of Heaven, and binds together 60,000,000 of human beings."

Morse was not forgotten. Despite his absence from the expedition, his name was widely invoked as its prophet and originator. Citizens of Poughkeepsie serenaded his house and raised a twenty-foot banner with the motto "*Our own Morse forever.*" Transparencies featured his likeness, such as the one displayed by a photographic supplies shop on Broadway:

MORSE, FIELD AND HUDSON [*Niagara's* captain] — THREE CABLE MATES —
HAVE MADE ALL NATIONS *The United States.*

The Christian evangelical press especially celebrated Morse as their own. As the *Western Episcopalian* put it, a humble Christian and man of God now held "the highest position ever attained by mortal man uninspired. . . . Kings and Emperors sink before him."

In Paris, seventy-five members of the American community hosted a testimonial dinner for Morse: "filled with enthusiastic admiration," the invitation read, "they desire to give to you some special mark of their exalted appreciation of your personal character, and of the achievements of your genius." Speakers and guests at the Trois Frères Provençaux turned the rejoicing over the Atlantic cable into a Morse love-feast, engulfing him in adulation and prolonged deafening applause: "every figure of rhetoric was exhausted in his praise," the New York *Times* reported; "no man ever received a greater ovation from his fellow-beings." Morse himself spoke for a half hour or more. "My dream of twenty years is realized," he said. He paid tribute to Franklin, Oersted, Steinheil, and others whose work had helped him during that time. Joseph Henry and Cyrus Field he left unmentioned, however, beyond observing that "at home there have been those in the past who, from whatever motive, have been disposed to harrass me."

A week after Morse's triumphant dinner, the extraordinary indemnity congress met again in Paris. All the governments involved, except the Netherlands, agreed to award him 400,000 francs. The contributors included Austria, Belgium, France, Piedmont, Russia, Sweden, Turkey, Tuscany—and the Vatican, one of the delegates being the nuncio of the Holy See. Their grants varied greatly in amount. France, with 462 Morse instruments in service, would give 144,000 francs; Tuscany, with only 14, would give 4400. England was not represented. The Board of Trade reasoned that since the British government owned no telegraph lines, it had no more reason to reward Morse than to reward any other inventor who had benefited the human race. Besides, if it gave Morse an indemnity, the like might justly be claimed by Wheatstone.

The homage paid him from on high moved Morse deeply. He sent thanks to the French government for its work on his behalf, "at a loss for language," he said, "adequately to express to them my feelings of profound gratitude." Promoted by Emperor Napoleon III, and conferred on him by representatives of ten continental countries, the award climaxed his long cultural-nationalist quest to gain European respect for his work as a product of American life. He ranked the indemnity as his grandest distinction, "an act of honor unprecedented in its lofty character, and extent of sympathy . . . specially conceived and carried into execution under the auspices of the highest dignitaries of the principle nations."

A month later, Morse and millions of others again shared a memorable experience. This time they marveled at one of the epic letdowns of modern Western history. Signals tapped out over the transatlantic cable had grown gradually weaker, perhaps owing to defective manufacture, damaged insulation, or the use of very high intensity currents. Whatever the cause, on October 20, having transmitted 732 messages during three months, the wizardly copper wires connecting the Old World and the New went dead. The last word they sent was "forward."

Rejoicing curdled into recrimination. A letter-writer to the Boston *Courier* called the venture a hoax: "*reliable* and *unimpeachable evidence is wanting,* that one solitary intelligible sentence ever passed upon the cable from either continent to the other." An oceanic cable was not commercially viable, some said: "a little cool judgment might save us from many extravagancies." Field was accused of staging a fake success in order to unload $375,000 worth of stock on a gullible market. Other scapegoats were named, other warnings issued, new proposals aired for different means of overseas telegraph communication.

The breakdown of the cable gave Morse the dismal satisfaction of feeling vindicated. He had prophesied that the cable could be laid and would work. "These points are successful," he said. What went wrong had nothing to do with his invention or his thinking, but with the shabby motives and faithlessness of others. While abroad he learned that two Canadians had been named Honorary Directors of Atlantic Telegraph, neither of whom were stockholders—confirming his belief that he had been "*ejected*" from the expedition deliberately. His removal and the breakdown of the cable had the same meaning, and the same cause—the detestable mentality of trade that saw transatlantic telegraphy as a speculation, a "*money matter.*" Mere money-making "was the great and I might almost say *exclusive* motive of Mr. Field. . . . The hasty, and unfair means he used to grasp too much, have resulted in utter failure."

Morse and Sarah spent the winter with Susan and her family in Arroyo, Puerto Rico. Enjoying the balmy weather, never in better health, he wore summer clothing in December and kept the windows open, chirped to sleep by crickets. The light pleased his painter's eye, the sky of "richest Claude blue," the spectacular sunsets "never exceeded in Italy for tender, rich & glowing tints."

Morse was impressed by his son-in-law's well-cultivated 1400 acres, rising two or three miles from the seashore to the mountains. And Edward's estate seemed to him quite as well governed as some German principalities he had seen, including the small army of slaves who worked the sugar plantations and served the elegant mansion house. He thought the slaves superior physically to the white laborers of Europe, but not mentally: "In intellect they are indeed inferior and for that reason and their low tastes and passions, and besetting vices, require the wholesome restraints of a master." Nor did he admire the *Arroyanos,* whom he found indulgent and profane: "No church privileges, no religion among the masses . . . the inhabitants of these rich hills, they are rather like the swine in their habits and enjoyments."

The island's commercial and political leaders treated Morse as a celebrity. The local *Bolletin Mercantil* reported his activities, and he passed an evening with the Governor of Puerto Rico. In February he organized and constructed a two-mile line between his son-in-law's house and place of business—the island's first telegraph. The government honored him with a public breakfast, attended by the American consul. A portrait of him was displayed, decorated with Spanish and American flags. Afterward the breakfasters, accompanied by a band of music, repaired to Don Eduardo's office on the bay to witness the telegraph in operation.

Morse viewed the line as a first step, the inauguration of a new enterprise in which he had become interested while in Paris. Outdoing his earlier fantasy of a cable from the Azores—and surpassing the ambitions of Cyrus Field—a transoceanic telegraph would be constructed uniting America with Europe by a South Atlantic route. The cable would pass from Madeira to the Canary Islands to the coast of Africa, thence by way of several islands to Brazil, island-hopping from there across the West Indies to Puerto Rico, and from there to Cuba and at last to Florida—a distance of nearly 7000 miles. The scheme had been gotten up in London, and some $2 million of the required $5 million had already been raised. Morse allowed his name to be used in a petition to the Spanish Queen as one of the projectors.

Morse and Sarah returned home in May to a surprise gala reception. Citizens of Poughkeepsie had not had the opportunity to express their pride in his contribution to the first oceanic transmission and his indemnity from the nations of Europe. They did so now. Hundreds of cheering townspeople met him and Sarah at the railroad station and followed them in carriages and on foot through town, amid ringing bells, waving flags, and schoolchildren let out for the day. As the procession reached the flower-wreathed gateways of Locust Grove, a band struck up "Sweet Home" and "Auld Lang Syne."

After Morse's ten-month absence, the house needed painting and puttying to become livable again, and a huge unanswered correspondence had accumulated. Feeling at first rather overwhelmed, he remained aglow over the indemnity, and even brightened as unexpected honors arrived from Europe. The Swedish Royal Academy of Sciences presented him with a diploma; the Portuguese government bestowed on him both its Cross of the Order of Christ and its Ancient and Noble Order of the Tower and Sword; the Queen of Spain made him Knight Commander (*Cavaliero Commandador*) of the 1st Class of the Order of Isabel the Catholic (!). He wrote to Madrid inquiring whether the form of address appropriate to the Order was "Your Excellence."

Homage poured in from America, too. Morse was made an honorary member of the New-York Historical Society, the Irving Literary Institute, the National Photographic Association, and the Washington Art Association. The New York Institution for the Deaf and Dumb, where Sarah had been a pupil, appointed him an Honorary Director; the Century Club elected him to membership, alongside John Jacob Astor, Jr., and the financier August Belmont. His patronage in great demand, he was sought for the presidency of the American Geographical and Statistical Society, asked to help organize a National Gallery of Art in Washington, invited to speak before the American Institute of Architects, as "a pioneer in the cause of Art Education." In at least one case, he again learned that his honors attracted not only do-gooders but also exploiters. Having agreed to serve as titular president of the Morse Insurance Company, he detected "suspicious doings" among his colleagues and hastily resigned.

Morse's $80,000 indemnity also beckoned. To his horror and disbelief, F. O. J. Smith claimed a contractual five-sixteenths interest in the amount, a third of which had already gone to the Paris agent Van den Broek. In Morse's view the money represented not payment but a gratuity, an award bestowed particularly on him, personally, "as *a mark of Honor*." Although accustomed to Smith's outrageous demands, this new one for some $16,000 startled him. "I cannot think you serious," he wrote to Smith. "I do not consider you either legally or equitably entitled to any share in any Testimonial." Smith at least agreed to have the issue arbitrated. Once again Morse collected documents and drew up lengthy briefs to support his case. "I have no apprehensions of the result," he told Kendall; "no intelligent just men could give a judgment against me, or in his favor."

The arbitration hearing, held in Boston, turned on the meaning of "otherwise." According to their 1838 contract, Smith would share in any profits that Morse earned in Europe by the sale of patent rights or "otherwise." The three referees judged Morse's indemnity an "otherwise." They awarded Smith five-sixteenths, after deducting Morse's expenses and payment to Van den Broek. Even so, Smith quibbled with Morse over the deductions and demanded interest on the award for the time it had been withheld from him. Morse scoffed at the decision as based on a legal technicality: "I ought, perhaps, with my experience to learn for the first time that *Law* and *Justice* are not synonyms." In the end, he paid Smith about $7000.

Morse saw in the situation, however, his best-ever chance, after so many best chances, to rid himself of Smith forever. He gave Smith an additional $500 for agreeing to sign a "General Release." Seemingly comprehensive, the document resolved all unsettled claims between them—"all manner of actions, causes of action, suits, debts, dues, sums of money, accounts, reckonings, promises, variances, trespasses, damages, judgments, decrees, executions, claims and demands whatsoever." Morse rejoiced in at last escaping from his tormented captivity to Smith, "bound hand and foot . . . to a corpus mortuum, to a body not merely dead but corrupted." The release ended, he said, "twenty two years of *apprehension,* like that of being in a den of rattlesnakes."

The much-reduced indemnity shrank some more as the family of Alfred Vail also claimed part of it. While in Puerto Rico, Morse had received news of his former student's death, at the age of fifty-two. He had worked closely if uncomfortably with Vail for a dozen years, experiencing with him such awesome breakthroughs as the construction of the original Baltimore-Washington line. Saddened by the news, he praised Vail as a pious if sometimes cranky Christian: "his intentions were good, and his faults were the result more of ill-health, a dyspeptic habit, than of his heart."

Vail died poor, having remarried and sold most of his telegraph stock in struggling to support his family. Before dying, however, he told his brother George that the Vails were contractually entitled to one-eighth of the indemnity. Morse paid over some $5000 to Vail's widow, Amanda, saying he had always intended to give her husband a portion. Anxious nevertheless to cut loose from the Vails as well as from Smith, he worked out a similar "General Release" with Amanda Vail and with Vail's brother. This release—to look ahead—also gave no release.

The various settlements left Morse with less than half the amount of the indemnity, plus of course the honor. But that, too, suffered new indignities. The first came when he applied for a seven-year extension of the 1846 patent covering his receiving magnet, the part of his system that actuated registers at telegraph stations along the main line. His onetime associate Charles Page printed up and issued what Page called a "manifesto," proclaiming that credit for the receiving magnet—the "life and soul" of Morse's system, he said—belonged to Charles Wheatstone, Joseph Henry, and himself: "the Invention claimed under the Patent of 1846 is not Morses and . . . he is entitled to no credit whatever in this connection."

Astonished, Morse added Page to his long list of traitors, having counted him a friend. Not only that, Page's assault represented an inexplicable change of opinion: when serving as an examiner in the Patent Office in 1846, he had approved Morse's application. What motivated Page to now challenge the very same patent is unclear. An inventor himself, he had helped Morse to miniaturize the cumbersome receiving magnet. But he had been paid for the work and had sought no further recognition for it. As Morse put it, Page may simply have "had some 'human nature' in him," envious that Morse had become world famous as an inventor. Morse protested to him the many misstatements in the manifesto, particularly the spurious charge that he had brought from abroad and put into use one of Wheatstone's receiving magnets. Another avenging angel also reappeared—Henry O'Reilly, informing Morse that he too planned to oppose the extension. And Morse suspected that the supposedly vanquished F. O. J. Smith had joined the campaign—as Smith had.

Morse went to Washington in April 1860 for the hearing on his case. In a thirty-two-page decision, the Patent Commissioner ruled that his receiving magnet differed utterly from Wheatstone's, and that its "combination of devices" was unique, "not to be found in any patent, or invention, or in any printed publication, or in public use, prior to its date; but that Morse is the original and first inventor thereof." The Patent Office granted the extension.

But then there was Joseph Henry. Morse's quarrel with him had erupted afresh every few years for a decade. And he heard that after four years of silence Henry would soon reply to his free-swinging ninety-page *Defence* ("*Attack!*"). Among other affronts, Morse's tract denied Henry any part in developing the Morse system and questioned his originality and credibility. Deeply offended, Henry damned the work as "wanton foolish and libellous" and privately called Morse a coward. To deflect the blow when it came, Morse suggested to brother Sidney that the *Observer* mention his diploma from the Swedish Academy of Sciences and his gold medals for science from the King of Prussia and the Emperor of Austria.

But Henry replied on a scale Morse had not imagined. He submitted his case to the Regents of the Smithsonian Institution, asking them to investigate and issue a report: "regard to my own memory, to my family, and to the truth of history," he explained, "demands that I should lay this matter before you." To evaluate the many letters and documents Henry presented, the Regents appointed a committee of inquiry that included two U.S. senators and the president of Harvard College.

The Smithsonian committee acquitted Henry of every failing and wrongdoing alleged in Morse's *Defence*. They denounced the tract as nothing more than character assassination, "a disingenuous piece of sophisticated argument, such as an unscrupulous advocate might employ to pervert the truth, misrepresent the facts, and misinterpret the language in which the facts belonging to the other side of the case are stated." Carefully documented and widely cited, the Smithsonian report made its way overseas, too. A leading Paris scientific journal, it infuriated Morse to learn, took up Henry's cause: "Morse is in effect the legal inventor [*l'inventeur legal*] of the electric Telegraph. The patents are in his name, the honors & rewards have fallen to him, but the real inventor [*l'inventeur réal*] is Professor Henry, director of the Smithsonian Institution of Washington."

The detailed case that Henry presented to the Regents belongs to his biography rather than to Morse's. It should be said, however, that it gave Morse no credit for the restless, thoughtful, continual tinkering and experiment by which he had devised and improved his telegraph. Morse viewed the report as snobbish and politically inspired. It placed Henry "in that superhuman class of *men of mind,* while I am treated as belonging to the *mechanical class.*" It issued, too, from a Washington clique composed of members of the Coast Survey, the Smithsonian, and the American Association for the Advancement of Science, of which Henry had been president. Many talented men belonged to these organizations, to be sure, but also many "toadies and pretenders" who sought advancement by kowtowing to Henry. "Henry is King on the Smithsonian throne, and as I have committed treason in their eyes by daring to inculpate this Sovereign, I am to be decapitated."

Morse began preparing an answer but put it aside, perhaps in frustration. One moment he was being singled out for exalted honors by "the highest scientific minds of Europe, and . . . the principal governments of the Old World." The next moment his indemnity was being raided, his patents besieged, himself "*arraigned, tried* and *condemned*" by Regents and Senators. The sequence demonstrated once again how his life took shape as reversals and contradictions. Gain became loss, reward was punishment: "when any special and marked honor has been conferred upon me there has immediately succeeded, some event of the envious or sordid character." Brooding on the matter, he speculated that it might be the moral equivalent of the physical law of equilibrium. Take for instance the antagonism between the opposite poles of a magnet: "if the positive be strengthened, the negative is also in an equal degree strengthened and visa [*sic*] versa." Similarly, "If upon anyone reputation and honors increase, on the one hand, detraction and slander in an equal degree are sure to be found on the other."

Morse reasoned that such physical and moral patterns could hardly be accidental. Events that seemed cursed, ultimately showed the workings of Providence. In his own case, Providence in its infinite wisdom was drawing him away from earthly honors to the enduring honor that comes only from God. "The mixed cup is best," he concluded, "for then honor will not puff up."

A business deal in the fall of 1859 changed Morse's life dramatically. The six "nations" of the North American Telegraph Association had excluded "Magnetic Telegraph," his first company, when they banded together a year and a half earlier. But they wanted to bring peace to the expensively contentious telegraph industry. In a turnaround, they now invited Magnetic Telegraph to consolidate with them.

Morse favored the idea, largely because his original telegraph patent (1840) and its seven-year extension had only about a year to run. After that, rivals would be free to build competing lines unrestrained, without fear of infringement: "in this view I would make much sacrifice, especially of feeling." In just such a sacrifice, he tried—warily—to mend his broken relationship with Cyrus Field. Field was stubbornly resolved on making a third attempt to engineer a transatlantic telegraph, and offered him a place on the Advisory Committee in America. Morse accepted, but his wariness proved to be justified. All the experimental work on the cable and machinery, he discovered, was being performed in England; the American advisory committee amounted to window dressing. He soon resigned the nonposition—preoccupied with other duties, he said.

Kendall handled the negotiations for union. Tortuously complex, the bargaining repeatedly broke down. The parties wrangled over pending litigation, the leasing of western lines, requests for representation by the Associated Press, the extortionate demand by F. O. J. Smith of over $300,000 for his patent rights and stocks. Still, the negotiations ended with a series of agreements in October 1859. Smith got his $300,000, mostly in interest-bearing bonds. "How the dog in the manger," Morse jeered, "must relax his defiant display of teeth into a grin of delight." Morse, Kendall, and their colleagues gave their unsold patent rights to the North American Telegraph Association in exchange for $107,000 of stock in Field's American Telegraph Company. They also exchanged some $369,000 of Magnetic stock for $500,000 of American stock. And together with Kendall, Morse was seated on the board of directors of Field's company, which now firmly controlled telegraph operations along the entire Atlantic seaboard from Newfoundland to New Orleans.

Morse's profit from the consolidation can only be estimated. But it provided material comfort and financial security for the rest of his life. The reorganized American Telegraph Company did well, netting in its first six months of operation over $100,000. Morse also continued to receive dividends from lines in the South and West, which were not included in the consolidation—sometimes a few dollars, sometimes a few thousand. His income tax returns for 1863, three years later, survive, and show earnings after taxes of $29,928—about $5000 more than the annual salary of the President of the United States.

However much Morse acquired in cash and property, and whatever his annual income from dividends, he thought it enough: "such a competence . . . as should satisfy the desires of any reasonable man." At the same time, by consigning most of his interest in his patents he virtually ended his active participation in the telegraph business. Probably to his relief, for he was now nearing seventy, had once more lamed himself by spraining his foot, and felt burdened, "overloaded," he said, "at a time of life when age is creeping on me with its train of incapacities physical and intellectual."

Morse marked his new prosperity by purchasing a stylish town house in New York City. He planned to spend the winters there and return to Locust Grove on May 1. The city had become the dynamo of the northeastern United States. Huge amounts of money circulated through its many banks and insurance companies, its one million inhabitants supported 104 newspapers, its mass transit system carried more than 50 million passengers a year. Morse's house and its two adjoining lots stood at No. 5 West 22nd Street, in the fashionable Gramercy Park section. One block away rose the brand-new Fifth Avenue Hotel, described by a British newspaperman as larger and handsomer than Buckingham Palace. Employing four hundred servants, it had its own telegraph office—one of fourteen American Telegraph Company stations now operating in the city.

Morse's house was a four-story brownstone, its front matted by a

Morse in his New York City study
(The Library of Congress)

spreading wisteria vine. The interior offered such comforts as a con-
servatory for plants, a library with bookcases of black walnut, and a
topfloor gymnasium. Morse bought a new piano and a burglar-proof
safe. Although "no great connoisseur in wines, and no great consumer
of them," he admitted, he ordered six cases from a city merchant and
sent to France for six cases of champagne. In the adjacent vacant lots
he had a spacious study built for himself, and a story-high picture
gallery.

Morse continued to house Sarah's mother; Sarah's sister and her
family had rooms in the neighborhood and called almost every
evening. Richard and Sidney had recently sold the *Observer*, and to

Morse's great satisfaction they both lived nearby. Restless as ever, Richard had trekked to Canton, Macao, and Java, learning Portuguese and translating a history of French literature. Well aware that he had never settled down, he felt he had done the best he could, "an inglorious life, but yet a prosperous & happy one." Morse joined his brothers in erecting a monument to their father in the New Haven cemetery, a twenty-foot granite shaft topped by a globe emblematic of The Geographer. Morse contributed most of the cost. In the past, when he was poor, his brothers had helped support him: "I am now, through the loving kindness and bounty of our Heavenly Father, in such circumstances that I can afford this small testimonial to their former fraternal kindness."

With Morse's fine house came standing in New York society. As a member of the upper crust he was elected to a committee appointed to arrange the social event of the year—a public banquet and ball honoring the visit of Queen Victoria's nineteen-year-old son, the Prince of Wales. He extended a fulsome personal invitation for the "illustrious Prince" to stop by Locust Grove, to see American country life "as it were, en dishabille." The offer was politely declined ("Every hour of our time is fully engaged"). But he apparently had a brief interview with the Prince in the New York University chapel, where he also delivered an address of welcome on behalf of the faculty.

With a momentous national election coming up in November 1860, friends tried to put Morse's name forward as a possible candidate for the presidency. He appreciated the gesture but declined, citing his advancing age, his lack of qualification, and the thankless vexations the office brought with it. "I have no taste for its duties, and its honors have no attraction for me." But the outcome of the election worried him. All eighteen free states except New Jersey—a majority of the electoral college—chose a possibly divisive candidate, Abraham Lincoln. And only six weeks later, the state of South Carolina voted in convention to secede from the Union. "The tea has been thrown overboard," the Charleston *Mercury* announced, "the revolution of 1860 has been initiated."

COMMANDADOR

Beat! beat! drums!—blow! bugles! blow!
Through the windows—through doors—burst like a ruthless
force

       —Walt Whitman, "Beat! Beat! Drums!" (1861)

It is stated on good authority that the vintages of Los Angeles
County will this year produce one million and a half gallons
of wine.

       —New York *Times*, December 20, 1868

Samuel F. B. Morse, at about seventy-two
(The Library of Congress)

SEVENTEEN

Is This Treason?
Is This Conspiracy?

(1860–1865)

OR SAMUEL F. B. MORSE, the Civil War was a surreal nightmare
that transfigured fifty years of hope and belief. In the half century
since his earliest trip to England, during the War of 1812, he had
often written and spoken out passionately against the wishful view
abroad that the United States, like all other republics, was inherently
unstable and likely to break apart. But in the first months of 1861, he
saw the states of Mississippi, Florida, Alabama, Georgia, and Louisiana
follow South Carolina out of the Union. Early in February, delegates
of the seceding states met in Montgomery, Alabama, and formed a
separate nation, the Confederate States of America, with its own president, Jefferson Davis. "We are now," Morse lamented, "the scorn of
the world."

The breakdown of the Union left Morse with conflicting loyalties.
He often said that he identified with no region, "an American who
knows no North nor South nor East nor West, but who feels that every
one within the United States is his fellow countryman." But he had
strong ties of kinship and memory with the South. Members of his
mother's family, the Finleys, had lived in Charleston; he had spent
years there himself, as a painter. Sarah had lived in New Orleans, as
her brother still did, the proprietor of a well-known sword-making
company.

These connections and his loathing of the disruptive Abolitionists
drew Morse's sympathies to the South—"especially with the Christian
Slaveholder," he said. Mostly he hoped and believed that the "Almighty

arm" would prevent war. Neither side could rejoice in shedding the blood of brethren: "There is something so unnatural and abhorrent in this outcry of *arms,* in our great family that I cannot believe it will come to a decision by the sword."

To do what he could toward reconciling the sections, Morse hosted discussions at his town house, inviting ministers, missionaries, and other "warmhearted praying conscientious Christians." With some New York friends he also formed an American Society for Promoting National Unity. There was much sympathy for the South in the city, whose port had flourished for years on the cotton-carrying trade. Morse's Society aimed at showing Southerners that they still had allies in the North. It would do so by exposing the Abolitionists as crackbrained, the sole cause of America's woes—"freedom-shriekers, Bible-spurners," Morse called them, "fierce, implacable, headstrong, denunciatory, Constitution and Union haters, noisy, factious, breathing forth threatenings and slaughter."

Morse's group held meetings at the Bible Society building, printed up a constitution, and appointed him President. But it lasted only about three months, dissolving in a sense of futility after 4:30 a.m. on April 12, 1861. At that moment the Confederate army began a thirty-three-hour bombardment of Fort Sumter in Charleston harbor, forcing the federal garrison there to surrender. With many New Yorkers now turning against the South, recruitment for the Union army began at once. Regiments formed, tents and wooden barracks went up in Central Park. Morse felt no sympathy for the war fever on either side. He refused to contribute to a fund for equipping Union volunteers, horrified by the vision of America at its own throat: "No one can tell the agony of mind which deprives me of sleep at night, and happiness by day, caused by this most deplorable civil strife, this war among brethren."

Morse's agony deepened to despair as other Southern states seceded—Virginia, Arkansas, North Carolina, Tennessee. Much as he believed the South had acted in torment, "maddened by the incessant outpouring of Abolition abuse," he thought Secession rash and unjustifiable, a surrender of principle. Instead of trusting that the rightness of its cause would eventually triumph, the South had played into the hands of Northern fanatics, conceding to them all the cherished tokens and axioms of national honor: "the prestige of the flag of the

Union, the war cry of liberty, the enthusiasm of Revolutionary recollections, the plausibility of defence of Government."

Morse recalled bitterly that his pleasure in the honors lavished upon him had always come from the thought that not he but his country was being honored. So now his honors meant nothing: "I have no country; the dismembered limbs of a convulsed and dying body, do not constitute my country." Having no country he might as well for his family's safety settle in more peaceful Europe. He had once before thought of retiring permanently to the Continent, but the irony of the temptation now seemed excruciating: "to flee for refuge, from the world's great city of refuge, to flee for safety from the boasted land of freedom, to despotic Europe! What a change! what an anomaly!"

Instead of fleeing, Morse entered more fully than ever into national politics, hoping to avert all-out war. He wished to personally confer with the governments at Washington and Richmond about ways of ending the conflict. Physically he did not feel up to carrying out such a mission. But he sent a paid representative (unnamed), who did manage to discuss the subject with both President Lincoln and President Jefferson Davis. Meanwhile he returned to political journalism. He tried to convince both sides that the calls to arms envenoming the country did not issue from "the American truly Christian heart."

Morse first presented his case in a series of newspaper articles, soon republished as a forty-page pamphlet entitled *The Present Attempt to Dissolve the American Union, A British Aristocratic Plot* (1862). He revealed that the North and the South had been tricked, turned against each other by a scheme "long-concocted and skilfully planned" to weaken the country by stirring up sectional animosity. Among much other evidence, he cited the activities in America of George Thompson, a fire-eating British Abolitionist who allegedly was awarded a seat in Parliament for exhorting slaves to cut their masters' throats. He also quoted damning speeches by British officials such as the Earl of Shaftesbury: "I, in common with almost every English statesman, *sincerely desire the rupture of the American Union. . . .* With a population of thirty millions, they will soon, if *not checked,* overshadow Great Britain." (Shaftesbury denied having made the remark.) Morse called on Americans to forget their domestic quarrel and attend to the external danger that contrived it: "Where are the *people?* why do they sleep when incendiaries have fired the house?" Plenty of people evidently heard him, however. Distributed by the New York publisher Daniel Appleton, the pamphlet found enough readers to justify a second printing.

As Morse pointed out, *The Present Attempt* repeated what he had written in his tract *Foreign Conspiracy* (1835), and had often prophesied. "I have for thirty years watched these foreign intrigues . . . predicting that if the warning were not heeded, or was looked upon as a false alarm, the Union would be dissolved. It was nevertheless unheeded, it was ridiculed as visionary, and the event has occurred as I predicted." His warnings took in French Infidelity and a more recent threat, German Transcendentalism. His focus on England of course reflects a lifetime of distrustfully contemptuous Anglophobia, intensified by the British government's unwillingness to contribute to his indemnity. Although publicly sworn to work for peace, he suggested privately that the Union and the Confederacy might be reconciled by joining forces to fight England: "Deplorable as war is . . . yet when we are compelled to choose between *two wars,* we may be allowed to express our preference for a *foreign* over a *domestic* war."

Morse's alarums about the "*British Aristocratic Plot*" did not express mere personal vendetta. The notion that Abolitionists were pawns of British imperialism, that Great Britain promoted an end to slavery in order to cripple its commercial rivals, had been widespread in America since the 1830s. Nor should Morse's warnings about foreign intrigue be seen as unfounded political paranoia. Anti-democratic elements in England and Europe did fear popular education, separation of church and state, and other forms of Americanization. And whatever Shaftesbury may or may not have said, the Earl of Shrewsbury did remark that "men now before me will live to see an aristocracy established in America." News and rumors abounded of foreign designs to exploit the divisions within the United States—of France outfitting warships in response to a possible Union blockade of Southern ports, of Spain sending troops to the Gulf of Mexico, looking to reassert its position in the Americas. A Boston newspaper alerted its readers to the gathering of the European vultures: "The terror of the American name is gone, and the Powers of the Old World are flocking to the feast from which the scream of our eagle has hitherto scared them."

Not surprisingly, for his efforts to bring North and South together against a common enemy Morse was seen by both as a turncoat. "I am charged by the administration with '*Secession*' proclivities, and at the

South with '*abolition*' sentiments." Of the two accusations, the Southern hurt more, deepened by a sense of betrayal. Morse learned that the Confederate government, under a sequestration law enacted by the Confederate Congress, had seized his investments throughout the region, identifying him as a resident of the United States of America, therefore an "Alien Enemy." Some $40,000 of his stock in Southern telegraph companies was declared null and void, and transferred to the Confederate States of America. "I am no '*alien enemy*,'" Morse howled; "Is this the return for my confidence reposed in the honor of the South? Is this the return for my sympathy with Southern wrongs, and my efforts to stem the torrent of evils which threaten to involve all in a common ruin?"

The eruption of full-scale combat left Morse in stunned anguish: "two armies, more numerous each than have met face to face in all the European wars at least for a century, are at this moment opposite to each other . . . to enact the bloodiest battle that civilization (?) has ever witnessed." Just how staggeringly bloody began making itself known after April 1862: 3500 killed, 16,500 wounded at Shiloh on the Tennessee River; 3100 killed, 16,000 wounded at the second Battle of Bull Run, Virginia; nearly 5000 killed and 20,000 wounded at Antietam Creek, Maryland; another 13,000 troops missing. To Morse the bloodbath seemed a delusional orgy of self-destruction, a communal madness he often compared to the Salem witchcraft crisis: "fight it out, kill, burn, devastate . . . misrepresent, exasperate, exaggerate, vituperate; fight the devil with fire, lie against lie . . . and gild the whole with the name of *Patriotism*."

Morse told Kendall that he felt unusually depressed: "I see no hope of Union. We are two countries, and what is most deplorable two hostile countries. Oh how the nations with England at their head crow over us." Foreign predators would find the torn corpse of the United States a helpless prey, too. American children now living might well grow into adulthood under the rule of a king or emperor: "I leave . . . this prophecy in black and white."

For Morse as for millions of other Americans, a turning point in the war came on September 22, 1862, when President Lincoln issued his preliminary Emancipation Proclamation. On the first day of the new year, it said, all slaves in the rebellious states would be declared "forever free." Morse regarded the Proclamation as both unconstitutional and fatal to the South. "I read it with astonishment," he said; "I thought it infamous, and ridiculous if it were not so wicked." Lincoln had seemed tolerable during his first days, prosecuting the war not to end slavery but to preserve the Union. But the war aims he now proposed were contradictory, Morse thought, "the one legitimate, *the establishment of the authority of the Constitution,* the other illegitimate, *the emancipation of the negros.*" Turning the fight against Secession into an Abolitionist crusade, the Proclamation was "outrageous," a "mad scheme," an "abominable hallucination."

Unless, Morse thought, the President had acted with subtle shrewdness. He saw sense in the view of some nonabolitionists in the North who discounted the edict as a *brutum fulmen,* an impotent threat that "freed" only those slaves beyond the federal government's reach. Lincoln, Morse surmised, had come under increasing pressure from ultra-abolitionists in his cabinet demanding that he end slavery. To head them off he made a show of yielding. "Look at it," Morse told a friend. "It is only a proclamation of his *intention,* at a future day, of proclaiming emancipation. That day is the first of Jany. 1863. Now what is to happen before that date? The *Elections.*" Elections for Congress, that is, would be held in November, certain to purge the legislature of radicals from Lincoln's Republican party. The President could then say that the people had declared their will against Abolition, and could withdraw the Proclamation.

Morse's fantasy proved half right. The 1862 midterm elections produced heavy Republican losses that some blamed on Lincoln's preliminary Proclamation. Just the same, shortly after noon on January 1, 1863, the President signed the final Proclamation, ending slavery in the United States. Portentously, the document also authorized the service of freed slaves in the United States Army. "Rabid bloodthirsty radicals," Morse decided, "seem to have got into the places of power."

Morse found some hope in a group of influential conservative Democrats. Early in February he accepted their invitation to chair an exclusive meeting at Delmonico's, a posh Fifth Avenue restaurant that offered the latest in Paris cuisine (at a price, *Harper's* noted, that could "support a soldier and his family for a good portion of the year"). The guest list consisted of twenty-four powerful New York business and professional men, including Horatio Seymour, the newly elected Democratic Governor of New York; the corporation lawyer Samuel

Tilden; and Morse's fellow Centurion August Belmont, head of the Democratic National Committee, who apparently called the meeting.

What drew these luminaries together was a desire to revoke the Emancipation Proclamation. They would work toward that end by appealing over the President's head directly to The People, gathering Northern support for the idea of preserving the Union without making Unionism a vehicle for Abolition. A program would be devised and financed to educate the public about which powers and rights the Constitution granted to the federal government, and which to the people and the states. The group appointed a committee to draft its own constitution, and resolved to call itself the New-York Society for the Diffusion of Political Knowledge.

The wealth and prominence of Belmont, Morse, and the others involved made the Delmonico's meeting headline news. William Cullen Bryant's *Evening Post,* which had long urged immediate emancipation, sent or smuggled a reporter into the restaurant and published several accounts of what transpired. The paper shocked its readers by depicting a revolutionary cabal—a "reactionist conspiracy," a "secret caucus," a "brotherhood of Carbonari." There on the "luxurious seats of parlor No. 4" were August Belmont, "a Hebrew from Germany," and Samuel F. B. Morse, "artist and inventor, born at Charlestown, Massachusetts"—a traitor, the tag implied, to the patriotic heritage of New England.

The paper gave a sinister version of the Society's aims: "The rich men of New York are to supply the money . . . for an active and unscrupulous campaign against the government of the nation, and in the behalf of a body of rebels now in arms." A huge fund would be amassed, not to disseminate knowledge of constitutional principles but "to hand the government over, if they can, to the malignant slave-holding oligarchs who for nearly two years have been slaughtering our sons." Many other papers picked up the story, including one in Pough-keepsie, which reported that the town's leading citizen "figured among the infamous gang of conspirators," meanwhile "making thousands out of the government through his telegraph."

The Society convened again at Delmonico's a week later and elected Morse its president. He took up his new role vigorously. Addressing the group, he observed that the press had charged the S.D.P.K. with disloyalty. He answered by restating in terms of democratic ideals its aim of appealing beyond the President and the legislatures directly to citizens of America. "Can we overlook the great truth that the very foundation of our governmental system is based on the sovereignty of the people?" he asked. "Is this treason? Is this conspiracy?" In working to realize the S.D.P.K.'s program, Morse hosted private brainstorming sessions in his library, and promoted the organization of auxiliary societies throughout the North and as far west as Iowa. He contributed $500 to maintain the publication of the *Knickerbocker* magazine, which the Society used as an outlet for writings by its members and supporters. He corresponded with many like-minded people, stressing that a peaceful reunion with the South could not be achieved before the Emancipation Proclamation was repealed: "We must first retract our own wrong, and show our respect for the Constitution ourselves."

Morse also helped to oversee the Society's major educational effort, the publication of *Papers from the Society for the Diffusion of Political Knowledge*. This series of twenty pamphlets issued from the Society's office at 13 Park Row in New York City, bearing the motto "READ—DISCUSS—DIFFUSE." Several pamphlets dealt directly with Emancipation, others presented the views of conservative ministers and legislators on civil liberties, states' rights, and related topics. Being "backed up by millionaires," as Morse said, the Society could offer its *Papers* for fifty cents a thousand, distribute them in colleges, and publish some in German as well as English.

In trying to reach "the christian mind of the country" personally, Morse became an eminent propagandist and apologist for slavery. He read widely in the heaps of pro-slavery and Abolitionist literature of the day, and closely followed the debate as it unfolded in the press. He made his views known in a steady stream of articles, letters, introductions to such kindred works as the Reverend Thornton Stringfellow's *Slavery: Its Origin, Nature, and History* (1861). He contributed to two of the S.D.P.K. pamphlets and wrote the whole of one himself, entitled *An Argument on the Ethical Position of Slavery in the Social System, and its Relation to the Politics of the Day.*

Morse wrote from experience. He had lived in a slave society while painting in Charleston, and black people had been a near presence in his youth. A black boy named Abraham had lived with the family in Charlestown, taking care of the horse and cow. Jedediah had ministered to the black population of Boston. He gave them a two-year course of weekly lectures and helped to start a black church and a school for black children. He condemned the slave trade, called for its abolition, and in some of his geographies denounced slavery as inconsistent with republican principles.

Morse himself had contributed money to the building of black churches and schools. But in looking back on his father's views from the current political crisis, he thought them misguided, "benevolently intended, but even then not soundly based." Moreover the Abolition monster had sprung into being since his father's death. Jedediah would surely have seen it as the hideous progeny of religious liberalism, "that Apostacy from the faith against which he battled so nobly during his life." Jedediah's views mattered to Morse not only in being his father's, but also because he regarded the religious issue as crucial. To save the country from destruction, what desperately needed confutation was the notion—a rallying cry of the Abolitionists—that Slavery Is Sin. "This monstrous heresy lies at the root of all the fanatical outbreaks . . . the definite settlement of that fundamental point is vital."

Morse himself tried to settle the point. After much "careful and prayerful" study of the Bible he undertook an analysis of slavery not as politics but as Scripture and theology. His many writings on the subject are repetitious, inviting collective summary rather than individual treatment. But they all present slavery as ordained by God, sanctioned in the Old and New Testaments, justified by Nature, and beneficial to the slave.

As Morse explained, the key to understanding slavery as an essential feature of divine governance is The Fall. Man was created in the image of God, partaking of the Divine Nature, but by his first Disobedience assumed the image of Satan. To help restore man to his original state, God arranged society as a "*system of restraints*" on man's proud will. He instituted four relationships: civil government, marriage, parenthood, and servility. Each relation consists of a superior and an inferior party: ruler and ruled, husband and wife, parent and child, master and slave. All four share "the one great central idea in Man's Redemption, to wit, *Obedience*, the natural antidote to *Disobedience*." The enslavement of blacks is no less legitimate or moral than marriage, a system of divinely decreed educational and disciplinary restraint: "God, in his wisdom and far-sighted benevolence, has ordained that despised and vilified *relation* as the means of bringing that race home to himself. This is the Bible theory."

That this view of slavery did represent "the Bible theory," Morse demonstrated by numerous citations of Scripture, and forays into philology and hermeneutics. For instance, against claims that the Bible spoke of "servants" but not of "slaves," he argued that the Hebrew word *ebed*, often translated as "servant," literally meant "bond slave." So where the King James version of Genesis 25 rendered Noah's words as "Cursed be Canaan, a servant of servants shall he be," a more correct translation would read "Cursed be Canaan, a *slave of slaves shall he be.*" In a typical bit of hermeneutics, Morse offered scriptural evidence implying that God ordained the continuance of slavery until the end of time. Regarding matrimony, one of the four "servile relations," Jesus says in Mark 12:25: "when they shall rise from the dead, *they neither marry nor are given in marriage.*" Since the New Testament foretells no end to matrimonial servility until the Resurrection, there is likewise no reason to suppose that God contemplates an end to the servility of slavery before the Last Day: "The *time* when this relation [marriage] is to cease may I think be assumed for all the others 'when they shall rise from the dead.'"

Morse tried to account for the acceptance in America of quite contrary, unscriptural ideas of human government. Much of the ideological corruption he traced to the Infidelity that had muddled Western thought since the French Revolution, had been fought by his father, and continued at present to inspire antislavery Unitarians, Transcendentalists, and other religious liberals—"the Christ rejecting humanitarian, the Bible spurning infidel, the pseudo merciful universalist, and the nothingarian." They all spoke and acted as if man were not a fallen, degenerate being, but still innocent and obedient to God's will. Atheists at heart, they secularized and thus debased the scriptural understanding of freedom as Freedom from Sin, "giving *freedom & liberty* an earthly, low, civil & political sense, as if an indiscriminate social & political liberty of every human being were the scope and end of man's redemption."

Despite his devotion to the cult of George Washington, Morse did not exempt the Revolutionary generation itself from fostering "the miserable delusion of *negro freedom.*" Some of its members had been contaminated by the rampant godlessness of the age:

> I cannot shut my eyes to the fact that the time, when that Declaration was made, favored the infidel views of some eminent minds who were parties to the promulgation of *fundamental error.* . . .

The so styled self evident truths are not all *truths.* Some are self evident falsehoods.

The untruths included a supposedly inalienable right to liberty, which actually had been lost to man by the rebellion in Eden. "*Slavery,* the subjection of one's will to the will of another, since the fall of man, is the rule, and not *liberty.*" And having introduced into American culture ideas inconsistent with Scripture, the Declaration had now become enthroned as an idol: "the Gospel of Peace has been cast out of its proper temples, to give place to a religion, whose *Bible* is the *Declaration of Independence.*" Indeed the present crisis might be God's way of humbling the country for deifying Liberty instead of Him.

Nature as well as Scripture warranted slavery, Morse observed, blacks being a "weak and degraded race." The opinion was not recent; his earlier papers contain many such slurs. Lecturing on art in 1826, for instance, he told his New York audience that on the chain of being, blacks ranked with beasts: "witness the negro, the ouran outan, the baboon, the monkey by gradual and downward steps blending the human face divine, with the unseemly visage of the brute." Now he defended the "cornerstone doctrine," named after some much-quoted remarks in an address by Alexander Stephens, vice president of the Confederacy. Stephens said that the "corner stone" of the new Southern nation was racial superiority, "the great truth that the negro is not equal to the white man; that slavery, subordination to the superior race, is his natural and normal condition." Morse agreed. Divinely ordained physical differences, he said, dictated the domination of blacks by whites: "Nothing is clearer to my mind than that the status of the African in the compound of the Caucasian & the African, is that of *subjection* to the superior race, and this is best for both races."

Morse emphasized this "best" in all his arguings, stressing the benefits of slavery to the slave. The institution had produced examples of domestic contentment rarely known in this fallen world: "Protection and judicious guidance and careful provision on the one part; cheerful obedience, affection, and confidence on the other." The apostle Paul himself had advised a slave to prefer slavery to freedom, even given a chance to become free. And missionary experience confirmed the wisdom of Paul's advice, Morse commented. After fifty years' labor the American missionary churches overseas could count only about 44,500 conversions among free blacks. By contrast, churches in the

South could boast more than 500,000 converts among enslaved blacks. The salutary message was dramatically clear: "CHRISTIANITY HAS BEEN MOST SUCCESSFULLY PROPAGATED AMONG A BARBAROUS RACE, WHEN THEY HAVE BEEN ENSLAVED TO A CHRISTIAN RACE. *Slavery* to them has been *Salvation,* and *Freedom, ruin.*"

Like Morse's warnings of foreign conspiracy, his defense of slavery, summarized above, offered his readers few unfamiliar ideas. Pro- and anti-slavery writings of the time were a sort of community product, its authors taking different approaches but arriving at the same conclusions. Both sides cited Scripture. Pro-slavery biblicists often contended that Abraham, Isaac, and Jacob were slaveholders and that Paul in several of his epistles admonished slaves to obey their masters. Many writers also attacked the Declaration's axioms about Liberty, antebellum experience having shown clearly enough that men were not born free and equal. And belief in the racial inferiority of blacks permeated American culture. It gained sanction from the claim of nineteenth-century ethnological pseudo-scientists that the various races constituted separate species, with blacks at the bottom of the scale.

What distinguishes Morse's treatment of these common themes is his neo-Puritan vision of their historical connection and continuity, beginning with the rebellion in Eden. "My fundamental axiom," he said, "is the *degeneracy of man.*" He had of course remained a pious Christian all his life. But the remark suggests that he steadied himself against the upheavals of war by embracing with new intensity the rigorous Calvinist-Federalist principles of his childhood. As he put it, "I have chosen to remain in the Sentiments of my early education." From this vantage point he saw that fallen man's impulse to resist divine government had been perpetuated in unchristian ideas of freedom among the founding fathers, aggravated by unceasing British and European designs to destabilize the country, and fatally preached as a gospel of individualism by liberals in the American churches. Begun in original sin, the train of misrule had brought the United States to its present moment of dissolution.

Sidney Morse shared his brother's thinking and echoed it. He published several pro-slavery articles and pamphlets, similarly affirming that the Bible sanctioned slavery, that slaveholding was as much a God-given right as government, that only infidels considered all men entitled to liberty: "Is not this deification of liberty, this apotheosis of the will of the negro, the most insulting of all violations of the first commandment of the decalogue?" Richard Morse, always a free spirit, announced that he intended to vote for the reelection of Lincoln. His brother Samuel tried to reason with him but gave up: "I pray you . . . may be delivered from the delusions which have pursued you."

It gratified Morse that his defense of slavery reached a large and appreciative audience, "some of the most pious, as well as distinguished, intellectual minds in the country." The West Virginia *Intelligence,* for instance, praised him as a communicator—first technological and now political:

> There is a great fitness that the distinguished originator of the American Magnetic Telegraph, whose genius has chained the lightning and made it an obedient messenger to carry information with the rapidity of thought from end to end of the land, should be among the foremost to flash the light of political knowledge into the minds of his fellow countrymen.

His S.D.P.K. pamphlet on *The Ethical Position of Slavery* sold so well he was hard put to find extra copies, "to supply the constant demand upon me for them."

But Morse's writing also brought him much vituperative criticism. "Oh my Brother," his former pastor wrote to him, "what a work of repentance, deep bitter repentance, have you made for yourself." The New York *Times* mocked his views on human equality, not for holding that one body of men might be less able than another, but for deducing that in such a case "it is the right of the latter to rob, beat and sell the former." The prestigious *North American Review* derided as "worthless and shallow" his treatment of slavery as merely a form of government, his endorsement of the cornerstone doctrine, his sneers at the Declaration. The journal attributed these and his other notions to "the self-conceit of a weak man." A Boston newspaper recommended that he be imprisoned.

Morse did not comment on the fact, but within the whistling of bullets on American battlefields could be heard the click of his invention. Both armies extensively telegraphed military information. The Confederacy used private telegraph companies, the Union organized a

Military Telegraph Department that transmitted some six and a half million dispatches. Over the course of the war a shortage of wire and other supplies silenced many of the South's lines. Meanwhile the North strung 15,000 additional miles of wire and laid a twenty-mile submarine line across Chesapeake Bay, using a section of Cyrus Field's abandoned 1858 Atlantic cable.

Morse's telegraphs put strategic decisions in motion. The web of circuits allowed commanders to coordinate troop movement at a distance from their forces. Atop the chain of command, President Lincoln visited the telegraph office at the War Department several times a day to receive reports from the front and send orders to his generals, sometimes staying late at night. General U. S. Grant, during his final campaign, telegraphed daily orders from his headquarters to all the Union forces engaged over thousands of square miles. As the head of the Military Telegraph Department described the potent efficiency of Morse's invention, "orders are given—armies are moved—battles are planned and fought, and victories won with the assistance of this simple, yet powerful aide-de-camp." To this extent Morse had wrought a techno-utopian Frankenstein that far from promoting national community and peace, as he hoped, hardened division and facilitated bloodshed.

The blare of the war and war news obscured some momentous events in very long distance telegraphy. In the spring and early summer of 1861, telegraph work gangs and wagon trains set out toward each other east from Sacramento and west from Omaha. They planned to link up at Salt Lake City to form a transcontinental line stretching 5500 miles from San Francisco to St. John's, Newfoundland. In just over four months they spanned the vast prairie and the Sierra Nevada mountains. On October 24 the Chief Justice of California sent the first transcontinental message, wiring Abraham Lincoln to express his state's loyalty to the Union. Morse telegrammed his congratulations to California, rejoicing in a feat of "indomitable perseverance and consummate skill."

Morse applauded a still more audacious plan by the Russian government, in cooperation with the Western Union Telegraph Company, to construct an overland line from Russia to the United States. The Russian superintendent of the project visited him at Locust Grove and gave him a map of the proposed route. It showed the line moving eastward from St. Petersburg through Siberia across the thirty-six-mile Bering Strait to Alaska, thence to San Francisco, where it could hook up with the transcontinental American line. Morse invested $30,000 in the venture and enthusiastically publicized it. By the spring of 1862 the Siberia-America line had already crossed the Ural Mountains. Its robust telegraph workers advanced on snowshoes, dogsleds, and sealskin-covered umiaks. For nourishment they survived on white rum, dried woodchucks, and Siberian *Manyalla*—frozen loaves of clotted reindeer blood.

The vastly long lines made actual what Morse had long ago envisioned: "Early in the History of the invention in forecasting its future, I was accustomed to predict with confidence, 'it is destined to go round the world,' but I confess I did not expect to live to see the prediction fulfilled." A telegraph convention in Paris, attended by representatives of twenty governments, provisionally voted to adopt his apparatus for all international telegraphy. Against many competitors and with little modification, it pleased Morse to think, his system was coming into universal use, providing a single common world language of electrical communication.

As the war raged, Morse kept in touch with his American telegraph interests mostly through Amos Kendall. Now in his mid-seventies, Kendall wrote in a hand sometimes illegible for its trembling. And typhoid fever had taken his second wife and another son. As always he carried on: "It is my religion as well as my philosophy to submit to the dispensations of Providence without repining." His political views essentially matched Morse's: "We are both for the Union to the last," he said. A former slaveowner, he detested Abolition, but had no sympathy with Secession either. He wrote to President Lincoln, urging him to punish the secessionists for the "pride of wealth and . . . lust for power" bred in them by the cotton monopoly. He proposed that as Union armies advanced in the South, the federal government should confiscate slaves abandoned by their masters, set them free, and surrender their masters' lands to them for cultivation.

Morse and Kendall kept particularly close watch on the consolidation movement, which had continued actively despite the war. The aggressive directors of the Western Union Telegraph Company strove to overtake Cyrus Field's American Telegraph and seize control of all the major American telegraph associations. They scooped up several independent companies in which Morse had large investments. Such mergers, according to the New York *Tribune,* were making telegraphy "the most profitable business in the country."

Wealthy already, Morse became wealthier. He owned 7500 shares in Western Union, as the powerhouse more simply became known. This and his other holdings of telegraph stock and government bonds became so valuable that he employed a New York stockbroker to look after them. He had daily price reports telegraphed to him, using a word-number code in which "fire," for example, might mean 9: "You wish to tell me that W.U. stock is 185, you therefore send me the words, '*home, mat, run.*' " As the price of Western Union zoomed, in one case rising 25 percent over a few days, he sold off hundreds of his shares. Having money to spare—the *Tribune* spoke of his "regal income"—he invested in a petroleum company, an insurance company, western copper mines, California gold mines. Always generous when he could afford to be, he subscribed $10,000 toward erecting a Theological Hall at Yale. He also sent money to aid Philadelphia's deaf mutes, build hospitals, and help out strangers in financial distress because of the war.

To Morse's delight, the wealth produced by his telegraph also enabled others to carry out large philanthropic works. Kendall gave money and land to create the famed Columbia Institution for the Deaf and Dumb in Washington, D.C., the world's only college for deaf mutes. Ezra Cornell had returned to farming in Ithaca, New York, but kept his telegraph stock. He became the largest stockholder in Western Union. His telegraph income allowed him to donate a half-million dollars plus three hundred acres of land to build and endow a nonsectarian school in Ithaca—Cornell University. "I have viewed his course with great gratification," Morse said, "as the evidence of God's blessing on *what He hath wrought.*"

At the time Southern troops fired on the federal garrison at Fort Sumter, Morse was seventy years old, the father of seven children ranging in age from four to forty-two. The youngest and most recent was named Edward Lind Morse, in honor of his son-in-law, the Puerto Rico planter Edward Lind. Of his three other children with Sarah he confessed feeling some special warmth toward Lela (Cornelia) because of the "artlessness" natural to her sex. But he meant to give all of them the benefits of his wealth and what he called "the position I hold before the world."

Morse sent his sons Arthur and Willie to Newport for schooling, got them French lessons, treated them to a terrier and a pony. In return for his generosity he demanded submission, gratitude, and achievement, as Jedediah had demanded of him: "you must remember you are a *Morse* and that your grandfather was the Father of American Geography." He covered his lengthy letters to the boys with Jedediah-like instructions and maxims—diligence in studies, kindness to others, control of temper: "When you write, *fill your paper. . . .* be strictly obedient to all the directions of your teachers . . . guard against *Slang.*" Above all, he expected his children to be prayerful Christians, to follow "the old orthodox paths" in asking God to guide them through life and direct their way. It saddened him to think he would not live to know them as adults, but there would be time enough in the afterlife: "Then shall we meet," he told them, "where we shall know each other forever."

Morse's adult children were entering middle age, each in a different way blighted. That does not seem surprising, given the early death of their mother, and their abandonment to relatives, family friends, and paid caretakers as their father struggled to become a famous history painter. Approaching forty, Finley remained childlike. He now permanently lived in the Adirondack Mountains, where he passed the time gardening and fishing, looked after by Morse's cousins, the Davises. Morse paid for his upkeep, but found one excuse after another not to write to him, and asked the Davises to explain: "Please say to Finley that I received his letter, and would have replied . . . but the truth is I am so overwhelmed with cares just now." At least once, he himself tried to explain:

My dear Son,

Perhaps you think it strange that I have not written you, but the truth is, that unless I have something very important to say, I am obliged to employ my pen from morning till night on matters which require my whole attention. . . .

Morse may have found Finley's mental incompetence too distressing to face, much less manage. He told himself and others that his son was the happiest member of the family despite his "unfortunate" condition—"catches sometimes a dozen fish in a day as long as your finger, and is as happy as if they were whales."

Susan, now in her mid-forties, stayed at Locust Grove during the summers and for other periods as well. Frail, she slept poorly, suffered from fevers, and had taken several falls that may have injured her spine. While at Locust Grove she underwent some unspecified "treatment," seemingly an early form of psychotherapy for what Morse termed her "mental condition," her "*nervousness*." The decline of her husband's sugar business in Puerto Rico because of the war deeply worried her. Morse loaned Edward $14,000 to help him out of debt, and tried to persuade him to quit his plantation and join Susan in Poughkeepsie, perhaps permanently. Otherwise, he said, "we fear her health if not her life may seriously suffer."

Charles, too, was now in his forties, and in Morse's eyes could do nothing right. Charles had gone west to work with a federal surveying party among the Sioux nation. He came back financially ruined, "the victim of dishonest sharpers," Morse said, "who owe him money and will not or can not pay him." He scolded Charles for having remained gullible in business dealings—a shortcoming in which Charles resembled no one so much as himself, although he did not say so. Instead he attributed Charles' too-trusting nature to idiocy. "I sometimes think there must be a constitutional mental defect in you, in some respects like that of your brother Finley's."

Charles was much discouraged, unable to pay his rent or feed his family. Morse helped him out financially, giving him over four or five years some $30,000—along with a barrage of criticism: "You are too easy and good natured. . . . you should put on a bolder attitude. . . . you act upon very loose principles of disbursement." He provided a hundred-dollar-a-month allowance for Charles' wife, Manette, when Charles headed west again, this time for Central City, Colorado, to find work in local mining operations. A gifted writer, Charles sent home vivid descriptions of dust-begrimed bull-whackers, charred bodies of teamsters massacred by Indians, carcasses of oxen putrefying in the sun.

To Morse's displeasure, Charles' grim picture of frontier life upset Manette, suggesting that her husband was unhappy with his situation. "I do hope you will not give way to any weak longings for home," Morse wrote to him. "Love to your wife and family can be better shown by persevering effort to provide for them, and be an independent man, even if you have to be absent for years. . . . You must be more manly." But Charles became ill and depressed in Colorado and soon declared bankruptcy: "all I have done for him," Morse brooded, "seems to be like throwing it into the sea."

Both Charles and his sister Susan had presented Morse with grandchildren. Charles and Manette's son Bleecker sometimes stayed at Locust Grove, "quite a favorite with us," Morse said. With Charles away in Colorado, Morse inquired after Bleecker's "standing and moral character" at school, and with "real joy" attended his formal admission to communion in a Brooklyn church. Susan's son, also named Charles, came with her when she visited Locust Grove and as a teenager remained in the United States to enroll at Union College, Schenectady. Proud of his grandson's unmistakable talent for painting, Morse paid for his education and looked forward to his someday setting up professionally in New York City. "Artists are now in high esteem," he told the boy, "and their general character both as to talent and moral elevation is of a vastly superior type compared with that which belonged to them when I first came to New York." He wrote off to Puerto Rico urging Edward Lind to allow Charles to study painting in Europe.

It may have been his grandson's promise that stirred old longings in Morse, "many yearnings," he confided to a friend, "towards painting & sculpture." When he tried to draw, however, he found that his perpendicular lines went awry: "I could place no confidence in my *eyes*." In the spring of 1861, Asher B. Durand, W. S. Mount, Albert Bierstadt, and other leaders of the National Academy of Design asked him to serve once again as president, as he had for eighteen years. His long absence from the art world made him reluctant to do so, but many members told him that vital interests of the Academy were at stake. He gave in partway, agreeing to act as president until the next annual election: "the feeling of paternity is strongly revived in my heart, and I cannot forget the early travail with my honored associates, which brought into existence the National Academy of Design."

Morse's duties apparently amounted to little more than lending the N.A.D. his lustrous name. But during his term and over the next few years he also served as a benefactor. He contributed $500 toward purchasing for the Academy Charles Leslie's portrait of Washington

Allston, "my Master in Art." For $7000 he bought as a gift to the Yale Art Gallery Allston's seven-by-eight-foot *Jeremiah Dictating His Prophecy of the Destruction of Jerusalem* (1820). And recalling the "darkness and desolateness" of his own early painting career he donated shares of telegraph stock to the Artists' Fund Society: "I still have an Artist's heart, while deprived by long disuse of an Artist's skill."

On Independence Day 1863, telegraphed accounts appeared in New York City newspapers of the third and last day of hellish combat at Gettysburg, Pennsylvania. The *Times* did not exaggerate in calling the battle "sanguinary in the extreme." Of about 150,000 troops engaged, some 33,000 were killed or wounded. Hundreds of the survivors streamed into New York's hospitals.

Scarcely ten days later, the city itself became a killing ground. A wild mob took to the streets on July 13 to protest the National Conscription Act, passed by Congress to draft troops for the Union army. Over three days of the worst rioting in the nation's history, the horde broke into gun-shops to arm themselves, tore out railroad tracks and telegraph poles, sacked Fifth Avenue mansions, and beat up policemen and soldiers, the agents of federal power. Especially they hunted the black population. With cries of "Burn the niggers nest," a mostly Irish pack of hundreds stormed the Colored Orphan Asylum, looted it, and torched the building. Black men were hanged from lampposts or drowned, the bodies burned or mutilated.

Spending the summer as usual at Locust Grove, Morse anxiously stayed informed about the battles in both Manhattan and Gettysburg. The anti-draft riots brought him down to the city in July to check the security of his town house. In the Pennsylvania fighting he saw an aspect of hope. General Robert E. Lee's "fatal mistake" of leading his army into Pennsylvania—seen by many other Northerners as the great Union victory at Gettysburg—might hasten negotiations to end the war. Morse's hope vanished when President Lincoln repulsed a peace feeler from Jefferson Davis. He found every occasion to revile the President as "illiterate," "inhuman," "wicked," above all "*irreligious*"—"a coarse, vulgar, uncultivated man, an inventor or re-teller of stories so low and obscene, that no decent man can listen to them without disgust." The great barrier to restoring peace was the administration in Washington. Nothing it did showed statesmanship, justice, or humanity, least of all magnanimity: "What can be expected of a President without brains."

The country's one hope of peace, Morse believed, lay in preventing Lincoln's reelection in 1864. His candidate, favored by most members of the Society for the Diffusion of Political Knowledge, was General George B. McClellan. The "Little Napoleon," as his admirers called him, was only thirty-seven years old and had no political experience. But as commander of the Army of the Potomac he had gained a national military reputation in September 1862 by turning back Lee's army at Antietam. Lincoln otherwise thought him indecisive and slow to act, and later the same year removed him from command.

Morse backed McClellan because the general promised to seek peace on the basis of Union not Abolition, readmitting the Southern states with slavery unchanged. Morse had reservations about electing a military man. But there was Washington, of course, and McClellan's martial spirit seemed well disciplined, "under the control of a Christian heart, a heart devoted to God, and so restrained within proper bounds." Besides, military reputation appealed to the masses and would win votes: "I see no reason why we should not have the help of hero worshippers to put one in office whom we respect & honor for his Christian humility & devotion." What mattered was to get rid of Lincoln, "putting out of power, the present imbecile, & bloodthirsty administration." To aid McClellan's campaign, the S.D.P.K. voted to merge its operations with those of the Democratic National Committee. Morse contributed a thousand dollars toward the work of this hybrid organization and was appointed to the executive committee.

He looked ahead to the November elections uneasily. At times he felt certain that Lincoln had committed "political suicide" by insisting the South could purchase peace only by ending slavery: "He is politically dead, and . . . will certainly be defeated." Other times he feared that the administration might beat McClellan by a "corrupt and reckless" use of its powers. A "marked man" himself, he heard, Morse believed that his mail was being inspected at the post office; some letters came to him "opened and sealed again in the most slovenly matter." Having already invaded personal liberties—in some cases suspending habeas corpus—the administration might now try to control the votes of the troops under its command. The possibility of a second Lincoln term again raised for Morse the painful vision of fleeing his homeland for Europe. Better peaceable exile under an established despotism than continued turmoil under a despotism clawing its way into being, "fixing itself on its throne through years of anarchy & bloodshed, on the ruins of our Republic."

As the election neared, Morse made himself highly visible in McClellan's New York City campaign. On November 4 he presided over a Democratic rally at a crowded meeting hall on Thirty-fourth Street, introduced as "a gentleman who, by his scientific researches and discoveries, has made his fame and name immortal." Addressing the party faithful, he warned of administration efforts to trample the Constitution and the liberties of the people. Next evening he escorted McClellan to the balcony of the Fifth Avenue Hotel and presented him to the assemblage in the square below—"a dense mass of heads, as far as the eye could reach in every direction." A minutes-long shout went up, reminding him of the reception he had witnessed in London fifty years ago of European military leaders who had helped defeat Napoleon at Waterloo. With McClellan he watched the nearly three-hour torchlight parade up the avenue—banners, fireworks, hats tossed in the air. Afterward McClellan took his arm as they tried to maneuver through the crush in the hotel, as three policemen scarcely managed to make a way for them.

The hoopla came to nothing. As was a foregone conclusion, Lincoln lost New York City by a landslide, about 37,000 votes. But he solidly beat McClellan in the popular and electoral vote, and by about four to one in the military vote. Morse felt he had done what he could for the Democratic party. He retreated from politics, although with foreboding. "I retire from the conflict," he announced, "leaving the responsibility on those who have re-elected an administration from whose acts I augur only a prolongation of our civil war." He took up his Christian duty to now devote himself to relieving the misery the war continued to create, beginning with the "*so called* enemy." He chaired an informal association to collect money for the relief of captured Confederate troops in Northern prisons and personally tried to send them cold-weather clothing and blankets.

As Union troops moved decisively toward and then into Atlanta, Savannah, and Richmond, Morse seems to have fallen silent. He joined two hundred fellow New Yorkers in protesting plans by the Common Council to celebrate recent victories of the Union army. But his surviving papers contain no comments on General Sherman's march through Georgia, on newsboys shouting in the streets "Richmond Ours!," or any of the other closing scenes of the war. One of his sons later recalled being taken in the spring of 1865 to the second floor of a stable his father kept, a few blocks from the town house. From there he witnessed six gray horses covered with black cloth drawing through the city's streets the coffin of President Lincoln, shot in the head and killed a week after the Confederacy surrendered.

Morse grieved for the South in its defeat. He declined an invitation to take part in ceremonies at the Yale commencement honoring his alma mater's New England graduates who had served in the Union army. "I should as soon think of applauding one of my children for his skilful shooting of his brothers in a family brawl," he said. Mostly he wanted to erase the last four years from his own and the nation's consciousness and from the record of American history: "the whole era of the war is one I wish not to remember. I would have no other memorial than a black cross like those over the graves of murdered travellers to cause a shudder whenever it is seen."

But as Morse soon learned, the racial problems that had ignited the war survived it in new forms, terrible for him to contemplate. "The future of our country looks very dark," he thought. The president of Vassar College was hinting that he would teach miscegenation, "that he will prepare his female pupils to resist their so called '*prejudices*' of color, so as to be in readiness to receive graciously, the matrimonial offers of our 'citizens of African descent.' " The "*false philanthropy*" that had inspired the Abolitionists was growing not less but more bold, pressing now for black suffrage. And once freed, blacks felt helpless and angry, threatened with annihilation. Even as a constitutional amendment to abolish slavery was being offered to the states for ratification, two thousand freed slaves in Jamaica, impoverished by emancipation there, had taken over the town of Morant Bay, killing about twenty white militia, officials, and planters. "We look for the same result here," Morse said. "I fear it cannot be avoided."

Morse decided to remove himself and his family from the ominous scene by going abroad, for an extended stay of nearly two years. The children could study music and learn French and German, and the whole family would all enjoy the International Exposition to be held in Paris. Intending to take along Sarah's mother, a teenaged niece, a governess, a tutor, and ten or more trunks, he financed the recess by offering his town house for rent, at $6000 annually, and selling six hundred shares of his Western Union stock, for $35,475.

Before leaving, Morse sent a ten-page letter to Cyrus Field. A few months after the war ended, Field had tried again to lay a transatlantic cable, now using only one vessel—the 700-foot-long iron-sided *Great Eastern,* by far the largest ship afloat. Again the attempt failed. Leaving from Ireland, the *Great Eastern* was only about 600 miles from Newfoundland when the cable broke; 1200 miles of it were lost in the bottom of the sea. Unstoppable, Field planned to make still another attempt. Morse offered him a novel method of paying-out devised by Sidney Morse, and expressed the hope of meeting him abroad.

A week or so later, Morse received a letter from Finley. It asked permission to come down from the Adirondacks to see him and Sarah in the city before their departure. Once more he did not answer the boy-man. Instead he wrote to the Davises, Finley's caretakers, sending money for him but pleading that he must put off making a decision: "We should be glad of course to see him but it would be adding greatly to our care in the midst of our preparations."

EIGHTEEN

Visions of Receding Glory

(1866–1872)

IT REFRESHED MORSE to be once again in France. Lafayette, Arago, and other notables had always received him warmly; the nation had formally adopted his telegraph system; the Emperor himself had arranged his indemnity from the other European states. His appearance marked him for attention, a fact recorded in the bearded bemedaled image of himself he referred to as the "*family photograph portrait*".* His family had prodded him to have it taken, he often said. Some justification was needed. As a much younger man he had said he despised the "artificial distinctions" of the Old World, the "ribbons, and garters and crosses and other gewgaws that please the great babies of Europe." Now, however, when sending out copies of the picture he explained in detail the decorations on his chest, sometimes listing the many other honors he had received as well, as if relishing to simply name them all.

The Abrahamic beard was a recent growth—a breastbone-length frizzy white cloud declaring settled strength, wisdom, and, of course, old age. He felt close to the end of his journey, "daily more weaned from earth, and have my nightly & daily thoughts more & more fixed upon him alone who is my trust, my Savior, my Life." Neuralgia sometimes ached his face and head, but his five-foot-ten frame was still erect, his voice strong. His handwriting was tremorless, having retained for fifty years its crisp, steel-plate elegance.

Morse had always particularly loved Paris, now a city of nearly two million inhabitants, "the great centre of the world," he called it. He

*See p. 390.

found the place dramatically transformed since his last visit. Baron Georges Eugène Haussmann, the prefect of Paris, had overseen the destruction of the crowded medieval slums and open sewers, replacing them with handsome public spaces and sweeping tree-lined boulevards. "I used to think it the *dirtiest* city in Europe; now it is the *cleanest.*" And very grand. There were luxurious hotels, the nearly completed Théâtre de l'Opéra, the airy pavilions of Les Halles—everywhere "magnificent improvements in the multitude and beauty of the avenues and buildings."

Morse lent himself to the style of the new Metropolis. He rented the entire third floor of a six-story house at no. 10 avenue du Roi de Rome, an expensive neighborhood of embassies and fine private homes near the Arc de Triomphe. The cream-colored stone building, only a year old, was exquisitely ornamented with wrought-iron balconies, classical columns, and sculpted figures. Morse's apartment, elegantly furnished, provided him and his family a living room, two parlors, four bedrooms, and a dining room capable of seating twelve. There were three additional rooms for servants, which he presumably filled after engaging a valet, cook, chambermaid, and seamstress. And the rental entitled him to store his wine in the building's cellar. "So far as material comfort is concerned," he decided, "there is no place in the world that can equal Paris."

Morse enjoyed playing the part of an *haut bourgeois*. With Sarah and the children he often drove to the Bois de Boulogne in a two-horse barouche. They circled the lake, greeting friends and ogling the celebrities whose afternoon rides made the *tour du lac* a great public spectacle. They spent a "quite *gay*" winter attending Baron Haussmann's fete at the Hôtel de Ville and court balls at the Tuileries, mingling with princes and princesses, ex-queens, ambassadors, "the highest Society in the world." As he did in similar circumstances, he reasoned away the moral and political distance he had traveled from being the son of a Calvinist minister, born in the shadow of Bunker's Hill, to being a grandee in the flamboyant Paris of the Second Empire. "The evil does not lie in assembling in splendid rooms, and in wearing rich apparel," he reflected, "but in so setting the heart upon such scenes as to have no room there for the more substantial pleasures of ordinary duties, whether domestic or more purely religious. There is such a thing as *using* the world, and not *abusing* it."

Using the world very well indeed, Morse was presented at court—

the most splendid in all Europe—to the Emperor Napoleon III and the Empress Eugénie. With Paris becoming the world's fashion center, he had himself outfitted for the surpassing occasion in a resplendent full suit—*chapeau bras,* silk-lined coat embroidered with gold lace, cashmere vest with gilt buttons, white cravat, pantaloons with a broad stripe of gold lace, a small sword—"which last for a peaceable man like him," he admitted, "was a little out of character." He covered the breast of his coat with six of his orders and the plaque of *Cavaliero Commandador* of the Spanish Order of Isabella the Catholic(!), and hung around his neck his Nishan Iftichar, the diamonded gold brooch conferred upon him by the Sultan of Turkey. Standing in a receiving line among other brilliantly costumed notables, he got to meet the debonair mustachioed Emperor, as well as Eugénie, who said to him, he recalled, " 'we are greatly indebted to you, Sir, for the Telegraph,' or to that effect." He took some tempting-looking almonds and candies home for the children. To his surprise the bonbons turned out to be cunningly fashioned of fish.

From an even grander, historic event, however, Morse was painfully excluded. After thirteen years of single-minded perseverance, Cyrus Field at last succeeded in establishing telegraphic communication across the Atlantic Ocean, bringing London within minutes of New York and San Francisco.

On July 13, 1866, the 700-foot-long *Great Eastern* had once more taken off from the Irish coast, its iron hull scraped of a two-foot-thick crust of barnacles. Its paying-out machinery had been improved, the cable-insulation galvanized. After only one mishap at sea, when the cable fouled, the ship reached Newfoundland two weeks later and hooked its line onshore. Queen Victoria sent the first official transatlantic message, congratulating President Andrew Johnson on this new coupling of the United States and England. The immense promise of the cable was dramatized when Cyrus Field, in Newfoundland, received simultaneous messages from California and from Alexandria, Egypt. In a thrilling follow-up, the *Great Eastern* moved out six hundred miles to where its cable had snapped and sunk during the previous year's attempt. Grapnels were sent down, on rope a half-foot thick. After thirty tries, the lost cable was recovered and landed, making a second usable transatlantic telegraph line.

From Paris, Morse sent Field congratulations on this revolutionary boon to human intercommunication, to "the great system of nerves

that will make the world one great Sensorium." He would profit from
Field's success, too, owning 600 shares in the cable company. He
bought 200 more shares, speeding his order to New York across the
undersea line itself, at the steep cost of nearly $30 in gold. Just the
same, reading newspaper reports of the many London banquets and
celebrations and toasts to "England and America United," he felt left
out. The reports said nothing of him. "My name in connection with
the Atlantic cable, though it was my suggestion and built upon my
assurances of its feasibility, is carefully excluded from mention." Such,
he concluded, was public opinion. Years ago the public had doubted
his suggestion. Now it doubted that he ever made the suggestion.

As Morse had planned to do, he gave his family every advantage of
European travel and education. He took them all on excursions to
England, Scotland, Germany, and Switzerland. The children progressed in mastering French and German, learning to draw, and
becoming accomplished musicians. The often mischievous Arthur
played the violin in duets with his sister Lela, who was studying piano;
his teacher, a celebrated German violinist, remarked that he had
"extraordinary powers." Morse indulged his own fondness for music
by hearing performances in Dresden of Wagner's *Rienzi, The Flying
Dutchman,* and *Tannhäuser.*

Morse took particular delight in his grandson Charles Lind. As a
child in Puerto Rico, Charles had shown an aptitude for drawing. By
now he maintained his own atelier in Paris, studying painting at
Julien's Academy and readying some pictures to be shown at the exposition. Morse invited the young man to dine with the family once or
twice a week, and to visit often, proud that his own daughter's son
seemed determined to become a first-rate painter: "I tell him the mantel [*sic*] is going into the Lind branch."

Despite the seductions of Paris and his advanced age, Morse spent
most of his time working. "I have so many irons in the fire that I fear
some must burn. But father's motto was, 'better *wear* out, than *rust*
out.'" As one way of staying busy he represented a group called the
American Asiatic Society. With the Suez Canal under construction,
promising greatly increased commerce between East and West, the
Society hoped to persuade maritime nations to join in encouraging
global trade. The Society had in view, for instance, tapping the poten-

tially lucrative resources of undeveloped regions like eastern Africa. As President of the group, Morse undertook to personally present a memorial to the Emperor, requesting that he convene during the Paris Exposition an international conference on world commerce.

However flatteringly received at court in his medals and *chapeau bras,* Morse found the Emperor unreachable. He got a runaround from officials, and was hampered by his inability, still, to speak French. Anyway, Napoleon was tied up in cabinet meetings, preoccupied with the current war between Austria and Prussia, which threatened to engulf the Continent. When he at last replied to Morse, through the Minister of Foreign Affairs, he said that he looked favorably on the Society's project. But he declined calling a congress. Unable to get anywhere, Morse resigned his presidency.

Much other time Morse spent writing. The ever-present desire to prove his claim of priority had become obsessive as he aged. The need to do so in Europe was urgent, for the counterclaims that Dr. Charles Jackson had submitted to the Académie des Sciences decades ago remained unchallenged in the academy's records and continued to circulate: "How slander sticks!" In Germany, the author of a *Handbuch der angewandten Elektricitätslehre* fully retold Jackson's version of The *Sully* Story and summed up what it revealed: "we involuntarily arrive at the conclusion that Morse's attention was first directed to the subject of the electric telegraph and the employment of electro-magnetism, through Jackson's ideas." Morse bought up many other new books and articles on the history of telegraphy that in his view perpetuated errors and lies about his originality. He filled the margins with protests: "Infamous! . . . Is this a fair statement? . . . Was there ever such barefaced falsehoods crowded into so small a space as in this note?!!"

Morse labored to set the record straight, "the pen in my hands from early morning to late at night." He published two pamphlets in Paris, the first a reissue of Amos Kendall's *Full Exposure . . . of Dr. Charles T. Jackson,* published in America in 1850. Undying trust in Jackson's mendacities, he explained, demanded the "exhumation"—for which he wrote a new preface. Out of a mass of books and papers brought from home he also composed and published an elaborate self-defense, *Modern Telegraphy. Some Errors of Dates of Events and of Statement in the History of Telegraphy Exposed and Rectified.* The pamphlet consists of a fifty-page narrative of his early work on the telegraph, valuably illustrated with detailed drawings, plus thirty-eight pages of letters and depositions from people who had observed his work first-hand at the time. He based his defense on what he called the "philo-logical position"—the literal meaning of the Greek *tele graphos:* "I WRITE, AT A DISTANCE." All telegraphs before his own, that is, had been semaphores, designed to communicate information but not to record it. He sent dozens of copies of his pamphlets to highly placed persons in Paris and in England, and planned to take three or four hundred back with him to America.

Morse took on additional work at the International Exposition. He accepted a federal appointment to the show as Honorary Commissioner of the American government. This involved writing a substantial report for the State Department on the telegraph display. He and his family watched the opening grand review of the French army from the Emperor's own gallery—an unbeatable view of the 60,000 Zouaves, grenadiers, and foot soldiers colorfully defiling below. Afterward they mingled at a reception given by the City of Paris at the Hôtel de Ville for visiting dignitaries, including Bismarck and the King of Prussia, awesomely lighted by 70,000 candles.

Morse had plenty of company at the Exposition. Between April and October 1867 the fair drew over six million spectators. They included the crowned heads of state large and small—"as much of this world's glory," he said, "as has been seen in one spot since Solomon's time." The fairground stood on the Champs de Mars, in easy walking distance of his house, pennants everywhere flying from tall poles. The vast exhibition building was laid out as seven concentric iron, brick, and glass ovals, something like nested racetracks. Inside, the various national pavilions offered thousands of displays of arts and industry— "the world in epitome," Morse said. Despite the overtones of a universal common bond—the gold prize medals were stamped "Social Harmony"—some criticized the Exposition as vulgarly materialistic and socially conservative. Little could be seen there of the hordes of urban poor, the quite other Paris of ragpickers, beggars, and teenaged prostitutes. Emile Zola called the event an "extravaganza of lies."

Morse however found it all intensely interesting, not least the strong showing of Albert Bierstadt, Frederick Church, John Frederick Kensett, and other American painters in the art section. He also reported to Sidney on the display of the "Morse Bathometer" his brother had invented, though with discouraging news about its reception. Mostly he inspected the huge array of telegraphic apparatus laid out by seventy-five exhibitors—transmitters, receivers, batteries, magnets, insulation, and the like submitted by inventors and manufacturers not only from Europe, America, and Great Britain but also from Scandinavia, Turkey, Egypt, and Russia.

Press reaction to the display of recently invented telegraphs was divided. One French newspaper remarked that the new devices "function satisfactorily, but can't supplant Morse." Contrarily, the Paris *Moniteur* observed that years earlier Morse's telegraph would have dominated the Exposition, but no longer did. "*Ce n'est sans doute plus qu'un roi détrôné*"—the Morse system is now nothing more than an overthrown king. For himself, Morse saw in the new instruments nothing so much as the features of his own. He could pass by scarcely any of them, he said, "that I do not hear the cry of *father.*"

Morse attended the award ceremony at the close of the Exposition, held before 20,000 persons including the Emperor, the Sultan of Turkey, and the Prince of Wales. In the telegraph section, one Grand Prize went to Cyrus Field for his transatlantic cable. Morse felt a fresh pang of resentment and exclusion when another Grand Prize went to the Kentucky music teacher David Hughes, for an improved version of his piano-like printing telegraph—the device that Field's company had threatened to use in competition with Morse lines. "Many of my friends," Morse commented, "think I ought to have received some prize of the kind as the original Inventor of the Recording Telegraph." Adept at preserving his pride, however, he reasoned that he had received a "*Grander Prize*" in his indemnity from the nations of Europe, and the provisional adoption of his system on all international lines. "An Honorary notice would of course [have] been agreeable, but in my case would be *supererogatory.*"

Getting started on his report to the State Department, Morse obtained a catalog of all the telegraphic apparatus and supplies at the Exposition, covering the displays of dozens of manufacturers. He also collected statistics about the use of the telegraph in various countries. This sometimes meant having the information translated into English from scientific journals in German and other languages. Assimilating the material and writing it up while abroad, in time for the next session of Congress, proved to be exhausting: "I shall think myself fortunate if I do not break down under this load." To escape the summer heat of Paris he rented a six-room cottage on the Isle of Wight, hoping to write there as he and his family enjoyed the fine air and the sea bathing. He could not get around the pile of documents, however. In frustration, he resigned himself to completing the report when he returned to America.

Morse did return. Although he sometimes spoke of his life in Paris as "my exile" and thought of settling there, the dissipation of European society began to wear on him. He longed again for the quiet of Locust Grove and a Sunday at New York's Madison Square Church, "the steady, rational, religious habits of our own Countrymen." Since adolescence the Son of The Geographer had yearned to travel. Heading home he was nearly eighty years old, and crossing the Atlantic for the sixteenth time: "my age admonishes me that, in all probability, I shall never again visit Europe."

Although more than a quarter century in use, Morse's telegraph remained for many people an astonishment—"the greatest triumph of the human mind," as one newspaper put it, "the most direct proof of man's conquest of nature." It had spread ever more rapidly, too; the more stations that became connected the faster the network grew. And telegraphy now reached Asia. In 1870 a line went up in the Mikado's palace and sent the first message in Japan, reading: "The Emperor is highly pleased with the wonderful Western invention." The Chinese government had been wary of the telegraph as a threat to its sovereignty, a means of prying the country open to foreign influence. But in 1871, after much public and official resistance, a four-digit code representing Chinese characters began whizzing through the *dianxian*, "lightning wires."

Morse's globe-circling invention gave him a quasi-mythical stature not much less fabulous than that of Washington. Engravings of him hung in many American homes, based on Christian Schussele's famous *Men of Progress* (1862), a group portrait that imagines nineteen American inventors gathered in one room. Morse sits at the central table beside his telegraph, the focal point of the scene. Visitors to the U.S. Capitol who peered upward to the dome, now frescoed by Constantino Brumidi's *Apotheosis of Washington* (1866), saw a giant Raphaelesque Morse, in company with Benjamin Franklin, Robert Fulton, and Minerva, goddess of the arts. Americans in all stations of life sent worshipful fan letters: "I can hardly tell how to express myself to you of the great obligation the People are under to you for the perciveriance in your worke [*sic*]." Other letters reached Morse's town house with no more address than "Inventor of the Telegraph/New York City." A photograph arrived from a couple he did not know, showing the child they had christened "S. F. B. Morse Ebbinghaus."

Christian Schussele, *Men of Progress*
(National Portrait Gallery)

Despite his fabulous renown, Morse's last four years were a grim crescendo of unhappiness and abuse. Immediately upon his return to the United States, he discovered that Locust Grove had been burglarized, the locks broken. His town house, mistreated by its tenants, needed thousands of dollars in repairs. Pictures he stored in the cellar had been eaten through by rats.

Four months later Morse learned that his brother Richard was gone. Richard had never overcome what he called his "mental depression arising from ill health." Wandering as usual, he had died in

Bavaria of liver cancer. "And so *the triple cord is broken*," Morse wrote, "the youngest, is the first of us to pass the dark valley." He felt the blow more than he supposed possible.

The political situation distressed him, too, hardly less so than when he had left the country. The House had voted to impeach President Andrew Johnson. The vice presidential candidates in the November 1868 election were accused of corruption and drunkenness. Europeans would think the country depraved, "that our choice of Rulers is made from a class more fitted for the State's prison than the State thrones."

Even occasions that should have comforted Morse became trials. He had, of course, often been feted, but never before on the scale of the gargantuan six-hour banquet given in his honor by Western Union. The *Times* devoted virtually its entire front page to reporting what it called "one of the most magnificent affairs of the kind that ever took place in this City." For the event, on the evening of December 29, Delmonico's restaurant exuberantly sprouted profusions of flowers and flags, a representation of Franklin's kite experiment, a statue of Jove launching bolts of lightning, among much else. A sixteen-piece orchestra played such operatic selections as "Barbe Bleu" and "La Grande Duchesse."

The many eminences among the more than two hundred diners included the presidents of Yale and Columbia, the British ambassador to America, the Attorney General of the United States, and Salmon P. Chase, Chief Justice of the United States Supreme Court. Morse's family and friends attended—Sarah and their daughter Lela, Sidney Morse, Amos Kendall, Cyrus Field, Asher B. Durand, William Cullen Bryant. Telegrams arrived from Admiral David Farragut ("Damn the torpedoes") and from President-elect Ulysses S. Grant. The menu, adorned with an engraving of Morse bemedaled, offered ten courses of *Escaloppes de bass, aux éperlans dauphins, Grouses en salmis aux truffles,* and *Pain de faisans à la Chantilly,* with six courses of wine and champagne, not to mention oysters, sorbets, sweets, and desserts. The guests hoisted sixteen toasts during the evening, with lengthy responses and speeches that heaped praise on Morse until after midnight.

But the regal blowout was not exactly the tribute it seemed. Western Union very probably dreamed up the event to win public support for itself. By now Western Union had absorbed all the chief American telegraph companies. Using Morse's system, it commanded 37,000

miles of telegraph line and administered over 2000 stations. For this
the transcontinental corporate giant was denounced by reformers and
politicians who considered monopolies unhealthy in American economic life. At the time of the banquet, Congress was looking into proposals for the government to build and operate its own telegraph
system under the Post Office Department, in competition with Western
Union; or, alternatively, to buy out and operate all existing telegraph
lines. And Western Union fought every move toward government control, publishing countless pamphlets in its own defense and lobbying
vigorously in Washington.

Surely by no accident, a key speaker at Delmonico's was William
Orton, the tall, dignified president of Western Union. No one had
been more energetic than he in speechmaking and testifying before
congressional committees to oppose plans for federal intervention. In
addressing the banqueters he attacked such plans as unconstitutional,
amounting to government interference with free enterprise. "The
American telegraph is on its trial," he said, "and it feels honored on
this occasion that that trial is in the presence of the Chief-Justice of the
United States . . . and the distinguished Attorney-General of the
United States."

When Morse rose to speak, introduced by Chief Justice Chase, the
two hundred guests stood up to give cheer after cheer. When the
applause subsided a little it broke out again and again. He spoke for at
least an hour, mostly explaining once more the grounds of his and
America's claims to priority. But indirectly he also addressed the issue
of government control, by relating his experiences with Congress a
quarter century ago. When he applied for an appropriation to erect
an experimental line, he recalled, some House members ridiculed his
invention, saying half the money should be given to experiments in
mesmerism. And after the demonstrated success of his Washington-
Baltimore line, he had offered his invention to the government for
$100,000—and got no response, the then–Postmaster General having
informed Congress that the telegraph would never produce revenue.
He told the distinguished audience that he neither advocated nor
opposed the plans now before Congress. He merely offered his
remarks as timely, "useful to remember in endeavoring to reach a just
judgment in the matter."

Morse's recollections, however, can have left little doubt about
how far Congress could be entrusted with the future of American

telegraphy. He did not escape brutal criticism for his remarks, especially in James Gordon Bennett's *Herald,* which favored government
control. In several editorials the *Herald* questioned the intent of the
banquet: "It is difficult . . . to resist the conviction that the affair was
got up less for the purpose of honoring Professor Morse than of
advancing the interests of the Western Union Telegraph Company." If
proof were needed, the *Herald* said, William Orton's "execrable"
remarks made it clear that the homage to Morse was propaganda for
an offensive, "a decoy duck to affect a great lobby movement upon
Congress." The revered guest and the influential diners had been
bought off, "to spread abroad the erroneous impression that the Professor and the company assembled to meet him were all opposed to
the absorption of the telegraph in the postal system."

Whether Morse understood that the *Pain de faisans* was in reality
decoy duck is debatable. He may have conspired with Western Union,
willing to endorse its cause. He approved the company's drive for
power, having always believed that only under a single management
could the nation's telegraph network provide efficient and reliable
communications: "[Western Union] is becoming, doubtless, a *monopoly,*" he told Kendall, "but . . . its unity is in reality a public advantage."
And he had a large stake in the company's success. All of his patents
having expired in 1867, he could no longer look to them for income.
Instead he had sunk his money in Western Union, making it "the *basket* in which I *have all* my *eggs*"—eggs here being stocks apparently
worth $400,000. On the other hand, Morse may simply have been
gulled. Western Union would not have been the first seeker after
power and respectability to play on his hunger for medals, diplomas,
honorary titles, and testimonial dinners.

Morse's hefty report to the State Department turned out to be not
much more welcome than his speech at Delmonico's. Between the
writing and the arduous collection or making of diagrams, maps, photographs, and statistical tables, the work only crept along. He failed to
meet several deadlines: "I fear I have assumed at my age, a task above
my strength." As he labored, too, the report became less a review of
the Paris Exposition than a personal testament, "to settle once for all
the disputed claim of my right to be considered the Inventor of the
Telegraph proper."

Morse's claim, however, had expanded. Although his telegraph
entitled him to be considered the most influential inventor America

had so far produced, he had come to call his own almost every feature of its development, as if conceding one conceded them all. "I assert a truth, when I say that the Telegraphic system which I devised in 1832 . . . has had no essential improvement added to it, to this day." He granted importance to advances in conducting wires, batteries, and the like. But whenever he received suggestions for some improving modification of his basic apparatus he bluntly repulsed them as attempts to question his priority and nibble away at his reputation. "In regard to the '*Electro-magnetic conductor*' of which you inquire my opinion . . . I really see nothing new or particularly useful in the plan." "The idea of such railroad telegraphing is not new. I patented in France in 1838 a system of Railroad telegraphing." "An arrangement for prolonging the *sound* of the *dash* in two ways, differing from yours, I put in operation as far back as 1844."

Morse completed the 300-page manuscript around June 1869. He sent it on to Washington, where it was vetted by Professor W. P. Blake, general editor of the government reports. Surprised and disappointed by what Morse submitted, he twice wrote back tactfully asking for revisions. He recommended large cuts in the material on priority. Morse should take it for granted that he had invented "*the*" telegraph: "For you to argue it . . . implies, at the least, that there is room for explanation and discussion." Blake also asked for revision of another matter, "upon which I know that you are sensitive." Scientists generally acknowledged the "radical importance and value" to the telegraph of the experiments of Joseph Henry, who went unmentioned in the report.

Morse conceded that on the priority issue he had been "too weakly sensitive." But he more than ever had it in for Henry. He now believed that the influential attack on him published a decade ago by a prestigious committee of the Smithsonian Institution had actually been written by Henry himself, deceptively "prepared for the Committee to father." Blake's criticism caused him much puzzled distress. He drafted memo after memo and note after note, trying again and again to come up with some innocuous way of bringing Henry into the report.

Late in November the Government Printing Office issued Morse's work, as *Examination of the Telegraphic Apparatus and the Processes in Telegraphy*. Whatever he may have cut from the manuscript, the 162-page published report remained largely a brief for himself, his final and fullest attempt to compile an unassailable historical record of his invention. "The Morse system was the introduction and the addition of a new art to the means of communicating at a distance. . . . It was emphatically the first realization of a telegraph." In discussing the recently created telegraphs exhibited in Paris he explained that people tend to mistake modifications for entirely new things. "It will not be deemed egotistical on the part of an inventor," he wrote, "if in the attempts of others to improve his invention he should now and then recognize the familiar features of his own offspring, and claim the paternity." He therefore traced back to himself most of the "improvements" on display, including the invention of the "acoustic semaphore" (i.e., his sounder) and of submarine telegraphy. In passing he mentioned Henry's work on the lifting power of electromagnets, slyly putting Henry down as someone who demonstrated "the practicability of ringing a bell by means of electro-magnetism at a distance."

Morse's difficulty in completing the report made up the lesser part of his misery at the time. He was forced to do some of his writing in bed, having injured his leg worse than ever before. Slipping on the stairs at Locust Grove, he fell with his whole weight and broke the leg in two places below the knee. Given his age, some feared he would not survive the shock. The injury laid him up for more than three months. After that, grown pale, he managed to hobble about on two sawhorse-like supports.

In August, having sent in his report but apparently still bedridden, Morse was confronted by a family crisis. Susan, Charles, and Finley, the children of his first marriage, had turned out to be helpless adults—gullible, sickly, or disabled. Two of the boys from his second marriage were turning out to be scoundrels. Twenty-year-old Arthur, for all his promise as a violinist, had a weakness for bad companions, a "*disgusting filthy*" habit of chewing tobacco, and little self-control. While abroad, in Dresden, he had nearly gotten into a duel with some young German army officers. His "rude brusqueness," Morse lamented, belonged not to the family's ideal of the Christian Gentleman but to "corner grocery New York rowdies."

That August, Arthur got into serious trouble—serious enough for Morse to book him passage on a ship bound for Valparaiso. Hustling Arthur out of the country to Chile seems a desperate move, suggesting some offense on the order of fathering an illegitimate child. Whatever the trouble, it left Morse "greatly depressed." He asked Sidney to come to Locust Grove to discuss the situation. Perhaps worse, Christmas Day came and went without a letter from Arthur or report of him. Morse and Sarah wept, hoping he was safe. "We cannot forget him," Morse said, "although he has given us such great pain & anxiety." After more than five months he still had not heard from Arthur and felt unstrung: "No one, not even any in the family, can know the secret yearnings of my heart towards him. Many are the hours when I am in bed that I think of him, and pray for him."

Morse worried that Arthur's brother Willie, now seventeen, might also be headed for some Valparaiso. Morse had sent him for schooling to Phillips Academy in Andover, where he had been sent himself. There Willie showed a taste for vulgar "Velocipede rinks," patronized by "low company." The school notified Morse that the boy had played hookey, too. "See what evil it has already brought upon your poor brother Arthur, and what grief it has caused us all," Morse wrote to him; "Oh, my dear Willie, are you going to be also a source of grief to us." He had greatly desired the boy to master Greek and Latin, and to follow his father and grandfather into Yale. But he began thinking it might do Willie more good to expect something different from him. The boy was "unusually strong" and might succeed in some profession that called on his physical gifts.

In November 1869, just as his government report appeared and as he waited anxiously to hear from Arthur, Morse had one more shock. Amos Kendall was dead. He died in Washington, a wealthy man but desolate. He left unfinished the biography of Andrew Jackson he had worked on for years. No complainer in his lifetime, he brooded near the end over the anguish he had endured, including the deaths of nine siblings, the murder of one son, and the deaths by typhoid of another son and a wife. "My first marriage was into a family consisting of a father, mother, four sons, and three daughters. They are all dead. My second marriage was into a family consisting of a father, mother, two sons, and two daughters. They are all dead. I have had two wives, five sons, and nine daughters. The wives and the sons are all gone, and only four daughters are left."

Kendall had been declining for three months, so his passing was not unexpected. Morse nevertheless felt bereft and damaged. He had confided in Kendall as in a father. Unlike many others, Kendall had never manipulated him or betrayed his trust. Thankful, too, for Kendall's sound business sense and untiring effort, he grieved that he had lost his one necessary friend—"to whose energy & skill . . . I owe (under God) the comparative comfort which a kind Providence has permitted me to enjoy in my advanced age."

The record of Morse's life is scanty for the fifteen or so months between the end of 1869 and the summer of 1871. He complained of weakness, and in answering his correspondence sometimes used an amanuensis. Commuting between two residences had become wearying. He considered selling Locust Grove, although parting with it, he said, "is like amputating my right arm." Items in the press occasionally announced that his health was failing.

Morse tried to keep up his many interests. He followed political movements abroad; endorsed Cyrus Field's proposal for laying a San Francisco–to–Yokohama transpacific cable; agreed to serve as a vice president of the just-launched Metropolitan Museum of Art, with no duties to perform. The best of his remaining energy he devoted to Christian charities and evangelical work: "if I can use the little strength, and the few years that remain in furthering the cause of our Divine Master, I ought perhaps to rouze myself." He found strength enough at least to address a convention of the Y.M.C.A., and draft a memorial to Czar Alexander II on behalf of persecuted Protestants in the Baltic provinces. He happily gave consent to Finley—now forty-five and seeming to him "old & sunburnt"—to become confirmed in the Episcopal church, whose clergy he had always respected.

For many years Morse had fought foreign conspiracies against America, as he and others viewed anti-democratic forces abroad. But unknown to him, a cabal was now forming at home to make his last days a torment. It grew out of widely publicized plans for erecting two statues of him. The National Monument Association proposed placing his figure on the pedestal of a huge sculptured memorial to the telegraph, in Washington. Western Union also proposed a statue, to be raised in New York City. As President William Orton explained in a company circular,

> The venerable "Father of all the Telegraphs" . . . is nearing rapidly the verge of that dark river from whose further shore no message ever comes. It becomes, therefore, all those who know and love him . . . not to delay their tributes of respect and affection.

Maybe so, but with Congress now debating a bill for establishing a federal postal telegraph system, Morse had good reason to be wary of further homage from Western Union. He managed to think of the statue as a gesture of friendship. "I rather shrink from the notoriety while I cannot but feel gratified at the kind feeling manifested to me personally."

Western Union telegraphed a message through its nationwide network, soliciting $1 contributions from the company's superintendents, operators, and messengers. The $5000 statue was fashioned by a sculptor named Byron Pickett. He rendered Morse eight feet tall in bronze, bearded and frock-coated, standing beside a waist-high column supporting a telegraph receiver. Given a preview, Morse thought the figure both successful aesthetically and a faithful likeness.

Western Union got permission from local officials to place the statue at a prominent, indeed celebrated point in New York City, the Central Park Mall. Monuments to Shakespeare and Schiller already ornamented this promenade, but Morse was the first American to be honored there. The statue was raised on a seven-foot-high granite pedestal, the name **MORSE** boldly chiseled into the block. It was unveiled on June 10, 1871, a cool sunny day, before a crowd estimated at ten thousand persons. The sea of top hats, bustles, and parasols included a thousand or so telegraph workers who had come from around the country. After William Orton and the Governor of Massachusetts threw aside the drapery, a military band played "The Star-Spangled Banner." Then William Cullen Bryant addressed the throng, remarking that the statue could be deemed unnecessary: "the great globe itself has become his monument."

Morse did not attend the unveiling—out of modesty, some said. But he did come to the follow-up ceremony the same evening, held at the plush Academy of Music. Opened in 1854 as the largest opera house in the world, the hall seated 4000 but was packed for the occasion. In the dramatic highlight of the evening, the telegraph instruments used on the original Washington-Baltimore line were placed at center stage, but set up to connect with lines all over the world. A young female operator clicked off to the global telegraph community a greeting chosen by Morse, the same one he had selected for the opening of the transatlantic cable: "Glory to God in the highest, on earth peace, good will to men." As she left the table, Morse approached it,

Morse statue in Central Park
(Princeton University Library)

escorted by Orton. The tremendous applause ceased as his hand touched the key and began slowly tapping the letters of his name in the dotdash code. As he came to the final *e*, a single dot, the telegraphers in the audience stood up, cheering and waving handkerchiefs. Speaking from the stage, Orton commented to the crowd, "Thus the Father of the Telegraph bids farewell to his children."

Responses to Morse's message began coming in to the Academy of Music from all over the earth. They arrived first from nearby cities, then from New Orleans, Quebec, San Francisco, lastly from Hong Kong and Bombay. Morse was almost overcome with emotion. By one account, he sat for some time with his head in his hands, weeping, trying to regain his self-control.

The tribute left Morse feeling washed out for days afterward: "I

Morse Celebration at the Academy of Music
(*Frank Leslie's Illustrated Newspaper,* July 1, 1871)

find it more difficult to bear up with the overwhelming praise that is poured out without measure, than with the trials of my former life. . . . the effect on me, strange as it may seem, is rather depressing than exhilirating." Others also found the event depressing, but for different reasons. Amanda Vail—Alfred's second wife, now his widow—was present at the Academy, together with Vail's three sons, her stepsons. It angered her that Morse's valedictory address to the audience allowed Alfred but a single sentence, thanking him and his family for their financial aid. She considered the acknowledgment "*meagre.*" Her dead husband, after all, had made many improvements in Morse's apparatus, and in her view had also invented the dotdash code and suggested the submarine cable. Altogether he had been Morse's "truest, best, most faithful, most efficient friend." And having made Morse and Kendall rich, Alfred died poor. On hearing her husband merely alluded to, she said, and only for his financial aid, "my whole soul filled with indignation."

Amanda Vail confronted Morse at his town house two days after the event. The interview is known only through her account of it, which depicts Morse's behavior as glib and hypocritical. Morse ushered her into his library cordially, she recorded, but was embarrassed to see her. She frankly told him that his remarks at the Academy "greatly disappointed" her, they said so little about Alfred:

> "Professor Morse you know that I have in my house an immense amount of manuscript, letters, journals, drawings left by Mr. Vail and I have heard him say that some of the most important parts of the telegraph were his invention and the proof of it existed in these papers."

By her account, Morse evaded the accusation:

> "Oh yes, Mr. Vail preserved his letters and papers just as I did. I know I intended to have gone out to Morristown and seen them."

With this, Morse went to a cabinet, took out a box, and showed her what it contained—his medals, the glittering gifts of foreign courts and potentates. "Some of these belong to you," he said. "I am going to have some of these jewels set for you. I have for some time been intending to have it done."

But Vail doubted that Morse would ever do so. It seemed to her that he handled the medals as if unable to part with them, "regarding with eye intent these gifts of God he had so long worshipped!" At that moment, some new guests entered, giving him an excuse to get rid of her. "I am glad to have seen you," he said, handing her a photograph of himself. So ended what she called "this *unsatisfactory* visit to Professor Morse the *Inventor!* of the telegraph."

Whatever Amanda Vail may actually have said to Morse, it hardly suggested the depth of her bitterness. Unknown to him, she had for some time been gathering supporters to prove her dead husband the driving force behind the telegraph, the man "to whom he owed his *fame* and *fortune*." She sent extracts from Alfred's letters and other papers to everyone who wrote about the telegraph or about American technology, pressing them to give Vail the credit she believed he deserved. She was listened to. Morse had never lacked critics, and since Western Union's Delmonico banquet, several had grown increasingly irritated by the public attention lavished upon him.

In two of Morse's former associates, Amanda Vail found especially willing allies—the much-scarred Henry O'Reilly and ever-vengeful F. O. J. Smith. Since his failure in the telegraph business, O'Reilly had moved on to other, also unsuccessful ventures: a machine called the Terracultor, meant to replace the plow by pulverizing soil; the National Anti-Monopoly Cheap Freight Railway League. The ex-"Napoleon of the Telegraph" had been constantly in debt, and one of his sons, a Union soldier, had been killed during the Civil War. His grudge against Morse took in both past defeats at court and present neglect. "I projected, constructed and organized the first great range of about eight thousand miles," he boasted. Yet neither in print nor before an audience did Morse ever mention him. He responded eagerly to Vail's campaign to disabuse the public. "Never was greater fraud & humbug about any inventions or patents," he wrote; "it is high time that one of the most monstrous humbugs and frauds of the age should be thoroughly blown up."

Fog Smith needed no prodding to join Vail and O'Reilly. He was, as an associate correctly remarked, "one of the most heartless and vindictive villains that ever trod in shoe leather." Involved the past few years in water companies, railroads, and numerous other business projects—and many more lawsuits—he had been indicted by a grand jury in 1864 for six cases of adultery, and convicted the following year of subornation of perjury. He encouraged Amanda Vail to think that her husband had transformed "*very nearly the entire mechanism*," turning a gadget into a practicable invention: "the absolute monopoly . . . to which Professor Morse aspires, must become divided, when the public shall possess the actual truths of history." He particularly wanted to expose the testimonials to Morse as undeserved and self-serving charades staged by William Orton: "the world will be astonished at the *humbuggery* that has been practiced from *sordid motives*, principally by the instrumentalities of the Western Union Telegraph Company in and with the name of Professor Morse as inventor of the telegraph."

During the last six months of 1871, Vail, O'Reilly, and Smith made a concerted effort to destroy Morse's reputation. For ammunition they had at their disposal the depositions and other testimony in voluminous court records, and several hundred personal letters Morse had written to them over the years. These they now exchanged with each other, collated, and reassembled to build a ruinous case against him. Using such material, O'Reilly and Smith had already been composing what they called a *Colloquial History* of the telegraph—dedicated, for extra punch, to Joseph Henry. "Professor Morse," they announced in their preface, "has been too ambitious of realising and enjoying prematurely, a pretension to immortality as one of the great creative, original minds among men." In reality, his pretensions as an inventor were "groundless, and hollow, as soap bubles [*sic*] which amuse frolicksome childhood."

Vail was not through. She put O'Reilly and Smith in touch with her cousin Lyman W. Case, who was writing a chapter on telegraphy for a forthcoming encyclopedic volume entitled *Great Industries of the United States*. O'Reilly and Smith promised to supply him with evidence of "the gross deception which this Morse has practised upon the world." Vail also joined Smith in protesting to the National Monument Association its plan to cap the proposed telegraph memorial in Washington with a statue of Morse. "Prof. Morse cannot justly claim, nor will authentic history sustain such pre-eminence for himself," Smith wrote; "it is my conviction, that the statue most worthy to stand upon the pedestal of such monument would be, that of the man of true science . . . and that man is, Professor Joseph Henry."

The results of this cabal began to reach Morse in mid-January 1872. At the time he was uniquely vulnerable. A few weeks earlier, on December 23, his brother Sidney had died at the age of seventy-eight, following a stroke or heart attack. By one account Morse sat beside him as he lay paralyzed on his bed, speaking into his ear, but Sidney gave no sign that he heard. Morse found consolation in knowing that his brother—a deeply religious man, equal to him in piety—was now "a happy spirit in the presence of his Savior." But he and Sidney had always been extremely close and, as the minister of his congregation put it, he "began to die also." Feeble and lame, his head pains growing more intense, he became housebound.

It was in this deteriorated condition that Morse came upon articles in the press with outworn titles like "Who Invented the Telegraph."

The impulse to freshen such stale news, he discovered, came from Fog Smith's letter to the Monument Association, calling on it to honor Henry, not Morse, on the telegraph memorial. Smith cared nothing for Henry, Morse believed: "It is simply a matter of spite, carrying out his intense & smothered antipathy to me." But Smith's protests, and those of Vail and O'Reilly, succeeded in scaring off the memorial committee and, according to one of its members, "killed the project." No statue of Morse was erected in Washington. "I plead guilty," Smith said, contented.

In February—perhaps the most harrowing month of his life—Morse received advance sheets of "The American Magnetic Telegraph," a sixteen-page chapter from the forthcoming *Great Industries of the United States*. It seemed to him the monstrous climax to a lifetime of slanders, "the most atrocious and vile attack upon me, which has ever appeared in print." The writer wiped him from the record as an unscrupulous charlatan, eliminated him as an utter fake:

> In the whole range of "pious frauds," romantic imaginings, and spurious pretences of all kinds, perhaps there never was a more ludicrous and lamentable delusion practised than that which . . . has been practised upon the credulous masses, causing them to believe that Prof. Morse is the inventor of the practical telegraph known by his name.

Morse could not have produced the so-called Morse telegraph, the writer went on, because he lacked the requisite scientific knowledge, mechanical skill, and entrepreneurial ability. These had been supplied by its actual inventors: by Joseph Henry, "the legitimate father of the American electro-magnetic telegraph"; by Alfred Vail, "the brains of the mechanical portion"; and by F. O. J. Smith, who "made it a commercial success." The writer also trashed the "almost divine honors" recently bestowed on Morse by the crowds of dupes Western Union had lured to Central Park and the Academy of Music, "as the necessary stock actors in a play."

Morse sidelined and annotated passage after passage of the proof sheets: "false. . . . false. . . . false. . . . false. . . . oh!" He wrote to the publishers—Burr and Hyde, in Hartford—asking them to withhold the chapter from the published volume, as being "spiteful, distorted and untrue." Probably because the chapter contained information from his private correspondence with Smith and O'Reilly, he believed it to be the work of these "ancient enemies." For confirmation he wrote repeatedly and urgently to Lyman Case, editor of the volume, unaware that Case had written the chapter himself, from material supplied by Smith and O'Reilly and by his cousin Amanda Vail.

Case again and again fended off Morse's inquiries. He said that the name or names of the author(s) might be given out later; that the "chief author" was little known; that he was too busy to reply. Morse never learned how the information in the chapter was collected, or who shaped it into a murderous assault on his reputation. Nor was the chapter suppressed. The popular volume in which it appeared, a celebration of American technology, quickly sold 10,000 copies.

February brought another jarring surprise from the past. Upon the death of Archbishop M. J. Spalding of Louisville, the New York *Herald* published a eulogistic letter to the editor recalling the prelate's newspaper duel with Morse eighteen years before. Morse had attributed to Lafayette the remark that "*American liberty can be destroyed only by the Popish clergy.*" Spalding had countered with a pamphlet and newspaper articles claiming that the partial quotation reversed the meaning of Lafayette's full statement, which was that Americans had no reason to fear Catholicism. His admirer in the *Herald* now recalled that Spalding's powerful arguments, "the rude force with which his blows fell," had compelled Morse to retract. Morse saw the letter and in his greatly weakened state wrote a five-and-a-half-page retort—a full column of print presenting a detailed case for the attribution. "I retracted nothing," he said. He mocked Spalding's eulogist for thinking that attempts to defame him would go unnoticed: "He may have supposed I was dead."

During the same few weeks Morse received a troubling letter from his son Willie, in New Orleans. Having apparently quit or been withdrawn from school at Andover, Willie had headed west to seek his fortune in Texas. "We part with him with great anxiety for his welfare," Morse said. There was reason to worry, for the physically powerful young man was turning out to be much like his brother Arthur, impulsive and hot-tempered. Morse had sent him off with money to start a business, but the letter asked for more money. He feared that instead of settling down, Willie was dawdling with his much-loved dogs and gun, and reaching for the bottle. "I hope you keep rigidly to your resolution not to touch for drink any alcoholic liquor," he wrote to him; "we pray for you that you may be kept from temptation."

Ill and besieged, Morse at the same time tried futilely to reach a man named John Lindsay, to whom he had handed over more than $25,000. The nervewracking predicament arose from his son Charles' continued inability to support himself and his family. "There is a 'screw loose' somewhere," Morse told him, "with all my efforts to help you, you are just where you were years ago." Making one more effort, he had set Charles up as manager of a store near Wall Street, the Lippiatt Silver Plate Company. He arranged for the job by purchasing stock in the company and allowing his name to be used as President. To his grief, he had learned a few months earlier that as President he was liable for Lippiatt's many debts. This Lindsay, an acquaintance of Charles, had persuaded him that his best strategy was to acquire the company.

Now, having given Lindsay $25,000 to buy Lippiatt Silver Plate, Morse was unable to reach him. He had nothing to show for his money but dread, "a state of anxiety which is seriously affecting my health." He died without learning that the swindler—later arrested for fraud—had bought the company for less than half the money and kept the rest for himself.

In March, Morse suffered severe head pains and became so weak that he had to remain in bed. All but one of his last few letters are in the hand of his son Arthur, his physician having forbidden him to read or write. He apparently defied both orders, however. He probably read Fog Smith's latest anti-Morse tract, *History Getting Right on the Invention of the American Electro-Magnetic Telegraph*. And he wrote in his own hand what seems to be his final letter, dated March 14. It begins: "I should be much gratified to know what part Prof. Henry has taken, if any, in this atrocious & absurd attack of F. O. J. S."

By the end of March, Morse was comatose. He briefly regained consciousness on April 1 and smiled at Sarah, but could not speak. He died just before 8 p.m. the next evening, three weeks short of his eighty-first birthday. As his death was recorded in the family Bible at Locust Grove, he "entered into life on the 2nd of April 1872."

According to his death certificate, Morse died of "Subacute Cerebral Meningitis." But his physician added a note to the document, naming a secondary or complicating cause: "Unusual anxiety & exertion of brain for some months past."

Others also understood that in his debilitated physical condition, Morse had been subjected to a punishing psychological ordeal. The

New York *Times* speculated that "the vexations and annoyances, the troubles and sorrows of the last few weeks of his life . . . contributed, in a great degree, to bring on his last fatal attack." F. O. J. Smith agreed. With rabid ill will, he told Amanda Vail that he had greatly desired Morse to live longer—to cope with the many new charges they and O'Reilly had brought against him. "But I was fearful that the strong visions recently opened to him, of *receding glory*, would overload his brain as I doubt not they did."

Coda: 1872–2000

No technological project is technological first and foremost.

—Bruno Latour, *Aramis or The Love of Technology* (1993)

B ORN TWO YEARS after the inauguration of George Washington, Samuel F. B. Morse lived through the Civil War and the first administration of President Ulysses S. Grant. In that time, the land area of the United States quadrupled and its population grew tenfold, from four to forty million people. The nation's newspapers printed front-page obituaries and lead editorials reviewing his long eventful life and assessing its significance. Many declared him one of the great men of American, perhaps of human, history. "If it is legitimate to measure a man by the magnitude of his achievements, the greatest man of the nineteenth century is dead" (Louisville *Courier-Journal*). "The first inventor of his age and century is dead!" (*Patent Right Gazette*). "Morse was, perhaps, the most illustrious American of his age" (New York *Herald*).

The encomia that followed praised Morse as, above all, a courageous benefactor. He had defied insult and injury to advance commerce, politics, journalism, and other everyday affairs—to better civilization itself. Only a few papers mentioned his influential career in painting and photography. And only a very few seem to have criticized his outspoken suspicion of immigrants and hatred of Catholics. The New York *Golden Age,* a weekly, recalled that he had passionately defended the right of one human being to hold another human being in chattel bondage: "Among the many . . . apologies for American slavery are some shameful passages from his pen."

On April 5, Morse was buried beside his brothers Sidney and Richard amid the picturesque statuary and foliage of Brooklyn's Green-Wood Cemetery, on a height overlooking the bay of New York City. His funeral occasioned a national day of mourning. Flags flew at half-mast. Telegraph operators draped their instruments in black. The New York Stock Exchange adjourned. Presses struck off elegies on Morse and Morse funeral marches. Artists gathered to express their debt for his founding of the National Academy of Design. Commenting on the nationwide outpouring of affection and praise, a speaker in Poughkeepsie offered what would have been for Morse the ultimate compliment: "Never since Washington died has such sympathetic unanimity been witnessed."

The most imposing ceremony took place on April 16 at the House of Representatives. From its gallery hung an evergreen-wreathed portrait of Morse. Members of his family sat in the semicircle facing the Speaker's desk, along with President Grant, his Cabinet, and justices of the United States Supreme Court. Throughout the memorial, receivers clicked off messages coming in from simultaneous meetings around the world—from telegraphers in London and in Java, Brigham Young in Salt Lake City, ex-President Millard Fillmore in Buffalo, the aldermen of Galveston, Texas. Typical was the telegram sent from a San Francisco gathering led by the city's mayor: "*Resolved.* That, on behalf of the citizens of San Francisco and of the people of California, we recognize the inestimable services of Professor Samuel F. B. Morse. . . . His vast conception of enlisting electricity in the work of civilization was the grandest thought of time." The collected telegrams and speeches, later published by the Government Printing Office, made a volume of 359 pages.

The often cruel controversy that had surrounded Morse's invention lingered, mostly as a family feud. Amanda Vail hunted him for the next twenty years. Next to caring for Alfred's children, she said, "I resolved that my life work . . . should be to rescue the memory of my dear husband in connection with his great work, from the oblivion into which Professor Morse had cast it." She studied Vail's voluminous papers and drawings, interviewed his co-workers, continued to exchange supposedly damning evidence against Morse with F. O. J. Smith and Henry O'Reilly.

Smith died in 1876, bankrupt and unlamented; O'Reilly died ten years later, an invalid. But Vail pressed on until her own death in 1894.

Her accusations recent and old still made news, especially her ever more vigorous claim that Alfred had devised the dotdash code. This is extremely unlikely. In his pamphlet *The American Electro Magnetic Telegraph* (1845), Alfred Vail himself remarked that the alphabet of "dots, lines and spaces" was created "on board the packet Sully, by Prof. Morse."

The feud survived into the next generation and the new century. In 1891 a Senate committee introduced a bill appropriating $10,000 to buy the "original telegraph"—invented, the committee said, by Alfred Vail. Forty-year-old Lela Morse wrote to the committee protesting the form of the bill, "as the daughter of Professor Samuel F. B. Morse, the inventor of the original telegraph instrument." Two years later, officials of the World's Columbian Exhibition in Chicago set a medallion of Vail on a frieze around the Electrical Building, beside one of Morse. Objections from Morse's family persuaded them to remove it. As late as 1912, Morse's youngest son, Edward, publicly traded charges and countercharges with Vail's son J. Cummings Vail, in the *Century* magazine.

By that time, Morse had few immediate descendants to defend his name. For his legacy to them was not only his renown but also his neglect and inner turbulence. Of the children by his first marriage, Susan, motherless since before the age of six, had been in poor health most of her adult life, afflicted by what Morse had called "*nervousness.*" "I feel sometimes as if I had no desire whatever to live," she once wrote to him. She became estranged from her husband, the Puerto Rico planter Edward Lind. Their son, Charles, the gifted young painter who was Morse's favorite grandson, committed suicide in 1880, while in his twenties. Five years later Susan followed him into the void. Sixty-six years old, she boarded a Spanish steamer en route to Havana and disappeared. "It is supposed," the New York *Times* reported, "she threw herself into the sea in a temporary fit of mental aberration."

Morse's son Charles, long unable to support his family, worked for Western Union during the last few years of his life. He died in 1887, having helped to establish the Morse system in Venezuela. A dozen years later, his son Bleecker, Morse's grandson, committed suicide, at the age of fifty-one. Depressed after being let go from his job in a telephone and telegraph company, he hanged himself from a rope tied to his children's swing.

Of the fate of Morse's disabled son Finley there is little account, beyond his having passed away in old age, living with a relative, as he had almost his entire life.

Of Morse's four children from his second marriage, Arthur, the once-promising violinist, died brutally in New Orleans in 1876, at the age of twenty-seven. The city's *Daily Picayune* reported that on the evening of July 17 he fell (jumped?) from the platform of a car on the Pontchartrain railroad. Seeing him about to go over the guardrail, a fellow passenger grabbed at his trousers but could not hold him. Arthur dropped onto the tracks between cars. The train rolled over him, the newspaper said, "crushing one of his arms, his leg, and shattering his skull, leaving the mask only."

Morse's powerful, liquor-and-gun-loving son Willie made his way to Comanche territory in Texas. Around 1910 he spent eighty-four days in jail for shooting to death an Indian named Juan Amador, in Valle La Trinidad, Mexico. Released when it was proved he had acted in self-defense, he joined Buffalo Bill's Wild West show, as a cowboy.

Morse's daughter Lela and his son Edward perpetuated him less destructively. Edward became a modestly successful painter. After studying in Paris with the vastly popular artist Adolphe Bouguereau, he taught for a while at the Art Students League before settling in Pittsfield, Massachusetts, where he died in 1923. Lela married a British concert pianist, Franz Rummel, and became an expatriate. For some time she lived in Berlin. Sarah Morse, her mother, died while visiting her there in 1901, having recently sold Locust Grove. Lela moved permanently to Paris, where she died in 1937.

Morse's lightning out-survived her, but not much longer. In May 1944, Allied armies were poised to advance on Rome and to land the largest invasion force in history on the beaches of Normandy. Yet on May 15, Congress paused to commemorate the opening of the country's first telegraph line in the same month one hundred years earlier. On that astonishing occasion, Samuel F. B. Morse, in the chamber of the Supreme Court, had tapped out to Alfred Vail in Baltimore the text of Numbers 23: 23—"What hath God wrought!" The event was faithfully reenacted in 1944 with operators at the same places, and broadcast nationally over CBS and NBC. The Army Signal Corps and the Navy picked up the Washington-Baltimore message and transmitted it in two directions around the world.

Americans found many other ways of remembering. The Post Office Department issued a Morse commemorative stamp. The Metropolitan Museum of Art opened an exhibition of Morse's paintings. A new Liberty ship was launched, christened *Samuel F. B. Morse.* New York University dedicated a Morse Study Hall. Topical questions were posed to contestants on such popular radio quiz shows as *Dr. I. Q., Double or Nothing,* and *Take It or Leave It:* Which came first, the telegraph or the telephone?

At the time, some two hundred million telegraph messages were being sent annually in the United States. But the telephone and Teletype had already taken over much of the work of the telegraph. And after the war telegraphy largely disappeared as an important information technology. Western Union sent its last Morse telegram in 1960. Scores of transatlantic cables had been laid since Cyrus Field's first success. But the last of them was abandoned in 1966, the insulated copper conducting wires giving way to digital fiber-optic cables of vast capacity capable of transmitting live TV and e-mail.

In the 1990s the U.S. military and coast guard phased out Morse code in their operations. Eliminating human watchkeepers, they replaced it with the Global Maritime Distress and Safety System (GMDSS), using satellites and computers. Commercial Morse in North America—dotdash messages between ships and coastal stations—ended in 1999.

In the new millennium, the code continues in use among radio amateurs. And it is being revived as a means of communication for persons who have little or no ability to move, or who cannot speak or sign—who are ventilator-dependent or who suffer from severe cerebral palsy or some other devastating impairment.

Documentation

In quoting printed and manuscript sources I have generally retained the spelling, punctuation, and typography of the originals. In fitting short quotations grammatically into my own sentences, however, I have occasionally had to capitalize or lower-case the first letter of the original.

The following abbreviations appear frequently in the documentation, representing the chief collections of primary material by and about Morse:

C: Ezra Cornell Papers, Cornell University Library

ELM: *Samuel F. B. Morse: His Letters and Journals,* ed. Edward Lind Morse, 2 vols. (1914; rpt. New York, 1973)

HORLB: Henry O'Reilly Letterbooks, New-York Historical Society

HORP: Henry O'Reilly Papers, New-York Historical Society

HORSB: Henry O'Reilly Scrapbooks, New-York Historical Society

LHL: Samuel F. B. Morse journal, Linda Hall Library, Kansas City, Mo.

M: Samuel F. B. Morse Papers, Library of Congress. The abbreviation is followed by a number that indicates the relevant reel in the library's microfilm edition. Thus M32 stands for reel 32 of the microfilm edition of the Morse Papers. The abbreviation "fr." indicates the frame number in the reel.

N: Edward Julian Nally Papers, Princeton University Library

N-YO: *New-York Observer*

P: Samuel Irenaeus Prime, *The Life of Samuel F. B. Morse, LL.D.* (New York, 1875)

S: Francis O. J. Smith Papers, Maine Historical Society

V: Vail Telegraph Collection, Smithsonian Institution Archives

V-NYHS: Alfred Vail Transcripts, New-York Historical Society

WU: Western Union Collection, National Museum of American History

XM: "Samuel F. B. Morse and other members of the Morse and Walker families 1816–1869," microfilm, Library of Congress

Y: Morse Family Papers, Yale University Library

I have also abbreviated the names of frequently mentioned persons as follows:

447

AK = Amos Kendall; AV = Alfred Vail; EC = Ezra Cornell; EM = Elizabeth Morse; FOJS = Francis O. J. Smith; HOR = Henry O'Reilly; JM = Jedediah Morse; LWM = Lucretia Walker Morse; RM = Richard Morse; SFB = Samuel F. B. Morse; SM = Sidney Morse.

The following, mostly secondary works are all cited in the documentation, usually by the author's last name alone:

Adkins, Nelson Frederick. *Fitz-Greene Halleck: An Early Knickerbocker Wit and Poet.* New Haven, Conn., 1930.

Allston, Washington. *The Correspondence of Washington Allston,* ed. Nathalia Wright. Lexington, Mass., 1993.

Anbinder, Tyler. *Nativism and Slavery: The Northern Know Nothings and the Politics of the 1850s.* New York, 1992.

Baark, Erik. *Lightning Wires: The Telegraph and China's Technological Modernization, 1860–1890.* Westport, Conn., 1997.

Baker, Paul R. *The Fortunate Pilgrims: Americans in Italy 1800–1860.* Cambridge, Mass., 1964.

Barger, M. Susan, and William B. White. *The Daguerreotype: Nineteenth-Century Technology and Modern Science.* Baltimore, 1991.

Bates, David Homer. *Lincoln in the Telegraph Office.* 1907; rpt., Lincoln, Nebr., 1995.

Beauchamp, Ken. *History of Telegraphy.* London, 2001.

Bektas, Yakup. "The Sultan's Messenger: Cultural Constructions of Ottoman Telegraphy, 1847–1880." *Technology and Culture* 41 (October 2000): 669–96.

Beniger, James R. *The Control Revolution: Technological and Economic Origins of the Information Society.* Cambridge, Mass., 1986.

Bergen, Fons Vanden. *Classics of Communication.* Brussels, 1999.

Berkeley, G. F.-H. *Italy in the Making 1815 to 1846.* 1932; rpt., Cambridge, England, 1968.

Bijker, Wiebe E., et al. eds. *The Social Construction of Technological Systems.* Cambridge, Mass.,1987.

Billington, Ray Allen. *The Protestant Crusade.* New York, 1938.

Bjelajac, David. *Millennial Desire and the Apocalyptic Vision of Washington Allston.* Washington, D.C., 1988.

Blied, Benjamin J. *Austrian Aid to American Catholics 1830–1860.* Milwaukee, 1944.

Blondheim, Menahem. *News over the Wires: The Telegraph and the Flow of Public Information in America, 1844–1897.* Cambridge, Mass., 1994.

———. "When Bad Things Happen to Good Technologies: Three Phases in the Diffusion and Perception of American Telegraphy," in *Technology, Pessimism, and Postmodernism,* ed. Yaron Ezrahi, et al. (Dordrecht, Netherlands, 1994), 77–92.

Boase, T. S. R. *English Art 1800–1870.* Oxford, England, 1959.

Bowers, Brian. *Sir Charles Wheatstone FRS 1802–1875.* London, 1975.

Briggs, Charles F., and Augustus Maverick. *The Story of the Telegraph, and a History of the Great Atlantic Cable.* New York, 1858.

Bright, Charles. *The Story of the Atlantic Cable.* New York, 1903.

Brown, Charles H. *William Cullen Bryant.* New York, 1971.

Brown, Ralph H. "The American Geographies of Jedediah Morse." *Annals of the Association of American Geographers* 31, no. 3 (September 1941): 145–217.

Bruce, Robert V. *The Launching of Modern American Science 1846–1876.* New York, 1987.

Burchell, S. C. *Imperial Masquerade: The Paris of Napoleon III.* New York, 1971.

Burnham, M., and Lucretia Hoover Giese, eds. *Redefining History Painting.* New York, 1995.

Burrows, Edwin G., and Mike Wallace. *Gotham: A History of New York City to 1898.* New York, 1999.

Butrica, Andrew J. "From *Inspecteur* to *Ingénieur:* Telegraphy and the Genesis of Electrical Engineering in France, 1845–1881." Ph.D. diss., Iowa State, 1986.

Cain, Robert J. "Telegraph Cables in the British Empire, 1850–1900." Ph.D. diss., Duke, 1971.

Carré, Patrice A. *Télégraphes: Innovations techniques et société au 19e siècle.* Paris, 1996.

Carter, Samuel, III. *Cyrus Field: Man of Two Worlds.* New York, 1968.

Cavanaugh, Cam, et al. *At Speedwell in the Nineteenth Century.* Morristown, N.J., 1981.

Church, Clive H. *Europe in 1830: Revolution and Political Change.* London, 1983.

Clark, Eliot. *History of the National Academy of Design 1825–1953.* New York, 1954.

Cooper, James Fenimore. *Gleanings in Europe: France,* ed. Thomas Philbrick and Constance Ayers Denne. Albany, N.Y., 1983.

———. *Letters and Journals of James Fenimore Cooper,* ed. James Franklin Beard, vols. 2, 3, 5, 6. Cambridge, Mass., 1960, 1964, 1968.

Coulson, Thomas. *Joseph Henry: His Life and Work.* Princeton, N.J., 1950.

Cowdrey, Mary Bartlett, et al. *American Academy of Fine Arts and American Art-Union.* New York, 1953.

Crook, D. P. *The North, the South, and the Powers 1861–1865.* New York, 1974.

Crosland, Maurice. *The Society of Arcueil: A View of French Science at the Time of Napoleon I.* London, 1967.

Cummings, Thomas S. *Historic Annals of the National Academy of Design.* 1865; rpt., New York, 1969.

Cunningham, Noble E., Jr. *The Presidency of James Monroe.* Lawrence, Kans., 1996.

Czitrom, Daniel J. *Media and the American Mind: From Morse to McLuhan.* Chapel Hill, N.C., 1982.

Davis, David Brion. *The Slave Power Conspiracy and the Paranoid Style.* Baton Rouge, La., 1969.

Dearinger, David B. "Annual Exhibitions and the Birth of American Art Criticism to 1865," in Dearinger, ed., *Rave Reviews: American Art and Its Critics, 1826–1925* (New York, 2000), 53–91.

Dibner, Bern. *The Atlantic Cable,* 2d ed. New York, n.d.

Dobyns, Kenneth W. *The Patent Office Pony: A History of the Early Patent Offices.* Fredericksburg, Md., 1997.

Dorf, Philip. *The Builder: A Biography of Ezra Cornell.* New York, 1952.

Droz, Jacques. *Europe Between Revolutions 1815–1848,* trans. Robert Baldick. New York, 1967.

Du Boff, Richard B. "Business Demand and the Development of the Telegraph in the United States, 1844–1860." *Business History Review* 44, no. 4 (Winter 1980): 459–79.

Dunlap, William. *A History of the Rise and Progress of the Arts of Design in the United States,* 2 vols. 1834; rpt., New York, 1969.

———. *Diary of William Dunlap,* 3 vols. New York, 1931.

Faust, Drew Gilpin. "Introduction," in Faust, ed., *The Ideology of Slavery: Proslavery Thought in the Antebellum South, 1830–1860* (Baton Rouge, La., 1981), 1–21.

Feller, Daniel. *The Jacksonian Promise: America, 1815–1840.* Baltimore, 1995.

Field, Henry M. *History of the Atlantic Telegraph.* New York, 1866.

Flagg, Jared B. *The Life and Letters of Washington Allston.* New York, 1892.

Fleming, Donald. *John William Draper and the Religion of Science.* Philadelphia, 1950.

Foresta, Merry A., and John Wood. *Secrets of the Dark Chamber: The Art of the American Daguerreotype.* Washington, D.C., 1995.

Fox, Robert. *The Culture of Science in France, 1700–1900.* Great Yarmouth, England, 1992.

Fraser, Walter J., Jr. *Charleston! Charleston! The History of a Southern City.* Columbia, S.C., 1989.

Frusciano, Thomas J., and Marilyn H. Pettit. *New York University and the City: An Illustrated History.* New Brunswick, N.J., 1997.

Fryd, Vivien Green. *Art & Empire: The Politics of Ethnicity in the United States Capitol, 1815–1860.* New Haven, Conn., 1992.

Gaffney, Thomas L. "Maine's Mr. Smith: A Study of the Career of Francis O. J. Smith, Politician and Entrepreneur." Ph.D. diss., Maine, 1979.

Geisst, Charles R. *Wall Street: A History.* New York, 1997.

Gerdts, William H., and Theodore E. Stebbins, Jr. *"A Man of Genius": The Art of Washington Allston.* Boston, 1979.

Gerdts, William H., and Mark Thistlethwaite. *Grand Illusions: History Painting in America.* Fort Worth, Tex., 1988.

Gernsheim, Helmut, and Alison Gernsheim. *L. J. M. Daguerre.* London, 1956.

Greenough, Horatio. *Letters of Horatio Greenough American Sculptor,* ed. Nathalia Wright. Madison, Wis., 1972.

Headrick, Daniel R. *The Invisible Weapon: Telecommunications and International Politics 1851–1945.* New York, 1991.

Henry, Joseph. *The Papers of Joseph Henry,* ed. Nathan Reingold. Washington, D.C., 1972– .

Hershkowitz, Leo. "The Native American Democratic Association in New York City, 1835–1836." *New-York Historical Society Quarterly* 46 (January 1962): 41–59.

Hochfelder, David Paul. "Electrical Communication, Language, and Self," in Chris Hables Gray, ed., *Technohistory* (Malabar, Fla., 1996), 119–39.

———. "Taming the Lightning: American Telegraphy as a Revolutionary Technology, 1832–1860." Ph.D. diss., Case Western, 1999.

Holt, Michael F. *The Rise and Fall of the American Whig Party: Jacksonian Politics and the Onset of the Civil War.* New York, 1999.

Holzmann, Gerard J., and Björn Pehrson. *The Early History of Data Networks*. Los Alamitos, Calif., 1995.

Hone, Philip. *The Diary of Philip Hone 1828–1851*, ed. Allan Nevins, 2 vols. New York, 1927.

Howarth, T. E. B. *Citizen-King: The Life of Louis-Philippe*. London, 1961.

Hunnewell, James F. *A Century of Town Life: A History of Charlestown, Massachusetts, 1775–1887*. Boston, 1888.

Hutchison, Sidney C. *The History of the Royal Academy 1768–1986*. London, 1986.

Hyman, Harold, ed. *Heard Round the World: The Impact Abroad of the Civil War.* New York, 1969.

Israel, Paul. *From Machine Shop to Industrial Laboratory: Telegraphy and the Changing Context of American Invention, 1830–1920*. Baltimore, 1992.

Israel, Paul, and Keith Nier. "The Transfer of Telegraph Technologies in the Nineteenth Century," in David J. Jeremy, ed., *International Technology Transfer: Europe, Japan and the USA, 1700–1914* (Hampshire, England, 1991), 95–121.

Jaffe, Irma B. *John Trumbull: Patriot-Artist of the American Revolution*. Boston, 1975.

———, ed. *The Italian Presence in American Art, 1760–1860*. New York, 1989.

Jepsen, Thomas C. *My Sisters Telegraphic: Women in the Telegraph Office, 1846–1950*. Athens, Ohio, 2000.

John, Richard R. "Recasting the Information Infrastructure for the Industrial Age," in Alfred D. Chandler, Jr., and James W. Cortada, eds., *A Nation Transformed by Information* (New York, 2000), 55–106.

———. "Private Enterprise, Public Good? Communications Deregulation as a National Political Issue, 1839–1851," unpublished.

Johnson, Paul. *The Birth of the Modern: World Society 1815–1830*. New York, 1991.

Jones, Alexander. *Historical Sketch of the Electric Telegraph*. New York, 1852.

Jones, Theodore Francis. *New York University, 1832:1932*. New York, 1933.

Katz, Irving. *August Belmont: A Political Biography*. New York, 1968.

Kendall, Amos. *Autobiography of Amos Kendall*, ed. William Stickney. Boston, 1872.

Khan, Bibi Zorina. " 'The progress of science and the useful arts': Inventive activity in the antebellum period." Ph.D. diss., UCLA, 1991.

King, Thomas Wayne. *Modern Morse Code in Rehabilitation and Education*. Boston, 2000.

King, W. James. "The Development of Electrical Technology in the 19th Century: The Telegraph." *Contributions from the Museum of History and Technology*, Bulletin 228 (Washington, D.C., 1962).

Knobel, Dale T. *Paddy and the Republic: Ethnicity and Nationality in Antebellum America*. Middletown, Conn., 1986.

Kramer, Lloyd. *Lafayette in Two Worlds: Public Cultures and Personal Identities in an Age of Revolution*. Chapel Hill, N.C., 1996.

Langer, William L. *Political and Social Upheaval 1832–1855*. New York, 1969.

Lee, Basil Leo. *Discontent in New York City 1861–1865*. Washington, D.C., 1943.

Leonard, Ira M. "New York City Politics, 1841–1844: Nativism and Reform." Ph.D. diss., New York University, 1965.

Leonard, Ira M., and Robert D. Parmet. *American Nativism, 1830–1860*. New York, 1971.

Levenstein, Harvey. *Seductive Journey: American Tourists in France from Jefferson to the Jazz Age*. Chicago, 1992.

Lindley, Lester G. "The Constitution Faces Technology: The Relationship of the National Government to the Telegraph, 1866–1884." Ph.D. diss., Rice, 1971.

London—World City 1800–1840, ed. Celina Fox. New Haven and London, 1992.

Long, E. B. *The Civil War Day by Day*. New York, 1971.

Lundeberg, Philip K. *Samuel Colt's Submarine Battery: The Secret and the Enigma*. Washington, D.C., 1974.

Mabee, Carleton. *The American Leonardo: A Life of Samuel F. B. Morse*. New York, 1943.

Marland, E. A. *Early Electrical Communication*. London, 1964.

Martineau, Harriet. *Retrospect of Western Travel*, ed. Daniel Feller. Armonk, N.Y., 2000.

Mattelart, Armand. *The Invention of Communication*, trans. Susan Emanuel. Minneapolis, 1996.

Mayer, Henry. *All on Fire: William Lloyd Garrison and the Abolition of Slavery*. New York, 1998.

McKay, Ernest A. *The Civil War and New York City*. Syracuse, N.Y., 1990.

McNamara, Brooks. *Day of Jubilee: The Great Age of Public Celebrations in New York, 1788–1909*. New Brunswick, N.J., 1997.

McPherson, James M. *The Struggle for Equality: Abolitionists and the Negro in the Civil War and Reconstruction*. Princeton, N.J., 1964.

Memorial of Samuel Finley Breese Morse. Washington, D.C., 1875.

Meyer, Herbert W. *A History of Electricity and Magnetism*. Cambridge, Mass., 1971.

Miller, Lillian B. *Patrons and Patriotism: The Encouragement of the Fine Arts in the United States 1790–1860*. Chicago, 1966.

Morse, Samuel F. B. *Lectures on the Affinity of Painting with the Other Fine Arts by Samuel F. B. Morse*, ed. Nicolai Cikovsky, Jr. Columbia, S.C., 1983.

Morus, Iwan R. "Telegraphy and the Technology of Display: The Electricians and Samuel Morse." *History of Technology*, 1991, 20–40.

———. *Frankenstein's Children: Electricity, Exhibition, and Experiment in Early Nineteenth-Century London*. Princeton, N.J.,1998.

Moss, Richard J. *The Life of Jedediah Morse: A Station of Peculiar Exposure*. Knoxville, Tenn., 1995.

Moyer, Albert E. *Joseph Henry: The Rise of an American Scientist*. Washington, D.C., 1997.

Mullaly, John. *The Laying of the Cable*. New York, 1858.

Neal, John. *Observations on American Art*, ed. Harold Edward Dickson. State College, Pa., 1943.

The New American State Papers: Science and Technology, 8. Wilmington, Del., 1973.

Newman, John. *Somerset House*. London, 1990.

Nickles, David. "Telegraph Diplomats: The United States' Relations with France in 1848 and 1870." *Technology and Culture* 40, no. 1 (January 1999): 1–25.

Niven, John. *Martin Van Buren: The Romantic Age of American Politics*. New York, 1983.

Noll, Mark A. "The Bible and Slavery," in *Religion and the American Civil War,* ed. Randall M. Miller, et al. (New York, 1998), 43–73.

Nonnenmacher, Thomas W. "Law, Emerging Technology and Market Structure: The Development of the Telegraph Industry: 1838–1868." Ph.D. diss., Illinois, 1996.

Nye, David E. "Shaping Communication Networks: Telegraph, Telephone, Computer." *Social Research* 64, no. 3 (Fall 1997): 1067–91.

Overmyer, Grace. *America's First Hamlet.* Westport, Conn., 1957.

Perkins, Bradford. *Prologue to War: England and the United States 1805–1812.* Berkeley, Calif., 1961.

Perkins, Dexter. "Henry O'Reilly." *Rochester History* 7, no. 1 (January 1945): 1–24.

Pessen, Edward. *Jacksonian America: Society, Personality, and Politics,* rev. ed. Chicago, 1985.

Peters, John Durham. *Speaking into the Air: A History of the Idea of Communication.* Chicago, 1999.

Phillips, Joseph W. *Jedediah Morse and New England Congregationalism.* New Brunswick, N.J., 1983.

Pilbeam, Pamela. *The 1830 Revolution in France.* New York, 1991.

Pinkney, David H. *Napoleon III and the Rebuilding of Paris.* Princeton, N.J., 1958.

Plum, William R. *The Military Telegraph during the Civil War in the United States.* 1882; rpt., New York, 1974.

Post, Robert C. *Physics, Patents, and Politics: A Biography of Charles Grafton Page.* New York, 1976.

Potter, David M. *The Impending Crisis 1848–1861.* New York, 1976.

Prescott, George B. *History, Theory, and Practice of the Electric Telegraph,* 4th ed. Boston, 1866.

Rebora, Carrie J. "The American Academy of the Fine Arts, New York, 1802–1842." Ph.D. diss., New York University, 1990.

Remini, Robert V. *Andrew Jackson: The Course of American Democracy, 1833–1845.* Baltimore, 1984.

Report of the Commissioner of Patents for the Year 1849. Washington, D.C., 1850.

Root, M. A. *The Camera and The Pencil: or the Heliographic Art.* Philadelphia, 1864.

Rudé, George. *Debate on Europe 1815–1850.* New York, 1972.

Russell, R. W. *History of the Invention of the Electric Telegraph Abridged from the Works of Lawrence Turnbull, M.D.* New York, 1853.

Samuel F. B. Morse Educator and Champion of the Arts in America. New York, 1982.

Saward, George. *The Trans-Atlantic Submarine Telegraph.* London, 1878.

Schudson, Michael. *Discovering the News: A Social History of American Newspapers.* New York, 1978.

Scisco, Louis D. *Political Nativism in New York State.* New York, 1901.

Sellers, Charles. *The Market Revolution: Jacksonian America, 1815–1846.* New York, 1991.

Shoptaugh, Terry L. "Amos Kendall: A Political Biography." Ph.D. diss., New Hampshire, 1984.

Siemens, Werner. *Personal Recollections of Werner von Siemens,* trans. W. C. Coupland. New York, 1893.

Smith, Tony. "Who Was Prof. Daubeny?" *Morsum Magnificat,* no. 49 (Christmas 1996): 18–19.

Snyder, Alan K. "Foundations of Liberty: The Christian Republicanism of

Timothy Dwight and Jedediah Morse." *New England Quarterly* 56, no. 3 (September 1983): 382–97.

Spann, Edward K. *The New Metropolis: New York City 1840–1857.* New York, 1981.

Staiti, Paul J. "Samuel F. B. Morse in Charleston 1818–1821." *South Carolina Historical Magazine* 79, no. 2 (April 1978): 87–112.

———. "God, Family, and Art: *Unpublished Letters from Samuel F. B. Morse.*" *Archives of American Art Journal* 25, no. 4 (1985): 10–15.

———. *Samuel F. B. Morse.* Cambridge, Mass., 1989.

Stebbins, Theodore E., Jr., ed. *The Lure of Italy: American Artists and the Italian Experience.* New York, 1992.

Stephens, Carlene E. "The Impact of the Telegraph on Public Time in the United States, 1844–1893." *IEEE Technology and Society Magazine,* March 1989, 4–10.

Strong, George Templeton. *The Diary of George Templeton Strong . . . 1850–1859,* ed. Allan Nevins and Milton Halsey Thomas. New York, 1952.

Tatham, David. "Samuel F. B. Morse's *Gallery of the Louvre:* The Figures in the Foreground." *American Art Journal* 13, no. 4 (Autumn 1981): 38–48.

Thayer, Donald R. "Art Training in the National Academy of Design, 1825–1835." Ph.D. diss., Missouri, 1978.

Thompson, Robert Luther. *Wiring a Continent: The History of the Telegraph Industry in the United States 1832–1866.* Princeton, N.J., 1947.

Waples, Dorothy. *The Whig Myth of James Fenimore Cooper.* New Haven, Conn., 1938.

Watts, Steven. *The Republic Reborn: War and the Making of Liberal America, 1790–1820.* Baltimore, 1987.

Welling, William. *Photography in America: The Formative Years 1839–1900.* New York, 1978.

Whitman, Walt. *The Journalism,* 1, ed. Herbert Bergman. New York, 1998.

Wood, John, ed. *America and the Daguerreotype.* Iowa City, Iowa, 1991.

Wright, Conrad. "The Controversial Career of Jedediah Morse." *Harvard Library Bulletin* 31, no. 1 (Winter 1983): 64–87.

Wright, Nathalia. *Horatio Greenough: The First American Sculptor.* Philadelphia, 1963.

———, ed. *Letters of Horatio Greenough, American Sculptor.* Madison, Wis., 1972.

In the documentation that follows, I have used the first few words of each paragraph in the text, printed in boldface, to group citations for that paragraph. Individual citations are keyed to a prominent word in the relevant sentence of the paragraph:

ONE: GEOGRAPHY

On April 30/ Sufficient: JM to his father, 6 Nov 1786, Y. On JM generally see R. Brown, Moss, Phillips, and C. Wright. **And for Jedediah/** Greatest: JM to his father, 29 Nov 1786, Y. **Two weeks after/** Dwarf: ELM, I, 173. Pattern: JM to EM, 5 Sep 1796, Y. **Jedediah became prominent/** Whirlpool: JM to his father, 28 Feb 1794, Y. **Such ominous/** See, for instance, JM, *Sermon Preached at Charlestown, November 29, 1798, on the Anniversary Thanksgiving* (1799). **Jedediah's fiery/** Unhappy: JM to John Jay, 23 May 1800, Y. **Concerned above/** Rise: "Directions for the behaviour of Samuel Finley Breese Morse, by his Father," 1 Nov 1799, Phillips Academy. Observe: JM to

SFB, 19 Dec 1800, Y. **Settled in the**/ Retire: SFB to JM, 19 Aug 1799, Historical Society of Pennsylvania. Daily: EM to her sons, 11 Feb 1804, Phillips Academy. **The long-distance**/ Vary: JM to his sons, 12 Feb 1804, Phillips Academy. Vulgar: various letters from JM to SFB, 1799–1805, Phillips Academy. **The letters Finley**/ Character: JM to SFB, 7 Mar 1801, Y. Indulgence: JM to SFB and SM, 3 Nov 1802, Y. **Jedediah rarely**/ Peculiar: JM to [unidentified], 17 Nov 1800, Y. **And Jedediah and**/ Remember: Oliver Brown to SFB, 18 Sep 1801, Phillips Academy. **Once Finley left**/ Preceptor: JM to his sons, 1 Aug 1803, Y. Omitted: JM to his sons, 12 Mar 1804, Phillips Academy. **And Finley's improvement**/ Hills: JM to SFB, 17 Oct 1804, Phillips Academy. **Of Finley's improvement**/ Prepared: SFB to SM and RM, 15 Mar 1805, M1. **While becoming more**/ Instructions: JM to his father, 25 Oct 1802, Y. Amusement: JM to his sons, 1 Oct 1804, Phillips Academy. Manly: JM to SFB and SM, 3 Nov 1802, Y. **Finley now learned**/ Stranger: ELM, I, 9. **Finley felt belittled**/ Anxious: JM to SFB, 18 Nov 1805, M1. **When Finley at last**/ Amusements: EM to SFB, 23 Nov 1805, M1. **The question of**/ Homesick: SFB to his parents, 25 Dec 1805, M1. Determine: EM to SFB, 27 Dec 1805, M1. **Finley retaliated**/ Brevity: SFB to JM, 20 Jan 1806, M1. Segars: EM to SFB, 1 Feb 1806, M1. **The last condition**/ Absent: SFB to his parents, 7 Jun 1807, M1. Exercise: SFB to his parents, 13 May 1807, M1. **Around the fall**/ Careful: EM to SFB, 1 Feb 1806, M1. Expend: SFB to his parents, 22 Oct 1805, M1. **But Finley found**/ Gluttons: EM to SFB, 1 Feb 1806, M1. Promised: EM to SFB, 23 Nov 1805, M1. **Finley knew that**/ Pocketbook: SFB to his brothers, 1 Jun 1809, M1. Blaming: SFB to his parents, 6 Mar 1808, M1. **Jedediah and Elizabeth**/ *Disappointed:* SFB to his parents, 9 Jan 1809, M1. **Finley's lusterless**/ Whim: EM to SFB, 23 Nov 1805, M1. Steady, Fondness: P, p. 14; JM to SFB, 15 Jan 1806, M1. **But at Yale**/ Blow: P, p. 22. **Finley developed**/ Contents: SFB to his parents, 30 Jun 1807, M1. *Trash:* SFB to his parents, 25 Jan 1808, M1. Forever: document of 4 Mar 1808, Y. **Jedediah and Elizabeth badly**/ Prayers: EM to her sons, 13 Nov 1808, Y. Mortify: JM to "Dr. Green," 24 Dec 1805, M1. **The world outside**/ Dissolves: JM to Joseph Lyman (copy), 15 Jun 1805, Y. Fountain: JM to Joseph Lyman, 19 Feb 1805, M1. Jesus: JM to "Dr. Osgood," 3 Apr 1805, M1. **The political situation**/ Fallen: JM to Joseph Lyman, 22 Apr 1806, M1. **Finley's graduation**/ Heart: SFB to Jennette Hart (copy), 30 May 1813, M2. **The misery arose**/ Admire: P, p. 25. **Jedediah put off**/ Best: ELM, I, 22. **After learning the plan**/ Determined: ELM, I, 23. **Finley's training**/ Designed: JM to [unidentified], 18 Jul 1811, M1. **Having consented**/ Solicitude: JM to [unidentified], 18 Jul 1811, M1. **With two piano-playing**/ Singularly: ELM, I, 33.

TWO: NO ONE UNINSPIRED BY THE MUSES MAY ENTER

The honored place/ Recommended: SFB to [unidentified], 17 Sep 1811, M1. **Finley took rooms**/ Reference: P, p. 41. SFB and Leslie later moved to 8 Buckingham Place. **Many other artists**/ Perfection: SFB to Jennette Hart, 30 May 1813, M2. Angel: SFB to his parents, 30 May 1813, M2. On Allston's work see Gerdts, "*A Man of Genius.*" **Through Allston**/ Rubens: P, p. 36. Finley also visited fellow New Englander John Singleton Copley, expatriated, now in his seventies, and infirm: "his powers of mind have almost entirely left him; his late paintings are miserable." ELM, I, 47. **Only a few days**/ Voyage: SFB to [unidentified], 17 Sep 1811, M1. **With an introduction**/ Admittance: P, p. 35. On the Royal Academy see Hutchison and Newman. **Finley first decided**/ Difficult: SFB to his parents, 21 Oct 1811, M1, and cf. P, p. 40. **Allston oversaw**/ Mortifying: SFB to his parents, 25 May 1812, M2. **With Finley's**

growing/ Poets: SFB to Jennette Hart, 30 May 1813, M2. Color: SFB to his parents, 28 Feb 1812, M1. Preëminent: P, p. 46. **Finley was not daunted**/ Passion: P, p. 47. **Finley took time**/ Novels: Charles King to SFB and Charles Leslie, 3 Jan 1812, M1. Kindness: ELM, I, 46. Happy: SFB to Washington Allston, 10 Apr 1816, M3. **Once settled**/ Bloated: P, p. 45. Extensively: SFB to his parents, 20 May 1812, M2. **Through Allston**/ Pleased: SFB to his parents, 12 Jun 1813, M2. On Payne see Overmyer. **Finley became an ardent**/ Actress: P, p. 45. Confessed: ELM, I, 130. **Finley's new way**/ Agreeable: SFB to his parents, 28 Feb 1812, M1. Capricious: P, p. 47. **But to Elizabeth**/ Absorb'd: EM to SFB, 15 May 1812, Y. Acquisition: JM to SFB, 4 Mar 1814, M2. Pure: ELM, I, 118. **Parents and child**/ Dainties: P, p. 56. Respectable: ELM, I, 108. **Finley stayed in touch**/ Habitually: SFB to his parents, 28 Feb 1812, M1. **Jennette Hart**/ *Friend:* SFB to Jennette Hart, 24 Jun 1814, M2. Reserve: SFB to Samuel Jarvis, 9 Sep 1814, Y. Small: P, p. 86. **Born in the shadow**/ Suffer: P, p. 49. **No admirer**/ Cease: SFB to his parents, 1 Nov 1812, M2. Servility: B. Perkins, 292. Scorn: Watts, 223. **Over the first**/ Alarming: P, pp. 43–44. **One month later**/ *Chinese:* SFB to his parents, 1 Nov 1812, M2. Bravo!: SFB to E. D. Cushing, 24 Sep 1812, Y. Insolent: Edward L. Morse, "Letters of Samuel F. B. Morse—1812," *North American Review* 196 (1912): 122. **Jedediah and Elizabeth did**/ Mad: EM and JM to SFB, 28 Jun 181[2?], M2. **But for Finley**/ Beating: SFB to his parents, 1 Nov 1812, M2. Raptures: Edward L. Morse, "Letters of Samuel F. B. Morse—1812," *North American Review* 196 (1912): 120. **Finley dismissed**/ Spirit: SFB to his parents, 1 Nov 1812, M2. **Finley's parents**/ Maintain: JM to SFB, 17 Nov 1813, M2. **Now a student**/ Twenty: SFB to his parents, 1, 12, and 14 Mar 1814, M2. **Finley worked on**/ Compliment: P, p. 47. **The judges**/ Merit: Dunlap, *History,* 311. On the exhibition see also Boase, 152. **Finley's parents had long**/ Likeness: EM to SFB, 13 Jun 1814, M2. Proficiency: Ward Safford to SFB, 13 Jun 1814, M2. Modesty: ELM, I, 113. **Finley decided that**/ Mammon: ELM, I, 164. Fie!: SFB to his parents, 22 Dec 1814, M2. **Finley drew a second**/ *Conquest:* ELM, I, 153. **Outraged, Finley**/ Washington: ELM, I, 152–53. Hate: ELM, I, 163. **Finley appealed**/ Intellectual: ELM, I, 133. On history painting see Gerdts and Thistlethwaite, *Grand Illusions.* Grieve: Washington Allston to JM, 15 Mar 1814, M2. **Jedediah's reply**/ Portraits: ELM, I, 159. Farrand: EM to SFB, 3 Aug 1814, M2. In addition, Jedediah was involved in a decades-long fracas with a writer named Hannah Adams. See Phillips, 152 ff. **Finley did not help**/ Despotism: P, pp. 62, 67. **Finley explained**/ Louvre: SFB to his parents, 11 Oct 1814, M2. Desponding: ELM, I, 134. **But to Elizabeth**/ Schemer: ELM, I, 154. Educations: JM to SFB, 25 Jan 1815, M2. **Late in December**/ Approved: JM to SFB, 19 Jul 1815, M2. **Finley's pleasure**/ Mutually: SFB to Samuel Jarvis, 8 Feb 1815, Y. Bereft: P, p. 81. Leslie implies that Allston became suicidal. Revealed: Allston, 625. **Finley still fretted**/ Storm: ELM, I, 172. Success: Edward L. Morse, "Letters of Samuel F. B. Morse—1812," *North American Review* 196 (1912): 122. **During the year**/ Dread: Washington Allston to JM, 4 Aug 1815, Historical Society of Pennsylvania. See also Dunlap, *History,* 312–13. **In depicting Marpessa's**/ Recollect: SFB to his parents, 23 Apr 1815, M2. **Finley's manifesto**/ Advice: ELM, I, 182; EM to SFB, 1 Jun 1815, M2. **Jedediah returned**/ Profession: ELM, I, 183. **Although Finley considered**/ Taste: SFB to his parents, 1 Mar 1814, M2. Endeavor: M32, fr. 40. **The speed of**/ Loss: SFB, journal for Jul–Aug 1811, M32. **Finley sailed from**/ Terror: SFB, journal for Aug–Sep 1815, M32. **But on October**/ Providence: SFB to his parents, 18 Oct 1815, M25.

THREE: A TERRIBLE HARUM-SCARUM FELLOW

Finley's exhibition/ Accomplished: Staiti, *Samuel F. B. Morse*, 37. Uncommon: J. S. Dorsey to SFB, 27 May 1816, M3. **With his most**/ Hovel: SFB to LWM, 12 Jan 1820, M3. *Drunkenness:* SFB to his parents, 3 Oct 1816, M3. **In getting about**/ Undeceived: SFB to Samuel Jarvis, 10 Nov 1815, Y. **Far from doing**/ Celebrated: LWM to Sarah Livermore, 10 Aug 1816, M25. **In fact, Finley**/ Moon: SFB to LWM, 3 Sep 1816, Y. **Considering that**/ Fellow: ELM, I, 202. Remember: ELM, I, 206. Slutt: EM to RM, 6 Feb 1819, Y. **One thing about**/ Gay: SFB to his parents, 7 Sep 1816, M3. Gospel: SFB to his parents, 14 Dec 1816, M3. **As Finley's qualms**/ Impressions: JM to SFB, 9 Aug 1816, M3. Pleasure: JM to his parents, 20 Feb 1781, Y. **While undergoing**/ Coldness: SFB to LWM, 7 Jan 1817, Y. Endless: SFB to LWM, 17 Aug 1817, Woodruff Library, Emory University. **Finley found Lucrece**/ Pray: SFB to LWM, 18 Feb 1817, Y. Renewed: SFB to LWM, [probably Nov 1816], M25. **Lucrece dutifully**/ Depravity: LWM to SFB, 24 Feb 1817, XM. Folly: LWM to SFB, 20 Feb 1817, M3. **To foster Lucrece's**/ Relishes: JM to SFB, 8 Mar 1817, Woodruff Library, Emory University. Amiable: LWM to SFB, [no day] Mar 1817, Woodruff Library, Emory University. Talents: JM to SFB, 8 Mar 1817, Woodruff Library, Emory University. **Five months later**/ Professor: SFB to LWM, 3 Jul 1817, M25. Sinner: LWM to SFB, 11 Jul 1817, Y. **While Finley's spiritual**/ Disapproved: Joseph Delaplaine to SFB, 4 Apr 1817, M3. **Finley tried invention**/ Pricks: Feller, 29. Research: SFB to LWM, 27 Mar 1817, Y. On "improvements" at the time see, for instance, *Report of the Commissioner.* **Experimenting together**/ Metallic: P, p. 104. **Finley's and Sidney's**/ Fortunes: SFB to his parents, 25 Aug 1817, M3. **But at the same**/ Intelligence: SFB to LWM, [no day] May 1817, Y. Forgiveness: SFB to Henry Bromfield, 1 May 1819, Huntington Library. Opposed: Dunlap, *Diary*, III, 659. **In the summer**/ *Change:* SFB to LWM, 3 Jul 1817, M25. Salvation: SFB to LWM, 17 and 10 Jul 1817, M25. **Finley planned**/ *Clergyman:* SFB to LWM, 22 Jul 1817, M25. **Lucrece had affectionately**/ *Fickle:* SFB to LWM, 13 Sep 1817, M25. **To restart**/ Lists: James E. B. Finley to JM, 5 Apr 1815, New-York Historical Society. **Finley timed**/ Slave: SFB to LWM, 31 Dec 1819, M25. Torrent: SFB to LWM, 17 Feb 1818, M3. On Charleston see Fraser, 191–98. **With his first**/ Pouring: SFB to his parents, 7 Apr 1818, M3. **Capable now**/ Yields: P, p. 108. Engines: LWM to SFB, 10 Jul 1818, XM. **Finley's plentiful**/ Exposed: Staiti, *Samuel F. B. Morse,* 54. **Finley did tend**/ Pointed: M3, fr. 120. **During Finley's**/ Overcome: LWM to SFB, 10 Jul 1818, XM. **As their separation**/ Idolise: SFB to LWM, 15 Jul 1818, XM. Blessing: LWM to SFB, 18 Jul 1818, XM. **Marriage also**/ *Fix:* LWM to SFB, 17 Jul 1818, XM. Careth: SFB to LWM, 16 Jul 1818, XM. **Finley and Lucrece**/ *Belle:* SFB to RM, 21 Dec 1818, Y. **The new social**/ *Fashion:* SFB to his parents, 26 Feb 1819, M25. Academy: P, p. 118. **The basis of**/ Discourse: Phillips, 197. Hue: EM to RM, 26 Mar 1819, Y. **Finley encouraged**/ Meanest: SFB to his parents, 26 Feb 1819, M25. *Hydra:* ELM, I, 223. **But to Finley's**/ Speedily: SFB to JM, 26 Oct 1819, M3. **Over the summer**/ Last: ELM, I, 197. Sun: Dunlap, *Diary*, III, 742. **Probably inspired**/ Deal: Staiti, *Samuel F. B. Morse,* 56. **The addition of**/ Care: SFB to his parents, 23 Dec 1819, M3. *Aspect:* SFB to LWM, 8 Dec 1819, M25. **Finley managed**/ Graceful: [M.?] Robertson to SFB, 1 Nov 1820, M4. **Finley discovered**/ Divide: ELM, I, 229. Husband: LWM to SFB, 14 Jan 1820, XM. On the economic depression see, for instance, Sellers and Watts. **Lucrece also reported**/ Longings: SFB to LWM, 7 Jan 1820, XM. **Finley's discontent**/ Moping: RM to his parents, 21 Jan 1819, Y. Quere: EM to JM, 14 Jan 1820, M3. Confidence: SFB to RM, 20 Nov 1818, Y. Enemy:

RM, Day-book for 1819–22, Y. **At the end**/ Wish: LWM to SFB, 7 Mar 1820, XM. **Only a few months**/ Beings: JM to "Dr. Campbell" (copy), 26 Feb 1820, M4. **Jedediah's appointment**/ *Cruel:* EM to SM, 16 Jun 1820, XM. Depression: JM to "Miss Bradstreet," 30 Apr 1820, M4. **Finley tried one**/ Rice: SFB to LWM, 21 Feb 1821, XM. Established: SFB to LWM, 18 Feb 1821, M4. **Finley realized that**/ Branches: SFB to LWM, 21 Jan 1821, XM. **Perhaps simply**/ Sanguine: SFB to LWM, 18 Feb 1821, M4. On the Academy see Miller, 123–24. **Finley had planned**/ *Trial:* LWM to SFB, 12 Mar 1821, XM. Short: SFB to LWM, 25 Mar 1821, M25. **Still without a home**/ Bed: LWM to SFB, 18 Sep 1821, XM. **During his tour**/ Popular: SFB to LWM, 9 Dec 1821, N. **Finley began the work**/ Pleased: SFB to LWM, 14 Nov 1821, N. Splendid: SFB to LWM, 9 Dec 1821, N. **Yet the painting**/ Herculean: SFB to LWM, 20 Dec 1821, N. Grace: SFB to LWM, 9 Dec 1821, N. Certain: SFB to LWM, 2 Dec 1821, N. **Lucrece had expected**/ Decide: SFB to LWM, 2 Jan 1822, M25. Absence: LWM to SFB, 9 Jan 1822, XM. **He saw encouraging**/ Talents: *Quarterly Christian Spectator* 4 (1822): 383. **After displaying**/ Beautiful: Allston, *Correspondence*, 206. **The Boston exhibition**/ Success: SFB to LWM, 21 Feb 1823, M4; 14 Feb 1823, XM. **Allston urged Finley**/ Classes: Washington Allston to SFB, 15 Apr 1823, M4. **At the end**/ Predict: SFB to LWM, 10 May 1823, Y. **Under Pratt's**/ Multiplied: Henry Pratt to SFB, [5?] and 19 Jun 1823, M24. **Lucrece worried**/ Submit: LWM to SFB, 30 Nov 1823, XM. Merit: *United States Review and Literary Gazette* II, no. 4 (Jul 1827): 251. Meant: SFB to "Mr. Poinsett" (draft), [ca. Dec 1823], M5. Morse shipped the *House of Representatives* to Charles Leslie in England, where it was sold. It turned up twenty years later in New York, however, rolled up, dirty, and cracked. It was salvaged by Morse's student Daniel Huntington, from whose estate it was purchased in 1911 by the Corcoran Gallery of Art.

FOUR: AN AFFECTION OF THE HEART

The failure/ Tune: P, p. 129. Business: SFB to LWM, 8 Dec 1823, M4. Wait: SFB to LWM, 6 Jan 1824, M5. **Finley tried to revive**/ Sculptor: SFB to LWM, 16 Aug 1823, M4. Leaving: SFB to "Mr. Poinsett" (draft), [ca. Dec 1823], M5. **Finley's latest scheme**/ Consent: ELM, I, 253. Health: LWM to SFB, 26 Aug 1823, XM. **The first week**/ Farewell: P, p. 137. **A week later**/ Hazard: SFB to LWM, 22 Apr 1824, M5. **Finley went back**/ Desert: SFB to LWM, 27 Jun 1824, Y. **Whatever the cause**/ Gloomy: SFB to LWM, 22 Jun 1824, M25. **For a few months**/ Poverty: SFB to his parents, 16 Aug 1824, M5. On New York see Burrows, 450. **Unlike Finley**/ Service: RM to SM, 10 Apr 1823, Y. Schemes: SM to EM, 11 Aug 1824, Y. **Finley settled**/ Wonder: ELM, I, 258. Storms: P, p. 138. **"We must begin"**/ Rational: LWM to SFB, 6 Jan 1825, M25. Safely: LWM to SFB, 5 Dec 1824, Y. On the reception of Lafayette see Cunningham, Kramer, and McNamara. **On first shaking**/ Revolution: P, p. 140. **Finley not only heard**/ Nobleness: P, p. 141. **Excited at being**/ Sorrowful: P, p. 142. **Just twenty-five**/ Affection: JM to Samuel S. Breese, 2 Mar 1825, Archives of American Art. See also LWM's obituary in N-YO, 19 Feb 1825. **Finley received the agonizing**/ Blow: P, pp. 144–45. **And what would**/ Darkest: SFB to his parents, 5 May 1825, M5. Dare: SFB to his parents, 1 Dec 1825, M5. **As he tried to**/ Ready: P, p. 148. Shake: SFB to his parents, 18 Apr 1826, M5. **Although still uncompleted**/ Pumping: SFB to his parents, 3 Nov 1825, M5. **Finley's commission**/ Intensity: SFB to his parents, 5 May 1825, M5. **Trumbull had liabilities**/ Shoemaker: Jaffe, *John Trumbull,* 270. **In October**/ Beggars: Dunlap, *History,* 280. **Finley was pleased**/ Harmony: ELM, I, 282. See also Thayer, 58 ff. **Finley seems not to**/ Stately: Cummings, 22. **Finley led an effort**/ Ensuring: SFB, undated committee report, New-York Historical Society. **Finley's peacemaking**/ I have glided over the many complexities in this matter, which also involved the payment of a stockholders' fee by artists who were elected to the board of directors. For a fuller account see Rebora, esp. 273–80. **Four days after**/Assumed: Cummings, 26, 29. **The members elected**/ Rallying: SFB to John L. Morton, 18 Apr 1831, National Academy of Design. Freedom: SFB to Henry Pratt, 26 Mar 1833, Massachusetts Historical Society. Balance: ELM, I, 284. Shrink: SFB to his parents, 15 Jan 1826, M25. On the later development of the N.A.D. see especially Clark and *Samuel F. B. Morse Educator.* **The idea of lecturing**/ Alone: SFB, *Lectures on the Affinity*, 14. All the quotations in the next four paragraphs are from this volume. **According to Finley**/ Solely: Cummings, 35. On this and other exhibitions at the Academy see Dearinger. **Probably only a day**/ Cares: EM to her sons, 10 May 1826, in RM's MS life of his father, Y. Look: ELM, I, 286. Gratified: EM to her sons, 12 May 1826, in RM's MS life of his father, Y. Imperious: SFB to his parents, 11 Jun 1826, XM; ELM, I, 286–87. **At one moment**/ Foretaste: RM's MS life of his father, Y. Gloom: SFB to J. M. Mathews, 10 Jun 1826, Historical Society of Pennsylvania. Mark: SFB to Stephen Van Rensselaer, 10 Jun 1826, Historical Society of Pennsylvania. **But Jedediah's end**/ Mortify: EM to JM, 26 Feb 1822, Y. Published at his own expense, Jedediah's *Report to the Secretary of War . . . On Indian Affairs* appeared in New Haven in 1822, containing much still-valuable information on Native American life at the time. **Jedediah's will**/ Motherless: Moss, 140. **Throughout Finley's life**/ Sensation: Thomas Sully to SFB, 4 Mar 1828, Historical Society of Pennsylvania. Qualified: John Neagle to SFB, 15 May 1828, M5. Great: Allston, *Correspondence*, 231. **Finley's completed**/ SFB's explanation appears in *United States Review and Literary Gazette* II, no. 4 (Jul 1827): 248. The reviewer was quite certainly SFB himself. **Finley's *Lafayette***/ Better: Neal, 44. Unskillful: Adkins, 226. Common: C. Brown, 181. P.N.A.: Cummings, 47. **Without meaning to**/ Pretension: Cummings, 49, 55. **Finley's pamphlet provoked**/ Eloquence: *North American Review* 26 (1828): 218. **Finley published**/ Civilization: Cummings, 64–65. **One side attacked**/ Principle: Cummings, 85 ff. **This "Exposé**/ Wretched: Cummings, 105. **Finley remained calm**/ Promotion: Cummings, 107. **The controversy died**/ Daubings: SFB to DeWitt Bloodgood, 26 Dec 1828, Historical Society of Pennsylvania. **The atmosphere**/ Evolvement: MS Minutes of the Sketch Club, Century Association, New York City. **Finley had done**/ *Naked:* N-YO, 3 Mar 1825. Pander: See SFB's letter to the N.Y. *Herald*, undated but ca. 1835, M24. Freely: SFB to Lafayette (copy), [no day] Jul 1825, M5. Magic: ELM, II, 495. **Finley also found time**/ Exquisite: SFB to Sir Walter Scott, [1829?], M5. **Finley thought often**/ Gloves: SFB to Margaret Breese, 8 Dec 1828, University of Rochester Library. **Such a moment**/ Different: Catherine Pattison to SFB, 24 May 1837, M6. **But Catherine's father**/ Explain: SFB to Margaret Breese, 8 Dec 1828, University of Rochester Library. **Although tempted**/ Account: SFB to Margaret Breese, 2 Jan 1829, University of Rochester Library. **Securing a commission**/ Preparing: SFB to Robert Hayne (draft), 9 Jan 1829, M5. **As to leaving**/ Accuse: SFB to EM, 9 Nov 1826, M5. Gratify: SFB to Elizabeth Breese, 20 Jan 1827, Archives of American Art. Danger: SFB to Margaret Breese, 8 Dec 1828, University of Rochester Library. **Following the deaths**/ First: ELM, I, 291, 292. Graves: SFB to Margaret Breese, 8 Dec 1828, University of Rochester Library. **After Elizabeth's death**/ Unusual: SFB to EM, 20 Sep 1826 and 6 May 1828, M5. Expence: SFB to EM, 11 Feb 1828, M5. **The couple considered**/ Commanded: Susan Pickering to

SFB, 25 Sep 1828 and 7 Apr 1829, M5. Remember: Susan Morse to SFB, 7 Apr 1829, M5. **Finley was not deaf**/ Severely: SFB to Margaret Breese, 8 Dec 1828 and 2 Jan 1829, University of Rochester Library. Depression: SFB to DeWitt Bloodgood, 24 Aug 1830, New-York Historical Society.

FIVE: *IL DIAVOLO*

After a twenty-six/ Low: SFB to Margaret Breese, [Jan 1830], M5. Unless otherwise noted, all quotations in this chapter are from the diaries SFB kept while in Europe, in M32. **Then, Rome**/ Classic: SFB, "Sketches of France, Italy and Switzerland," N-YO, 6 Jul 1833. On American painters in Italy see Jaffe, *Italian Presence,* and Stebbins. **When he could**/ Desired: SFB to DeWitt Bloodgood, 24 Aug 1830, New-York Historical Society. **Thorwaldsen presented**/ PRESENTS: Cummings, 123. **Apart from the superb**/ Imitates: SFB, "Sketches of France, Italy and Switzerland," N-YO, 17 Aug 1833. **Like his compatriots**/ Bows: P, p. 198. On American travelers in Italy see Baker. **But much in Catholic**/ Gorgeous: "Sketches of France, Italy and Switzerland," N-YO, 6 Jul 1833. **Such uncomfortable reminders**/ Frivolity: SFB, "Sketches in France," N-YO, 2 Mar 1833. **In the time between**/ The discussion of the European political situation here and throughout the chapter is based on Berkeley, Church, Droz, Langer, Pilbeam, and Rudé. **Morse welcomed**/ Contention: SFB to G. L. Verplanck, 2 Jan 1832, New-York Historical Society. **Morse admired Greenough**/ *Excellence:* SFB to John L. Morton, 18 Apr 1831, National Academy of Design. Depravity: Horatio Greenough to SFB, 23 Apr 1832, M5. Ballast: ELM, I, 413–14. Primed: N. Wright, *Horatio Greenough,* 81. **During his year in Paris**/ Slaves: Horatio Greenough to SFB, 24 Aug 1834, M6. Ding: Horatio Greenough to SFB, 23 Apr 1832, M5. On Paris see Cooper (*Gleanings*), Pinkney, and Levenstein. **Members of the American**/ Fellow-citizen: M6, fr. 138; see also unidentified newspaper clipping reprinted from the *Daily Advertiser,* Leila Morse scrapbooks, Columbia University Library. **Practically every evening**/ Unconciliating: Waples, 122, 133, 134. **Morse admired Cooper**/ Taunt: SFB to Margaret Breese, 8 Dec 1828, University of Rochester Library. Cherished: SFB to Benjamin Silliman, 12 Jul 1832, Silliman Papers, Yale University Library. **For his part**/ Fellow: Cooper, *Letters and Journals,* III, 239. Captivate: Cooper, *Letters and Journals,* III, 375. **Nevertheless, the rumor**/ Dignity: SFB to DeWitt Bloodgood, 24 Aug 1830, New-York Historical Society. Conscience: ELM, I, 413. **Through Cooper and Lafayette**/ Price: ELM, I, 405. Influence: ELM, I, 406. On Louis-Philippe see Howarth. **Cooper thought otherwise**/ Mummery: Cooper, *Letters and Journals,* III, 79. Volcano: Cooper, *Letters and Journals,* III, 240. **Parisians protested**/ Dashed: P, p. 227. **Morse became an active**/ Cavalier: P, p. 229. See also Kramer, 253–73. **Morse also wrote**/ Outcasts: *Badger's Weekly Messenger,* 29 Feb 1832. **The museum's mammoth**/ Mist: SFB to Margaret Breese, 25 Dec 1829, University of Rochester Library. Numerous: Staiti, *Samuel F. B. Morse,* 244. **Morse painted**/ Yellow: Cooper, *Letters and Journals,* II, 163, 238. Pains: P, p. 715. **Sometime around the new**/ Closest: P, p. 228. Interested: SFB to James Fenimore Cooper (typed transcript), 6 Sep 1832, M6. Danger: Staiti, "God, Family, and Art," 14. **Morse considered his *Grand Gallery*/** *Correct:* SFB to his brothers, 18 Jul 1832, M6. Sensation: Cooper, *Letters and Journals,* III, 172. **Morse planned to complete**/ Intimacy: James Fenimore Cooper to SFB, 21 Sep 1832, Morristown National Historical Park. On the completed painting see Tatham. **As he got ready**/ Boiling: SFB to [his brothers?], undated fragment ca. Apr 1830, M26. *Sword:* SFB,

"Sketches of France, Italy and Switzerland," N-YO, 2 Mar 1833. **Morse also appreciated**/ *Persuasion:* SFB to the Marquis de Lafayette, 5 Mar 1833, American Antiquarian Society. **Morse had also come**/ Patriots: SFB to G. L. Verplanck, 2 Jan 1832, New-York Historical Society. Many Americans who had not been abroad of course shared Morse's view. **But three months**/ *Never:* SFB to the Marquis de Lafayette, 26 Jan 1833, American Antiquarian Society. **When he left America**/ Tormented: SFB to DeWitt Bloodgood, 24 Aug 1830, New-York Historical Society. Dribbled: N. Wright, *Letters,* 125. **Where was** *his*/ Stake: P, p. 288. Hang: N. Wright, *Letters,* 144. **But hanging on**/ Wasted: SFB to G. L. Verplanck, 2 Jan 1832, New-York Historical Society.

SIX: ANOMALOUS, NONDESCRIPT, HERMAPHRODITE

Morse's return to New/ On New York University see T. Jones, Frusciano and Pettit, and SFB documents at NYU Archives, Bobst Library, New York University. **Shortly after resuming**/ Absurd: SFB to John L. Morton, 19 Oct 1830, National Academy of Design. **In January 1833**/ Violation: see Rebora, 309–17. **Morse spent two**/ Incubus: SFB to Henry Pratt, 26 Mar 1833, Massachusetts Historical Society. **Returning to his easel**/ Italy: Jaffe, *Italian Presence,* 196–97. *Imitation:* SFB, *Lectures on the Affinity,* 59. Imagination: Hone, I, 92–93. **However Morse's European**/ *Feeling:* SFB to James Fenimore Cooper, 21 Feb 1833, M6. Principles: SFB to Henry Pratt, 26 Mar 1833, Massachusetts Historical Society. Herculean: Staiti, *Samuel F. B. Morse,* 199. **Despite his professorship**/ Mental: SFB to DeWitt Bloodgood, 29 Dec 1833, Historical Society of Pennsylvania. Fits: SFB to James Fenimore Cooper (typed transcript), 21 Feb 1833, M6. **He decided not**/ *Beggar:* SFB to DeWitt Bloodgood, 29 Dec 1833, Historical Society of Pennsylvania. **Perhaps to begin**/ Property: George Clarke to SFB, 9 Aug 1834, M6. **Morse's domestic situation**/ Unnatural: RM to SM, 19 Jul 1854, Y. The bequests provided $4500 for each child. **Morse visited Susan**/ Surprise: Susan Morse to SFB, 13 Oct 1834, M6. Haste: SFB to Susan Morse, 26 Sep 1836, M6. **Morse still felt**/ Wounds: SFB to P. Van Rensselaer (copy), 20 Jun 1835, M6. Forbidden: SFB to "Dear friend Mary," 28 Apr 1837, M6. Fawn: SFB to Catherine Pattison, 22 Oct 1836, M6. *Destiny:* Catherine Pattison to SFB, 24 May 1837, M6. **Morse found a more**/ Laughed: Cooper, *Letters and Journals,* III, 228–29. **Morse's experience**/ Invaded: *Commercial Advertiser,* 27 Apr 1833. **Morse tried to show**/ Antidote: SFB, unsigned article in *Journal of Commerce,* 14 Jan 1836. **Morse's encounter**/ Communicants: N-YO, 29 Jun 1833. On anti-Catholicism see Billington. **Morse deplored**/ Outrage: SFB, *Foreign Conspiracy against the Liberties of the United States* (1835), 182–83. **The Pope, Morse**/ Superadded: SFB, *Imminent Dangers to the Free Institutions of the United States* (1835), 10. On the Leopold Foundation see Blied. **At stake for America**/ Support: Snyder, 382. **Morse's** *Foreign*/ *Unconsciously:* SFB to A. S. Willington (draft), 13 Apr 1835, M6. Persuasion: SFB to J. R. Poinsett, 2 Jun 1835, Historical Society of Pennsylvania. **Morse soon began**/ Document: SFB, *The Proscribed German Student* (1836), 19. **Some of Clausing's fellow**/ On the Clausing war see 1836–37 items from the *New Era* and *Brooklyn Advocate* in SFB scrapbook, WU. **A sort of male**/ Overflows: M34, fr. 684 (MS version of the *Confessions*). **America, in Morse's**/ Filthy: SFB, *Foreign Conspiracy,* 178. The discussion of immigration and nativism draws on Hershkowitz, Leonard, Pessen, and Scisco. **Morse's visceral**/ Stomach: Strong, 94. Ocean: Hone, I, 209. **Among the national**/ Firebrand: SFB to the Marquis de Lafayette, 6 Aug 1833, Cornell University Library. On Garrison and

O'Connell see Mayer, 161. Although the nativist groups professed to oppose all foreign influence, they singled out Irish Catholics especially, who in the 1830s made up about a third of all immigrants. See Knobel. **In addition to his influential/** Insolence: SFB scrapbook, p. 23, WU. Ignorant: N-YO, 27 Dec 1834. **In the spring of 1836/** Sacrifice: Mabee, 170. **Morse quickly got/** *Designing:* Mabee, 171. **Morse's explanation/** Fellow: Cooper, *Letters and Journals,* III, 220. **The beating Morse/** Outrage: unidentified newspaper clipping, 11 Mar 1837, SFB scrapbook, WU. **Morse's shift/** *Fix:* Cooper, *Letters and Journals,* V, 213. Powers: Allston, 364. Embody: Greenough, 179. **But in addition/** Dagger: Allston, 428. On the later development of history painting see Burnham and Giese. **But however behind/** Devoted: SFB to Senator Samuel Southard, 7 Mar 1834, Princeton University Library. **But the signs/** Eminence: Cooper, *Letters and Journals,* III, 81. On the rotunda paintings see also Fryd, 42–61. **For Morse, the decision/** Progress: *Journal of Commerce,* 21 Feb 1837. **But Morse felt humiliated/** Offence: SFB to Washington Allston (draft), 21 Mar 1837, M6. On Adams' dislike of JM see SFB to Senator Dix (draft), 7 Dec 1846, M10. **Rejected beyond hope/** Key Stone: Thomas Cole to SFB, 14 Mar 1837, M6. **But Morse felt battered/** Ill: Cooper, *Letters and Journals,* III, 259. Authorization: M33, fr. 638. See also clipping headed "Weary of Life," Vail scrapbook, V. **Morse's near-collapse/** Noble: SFB to Washington Allston (draft), 21 Mar 1837, M6. See also Cummings, 144 ff. **His depression lifting/** Constitution: see document of 17 Mar 1837, M6.

SEVEN: HIGH ATTRIBUTE OF UBIQUITY

In operation, then/ The account of SFB's 1837 telegraph is based on many different sources, but chiefly the draft of the caveat he prepared in Oct 1837. See M6, fr. 373 ff. **However crude/** Alluded: *Journal of Commerce,* 27 Apr 1837. **Whatever dismay Morse/** Graphy: M33, fr. 366. On the Chappe system see Holzmann and Pehrson., ch. 2. Telegraph: Marland, 19. **Morse soon learned/** Notice: *Journal of Commerce,* 28 Aug 1837. **Morse clipped/** Grandest: Poughkeepsie *Journal,* 13 Sep 1837. Other clippings appear in M33, fr. 369. **Such reports described/** Relative: SFB to Catherine Pattison, 27 Aug 1837, M6. **Morse set to work/** Excitement: SFB to Catherine Pattison, 27 Aug 1837, M6. **To confirm his suspicions/** The information and quotations in this and the next four paragraphs come from SFB's correspondence of Sep 1837 in M14, fr. 248 ff. **Some at least of Morse's account/** SFB's original sketchbook was consumed in a fire at the Supreme Court building in Washington. A certified copy of the sketchbook had been made before the fire, but apparently no longer exists. A certified copy of this certified copy, made in 1849, survives at the Electricity Division of the National Museum of American History, Washington. **Some of Morse's colleagues/** Grieved: P, p. 724. On the testimony of other witnesses to SFB's early experiments see his *Modern Telegraphy* (1867) and the statement of Robert Dodge, 9 Jan 1851, M14. **To further secure/** Conceived: *Journal of Commerce,* 27 Aug 1837. Successful: *Journal of Commerce,* 7 Sep 1837. **Suspecting that foreigners/** *Mutual:* Charles Jackson to SFB, 10 Sep 1837, M14. On Jackson see Bruce, 37–38. **"I lose no time/** Disabuse: SFB to Charles Jackson (copy), 18 Sep 1837, M14. **"I have always entertained/** Opinion: Charles Jackson to SFB, 7 Nov 1837, M14. **Too enraged to bother/** Claimants: SFB to Joshua Fisher (copy), 4 Nov 1837, M14. **Morse asked Rives/** *Manner:* SFB to William Pell, 29 Jan 1838, M14. Novelty:

William Rives to SFB, 1 Mar 1838, M14. Originator: William Pell to SFB, 1 Feb 1838, M14. **In sum, Morse/** Hint: SFB to Charles Jackson, 7 Dec 1837, M14. On what Morse may have learned from Jackson see Hochfelder, "Taming the Lightning," 63–66. The question of whether SFB sent Jackson a copy of the circular requires too elaborate demonstration to try to resolve here. But it may be added that on a copy of the circular he retained, SFB noted that he believed he sent a circular to Jackson, but was not certain he did so. See the circular of 28 Aug 1837, M14. **If nothing else/** Condition: ELM, II, 77. Intelligence: see SFB's draft of the caveat, M6, fr. 373 ff. **Gale knew how/** Surprise: See Gale's MS "Historical facts concerning Morse's Electro Mag. Telegraph" [1872], NYU Archives, Bobst Library, New York University. The archives house additional material on Gale. **With the powerful/** Proposed: *Journal of Commerce,* 4 Sep 1837. On Daubeny see Smith. **Morse described in detail/** Indebted: *New American State Papers,* 44–45. **Vail had been present/** *Delicate:* SFB, *Modern Telegraphy* (1867), 31–33, and Appendix, 17–18. **This so-called relay/** Creative: Prof. David Hochfelder, in a version he sent me of ch. 2 of his "Taming the Lightning." **Morse's description/** Disided: AV, untitled essay in his "Miscellaneous Telegraphy Papers," V. On the depression see Geisst, 26, and Remini, 427. **Morse and Vail signed/** *Proper:* copy of contract dated 23 Sep 1837, V-NYHS. On Vail generally see William Baxter, "Real Birth of the Electric Telegraph," MS, New-York Historical Society; Cavanaugh et al.; V; Vail Papers, New Jersey Historical Society, Newark; and Vail material at the NYU Archives. **At the same time/** Tedious: SFB to AV, 14 Oct and 11 Nov 1837, V-NYHS. *Fullest:* SFB to AV, 11 Oct 1837, V. A sample page of the dictionary survives in M6, fr. 404. **Morse had once before visited/** Facility: William Baxter, "Real Birth of the Electric Telegraph," MS, New-York Historical Society. **Returned to Speedwell/** Waiter: See Cavanaugh et al. Success: ELM, II, 73. Accounts of the demonstrations conflict. In one place SFB says he used about three miles of wire. SFB to William Vail, 31 Jan 1863, M29. **Two weeks later/** Witness: M34, fr. 454. ATTENTION: P, p. 331. **Morse demonstrated both/** Systems: Report of the Franklin Institute (copy), 8 Feb 1838, M6. Alphabet: AV to Stephen Vail, 7 Feb 1838, V-NYHS. This seems to me a crucial letter in the controversy over the origin of the Morse code. **Arriving at the capital/** Unwilling: AV to Stephen Vail, 7 Feb 1838, V-NYHS. Unknown to Vail himself, the bills were actually being paid by his brother George. Their father, Stephen Vail, apparently took a dislike to Morse and withdrew his support. **A week at Gadsby's/** Indisposed: AV to Stephen Vail, 7 Feb 1838, V-NYHS. See also AV to George Vail, 22 Jan 1837 and 20 Feb 1838, V-NYHS. **Morse's Washington demonstrations/** Enemy: AV to George Vail, 20 Feb 1838, V-NYHS. **But to Morse's delight/** Scouted: SFB to George Vail, 21 Feb 1838, V. Jefferson: AV to Stephen Vail, 17 Feb 1838, V-NYHS. **Looking further ahead/** Enterprising: *New American State Papers,* 60. See also John, "Private Enterprise." My thanks to Prof. John for allowing me to read his paper before publication. **The Committee on Commerce/** UBIQUITY: *New American State Papers,* 53. **Commissioner Ellsworth/** Slavish: SFB to FOJS (copy), 14 Apr 1838, S. On Smith see especially Gaffney and Shoptaugh. **In March, Morse/** see the Articles of Agreement, [no day] Mar 1838, M6. **Morse also gathered/** Honor: SFB to Hugh Legare, 14 Apr 1838, S. Arduous: ELM, II, 89. **Morse sent the subscribers/** Suspense: SFB to Thomas Cummings, 15 Mar 1838, M6; Cummings, 144–46. **Morse's brother Richard/** Nerves: RM to his wife, 2 Jul 1838, Y. **As he embarked/** Risking: SFB to AV, 20 Mar 1838, V-NYHS. Tide: P, p. 345.

EIGHT: TRAVELING ON A SNAIL'S BACK

Seeking a British/ Duped: SFB to [SM?], 3 Jul 1838, Y. Account of SFB's patent application based on his MS "History of proceedings in England to procure a Patent for my Telegraph," Y. **On the basis/** *National:* P, p. 359. **During his first interview/** Account of SFB's meetings with Wheatstone based on his MS "History of proceedings." On Wheatstone generally see Bowers. **During his seven weeks/** Imitation: P, pp. 358–59. See also Beauchamp, 33. Morse developed a cordial relationship with Steinheil, whose early telegraphs closely resembled his own but who conceded to him the priority. **Morse quickly obtained/** Monopoly: SFB to FOJS, 13 Feb 1839, S. Message: SFB to RM, 20 Aug 1838, Y. On the telegraph in France, with superb photos of European apparatus, see Carré. **It turned out to be/** Baby: P, p. 360. **The Academy met/** Account of SFB's demonstration at the Académie based on P, pp. 363–65. On Arago and on the state of electrical science in France see Butrica, Crosland, and Fox. **Full accounts/** Savant: M33, fr. 357. **Some of the journalists/** *Constructor: Courier Français,* 13 Sep 1838. **Morse enjoyed the publicity/** Superior: SFB to SM, 1 Oct 1838, V. Manifest: see *Journal of Commerce,* 6 Nov 1838. **The acclaim brought/** *Best:* SFB to FOJS (copy), 9 Oct 1838, S. **Having gained influential/** Portfolios: SFB to FOJS, 7 Jan 1839, S. Raptures: SFB to FOJS, 22 Nov 1838, S. **The problem, Morse/** Organ: P, p. 374. **There were other/** Associations: SFB to FOJS, 14 Nov 1838, S. **The directors of/** Patience: SFB to FOJS, 13 Oct 1838, S. Dilatory: SFB to FOJS, 22 Nov 1838, S. **Morse also tried/** Wagons: ELM, II, 133–34. **Despite his many/** Gentlemen: SFB to Baron Rothschild (draft), 28 Aug 1838, M6. On Chamberlain see MS "Memorandum of an agreement," 20 Sep 1838, Vermont Historical Society. **Morse had intended/** Dejection: RM to SFB, 24 Aug 1838, Y. Agreeable: RM journal for 1838, Y. **Morse now saw Smith/** Suggests: SFB to FOJS, 2 Feb 1839, S. Perpetual: SFB to RM, 13 Oct 1838, Y. Command: SFB to FOJS, 14 Nov 1838, S. Funds: SFB to FOJS (copy), 7 Jan 1839, S. **The stalled funds/** *Nothing:* SFB to RM, 20 Aug 1838, Y. *Blues:* SFB to James Fenimore Cooper, 21 Feb 1833, M6. Confidence: SFB to FOJS, 21 Jan 1839, S. **The black moods/** Orphans: ELM, II, 115–16. **Morse had cause/** Presents: Susan Morse to SFB, 19 Dec 1838, M6. *Exactly:* Susan Morse to SFB, 13 Dec 1838, New-York Historical Society. **Morse usually offered/** Wound: P, p. 361. Snug: SFB to Susan Morse, 11 Nov 1838, M6. Long: Susan Morse to SFB, 19 Dec 1838, M6. **However insensitive/** Unfit: SFB to SM, 6 Jan 1838, M6. Farmer: RM to SM, 31 Dec 1838, Y. **Sidney planned/** *Wanderers:* Susan Morse to SFB, 8 Dec 1838, M6. **With the New/** Snail's: SFB to FOJS (copy), 7 Jan 1839, S. **Morse got some further/** Fame: see SFB to FOJS (copy), 28 Jan 1839, S. Chamberlain apparently also demonstrated SFB's telegraph at the Royal Museum of Physics in Florence. **But Morse was beginning/** *Go-ahead:* SFB to FOJS (copy), 28 Jan 1839, S. Supplant: SFB to FOJS, 13 Feb 1839, S. **This depended, however/** Pretended: see N-YO, 2 Feb 1839. Deserve: SFB to Charles Jackson, 13 Feb 1839, M6. **Far from retracting/** Pained: M11, fr. 307–308. **In reopening/** Tide: P, p. 389. Advertisements: SFB to FOJS, 13 Feb 1839, S. **Toward the end of/** Author: SFB to FOJS, 21 Jan 1839, S. **Meyendorff's Czar/** Liberal: SFB, memo of interview with Baron Meyendorff, 9 Mar 1839, M7. **Morse immediately booked/** Energies: SFB to FOJS, 22 Feb 1839, S. **Daguerre's invention competed/** Wonders: SFB to FOJS (copy), 2 Feb and 2 Mar 1839, S. On Daguerre see Gernsheim and Gernsheim. **Morse was startled/** Delineation: P, pp. 400–402. **Probably a few days/** Delay: ELM, II, 126. **Morse was reluctant/** On the events that follow see SFB's MS "History of proceedings in England to procure a Patent for my Telegraph," Y.

NINE: BEWARE OF TRICKS

Having been gone/ Nominal: ELM, II, 114. Farthing: SFB to FOJS, 16 Apr 1839, S. **Morse wrote Henry**/ Obviate: Joseph Henry to SFB, 6 May 1839, M7. On Henry see Coulson and Moyer. **Morse expected to hear**/ Czar: P, p. 400. **While streamlining**/ Suspense: SFB to Baron Meyendorff (draft), 31 Jul 1839, M7. **The news finally**/ Rejected: C. B. Amyot to SFB (copy), 11 Jun 1839, M18. Nothing: SFB to George Vail, 20 Aug 1839, V. **Morse decided to**/ Wisdom: SFB to AV, 4 Nov 1839, V-NYHS. **Morse had kept**/ Remarkable: see the various early texts on the Web site of The Daguerrian Society, <www.daguerre.org>. Defense: P, p. 407. **Morse set to work**/ Beat: Wood, 111. On the various claims of priority see 1871 letter from SFB in *Philadelphia Photographer* 9, no. 97 (Jan 1872): 3–4; SFB to Fuller Walker, 14 Aug 1871, M31; Welling, 8 ff. **At first Morse used**/ Indifferent: Gernsheim and Gernsheim, 129. On Daguerre's procedures see Foresta and Wood. **During January and February**/ See SFB, "Memoranda of Daguerreotype," M33. **Morse was joined**/ Accordance: P, p. 404. On Draper see Fleming. **Morse and Draper**/ Likenesses: N-YO, 18 Apr 1840; cf. Gouraud in Boston *Daily Advertiser and Patriot*, 26 Mar 1840. *Open: Philadelphia Photographer* 9, no. 97 (Jan 1872): 3–4. See also SFB to Edward L. Wilson, 18 Nov 1871, M31. **Whoever did what**/ Valuable: Welling, 21. **How long Morse**/ Sanguine: SM to RM, 29 Jan 1841, Y. Outdoor: SFB to W. W. Horsford, 20 Nov 1840, Rensselaer Polytechnic Institute. In this letter SFB describes his lenses as "2 large achromatic 4 inches diameter, a plano convex, a double convex each 4 inches and a large double convex, 6 inches in diameter." **Morse worked hard**/ Tied: P, pp. 425–26. Introducer: Mathew Brady to SFB, 15 Feb 1855, M17. **Like all of Morse's**/ Daub: *New-Yorker*, 14 Dec 1839, 205. Ghost: Welling, 8. **Morse disputed such**/ See Root, 390–92. **No honor, however**/ On the SFB-Gouraud blowup recounted in this and the next four paragraphs see New York *Evening Star*, 27–29 Feb 1840; New York *American*, 24 Jun 1840; *Journal of Commerce*, 2 and 8 Jul 1840; Abel Rendu to [unidentified attaché], 22 Jul 1840, M7; SFB to Abel Rendu, 27 Oct 1840, M7; SFB to Nathan Hale, [ca. Oct 1840], M7; and newspaper clippings in the Morse scrapbook, WU, 50 ff. **Morse happened to meet**/ Cautious: SFB to SM, 26 Jun 1841, New-York Historical Society. **Governor William**/ Concerted: N-YO, 7 Nov 1840, 27 Feb 1841. On the school funding conflict see Billington, 142–65; Leonard, "New York City," 1–75, 129–42; Scisco, 32–38. **To Morse's relief**/ Recorded: SFB, *Our Liberties Defended* (1841), vii. Morbid: see document of Oct 1840, M7. **The political dirty**/ Principles: N.Y. *Sun*, 10 Apr 1841. **But the Whig**/ Diversion: *Commercial Advertiser*, 12 Apr 1841. Humbug: *Tribune*, 13 Apr 1841. **In the space**/ Withdraw: *Commercial Advertiser*, 13 Apr 1841. **The flimflam**/ Tricks: SFB, memo on 12 Apr 1841, M7. **But the Catholic**/ Perversion: Leonard, "New York City," 108. Slaves: N-YO, 11 Dec 1841. Denounced: N-YO, 31 Jul 1841. **The most notorious**/ Cunning: Whitman, 43. **For Morse and for**/ Mask: N-YO, 6 Nov 1841. **Two days after**/ Juggling: *Commercial Advertiser*, 2 Nov 1841. **Morse continued to**/ Citadel: N-YO, 16 Apr 1842. **Now fifty years**/ Prime: ELM, II, 159. Visits: SFB to Catherine Pattison (draft), 3 Apr 1841, M7. Healed: SFB to Alphonse Foy (draft), 25 Feb 1839, M6. **The shock of**/ Burnt: SFB to Catherine Breese, 14 Aug 1841, University of Rochester Library. Attitude: SFB to Catherine Pattison (draft), 28 Apr 1840, M7. **Uncertain how to**/ Effort: SFB to Catherine Breese, 30 Sep 1841, University of Rochester Library. Tickle: Mrs. A. C. Stevens to Sidney Breese, 12 Dec 1841, University of Rochester Library. Blue: SFB to Catherine and Helen Breese, 10 Feb 1842, Phillips Academy. **The Breese family**/ Expend: Staiti, "God, Family, and Art,"

14–15. Kindness: SFB to T. D. Woolsey, 29 Sep and 15 Oct 1842, Yale University Library. Wish: Charles Morse to SFB, 28 Nov 1842, M7. **Susan shuffled**/ Cheering: Susan Morse to SFB, 18 Jun 1841, M7. **Without meaning to**/ Abiding: Susan Morse to SFB, 18 Jun 1841, M7. Dream: SFB to Catherine Breese, 30 May 1842, Historic Northampton. **Having not painted**/ Neglect: ELM, II, 160. Precious: SFB to Edward Salisbury, 24 Feb 1841, M7. **Morse apparently had**/ Inquire: *Mirror,* 16 Oct 1841. **Wisely, Morse**/ Design: circular of 30 Nov 1841, M7. **A serious rival**/ Revenue: Cummings, 165. On the Art-Union see Cowdrey et al. **Morse remained proud**/ Centre: SFB to William H. Seward (draft), 20 Jun 1842, M7. **Morse learned that**/ Merit: P, p. 415. **Stung and worried**/ Secure: SFB to FOJS (copy), 23 Mar 1840, S. Deprive: P, p. 427. **Not only the English**/ Gigantic: Senate document #136, 30 Jan 1841, 26th Cong. 2d Session. **It was in part**/ Cheat: SFB to FOJS, 3 Dec 1841, S. **For a commission**/ Houses: Isaac Coffin to SFB, 24 Jun 1841, M7. **After two years of stagnation**/ Nibbles: SFB to AV, 16 Oct 1841, V-NYHS. Defraud: SFB to FOJS, 16 Aug 1841, S. **Taking advantage of**/ Waste: SFB to FOJS, 3 Dec 1841, S. **Smith, an experienced**/ Risk: Isaac Coffin to SFB, 10 Dec 1841, M7. Death: Isaac Coffin to SFB, 30 Nov 1841, M7. **After months of**/ Winds: SFB to FOJS, 3 Dec 1841, S. Postage: SFB to FOJS, 3 Dec 1841, in *Argument of Francis O. J. Smith . . . upon the Claim preferred by him against Prof Samuel F. B. Morse* (1860), 33. Era: SFB to FOJS, 19 Sep 1842, S. **Morse decided to start**/ Views: Henry, *Papers,* V, 141. Success: Moyer, 23. **Morse wrote the same**/ Expediency: *Memorial,* 77. Excite: W. W. Boardman to SFB, 7 Jan 1842, M7. **To create a stir**/ Early: SFB to Catherine and Helen Breese, 10 Feb 1842, Phillips Academy. Powerful: P, p. 438. **Morse exhibited**/ Wonderful: *Tribune,* 9 Aug 1842. Ingenuity: M33, fr. 367. **The Institute**/ Great: *Herald,* 12 Oct 1842. **In October, Morse**/ Bang: *Herald,* 19 Oct 1842. On Colt see Lundeberg. **Morse's public demonstration**/ Destined: ELM, II, 183. **Morse's new campaign**/ Well: SFB to FOJS, 16 Jul 1842, S. Sympathy: SFB to FOJS, 19 Sep 1842, S. Suspense: P, p. 434. **The worst of it**/ Stricken: AV to SFB, 28 Feb 1843, M7; P, p. 444. Engaged: SFB to FOJS, 19 Sep 1842, S. **Morse journeyed to**/ Power: AV to SFB, 28 Feb 1843, M7. **Morse believed that**/ Speculation: reprinted in N-YO, 24 Dec 1842. **On December 30**/ Superior: *New American State Papers,* 65–66. **Morse took a deep**/ Sentiment: ELM, II, 185.

TEN: HURRAH BOYS WHIP UP THE MULES

January and February/ Trying: SFB to SM, 27 Jan 1843, M7. *Define:* ELM, II, 190. **Morse tried to talk**/ Extreme: ELM, II, 191–92. **The suspense eased**/ Mesmeric: ELM, II, 194–95. **Two days later**/ Period: SFB to FOJS (copy), 23 Feb 1843, S. **On March 3**/ Deo: SFB to SM, 3 Mar 1843, British Library. **Morse wrote up**/ Million: *American Journal of Science* 45 (Oct 1843): 393. Morus, "Telegraphy and the Technology," remarks that the experiments were neither original nor unusual, being distinguished only by their scale. **In reporting his**/ Realised: SFB to John C. Spencer (copy), 10 Aug 1843, LHL. **While the insulated**/ *Foot:* SFB to John Spencer (copy), 29 Aug 1843, LHL. Yankee: SFB to FOJS (copy), 1 Sep 1843, LHL. **The trenching got under way**/ See EC to S. I. Prime, 28 Apr 1873, M23. On EC generally see Dorf. **Existing documents**/ Cold: SFB to James Fisher (copy), 2 Dec 1843, M8. **Sometime in early**/ Ascertain: reprinted in N-YO, 23 Dec 1843. **During the time-out**/ Discourage: ELM, II, 211. **Discouragement was not**/ Hearing: James Fisher to SFB, 1 Jan 1844, M8. Whistle: James Fisher to SFB, 22 Dec 1843, M8. **Though fond of**/ SFB to James Fisher (draft), 29 Dec 1843, M8. In the draft SFB has crossed out the comment about opinion in Washington, and may not have included it. Trifle: James Fisher to SFB, 19 May 1845, M10. **At the same time**/ Liar: Gaffney, 146. **Morse discovered**/ Fair: ELM, II, 212. **Morse's scrupulous sense**/ Dearer: SFB to FOJS, 21 Dec 1843, S. Scrutiny: FOJS to SFB, 21 Dec 1843, S; FOJS to EC, 20 Mar 1844, S. Much of Smith's behind-the-scenes maneuvering over the Bartlett contract is obscure, probably because he took care to cover his tracks. **Morse had been inclined**/ Regard: SFB to FOJS, 30 Dec 1843, S. **Morse declined**/ Cluster: SFB to SM, 16 Dec 1843, XM. Pursues: ELM, II, 213. **Vail roomed near**/ Wonder: AV to Jane Vail, 9 Jan 1844, V. **Cornell too read**/ Pay: EC to Mary Ann Cornell, 18 Aug 1844, C. **During the break**/ Error: FOJS to EC, 7 Apr 1844, C. **Smith also took sides**/ Current: see Leonard Gale to SFB, 1 Jun 1844, M8. Worthless: FOJS to EC, 17 Mar 1844, S. **Morse still hoped**/ Heartless: Gaffney, 488. In the original, "villains" appears as "villians." Exposure: FOJS to SFB, 3 Mar 1844, S. Superseded: AV Journal, 12 Jan 1844, V. **Morse replied to**/ Sensitive: ELM, II, 217. **Morse also understood**/ Sanguine: reprinted in N-YO, 6 Jan 1844. **Proceeding this time**/ No glass plates are mentioned, however, in Henry Rogers' description of the "very defective" insulation. See his unpublished history of the telegraph, Henry J. Rogers Papers, Smithsonian Institution. **Each day, as**/ Nitric: SFB, memo of 27 Apr 1844, M8. Tiptoe: AV to Jane Vail, 11 Apr 1844, V. **As the line neared**/ Rapidity: SFB to D. Ayerigg (draft), [8?] May 1844, M8. Language: SFB to AV, 29 May 1844, V. **As public curiosity**/ Wind: AV to Jane Vail, 28 Apr 1844, V-NYHS. Hallucination: SFB to FOJS, 17 May 1844, M8. Boar: ELM, II, 219. **Unfortunately, no graphic**/ See SFB to Catherine Livingstone Morse, [no day] Apr 1844, M25; SFB to SM, 24 May 1844, M25. **Morse generated**/ Begged: AV to SFB (copy), 3 Jun 1844, M8. Watch: *Herald*, 28 May 1844. **Those seeking**/ Transcripts in V, 19 May 1844. In the original, the identifying letters "M" and "V" appear at the end of the telegraphed sentences. **Morse created**/ Speed: *National Register*, 1 Jun 1844. **Vail intercepted news**/ Riots: Vail Telegraph Journals, 8 Jun 1844, V. Gazing: EC to Mary Ann Cornell, 10 Jun 1844, C. **In June, Morse**/ Mother: N-YO, 21 Dec 1844. Ease: *New American State Papers*, 88. **Morse had suggested**/ Accurately: Charles Wilkes to SFB, 13 Jun 1844, M9. See also Stephens. **Into the late**/ Sport: AV to George Vail, 14 Oct 1844, V. **In proving the**/ Substance: *Daily Times*, 14 Sep 1852. Hebrew: Cyrus Mendenhall to Charles Mendenhall, 4 Nov 1872, Cincinnati Historical Society. **Bafflement was**/ Supernatural: M33, fr. 550. Confused: *National Police Gazette*, 30 May 1846. Chained: M33, fr. 550. Climax: M33, fr. 497. Several quotations in the last two sections of this chapter are culled from SFB's scrapbook of newspaper clippings in M33. In cases where he does not give the source of the clipping, I have identified the quotation by frame number alone, as I occasionally do elsewhere in the documentation. On the ideology of communication see Mattelart, Nye, and Peters. **Just as bafflingly**/ Less: M33, fr. 527. Incomparably: *Report of the Commissioner*, 493. Species: M33, fr. 382. Here: *North American*, 15 Jan 1846. **But Morse's "magic**/ Doubt: *New American State Papers*, 115. Nerve: M33, fr. 552. **In forecasting**/ Revolution: *Sun*, 3 Nov 1847. **In this spirit**/ Fly: M33, fr. 551, 515. Blessing: *North American*, 15 Jan 1846. Blended: *National Telegraph Review*, Jul 1853, 107. Sensorium: *Christian Observor*, 20 Mar 1846. Future: *Herald*, 23 Mar 1846. On the blurring of boundaries between the nervous system and electrical communication see Hochfelder, "Electrical Communication." **In its more practical**/ Events: *North American*, 15 Jan 1846. Strength: Philadelphia *Dollar Newspaper*, 17 Jun 1846. Task: *National Police Gazette*, 30 May 1846. **Whatever their particular**/ Climax: Washington *Union*, 1 May 1845. Modern: N-YO, 12 Oct

1844. Effort: *De Bow's Review* 1 (1846): 136. **To its enthusiasts**/ Steam: M33, fr. 625. Improved: Thoreau, *Walden* (1854; New York, 1992). **In the "Lightning**/ Tablet: M33, fr. 382. The coupling of SFB and Franklin became commonplace. Temple: A. B. Quinby to SFB, 23 May 1846, M10. Eminent: M33, fr. 354. Forcible: *Home Journal,* 4 Feb 1848. **Invitations, honors**/ Sober: S. W. Chubbuck to SFB, 1 Jul 1844, M9. **Morse had always**/ Praises: ELM, II, 234. **Scarcely if at all**/ Opposed: ELM, II, 224. The belief that technology emanated from the Deity and served religion was widespread. "Inventors are Apostles of Nature, or rather of the Author of Nature," as the *Tribune* put it, "for the Sciences and Arts are Divine revelations." M33, fr. 518. **Not only failure**/ Christ: ELM, II, 234.

ELEVEN: MERE MEN OF TRADE

As one possible/ Business: ELM, II, 236. **Morse also weighed**/ Monopoly: *Union,* 1 May 1845. Knaves: *Mirror,* 15 Dec 1846. **With a half-dozen**/ Plans: AV to George Vail, 15 Aug 1844, V-NYHS. Inch: FOJS to EC, 19 Feb 1845, C. **Not that letters**/ Satisfied: SFB to FOJS, 20 Dec 1844, M9. **Their angriest**/ Determined: ELM, II, 219. **Morse may have**/ Mousing: FOJS to SFB, 10 Jun 1844, S. Sick: SFB to AV (copy), 11 Jun 1844, M9. Hatred: EC to Mary Ann Cornell, 10 Jun 1844, C. **Smith had other**/ Absurd: SFB, "Copy of Propositions to FOJS," 5 Jun 1844, M8; M9, fr. 471 ff. Accede: SFB to FOJS (draft), 6 Dec 1844, M9. **Morse's efforts**/ Family: AV Journal, 17 Aug 1844, V. **Morse's handling**/ Millions: AV to SFB, 3 Jun 1844, M8. Cunning: AV to George Vail, 15 Aug 1844, V-NYHS. Advantage: AV to George Vail, 10 Jul 1844, V-NYHS. Cheat: AV to George Vail, 1 Sep 1844, V-NYHS. **Vail probably**/ Friend: George Vail to AV, 7 Jul 1844, V-NYHS. **Staying in Washington**/ See AV to Stephen Vail, 25 Dec 1844, V-NYHS. On Page see Post. **Morse's experiments**/ Sound: N-YO, 31 Aug 1844. Hoped: see N-YO, 14 Sep 1844. **Morse and his assistants**/ See Rogers' unpublished history of the telegraph, Henry J. Rogers Papers, Smithsonian Institution. **As usual, Vail**/ Unfit: AV to Stephen Vail, 31 Jan 1848, V-NYHS. *Credit:* AV to George Vail, 20 Aug 1844, V-NYHS. **With Congress not**/ Disposition: SFB to SM (draft), 31 May 1844, M8. **Whether or not**/ Broken: SFB to SM, 18 Dec 1843, XM. **Sidney Morse vigorously**/ Favored: SFB to SM, 12 Oct 1847, M11. Crew: SFB to SM, [no day] Sep 1846, New-York Historical Society. **By contrast with**/ Indigestion: RM to SM, 21 Mar 1843, Y. Spirits: SFB to RM (copy), 1 Jul 1859, M26. **Although Morse surely**/ Keenly: P, p. 511. Scenes: SFB to Annie Ellsworth, [no day] Mar 1845, offered for sale in 1997 by the Philadelphia autograph dealer Catherine Barnes. Fondly: Susan Morse to SFB, 7 Jun 1845, M10. **Morse stayed in**/ Master: N-YO, 15 Jul 1843. See also SFB to Mrs. Washington Allston, 13 Jul 1843, Massachusetts Historical Society. **Savvy and cynical**/ Charity: FOJS to EC, 19 Feb 1845, C. Sinecure: FOJS to [Cave Johnson] (draft), 24 Mar 1845, M10. **On Morse's recommendation**/ Talent: SFB to Cave Johnson (draft), 18 Mar 1845, M10. Obstacles: SFB to [Cave Johnson] (draft), [Mar 1845], M10. **Morse's defeat brought**/ Greatness: undated circular for *Prominent Men of Business and Enterprise,* HORP. See also Sellers and Feller. **Morse did not share**/ Trifling: SFB to B. F. Mudgett (copy), 23 Oct 1857, M27. **Morse's deliverance**/ Whiffet: Shoptaugh, 1. See also AK's *Autobiography.* **Kendall became Jackson's**/ Marat: Sellers, 326. Dark: Martineau, 54. **Contemporaries of this**/ Honesty: Remini, 485. Suspicious: Rochester *Daily Advertiser,* 29 Sep 1848. Machine: Shoptaugh, 326. Trade: SFB to AK, 14 Feb 1857, M27. Desire: AK to SFB, 9 Mar 1847, WU. **No less important**/ Murmur: Kendall, *Autobi-*

ography, 657. **In a decision/** Manage: SFB to Leonard Gale, 11 Mar 1845, M10. Earthly: AK to SFB, 14 Mar 1847, WU. **One month after/** Complete: agreement of 14 Jul 1845, WU. Agency: AK to SFB, 4 Mar 1845, M10. **Morse's agreement/** Trade: FOJS to AK, 6 Aug 1845, S. **Kendall was also/** Heart: AK to FOJS, 12 Aug 1845, S. Folks: FOJS to EC, 17 Aug 1845, C. **Kendall drew up/** *Newer:* HOR to AK, 6 Sep 1845, V. On O'Reilly see also D. Perkins. **In his agreement/** Field: HOR to Henry Rogers, 18 Jun 1846, HORLB. On the various agreements see AK, *Morse's Telegraph and the O'Reilly Contract* (1848). **The high-risk/** Great: HOR to FOJS (copy), 26 Jul 1845, C. Soldier: HOR to AK (draft), 18 Aug 1846, HORSB. Brothers: HOR to AK, 17 Aug 1845, V. *Morsograph:* HOR to SFB, 4 Feb 1846, M10. **Kendall worried/** Outline: HOR to AK, 8 Jul 1845, HORLB. Field: AK to HOR, 12 Jul 1845, HORSB. **Although Kendall spoke/** Short: AK to FOJS, 31 Jul 1845, C. **Kendall admittedly/** Know: Kendall, *Autobiography,* 529. Calm: AK to FOJS, 25 Aug 1845, S. **At the moment/** Benevolent: P, p. 594. **Similar European/** Stay: SFB to AV, 26 Jul 1845, V-NYHS. Thousands: AV to SFB, 30 Jul 1845, M10. **Morse offered/** Nonsense: AV to George Vail, 13 Aug 1845, V-NYHS. Vail's book remains valuable for its information on the early history of Morse's invention and for its eighty-one woodcuts. **In setting out/** Command: SFB to AV, 8 Oct 1845, V. **London journals/** Informed: M9, fr. 319. Thefts: M33, fr. 365. **Morse had inspected/** Needle: *Pictorial Times,* 11 Oct 1845. **And as in Wheatstone's/** Advantage: SFB to AV, 1 Sep 1845, V. Adopted: SFB, memo dated 2 Oct 1845, M10. Truly: SFB to AV, 8 Oct 1845, V. **Morse was anxious/** Idea: SFB to SM, 29 Dec 1845, M10. Civil: ELM, II, 256. **Morse was well positioned/** Cock: SFB to SM, 1 Nov 1845, M10. On Bréguet's telegraph see also Butrica, 160–65; Holzmann and Pehrson, 92–94; and Israel and Nier, "The Transfer of Telegraph," 104–05. **On the last day/** *120:* SFB, memo dated 31 Oct 1845, M10. *Simpler:* SFB to Dominique Arago, 1 Nov 1845, Historical Society of Pennsylvania. **Arago arranged/** Defective: M11, fr. 307–308. Encroach: SFB to Robert Walsh, 11 Nov 1845, M10. **Metternich expressed/** Beautiful: P, p. 531. See also N-YO, 21 Mar 1846 and [Charles Fleischmann] to [unidentified], 14 Jan 1846, M26.

TWELVE: TANTALUS STILL

Returning to America/ *Millions:* AK to SFB, 9 Jan 1846, WU. **A massive physical/** Battery: M9, fr. 489. **Morse considered/** Hindrance: SFB to AV, 16 Jan 1846, V. **A different problem/** Botch-work: HOR to EC, 30 Dec 1845, HORSB. **Morse felt doublecrossed/** Bewitched: SFB to AV, 16 Feb 1846, V. Plague: SFB to AV, 12 Jan 1846, V-NYHS. See U.S. Patent No. 4453, 11 Apr 1846. Morse presented the application as an "improvement" on his original patent of June 1840. **With whatever difficulties/** Penman: M33, fr. 353. **A month later/** Parallel: *Union,* reprinted in an unidentified English journal preserved in Charles Bright's Telegraphic Notes, I, Institution of Electrical Engineers, London. Branch: unidentified clipping in Charles Bright's Telegraphic Notes, I, Institution of Electrical Engineers, London. **On June 27/** Boasting: SFB to AV (copy), 29 Aug 1846, M10. Satanic: SFB to SM, 24 Feb 1847, M11. **The first week/** Compliments, Feature: M10, fr. 522. **The publicity and acclaim/** Enterprize: AK to FOJS, 12 Feb 1846, S. *Millionaire: Articles of Agreement and Association, for the Formation of the Washington & New Orleans Telegraph Company* (1846). **Morse's new revelations/** Idol: P, p. 541. Yale described the degree as Naturae Artisque Legum Doctor—Doctor of Laws and Natural Arts. See also Bektas. **To the press and the public/** The date of the formation of the AP is much debated, but a convincing case for 1846 is made in Blondheim, *News*. See also Schudson. **Morse stayed aloof**/ Situated: SFB to RM, 5 Dec 1846, V. Pity: SFB to RM, 19 Dec 1846, Y. **Smith charged that**/ Form: HOR et al. to AK (copy), 19 Nov 1846, HORSB. Except: HOR to AK (draft), 13 Oct 1846, HORSB. Another time HOR acknowledged having given out what he called "orders for stock." **Whatever the truth**/ Storms: AK to HOR, 24 Oct 1846, HORSB. **They came, for**/ Crawl: HOR to Charles Oslere, 16 Nov 1846, HORLB. World: HOR to "Judge Selden," 27 Oct 1846, HORSB. **O'Reilly directed**/ Yield: HOR to Hervey Ely, 16 Oct 1846, HORLB. **Morse got drawn**/ Hands: HOR to Henry Selden, 25 Nov 1846, HORLB. *Morally:* SFB to AK (draft), 16 Feb 1847, M11. **Morse went to Philadelphia**/ Confess: ELM, II, 272. Allowance: SFB to AK, 16 Feb 1847, M11. Steps: ELM, II, 273. Suffer: SFB to J. D. Reid (copy), 21 Dec 1847, M11. **Morse got no**/ Stranger: judgment of 18 Feb 1847, HORSB. **The ruling jolted**/ Rights: SFB to AK (draft), 24 Feb 1847, M11. Worst: SFB to AV, 16 Mar 1847, V-NYHS. **Morse much needed**/ *West:* HOR to "Friend O'Connor," 19 Feb 1847, HORLB. Effect: SFB to AK (draft), 24 Feb 1847, M11. Ruin: HOR to Henry Rogers, 24 Oct 1846, HORSB. **Morse abhorred**/ Odium: ELM, II, 281–82. Target: ELM, II, 272. **O'Reilly had used**/ Superior: *Herald,* 9 Oct 1845. Genius: HOR to George Dawson, 2 Sep 1847, HORLB. On the House telegraph see W. J. King, "The Development," 301–302. **Morse examined**/ Humbug: SFB to AV, 17 Jul 1845, V-NYHS. *Backwards:* SFB to FOJS, 1 May 1846, S. Avail: SFB to [unidentified] (draft), 3 Apr 1846, M10. **Though he thought**/ *Would-be:* SFB to SM, 24 Feb 1847, M11. *Toys:* SFB to AV, 26 Apr 1847, V. **O'Reilly understood**/ Modes: HOR to "Friend Wallace," 8 Jan 1847, HORLB. Monopoly: printed broadside entitled "The Wire Party's Song," HORP. **Behind O'Reilly's**/ Robberies: SFB to Samuel Hazard (draft), 5 Mar 1850, M13. Obtained: Louisville *Journal,* 15 Aug 1848. **As Morse feared**/ Currency: SFB to SM, 12 Jan 1848, M11. Profit: SFB to SM, 27 Nov 1847, M11. Russian: *Tribune,* 6 Oct 1848. Editors: *Day Book,* 17 Feb 1849. **O'Reilly found other**/ Judges: Henry, *Papers,* VII, 175n. Vail's pamphlet sold well in the U.S.—apparently about 4000 copies—and also appeared abroad in French and Italian translations. **Greatly though he had**/ Cypher: HOR to John I. Rielly, 30 Jun 1849, HORP. Tears: HOR to "Major Downing" (copy), 13 Jul 1847, HORP. Invoke: HOR to Charles Jackson, 18 Jan 1847, HORLB. **Embroiled as he was**/ Knowledge: M33, fr. 541. Deprived: *Tribune,* 6 Oct 1848. On Jackson and ether see Bruce, 37–38. Jackson's claims were supported by his brother-in-law, Ralph Waldo Emerson. **Morse had no appetite**/ Vanity: ELM, II, 274. Mistake: SFB to AV, 10 Mar 1847, V-NYHS. **O'Reilly launched**/ Bull: HOR to H. R. Selden, 3 Sep 1847, HORLB. Failure: HOR to "Dr. Bell" (draft), [1848], HORP. Fraud: Louisville *Morning Courier,* 15 Feb 1848. **Even worse, O'Reilly**/ Motion: U.S. Patent Reissue 79, 15 Jan 1846. Glibly: HOR to "Friend Wallace," 2 Sep 1847, HORLB. **The press and public**/ Wheel: *Daily Post,* 30 Sep 1847. Nutmegs: Louisville *Morning Courier,* 15 Feb 1848. **Morse answered the attack**/ Hurra: HOR to Hervey Ely, 7 Dec 1847, HORLB. **O'Reilly paid a price**/ *Suffers:* HOR to S. Allen, 30 Jan 1849, HORP. Pining: HOR to Charles Moss, 8 Sep 1847, HORLB. Bitter: James D. Reid to HOR, 3 Dec 1847, HORP. **To Morse it seemed**/ Denounced: AK, *Morse's Telegraph and the O'Reilly Contract* (1848), 34. *Tantalus:* SFB to RM, 13 Dec 1846, Y. **A showdown**/ *Everywhere:* AK to FOJS, 3 Mar 1848, HORP. **On the New Orleans**/ IMPROVED: M33, fr. 376. Simple: HOR to Hervey Ely, 4 Dec 1846, HORLB. The high electrical resistance of House's telegraph made it impractical for use on long lines, though it was put into use on shorter ones. Greatest: M33, fr. 501. Minds: See [HOR], *To the People of Michi-*

gan, Indiana, Illinois and Wisconsin [1848], 17. **Probably so**/ Manifest: SFB to FOJS (copy), 11 Mar 1848, S. **By January 1848**/ Armed: Taliaferro Shaffner to SFB, 9 Jan 1848, M11. Sorrow: SFB to Taliaferro Shaffner, 21 Jan 1848, M11. See also Shaffner's quite different, later account of this episode in M35, fr. 329. **As the competing**/ Reptile: See clippings in Box 9C, V. Sympathy: Vail Scrapbook, p. 21, V. Nations: SFB to *Journal* (not in SFB's hand), 28 Jan 1848, M11. **Morse's genteel replies**/ Protect: Theodore Faxton to SFB, 10 Mar 1848, M12. Character: RM to SFB, 12 Mar 1848, M12. **By early spring**/ Infringers: SFB to FOJS (copy), 11 Mar 1848, M12. **For weeks Morse**/ Defense: ELM, II, 283. Adversary: AK to SFB, 27 Jun 1848, WU. Encounter: AK to SFB, 8 Dec 1848, WU. **The competing telegraphs**/ Jackdaw: HOR to James S. Wallace, 6 Sep 1848, HORP. On the trial see M33, fr. 539–46. **Judge Monroe rendered**/ Evasion: *Yeoman*, 14 Sep 1848. **O'Reilly did not**/ Dead: *Courier*, 12 Sep 1848. *Case:* HOR to editors of *American Mining Journal*, 16 Oct 1848, HORP. HOR's charge of conspiracy was not entirely fanciful. Quite unethically, Page had given Morse information about Royal House's application for a patent. **Morse had learned**/ Murder: SFB to RM, 25 Oct 1848, Y. **Morse's Order of Glory**/ Messiah: Vail Scrapbook, p. 86, V. Grateful: SFB to Secretary P. Marsh (draft), 15 Dec 1849, M13. *Titles:* SFB, *Foreign Conspiracy against the Liberties of the United States*, 66–67. **Morse discovered once**/ Citizen: See M33, fr. 385, 391. **And O'Reilly's**/ See HOR's Atlantic and Pacific Telegraph Range circular headed "Telegraphic and Letter-Mail Communication with the Pacific," New-York Historical Society. **Whatever Morse might**/ Married: Vail Scrapbook, p. 47, V.

THIRTEEN: THE GREAT TELEGRAPH CASE

Morse first saw Sarah/ Deportment: SFB to SM, 7 Aug 1848, M26. Sarah was SFB's second cousin on his mother's side. **Sarah had been deaf**/ Uttered: SFB to L. J. Anderson (draft), 24 Jan 1853, M16. Alfred Vail remarked that Sarah was "still Deaf." AV to George Vail, 1 Sep 1848, V. Anyone: SFB to Thomas Walker, 9 Jan 1852, M15. **Sarah's impairment**/ Excited: SFB to SM, 7 Aug 1848, M26. *Personal:* SFB to RM, 29 Jul 1848, Y. **Morse felt no less**/ Thwarted: SFB to RM, 27 Aug 1848, Y. **Sarah attended**/ Taught: SFB to Sarah Morse, 25 Dec 1852, M15. Summons: SFB to Sarah Morse, 25 Feb 1855, M17. **Morse brought Sarah**/ Variety: ELM, II, 280–81. **To manage the large place**/ Farmer: see M14, fr. 98. Friendless: P, pp. 669–71. **Morse gave his estate**/ Permitted: SFB to SM, 12 Sep 1847, M11. SFB seems to have paid $8000 down in cash, and to have taken a mortgage for the rest. Picturesque: A. J. Davis to SFB, 5 Sep 1852, M15. SFB had painted a frontispiece for Davis' book. Davis' evolving plans survive at the Metropolitan Museum of Art Library. **Morse and Sarah quickly**/ Sinner: SFB to George Wood, 2 Feb 1853, Historical Society of Pennsylvania. Souls: SFB to Sarah Morse, 2 Apr 1854, M16. **Morse's children by Lucrece**/ Kind: Charles Morse to SFB, 23 Nov 1847, M11. **Morse had little sympathy**/ Millions: SFB to SM, 18 Dec 1848, New-York Historical Society. **Finley too lived**/ Despair: SFB to SM, 19 Apr 1848, M1. **Susan—"my ancient**/ Horrid: Charles W. Lind to SFB, 30 Jun 1855, M17. **Morse had intently**/ Race: SFB to SM, 29 Oct 1846, M10. Operations: SFB to SM, 8 May 1847, M11. Thrashing: SFB to AV, 27 Mar 1847, V. **Like many other**/ Destiny: SFB to Dominique Arago (draft), [no day] Apr 1848, M12. Crushed: N-YO, 8 Jan 1852. On the revolutions see Langer and Rudé. **As for his aesthetic**/ Sadness: SFB to RM, 24 Feb 1848, Y. **His eyesight deteriorated**/ Destroyed: SFB to James Fenimore Cooper (typed transcript), 20 Nov 1849, M13.

Morse's disgust/ Continent: *Daily Freeman,* 6 Aug 1850. **They did not, but/** Gaze: "A Review of the Circular of L. L. Hill," *Photographic Art Journal* 5, no. 1 (1853): 38. **Hill wrote to Morse/** Systems: L. L. Hill to SFB, 7 Jun 1852, M15. Motto: L. L. Hill to SFB, 26 Apr 1852, M15. On Hill see Barger and White, 38 ff. **Despite the bunker/** Delusion: SFB to Editor of the *National Intelligencer* (draft), 4 Oct 1852, M26. Rejoiced: SFB to L. L. Hill (draft), 21 Jun 1851, M15. **Grateful for Morse's/** Actual: L. L. Hill to SFB, 29 Jan 1852, M15. Pounce: L. L. Hill to SFB, 26 Apr 1852, M15. Plagued: see N-YO, 26 Jun 1851. **That may or may not/** Remarkable: see N.Y. *Tribune,* 17 Jun 1851. **A second, more complex:** Angel: Dorf, 173. On the litigation see Khan, 195–96. **Morse's new legal/** Hotel: HOR to J. B. [Monnot?], 30 Oct 1851, HORP. **Burdened or not/** Outrage: HOR to George Dawson (draft), [ca. 1848], HORP. Highway: see HOR's Atlantic and Pacific Telegraph Range circular headed "Telegraph and Letter-Mail Communication with the Pacific" [1849]. **Morse saw in Bain's/** Chapter: SFB to AV (copy), 6 May 1848, M12. On the Bain telegraph and the subsequent lawsuit see the excellent discussion in Hochfelder, "Taming the Lightning." **Morse dug up/** *Complicated:* SFB to SM, 12 Jan 1848, M11. **Morse tried to stop/** Mark: SFB, patent application (copy), 20 Jan 1848, Maryland Historical Society. **Morse attended Bain/** The account of the trial is based on *Report of the Case of Alexander Bain, Apellant, vs. Samuel F. B. Morse* (1849); *Franklin Institute Journal,* 18, 3d ser. (1849); Baltimore *Sun,* 16 Mar 1849; AK to SFB, 26 Mar 1849, M12. **The press reargued/** Affair: Rochester *Daily Democrat,* 24 Mar 1849. Just: *Sun,* 6 May 1848. **In the patent granted/** Formidable: AK to SFB, 13 Apr 1849, M12. **Using Bain's system/** Loose: Circular of HOR's Atlantic and Pacific Telegraph Range, headed "Restoration of Louisville and New Orleans Line" (1849). **Morse and Kendall/** Sustained: See N.Y. *Tribune,* 28 Jun 1849. **In his handsome Tuscan/** Enjoyment: see part transcription of 1849 letter from SFB, *Autograph* (Apr 1999), 30. Almost: AK to SFB, 28 Jul 1850, M14. A current estimate held that for every dollar received for damages in cases of infringement, $99 was spent on legal fees. See M33, fr. 536. **Morse also faced/** Knowledge: Theodore Faxton to SFB, 17 Nov 1848, M12. **And try as he might/** Pirates: SFB to George Wood, 14 Jan 1851, A. S. W. Rosenbach Foundation. **The definition was crucial/** Conceived: M24, fr. 250. Principle: SFB to George Gifford, 1 Jan 1851, M14. Application: SFB to L. Bréguet (draft), 27 Oct 1846, M10. **It upset Morse/** Exalted: Henry, *Papers,* VII, 522. Trust: P, pp. 551–52. Coloured: Bruce, 275. Henry felt that his achievements had not been adequately recognized in Europe either. See Coulson, 217–20, and Moyer, 242 ff. **Morse's opponents used/** Original: Henry, *Papers,* VII, 600n. Forbear: SFB to AV, 15 Jan 1851, V. **And to deepen/** Worst: AK to "M. Ray," 27 Jan 1852, WU. On the agreement see *Deduction of Henry O'Rielly's* [*sic*] *Title to the use of Morse's Patents in Certain Regions* (n.d.). **As he usually did/** Distorts: SFB to AK, 23 May 1849, WU. Confirm: AK to SFB, 3 Jan 1850, M13. Suffer: SFB to AK (copy), 22 Dec 1849, WU. Allowance: SFB to FOJS, 15 May 1849, S. **But Smith allowed/** Judas: Theodore Faxton to SFB, 18 Jun 1852, M15. Smith justified the construction by calling it not a main line but a side line, passing through and serving such villages as Nunda and Dansville. See Dorf, 129–51. Prospects: *Herald,* 1 Feb 1850. Smith tried to make Morse see Kendall as an enemy too, by implying that Kendall was skimming sales receipts. **Kendall pleaded with/** Alternatives: AK to SFB, 4 Dec 1849, M13. Facts: SFB to FOJS, 4 Mar 1850, S. Fraudulent: FOJS to AK, 5 Mar 1850, S. F. O. G.: SFB to AK, 8 Mar 1850, WU. Fangs: SFB to RM, 26 Apr 1850, Y. **Smith wanted Morse/**

Feather: SFB to FOJS (copy), 13 Mar 1850, S. See also [AK], *Full Exposure of the Conduct of Dr. Charles T. Jackson* [1850?]. **Through a farcical**/ *Permit:* E. Fitch Smith to SFB, 17 Apr 1850, M14. **Smith threatened to break**/ Knife: AK to FOJS, 22 Apr 1850, S. Glory: FOJS to SFB, 15 Apr 1850, S. **Whether the decision**/ Bribed: SFB to SM, 22 Nov 1850, M14. Thorn: M33, fr. 527. For an excellent discussion of the Downing case see Hochfelder, "Taming the Lightning." **Having sided with**/ Foggy: SFB to AK (copy), 10 Jan 1853, M16. **To Morse, Smith's**/ Rascality: SFB to George Vail, 10 Mar 1852, V. Order: FOJS to AK, 9 Apr 1852, Amos Kendall Papers, Library of Congress. *Morse* v. *Smith*/ See *Samuel F. B. Morse, and Alfred Vail, against Francis O. J. Smith* (1852) and the judicial decision of 20 Nov 1852, M15. **Morse suffered**/ Crows: ELM, II, 319. **In reality, Smith**/ Lust: Gaffney, 428. Happiness: FOJS to "my friend Lucy," 25 Dec 1851, S. **Looking into the future**/ Corpse: SFB to Daniel Lord, 5 Aug 1854, M29. Cutting: SFB to AK (draft), 4 Jan 1851, M14. Downward: SFB to George Wood, 4 Jan 1851, A. S. W. Rosenbach Foundation. Crept: SFB to RM, 1 Jul 1852, Y. **Morse's expensive**/ Relentless: SFB to AK (draft), 4 Jan 1851, M14. *Cheap:* SFB to [unidentified], 12 Jul 1851, A. S. W. Rosenbach Foundation. Grave: SFB, draft of an article for N-YO, 7 Jan 1851, M14. **Becoming one of the most**/ *Obscurity:* SFB to J. E. Sherwood (draft), 14 Jan 1853, M16. **O'Reilly was in less**/ *Agony:* HOR to S. K. Zook, 18 Feb 1852, HORP. The Court agreed to hear the case in January 1852, but delayed until the end of the year. During the wait, a fire in a clerk's room at the Supreme Court destroyed many of Morse's important legal papers and evidence, including his *Sully* sketchbook. Fortunately he had prepared a certified copy. Pivot: George Wood to SFB, 20 Apr [1852], M15. **Morse's side tried**/ Object: see *Argument of George Gifford, Esq., Delivered in December, 1852, at Washington, before the Supreme Court* (1853). *Marking:* See *The Electric Telegraph. Substance of the Argument of S. P. Chase before the Supreme Court of the United States* (1853). **Morse considered the outcome**/ SFB to Sarah Morse, 25 Dec 1852, M15. **The decision would test**/ First: M17, fr. 120. **An editorial in**/ Grant: *Daily Times* (later the *New York Times*), 14 Sep 1852. Many contemporary historians of technology have challenged the nineteenth-century myth of the lone inventor. For most of them the story of the telegraph better fits the modern model of organized industrial research. See, for instance, *Social Construction* and Israel, *From Machine Shop*. **The Supreme Court spoke**/ For the Court's decision(s) see *Journal of The Franklin Institute* 27, 3d ser. (1854). **Kendall, in Washington**/ Signal: AK to SFB, 31 Jan 1854, M16. Utterly: SFB to EC (telegram), 8 Feb 1854, M16. World: SFB to Sarah Morse, 19 Feb 1854, M16. **Having narrowed**/ Anxieties: SFB to AK (copy), 20 Jun 1854, M29. **But Morse succeeded**/ See the opinion of Commissioner Charles Mason, 23 Jun 1854, M16. Reap: ELM, II, 324.

FOURTEEN: A TRUE SOCIAL FRATERNITY

The decade since/ On the effect of the telegraph on business see N.Y. *Herald*, 9 Jul 1855; Du Boff; Beniger; John, "Recasting the Information." **By 1855, the telegraph**/ Early duplex systems were invented by M. G. Farmer of Salem, Mass., in 1852, and by Gintl of Vienna in 1853. See Meyer, 111–12. Morse was enthusiastic for Gintl's process, and offered to secure a patent for it in the United States. See SFB to Charles F. Loosey, 8 Oct 1855, M27. **The occupation**/ Babel: Russell, 54. **The fifty or so**/ On consolidation see especially Blondheim, *News*, 191–92; Nonnenmacher; Thompson. **At the same time**/ Prussia: See Siemens, 108–09. Sweden: See material on Telemuseum Web site, <www.telemuseum.se/musinfo/telegrafi>. Australia: See Samuel McGowan to SFB, 3 Dec 1853, M16. India: Headrick, 54. **Field's oracular venture**/ Absurd: M33, fr. 559. Sublime: *Tribune*, 1 Jun 1855. History: N-YO, 7 Jun 1855. **Morse shared this**/ Future: P, p. 624. See also Dibner. **Morse tried to make**/ Project: SFB to Cyrus Field (draft), 11 Mar 1854, M16; cf. SFB to John C. Spencer (copy), 10 Aug 1843, LHL. Offended: SFB to Horatio Hubbell, 12 Jun 1854, Duke University Library. **Morse sent descriptions**/ Office: SFB to Michael Faraday (draft), 30 Sep 1854, M17. **Faraday did not reply**/ Induce: C. D. Archibald to SFB, 30 Oct 1854, M17. **Morse quickly learned**/ Consent: SFB to Cyrus Field, 22 Apr (draft) and 15 Apr (copy) 1854, M26. **Kendall too was disturbed**/ Enter: AK to SFB, 10 Jun 1854, M16. Sincerity: AK to SFB, 16 May 1854, M16. **But Morse felt**/ Priest: C. D. Archibald to SFB, 16 Sep 1854, M17. Folly: SFB to AK (copy), 13 Jun 1854, M29. **Not only O'Reilly**/ Care: AV to SFB, 21 Sep 1848, V-NYHS. Brain: AV to Daniel Griffin, 26 May 1849, V. **Vail returned**/ Crushing: AV to AK, 29 Jun 1852, V-NYHS. Bitter: see AV diary for 1851, New Jersey Historical Society. **Morse believed that**/ Annoyances: SFB to George Vail (copy), 15 Jul 1854, M29. Animal: SFB to AK, 24 Aug 1854, M29. **And Smith won**/ Swindle: ELM, II, 347. Element: SFB to AK (copy), 4 Dec 1855, M27. *Incubus:* SFB to T. R. Walker (copy), 8 Sep 1854, M29. Revolting: AK to SFB, 7 May 1856, M18. **Morse thought of disengaging**/ Relation: SFB to AK (copy), 22 Jun 1854, M29. Precarious: AK to SFB, 1 Nov 1854, M17. **Morse sent Kendall**/ Liable: SFB to AK, 26 Jun 1854, WU. **Morse's tone sounds**/ Complain: AK to SFB, 1 Oct 1855, M17. **In private, Morse**/ *Attack!* : SFB to AK, 6 Dec 1856, M27. **While at Locust**/ Cordially: SFB to Joseph L. Jones (copy), 18 Oct 1854, M29. Votes: SFB to N. Robinson, 14 Jun 1855, M29. **In the congressional**/ Platform: SFB to Joseph L. Jones (copy), 18 Oct 1854, M29. **Morse had always thought**/ Rabid: SFB to W. S. Tisdale (copy), 30 May 1855, M29. Good: SFB to S. M. Dorr, 1 Nov 1854, M29. Reckless: SFB to Tisdale. **Despite efforts by Morse**/ Shock: SFB to William B. Weiss (draft), 12 Feb 1852, M15. **Morse felt the effects**/ Savages: SFB to "Mr. Sherrell," 4 Apr 1849, M12. Cried: SFB to RM, 4 Apr 1849, Y. Wish: SFB to "Mr. Bokum" (copy), 18 Jul 1854, M29. **Morse became a rallying**/ *Jesuitism:* Joseph C. Morton to SFB, 17 Aug 1849, M13. **Although running**/ GOVERN: N-YO, 21 Jun 1855. Awake: SFB to Edward Beecher (copy), 9 Apr 1855, M29. On the Know-Nothings see Billington, chs. 11–12, and Holt, ch. 24. **About ten days before**/ See N-YO, 24 May 1855. **Soon Morse was trading**/ Festering: N-YO, 24 May 1855. Eel: SFB to Norman Robinson (copy), 21 Apr 1855, M29. **Morse's months**/ Moment: N-YO, 30 Aug 1855. Layed: J. Packarde to SFB, 11 Jul 1855, M17. Pilloried: see N-YO, 19 Jul 1855; here the name is spelled Spaulding. **Despite his passion**/ Ruinous: SFB to Stephen Clark (copy), 15 Sep 1855, M29. On abolition and nativism see Anbinder. **To a lengthening list**/ Ultraisms: SFB to Joseph L. Jones, 18 Oct 1854, M29. Platforms: SFB to Anna Ella Carroll (copy), 27 May 1856, M27. **On August 20**/ Bound: *Herald,* 3 Sep 1855. In describing the voyage I have summarized and tried to square conflicting accounts in Cain, Carter, Field, Mullaly, and N.Y. *Tribune,* 6 Sep 1855. **Field's sudden interest**/ Scruple: SFB to AK (copy), 7 Dec 1855, M27. On the Hughes telegraph see W. King, "The Development," 303; Prescott, 139–44. In its later modifications, Hughes' telegraph was used in Europe to the end of the century. **But two weeks later**/ Wonderful: *Herald,* 17 Nov 1855. **Morse knew about**/ Collision: SFB to AK (copy), 20 Nov 1855, M27. **Kendall was less**/ Friendship: AK to SFB, 7 Dec 1855, M17. **But Morse was by nature/** Unsuspicious: AK to SFB, 12 Feb 1850, WU. Enterprize: SFB to John W. Brett, 26 Dec 1855, M27. Business: SFB to AK (copy), 4 Dec 1855, M27. **Morse agreed to accompany/** Extent: SFB to George Harding, 7 May 1856, M27. Liberal: William Goodrich to SFB, 26 May [1855, but misdated 1850], M14. Farthing: SFB to [probably AK] (copy), 8 Jan 1855, M29. **But the spring months/** Wretch: SFB to T. R. Walker (copy), 16 Jan 1856, M27. Claim: AK to SFB, 20 Feb 1856, M18. **Morse made his uncomfortable/** Honorable: SFB to T. R. Walker (copy), 28 Feb 1856, M27. Warm: SFB to AK, 29 Feb 1856, M27. Undoing: SFB to Taliaferro Shaffner (copy), 8 Apr 1856, M27. **Morse may have undone/** Hostile: AK to SFB, 5 Mar 1856, M18. **Against his every wish/** Plan: SFB to AK, 20 May 1856, M27. Moment: SFB to AK (copy), 20 May 1856, M27. **Jedediah was much/** Malice: SFB to "Rev. Sprague" (copy), 24 May 1856, M27. **Morse and Sarah departed/** Fixed: Cyrus Field to SFB (telegram), 17 May 1856, M18. SFB's answer appears as a handwritten note on Field's telegram, seemingly intended for a telegram also.

FIFTEEN: CAN'T! SIR, CAN'T!

After about ten/ Chatting: SFB to SM (copy), 19 Jul 1856, Y. **Morse's journey north/** Passport: SFB to SM (copy), 19 Jul 1856, Y. Services: P, p. 612. **Morse considered his visit/** Foundation: ELM, II, 354–55. **Through the American minister/** On SFB's visit to St. Petersburg see ELM, II, 355–64, and M18, fr. 237–39. **The test results/** Resolved: P, p. 645. **After the downing/** The transcriptions of SFB's long speech in several newspapers differ substantially. I have relied chiefly on an official report of the dinner, M18, fr. 327. But see also the discrepant transcriptions and summaries in N-YO, 30 Oct 1856, and M33, fr. 579–80. **London newspapers reported/** Entitled: *European*, 22 Nov 1856. Progress: London *Times*, 13 Oct 1856. **F. O. J. Smith was suing/** Thorn: ELM, II, 371. KNIGHT: M33, fr. 567. **The assaults left Morse/** Depressed: SFB to AK (copy), 29 Dec 1856, M27. Money-worshipping: SFB to Charles Morse, 10 Jan [1859 but misdated 1858], M26. Nook: SFB to AK (copy), 29 Jan 1857, M27. **Morse sought relief/** Problems: SFB to Peter Cooper (copy), 21 Mar 1857, M27. Hostile: AK to SFB, 4 Jan 1857, M18. **Morse still hoped/** Onward: Peter Cooper to SFB, 10 Mar 1857, M18. **A few days later/** Duplicity: SFB to Peter Cooper, 14 Mar 1857, M27. **Field's non-offer/** Scheme: AK to SFB, 22 Feb 1857, M18. **Morse thanked Field/** Something: SFB to Cyrus Field, 13 Feb 1857, M27. Sacrifice: SFB to AK (copy), 14 Feb 1857, M27. **Morse's ever more desperate/** Sacred: AK to SFB, 23 Feb 1857, M18. Bluish: SFB to AK (copy), 14 Feb 1857, M27. **Morse anxiously longed/** Rupture: SFB to T. R. Walker (copy), 21 Mar 1857, M27. The bill for the appropriation provoked angry debate in the Senate. Southerners and westerners saw the transatlantic telegraph chiefly profiting traders and merchants in the industrial North. Others argued that, in case of war, the cable would greatly benefit England. See *The Arguments in Favor of the International Submarine Telegraph, in the Senate of the United States* (1857). **The offer cannot have/** Waived: SFB to Peter Cooper (copy), 21 Mar 1857, M27. **Morse did not say/** Satisfied: SFB to T. R. Walker (copy), 21 Mar 1857, M27. **As a world-historic/** GREAT: M33, fr. 681. Annals: N.Y. *Tribune*, 27 Aug 1857. Sublime: *Times and Messenger*, 23 Aug 1857. **Morse received extensive/** Can't: *Harper's Weekly*, 2 May 1857, 282. **Morse shipped for England/** *Falls:* SFB to Sarah Morse, 2 May 1857, M18. The following account of the laying of the transatlantic cable draws on Briggs and Maverick, Dibner, Field, Mullaly, and Saward, and on newspaper clippings in M33. **A serious problem**/ Splendid: SFB to Cyrus Field (copy), 15 May 1857, M27. **Morse enthusiastically approved**/ Conferred: SFB to Sarah Morse, 6 Jun 1857, M18. Ordinary: SFB to Frederic Van den Broek (copy), 2 Jun 1857, M27. **To reinforce the French**/ Withhold: SFB to SM, 15 Jun 1857, New-York Historical Society. **Providence in some**/ Jeopardy: Lewis Cass to John G. Mason, 31 Jul 1857, M19. **Morse spent the rest**/ Abused: SFB to Sarah Morse, 6 Jun 1857, M18. **Morse and his fellow**/ Delighted: SFB to Sarah Morse, 9 Jul 1857, M19. **Morse reboarded**/ Harbors: SFB to Sarah Morse, 28 Jul 1857, M19. Scholars: M33, fr. 705. **News that the historic**/ Fleet: *Herald,* 18 Aug 1857. For the sake of compression, I have connected parts of closely related sentences from two adjoining paragraphs. Glory: ELM, II, 376. **An immense coil**/ Steam-engines: ELM, II, 378. **The squadron had moved**/ *Occur:* SFB to SM, 7 Aug 1857, M19. **Operations resumed**/ Rumbling: ELM, II, 380. **Morse telegraphed**/ 214: SFB to [Edward Whitehouse], 10 Aug 1857, M19. Littleness: P, p. 659. **As the *Niagara* steamed**/ Thread: SFB to Sarah Morse (draft), 12 Aug 1857, M19. **Also lost overboard**/ Herculean: *Tribune,* 27 Aug 1857. Sanguine: M19, fr. 96. Disagreeable: *Scientific American,* 3 Oct 1857, 29. **Morse contributed**/ Fatal: *Scientific American,* 19 Sep 1857, 13. Demur: Briggs and Maverick, 114. **In fact, Morse's**/ Engage: SFB to John Mullaly, 23 Oct 1857, Morgan Library. **Meanwhile the company's**/ Providential: SFB to George Saward (draft), 18 Aug 1857, M19. **Having sent his recommendation**/ Tomorrow: SFB to Sarah Morse, 14 and 20 Aug 1857, M19. **Kendall gave Morse**/ Defiant: AK to SFB, 6 Jul 1857, M18. See also *Proceedings of the Principal Telegraph Companies in the United States* (1857). **Morse was already peeved**/ Adverse: SFB to Sarah Morse, 7 Sep 1857, M19. **A little relieved**/ Posted: SFB to Cyrus Field (draft), 1 Jun 1858, M19. **Morse's 140**/ Thinly: SFB to Sarah Morse, 19 Sep 1857, M19.

SIXTEEN: FORWARD

Kendall had obtained/ *Existed:* AK to SFB, 3 Oct 1857, M19. Morse's extant correspondence leaves it uncertain whether he learned of the events recounted in AK's important letter of 27 Aug 1857 (M19) before he left England or after he returned to the United States. My best judgment is that he learned of them after his return. See also Thompson, 310 ff. **Morse had had**/ Sacrifice: SFB to John Mullaly, 23 Oct 1857, Morgan Library. Suicide: SFB to AK, 20 Oct 1857, M27. **Field explained that**/ Violating: SFB to SM, 15 Mar 1858, M19. Exculpate: SFB to J. W. Brett (draft), 27 Dec 1858, M19. **Hurt and angry**/ Imparted: SFB to Cyrus Field (copy), 12 Mar 1858, M19. Perfidy: AK to SFB, 27 Aug 1857, M19. Inordinate: *New American State Papers,* 196. **Morse companies excluded**/ Africa: AK to SFB, 27 Aug 1857, M19. **Morse had always striven**/ Intriguants: SFB to AK, 20 Oct 1857, M27. **Field's exact part**/ Deserved: Cyrus Field to SFB (copy), [no day] May 1858, M19. **Morse replied by recalling**/ Blind: SFB to Cyrus Field (draft), 1 Jun 1858, M19. **"My faith in those**/ Misplaced: SFB to SM, 29 Dec 1857, New-York Historical Society. Contempt: AK to SFB, 5 Jun and 18 May 1858, M19. Gratuity: ELM, II, 395. COLUMBUS: N.Y. *Times,* 9 Sep 1858. **Morse and Sarah sailed**/ Right: SFB, "To the Conductors," 27 Nov 1857, Samuel Morse Historic Site, Poughkeepsie. **Morse had rarely**/ Pleasure: ELM, II, 397. Plants: SFB to Charles Morse, 10 Jan [1859 but misdated 1858], M26. Severe: SFB to E. D. Apthorp, 26 Jan 1857, M27. Punish: SFB to Arthur Morse (copy), 27 Dec 1858, M26. **Americans greeted**/ Neighborhood: M33, fr. 724. **New Yorkers closed**/ Orgasm: Strong, 412. On the celebration see the newspaper clippings gathered in M33, fr. 727–30. **Morse was not forgotten**/ *Forever:* M33, fr. 749. Uninspired: *Western Episcopalian,* 10 Sep 1858. **In Paris, seventy-five**/ Mark: John Munro et al. to SFB, [no day] Aug 1858, M19. Realized: *Times,* 9 Sep 1858. **A week after Morse's**/ On the Board of Trade see Earl Shelbourne to Board of Trade, 21 Nov 1857, Public Record Office, London. **The homage paid him**/ Gratitude: ELM, II, 394–95. Lofty: M20, fr. 157 ff. On Sep 27, SFB attended the ten-hour exhibition at the Café de la Régence, in which the young American chess wizard Paul Morphy defeated eight of the best players in Paris while blindfolded. **Rejoicing curdled**/ Solitary: *Courier,* 19 Jan 1859. Judgment: M33, fr. 743. On the cable failure see Bright and Dibner. **The breakdown**/ *Ejected:* SFB to J. W. Brett (draft), 27 Dec 1858, M19. Motive: SFB to [AK] (copy), 22 Dec 1858, M26. **Morse and Sarah spent**/ Claude: SFB to SM (copy), 12 Jan [1859 but misdated 1858], M26. **Morse was impressed**/ Inferior: SFB to RM (copy), 28 Dec 1858, M26; see also Leila Morse Rummel, TS "Souvenirs of Samuel F. B. Morse," Archives of American Art. Swine: SFB to Cornelia Goodrich (copy), 26 Jan 1859, M26. **After Morse's ten-month**/ Excellence: SFB to Robert Walsh, 28 Mar 1859, M26. **Homage poured in**/ Suspicious: SFB to Vice President and Directors of the Morse Insurance Company, 28 Oct 1860, M29. The invitation from the architects came later, in 1869. See Russell Sturgis to SFB, 12 Oct 1869, M23. **Morse's $80,000 indemnity**/ *Honor:* SFB to George T. Curtis (copy), 6 Jul 1860, M29. Serious: SFB to FOJS, 24 May 1860, M20. Favor: SFB to AK (copy), 3 Aug 1860, M29. **The arbitration hearing**/ Synonyms: ELM, II, 411–12. On the hearing see MS document of 31 Jul 1860, Y. **Morse saw in the situation**/ Demands: see "General Release," 3 Jun 1862, WU. Corpus: SFB to George Curtis (copy), 6 Jul 1860, M29. Den: SFB to RM, 7 Sep 1860, M29. **The much-reduced**/ Dyspeptic: ELM, II, 400. **The various settlements**/ Manifesto: see M20, fr. 224–26 and documents included in AK to Charles Page (not in Kendall's hand), 2 Apr 1860, M20. **Astonished, Morse**/ Human: SFB to Leonard Gale, 12 Apr 1869, M31. **Morse went to Washington**/ See *Decision of Hon. Philip F. Thomas, Commissioner of Patents, on the Application of Samuel F. B. Morse* (1860). **But then there was**/ Libellous: Moyer, 272. **But Henry replied**/ See pamphlet entitled "Extracts from the Proceedings of the Board of Regents of the Smithsonian Institution, in Relation to the Electro-Magnetic Telegraph" [1860?], copy in HORP. **The Smithsonian committee**/ Pervert: Coulson, 232. Legal: see F. M. Baudouin to SFB, 27 Nov 1860, M20. **The detailed case that Henry**/ Superhuman: SFB to SM, 12 Jan [1859 but misdated 1858], M16. Inculpate: SFB to RM, 16 Oct 1858, Y. **Morse began preparing**/ *Arraigned:* M20, fr. 161. **Morse reasoned that**/ Mixed: SFB to SM (copy), 23 Feb 1859, M26. **Morse favored the idea**/ Feeling: SFB to AK, 7 Jul 1859, M27. **Kendall handled**/ Manger: Thompson, 329. On the negotiations see also Blondheim, 118–29. **However much Morse**/ Competence: SFB to FOJS, 24 May 1860, M20. Creeping: SFB to Taliaferro Shaffner, 27 Jun 1860, M27. **Morse's house was**/ Consumer: SFB to H. S. Lansing (copy), 9 Aug 1860, M29. On New York City at the time see Burrows and Wallace, and Spann. **Morse continued to house**/ Inglorious: RM to SM, 31 Jul 1851, Y. Bounty: ELM, II, 421. **With Morse's fine**/ Dishabille: SFB to Duke of Newcastle (copy), 18 Aug 1860, M29. Engaged: Duke of Newcastle to SFB, 8 Oct 1860, M20; and see T. Jones, 86. **With a momentous**/ Attraction: SFB to "Mr. Reibart," 10 Jun 1859, M26. Overboard: Potter, 485.

SEVENTEEN: IS THIS TREASON? IS THIS CONSPIRACY?

For Samuel F. B. Morse/ Scorn: SFB to S. B. S. Bissell, 20 Sep 1861, M29. **The break-down/** Fellow: SFB to J. L. M. Curry, 16 Mar 1860, M27. **These connections/** Slave-holder: SFB to Robert Baird (copy), 16 Jul 1860, M29. Sword: SFB to George L. Douglas (copy), 12 Jan 1861, M29. **To do what he could/** Praying: SFB to H. G. Ludlow (copy), 13 May 1861, M29. Slaughter: SFB, "The Letter of a Republican," *Papers from the Society for the Diffusion of Political Knowledge*, no. 4 [1863]: 6. **Morse's group held/** Brethren: SFB to Cornelia Goodrich, 21 Apr 1861, New York Public Library. On the opening events of the war see Potter. **Morse's agony deepened/** Abuse: SFB to H. G. Ludlow (copy), 13 May 1861, M29. Prestige: SFB to James Wynne (copy), 2 May 1861, M26. **Morse recalled bitterly/** Anomaly: SFB to "Col. Hamilton" (copy), 10 May 1861, M29. **Instead of fleeing/** Heart: SFB to [unidentified] (copy), 5 Feb 1862, M29. **As Morse pointed out/** Deplorable: SFB to Charles Mason (copy), 27 Jan 1865, M28, referring to a letter of 1862. Some other Unionists also suggested that North and South could overcome their differences by joining to fight England, or England and Spain. See McKay, 107. **Morse's alarums/** Aristocracy: Hyman, 66. Terror: Crook, 54–55. See also Davis, 44–46. **Not surprisingly/** Charged: SFB to Edward Hyde (copy), [day illegible] Oct 1861, M29. Return: SFB to George L. Douglass (copy), 21 Apr 1862, M29. See also Thompson, 377. **The eruption of/** Armies: SFB to Edward Lind (copy), 22 Sep 1861, M29. Gild: SFB to James Wynne (copy), 12 Aug 1861, M29. Battle figures based on Long. **Morse told Kendall/** Crow: SFB to AK (copy), 23 Jul 1862, M29. Prophecy: SFB to T. R. Walker (copy), 27 Oct 1862, M29. **For Morse, as for/** Wicked: SFB to "Judge Caton" (draft), 18 Feb 1863, M21. Scheme: SFB to William Goodrich (copy), 17 Oct 1862, M29. On the Proclamation see McPherson, 118 ff. **Unless, Morse thought/** *Elections:* SFB to William Goodrich (copy), 17 Oct 1862, M29. **Morse's fantasy/** Rabid: SFB to Susan Morse, 12 Feb 1863, M29. **Morse found some hope/** Support: Burrows and Wallace, 879. **The paper gave a sinister/** Oligarchs: see *Evening Post*, 7, 9, 10, 14 Feb 1863. Infamous: Mabee, 348. See also Katz, 120–21. **The Society convened/** Treason: "The Constitution. Addresses of Prof Morse, Mr. Geo Ticknor Curtis, and Mr. S. J. Tilden, at the Organization," *Papers from the Society for the Diffusion of Political Knowledge*, no. 1 [1863?]. Retract: SFB to "Judge Caton," 18 Feb 1863, M21. On the S.D.P.K. see also Lee, 228–30, and McKay, 174–75. **In trying to reach/** Mind: SFB to Charles Mason, 14 Oct 1863, M29. **Morse himself had contributed/** Intended: SFB to H. G. Ludlow (copy), 13 May 1861, M29. Heresy: SFB to "Senator Bigler" (copy), 6 Feb 1861, M29. Morse also studied but wrote little about the constitutional issues, considering the main one settled: "The United States are forbidden to touch [slavery]. The *States* alone individually have the right to regulate the relation." SFB to RM (copy), 5 Nov 1864, M28. **As Morse explained/** See SFB, *An Argument,* passim. **That this view/** Cursed: SFB to Martin Hauser (copy), 21 Sep 1863, M29. Relation: SFB to Charles Mason (copy), 14 Oct 1863, M29. **Morse tried to account/** Rejecting: SFB to H. G. Ludlow (copy), 13 May 1861, M29. **Despite his devotion/** Delusion: SFB to "Mr. Luckey" (copy), 19 Nov 1862, M29. Declaration: SFB to H. G. Ludlow (copy), 17 May 1860, M27. Subjection: SFB, *The Present Attempt to Dissolve the American Union,* 40–41. Temples: SFB, *An Argument,* 3. **Nature as well/** Degraded: SFB, *An Argument,* 19. Baboon: SFB, *Lectures on the Affinity,* 64. Superior: McPherson, 61. Caucasian: SFB to Gideon S. Tucker (copy), 10 Apr 1863, M29. On the linking of pro-slavery biblical arguments with racialist arguments see Noll. **Morse emphasized/** Guidance: SFB, *An Argument,* 12. BARBAROUS: SFB, *An Argument,* 16. **What distinguishes**

Morse's/ Axiom: SFB to George Wood (copy), 5 Mar 1865, M28. Remain: SFB to RM (copy), 6 Jun 1865, M28. On the pro-slavery argument see especially Faust. **Sidney Morse shared**/ Deification: SM, *Premium Questions on Slavery* (1860), 13. Delusions: SFB to RM (copy), 9 Nov 1864, M28. **It gratified Morse**/ Pious: SFB to Stuart Robinson, 23 Nov 1863, M29. Fitness: M33, fr. 488. Demand: SFB to "Mr. Shedd" (copy), 22 Jul 1864, M28. **But Morse's writing**/ Repentance: H. G. Ludlow to SFB, 5 May 1861, M20. Former: *Times*, 29 Mar 1863. Shallow: *North American Review*, Jan 1864, 122, 126. **Morse's telegraphs put**/ Orders: Plum, II, 366. On the telegraph in the Civil War see also Bates. **The blare**/ Skill: SFB to Peter Cooper et al. (copy), 3 Mar 1863, M29. **Morse applauded**/ See D. Romanoff to SFB, 5 Apr 1862, M20. **The vastly long**/ Fulfilled: SFB to George Wood (copy), 25 Jun 1864, M26. **As the war raged**/ Repining: AK to SFB, 27 Dec 1861, M20. Union: AK to SFB, 12 Mar 1863, M21. Pride: see AK's fourth letter of 22 Feb 1862, Amos Kendall Papers, Library of Congress. **Morse and Kendall**/ Profitable: *Tribune*, 5 Dec 1865. **Wealthy already**/ Words: SFB to T. R. Walker (copy), 16 Mar 1864, M28. Regal: *Tribune*, 5 Dec 1865. **To Morse's delight**/ Evidence: ELM, II, 443. **At the time Southern**/ Artlessness: SFB to Sarah Morse, 19 Feb 1854, M16. Lela also sometimes appears in Morse's papers as Leila. Position: SFB to Charles Morse (copy), 10 Jan [1859 but misdated 1858], M26. **Morse sent his sons**/ Remember: SFB to Arthur Morse, [no day] Jul 1862, M29. Obedient: SFB to Arthur Morse, 30 Oct 1866, M30; to Arthur Morse, [no day] Jul 1862, M29; to M. Baudoin, 16 Oct 1866, M30. Paths: SFB to E. S. Salisbury, 11 Aug 1865, M21. Forever: SFB to his children, 10 May 1857, M18. **Morse's adult children**/ Cares: SFB to Mrs. H. L. Davis (copy), 11 May 1866, M28. Strange: SFB to Finley Morse (copy), 12 Mar 1870, M31. Whales: SFB to Arthur Morse (copy), 6 Sep 1868, M30. **Susan, now in her**/ Mental: SFB to Edward Lind, 22 Sep 1861, M29. *Nervousness:* SFB to Charles Lind, 19 Dec 1867, M30. Suffer: SFB to Edward Lind, 16 Jul 1861, M19. **Charles, too**/ Sharpers: SFB to SM, 29 Dec 1857, New-York Historical Society. Defect: SFB to Charles Morse (copy), 10 Jan [1859 but misdated 1858], M26. **Charles was much**/ Easy: SFB to Charles Morse, 8 Jan 1866 and 15 Jun 1863, M29. **To Morse's displeasure**/ Manly: SFB to Charles Morse (copy), 7 Oct 1865, M28. Sea: SFB to SM, 8 Aug 1867, XM. **Both Charles and his sister**/ Favorite: SFB to Charles Morse (copy), 25 Jun 1864, M26. Standing: SFB to "Rev. Dr. Hamill," 4 Oct 1865, M28. Joy: SFB to Charles Morse, 17 Mar 1866, M28. Esteem: SFB to Charles Lind (copy), 5 Nov 1865, M28. **It may have been**/ Eyes: SFB to Nathaniel Jocelyn (copy), 20 Jan 1864, M28. Revived: SFB to "Messrs Durand, Ingham & others," [Mar 1861], M29. **Morse's duties**/ Heart: SFB to Daniel Huntington (copy), 26 Dec 1864, M28. **Scarcely ten days**/ See McKay, 199–209. **Spending the summer**/ Illiterate: See various letters of SFB in 1863–64, M28 and M29. Brains: SFB to William Goodrich, 9 Jul 1863, Jacob Eliot Family Papers, Yale University Library. **Morse backed McClellan**/ Devotion: SFB to A. G. Jennings (copy), 10 Aug 1864, M28. **He looked ahead**/ Dead: SFB to Edward Lind (copy), 19 Aug 1864, M28. Sealed: SFB to RM (copy), 7 Nov 1864, M28. Throne: SFB to RM (copy), 29 Oct 1864, M28. **As the election**/ Immortal: N.Y. *Express*, 5 Nov 1864. Mass: ELM, II, 430–31. **The hoopla**/ Augur: SFB to [unidentified] (copy), 3 Dec 1864, M28. Enemy: SFB to Charles L. Chaplain, 15 Dec 1864, M28. **Morse grieved for**/ Applauding: SFB to E. S. Salisbury, 11 Aug 1865, M21. **But as Morse soon**/ Dark: SFB to Mrs. C. W. Griswold, 22 Sep 1866, M21. Pupils: SFB to RM (copy), 6 Jun 1865, M28. Avoided: SFB to Charles Lind (copy), 25 Nov 1865, M28. **A week or so**/ Adding: SFB to H. L. Davis (copy), 11 May 1866, M28.

EIGHTEEN: VISIONS OF RECEDING GLORY

It refreshed Morse/ *Portrait:* SFB to Edward Lind, 1 Nov 1863, M29. Gewgaws: SFB to his brothers (draft), 18 Jul 1832, M6. **The Abrahamic**/ Weaned: SFB to RM (copy), 29 Apr 1864, M28. **Morse had always**/ Centre: ELM, II, 454. *Cleanest:* SFB to John Thompson (copy), 4 Oct 1866, M30. **Morse lent himself**/ Comfort: SFB to SM (copy), 1 Oct 1866, M30. **Morse enjoyed playing**/ Evil: SFB to C. W. Griswold (copy), 8 Mar 1867, M30. **Using the world**/ Peaceable: SFB to Susan Morse (copy), 4 Feb 1867, M30. Indebted: SFB to "Cousin Mother," [Jan 1867], M30. **From Paris, Morse**/ Nerves: SFB to Cyrus Field, 12 Mar 1867, M30. Excluded: SFB to SM, 4 Oct 1866, M25. **As Morse had planned**/ Powers: SFB to SM, 1 Dec 1867, XM. **Morse took particular**/ Branch: SFB to SM, 16 Aug 1866, XM. **Despite the seductions**/ Irons: SFB to SM (copy), 27 May 1867, M30. **Much other time**/ Slander: SFB to SM (copy), 31 Jul 1867, M30. Conclusion: M23, fr. 150. Infamous: see SFB's annotations in his copy of the *History of the Invention of the Electric Telegraph. Abridged from the Works of Lawrence Turnbull, M.D.* (1853), Library of Congress. **Morse labored to set**/ Hands: SFB to Charles Morse (copy), 11 Jul 1868, M30. SFB conceded, however, that Steinheil invented a genuine telegraph—that is, an electromagnetic recording device—in 1836, independent of himself. The two men had stayed friendly over the years. **Morse had plenty**/ Spot: SFB to SM, 8 Jun 1867, M26. Epitome: ELM, II, 453. Lies: Mattelart, 123. On the Exposition see also Burchell, 123–38, and Levenstein, 90–91. **Press reaction**/ Supplant: M33, fr. 473. King: *Moniteur,* 5 Jun 1867. Cry: M22, fr. 243. Excellent photographs of several European adaptations of SFB's apparatus appear in Bergen. **Morse attended the award**/ Original: SFB to Sidney Morse, Jr. (copy), 18 Jun 1867, M30. Some Hughes telegraphs were in service in France. **Getting started on**/ Load: SFB to SM, 31 Jul 1867, Library of Congress. **Morse did return**/ Exile: SFB to H. G. Ludlow (copy), 30 Mar 1867, M30. Steady: SFB to "Dear Mother" (copy), 27 Feb 1868, M30. Never: ELM, II, 464. **Although more than a quarter**/ Proof: M33, fr. 474. Emperor: N.Y. *Herald,* 18 Nov 1870. On SFB's telegraph in China see Baark, 80 ff., and Headrick, 57. **Morse's globe-circling**/ Express: Horace Baker to SFB, 27 Mar 1871, M23. **Four months later**/ Mental: RM to Richard C. Morse, 25 Sep 1856, Clements Library, University of Michigan. Valley: SFB to SM, 26 Sep 1868, M26. **The political situation**/ Prison: SFB to "Col. Leslie," 2 Nov 1868, M30. **Even occasions**/ Affairs: N.Y. *Times,* 30 Dec 1868. See also the many newspaper clippings about the event in M34. **But the regal blowout**/ On Western Union and the government see Thompson and Lindley. **Morse's recollections**/ Decoy: N.Y. *Herald,* 30 Dec 1868 and 1 Jan 1869. Bennett argued that the telegraph was too powerful an instrument to be wielded by a monopoly, which could use it to rule the press and the country's business in general. **Whether Morse understood**/ Advantage: SFB to AK, 19 Mar 1866, M28. *Basket:* SFB to SM, 25 Jan 1867, M30. **Morse's hefty report**/ Task: SFB to W. P. Blake (copy), 4 Feb 1869, M31. Disputed: SFB to RM (copy), 25 Mar 1867, M30. **Morse's claim, however**/ Truth: SFB to A. S. Manton, 7 Apr 1862, M29. Opinion: SFB to David Burbank, 30 Mar 1860, M27. System: SFB to Denison Cheseboro, 22 Aug 1859, M27. *Sound:* SFB to Edwin F. Reynolds, 22 Mar 1860, M27. **Morse completed**/ Implies: W. P. Blake to SFB, 5 Aug 1869, M23. Radical: W. P. Blake to SFB, 21 Aug 1869, M23. **Morse conceded**/ Weakly: SFB to W. P. Blake (draft), 8 Aug 1869, M23. Father: SFB to AK (draft), 16 Sep 1868, M30. **In August, having**/ *Filthy:* SFB to Arthur Morse (copy), 7 Apr 1867, M30. Rowdies: SFB to J. R. Leslie, 10 Sep 1868, M30. **That August, Arthur**/ Depressed: SFB to SM (copy), 14 Aug 1869, M31. Anxiety: SFB to William Morse (copy), 31 Dec 1869, M31. Secret: SFB to the Linds (copy), 17 Jan 1870, M31. **Morse worried that**/ Rinks: SFB to William Morse (copy), 9 Nov 1869, M31. Grief: SFB to William Morse (copy), 21 Feb 1870, M31. Strong: SFB to Adele Roch (copy), 17 Jul 1870, M31. **In November 1869**/ Marriage: Shoptaugh, 381. **Kendall had been**/ Skill: SFB to William Stickney (copy), 12 Nov 1869, M31. **The record**/ Arm: SFB to John Thompson, 3 Mar 1871, M23. **Morse tried to keep**/ Rouze: SFB to J. Scudder, 8 Jul 1868, NYU Archives, Bobst Library, New York University. Sunburnt: SFB to Arthur Morse (copy), 26 Jun 1868, M30; SFB to S. B. Bostwick, 22 Jan 1870, M31. **For many years**/ Venerable: M34, fr. 308. Manifested: SFB to the Linds (copy), 21 Jan 1871, M31. **Western Union got**/ Globe: ELM, II, 484. Bryant at first had been unwilling to speak, resentful of Morse's Copperhead politics during the Civil War. **Responses to Morse's**/ On the two statue ceremonies see accounts in ELM; *Hearth and Home*, 1 Jul 1871; *Journal of the Telegraph*, 15 Jun 1871; P; and Leila Morse Rummel, TS "Souvenirs of Samuel F. B. Morse," Archives of American Art. From the beginning of commercial service, the industry had employed a few women as operators. Their number increased greatly during the Civil War, when they replaced male operators who entered the military. By 1870 there were some 350 women operators, about 4 percent of the total. See Jepsen. **The tribute left Morse**/ Strange: SFB to the Linds (copy), 14 Jun 1871, M31. Filled: Amanda Vail to John Horn, 6 Aug 1871, V-NYHS. **Amanda Vail confronted**/ See Amanda Vail's MS account of her visit, 12 Jun 1871, V-NYHS, and the TS copy of her "My interview with Professor Morse," V. **In two of Morse's**/ Projected: see F. O. J. Smith, *History Getting Right on the Invention of the American Electro-Magnetic Telegraph* [n.d.], 3. Frauds: HOR to L. W. Case, 12 Feb and 9 Nov 1872, V-NYHS. During the war HOR also edited a collection of antislavery tracts. **Fog Smith needed**/ Heartless: Gaffney, 488. Divided: FOJS to Amanda Vail, 29 Aug 1870, V-NYHS. *Sordid:* FOJS to L. W. Case, 2 Oct 1871, V-NYHS. **Vail was not through**/ Gross: FOJS to L. W. Case, 18 Oct 1871, V-NYHS. Pedestal: FOJS, *History Getting Right,* 5. **The results of this**/ Spirit: SFB to Adiel Sharwood (copy), 3 Jan 1872, M31. Began: unidentified newspaper clipping headed "Professor Morse's Funeral," Box 16, Y. **It was in this**/ Invented: M34, fr. 171. Spite: SFB to Leonard Gale, 25 Jan 1872, M31. Killed: Henry Rogers to Amanda Vail, 4 Apr 1873, V. Guilty: FOJS to Amanda Vail, 19 Jul 1872, V-NYHS. **In February**/ Vile: SFB to Aspinwall Hodge (copy), 26 Feb 1872, M31. See *Great Industries,* 1238–46. **Case again and again**/ See the correspondence between SFB and Case, M23. **February brought another**/ Retracted: M34, fr. 173. **During the same few**/ Welfare: SFB to Howard Parmele (copy), 29 Jan 1872, M31. Liquor: SFB to William Morse (copy), 28 Feb 1872, M31. **Ill and besieged**/ Screw: SFB to Charles Morse (copy), 11 Jul 1868, M30. **Now, having given**/ Anxiety: SFB to J. P. Lindsay (copy), 22 Jan 1872, M31. See account of Lindsay in M34, fr. 172. **In March, Morse**/ Atrocious: SFB to F. J. Mead (copy), 14 Mar 1872, M31. **According to his**/ SFB's death certificate is at the Samuel Morse Historic Site, Poughkeepsie. **Others also**/ Attack: M34, fr. 172. Overload: FOJS to Amanda Vail, 3 Apr 1872, V-NYHS.

CODA: 1872–2000

The encomia/ *Golden Age*, 13 Apr 1872. **On April 5**/ *Memorial*, 238. **The most imposing**/ California: *Memorial*, 193–94. **The often cruel**/ Resolved: Amanda Vail to C. H. Adams (copy), 18 Oct 1888, V-NYHS. **The feud survived**/ Daughter: Unidentified newspaper clipping of 1 Apr 1891, scrapbook entitled "Correspondence relating to Alfred Vail's connection with the Electric Telegraph," V. See also Cavanaugh, 56. **By**

that time/ Desire: Susan Morse to SFB, 18 Jun 1841, M7. Supposed: *Times*, 8 Dec 1885. **Morse's son Charles**/ See New Orleans *Times-Picayune*, 28 Jun 1900; New Orleans Health Department Death Certificates, vol. 122. **Of Morse's four children**/ Crushing: *Daily Picayune*, 18 and 19 Jul 1876. **Morse's lightning survived**/ On the centenary celebration see the documents and scrapbooks assembled by Leila Morse, Columbia University Library. **In the new millennium**/ On the present state of telegraphy see the current journal *Morsum Magnificat;* T. King, *Modern Morse Code;* and *Morsels*, the newsletter of the Morse 2000 Worldwide Outreach.

Acknowledgments

My liveliest thanks to

—the Library of Congress, the Maine Historical Society, the New-York Historical Society, the Olin Library of Cornell University, the Sterling Memorial Library of Yale University, and the Smithsonian Institution Archives, for preserving and allowing me to study their voluminous collections of the papers of Samuel F. B. Morse and his family and associates.

—the other unique libraries, historical societies, and museums that gave me access to their smaller but invaluable collections of Morse material, including the Académie des Sciences (Paris); American Antiquarian Society; Archives of American Art; Bobst Library of New York University; British Library (London); Century Association; Cincinnati Historical Society; Clements Library, University of Michigan; Columbia University Library; Duke University Library; Historic Northampton; Historical Society of Pennsylvania; Huntington Library; Institution of Electrical Engineers (London); Linda Hall Library; Maryland Historical Society; Massachusetts Historical Society; Metropolitan Museum of Art Library; Morgan Library; Morristown National Historical Park; Samuel Morse Historic Site; National Academy of Design; National Museum of American History (Western Union Collection); New Jersey Historical Society; New York Public Library; Phillips Academy Library; Princeton University Library; Public Record Office (London); Rensselaer Polytechnic Institute Library; University of Rochester Library; A. S. W. Rosenbach Foundation; Vermont Historical Society; Woodruff Library, Emory University.

—the many expert curators and librarians at these repositories, particularly Nancy Cricco and Joan Grant (Bobst Library), Margaret Heilbrun (New-York Historical Society), Bruce Kirby (Smithsonian Institution Archives), Jennifer Lee (New York Public Library), and Laura Linke (Olin Library).

—New York University, my longtime second home, for a Research Challenge Fund Grant.

—Beth Phillips, for her photographs; Professors Richard R. John, Jill Lepore, and Paul Magnuson, for helpful information about Morse's activities; and especially Professor David Hochfelder, assistant editor of the Thomas Edison Papers, for reviewing a draft of this biography, giving me the benefit of his precise technical understanding of Morse's telegraph system.

—friends and colleagues whose companionship has been a delight and a boost, both those I have thanked in previous books and those I acknowledge now: Stan Allen, Ann Birstein, Fred Brown, Ed Cifelli, Elam and Mary Lou Collins, Charles DeFanti, Michael Dellaira, Dr. Stuart Feder, Judy Feiffer, Diane Jacobs, Richard Kaufman, Herb Leibowitz, David Levering Lewis, Larry Lockridge, Bill Luhr, Patricia O'Toole, Arnold Rampersad, Carl Rollyson, Mark Rudman, Matthew Santirocco, George and Nina Schindler, Catharine R. Stimpson, Arthur Tannenbaum, Brenda Wineapple, and Meier Yedid.

—my ace literary agent, Hugh Rawson, and my superb editor at Alfred A. Knopf, Ann Close.

—Jane Mallison, *gloriosa donna de la mia mente*.

Kenneth Silverman
Washington Square and Highland Lake

Index

Illustration Credits

77. Samuel F. B. Morse, *DeWitt Clinton* (1826). Oil on canvas, 30$\frac{1}{16}$ × 25$\frac{3}{16}$ in. Metropolitan Museum of Art, Rogers Fund, 1909 (09.18). The Metropolitan Museum of Art. All rights reserved.

86. Samuel F. B. Morse, *The Marquis de Lafayette* (1825–26). Oil on canvas, 94 × 64 in. City Hall, New York. Courtesy of the Art Commission of the City of New York.

96. Horatio Greenough, *Samuel F. B. Morse* (1831). Marble, 19$\frac{1}{2}$ × 12 × 8$\frac{3}{4}$ in. Smithsonian Museum of American Art.

101. Samuel F. B. Morse, *Contadina of Nattuno at the Shrine of the Madonna* (1830). Oil on canvas, 21$\frac{1}{2}$ × 17$\frac{1}{4}$ in. © Virginia Museum of Fine Arts, Richmond. The Adolph D. and Wilkins C. Williams Fund.

120–21. Samuel F. B. Morse, *Grand Gallery of the Louvre* (1831–33). Oil on canvas, 73$\frac{3}{4}$ × 108 in. Terra Foundation for the Arts, Daniel J. Terra Foundation (1992.51). Photograph courtesy of Terra Foundation for the Arts, Chicago.

125. *New York University* (ca. 1835). New York University Archives, Bobst Library, New York University.

126. Samuel F. B. Morse, *Allegorical Landscape Showing New York University* (1836). Oil on canvas, 22$\frac{1}{2}$ by 36$\frac{1}{4}$ inches. Collection of the New-York Historical Society, #6326.

128. Samuel F. B. Morse, *The Reverend Thomas Harvey Skinner* (ca. 1836). Oil on paperboard, 29$\frac{1}{2}$ × 24$\frac{5}{8}$ in. Courtesy of the Museum of Fine Arts, Boston. Gift of Maxim Karolik for the M. and M. Karolik Collection of American Paintings, 1815–1865.

131. Samuel F. B. Morse, *The Muse—Susan Walker Morse* (ca. 1835–37). Oil on canvas, 73$\frac{3}{4}$ × 56$\frac{6}{8}$ in. The Metropolitan Museum of Art, bequest of Herbert L. Pratt, 1945 (45.62.1). The Metropolitan Museum of Art. All rights reserved.

149. Morse's original telegraph apparatus, ca. 1836. Samuel Irenaeus Prime, *The Life of Samuel F. B. Morse, LL.D.* (1875).

150. Reproduction of Morse's original port-rule. Smithsonian Institution, neg. #26, 811.

151. Chappe semaphore. Musée de la Poste, Paris.

155. Page from Morse's *Sully* sketchbook. Smithsonian Institution, neg. #17, 479C.

162. Alfred Vail. New York University Archives, Bobst Library, New York University.

163. Morse's 1837 relay plan. Samuel Irenaeus Prime, *The Life of Samuel F. B. Morse, LL. D.* (1875).

166. Speedwell factory building, Morristown, New Jersey. Smithsonian Institution, neg. #72-4315.

170. Francis O. J. Smith. Collections of the Maine Historical Society (Coll. #30).

176. Sir Charles Wheatstone. Science and Society Picture Library, Science Museum, London.

193. Joseph Henry. Chicago Historical Society (ICHi-10693). Photographer unknown.

235. Original register used in the Baltimore-Washington trials of 1844. Smithsonian Institution, neg. # 29, 651.

235. Telegraph key of the 1840s. Smithsonian Institution, neg. #27, 979.

248. Samuel F. B. Morse, ca. 1850. Edward Julian Nally Papers. Manuscript Division, Department of Rare Books and Special Collections, Princeton University Library.

259. Amos Kendall. Prints and Photographs Division, The Library of Congress (LC-USZ62-10501).

263. Ad for the Magnetic Telegraph Company. Washington *Republic,* February 1, 1852.

264. Henry O'Reilly. Courtesy of the Rochester Historical Society and Grace Cutler Rice.

270. Cooke-Wheatstone double-needle telegraph. Science & Society Picture Library, Science Museum, London.

284. House printing telegraph. Smithsonian Institution, neg. #30, 396.

298. *Samuel Morse's Wife and Daughter* (1848). Daguerreotype by Samuel F. B. Morse. Collection of the New-York Historical Society, #6878.

302. Alexander Jackson Davis, plan for Morse home at Locust Grove (1851). Metropolitan Museum of Art Library, Harris Brisbane Dick Fund, 1924.

328. Cyrus W. Field (ca. 1860). *Carte-de-visite* by Mathew Brady. Collection of the New-York Historical Society, #40401A.

361. Landing of cable from the stern of the *Niagara. Illustrated London News,* August 22, 1857.

363. Sectional view of the *Niagara* (ca. 1855). Engraving by unidentified artist. New-York Historical Society, #37471A.

386. Morse in his New York City study. Prints and Photographs Division, The Library of Congress (LC-BH8201-963).

390. Morse ca. 1863. Prints and Photographs Division, The Library of Congress (LC-USZ62-11302).

423. Christian Schussele, *Men of Progress* (1862). Oil on canvas, $51\frac{3}{8} \times 76\frac{3}{4}$ in. National Portrait Gallery (NPG. 65. 60), Smithsonian Institution.

432. Morse statue in Central Park. Edward Julian Nally Papers. Manuscript Division, Department of Rare Books and Special Collections, Princeton University Library.

433. Morse Celebration at the Academy of Music. *Frank Leslie's Illustrated Newspaper,* July 1, 1871.

A NOTE ABOUT THE AUTHOR

Born and raised in Manhattan, Kenneth Silverman is Professor Emeritus of English at New York University. His other books include *Timothy Dwight, A Cultural History of the American Revolution, The Life and Times of Cotton Mather, Edgar A. Poe: Mournful and Never-ending Remembrance,* and *HOUDINI!!!.* He is the winner of the Bancroft Prize in American History, the Pulitzer Prize for Biography, the Edgar Award of the Mystery Writers of America, and the Christopher Literary Award of the Society of American Magicians.

A NOTE ON THE TYPE

This book was set in Baskerville, a facsimile of the type cast from the original matrices designed by John Baskerville. The original face was the forerunner of the modern group of typefaces. John Baskerville (1706–1775) of Birmingham, England, was a writing master with a special renown for cutting inscriptions in stone. About 1750 he began experimenting with punch cutting and making typographical material, and in 1757 he published his first work, a Virgil in royal quarto. His types, at first criticized as unnecessarily slender, delicate, and feminine, in time were recognized as both distinct and elegant, and his types as well as his printing were greatly admired.